The 1st Amendment in the Classroom Series, Number 5

The Freedom to PUBLISH

EDITED BY HAIG A. BOSMAJIAN

NEAL-SCHUMAN PUBLISHERS, INC.
NEW YORK   LONDON

THE FIRST AMENDMENT IN THE CLASSROOM SERIES
Edited by Haig A. Bosmajian

The Freedom to Read Books, Films and Plays. The First Amendment in the Classroom Series, No. 1. Foreword by Ken Donelson. ISBN 1-55570-001-2.

Freedom of Religion. The First Amendment in the Classroom Series, No. 2. ISBN 1-55570-002-0.

Freedom of Expression. The First Amendment in the Classroom Series, No. 3. ISBN 1-55570-003-9.

Academic Freedom. The First Amendment in the Classroom Series, No. 4. ISBN 1-55570-004-7.

The Freedom to Publish. The First Amendment in the Classroom Series, No. 5. ISBN 1-55570-005-5.

Published by Neal-Schuman Publishers, Inc.
23 Leonard Street
New York, NY 10013

Copyright © 1989 by Neal-Schuman Publishers, Inc.

All rights reserved. Reproduction of this book, in whole or in part, without written permission of the publisher is prohibited.

Printed and bound in the United States of America.

Library of Congress Cataloging-in-Publication Data

The Freedom to publish / edited by Haig A. Bosmajian.
    p.   cm. — (The 1st Amendment in the classroom series ; no. 5)
    Includes bibliographical references.
    ISBN 1-55570-005-5
    1. Student newspapers and periodicals—Law and legislation—United States—Cases. 2. Freedom of the press—United States—Cases. 3. Student newspapers and periodicals—Censorship—United States—Cases. I. Bosmajian, Haig A. II. Series.
KF4165.A7F74 1989
342.73'0853—dc20   89-12724
[347.302853]   CIP

Contents

Preface	v
Constitutional Amendments	ix
Judicial Circuits	xi
Foreword	xiii
Introduction	1
Dickey v. *Alabama State Bd. of Education*, 273 F.Supp. 613 (1967)	11
Zucker v. *Panitz*, 299 F.Supp. 102 (1969)	15
Antonelli v. *Hammond*, 308 F.Supp 1329 (1970)	18
Korn v. *Elkins*, 317 F.Supp. 138 (1970)	24
Scoville v. *Board of Ed. of Joliet*, 425 F.2d 10 (1970)	30
Trujillo v. *Love*, 322 F.Supp. 1266 (1971)	35
Eisner v. *Stamford Bd. of Education*, 440 F.2d 803 (1971)	39
Lee v. *Board of Regents of State Colleges*, 441, F.2d 1257 (1971)	45
Quarterman v. *Byrd*, 453 F.2d 54 (1971)	48
Fujishima v. *Bd. of Education*, 460 F.2d 1355 (1972)	53
Shanley v. *Northeast Ind. School Dist.*, 462 F.2d 960 (1972)	57
Panarella v. *Birenbaum*, 296 N.E.2d 238 (1973)	68
Vail v. *Bd. of Ed. of Portsmouth Sch. Dist.*, 354 F.Supp. 592 (1973)	72
Sullivan v. *Houston Independent School Dist.*, 475 F.2d 1071 (1973)	80
Bazaar v. *Fortune*, 476 F.2d 570 (1973)	86
Joyner v. *Whiting*, 477 F.2d 456 (1973)	95
Baughman v. *Freienmuth*, 478 F.2d 1345 (1973)	103
Papish v. *University of Missouri Curators*, 410 U.S. 667 (1973)	107
Jacobs v. *Bd. of School Commissioners*, 490 F.2d 601 (1973)	112
Bayer v. *Kinzler*, 383 F.Supp. 1164 (1974)	119
Nitzberg v. *Parks*, 525 F.2d 378 (1975)	121
Mississippi Gay Alliance v. *Goudelock*, 536 F.2d 1073 (1976)	126
Gambino v. *Fairfax County School Bd.*, 429 F.Supp. 731 (1977)	140
Leibner v. *Sharbaugh*, 429 F.Supp. 744 (1977)	144
Trachtman v. *Anker*, 563 F.2d 512 (1977)	148
Commonwealth v. *Bohmer*, 372 N.E.2d 1381 (1978)	159
Frasca v. *Andrews*, 463 F.Supp. 1043 (1979)	165
Reineke v. *Cobb County School Dist.*, 484 F.Supp. 1252 (1980)	172
Williams v. *Spencer*, 622 F.2d 1200 (1980)	180
Nicholson v. *Bd. of Education*, 682 F.2d 858 (1982)	185
Stanton v. *Brunswick School Dept.*, 577 F.Supp. 1560 (1984)	190
San Diego Committee v. *Governing Bd.*, 790 F.2d 1471 (1986)	202
Hazelwood School Dist. v. *Kuhlmeier*, 108 S.Ct. 562 (1988)	213

Preface

THE *First Amendment in the Classroom Series* responds to the need for teachers, students, parents, and school board members to become more aware of how First Amendment rights apply to the classrooms of a free society. Those cherished rights, if they have any meaning, are directly relevant and essential to our schools. What is especially needed is a wider familiarity with and understanding of the arguments and reasoning used to reach judgments regarding First Amendment issues, so often controversial and divisive, affecting what goes on in the classroom. To be unfamiliar with those arguments is to be unprepared to defend the First Amendment rights of students and teachers. Those arguments will be found in this series devoted to (1) the banning of books, plays, and films; (2) religion and prayer in the classroom; (3) symbolic speech; (4) teaching methods and teachers' classroom behavior; and (5) school publications and underground newspapers. My earlier volume, *Censorship, Libraries, and the Law,* covers cases of school library censorship.

When United States District Judge Hugh Bownes declared unconstitutional a Portsmouth, New Hampshire, Board of Education rule forbidding "distribution of non-school sponsored written materials within the Portsmouth schools and on school grounds for a distance of 200 feet from school entrances," he declared in the order of the court that "this opinion and Order is to be posted on the school bulletin board in a prominent place, and copies of this opinion and Order are to be made available to the students in the school library."[1]

This was a reminder to students, teachers, and school board members—but especially to the students—that First Amendment rights applied to them. As the United States Supreme Court had put it exactly thirty years earlier in *Barnette,* the First Amendment rights need to be practiced in our schools "if we are not to strangle the free mind at its source and teach youth to discount important principles of our government as mere platitudes."[2]

While the actual decisions in the cases involving the First Amendment rights of students and teachers in the classroom are crucial, the arguments and reasoning in the opinions are equally important. *Why* did the court decide that students could not be prohibited from distributing their literature? *Why* did the court decide that students could not be compelled to salute the flag? *Why* could the teacher not be dismissed for using books containing "offensive" language? *Why* could not the school board dismiss the teacher for using "unorthodox" teaching methods? *Why* could not parents have sex education banned from the school? *Why* did the court decide that prayer in the classroom was unconstitutional? Understanding the "whys" leads to an understanding of the workings of a democratic society.

In 1937, when throughout the world democratic institutions were being threatened and some were being destroyed, John Dewey observed that wherever political democracy has fallen, "it was too exclusively political in nature. It had not become part of the bone and blood of the people in daily conduct of life. Democratic forms were limited to Parliament, elections, and combats between parties. What is happening proves conclusively, I think, that unless democratic habits of thought and action are part of the fibre of a people, political democracy is insecure. It cannot stand in isolation. It must be buttressed by the presence of democratic methods in all social relationships."[3]

When the students, teachers, school boards, and parents involved in these cases insisted on exercising their First Amendment freedoms, they learned that the principles of our democracy are not "mere platitudes." For the students especially, the cases helped demonstrate that the Bill of Rights and "democratic habits of thought and action are part of the fibre of a people." These cases show political democracy "buttressed by the presence of democratic methods" in one realm of our society—the classroom.

It has been clearly established at several levels of our judicial system that protecting the First Amendment freedoms of teachers and students is crucial in a free society. In *Barnette,* the United States Supreme Court declared: "The Fourteenth Amendment, as now applied to the States, protects the citizen against the State itself and all of its creatures—Boards of Education not excepted. These have, of course, important, delicate, and highly discretionary functions, but none that they may not perform within the limits of the Bill of Rights. That they are educating the young for citizenship is reason for scrupulous protection of Constitutional freedoms of the individual, if we are not to strangle the free mind at its source and teach youth to discount important principles of our government as mere platitudes."

In giving First Amendment protection to junior and senior high school students who had worn black armbands to school to protest U.S. involvement in the Vietnam War, the United States Supreme Court spoke most clearly in *Tinker* on the issue of the First Amendment rights of teachers and students. Justice Abe Fortas, delivering the opinion of the Court, said in 1969: "First Amendment rights, applied in light of the special characteristics of the school environment, are available to teachers and students. It can hardly be argued that either students or teachers shed their constitutional rights to freedom of speech or expression at the schoolhouse gate. This has been the unmistakable holding of this Court for almost 50 years."[4]

When in 1978 United States District Court Judge Joseph Tauro ordered school authorities to return to the high school library a book which had been removed because it contained a "dirty, filthy" poem, he reiterated in his own words what had been declared in *Tinker:* " . . . the First Amendment is not merely a mantle which students and faculty doff when they take their places in the classroom."[5]

On these pages are the stories of students and teachers who risked much to fight for their First Amendment rights in the classroom, who did not "shed their constitutional rights to freedom of speech or expression at the schoolhouse gate" and did not see the First Amendment as "merely a mantle which students and teachers doff when they take their places in the classroom." What is encouraging is that in almost all the cases appearing in this series, students and teachers have been given First Amendment protection by the courts.

The reasons given in the opinions on these pages are applicable to many of those First Amendment controversies which may never reach the courts. Edward Jenkinson, who has done much research and writing on censorship in the schools and who chaired the National Council of Teachers of English Committee Against Censorship has reported: "During the early seventies, approximately one hundred censorship incidents were reported to the ALA [American Library Association]'s Office for Intellectual Freedom each year. By 1976, the number had risen to slightly less than two hundred and climbed to nearly three hundred in 1977." Shortly after the 1980 Presidential election, Judith Krug of the American Library Association estimation a threefold increase in reported censorship incidents, "which would mean roughly nine hundred reported incidents a year." But as Jenkinson points out, the reported incidents "are only a small part of the censorship attempts each year. . . . After talking with teachers, librarians and administrators in meetings in 33 states, I believe that for every reported incident of censorship at least fifty go unreported."[6]

The First Amendment in the Classroom makes available the many substantial arguments that can be used by students, teachers, and parents involved in First Amendment controversies surrounding teachers and students in the classroom. The reasons given by the judges on these pages are there for students, teachers, and parents to use in their efforts to persuade school boards and others that the First Amendment applies to the school environment and that the "Fourteenth Amendment, as now applied to the States, protects the citizen against the State itself and all of its creatures—Boards of Education not excepted."

In his discussion of the nature and function of the judicial court opinion, legal scholar Piero Calamandrei has observed that "the most important and most typical indication of the rationality of the judicial function is the reasoned opinion." Of the need for the judge to present the reasoned opinion, Calamandrei says that

> "ever since justice descended from heaven to earth and the idea gained ground that the judge is a human being and not a supernatural and infallible oracle to be adored, whose authority is beyond question, man has felt the need of a rational explanation to give validity to the word of the judge." [The major function of the reasoned opinion, explains Calamandrei,] "is an explanatory or, one might say, a pedagogical one. No longer content merely to command, to proclaim a *sic volo, sic iubeo* [So I wish, so I command] from his high bench, the judge descends to the level of the parties, and although still commanding, seeks to impress them with the reasonableness of the command. The reasoned opinion is above all the justification of the decision and as such it attempts to be as persuasive as it can."[7]

Like the judge, neither supernatural nor infallible, we are asked for rational explanations to justify our decisions. The judicial opinions on these pages provide useful and persuasive reasons.

I hope that readers of the books in this series—students, teachers, school board members, parents, and others—will develop their appreciation for and commitment to the First Amendment rights of students and teachers in the classroom and will recognize the variety of arguments available to counter those who would not have the First Amendment apply to teachers and students. The First Amendment freedoms were put into the Bill of Rights to be used; the court opinions in this series demonstrate that teachers and students usually get First Amendment protection from the courts. We must recognize, however, that freedoms not exercised by the citizenry lose their vitality. Teachers and students, said Chief Justice Earl Warren, "must always remain free to inquire, to study and to evaluate, to gain new maturity and understanding; otherwise our civilization will stagnate and die."[8]

NOTES

1. *Vail v. Bd. of Ed. of Portsmouth School Dist.,* 354 F. Supp. 592 (1973).
2. *West Virginia State Bd. of Ed. v. Barnette,* 319 U.S. 624 (1943).
3. John Dewey, "Democracy and Educational Administration," *School and Society,* 45(April 3, 1937), p. 462.
4. *Tinker v. Des Moines School Dist.,* 393 U.S. 503 (1969).
5. *Right to Read Defense Committee v. School Committee, Etc.,* 454 F. Supp. 703 (1978).
6. Edward Jenkinson, "Protecting Holden Caulfield and His Friends from the Censors," *English Journal,* 74(January 1985), p. 74.
7. Piero Calamandrei, *Procedure and Democracy,* trans. John C. Adams and Helen Adams (New York: New York University Press, 1956), p. 53.
8. *Sweezy v. New Hampshire,* 354 U.S. 234 (1957).

Constitutional Amendments

ARTICLE I

Congress shall make no law respecting an establishment of religion, or prohibiting the free exercise thereof; or abridging the freedom of speech, or of the press; or the right of the people peaceably to assemble, and to petition the government for a redress of grievances.

ARTICLE XIV

All persons born or naturalized in the United States, and subject to the jurisdiction thereof, are citizens of the United States and of the State wherein they reside. No State shall make or enforce any law which shall abridge the privileges or immunities of citizens of the United States; nor shall any state deprive any person of life, liberty or property, without due process of law; nor deny to any person within its jurisdiction the equal protection of the law.

Judicial Circuits

Circuits	Composition
District of Columbia	District of Columbia
First	Maine, Massachusetts, New Hampshire, Puerto Rico, Rhode Island
Second	Connecticut, New York, Vermont
Third	Delaware, New Jersey, Pennsylvania, Virgin Islands
Fourth	Maryland, North Carolina, South Carolina, Virginia, West Virginia
Fifth	Louisiana, Mississippi, Texas
Sixth	Kentucky, Michigan, Ohio, Tennessee
Seventh	Illinois, Indiana, Wisconsin
Eighth	Arkansas, Iowa, Minnesota, Missouri, Nebraska, North Dakota, South Dakota
Ninth	Alaska, Arizona, California, Idaho, Montana, Nevada, Oregon, Washington, Guam, Hawaii, Northern Marianna Islands
Tenth	Colorado, Kansas, New Mexico, Oklahoma, Utah, Wyoming
Eleventh	Alabama, Georgia, Florida

Foreword

By David W. Kennedy

Students need look no further than very recent history to find too many examples of censorship of the press. When dictatorship prevails, the first thing to go is a free press. A press that refuses to report only authorized news or that expresses opinions at variance with the government's views threatens the continuation of the regime. Most tyrannies establish their own newspapers and radio and television stations in order to control the dissemination of ideas. Their version of the truth is all the populace ever sees, hears, or reads.

For example, when Chinese students were killed by government troops in June 1989, the world press was there to record the event. But the Chinese press was not allowed to report what really happened. The Chinese leaders used the press to tell their own people that nothing had occurred. As of this writing, the great majority of Chinese don't know the truth of Tiannamen square; they believed what they read.

We all tend to believe something we read more than something we are told. There is a certain majesty in the written word. Repressive governments understand this very well and use it to their advantage.

The power of the printed word explains why, even in a democracy, journalists are either reviled or revered. Because journalists strive to be tellers of the truth, dishonest officials revile them, while good citizens revere them.

In a democracy, journalists bear the responsibility for accurately reporting events that affect the citizens of their nation. They must separate fact from fiction, truth from falsehood, enabling readers to make informed decisions.

A free press is the life-support of a democratic society—a press that aggressively goes out after the truth. It was a free, uncensored press that exposed the crimes of Watergate. Compare this example to that of, say, Joseph Stalin's massacre of millions of Russian people. If the Soviet press had been able to uncover and report on his atrocities, history might have been different.

Sadly, American history, too, offers examples of censorship in the press. Some political and religious extremists—even some educators—evidently feel that one way to keep their followers on the straight and narrow is to restrict access to what they read. (Witness the recent call for suppression of an ultra-conservative publication at Dartmouth College). But the First Amendment to the Constitution is a strong defense against would-be censors.

As every student knows, the first ten Amendments to the U.S. Constitution are called the Bill of Rights, and they apply to all American citizens. It is significant that freedom of expression is the first Amendment. The framers

---

David W. Kennedy is President of the American Society of Journalists and Authors.

of the Constitution considered it to be the most important of all rights, and it should be considered so by all Americans today.

Among those who drew up the Bill of Rights were men who remembered censorship and the harm it can do. They understood that, to avoid repression, citizens had to be able to express whatever was in their minds, whether or not it conformed to the official view.

The First Amendment defines American democracy. Those powerful but simple words, "Congress shall make no law . . . abridging the freedom of speech, or of the press . . ." allow opinions of any and all stripes to flourish.

Imagine what America would be like without the diversity of opinion that gives our society its characteristic dynamism. We publish thousands of newspapers, magazines, and books in this country each year, and probably no two of them espouse exactly the same ideas, in exactly the same way.

When oppressed people talk about democracy, a good part of what they mean is the ability to speak and write freely. When you deprive people of their freedom to publish their thoughts, you are essentially depriving them of their humanity. Having the right to communicate thoughts, opinions, and beliefs to others is central to human dignity. In this country we call it "getting your two cents in," and whether we do it orally or in writing, it has something to do with our self-worth as individuals and as a people.

Suppression of writing, and hence ideas, is a recurring theme in history. Murdering people for publishing heretical ideas during the Inquisition and the wholesale burning of books during the Third Reich are only two examples of the extremes to which the suppression of ideas can lead. In the U.S. it is the courts—which make up the third part of our constitutional triad of Executive, Legislative, and Judicial branches—that are responsible for protecting those First Amendment rights. Time after time, the judges of the courts, who serve as the arbiters in our system, have ruled that students, not those acting in loco parentis to them, are entitled to those rights and must be given the freedom to exercise them. Like all Americans, students have the right to publish their opinions, including criticism of ideas and procedures in their schools.

The cases contained in this volume should give high school and college students comfort. They will learn that their rights are largely coterminus with those of older Americans. Simply put, students who publish newspapers are protected by the First Amendment.

It is unfortunate indeed that so many cases involving schools and colleges and student publications have come before our courts. Not only are educational institutions supposed to foster the interchange of ideas of all types, but student publications are the training ground for America's future journalists. They are also the voice of the student.

The courts have shown repeatedly that they respect the student voice. They have carefully and eloquently analyzed this fundamental right in many cases involving student publications, often citing the landmark *Tinker* v. *Des Moines* ruling that students do not "shed their constitutional rights to freedom of speech or expression at the schoolhouse gate."

When the courts of this land take student publications seriously, students should as well. Students should be able to express their opinion about what is going on around them without fear of censorship. That's their constitutional right.

Students have had to fight hard to maintain this freedom of expression. The college newspaper editor who wrote "Censored" in the blank where his editorial should have been saw his fight against censorship ultimately end in victory. Other students have had to fight to use graphic language or to report on controversial issues. Although they won many of these fights, today's students must be prepared to continue to defend their freedoms.

Publishing a newspaper is an exercise in democracy at its most fundamental level. Hundreds of thousands of Americans have lost their lives in wars to keep the freedom of expression alive, and it's incumbent on students as well as adults to keep that freedom alive by constantly testing its limits.

Students must be vigilant in protecting rights that may encompass the possibility of bringing a lawsuit. The freedom to publish, the freedom to tell the truth as one sees it, is so basic and vital to a democracy that it must be jealously guarded by each new generation.

We must understand the roots of censorship and why it occurs. Only then can we recognize it and challenge it. Only by this awareness can our First Amendment rights be preserved.

A country that tolerates censorship of the press cannot be truly free. Only when citizens can exercise their right and their responsibility to publish their thoughts in an unfettered manner can they claim to be truly free. It is a freedom worth going to court for.

Introduction

DURING the immediately preceding two decades before the United States Supreme Court in 1988 for the first time decided a high school newspaper censorship case, the lower courts consistently had been giving First Amendment protection to students whose publications were being censored or banned by school authorities. The lower courts for two decades had built a structure of law based on some recurring arguments that concluded with decisions supporting students' press and free speech rights. Those arguments, however, were either ignored or rejected as irrelevant by the five person majority of Supreme Court Justices in 1988 when they presented arguments heretofore unheard of from the High Court to justify its *Hazelwood* decision for school officials who had censored a high school newspaper.

In twenty five of the thirty three cases included in this volume, the courts upheld the First Amendment rights of students involved in editing, publishing or distributing newspapers at their schools. In some cases, the courts found the rules and regulations related to student publications to be vague and unreasonable. In other cases, the courts argued that procedural safeguards were lacking. In still other cases, especially after *Tinker* (1969), the courts argued that publication or distribution of the student newspapers did not involve any material and substantial interference with school work or discipline. Other courts argued that the student publications, while containing "offensive" articles and language, were not obscene. Further, it was argued that school officials were subjectively censoring material they found objectionable, an unconstitutional selective enforcement.

After the Supreme Court's *Tinker* decision in 1969, court after court relied on *Tinker* in deciding for students whose publications had been censored or banned. One year after *Tinker*, the United States Court of Appeals, Seventh Circuit, in deciding for high school students who had been expelled for distributing their publication *Grass High* to faculty and students, relied heavily on *Tinker*. "The authoritative decision, pertinent to the important issue before us," said the Court of Appeals, is *Tinker* v. *Des Moines School District* . . . *Tinker* is a high school 'armband' case, but its rule is admittedly dispositive of the case before us. The *Tinker* rule narrows the question before us to whether the writing of 'Grass High' and its sale in school to sixty students and faculty members could 'reasonably have led [the Board] to *forecast* substantial disruption of or material interference with school activities . . . or intru[sion] into school affairs or the lives of others . . . *Tinker* announces the principles which underlie our holding: High school students are persons entitled to First and Fourteenth Amendment protections. States and school officials have 'comprehensive authority' to prescribe and control conduct in the schools through reasonable rules consistent with fundamental constitutional safeguards." The Court of Appeals concluded: "We believe the discussion above makes it clear, on the basis of the admitted facts and exhibits, that the Board could not have reasonably forecast that the publication and distribution of this paper to the students would substantially disrupt or materially interfere with school procedures." (*Scoville*) The court thus applied the language and spirit of *Tinker* in giving constitutional protection to the students.

Again, the United States Court of Appeals, Seventh Circuit, relied on *Tinker* when it decided in 1972 for high school students who had been suspended for distributing their underground newspaper, *The Cosmic Frog,* before and between classes and during lunch breaks. The court struck down as unconstitutional a section of the rules of the Chicago Board of Education which read: "No person shall be permitted . . . to distribute on the school premises any books, tracts, or other publications . . . unless the same shall have been approved by the General Superintendent of Schools." The court argued: "Because section 6-19 requires prior approval of publications, it is unconstitutional as a prior restraint. This conclusion is compelled by combining the holding of *Near* v. *Minnesota* . . . and *Tinker* v. *Des Moines Independent Community School District* . . . . *Tinker* held that, absent a showing of material and substantial interference with the requirements of school discipline, schools may not restrain the full First Amendment rights of their students. *Near* established one of those rights, freedom to distribute a publication without prior censorship." As to that aspect of *Tinker* dealing with school officials "forecasting" substantial disruption of school activities, the court said: "The *Tinker* forecast rule is properly a formula for determining when the requirements of school discipline justify *punishment* of students for the exercise of their First Amendment rights. It is not a basis for establishing a system of censorship and licensing designed to *prevent* the exercise of First Amendment rights." (*Fujishima*)

The United States Court of Appeals, Fifth Circuit, in deciding for students who had been suspended for distributing near school premises an underground newspaper they had authored and published during out-of-school hours, metaphorized *Tinker* when it relied on the landmark decision to support its decision: "*Tinker's* dam to school board absolutism does not leave dry the fields of school discipline. This court has gone a considerable distance with the school boards to uphold its disciplinary fiats where reasonable . . . . *Tinker* simply irrigates, rather than floods, the fields of school discipline. It sets canals and channels through which school discipline might flow with the least possible damage to the nation's priceless topsoil of the First Amendment."

In deciding that a publications rule imposed on high school students constituted prior restraint and was void beause of vagueness and overbreadth, the United States Court of Appeals, Fourth Circuit, in 1975 referred to the widespread reliance on *Tinker:* " It is clear that Rule 5130.1(b) was intended to come within the exception to the ban on prior restraints suggested in *Tinker* . . . . There the Court appeared to recognize the right of school administrators to block the distribution of literature which would substantially disrupt school work and discipline. Despite the protest of commentators . . . , the Circuits which have dealt with the issue—with the exception of the Seventh—have accepted this interpretation of *Tinker.* . . . Applying this test, we find the challenged regulation to be improperly drawn in several respects." (*Nitzberg*)

The *Tinker* test, however, was found to be irrelevant when in 1988 the United States Supreme Court decided, 5-3, against high school students who had claimed their First and Fourteenth Amendment rights had been violated when the school principal deleted two pages from their high school newspaper *Spectrum*. While the five person majority noted that "students in the public schools do not 'shed their constitutional rights to freedom of speech or expression at the schoolhouse gate,' " it went on to assert that "the First Amendment rights of students in the public schools 'are not automatically coextensive with the rights of adults in other settings'... and must be 'applied in light of the special characteristics of the school environment.'" (*Hazelwood*)

Elements of the *Fraser* test were seen by the Supreme Court majority as controlling in *Hazelwood,* a test which the Court had established in 1986 when it decided against a high school student, Matthew Fraser, who had delivered at a school assembly a one minute nominating speech which contained "vulgar" language. Unlike the *Tinker* test which would not protect speech if it "substantially interfere[d] with the work of the school or impinge upon the rights of other students," *Fraser,* as noted by the Court in *Hazelwood,* declared that "a school need not tolerate student speech that is inconsistent with its 'basic educational mission.'" Continuing its reliance on *Fraser,* the Court said in *Hazelwood:* " We thus recognized that '[t]he determination of what manner of speech in the classroom or in school assembly is inappropriate properly rests with the school board . . . , rather than with the federal courts. It is in this context that respondents' First Amendment claims must be considered." (*Hazelwood*)

Fraser and *Hazelwood* lengthened the list of the types of speech which school officials could censor. With the lengthening of the list there also came an increase in the vagueness of the criteria to be used in determining what could be prohibited. The relatively limited "substantially interfere with the work of the school or impinge upon the rights of other students" of *Tinker* was expanded to the more amorphous aspects of the *Fraser* and *Hazelwood* tests. In *Hazelwood* the Court declared: "A school must also retain the authority to refuse to sponsor student speech that might reasonably be perceived to advocate drug or alcohol use, irresponsible sex, or conduct otherwise inconsistent with 'the shared values of a civilized social order.'" *Hazelwood* and *Fraser* gave school officials the power to censor still more types of speech: "Hence, a school may in its capacity as publisher of a school newspaper or producer of a school play ' disassociate itself,' *Fraser . . . ,* not only from speech that would "substantially interfere with [its] work . . . or impinge upon the rights of other students,' *Tinker . . . ,* but also from speech that is, for example, ungrammatical, poorly written, inadequately researched, biased or prejudiced, vulgar or profane or unsuitable for immature audiences." (*Hazelwood*)

It is one thing to prohibit speech which would "substantially interfere with the work of the school or impinge on the rights of others"; it is something else to place in the hands of school officials the power to censor speech or conduct which is "inconsistent with" the school's "basic educational mission" or which is "inconsistent with 'the shared values of a civilized social order'" or which is "vulgar or profane or unsuitable for immature audiences." With all of these amorphous, sometimes subjective, criteria come substantially greater censorship possibilities.

The dangers of such ambiguities were recognized by Justice Brennan in his *Hazelwood* dissenting opinion: "Official censorship of student speech on the ground that it addresses 'potentially sensitive topics' is, for related reasons, equally impermissible. I would not begrudge an educator the authority to limit the substantive scope of a school-sponsored publication to a certain, objectively definable topic, such as literary criticism, school sports, or an overview of the school year. Unlike those determinate limitations, 'potential topic sensitivity' is a vaporous non-standard . . . that invites manipulation to achieve ends that cannot permissibly be achieved through blatant viewpoint discrimination and chills student speech to which school officials might not object. In part because of those dangers, this Court has consistently condemned any scheme allowing a state official boundless discretion in licensing speech from a particular forum."

The *Hazelwood* test, drawing on *Fraser,* being so much more vague and less precise than the *Tinker* test, can easily lead to at least the following three results: (1) an increase in the types of language and articles that can be censored by school officials; (2) a chilling effect on freedom of expression inasmuch as one is not clear just exactly what is prohibited and hence one "steers far wider than the unlawful zone"; and (3) being less precise, the *Hazelwood* test can be applied in a more arbitrary manner by school authorities since the more vague the standard, the more is left up to the school officials interpreting the standard. When one must guess what utterance is going to be punished, one may become timid and steer clear of any imaginative language or controversial articles which school authorities would condemn as being "inconsistent with the basic educational mission of the school."

What the United States District Court stated in its 1970 decision for a teacher who had been dismissed for assigning Kurt Vonnegut's *Welcome to the Monkey House* to a high school English class, is relevant also to students: "Our laws in this country have long recognized that no person should be punished for conduct unless such conduct has been proscribed in clear and precise terms ... When a teacher is forced to speculate as to what conduct is permissible and what conduct is proscribed, he is apt to be overly cautious and reserved in the classroom. Such a reluctance on the part of the teacher to investigate and experiment with new and different ideas is anathema to the entire concept of academic freedom." [*Parducci* v. *Rutland,* 316 F. Supp. 352 (1970)]

To support its decision against the students in *Hazelwood,* the Court also argued that "the question whether the First Amendment requires a school to tolerate particular student speech—the question we addressed in *Tinker,* is different from the question whether the First Amendment requires a school *affirmatively* to promote particular student speech-sponsored publications, theatrical productions and other expressive activities that students, parents and members of the public might reasonably perceive to bear the imprimatur of the school." The majority argued that the public might believe that the school was giving its stamp of approval to the articles appearing in the school newspapers.

The implications of such an argument justifying censorship are disturbing. When teachers present unorthodox ideas in the classroom it does not follow that such ideas are being given the stamp of approval by the school. When school libraries purchase books to place on the school library shelves, that does not mean that the school is giving its imprimatur on all the ideas expressed in those books. Making ideas accessible to students does not necessarily imply that those ideas have received the imprimatur of the school.

Justice Brennan, in his dissenting opinion, rejected the Court's position that the ideas expressed in the newspaper might be "erroneously attributed to the school." In so doing he suggested that less wholesale censorship as practiced at Hazelwood East would have been more appropriate and that there were other means to achieve the disassociation: "Dissociative means short of censorship are available to the school. It could, for example, require the student activity to publish a disclaimer, such as the 'Statement of Policy' that *Spectrum* published each school year announcing that '[a]ll ... editorials appearing in this newspaper reflect the opinions of the *Spectrum* staff, which are not necessarily shared by the administrators or faculty of Hazelwood East,' App. 26; or it could simply issue its own response clarifying the official position on the matter and explaining why the student position is wrong. Yet, without so much as acknowledging the less oppressive alternatives, the Court approves of brutal censorship."

It was the position of the majority of the Court that the ideas in the divorce and pregnancy articles could be considered inappropriate for the less mature students; Justice White, writing for the majority, declared: "It was not unreasonable for the principal to have concluded that such frank talk [about divorce and pregnancy] was inappropriate in a school-sponsored publication distributed to 14-year-old freshmen and presumably taken home to be read by students' even younger brothers and sisters." In effect, the majority took the position that the fourteen year olds and the younger brothers and sisters at home, as potential readers of the high school newspaper, had to be kept in mind when senior high school students write and publish their school newspaper. This, of course, dictates that the content of the high school newspaper be reduced to the level of the most "susceptible" readers, any immature readers into whose hands the newspaper may fall.

This view, however, was not shared by the three dissenting Justices; Brennan wrote: "The Court's second excuse for deviating from precedent is the school's interest in shielding an impressionable high school audience from material whose substance is 'unsuitable for immature audiences.'" While Brennan agreed that "the educator may, under *Tinker,* constitutionally 'censor' poor grammar, writing or research because to reward such expression would 'materially disrupt' the newspaper's curricular purpose," he went on to argue that "the same cannot be said of official censorship designed to shield the *audience* or dissociate the *sponsor* from the expression. Censorship so motivated might well serve . . . some other school purposes. But it in no way furthers the curricular purposes of a student *newspaper,* unless one believes that the purpose of the school newspaper is to teach students that the press ought never report bad news, express unpopular views, or print a thought that might upset its sponsors. Unsurprisingly, Hazelwood East claims no such pedagogical purpose."

Reactions to the Supreme Court's *Hazelwood* decision varied from school officials and others who saw the decision as a welcome means for maintaining more control over students and their high school newspapers, to those who contended the decision would discourage serious students from studying journalism and would likely lead to an undesirable increase in the censorhsip of high school newspapers. The principal of Hazelwood East who had done the censoring expressed satisfaction with the Court's decision: "We're glad the court gave us control over the curriculum." (*Newsweek,* Jan. 25, 1988, p. 60) The attorney for the National Association of Secondary School Principals stated: "The only thing this will do is make principals feel more comfortable in exercising control when they see it as necessary." (*Time,* Jan. 25, 1988, p. 54) The *Chicago Tribune* (Jan. 15, 1988) editorialized that the ruling was correct but also declared the reasoning of the Court was faulty: "What the Court should have said is that the First Amendment rights to expression without censorship do not extend to editor-publisher relationships. No editors in our history have had a constitutionally guaranteed right to publish something in a newspaper that the publishers did not want in there. Editors who can't agree with publishers have to find a new job or become publishers themselves."

The dangerous implications and effects of *Hazelwood* were expressed by students directly involved in the case, various other journalists and legal scholars. Editor Cathy Kuhlmeier and Andrea Callow, the author of one of the censored articles, expressed their concern that the decision would have its chilling effects. Kuhlmeier's fear was that the decision might "turn kids off to journalism." She said: "We were trying to make a change with the school paper and not just write about the school proms, football games and piddly stuff." (*New York Times,* Jan. 14, 1988, A26) Callow's concern was that "if student journalists want to write about a subject like teen pregnancy, they are going to be hesitant." (*Time,* Jan. 25, 1988, p. 54)

Writing in the *St. Mary's Law Review* (vol. 19, p. 1139), Christopher Forbis expressed similar concerns: "The potential chilling effect *Hazelwood* will have on our aspiring student journalists seems very high. The decision creates a powerful tool for school officials, who now have less reason to weigh the benefits of publishing controversial articles in school papers against the dangers thereof." One of the concerns expressed by Jeffrey Smith in his *Virginia Law Review* (vol. 74, 860) article was the effect resulting from the Court's unwillingness to present clear guidelines: "[T]he failure of the Court in *Hazelwood* to provide definitive guidelines as to what is and is not protected by the

Constitution may significantly restrict the content of school newspapers. Educators armed with the broad discretion allotted to them by *Hazelwood* may limit school newspapers to mundane matters and cause students to ignore important, controversial issues." The concern that *Hazelwood* would result in school newspapers limiting themselves to "mundane matters" was shared by attorney and author Alan Levine who declared that high school newspapers would now become "more orthodox and bland." (*Newsweek,* Jan. 25, 1988, p. 60)

Discussing the "fallout from *Hazelwood,*" Laura Fraser, writing in the *Columbia Journalism Review* (May/June, 1988, p. 8), observed that "the Court's ruling severely limits the First Amendment rights of student journalists, and in general a principal now has the right to censor a story on any subject he or she deems unsuitable." Paul McMasters, deputy editorial director of *USA Today* and Chairperson of the Freedom of Information Committee of the Society of Professional Journalists, Sigma Delta Chi, concluded that "the Court's decision was no small defeat for the First Amendment" and he asked, "Why should we 'real' journalists care?" He answered: "Because the Court's decision means that many aspiring, now disgusted, journalists will turn their talents to careers built on a more solid base than the Court's interpretation of the First Amendment. Those who hang in will join our ranks well-schooled in cafeteria journalism, unwilling to question authority or challenge orthodoxy, and quite prepared to churn out stories that are often blind and always bland." (*The Quill,* March, 1988, p. 14)

A crucial difference that emerges from a close reading of the *Hazelwood* opinions and from an evaluation of the reactions to *Hazelwood* is the contrasting perceptions the proponents and opponents of the *Hazelwood* test have of the maturity of high school students, the functions of education, and the role of the state in controlling what language and ideas students shall be allowed to express and be exposed to. Justice Brennan did not want the students transformed into "closed-circuit recipients of only that which the State chooses to communicate"; he combined this metaphor from *Tinker* with his declaration that in its "capacity as educator the State may not assume an Orwellian 'guardianship of the public mind.'" He was responding to the majority's defense of school authorities justifying censorship to protect high school students, "immature audiences," from "potentially sensitive topics"; Brennan wrote: "The Court's second excuse for deviating from precedent is the school's interest in shielding an impressionable high school audience from material whose substance is 'unsuitable for immature audiences.' . . . Specifically, the majority decrees that we must afford educators authority to shield high school students from exposure to 'potentially sensitive topics' (like 'the particulars of teenage sexual activity') or unacceptable social viewpoints (like the advocacy of 'irresponsible se[x] or conduct otherwise inconsistent with 'the shared values of a civilized social order') through school-sponsored student activities."

During the two decades prior to *Hazelwood,* the lower courts generally took seriously the interests, needs, and concerns of high school students and argued that students must be free to discuss those needs and interests. In 1967, a group of New Rochelle High School (New York) students concerned about United States participation in the war in Vietnam, formed an "Ad Hoc Student Committee Against the War in Vietnam." They sought to place in the school newspaper a paid advertisement which read: "The United States government is pursuing a policy in Viet Nam which is both repugnant to moral and international law and dangerous to the future of humanity. We can stop it. We must stop it." While the editorial board of the newspaper approved publication of the advertisement, the principal "directed that the advertisement not be published." When the students took their case to a United States District Court in New York, the court concluded its opinion for the students by recognizing the importance of allowing students to express their views on subjects, controversial as they may be, which relate to the lives of the students: "This lawsuit arises at a time when many in the educational community oppose the tactics of the young in securing a political voice. It would be both incongruous and dangerous for this court to hold that students who wish to express their views on matters intimately related to them, through traditionally accepted nondisruptive modes of communication, may be precluded from doing so by that same adult community." (*Zucker*)

When the United States Court of Appeals, Fifth Circuit, decided in 1972 for students who had been suspended for distributing near school premises an "underground newspaper" called *Awakening,* the judges noted that the high school students needed to be taken seriously and not be looked upon as immature individuals who had to be protected from diversity: "Perhaps it would be well if those entrusted to administer the teaching of American history and government to our students begin their efforts by practicing the document on which that history and government are based. Our eighteen-year-olds can now vote, serve on juries, and be drafted; yet the Board fears the 'Awakening' of their intellects without reasoned concern for its effect upon school discipline. The First Amendment cannot tolerate such intolerance." (*Shanley*)

While the *Zucker* court recognized that the draft was a subject related to the interests of students and while in *Shanley* the court recognized that eighteen-year-olds could vote, serve on juries and be drafted, a United States District Court in Maine recognized in 1984 a student's serious interest in and concern about capital punishment when it decided against school officials who had banned from the high school yearbook the following quotation from *Time* magazine she wanted placed by her yearbook picture: "The executioner will pull this lever four times. Each time 2000 volts will course through your body, making your eyeballs first bulge, then burst, and then broiling your brains . . . ." In its opinion the court included her explanation of why she chose this quotation. She had read in her sophomore year in high school Truman Capote's *In Cold Blood* and the question of capital punishment was discussed at home. She went on to explain: "The reason I chose the quotation I selected was to possibly provoke some of my classmates to think a little more deeply than if I had written a standard butterfly quote. I wanted to make them aware of the realities that exist in today's world. The issue isn't that of capital punishment alone, but of those realities of which [sic] people prefer to avoid. It is important to think about these things because we are seniors and we are going to be on our own very soon."

In deciding for Stanton [the student], the United States District Court in Maine said: "Justice Frankfurter framed lucidly the pertinent calculus when he said that the right of free expression 'means not only informed and responsible criticism but the freedom to speak foolishly and without moderation . . . .' In the legitimate exercise of her right of free speech, this Plaintiff has the option to convey her conviction by the use of the most graphic language, even, if she so chooses, by language so physiologically stark that others may believe her to 'be a jerk.' Government has no legitimate nor compelling interest in preserving this lone woman from that fate if her own utterances shall visit it upon her." (*Stanton*)

Unlike the Supreme Court's *Hazelwood* majority, the United States Court of Appeals, Eighth Circuit, in deciding for Kuhlmeier in 1986, argued that the censored materials were not inappropriate for the high school audience. As to the pregnancy article and its relevance to students, the court said: "Nor is there evidence in this record to support the administrators' view that the article was inappropriate for publication in *Spectrum,* given the age and immaturity of some of its readers. Unfortunately, teenage pregnancy is a problem in nearly every high school in the United States, including Hazelwood East. The students in the high school, including the freshmen and sophomores, are aware of the problem, and it is most unlikely that anything in the articles would offend their sensibilities."

In deciding against the school officials, the Court of Appeals also argued that the subject of divorce was of direct relevance to high school students: "Underlying the deletion is the school district's feeling that these articles were inappropriate for high school students because: 'divorce is per se an inappropriate subject for high school newspapers.' Unfortunately, statistics reveal that a significant number of high school students have grown up in single parent homes due to divorce. Thus, a responsible treatment of this subject in the high school newspaper would not be shocking, or even new—it would be an outside and perhaps helpful, perspective on a well-known subject." [*Kuhlmeier* v. *Hazelwood Sch. Dist.*, 795 F.2d 1368 (1986)] In reversing the Court of Appeals' decision, the five member majority of the United States Supreme Court did not share this perception of high school students; instead, the majority of the Court argued: "It was not unreasonable for the principal to have concluded that such frank talk [in the pregnancy article] was inappropriate in a school-sponsored publication distributed to 14-year-old freshmen and presumably taken home to be read by students' even younger brothers and sisters." *Spectrum,* of course, was distributed also to sixteen, seventeen and eighteen year olds on the threshold of making important social, personal and political decisions.

Capital punishment, divorce, teenage pregnancy, the draft, war, drugs—all are seriously relevant to the lives of high school students, both seniors and the younger students. These are subjects discussed informally by students between classes and after school; subjects which are dealt with in various novels, plays and textbooks assigned by teachers; subjects which are the themes of books found on the high school library shelves; and perhaps, most important, subjects with which many of the students have had to deal in their own lives or will have to deal with in the future. It is too late in the day to deny students the right to write, edit, publish, and distribute their newspapers treating these subjects in a manner which possibly may offend the sensibilities of some school officials. The danger comes not from students having access to student writings on these subjects; the danger comes from school authorities attempting to shield high school students from the sometimes unorthodox, "offensive," and controversial treatment of these subjects, and others, in the student newspapers.

To deny high school students the opportunity to express through their newspapers their views on vital subjects and at the same time ask the students to not lose faith in our Constitutional principles may be asking too much. Justice Brennan, drawing on several now classic judicial pronouncements, summed it up in the conclusion of his *Hazelwood* dissenting opinion: "The Court opens its analysis in this case by purporting to reaffirm *Tinker's* time-tested proposition that public school students 'do not shed their constitutional right to freedom of speech or expression at the schoolhouse gate.' . . . That is an ironic introduction to an opinion that denudes high school students of much of the First Amendment protection that *Tinker* itself prescribed. Instead of 'teach[ing] children to respect the diversity of ideas that is fundamental to the American system' . . . and 'that our Constitution is a living reality, not parchment preserved under glass' . . . the Court today 'teach[es] youth to discount important principles of our government as mere platitudes.'"

The Constitution may indeed be seen by students as "only parchment preserved under glass" and not as "a living reality" when public school officials, including principals, as agents of the state, increasingly censor student publications. It is state censorship at its worst when it comes in the form of prior restraint, a form of censorship clearly rejected by the founders of this nation. Prior approval by school officials of student publications brings with it increased arbitrary censorship power to school authorities and further, since the speech and writings are banned before they are ever expressed, the public, including the student, is denied the opportunity to make a decision as to whether the censorship was justified.

To avoid having our youth "discount important principles of our government as mere platitudes" we must heed the principles enunciated by the United States Supreme Court when it decided in 1943 for students of the Jehovah's Witness faith who had been suspended from school because they refused to salute the flag; Justice Jackson, delivering the opinion of the Court, declared: "Such Boards [Boards of Education] are numerous and their territorial jurisdiction often small. But small and local authority may feel less sense of responsibility to the Constitution, and agencies of publicity may be less vigilant in calling it to account .... There are village tyrants as well as village Hampdens, but none who act under color of law is beyond the reach of the Constitution." In giving constitutional protection to the students, Justice Jackson eloquently concluded: "If there is any fixed star in our constitutional constellation, it is that no official, high or petty, can prescribe what shall be orthodox in politics, nationalism, religion, or other matters of opinion or force citizens to confess by word or act their faith therein." [*West Virginia State Bd. of Ed.* v. *Barnette,* 319 U.S. 624 (1943)]

A United States District Court in Alabama decides for a college student who had been "suspended" for one academic year because he had placed in the space ordinarily occupied by an editorial in the school paper a blank space with the word "Censored" written across it; he then sent the banned editorial which was "critical" of state legislators to a Montgomery newspaper. In ordering that the student be immediately reinstated as a student in Troy State College, the Court said: "A state cannot force a college student to forfeit his constitutionally protected right of freedom of expression as a condition to his attending a state-supported institution. State officials cannot infringe on their students' right of free and unrestricted expression as guaranteed by the Constitution of the United States where the exercise of such right does not 'materially and substantially interfere with requirements of appropriate discipline in the operation of the school.' ... The attempt to characterize Dickey's conduct, and the basis for their action in expelling him, as 'insubordination" requiring rather severe disciplinary action, does not disguise the basic fact that Dickey was expelled from Troy State College for exercising his constitutionally guaranteed right of academic and/or political expression."

Dickey v. Alabama State Bd. of Education, 273 F. Supp. 613 (1967)

JOHNSON, Chief Judge.

Gary Clinton Dickey, a citizen of the United States and a resident of this district, was, for the 1966-67 school year, a student in good standing at Troy State College, a state-operated public institution of higher learning located at Troy, Alabama, which is controlled and supervised by the Alabama State Board of Education.[1] Dickey had earned as of the end of the school year in June, 1967, 147 quarter hours toward a degree in English, which degree requires 192 quarter hours, according to Troy State standards. He made known his wishes to attend Troy State College for the school year 1967-68, commencing September, 1967, by giving written notice as required by the institution. On July 18, 1967, Dickey received "Official Notice of Admission" from the college, admitting him to the undergraduate division of said college for the fall quarter 1967. On August 11, 1967, Dickey received a certified letter from Troy State College, signed by the Dean of Men, advising him that the Student Affairs Committee at said college had voted not to admit him "at this time."

Upon the verified complaint filed with this Court on August 16, 1967, and the matters alleged therein, this Court observed that, in cases involving suspension or expulsion of students from a tax-supported college or university, due process requires notice and some opportunity for a hearing before suspension or expulsion. *Dixon v. Alabama State Board of Education,* 294 F.2d 150 (5th Cir. 1961). It was further observed in said order that, upon Dickey's verified allegations of deprivation of constitutionally guaranteed rights and where there is factual evidence of a clear and imminent threat of irreparable injury, judicial action was required. Accordingly, the defendants were, by formal order made and entered on August 17, 1967, directed to rescind the action suspending or expelling Dickey without any notice of hearing and to afford him an administrative hearing as required by the constitutional principle of due process. Following the order of the Court, the defendants on August 21, 1967, caused to be rescinded the action taken by the Student Affairs Committee that resulted in Dickey's suspension, and at that time advised Dickey that he would be afforded an opportunity to be heard "on the charge of insubordination resulting from his refusal to comply with specific instructions of his Faculty Advisor in defiance of such instructions" and that such a hearing would be conducted on Friday, August 25, 1967. A full hearing was afforded Dickey before the Student Affairs Committee on that date. Dickey was present with his attorney, and witnesses appeared and were examined. On August 28, 1967, Troy State College, acting through its Dean of Men, advised Dickey that it was the decision of the Student Affairs Committee that he not be admitted to Troy State College for one academic year (nine months), beginning with the fall quarter of 1967. Upon receipt of this notice, Dickey moved for a preliminary injunction on the theory that his substantive rights of due process had been and were being deprived by reason of his expulsion and/or suspension from Troy State College.[2] Jurisdiction of this Court was invoked pursuant to 28 U.S.C. § 1331. Due notice of the hearing upon the plaintiff's motion was given the defendants, and the matter is now submitted to this Court upon the pleadings and the evidence taken orally before the Court.

During the early part of the 1966-67 school year, Gary Clinton Dickey, while a full-time student at Troy State College, was chosen as an editor of the Troy State College student newspaper, *The Tropolitan*. It appears that Dickey was an outstanding student, as he was also chosen as editor-in-chief of the Troy State College literary magazine; was copy editor of the college's annual student yearbook, and was editor-in-chief of the student handbook. He was also a member of a national honorary journalism fraternity.

In early April, 1967, Dr. Frank Rose, President of the University of Alabama, came under attack by certain Alabama state legislators for his refusal to censor the University of Alabama student publication, "Emphasis 67, A World in Revolution." "Emphasis 67," as published for the University of Alabama, served as the program for a series of guest speakers and panel discussions held in March at the University of Alabama. The publication contained brief biographical sketches of the participants, which included Secretary of State Dean Rusk, James Reston of *The New York Times*, and Professor Robert Scalapino, a leading authority on Asian politics. The theme of the "Emphasis" program was a "World in Revolution." In carrying out this theme, "Emphasis" published excerpts from the speeches of Bettina Aptheker, a Communist who gained notoriety at the University of California, and Stokely Carmichael, President of the Student Nonviolent Coordinating Committee and an incendiary advocate of violent revolution. To give a balanced view of a "World in Revolution," "Emphasis" carried articles by leading antirevolutionaries such as General Earl G. Wheeler, Chairman of the Joint Chiefs of Staff. After public criticism by certain Alabama legislators, Dr. Rose, in the exercise of his judgment as President of the University of Alabama, took a public stand in support of the right of the University students for academic freedom. Criticism of Dr. Rose for this position by certain state legislators became rather intense. The newspapers widely publicized the controversy to a point that it became a matter of public interest throughout the State of Alabama.

Editor Dickey determined that the Troy State College newspaper, *The Tropolitan*, should be heard on the matter. He prepared and presented to the faculty adviser an editorial supporting the position taken by Dr. Rose. He was instructed by his faculty adviser not to publish such an editorial. Dickey then took the editorial to the head of the English Department at Troy State College. The head of this department approved the publication of Dickey's proposed editorial. Upon returning to the faculty adviser, Dickey was again informed that the editorial could not be published. Dickey then went directly to the president of the college, Ralph Adams, who also determined that the editorial could not be published. It is without controversy in this case that the basis for the denial of Dickey's right to publish his editorial supporting Dr. Rose was a rule that had been invoked at Troy State College to the effect that there could be no editorials written in the school paper which were critical of the Governor of the State of Alabama or the Alabama Legislature. The rule did not prohibit editorials or articles of a laudatory nature concerning the Governor or the Legislature. The rule has been referred to in this case as the "Adams Rule." The theory of the rule, as this Court understands it, is that Troy State College is a public institution owned by the State of Alabama, that the Governor and the legislators are acting for the owner and control of the purse strings, and that for that reason neither the Governor nor the Legislature could be criticized. The faculty adviser furnished substitute material concerning "Raising Dogs in North Carolina" to be published in lieu of Dickey's proposed editorial. Upon being furnished the editorial on the North Carolina dogs, Dickey, as editor of *The Tropolitan*, determined that it was not suitable, and, acting against the specific instructions of his faculty adviser and the president of the college, arranged to have—with exception of the title, "A Lament for Dr. Rose"—the space ordinarily occupied by the editorial left blank, with the word "Censored" diagonally across the blank space. In addition to this conduct, Dickey mailed the censored editorial[3] to a Montgomery newspaper. All parties in this case concede that the editorial is well written and in good taste. However, the evidence in this case reflects that solely because it violated the "Adams Rule," Dickey's conduct, in acting contrary to the advice of the faculty adviser and of President Adams, was termed "willful and deliberate insubordination."

This insubordination is the sole basis for his expulsion and/or suspension.

It is basic in our law in this country that the privilege to communicate concerning a matter of public interest is embraced in the First Amendment right relating to freedom of speech and is constitutionally protected against infringement by state officials. The Fourteenth Amendment to the Constitution protects these First Amendment rights from state infringement, *Thornhill* v. *State of Alabama,* 310 U.S. 88, 60 S.Ct. 736, 84 L.Ed. 1093, and these First Amendment rights extend to school children and students insofar as unreasonable rules are concerned. *West Virginia State Board of Education* v. *Barnette,* 319 U.S. 624, 63 S.Ct. 1178, 87 L.Ed. 1628. Boards of education, presidents of colleges, and faculty advisers are not excepted from the rule that protects students against unreasonable rules and regulations. This Court recognizes that the establishment of an education program requires certain rules and regulations necessary for maintaining an orderly program and operating the institution in a manner conducive to learning. However, the school and school officials have always been bound by the requirement that the rules and regulations *must be reasonable.* Courts may only consider whether rules and regulations that are imposd by school authorities are a reasonable exercise of the power and discretion vested in those authorities. Regulations and rules which are necessary in maintaining order and discipline are always considered reasonable. In the case now before this Court, it is clear that the maintenance of order and discipline of the students attending Troy State College had nothing to do with the rule that was invoked against Dickey. As a matter of fact, the president of the institution, President Adams, testified that his general policy of not criticizing the Governor or the State Legislature under any circumstances, regardless of how reasonable or justified the criticism might be, was not for the purpose of maintaining order and discipline among the students. On this point, President Adams testified that the reason for the rule was that a newspaper could not criticize its owners, and in the case of a state institution the owners were to be considered as the Governor and the members of the Legislature.

With these basic constitutional principles in mind, the conclusion is compelled that the invocation of such a rule against Gary Clinton Dickey that resulted in his expulsion and/or suspension from Troy State College was unreasonable. A state cannot force a college student to forfeit his constitutionally protected right of freedom of expression as a condition to his attending a state-supported institution. State school officials cannot infringe on their students' right of free and unrestricted expression as guaranteed by the Constitution of the United States where the exercise of such right does not "materially and substantially interfere with requirements of appropriate discipline in the operation of the school." *Burnside* v. *Byars,* 363 F.2d 744 (5 Cir. 1966). The defendants in this case cannot punish Gary Clinton Dickey for his exercise of this constitutionally guaranteed right by cloaking his expulsion or suspension in the robe of "insubordination." The attempt to characterize Dickey's conduct, and the basis for their action in expelling him, as "insubordination" requiring rather severe disciplinary action, does not disguise the basic fact that Dickey was expelled from Troy State College for exercising his constitutionally guaranteed right of academic and/or political expression.

The argument by defendants' counsel that Dickey was attempting to take over the operation of the school newspaper ignores the fact that there was no legal obligation on the school authorities to permit Dickey to continue as one of its editors. As a matter of fact, there was no legal obligation on the school authorities to operate a school newspaper. However, since this state-supported institution did elect to operate *The Tropolitan* and did authorize Dickey to be one of its editors, they cannot as officials of the State of Alabama, without violating the First and Fourteenth Amendments to the Constitution of the United States, suspend or expel Dickey from this state-supported institution for his conduct as that conduct is reflected by the facts presented in this case.

As the Supreme Court stated in *West Virginia State Board of Education* v. *Barnette, supra:*

"The Fourteenth Amendment, as now applied to the States, protects the citizen against the State itself and all of its creatures—Boards of Education not excepted. These have, of course, important, delicate, and highly discretionary functions, but none that they may not perform within the limits of the Bill of Rights. That they are educating the young for citizenship is reason for scrupulous protection of Constitutional freedoms of the individual, if we are not to strangle the free mind at its source and teach youth to discount important principles of our government as mere platitudes."

Defendants' argument that Dickey's readmission will jeopardize the discipline in the institution is superficial and completely ignores the greater damage to college students that will result from the imposition of intellectual restraints such as the "Adams Rule" in this case. The imposition of such a restaint as here sought to be imposed upon Dickey and the other students at Troy State College violates the basic principles of academic and political expression as guaranteed by our Constitution. Dr. Rose recognized the importance of this academic and constitutional principle when he determined that as to the University of Alabama, such freedoms must be permitted to flourish. As the Supreme Court stated in *Sweezy* v. *State of New Hampshire,* 354 U.S. 234, 250, 77 S.Ct. 1203, 1211, 1 L.Ed.2d 1311 (1957):

> "We believe that there unquestionably was an invasion of petitioner's liberties in the areas of academic freedom and political expression—areas in which government should be extremely reticent to tread.
>
> "The essentiality of freedom in the community of American universities is almost self-evident. No one should underestimate the vital role in a democracy that is played by those who guide and train our youth. To impose any strait jacket upon the intellectual leaders in our colleges and universities would imperil the future of our Nation. No field of education is so thoroughly comprehended by man that new discoveries cannot yet be made. Particularly is that true in the social sciences, where few, if any, principles are accepted as absolutes. Scholarship cannot flourish in an atmosphere of suspicion and distrust. Teachers and students must always remain free to inquire, to study and to evaluate, to gain new maturity and understanding; otherwise our civilization will stagnate and die."

In accordance with the foregoing, it is the order, judgment and decree of this Court that the action taken by Troy State College, acting through its Student Affairs Committee, on Friday, August 25, 1967, which action denies to Gary Clinton Dickey admission to Troy State College beginning with the fall quarter of 1967, be and the same is hereby declared unconstitutional, void, and is rescinded.

It is further ordered that the defendants immediately reinstate Gary Clinton Dickey as a student in Troy State College, commencing September 11, 1967.

It is further ordered that the defendants, and each of them, their agents, servants, employees, and others acting in concert or participation with them, be and each is hereby enjoined and restrained from denying, upon the basis of his conduct as herein discussed, Gary Clinton Dickey admission to Troy State College as a student and from refusing to allow him to attend as such for the academic year commencing September 11, 1967.

It is further ordered that the costs incurred in this proceeding be and they are hereby taxed against the defendants, for which execution may issue.

NOTES

1. Title 52, § 14 and § 438, Code of Alabama (1940) (Recomp.1958).
2. Counsel for Dickey acknowledged orally in open court that his client had been, after this Court's order of August 17, 1967, accorded procedural due process by the Troy State officials.
3. The complete text of the editorial, "A Lament for Dr. Rose," is as follows:

    "Dr. Frank Rose, president of the University of Alabama, is currently under attack by certain state legislators for his refusal to censor a student publication. The publication entitled, 'Emphasis 67, A World in Revolution,' served as the program for a series of guest speakers and panel discussions held on March 16 and 17 at the University. The publication contained brief biographical sketches of each of the participants, which included Secretary of State Dean Rusk, James Reston of *The New York Times*, and Professor Robert Scalapino, a leading authority on Asian politics.

    "The theme of the 'Emphasis' program was a 'World in Revolution.' In keeping with this theme, the publication carried excerpts from the speeches of Bettina Aptheker, a Communist who gained notoriety at the University of California, and Stokely Carmichael, president of the Student Non-Violent Coordinating Committee, and the incendiary advocate of violent revolution and 'black power.'

    "To give a balanced view of 'A World in Revolution,' the 'Emphasis' publication carried articles by leading antirevolutionaries such as Gen. Earl G. Wheeler, chairman of the Joint Chiefs of Staff, and Roy Wilkins, president of the NAACP and a supporter of nonviolent moderate change.

    "Some of the legislators have read into this publication an attempt by President Rose to condone and abet revolutionary and subversive activity at the University.

    "*The Tropolitan* feels that these legislators have sadly misinterpreted the intent of the publication.

    "Surely, they cannot seriously consider Gen. Wheeler, the highest military officer in the United States, a subversive. Surely, Secretary of State Dean Rusk, who was brought to the University as the keynote speaker on the 'Emphasis' program, and who is currently conducting a war of diplomacy and bullets against Communist subversion in Asia, cannot be labeled a subversive. The very purpose of including excerpted speeches by revolutionaries Carmichael and Aptheker was not to endorse their views, but to present a backdrop against which the phenomenon of revolution could be studied and the problems and the role of the United States in a world in revolution could be defined.

    "*The Tropolitan*, therefore, laments the misinterpretation of the 'Emphasis' program by members of the legislature, and the considerable harassment they have caused Dr. Rose. It is our hope that this episode does not impair his effective leadership at the University or discourage him in his difficult task."

A United States District Court in New York decides for students who had been prohibited by the New Rochelle High School (New York) principal from placing in the school paper an advertisement in opposition to the United States participation in the war in Vietnam. In deciding for the students, the District Court stated: "We have found, from review of its contents, that within the context of the school and educational environment, it is a forum for the dissemination of ideas.... Here, the school paper appears to have been open to free expression of ideas in the news and editorial columns as well as in letters to the editor. It is patently unfair in light of the free speech doctrine to close to the students the forum which they deem effective to present their ideas.... This lawsuit arises at a time when many in the educational community oppose the tactics of the young in securing a political voice. It would be both incongruous and dangerous for this Court to hold that students who wish to express their views on matters intimately related to them, through traditionally accepted nondisruptive modes of communication, may be precluded from doing so by that same adult community."

Zucker v. Panitz, 299 F.Supp. 102 (1969)

METZNER, District Judge:

This action concerns the right of high school students to publish a paid advertisement opposing the war in Vietnam in their school newspaper. The action is brought under 42 U.S.C. §§ 1981 and 1983 declaratory judgment and injunctive relief prohibiting violation of plaintiffs' freedom of speech by the principal of New Rochelle High School, the president of the New Rochelle Board of Education, and the New Rochelle Superintendent of Schools.

Plaintiffs move in the alternative for judgment on the pleadings, summary judgment granting an injunction enjoining interference with the right of students in the high school to place advertisements in the school newspaper or otherwise to express their views on public issues, an injunction *pendente lite* restraining interference with publication of the proposed advertisement, or such other relief as the court deems proper.

A group of New Rochelle High School students, led by plaintiff Richard Orentzel, formed an *Ad Hoc Student Committee Against the War in Vietnam.* The group sought to publish an advertisement in opposition to the war in the student newspaper, *The Huguenot Herald,* in November 1967, offering to pay the standard student rate. The text of the proposed advertisement is as follows: "The United States government is pursuing a policy in Viet Nam which is both repugnant to moral and international law and dangerous to the future of humanity. We can stop it. We must stop it." The editorial board of the newspaper, which was then headed by plaintiff Laura Zucker, approved publication of the advertisement, but the principal of the school, Dr. Adolph Panitz, directed that the advertisement not be published. The affidavit of plaintiff Orentzel alleges that the committee still desires to publish the advertisement and has been informed that the newspaper would accept it but for the directive of the principal.

The gravamen of the dispute concerns the function and content of the school newspaper. Plaintiffs allege that the purpose of the *Huguenot Herald* is *inter alia,* "to provide a forum for the dissemination of ideas and information by and to the students of New Rochelle High School." Therefore, prohibition of the advertisement constitutes a constitutionally proscribed abridgement of their freedom of speech.

The defendants take issue with this characterization of the newspaper. They advance the theory that the publication "is not a newspaper in the usual sense" but is a "beneficial educational device" developed as part of the curriculum and intended to inure primarily to the benefit of those who compile, edit and publish it.[1] They assert a longstanding policy of the school administration which limits news items and editorials to matters pertaining to the high school and its activities. Similarly, "no advertising will be permitted which expresses a point of view on any subject not related to New Rochelle High School." Even paid advertising in support of student government nominees is prohibited and only purely commercial advertising is accepted. This policy is alleged to be reasonable and necessary to preserve the journal as an educational device and prevent it from becoming mainly an organ for the dissemination of news and views unrelated to the high school.

In sum, defendants' main factual argument is that the war is not a school-related activity, and therefore not qualified for news, editorial and advertising treatment. They have submitted issues of the newspaper from September 1968 to April 1969 to illustrate school-related subjects and the absence of other than purely commercial advertising.

If the *Huguenot Herald's* contents were truly as flaccid as the defendants' argument implies, it would indeed be a sterile publication. Furthermore, its function as an educational device surely could not be served if such were the content of the paper. However, it is clear that the newspaper is more than a mere activity time and place sheet. The factual core of defendants' argument falls with a perusal of the newspapers submitted to the court. They illustrate that the newspaper is being used as a communications media regarding controversial topics and that the teaching of journalism includes dissemination of such ideas. Such a school paper is truly an educational device.

For instance, on October 18, 1968, an article on draft board procedures, including discussion of the basis for graduate deferments as well as problems of initial registration appeared, as well as an article concerning a poll of high school students on national political candidates and the war. On January 31, 1969, the paper included an item that the principal had placed literature on the draft in the school library. On April 25, 1969, the paper reported on a draft information assembly and informed its readers of the availability of draft counseling outside the school. Moreover, items have appeared on the following: the grant of money by the students' General Organization to Eldridge Cleaver to speak at Iona College (vetoed by the principal); school fundraising activities for Biafra; federal aid for preschool through high school education; meeting of a YMCA-sponsored group whose purpose is discussion of such issues as racial change, violence and political action possibilities; a state assemblyman's proposal for an elected Board of Education; the proposal of several educators for community involvement as part of the educational process; types of narcotics and their effects; high school drug use; community treatment facilities; establishment of a new anti-Establishment high school newspaper; and a letter to the editor that a poll should be held to determine whether the newspaper should serve more than its present function and become an instrument and advocate of student power.

The presence of articles concerning the draft and student opinion of United States participation in the war shows that the war is considered to be a school-related subject. This being the case, there is no logical reason to permit news stories on the subject and preclude student advertising.

Defendants further argue that since no advertising on political matters is permitted, the plaintiffs have no cause for discontent. It is undisputed that no such advertising has been permitted, but this is not dispositive. In *Wirta* v. *Alameda-Contra Costa Transit District,* 68 Cal.2d 51, 64 Cal. Rptr. 430, 434 P.2d 982 (1967) (*en banc*) (rehearing denied 1968), the court held that where motor coaches were a forum for commercial advertising, refusal to accept a proposed peace message violated the First Amendment guarantee of free speech.[2] It said:

"[D]efendants, having opened a forum for the expression of ideas by providing facilities for advertisements on its buses, cannot for reasons of administrative convenience decline to accept advertisements expressing opinions and beliefs within the ambit of First Amendment protection." Id. 64 Cal.Rptr. at 433, 434 P.2d at 985.

* * *

"Not only does the district's policy prefer certain classes of protected ideas over others but it goes even further and affords total freedom of the forum to mercantile messages while banning the vast majority of opinions and beliefs extant which enjoy First Amendment protection because of their non-commercialism." Id., 64 Cal.Rptr. at 434, 434 P.2d at 986.

Cf. *Danskin* v. *San Diego Unified School District,* 28 Cal.2d 536, 171 P.2d 885 (1946).

Defendants would have the court find that the school's action is protected because plaintiffs have no right of access to the school newspaper. They argue that the recent Supreme Court case of *Tinker* v. *Des Moines Independent Community School District,* 393 U.S. 503, 89 S.Ct. 733, 21 L.Ed.2d 731 (Feb. 24, 1969), held only that students have the same rights inside the schoolyard that they have as citizens. Therefore, since citizens as yet have no right of access to the private press, plaintiffs are entitled to no greater privilege.³ In *Tinker,* the plaintiffs were suspended from school for wearing black armbands to protest the war in Vietnam. The Court held that the wearing of armbands was closely akin to pure speech and that First Amendment rights, *"applied in light of the special characteristics of the school environment,* are available to teachers and students." Id. at 506, 89 S.Ct. at 736 (emphasis added). The principle of free speech is not confined to classroom discussion:

"The principal use to which the schools are dedicated is to accommodate students during prescribed hours for the purpose of certain types of activities. Among those activities is personal intercommunication among the students. This is not only an inevitable part of the process of attending school. *It is also an important part of the educational process.* A student's rights therefore, do not embrace merely the classroom hours. When he is in the cafeteria, or on the playing field, or on the campus during the authorized hours, he may express his opinions, even on controversial subjects like the conflict in Vietnam, if he does so without 'materially and substantially interfer[ing] with the requirement of appropriate discipline in the operation of the school' and without colliding with the rights of others." Id. at 512, 89 S.Ct. at 739 (emphasis added).

Defendants have told the court that the *Huguenot Herald* is not a newspaper in the usual sense, but is part of the curriculum and an educational device. However, it is inconsistent for them to also espouse the position that the school's action is protected because there is no general right of access to the private press.⁴

We have found, from review of its contents, that within the context of the school and educational environment, it is a forum for the dissemination of ideas. Our problem then, as in *Tinker,* "lies in the area where students in the exercise of First Amendment rights collide with the rules of the school authorities." Id. at 507, 89 S.Ct. at 737. Here, the school paper appears to have been open to free expression of ideas in the news and editorial columns as well as in letters to the editor. It is patently unfair in light of the free speech doctrine to close to the students the forum which they deem effective to present their ideas.⁵ The rationale of *Tinker* carries beyond the facts in that case.

Tinker also disposes of defendants' contention that cases involving advertising in public facilities are inapposite because a school and a school newspaper are not public facilities in the same sense as buses and terminals (see *Wirta, Kissinger* and *Wolin,* cited herein)—that is, they invite only a portion of the public.

This lawsuit arises at a time when many in the educational community oppose the tactics of the young in securing a political voice. It would be both incongruous and dangerous for this court to hold that students who wish to express their views on matters intimately related to them, through traditionally accepted nondisruptive modes of communication, may be precluded from doing so by that same adult community.⁶

Plaintiff's motion for summary judgment is granted. Settle order.

NOTES

1. Defendants' argument that the journal would be just as valuable an educational tool if it were compiled and then consigned to the files without publication is without merit, since in fact the paper is published and sold at 10 cents per copy or $2 per subscription. Moreover, the paper includes letters to the editor, clearly a part of the journalistic experience which would be truncated were the newspaper merely a dummy.
2. See also *Kissinger* v. *New York City Transit Authority,* 274 F.Supp. 438 (S.D.N.Y.1967); *Wolin* v. *Port of New York Authority,* 268 F.Supp. 855 (S.D.N.Y.1967), aff'd, 392 F.2d 83 (2d Cir. 1968).
3. See generally Barron, Access to the Press—A New First Amendment Right, 80 Harv.L.Rev. 1641 (1967).
4. Different policy considerations govern whether a privately owned newspaper has an affirmative duty to grant access to its pages, and whether a school newspaper has such a duty. For instance, there would be involved the thorny issue of finding state action, a problem which does not exist regarding a school newspaper.
5. The argument that alternative modes of expression exist—for instance, conversations or armbands—thus permitting suppression of the chosen mode, is without merit and has been consistently disregarded by the courts. See, e.g., *Tinker* v. *Des Moines Independent Community School District,* 393 U.S. 503, 89 S.Ct. 733, 21 L.Ed.2d 731 (Feb. 24, 1969); *Wirta* v. *Alameda-Contra Costa Transit District,* 68 Cal.2d 51, 64 Cal.Rptr. 430, 434 P.2d 982 (1967).
6. In *Tinker,* the Court noted that "the meeting at which the school principals decided to issue the contested regulation was called in response to a student's statement to the journalism teacher in one of the schools that he wanted to write an article on Vietnam and have it published in the school paper. (The student was dissuaded.)" 393 U.S. at 510, 89 S.Ct. at 738.

A United States District Court in Massachusetts decides for a college student who had challenged a Fitchburg State College policy that required issues of the campus newspaper be submitted to an advisory board composed of two faculty members for prior approval. In deciding for Antonelli, an editor-in-chief of the college newspaper, the District Court concluded: "Since (a) there is no right to editorial control by administration officials flowing from the fact that *The Cycle* [the college newspaper] is college sponsored and state supported, and (b) defendant has not shown that circumstances attributable to the school environment make necessary more restrictive measures than generally permissable under the First Amendment, the Court holds and declares that the prior submission to the advisory board of material intended to be published in *The Cycle*, in order that the board may decide whether it complies with 'responsible freedom of the press' or is obscene, may not be constitutionally required either by means of withholding funds derived from student activity fees or otherwise."

Antonelli v. *Hammond,* 308 F.Supp. 1329 (1970)

GARRITY, District Judge.

This action is brought under 42 U.S.C. § 1983 and its jurisdictional counterpart 28 U.S.C. § 1343(3). Plaintiff is John Antonelli, a student at Fitchburg State College, a state-supported school of higher education in the Commonwealth of Massachusetts.[1] He was the editor-in-chief of *The Cycle*, the campus newspaper, when a dispute as to the control of the newspaper arose between the student editorial staff and the college president, defendant James J. Hammond. The complaint in substance is that the defendant Hammond through his power over the purse is censoring the material for publication by subjecting it to the prior approval of a faculty advisory committee. It is also alleged that president Hammond refused to release the usual funds to pay for the printing of an issue of *The Cycle* containing an article the defendant felt was obscene. Contending that this action is in violation of the First and Fourteenth Amendments to the Constitution of the United States, plaintiff is seeking injunctive relief and a declaratory judgment under 28 U.S.C. §§ 2201 and 2202. The case was tried without jury; several witnesses testified for both parties and the court received memoranda of law, affidavits and certain stipulated facts.

Findings of Fact

1. In the spring of 1969 plaintiff Antonelli was duly elected by the student body of Fitchburg State College to serve for one year as the editor-in-chief of the campus newspaper. At the start of the fall semester in September 1969 Antonelli changed the name of the paper from *Kampus Vue* to *The Cycle*. The change in name was indicative of a change in policy and format. While *Kampus Vue's* focus had been primarily on student news and events on campus, *The Cycle* sought to explore and comment upon areas of broader social and political impact.

2. *The Cycle* is not financially independent. It depends on an allocation of a portion of revenues derived from compulsory student activity fees. In accordance with Mass.G.L. c. 73, § 1B, these fees and any receipts from the student activities themselves are retained in a revolving fund to be expended "as the president of the college may direct in furthering the activities from which the fees and receipts were derived...." Prior to the present dispute, the publication costs and other bills of the student newspaper at Fitchburg State College had been consistently paid from this fund. Without this money the campus newspaper cannot be published on a regular basis.

3. On September 21, 1969 an article entitled "Black Moochie" written by Eldridge Cleaver and originally appearing in *Ramparts Magazine,* Vol. 8, No. 4, October 1969, was included in the material for Vol. 1, No. 3, of *The Cycle* submitted to Raymond Plante, the paper's usual printer. Mr. Plante, whose daughter is a student at the college, strenuously objected to the theme of and four-letter words generously used in the text of "Black Moochie." He refused to print the article, preferring to smash his presses first, and he telephoned president Hammond to inform him of the content of the edition which the students were asking him to print. Soon thereafter the defendant came to Plante's office and expressed his own displeasure at the proposed issue of *The Cycle.* He felt that the "Black Moochie" article was "garbage" and obscene and not fit for publication in the campus newspaper. President Hammond had not been pleased with the change in the focus and format that previous issues of *The Cycle* had brought to the campus newspaper. He stated that publication should provide an opportunity for students to develop skills in journalism, should not consist primarily of compilations published previously elsewhere and should not serve as a vehicle for the dissemination of obscene material.[2] On this occasion and thereafter the defendant indicated to the plaintiff and others that he felt morally obligated to use his powers over the allocation of funds for student activites under G.L. c. 73, § 1B, to see that the money was spent properly and to prevent its expenditure on the publication of such "trash" as "Black Moochie." He stated that therefore he would not consider paying for articles like "Black Moochie" and would refuse to allow future editions of *The Cycle* to be published unless he or someone acting with his authority approved of all the matter to be included in the newspaper prior to its being printed.

4. In order that some form of student publication continue during the pendency of these proceedings, and under protest, plaintiff agreed to cooperate with an advisory board of two faculty members, Drs. Greene and Quigley, who were appointed by the defendant to exercise their judgment as to the "responsible freedom of the press" in the student newspaper. Under president Hammond's plan, funds from student fees would not be forthcoming for future issues until the issues were approved by the advisory board. Drs. Greene and Quigley were authorized by the defendant to certify the necessary expenditures and approve their payment only after they exercised their judgment as to the "responsible freedom of the press" in the student newspaper. President Hammond expressed his willingness to abide by the judgment of the advisory board.

5. The primary function of the advisory board is to pass on the acceptability of material intended to be published in *The Cycle* and to prevent the printing of articles which the administration feels are not fit for the campus newspaper. No guidelines of acceptability were established and no standards limit the discretion of the two faculty members as they pass judgment on the material submitted to them. No procedure was designed whereby the reasonableness or validity of a board decision might be tested or reviewed.

6. Prior to the present controversy, the officials at Fitchburg State College had left control over the content of the campus newspaper entirely to the student editors. Only with the attempted publication of "Black Moochie" did president Hammond feel it necessary to interpose administrative control in the form of the advisory board.

7. The issue of *The Cycle* containing the article entitled "Black Moochie" was in fact printed and widely circulated both at Fitchburg State College and elsewhere. A different printer did the printing and the costs were not paid for from the student activity funds. President Hammond never authorized payments relating to this issue of *The Cycle.* The publication came about through the combined efforts of the editors of the newspapers of five Massachusetts state colleges, including Fitchburg. There was no evidence that any of the funds expended in connection with this issue belonged to plaintiff or that he has any legal liability with respect to them.

8. On November 7, 1969 plaintiff repudiated his agreement to cooperate with the advisory board and he and the entire editorial board submitted their resignations. This action was announced in the one issue of *The Cycle* published under the control of the advisory board, Vol. 1, No. 4. It was prompted by disputes with the two faculty members as to the newspaper's financial responsibility and budgetary mechanics.

9. Although the conflict leading to the resignations did not concern material submitted for publication and although the board neither rejected nor censored in any way any of the material actually proposed for the one issue printed under its auspices, the controversy over censorship still colored the relationship of the student editors and representatives of the administration.

10. On November 20, 1969 the resignations were accepted by the student government association of the college. However, in an attempt to avoid the threat of mootness, a special meeting of the student government was called on November 25, 1969 and the previous recognition of the resignations was unanimously withdrawn. The acceptance of the resignations was now to be deemed effective December 17, 1969 rather than November 20.

11. This is not the only indication of support that the student government association has shown for *The Cycle* and the plaintiff in the dispute over the control of the content of the campus newspaper. On October 14, during a time of cessation in publication, an open meeting of the student government association was held and a motion was debated that another publication, edited by one who opposed *The Cycle*, be given funds from the newspaper budget to publish a weekly newsletter until the fate of *The Cycle* was decided. This motion was virtually unanimously defeated.

12. *The Cycle* has not been published since the announcement of the resignations on November 7. The office of editor-in-chief will have been officially vacant since December 17, 1969. Although he would have to be reelected by the student body, Antonelli testified that he would be willing to run again and serve as editor-in-chief if the advisory board were eliminated.

13. At no time has any disciplinary action been taken by Fitchburg State College against the plaintiff or any other student in connection with the publication of *The Cycle*.

Conclusions of Law

The first question for decision is whether the case is moot. "Simply stated, a case is moot when the issues presented are no longer 'live' or the parties lack a legally cognizable interest in the outcome. See E. Borchard, Declaratory Judgments 35–37 (2nd ed. 1941)." *Powell* v. *McCormack*, 1969, 395 U.S. 486, 496–497, 89 S.Ct. 1944, 23 L.Ed.2d 491. See also *Maryland Casualty Co.* v. *Pacific Coal and Oil Co.*, 1941, 312 U.S. 270, 273, 61 S.Ct. 510, 85 L.Ed. 826; *Golden* v. *Zwickler*, 1969, 394 U.S. 103, 108, 89 S.Ct. 956, 22 L.Ed.2d 113. As argued by the defendant, there has been full publication and circulation of Vol. 1, No. 3 of *The Cycle* including Eldridge Cleaver's "Black Moochie"; plaintiff did not spend any of his own money and is not liable in law to anyone for the expenses of such publication; the advisory board has not in fact censored any material submitted to it nor denied funds concerning the printing of any article; plaintiff has resigned as editor-in-chief and *The Cycle* has not functioned since the announcement of his resignation. Under these circumstances, the court rules that plaintiff has no legally cognizable interest in a decision by this court as to the constitutionality of president Hammond's efforts to prevent publication of the issue of *The Cycle* containing "Black Moochie."

However, plaintiff asserts a further and continuing interest, i.e., the right to be free from the burden of submitting future issues of *The Cycle* to the advisory board for its prior approval. The nature of the legal interest inherent in this claim is such that it is not affected by the factors which moot his other claims. This is true notwithstanding plaintiff's resignation, which was largely due to his unwillingness to "clear" the contents of *The Cycle* with the advisory board. The prospect of his reelection as editor is not at all insubstantial, considering that he was unopposed last year and has enjoyed the overwhelming support of the student government association. "There is and there ought to be no rule of constitutional standing that, in order to construct a justiciable 'case,' a plaintiff must submit to the very burden whose validity he wishes to attack." Bickel, Foreword: The Passive Virtues, The Supreme Court, 1960 Term, 75 Harv.L. Rev. 40, 52–53. See *Staub* v. *City of Baxley*, 1958, 355 U.S. 313, 78 S.Ct. 277, 2 L.Ed.2d 302; *Times Film Corp.* v. *City of Chicago*, 1961, 365 U.S. 43, 81 S.Ct. 391, 5 L.Ed.2d 403. We conclude that plaintiff has a continuing personal stake in the outcome of these proceedings[3] and that the case is not moot.

Turning to the merits of the plaintiff's claim to freedom from censorial supervision by the advisory board, we note first the absence of any express limitation on the board's powers to review and approve. All manner of intended publication must be submitted; there is no exception, so there is nothing that does not come within the censor's purview. Therefore, the powers actually conferred could presumably be used, without change in form or need for expansion, to achieve complete control of the content of the newspaper. However, there is no indication of an intention to go beyond excising obscenity, and in any event, for purposes of this case, we must construe the powers conferred upon the advisory board by the defendant in the narrowest light possible, i. e., censorial only over the obscene. This is essential because the plaintiff claims freedom from an obligation to submit anything for prior approval.[4]

No matter how narrow the function of the advisory board, it constituted a direct previous restraint of expression and as such there is a "heavy presumption against its constitutional validity." *Bantam Books, Inc.* v. *Sullivan*, 1963, 372 U.S. 58, 70, 83 S.Ct. 631, 639, 9 L.Ed.2d 584, and cases there cited. The general rules are clear, " . . . [L]iberty of the press, historically considered and taken up by the Federal Constitution, has meant, principally although not exclusively, immunity from previous restraints or censorship." *Near* v. *Minnesota*, 1931, 283 U.S. 697, 716, 51 S.Ct. 625, 631, 75 L.Ed. 1357. Any limitation on the constitutional immunity from prior restraints "is the exception; it is to be closely confined so as to preclude what may fairly be deemed licensing or censorship." *Kingsley Books, Inc.* v. *Brown*, 1957, 354 U.S. 436, 441, 77 S.Ct. 1325, 1328, 1 L.Ed.2d 1469.

It is true that the advisory board proposes to suppress only obscene writings and that obscenity does not fall within the area of constitutionally protected speech or press, see, e. g., *Alberts* v. *California,* decided with *Roth* v. *United States,* 1957, 354 U.S. 476, 485, 77 S.Ct. 1304, 1 L.Ed.2d 1498. However, the manner and means of achieving the proposed suppression are of crucial importance. Cf. *Curtis Publishing Co.* v. *Butts,* 1967, 388 U.S. 130, 149, 87 S.Ct. 1975, 18 L.Ed.2d 1094. Whenever the state takes any measure to regulate obscenity it must conform to procedures calculated to avoid the danger that protected expression will be caught in the regulatory dragnet. See, e g., *Marcus* v. *Search Warrants,* 1961, 367 U.S. 717, 731, 81 S.Ct. 1708, 6 L.Ed.2d 1127; *Bantam Books, Inc.* v. *Sullivan, supra; Quantity of Copies of Books* v. *Kansas,* 1964, 378 U.S. 205, 84 S.Ct. 1723, 12 L.Ed.2d 809. See generally, Monaghan, First Amendment Due Process, 1970, 83 Harv. L.Rev. 518. Such procedures are constitutionally required themselves—going to the very nature of the First Amendment rights. "It is characteristic of the freedoms of expression in general that they are vulnerable to gravely damaging yet barely visible encroachments. Our insistence that regulations of obscenity scrupulously embody the most rigorous procedural safeguards . . . is therefore but a special instance of the larger principle that the freedoms of expression must be ringed about with adequate bulwarks." *Bantam Books, Inc.* v. *Sullivan, supra,* 372 U.S. at 66, 83 S.Ct. at 637.

The type of procedural safeguards required by the First Amendment was indicated in *Freedman* v. *Maryland,* 1965, 380 U.S. 51, 85 S.Ct. 734, 13 L.Ed.2d 649. There the appellant had been convicted for exhibiting a motion picture without submitting it to the Maryland State Board of Censors for prior approval. In sustaining the challenge to the constitutionality of the licensing system because of procedural inadequancies, the Supreme Court listed three minimal requirements: first, that the censor bear the burden of showing the film to be obscene; second, that the requirement of advance submission not be so administered as to give an effect of finality to the censor's adverse determination; and third, that the procedure ultimately assure a prompt final judicial determination.[5]

Nothing of the sort is included in the system devised by the defendant for passing upon the contents of *The Cycle*. It lacks even the semblance of any of the safeguards the Supreme Court has demanded.[6] The advisory board bears no burden other than exercising its judgment; there is no appeal within the system from any particular decision; and there is no provision for prompt final judicial determination. Cf. *Kingsley Books, Inc.* v. *Brown, supra.*

Indeed, final responsiblity rests with two faculty members, serving at the pleasure of the defendant, who so far as the evidence showed are wholly unfamiliar with the complex tests of obscenity established by the Suprme Court in cases such as *Roth* v. *United States,* 1957, 354 U.S. 476, 77 S.Ct. 1304, and the *Memoirs, Ginzburg* and *Mishkin* cases, 1966, 383 U.S. 413–518, 86 S.Ct. 975, 942, 958, 16 L.Ed.2d 1, 31, 56. Accordingly, the court concludes that the defendant's establishment of the advisory board is prima facie an unconstitutional exercise of state power.

If the advisory board of *The Cycle* is to withstand constitutional challenge, it can only be because there is something either in the institutional needs of a public university or in the nature of a newspaper funded from student activity fees that justifies a limitation of free expression and thereby permits an exercise of state power plainly unwarranted if applied to the press generally.

Free speech does not mean wholly unrestricted speech and the constitutional rights of students may be modified by regulations reasonably designed to adjust these rights to the needs of the school environment. The exercise of rights by individuals must yield when they are incompatible with the school's obligation to maintain the order and discipline necessary for the success of the educational process. However, any infringement of individual constitutional freedoms must be adequately related to this legitimate interest. See, e. g., *Tinker* v. *Des Moines School Dist.,* 1969, 393 U.S. 503, 89 S.Ct. 733, 21 L.Ed.2d 731; *Burnside* v. *Byars,* 5 Cir. 1966, 363 F.2d 744; *Brooks* v. *Auburn University,* 1969, M.D.Ala., 296 F.Supp. 188.

No such justification has been shown in the instant case. Obscenity in a campus newspaper is not the type of occurrence apt to be significantly disruptive of an orderly and disciplined educational process. Furthermore, assuming that a college administration has a sufficient educationally oriented reason to prevent the circulation of obscenity on campus, there has been no showing that the harm from obscenity in a college setting is so much greater than in the public forum that it outweighs the danger to free expression inherent in censorship without procedural safeguards. If anything, the contrary would seem to be true. The university setting of college-age students being exposed to a wide range of intellectual experience creates a relatively mature marketplace for the interchange of ideas so that the free speech clause of the First Amendment with its underlying assumption that there is positive social value in an open forum seems particularly appropriate. See *Brooks* v. *Auburn University, supra,* 296 F.Supp. at 192.

There is an added element in the present case: the expenses of publishing *The Cycle* are payable by the college from funds received from compulsory student activity fees. Does this circumstance significantly alter either the rights of the students or the powers of the college president over the campus press? We think not. Contrary to the defendant's contention, Mass.G.L. c. 73, § 1B, does not make him ultimately responsible for what is printed in the campus newspaper. Under that section, student activity fees "shall be expended as the president of the college may direct in furthering the activities from which the fees and receipts were derived;"

* * *

This imposes no duty on the president to ratify or to pass judgment on a particular activity. The discretion granted is in the determination whether the funds to be expended actually further the activities to which they are inteded to be applied. Once that determination has been made, the expenditure is mandatory.

We are well beyond the belief that any manner of state regulation is permissible simply because it involves an activity which is a part of the university structure and is financed with funds controlled by the administration. The state is not necessarily the unrestrained master of what it creates and fosters. Thus in cases concerning school-supported publications or the use of school facilities, the courts have refused to recognize as permissible any regulations infringing free speech when not shown to be necessarily related to the maintenance of order and discipline within the educational process. See, e. g., *Dickey* v. *Alabama State Board of Education,* 1967, M.D. Ala., 273 F.Supp. 613; *Snyder* v. *Board of Trustees of University of Illinois,* 1968, N.D.Ill., 286 F.Supp. 927; *Brooks* v. *Auburn University,* 1969, M.D.A.a., 296 F.Supp. 188; *Zucker* v. *Panitz,* 196, S.D.N.Y., 299 F.Supp. 102; *Smith* v. *University of Tennessee,*1969, E.D. Tenn., 300 F.Supp. 777; *Close* v. *Lederle,* 1969, D.Mass., 303 F.Supp. 1109.

These decisions do not stand for the proposition that a state college adminstration has no more control over the campus newspaper than it would have over a private publication disseminated on campus. In the very creation of an activity involving media of communication, the state regulates to some degree the form of expression fostered. But the creation of the form does not give birth also to the power to mold its substance. For example, it may be lawful in the interest of providing students with the opportunity to develop their own writing and journalistic skills, to restrict publication in a campus newspaper to articles written by students. Such a restriction might be reasonably related to the educational process. See generally, Developments in The Law—Academic Freedom, 1968, 81 Harv.L.Rev. 1045, 1128–1134. But to tell a student what thoughts he may communicate is another matter. Having fostered a campus newspaper, the state may not impose arbitrary restrictions on the matter to be communicated. See *Zucker* v. *Panitz, supra.* What was said in *Tinker* v. *Des Moines School Dist., supra,* where the form of expression was the wearing of black armbands, is equally applicable here. "In our system, students may not be regarded as closed-circuit recipients of only that which the State chooses to communicate. They may not be confined to the expression of those sentiments that are officially approved. In the absence of a specific showing of constitutionally valid reasons to regulate their speech, students are entitled to freedom of expression of their views." 393 U.S. 511, 89 S.Ct. 739.

Because of the potentially great social value of a free student voice in an age of student awareness and unrest, it would be inconsistent with basic assumptions of First Amendment freedoms to permit a campus newspaper to be simply a vehicle for ideas the state or the college administration deems appropriate. Power to prescribe classroom curricula in state universities[7] may not be transferred to areas not designed to be part of the curriculum.

Accordingly, since (a) there is no right to editorial control by adminstration officials flowing from the fact that *The Cycle* is college sponsored and state supported, and (b) defendant has not shown that circumstances attributable to the school environment make necessary more restrictive measures than generally permissible under the First Amendment, the court holds and declares that the prior submission to the advisory board of material intended to be published in *The Cycle,* in order that the board may decide whether it complies with "responsible freedom of the press" or is obscene, may not be constitutionally required either by means of withholding funds derived from student activity fees or otherwise.

The court declines at this time to issue any injunctive relief. Defendant is a highly placed and responsible public official, and there is no reason to believe that he will not abide by the law as herein declared. Cf. *Smith* v. *University of Tennessee, supra.*

NOTES

1. The complaint was originally brought also in the name of the paper's editorial board. After hearing the court allowed defendant's motion to strike the editorial board as a plaintiff. The board exists solely at the fiat of the editor-in-chief who alone is elected by the student body. The members of the board are merely agents of the editor chosen by him to assist in publishing the campus newspaper.
2. At the trial, defendant, apparently instructed by his attorney, no longer contended that the "Black Moochie"

article was obscene. In this he was correct. See, e. g., *Keefe* v. *Geanakos*, 418 F.2d 359, 1 Cir., Nov. 12, 1969.
3. In view of this ruling, there is no need to elaborate on the possible relaxation of this standard when, as here, constitutional claims are raised. See, e. g., *Marchand* v. *Director, U.S. Probation Office,* 421 F.2d 331, 1 Cir., Jan. 13, 1970; *Esteban* v. *Central Missouri State College,* 8 Cir. 1969, 415 F.2d 1077, 1079 n. 1; *Sibron* v. *New York,* 1968, 392 U.S. 40, 88 S.Ct. 1889, 20 L.Ed.2d 917.
4. It follows that plaintiff's claim cannot succeed unless the imposition of any prior restraint by this board is impermissible. Cf. *Times Film Corp.* v. *City of Chicago,* 1961, 365 U.S. 43, 81 S.Ct. 391.
5. If anything, safeguards are more essential to protect publishers of a student newspaper than distributors of a motion picture. There the substantial investment involved in producing a movie proves an obvious impetus for the pressing of constitutional claims which is absent in the context of a student newspaper. Therefore the effective finality of a censor's decision regarding the content of a student newspaper is all the more probable and consequently so is the danger that protected expression will be suppressed.
6. Under the circumstances, we need not decide whether adequate procedural safeguards could ever be formulated supporting prior restraint of a weekly newspaper. It is extremely doubtful. Newspaper censorship in any form seems essentially incompatible with freedom of the press.
7. There is, of course, no occasion here to examine the nature and extent of the power of a state university over its curriculum. See generally, Developments in the Law—Academic Freedom, *supra* at 1051–1054. See also *Keyishian* v. *Board of Regents,* 1967, 385 U.S. 589, 87 S.Ct. 675, 17 L.Ed.2d 629; *Epperson* v. *Arkansas,*1 968, 393 U.S. 97, 89 S.Ct. 266, 21 L.Ed.2d 228.

A United States District Court in Maryland decides for University of Maryland students who had challenged the University's refusal to permit the publication of an issue of *Argus,* the University's student feature magazine, with a picture upon its cover of a burning American flag. In concluding that the Maryland flag desecration statute could not be applied by University officials to prohibit future publication of *Argus* containing "contents of the type excised from the December, 1969 issue," the District Court asserted: "While the student press may not 'enjoy the same privilege of nonmalicious misreporting afforded to critics of public figures under *The New York Times* decision and its progeny,' . . . there must be a showing that suppression of the contents of a student magazine is necessary to preserve order and discipline before such suppression can constitutionally be permitted. . . . In the total absence of any such showing, we hold that the Maryland statute involved in this case was unconstitutionally applied when the University officials, upon advice of Maryland's Attorney General, prohibited the use of the proposed cover."

Korn v. *Elkins,* 317 F.Supp. 138 (1970)

KAUFMAN, District Judge

No person shall publicly mutilate, defile, defy, trample upon, or by word or act cast contempt upon any such flag, standard, color, ensign or shield [of the United States or of the State of Maryland].
Md. Ann. Code art. 27, § 83 (1967 Repl. Vol.). The definition of "flag, standard, color, ensign or shield" includes any "copy, picture or representation thereof." Md. Ann. Code art. 27, § 81 (1967 Repl. Vol.). Similar statutes have been enacted by the federal government, 18 U.S.C. § 700, and by each of the states. Prosser, Desecration of the American Flag, 3 Ind. Legal Forum 160, 198–99 n. 208 (1969).

Plaintiffs, undergraduate students attending the College Park campus of the University of Maryland, and officers or members of the Editorial Board of *Argus,* the University's student feature magazine, challenge herein the refusal of the University to permit the publication of an issue of *Argus* with a picture upon its cover of a burning American flag. Jurisdiction is founded upon 28 U.S.C. § 1343. This three-judge court was convened pursuant to 28 U.S.C. §§ 2281 and 2284 to consider plaintiffs' request for declaratory and injunctive relief based on plaintiffs' contention that the aforesaid Maryland statute is unconstitutional.[1] Defendants, respectively the President, Vice-President for Administrative Affairs, and Director of Procurement of the University, have moved to dismiss the within action and have submitted in support of that motion an affidavit of the University's President, Dr. Elkins, categorically denying that there is any rule, regulation or custom of the University of Maryland prohibiting a student publication from containing a photograph or other depiction of a burning United States flag. Since the parties have stipulated in open court that there is no genuine issue as to any material fact, this Court will render summary judgment, pursuant to Rules 12(b) and 56 of the Federal Rules of Civil Procedure.

Publication of the magazine *Argus* is the responsibility of its student editors. Four issues of the magazine are published each year and distributed free of charge on the College Park campus of the University of Maryland. The magazine is financed from funds collected as "student activity fees," which each student attending the University of Maryland at College Park is required to pay, and also from the sale of commercial advertising which appears in the magazine. Funds collected as student activity fees are allocated to various student activities by the Student

Government Administration of the University, and checks in payment of the activities are drawn by the University on those funds which are deposited in the custody of the Comptroller of the State of Maryland. The amount allocated to *Argus* for the 1969–70 school year was approximately $12,000. In October, 1969, plaintiffs met with a representative of the defendant Plummer, Director of Procurement, Purchasing Department of the University, to arrange for a printer for *Argus*. Bids were received and a contract for the printing was awarded to Guthrie Lithograph Company, Washington, D. C. In November, 1969, after the "paste-ups" for the first 1969–70 issue of Argus were delivered to Guthrie Lithograph by the magazine editors, Guthrie refused to print the issue because it objected to the photographs on the cover and in the photograph feature section. Guthrie informed the University purchasing department that Guthrie believed that printing such material would subject it to criminal prosecution under the above-quoted Maryland statute.

The University purchasing department proceeded to procure another printer, McGregor & Werner, Inc. However, shortly thereafter, on December 5, 1969, defendant Plummer informed plaintiffs that the Attorney General of Maryland had advised Dr. Elkins that the publication of the cover would constitute a violation of the state statute prohibiting desecration of the flag of the United States, and could subject "those persons responsible to the prescribed criminal penalty." The only part of the magazine submitted to the Attorney General was the cover. Plummer also called McGregor & Werner and effectively stopped the printing of the cover by indicating that the University would not pay for the work if the cover were printed. No boards, committee, faculty member, or administrator of the University had ever, prior to the afore-related developments, censored *Argus* in any way. Not wishing to delay publication, plaintiffs then revised the cover. On or about December 17, 1969, the first 1969–70 issue of *Argus* appeared bearing the word "censored" across a plain white cover. No disciplinary action of any kind has been taken against any of the plaintiffs by the University.

In *Street* v. *New York,* 394 U.S. 576, 89 S.Ct. 1354, 22 L.Ed.2d 572 (1969), the Supreme Court reversed a criminal conviction under a New York statute containing language almost identical with that in the Maryland statue involved herein. In *Street,* the defendant, upon hearing of the shooting of James Meredith, the civil rights leader, burned an American flag on a street corner of New York City and made statements to the crowd which gathered, such as: "If they let that happen to Meredith, we don't need an American flag." (at 579, 89 S.Ct. at 1359). Mr. Justice Harlan, writing for the majority, stated that it was "unnecessary to consider" Street's contentions that the statute was facially unconstitutional since the statute had been "unconstitutionally applied... because it permitted him to be punished merely for speaking defiant or contemptuous words about the American flag" (at 581, 89 S.Ct. at 1360); that the record was "insufficient to eliminate the possibility either that [Street's] words were the sole basis of his conviction or that [Street] was convicted for both his words and his deed" (at 590, 89 S.Ct. at 1364); and that the records did not "constitutionally justify [Street's] conviction" (at 591, 89 S.Ct. 1354) under any of "four governmental interests which might conceivably have been furthered by punishing [Street] for his words" (at 591, 89 S.Ct. at 1365). Those four interests are:

... (1) vocally inciting others to commit unlawful acts; (2) an interest in preventing appellant from uttering words so inflammatory that they would provoke others to retaliate physically against him, thereby causing a breach of the peace; (3) an interest in protecting the sensibilities of passers-by who might be shocked by appellant's words about the American flag; and (4) an interest in assuring that appellant, regardless of the impact of his words upon others, showed proper respect for our national emblem. [at 591, 89 S.Ct. at 1365].

With regard to (1), Mr. Justice Harlan stated that Street's "words, taken alone, did not urge anyone to do anything unlawful." (at 591, 89 S.Ct. at 1365). With regard to (2), the Justice wrote that "we cannot say that [Street's] remarks were so inherently inflammatory to come within that small class of 'fighting words' which are 'likely to provoke the average person to retaliation, and thereby cause a breach of the peace.' *Chaplinsky* v. *New Hampshire,* 315 U.S. 568, 574, 62 S.Ct. 766, 86 L.Ed. 1031 (1942)." (at 592, 89 S.Ct. at 1365). With regard to (3), the majority opinion notes that "any shock effect of [Street's] speech must be attributed to the ideas expressed," and that:

... It is firmly settled that under our Constitution the public expression of ideas may not be prohibited merely because the ideas are themselves offensive to some of their hearers.... [at 592, 89 S.Ct. at 1366].

With regard to (4), after citing and quoting from *West Virginia State Board of Education* v. *Barnette,* 319 U.S. 624, 63 S.Ct. 1178, 87 L.Ed. 1628 (1943), Mr. Justice Harlan concluded (394 U.S. at 593, 89 S.Ct. at 1366):

We have no doubt that the constitutionally guaranteed "freedom to be intellectually... diverse and even contrary," and the "right to differ as to things that touch the heart of the existing order," encompass the freedom to express publicly one's opinions about our flag, including those opinions which are defiant or contemptuous. [quoting as from *Barnette* at 641–642, 63 S.Ct. at 1186–1187].

In *People* v. *Radich,* 26 N.Y.2d 114, 308 N.Y.S.2d 846, 257 N.E.2d 30 (Feb. 18, 1970), the Court of Appeals of New York, in a five-to-two decision, upheld the conviction, under the same statute at issue in *Street,* of a proprietor of a New York City art gallery at which were exhibited art works displaying the flag in sexual and other contexts which the majority characterized as "acts dishonoring the flag" (26 N.Y.2d p. 123, 308 N.Y.S.2d p. 853, 257 N.E.2d p. 35). In the dissent, Chief Judge Fuld, the author of the opinion upholding Street's conviction before the latter was reversed by the Supreme Court, concluded that no "sufficient legitimate public interest is served by preventing the sale and exhibition of the works of art" so as "to justify interference with [Radich's] right to free expression" (26 N.Y.2d at p. 125, 308 N.Y.S.2d at p. 854, 257 N.E.2d at p. 36); that nothing in the opinion of the Court of Appeals of New York in *Street* "suggests that the mere fact that a person chooses *to express himself by other than verbal means* removes him entirely from the protection of the First Amendment" (26 N.Y.2d at p. 127, 308 N.Y.S.2d at p. 855, 257 N.E.2d at p. 37, emphasis added); and that "the State may not legitimately punish that which would be constitutionally protected if spoken or drawn simply because the idea has been expressed, instead, through the medium of sculpture" (26 N.Y.2d at p. 127, 308 N.Y.S.2d at p. 856, 257 N.E.2d at p. 38).

In *Cowgill* v. *California,* 396 U.S. 371, 90 S.Ct. 613, 24 L.Ed.2d 590 (1970), in which the Supreme Court noted its denial of the appeal, Mr. Justice Harlan, joined by Mr. Justice Brennan, wrote:

> While I am of the view this appeal should be dismissed, I deem it appropriate to explain the basis for my conclusion since the issue tendered by appellant—whether symbolic expression by displaying a "mutilated" American flag is protected from punishment by the Fourteenth Amendment—is one that I cannot regard as insubstantial. See *Street* v. *New York,* 394 U.S. 576, 594, 89 S.Ct. 1354, 22 L.Ed.2d 572.
>
> The record before us is not in my judgment suitable for considering this broad question as it does not adequately flush the narrower and predicate issue of whether there is a recognizable communicative aspect to appellant's conduct which appears to have consisted merely of wearing a vest fashioned out of a cutup American flag. Such a question, not insubstantial of itself, has been pretermitted in the Court's previous so-called "symbolic speech" cases where the communicative content of the conduct was beyond dispute. . . . The Court has, as yet, not established a test for determining at what point conduct becomes so intertwined with expression that it becomes necessary to weigh the State's interest in proscribing conduct against the constitutionally protected interest in freedom of expression. [at 371-372, 90 S.Ct. at 614; citations omitted; footnote omitted].[2]

In the case at bar, there were no acts other than the creation of the cover illustration and its attempted publication. Here, we are not faced with any intertwining of conduct and expression. Nor is there anything in the record in this case to suggest that any one or more of the "four governmental interests" set forth in *Street* have been offended. Here, we have only expression in the form of art. The teachings of *Street* clearly require the protection of the expression attempted herein. The Maryland Statute cannot constitutionally be applied to curtail freedom of expression as such.

While the student press may not "enjoy the same privilege of nonmalicious misreporting afforded to critics of public figures under the *New York Times* decision[3] and its progeny," Developments in the Law—Academic Freedom, 81 Harv.L.Rev. 1045, 1130 (1968), there must be a showing that suppression of the contents of a student magazine is necessary to preserve order and discipline before such suppression can constitutionally be permitted. See *Dickey* v. *Alabama State Board of Education,* 273 F.Supp. 613, 618 (M.D.Ala.1967). In the total absence of any such showing, we hold that the Maryland statute involved in this case was unconstitutionally applied when the University officials, upon the advice of Maryland's Attorney General, prohibited the use of the proposed cover. In so holding, we do not reach the question of whether that statute is or is not facially unconstitutional. See *Street, supra* 394 U.S. at 581, 89 S.Ct. 1354.[4]

The fact that the University is involved in the financing of *Argus* does not permit its officials to apply a statute unconstitutionally. In *Antonelli* v. *Hammond,* 308 F.Supp. 1329 (D.Mass. February 5, 1970), University officials claimed the right to censor contents, concededly not unconstitutionally obscene, in a student publication of a Massachusetts state college, the expenses of which publication were payable by the college from funds received from compulsory student-activity fees. Holding such censorship constitutionally impermissible, Judge Garrity wrote (at p. 1337):

> We are well beyond the belief that any manner of state regulation is permissible simply because it involves an activity which is part of the university structure and is financed with funds controlled by the administration. The state is not necessarily the unrestrained master of what it creates and fosters. Thus in cases concerning school-supported publica-

tions or the use of school facilities, the courts have refused to recognize as permissible any regulations infringing free speech when not shown to be necessarily related to the maintenance of order and discipline within the educational process. See, e.g., *Dickey* v. *Alabama State Board of Education,* 1967, M.D.Ala., 273 F.Supp. 613; *Snyder* v. *Board of Trustees of University of Illinois,* 1968, N.D.Ill., 286 F.Supp. 927; *Brooks* v. *Auburn University,* 1969, M.D.Ala., 296 F.Supp. 188; *Zucker* v. *Panitz,* 1969, S.D.N.Y., 299 F.Supp. 102; *Smith* v. *University of Tennessee,* 1969, E.D.Tenn., 300 F.Supp. 777; *Close* v. *Lederle,* 1969, D.Mass., 303 F.Supp. 1109.[5]

Nor does the fact that the University officials themselves, as persons at least to some extent involved in the printing, publication and/or distribution of *Argus,* may perhaps have been subject to prosecution, as was the exhibitor in *Radich,* permit them to apply the Maryland flag desecration statute unconstitutionally.

The within case poses a justiciable controversy which is not rendered moot by the fact that the issue in question of *Argus* has been published, since there is a continuing problem in connection with future issues of *Argus,* and whether those issues will be permitted by the University officials to contain contents identical or similar to the excised portions of the December, 1969 issue. *Antonelli* v. *Hammond,* 308 F.Supp. at 1334 *supra.* Further, this is not a case in which this Court should abstain at this time from exercising its jurisdiction until a Maryland court can have the opportunity to pass upon the constitutional question presented, since no state interpretation or construction of the Maryland flag desecration statute can eliminate the constitutional defect inherent in the application of the statute attempted in this case. *See Anderson* v. *Solomon,* 315 F.Supp. 1192, at p. 1195 (D. Md. August 11, 1970), and cases cited therein.

This Court hereby declares that the Maryland flag desecration statute cannot be applied by officials of the University of Maryland to prohibit future publication of issues of *Argus* containing contents of the type excised from the December, 1969 issue. Because this Court has no doubt that defendants, as responsible public officials, will abide by this opinion, this Court hereby declines to issue any injunction at this time. *Antonelli* v. *Hammond, 308 F.Supp. at 1338 Supra; Smith* v. *University of Tennessee,* 300 F.Supp. 777, 783 (E.D.Tenn. 1969).

NORTHROP, District Judge (concurring in part and dissenting in part).

I agree with the majority that the action of the defendants as to this issue of *Argus* magazine was constitutionally impermissible, but I do so for a different reason. In this instance, well aware that the contents of the *Argus* magazine before us were just as questionable as the cover, the defendants nevertheless procured its publication, and such uneven application of prior restraint would seem to me to be constitutionally impermissible and a proper subject for declaratory relief. However, it is my feeling that if the censorship had gone to the contents as well as the cover of the publication, the university officials would have been exercising a constitutionally permissible prior restraint. I cannot subscribe to the view that the administration or the faculty must submit to possible criminal prosecution by the State in order to sustain the right of freedom of speech of a small minority of militant students. While a state university may not exercise censorship over the contents of a magazine merely by virtue of its proprietary interest, as was held in *Dickey* v. *Alabama State Board of Education,* 273 F.Supp. 613 (M.D.Ala.1967), and more recently in Antonelli v. *Hammond,* 308 F.Supp. 1329 (D.Mass.1970), it does not make sense to say that in no instance, particularly when advised by their legal counsel (in this instance, the Attorney General), that they must permit students to force them to violate the law.

Here their proprietary interest could subject them, as persons responsible, to the prescribed criminal penalty, and they were so advised by the Attorney General with reference to the cover of *Argus,* which was the only part of that magazine submitted to the Attorney General. They were also advised by the first printer that his attorney had found not only the cover but the contents to be violative of the so-called uniform "flag desecration" statute. In *People* v. *Radich,* 26 N.Y.2d 114, 308 N.Y.S.2d 846, 257 N.E.2d 30 (Feb. 18, 1970), the proprietor of an art gallery exhibiting the works of an artist was found guilty of flag desecration. And a publisher, as well as the art director and editor of a magazine in *People* v. *Von Rosen,* 13 Ill.2d 68, 147 N.E.2d 327 (1958), were submitted to criminal prosecution, though their conviction was ultimately reversed for insufficiency of the evidence. Other cases that constituted desecration of the flag were *Halter* v. *Nebraska,* 205 U.S. 34, 27 S.Ct. 419, 51 L.Ed. 696 (1907), involving use of the flag on a beer bottle; *State* v. *Schlueter,* 127 N.J.L. 496, 23 A.2d 249 (1941), tearing and crumbling a flag before a group; and more recently, *Hoffman* v. *United States,* 256 A.2d 567 (D.C. Court of Appeals 1969), wearing a shirt resembling an American flag en route to a Congressional hearing. While the United States Supreme Court has held that one need not honor the flag of the United States, it has not yet held that it is permissible to desecrate it. In *Street* v. *New York,* 394 U.S. 576, 89 S.Ct. 1354, 22 L.Ed.2d 572 (1969), at least four Justices, former Chief Justice Warren, and Justices Black, White and Fortas, indicated that the uniform flag desecration statute, which is the statute in question here, is facially constitutional. Former Chief Justice Warren stated categorically: "I believe that the States and the Federal Government do have the power to protect the flag from acts of desecration and disgrace." Id. at 605, 89 S.Ct. at 1372. Justice Fortas characterized the flag as "a special kind of personality" and stated further: "(i)ts use is traditonally and universally subject to special rules and regulation" and when it is used for the purpose of protest, its use "does not immunize the violator." It is not every type of symbolic speech that is constitutionally protected. *See United States* v. *O'Brien,* 391 U.S. 367, 88 S.Ct. 1673, 20 L.Ed.2d 672 (1968). While freedom of expression is certainly the hallmark of academic freedom, with the university community one crucible in which ideas and possible solutions to our complex civilization can be ground out for the betterment of all mankind, freedom of expression cannot and should not be the instrument by which a small minority seeks to bring down our civilization.

The administration of the university has every right to reduce a point of friction in the interests of accomplishing educational ends. In *Tinker* and *Antonelli,* and the cases cited therein relating to freedom of speech on the campus, it is recognized that regulations restricting speech are permissible when they relate to the maintenance of order and discipline in the educational process. *Tinker* v. *Des Moines Independent Community School Dist.,* 393 U.S. 503, 513, 89 S.Ct. 733, 740, 21 L.Ed.2d 731 (1968). Recent events on campuses throughout the country clearly indicate that unrestrained protestations characterized as "symbolic speech" have escalated the "protestations" into violence and disrupted the vast majority of the students' pursuit of education. We judges often, in our charges to the jury, term the law as "common sense." Can it be said that it is common sense to force the university to walk the tight rope of "imminent danger" for the sake of rhetorically extending logic to its breaking point? Certainly recent events on the University of Maryland's campus do not warrant this court in circumscribing the University in its sincere endeavor to eliminate "protestations" calculated to bring on disruption. The defendants are in a better position than this court to determine what printed matter, and under what circumstances that printed matter, might disrupt the order and discipline necessary to the educational process. I think the declaratory relief of the majority is over-broad, and I would not restrict the defendants from promulgating regulations of censorship and exercising them, even as to the uniform flag desecration statute.

NOTES

1. Plaintiffs, in their complaint herein, have also sought damages under 42 U.S.C. § 1983, but they have neither pressed, nor established any factual basis for, that claim. Consequently, that claim is hereby denied.
2. See also the discussion of lower court opinions in *Street* and *Radich* in Note, Constitutional Law—Freedom of Speech—Desecration of National Symbols as Protected Political Expression, 66 Mich.L.Rev. 1040 (1968).
3. *New York Times Co.* v. *Sullivan,* 376 U.S. 254 [84 S.Ct. 710, 11 L.Ed.2d 686] (1964).
4. *But see Hodson* v. *Buckson,* 310 F.Supp. 528 (D.Del.1970), in which a three-judge court held the Delaware flag statute facially unconstitutional.
5. In *Dickey,* Chief Judge Johnson wrote (273 F.Supp. at 618):

* * *

A state cannot force a college student to forfeit his constitutionally protected right of freedom of expression as a condition to his attending a state-supported institution. State school officials cannot infringe on their students' right of free and unrestricted expression as guaranteed by the Constitution of the United States where the exercise of such right does not "materially and substantially interfere with requirements of appropriate discipline in the operation of the school." *Burnside* v. *Byars,* 363 F.2d 744 (5 Cir. 1966).

* * *

See also Developments in the Law—Academic Freedom, 81 Harv.L.Rev. *supra* at 1129:

* * *

The notion that the state can condition the grant of a privilege on the surrender of a constitutional right without compelling justification has been descredited by the Supreme Court in other areas, and by several lower federal courts in the context of student rights. With the removal of this obstacle to judicial relief, school regulations restricting student extracurricular speech and association will be subjected to the requirements of the first amendment. [Citations omitted.]

See also the following comments of Judge Garrity in *Antonelli* (308 F.Supp. at 1337):

These decisions do not stand for the proposition that a state college administration has no more control over the campus newspaper than it would have over a private publication disseminated on campus. In the very creation of an activity involving media of communication, the state regulates to some degree the form of expression fostered. But the creation of the form does not give birth also to the power to mold its substance. For example, it may be lawful in the interest of providing students with the opportunity to develop their own writing and journalistic skills, to restrict publication in a campus newspaper to articles written by students. Such a restriction might be reasonably related to the educational process. See generally, Developments in The Law—Academic Freedom, 1968, 81 Harv.L.Rev. 1045, 1128–1134. But to tell a student what thoughts he may communicate is another matter. Having fostered a campus newspaper, the state may not impose arbitrary restrictions on the matter to be communicated. See *Zucker v. Panitz, supra.* What was said in *Tinker v. Des Moines Independent Community School Dist., supra* [393 U.S. 503, 89 S.Ct. 733, 21 L.Ed.2d 731] where the form of expression was the wearing of black armbands, is equally applicable here. "In our system, students may not be regarded as closed-circuit recipients of only that which the state chooses to communicate. They may not be confined to the expression of those sentiments that are officially approved. In the absence of a specific showing of constitutionally valid reasons to regulate their speech, students are entitled to freedom of expression of their views." 393 U.S. 511, 89 S.Ct. 739.

Because of the potentially great social value of a free student voice in an age of student awareness and unrest, it would be inconsistent with basic assumptions of First Amendment freedoms to permit a campus newspaper to be simply a vehicle for ideas the state or the college administration deems appropriate. Power to prescribe classroom curricula in state universities may not be transferred to areas not designed to be part of the curriculum. [Footnote omitted.]

THE United States Court of Appeals, Seventh Circuit, decides for high school students who had been expelled from school "after writing, off the school premises, a publication which was distributed in school and which contained among other things, material critical of school policies and authorities." In deciding for the students, the Court declared: "Plaintiffs' freedom of expression was infringed by the board's action, and defendants had the burden of showing that the action was taken upon a reasonable forecast of a substantial disruption of school activity. No reasonable inference of such a showing can be drawn from the complaint which merely alleges the fact recited in the beginning of this opinion.... While recognizing the need of effective discipline in operating schools, the law requires that the school rules be related to the State interest in the production of well-trained intellects with constructive critical stances, lest students' imaginations, intellects and wills be unduly stifled or chilled. Schools are increasingly accepting student criticism as a worthwhile influence in school administration."

Scoville v. *Board of Ed. of Joliet,* 425 F.2d 10 (1970)

KILEY, Circuit Judge.

The plaintiffs, minors, were expelled from high school after writing, off the school premises, a publication which was distributed in school and which contained, among other things, material critical of school policies and authorities. This civil rights action was brought for declaratory judgment, injunctive relief, and damages,[1] alleging violation of First and Fourteenth Amendment rights, as well as an unconstitutional application of an Illinois statute. The district court dismissed the suit for failure to state a claim upon which relief could be granted. A panel of this court, in an opinion (one judge dissenting) issued September 25, 1969, affirmed the district court's judgment dismissing the complaint. Subsequently, this court granted plaintiffs' petition for rehearing *en banc.* We now reverse the district court's judgment and remand for further proceedings.

The plaintiffs are Raymond Scoville and Arthur Breen, students at Joliet Central High School, one of three high schools administered by the defendant Board of Education. Scoville was editor and publisher, and Breen senior editor, of the publication *Grass High.* They wrote the pertinent material. *Grass High* is a publication of fourteen pages containing poetry, essays, movie and record reviews, and a critical editorial. Sixty copies were distributed to faculty and students at a price of fifteen cents per copy.

On January 18, 1968, three days after *Grass High* was sold in the school, the dean advised plaintiffs that they could not take their fall semester examinations. Four days thereafter plaintiffs were suspended for a period of five days. Nine days after that Scoville was removed as editor of the school paper, and both he and Breen were deprived of further participation in school debating activities.

The dean then sent a report to the superintendent of the high schools with a recommendation of expulsion for the remainder of the school year. The superintendent wrote the parents of plaintiffs that he would present the report, together with the recommendation, to the Board of Education at its next meeting. He invited the parents to be present. Scoville's mother wrote a letter to the Board (plaintiffs' Exhibit 2, appended to the complaint) expressing plaintiffs' sorrow for the trouble they had caused, stating that they had learned a lesson, that they were worried and upset about possible interruption in their education and that the parents thought the boys had already been adequately punished. Neither plaintiffs nor their parents attended the Board meeting. The

Board expelled plaintiffs from the day classes for the second semester, by virtue of the Board's authority under Ill.Rev.Stat.Ch. 122, Sec. 10-22.6 (1967), upon a determination that they were guilty of "gross disobedience [and] misconduct." The Board permitted them to attend, on a probationary basis, a day class in physics, and night school at Joliet Central. The suit before us followed.

Upon defendants' motion to dismiss, the district court decided that the complaint, on its face, alleged facts which "amounted to an immediate advocacy of, and incitement to, disregard of school administrative procedures," especially because the publication was directed to an immature audience. In other words, the court implicitly applied the clear and present danger test, finding that the distribution constituted a direct and substantial threat to the effective operation of the high school. At no time, either before the Board of Education or in the district court, was the expulsion of the plaintiffs justified on grounds other than the objectionable content of the publication. The Board has not objected to the place, time or manner of distribution. The court found and it is not disputed that plaintiff's conduct did not cause any commotion or disruption of classes.

No charge was made that the publication was libelous, and the district court felt it unnecessary to consider whether the language in *Grass High* labeled as "inappropriate and indecent" by the Board could be suppressed as obscene.[2] The court thought that the interest in maintaining its school system outweighed the private interest of the plaintiffs in writing and publishing *Grass High*. The basis of the court's decision was an editorial entitled "My Reply" (a copy of which is appended to this opinion) which—after criticizing the school's pamphlet, "Bits of Steel," addressed to parents—urged the students not to accept "in the future," for delivery to parents, any "propaganda" issued by the school, and to destroy it if accepted.

I

Plaintiffs contend that the expulsion order violated their First and Fourteenth Amendment freedoms. The same cases are cited by plaintiffs and defendants in support of their arguments on this contention. The authoritative decision, pertinent to the important[3] issue before us, is *Tinker* v. *Des Moines School District*, 393 U.S. 503, 89 S.Ct. 733, 21 L.Ed.2d 731 (1969).[4] *Tinker* is a high school "arm band" case, but its rule is admittedly dispositive of the case before us.[5]

The *Tinker* rule narrows the question before us to whether the writing of *Grass High* and its sale in school to sixty students and faculty members could "reasonably have led [the Board] to *forecast substantial disruption of or material interference with school activities . . . or intru[sion] into the school affairs or the lives of others.*"[6] *Tinker* v. *Des Moines School District*, 393 U.S. at 514, 89 S.Ct. at 740. (Emphasis added.) We hold that the district court erred in deciding that the complaint "on its face" disclosed a clear and present danger justifying defendants' "forecast" of the harmful consequences referred to in the *Tinker* rule.

Tinker announces the principles which underlie our holding: High school students are persons entitled to First and Fourteenth Amendment protections. States and school officials have "comprehensive authority" to prescribe and control conduct in the schools through reasonable rules consistent with fundamental constitutional safeguards. Where rules infringe upon freedom of expression, the school officials have the burden of showing justification. See also *Burnside* v. *Byars,* 363 F.2d 744 (5th Cir. 1966); *Blackwell* v. *Issaquena Co. Board of Education,* 363 F.2d 749 (5th Cir. 1966); *Soglin* v. *Kaufman,* 418 F.2d 163 (7th Cir. Oct. 24, 1969); *Breen* v. *Kahl,* 419 F.2d 1034 (7th Cir. Dec. 3, 1969); *Dickey* v. *Alabama State Board of Education,* 273 F.Supp. 613 (M.D.Ala.1967); *Jones* v. *State Board of Education,* 279 F.Supp. 190 (M.D.Tenn.1968). There is no dispute here about the applicable principles or decisional rules.

Plaintiffs' freedom of expression was infringed by the Board's action, and defendants had the burden of showing that the action was taken upon a reasonable forecast of a substantial disruption of school activity. No reasonable inference of such a showing can be drawn from the complaint which merely alleges the facts recited in the beginning of this opinion. The criticism of the defendants' disciplinary policies and the mere publication of that criticism to sixty students and faculty members leaves no room for reasonable inference justifying the Board's action. While recognizing the need of effective discipline[7] in operating schools, the law requires that the school rules be related to the state interest in the production of well-trained intellects with constructive critical stances, lest students' imaginations, intellects and wills be unduly stifled or chilled. Schools are increasingly accepting student criticism as a worthwhile influence in school administration.[8]

Absent an affirmative showing by the defendants, the district court, faced with the motion to dismiss, inferred from the admitted facts in plaintiffs' complaint and the presented exhibits that the Board action was justified. However, the district court had no factual basis for, and made no meaningful application of, the proper rule of balancing the private interest of plaintiffs' free expression against the state's interest in furthering the public school system.

Burnside v. *Byars,* 363 F.2d at 748. No evidence was taken, for example, to show whether the classroom sales were approved by the teachers, as alleged; of the number of students in the school; of the ages of those to whom *Grass High* was sold; of what the impact was on those who bought *Grass High;* or of the range of modern reading material available to or required of the students in the school library. That plaintiffs may have intended their criticism to substantially disrupt or materially interfere with the enforcement of school policies is of no significance per se under the *Tinker* test.

The *Grass High* editorial imputing a "sick mind" to the dean reflects a disrespectful and tasteless attitude toward authority. Yet does that imputation to sixty students and faculty members, without more, justify a "forecast" of substantial disruption or material interference with the school policies or invade the rights of others? We think not. The reference undoubtedly offended and displeased the dean. But mere "expressions of [the students'] feelings with which [school officials] do not wish to contend" (*Tinker* v. *Des Moines School District,* 393 U.S. at 511, 89 S.Ct. at 739; *Burnside* v. *Byars,* 363 F.2d at 749) is not the showing required by the *Tinker* test to justify expulsion.

Finally, there is the *Grass High* random statement, "Oral sex may prevent tooth decay." This attempt to amuse comes as a shock to an older generation. But today's students in high school are not insulated from the shocking but legally accepted language used by demonstrators and protestors in streets and on campuses and by authors of best-selling modern literature. A hearing might even disclose that high school libraries contain literature which would lead students to believe the statement made in *Grass High* was unobjectionable.[9]

We believe the discussion above makes it clear, on the basis of the admitted facts and exhibits, that the Board could not have reasonably forecast that the publication and distribution of this paper to the students would substantially disrupt or materially interfere with school procedures.

II

The sole authority for the Board's action is Ill.Rev.Stat. Ch. 122, Sec. 10–22.6 (1967), which gives the School Board the power "to expel pupils guilty of gross disobedience or misconduct." In view of our conclusion that the complaint "on its face" discloses an unjustified invasion of plaintiffs' First and Fourteenth Amendment rights, it follows that we agree with plaintiffs that the Board applied the Illinois statute in an unconstitutional manner.

We conclude that absent an evidentiary showing, and an appropriate balancing of the evidence by the district court to determine whether the Board was justified in a "forecast" of the disruption and interference, as required under *Tinker,* plaintiffs are entitled to the declaratory judgment, injunctive and damage relief sought.

The cause is remanded for further proceedings.
Reversed and remanded.

CASTLE, Senior Circuit Judge (dissenting).

I find myself constrained to disagree with the majority's conclusion that *Tinker* v. *Des Moines School District,* 393 U.S. 503, 89 S.Ct. 733, 21 L.Ed.2d 731, and the other cases relied upon, dictate that in the circumstances of this particular case an evidentiary hearing was a prerequisite to the District Court's implicit finding and conclusion that the disciplinary action taken by the school board was justified. Here, there was admitted action by the minor plaintiffs, through the medium of their publication *Grass High,* calling upon their fellow students to flaunt the school's administrative procedure by destroying, rather than delivering to their parents, materials delivered to the students for the latter purpose.

I perceive no occasion here for the court to hear evidence bearing on the actual or likely success or effect of such advocacy as a prerequisite to a "balancing of the private interests" of these adolescent plaintiffs' "free expression" against the state's interest in conducting an efficient system of public schools. In my view, plaintiffs' advocacy of disregard of the school's procedure carried with it an inherent threat to the effective operation of a method the school authorities had a right to utilize for the purpose of communicating with the parents of students.

I would affirm the judgment of the District Court.

APPENDIX

MY REPLY

Recently, we students at Joliet Central were subjected to a pamphlet called "Bits of Steel." This occurrence took place a few weeks before the Christmas vacation. The reason why I have not expressed my opinions on this pamphlet before now is simple: being familiar with the J-HI Journal at Central, I knew that they would not print my views on the subject.

In my critique of this pamphlet I shall try to follow the same order in which the articles were presented.

The pamphlet started with a message from the principal, David Ross. This is logical because the entire pamphlet is supposed to be "The Principal's Report to Parents." In this article Ross states why the pamphlet was put out and the purpose it is supposed to accomplish, namely, the improvement of communication between parents and administration. He has to be kidding. Surely, he realizes that a great majority of these pamphlets are thrown away by the students, and in this case that is how it should have been. I urge all students in the future to either refuse to accept or destroy upon acceptance all propaganda that Central's administration publishes.

The second article told about the Human Relations committee which we have here at Central. It told why the committee was assembled and what its purpose is. It also listed the members of the committee who attend school here at Central. All-in-all this was probably the best article in the whole pamphlet, but never fear the administration defeated its own purpose in the next article which was a racial breakdown of the Central campus. As far as I could see this article served no practical purpose. By any chance did the administration feel that such a breakdown would improve racial relations? I think not. This article had such statements as: Spanish American students were included with the white students. Well, wasn't that nice of the administration. In other words, the only difference noted was whether the student was white or Negro.

This was followed by an article called "Did you Know?" This was, supposedly, to inform the parents of certain activities. Intertwined throughout it were numerous rules that the parents were to see their children obeyed. Quite ridiculous.

Next came an article on attendance. There's not much I can say about this one. It simply told the haggard parents the utterly idiotic and asinine procedure that they must go through to assure that their children will be excused for their absences.

Questions from the parents was the next in the line of articles. This consisted of a set of three questions written by the administration and then answered by the administration. The first question was designed to inform the reader about the background of the new superintendent. The second was about the paperbacks which were placed in the dean's office. They state that the books were put there "so that your sons and daughters may read while they wait. The hope is that no moment for learning will be lost." Boy, this is a laugh. Our whole system of education with all its arbitrary rules and schedules seems dedicated to nothing but wasting time. The last question concerned the Wednesday Que-ins. It was followed by a quote: "Sometimes we, parents and schoolmen must seem cruel in order to be kind to the children placed in our care." Do you think that the administration is trying to tell us something about the true purpose of the Wednesday Que-ins?

The next gem we came across was from our beloved senior dean. Our senior dean seems to feel that the only duty of a dean or parent is to be the administrator of some type of punishment. A dean should help or try to understand a student instead of merely punishing him. Our senior dean makes several interesting statements such as, "Proper attitudes must be part of our lives and the lives of our children." I believe that a person should be allowed to mold his own attitudes toward life, as long as they are not radically anti-social, without extensive interference from persons on the outside, especially those who are unqualified in such fields. Another interesting statement that he makes is "Therefore let us not cheat our children, our precious gifts from God, by neglecting to discipline them!" It is my opinion that a statement such as this is the product of a sick mind. Our senior dean because of his position of authority over a large group of young adults poses a threat to our community. Should a mind whose only thought revolves around an act of discipline be allowed to exert influence over the young minds of our community? I think not. I would urge the Board of Education to request that this dean amend his thinking or resign. The man in the dean's position must be qualified to the extent that his concern is to help the students rather than discipline or punish them.

This pamphlet also contained an article from the freshman dean. I should like to say that Dean Engers, in his article, shows a great deal of promise. He appears to be genuinely interested in the problems of the students entrusted to him. All I can say to him is to keep up the good work.

The last thing of any interest in the pamphlet was about the despicable and disgusting detention policy at Central. I think most students feel the same way as I about this policy. Therefore I will not even go into it.

In the whole pamphlet I could see only one really bright side. We were not subjected to an article written by Mr. Diekelman.

Senior Editor
GRASS HIGH

NOTES

1. The period of expulsion has ended and plaintiffs were readmitted to Joliet Central High School as seniors for the school year 1969–70. This fact renders moot the question of injunctive relief against the Board of Education's order. Remaining are the questions of

declaratory judgment, injunctive relief with respect to restraining defendants from sending information of the expulsion to colleges and prospective employers of plaintiffs, and with respect to expunging the expulsions from the school record.

2. The Board found sufficient to justify expulsion that the action of plaintiffs

(1) constitutes a public use of inappropriate and indecent language, (2) constitutes a violation of established rules of said school district, (3) constitutes a disregard of and contempt for the authorities charged with the administration of said Central Campus and said school district, (4) encourages the disregard and disobedience of orders promulgated by the duly constituted authorities of said Central Campus and said school district, (5) involves other students as parties to the preparation and distribution of the aforesaid writing who were in fact not parties thereto.

Board resolution, plaintiffs' Exhibit 3, appended to the complaint.

There is a risk with respect to (4) above. "But our Constitution says we must take this risk." *Tinker* v. *Des Moines School District,* 393 U.S. 503, 508, 89 S.Ct. 733, 737 (1969).

The Board relied upon an unwritten policy which was presumably applied ex post facto to the plaintiffs.

3. "High school underground newspapers are spreading like wildfire in the Chicago area." *High School Students Are Rushing into Print—and Court,* Nation's Schools, Jan. 1969, p. 30. See also Nahmod, *Black Arm Bands and Underground Newspapers: Freedom of Speech in the Public Schools,* 51 Chicago Bar Record 144 (Dec. 1969).

4. The Supreme Court decision in *Tinker* was not filed until after the district court decided the case before us and after plaintiffs' original brief was filed. *Tinker* was cited and discussed in defendants' brief and in plaintiffs' reply brief.

5. The closest case factually which gives support to plaintiffs is the university publication case of *Dickey* v. *Alabama State Board of Education,* 273 F.Supp. 613 (M.D.Ala.1967)—also decided before *Tinker.* The fact that it involved a university is of no importance, since the relevant principles and rules apply generally to both high schools and universities.

We think the district court should not have been too concerned over the immaturity of the student readers of *Grass High.* Professor Charles Alan Wright has noted, however: "It is likely that the tolerable limit for student expression in high school should be narrower than at college or university level." Wright, *The Constitution on the Campus,* 22 Vand.L.Rev. 1052, 1053 (1969).

6. This "forecast" rule is an extension of the "substantial disruption or material interference" rule applied in the leading decision of *Burnside* v. *Byars,* 363 F.2d 744 (5th Cir. 1966), in favor of students, and in *Blackwell* v. *Issaquena Co. Board of Education,* 363 F.2d 749 (5th Cir. 1966), against students' conduct.

7. Ill-considered suppression carries its own dangers. For example, in *Blackwell* v. *Issaquena Co. Board of Education,* 363 F.2d at 751, it is said that three students wore the challenged freedom buttons on Friday. They were taken to the principal who ordered the buttons removed. The three refused to do so and were suspended. On Monday 150 students wore the buttons.

8. The Harvard Law Review states "[R]esponsible student criticism of university officials is socially valuable since in many instances the students are peculiarly expert in campus issues and possess a unique perspective on matters of school policy." *Developments in the Law-Academic Freedom,* 81 Harv.L.Rev. 1045, 1130 (1968). Prudent criticism by seventeen-year-old high school juniors may also have value.

9. See Nahmod, *Black Arm Bans and Underground Newspapers: Freedom of Speech in the Public Schools,* 51 Chicago Bar Record, 144, 152 n. 4 (Dec. 1969).

A United States District Court in Colorado decides for a Southern Colorado State College student who had been suspended from her position as Managing Editor of the *Arrow*, the college newspaper, after she had written a "controversial" editorial objected to by the faculty adviser. In deciding for the student, the District Court declared that the *Arrow* served as a student forum and the restraints placed on the student's writing "did abridge her right of free expression, and her suspension was an impermissible punishment for the exercise of that right." In ordering school officials to reinstate the student, with back pay, to her position as Managing Editor of the *Arrow*, the District Court stated: "The state is not necessarily the unfettered master of all it creates. Having established a particular forum for expression, officials may not then place limitations upon the use of that forum which interfere with protected speech and are not unjustified by an overriding state interest. . . . In the context of an educational insititution, a prohibition on protected speech, to be valid, must be 'necessary to avoid material and substantial interference with schoolwork or discipline.' . . . No such justification has been offered here."

Trujillo v. *Love*, 322 F.Supp. 1266 (1971)

MEMORANDUM OPINION AND ORDER

ARRAJ, Chief Judge.

Plaintiff is a student at Southern Colorado State College who in the fall of 1970 was suspended from her position as managing editor of the college newspaper, the SCSC *Arrow*, after some disagreements with the newspaper's faculty adviser. Plaintiff brought this action seeking a declaration that defendants' conduct in "censoring" her writing and suspending her was an unconstitutional interference with her rights as guaranteed by the first amendment to the United States Constitution. She seeks reinstatement to the position of managing editor, with back pay, and temporary and permanent injunctions restraining defendants from interfering with her freedom of speech. Briefs were submitted and a hearing held on plaintiff's request for a preliminary injunction. The parties have agreed to regard our decision on the preliminary injunction question as dispositive of the merits of the case. The issues are now before us for final determination.

In July, 1970, two events occurred at Southern Colorado State College which, though seemingly unrelated, were to give rise in part to difficulties between plaintiff and members of the SCSC faculty and administration. The first event was the mass communication department's appointment of plaintiff Trujillo, then an *Arrow* staff member, to managing editor of the newspaper. The managing editor's salary was $75 a month and a tuition waiver. In addition, plaintiff Trujillo earned $20 a month as an engraver. The second event was an agreement between SCSC President J. Victor Hopper, a defendent in this action, and representatives of the student government concerning financial support for the newspaper, which, prior to July, 1970, had been financed with student activity fees. Because the students wished to allocate a greater percentage of their fees to other enterprises, Dr. Hopper agreed that the college would assume the cost of printing the *Arrow* and would help with bill collecting. The student government agreed to pay for staff salaries and some supplies. Dr. Hopper announced at a budget meeting that summer that the college was taking over the role of *Arrow* publisher and that the mass communications department would supervise operation of the *Arrow* as an "instructional tool." While Dr. Hopper testified that the administration and faculty had always "indirectly controlled" the *Arrow* and

35

regarded it as a "laboratory course," neither his testimony nor the testimony of any other witness at the hearing even suggested that this fact was generally known among students or faculty.

The first difficulty occurred after the *Arrow* staff had sent its Welcome Week edition to the printer in the fall of 1970. Thomas W. McAvoy, a teacher in the mass communications department and faculty adviser to the *Arrow*, had visited the printer on a mission unrelated to the subsequent troubles. While reading proof for the Welcome Week edition, he came upon an item by plaintiff Trujillo entitled "Comment—Hopper skirts Coors issue," which concerned the president's decison to close campus "pubs." Accompanying the commentary was a cartoon of President Hopper and below it, in boldface type, the following:

I will not give in to threats of violence. I shall continue my policy of indecision. I must reiterate that I will not be persuaded by threats of violence. I will follow the will of the student body or any group of them.

This is my school and if you don't like it, I'll change my mind.—J. V. Hopper (art by Wisner)

Defendant McAvoy, persuaded that the caption was potentially libelous and a violation of journalism's canons of ethics, consulted with other faculty members. The acting chairman of the department then ordered the printer to delete the page containing the cartoon and caption. The decision to delete, rather than reset, the page was based upon cost, defendant McAvoy testified.

About a month later plaintiff Trujillo submitted to Mr. McAvoy a proposed editorial on campus parking problems and a proposed column discussing the Colorado attorney general's race then under way. The parking editorial commented upon a request by the SCSC Board of Trustees to the Pueblo City Council asking that the latter authorize SCSC security police to write city parking tickets. Plaintiff called this a "flagrant attempt" to harass students and took issue with the wisdom of placing SCSC parking problems in the hands of a municipal judge: "The judge of Municipal Court is not capable of comprehending the magnitude of the parking problem at SCSC," she wrote. "It's like asking a small-town farmer to solve the transportation problem in New York City—he simply isn't acquainted with the facts." Defendant McAvoy took issue with these statements, again on grounds of libel and ethics, and plaintiff Trujillo and the editor-in-chief of the *Arrow* agreed to revise the editorial. However, in the meantime, Mr. McAvoy suspended the managing editor and the parking editorial was subsequently printed as revised by Mr. McAvoy. The proposed column never appeared in the *Arrow*. Mr. McAvoy testified that he held up publication pending an investigation of certain statements of fact, and, after Miss Trujillo had been suspended, publication was dropped.

The suspension of plaintiff Trujillo caused a considerable stir on the campus. The editor-in-chief, Miss Teddy Incerto, resigned to show support for Miss Trujillo. The Associated Student Government provided funds to finance a single issue of the *Broadside*, a newspaper edited by Miss Incerto and Miss Trujillo. The *Broadside* published the cartoon of Dr. Hopper and the caption, without, however, the president's name attached. The issue also contained the column and parking editorial, without reference to "the" municipal judge as a "small-town farmer." In addition, the Associate Student Government voted to stop any transfer of student activity fees to the *Arrow*. However, the business manager "overruled" the students on the ground that it would be illegal to hold up transfer of funds. In November, 1970, the College Senate, composed predominately of faculty members, promulgated a publications policy to guide the faculty adviser in his relations with the *Arrow* staff.

The most important testimony at the hearing concerned the understanding of those involved in the disagreements as to the function of the *Arrow*. Plaintiff Trujillo testified that prior to July, 1970, the newspaper had been a student enterprise. Miss Incerto, former editor-in-chief, confirmed this view, and, indeed, no evidence was offered which showed that either "direct" or "indirect" control was exerted over student writing prior to the events which are the subject of this lawsuit. Plaintiff also testified that she was informed of the policy change only after the Welcome Week incident. Her understanding of the change was that the *Arrow* staff had a duty to submit to defendant McAvoy any writing which the students judged to be "controversial." She stated that she did not know what "controversial" meant and she knew of no standards which the faculty intended to use in judging the acceptability of student work. The administration's new policy was not discussed in any of her summer journalism classes, Miss Trujillo said, nor were the canons of ethics ever thoroughly discussed or related to the work of the *Arrow* staff.

Mr. McAvoy testified that, when he was appointed faculty adviser to the *Arrow* in the summer of 1970, he was told to use his professional experience and the canons of ethics in judging student work. The idea of the policy change, he said, was to prepare students for a career in journalism. He confirmed that the *Arrow* staff was instructed to submit only "controversial" material and that he had made no effort to define "controversial." He denied that the policy was one of censorship or that student rights of free speech had been diminished. All of the changes proposed or made were changes in form, not substance, he stated. When asked why he had not informed Miss Trujillo of the policy change before the publication of the Welcome Week edition, Mr. McAvoy replied that Miss Incerto had been informed and he had assumed she would explain the matter to her staff. Mr. McAvoy also testified that he suspended Miss Trujillo because she seemed unwilling to learn and he "couldn't do any more for her."

Miss Incerto confirmed that she had not explained the policy change to her staff and that she too had been confused about the policy and her responsibility. The president of the student body testified that he was not told of any policy change during discussions about finances but he understood that some change might take place in the future.

We do not doubt the good faith of any of the parties who testified at the hearing. Little of the evidence was contradictory. What the testimony rather emphatically revealed is that the SCSC administration and faculty, on one hand, and students, on the other, have been living in separate worlds. Because they control *Arrow* financing, the former have assumed that they are free to change the function of the newspaper. They believe that a change has been carried out. Defendant McAvoy clearly regarded it as his duty to superintend production of the *Arrow* and he viewed plaintiff Trujillo's opposition as evidence that she was unwilling to learn. Plaintiff Trujillo assumed, at least prior to the fall of 1970, that she was free, within the limits of protected speech, to write as she pleased. In September she learned of a change in policy but did not know what to make of it and apparently disapproved.

We begin by noting what we are not required to decide. The question presented is not whether Southern Colorado State College may prohibit entirely the independent expression of student opinion on campus. *Cf. Tinker v. Des Moines Independent School District,* 393 U.S. 503, 89 S.Ct. 733, 21 L.Ed.2d 731 (1969). The college made no effort to squelch the student-financed *Broadside* and we trust that plaintiff has been and still is free to take to the soapbox or handpress to express her views. In addition, we find it unnecessary to decide whether a state-supported college is free to establish a newspaper which it places under the control of its journalism department, whether such a college may decline to finance a newspaper for the expression of student opinion or whether, once established, such a project may be abandoned. We need not decide these questions because we have concluded from the evidence that prior to the summer of 1970 the *Arrow* did serve as a forum for student expression and the new policy of administration and faculty was not thereafter put into effect with sufficient clarity and consistency to alter the function of the newspaper. As a result, we find, the *Arrow* continued to serve as a student forum, the restraints placed on plaintiff's writing did abridge her right of free expression, and her suspension was an impermissible punishment for the exercise of that right.

The faculty adviser's testimony by itself indicates the depth of inconsistency and confusion about the function of the *Arrow*. The idea of the policy change, Mr. McAvoy testified, was to prepare students through supervised *Arrow* work for a career in journalism. Yet student writing was not supervised. No advice or help was extended to the *Arrow* staff either directly or in journalism classes. No standards were promulgated until after the Welcome Week edition had been unilaterally altered and even then staff members were only put on warning that they must secure approval for "controversial" material. Coming as it did upon the heels of a censorship, this instruction no doubt suggested that the faculty adviser would take a serious interest in the student work, yet the *Arrow* editors were told that they themselves should judge what is "controversial." We find it anomalous to urge, on one hand, that the *Arrow* was to serve as an instructional tool, and also maintain, in effect, that students were to decide what education they ought to receive. Perhaps defendant McAvoy himself saw no inconsistency between the *Arrow* as a teaching device and as a forum for student expression. He testified that the *Arrow* had always been such a forum and that plaintiff Trujillo's writings had not been censored. By this he meant that she was permitted to write upon subjects she had chosen and he regarded his own suggestions as going to "form" rather than "content." To recommend that an editorial written in a prose line be rendered in iambic pentameter *may* be a suggestion concerning form, but the deletion of a cartoon and caption and the recommendation that a reference to a judge as a small-town farmer be dropped obviously concern content. The right of free expression would have little meaning if otherwise protected speech could be so altered.

The state is not necessarily the unfettered master of all it creates. Having established a particular forum for expression, officials may not then place limitations upon the use of that forum which interfere with protected speech and are not unjustified by an overriding state interest. *Antonelli v. Hammond,* 308 F.Supp. 1329 (D.Mass.1970); *Zucker v. Panitz,* 299 F.Supp. 102 (S.D.N.Y.1969); *Dickey v. Alabama State Board of Education,* 273 F.Supp. 613 (M.D. Ala.1967); *Wirta v. Alameda-Contra Costa Transit District,* 68 Cal.2d 51, 64 Cal.Rptr. 430, 434 P.2d 982 (1967). In the context of an educational institution, a prohibition on protected speech, to be valid, must be "necessary to avoid material and substantial interference with schoolwork or discipline." *Tinker v. Des*

Moines Independent Community School District, 393 U.S. 503, 511, 89 S.Ct. 733, 21 L.Ed.2d 731, 739 (1969). No such justification has been offered here. While Mr. McAvoy did suggest that he was concerned about libel, defendants made no effort to prove that plaintiff Trujillo's writings were libelous as a matter of Colorado law and also unentitled to first amendment protection as a matter of federal law. *Cf. New York Times Co.* v. *Sullivan,* 376 U.S. 254, 84 S.Ct. 710, 11 L.Ed.2d 686 (1964).

We appreciate that school officials have authority "to prescribe and control conduct in the schools," but this authority must be exercised so as not to intrude upon "fundamental constitutional rights." *Tinker* v. *Des Moines Independent Community School District, supra,* 393 U.S. at 507, 89 S.Ct. at 737. The faculty advisor's conduct had the effect of reining in on the writings of plaintiff Trujillo while leaving the work of the *Arrow* writers unexpurgated. As the testimony of everyone made clear, the rubric "controversial" was ill-suited to justify this difference in treatment. Nor can we uphold such conduct merely because it comes labeled as "teaching," when in fact little or no teaching took place. The administration and faculty may have had the best of intentions concerning the *Arrow's* future, but it is clear to us that they did not carry out their plans.

Had the *Arrow* not served as a student newspaper prior to the summer of 1970, the questions posed by this litigation might never have arisen. This decision only requires that school officials make a clear choice. That much, we think, will be salutary both for faculty and students. Experience shows, and the *Broadside* is but an example, that when one forum for the free expression of beliefs is shut off, students will find another.

The foregoing constitutes the required findings of fact and conclusions of law.

It is therefore

Ordered that defendants reinstate plaintiff, with back pay, to her position as managing editor of the Southern Colorado State College *Arrow.*

THE United States Court of Appeals, Second Circuit, finds parts of the Stamford, Connecticut Board of Education's policy on "Distribution of Printed and Written Matter" deficient and unenforceable. Arguing that the Board's policy did not ensure an expeditious review procedure, the Court said: "The policy as presently written is wholly deficient in this respect for it prescribes no period of time in which school officials must decide whether or not to permit distribution. To be valid, the regulation must prescribe a definite brief period within which review of submitted material will be completed. The policy is also deficient in failing to specify to whom and how material may be submitted for clearance." "Finally," concluded the Court, "we believe that the proscription against 'distributing' written or printed material without prior consent is unconstitutionally vague. We assume that by 'distributing' the board intends something more than one student passing to a fellow student his copy of a general newspaper or magazine. Indeed, this assumption underpins most of our discussion concerning the constitutional validity of the policy statement, apart from the deficiences we describe here. If students are to be required to secure prior approval before they may pass notes to each other in the hallways or exchange *Time, Newsweek* or other periodicals among themselves, then the resultant burden on speech might very likely outweigh the very remote possibility that such activities would ever cause disruption."

Eisner v. *Stamford Bd. of Education,* 440 F.2d 803 (1971)

Irving R. Kaufman, Circuit Judge:
The deceptively simple facts in this case generate legal problems which summon up many centuries of political and social thought and action concerning the relation between the rights and powers of men, women, and children, and their government. To resolve this problem we are required to consider principles and concepts which courts have fashioned over several decades of this century, giving concrete effect to the proscription of the First Amendment against any law abridging freedom of expression, and apply them to the unique social structure prevailing in a public system of secondary schools.[1]

The Board of Education of the city of Stamford, Connecticut, on November 18, 1969, adopted the following "policy":

"Distribution of Printed or Written Matter
"The Board of Education desires to encourage freedom of expression and creativity by its students subject to the following limitations:

"No person shall distribute any printed or written matter on the grounds of any school or in any school building unless the distribution of such material shall have prior approval by the school administration.

"In granting or denying approval, the following guidelines shall apply.

"No material shall be distributed which, either by its content or by the manner of distribution itself, will interfere with the proper and orderly operation and discipline of the school, will cause violence or disorder, or will constitute an invasion of the rights of others."

Plaintiffs are students at Rippowam High School in Stamford. They wish to distribute free of the restraint imposed by the quoted policy, or of any other similar restraint, a mimeographed newspaper of their own creation and other printed and written literature. The district court agreed with their contention that the Board's policy violates their right to freedom of expression. Limiting the issue to the constitutional validity of the requirement that the *contents* of "the literature be submitted to school officials for approval prior to distribution" (the validity of reasonable regulation concerning time, place, and manner of distribution being conceded by plaintiffs), the court reasoned that the policy imposed a "prior restraint" on student speech and press, invalid under *Near* v. *Minnesota ex. re. Olson,* 283 U.S. 697, 51 S.Ct. 625, 75 L.Ed. 1357 (1931), in the absence of even "a scintilla of proof which would justify" the restraint. As an independent ground for granting plaintiffs' and denying defendants' motions for summary judgment, the court found the policy fatally defective for lack of "procedural safeguards," citing *Freedman* v. *Maryland,* 380 U.S. 51, 85 S.Ct. 734, 13 L.Ed.2d 649 (1965). Specifically, Judge Zampano faulted the policy because it does "not specify the manner of submission, the exact party to whom the material must be submitted, the time within which a decision must be rendered; nor . . . provide for an adversary proceeding of any type or for a right of appear." The court therefore declared the policy unconstitutional and enjoined defendants from enforcing any requirement that students obtain prior approval before publishing or distributing literature within the Stamford public schools.

We affirm the decision below, 314 F.Supp. 832 (1970), insofar as it declares unconstitutional and enjoins the enforcement of the Board's policy of November 18, 1970, but we do so, as will shortly appear, with some reservations and for reasons significantly different from those advanced by the court below. In sum, we agree that *Freedman* v. *Maryland* delineates precisely why the policy here is defective. We do not agree with the district court, however, that reasonable and fair regulations which corrected those defects but nevertheless required prior submission of material for approval, would in all circumstances be an unconstitutional "prior restraint."

I.

Consideration of the judicial interpretations enunciated over the years in this highly complex free speech-press area are a necessary backdrop to our discussion. In *Near,* the Supreme Court struck down a statute which if analogized to the instant case would place a prior restraint upon distribution of literature by any student who had in the past regularly distributed material deemed by school authorities to be obscene, lewd, and lascivious, or malicious, scandalous, and defamatory. The law held unconstitutional in *Near* permitted such a broad restraint to be imposed by county courts upon publishers of newspapers and periodicals in the state of Minnesota. The Court considered such a scheme to be "of the essence of censorship" and in strong terms, gave expression to the enmity reflected in the First Amendment toward "previous restraints upon publication." 283 U.S. at 713, 51 S.Ct. 625. The Court's particular concern was directed at that aspect of the law under which crusading newspaper publishers would hazard not only libel actions, but the utter abatement of their publications and consequently the squelching of their campaigns, if they should attempt systematically to expose the derelictions of public officials. But Chief Justice Hughes made it clear that his opinion was not to be read as invalidating all "previous restraints." He took pains to catalogue several varieties of "exceptional cases" which would justify a "previous restraint." Thus, it was well established then as it is now that "[t]he constitutional guaranty of free speech does not 'protect a man from an injunction against uttering words that may have all the effect of force'." Nor did it question that "the primary requirements of decency may be enforced against obscene publications." 283 U.S. at 716, 51 S.Ct. at 631.

A listing of permissible prior restraints did not have its genesis nor end in *Near.* We are aware of the warning sounded in *Kingsley Books, Inc.* v. *Brown,* 354 U.S. 436, 441, 77 S.Ct. 1325, 1 L.Ed.2d 1469 (1957), quoted and put to use by *Times Film Corp* v. *City of Chicago,* 365 U.S. 43, 49, 81 S.Ct. 391, 394, 5 L.Ed.2d 403 (1961), that "[t]he phrase 'prior restraint' is not a self-wielding sword. Nor can it serve as a talismanic test." In *Times Film,* the Court instructed that the First Amendment does not guarantee "complete and absolute freedom to exhibit, at least once, any and every kind of motion picture," relying in part on the dictum in *Chaplinsky* v. *New Hampshire,* 315 U.S. 568, 571–572, 62 S.Ct. 766, 86 L.Ed. 1031 (1942), that governments may with appropriate measures either punish or prevent the dissemination of "the lewd and obscene, the profane, the libelous, and the insulting or 'fighting' words—those which by their very utterance inflict injury or tend to incite an immediate breach of the peace." The earlier dictum and the holding in *Times Film* were sifted and refined again in *Freedman* v. *Maryland,* 380 U.S. 51, 85 S.Ct. 734, 13 L.Ed.2d 649 (1965), when the Court laid down three specific procedural safeguards "designed to obviate the dangers of a censorship system," safeguards which we shall shortly discuss in more detail.

The sensitive analysis of the constitutional validity of previous restraints of speech suggested by these cases requires that we address ourselves to the following questions: First, is the Board's policy justified as included within one or more of the categories of exceptional cases to which previous restraints are permissible? Second, is the policy as narrowly drawn as may reasonably be expected so as to advance the social interests that justify it or, to the contrary, does it unduly restrict protected speech, to an extent "greater than is essential to the furtherance of" those interests? See *United States* v. *O'Brien,* 391 U.S. 367, 377, 88 S.Ct. 1673, 20 L.Ed.2d 672 (1968). In light of *Freedman,* the latter question might usefully be addressed, alternatively, to the substantive and to the procedural aspect of the policy—that is, first to the criteria by which school officials are permitted to bar literature from the school and second to the means by which the bar is to be effected.

II.

We agree with the appellants that we need not and should not concern ourselves with the content or disruptive potential of the specific issue of the newspaper which plaintiffs sought unsuccessfully to distribute on school property. The students are challenging the policy "on its face" and not as applied to their particular publication.

Moreover, we cannot ignore the oft-stressed and carefully worded dictum in the leading precedent, *Tinker* v. *Des Moines School District,* 393 U.S. 503, 514, 89 S.Ct. 733, 740, 21 L.Ed.2d 731 (1969) that protected speech in public secondary schools may be forbidden if school authorities reasonably "forecast substantial disruption of or material interference with school activities." In an apparent reformulation of that dictum, the *Tinker* Court dissociated its holding that school authorities may not prohibit entirely non-disruptive student speech from cases involving "speech or action that intrudes upon the work of the schools or the rights of other students." 393 U.S. at 508, 89 S.Ct. at 737.[2]

Many cases, following in the choppy waters left by *Tinker,* have applied the quoted language either to validate or to restrain a school's attempt to prevent students from engaging in constitutionally protected activity.[3] Nor need we search far for a theoretical underpinning for the authority of school officials to control disruptive speech, in view of the unassailable power of the state to suppress "words ... which by their very utterance inflict injury or tend to incite an immediate breach of the peace." *Chaplinsky* v. *New Hampshire, supra,* or words which "have all the effect of force." *Near* v. *Minnesota,* 283 U.S. at 716, 51 S.Ct. at 631. These phrases have a venerable ancestry, descending from the principle at least as old and as formidable as *Schenck* v. *United States,* 249 U.S. 47, 52, 39 S.Ct. 247, 249, 63 L.Ed. 470 (1919), that "[t]he question in every case is whether the words are used in such circumstances and are of such a nature as to create a clear and present danger that they will bring about the substantive evils that Congress has a right to prevent."

The potential "evil," the School Board urges, is the disruption of the effort by the State of Connecticut through its system of public schooling, to give its children "opportunities for growth into free and independent well-developed men and citizens." *Prince* v. *Massachusetts,* 321 U.S. 158, 165, 64 S.Ct. 438, 442, 88 L.Ed. 645 (1944). As the *Tinker* court recognized, it has "repeatedly emphasized the need for affirming the comprehensive authority of the States and of school officials ... to prescribe and control conduct in the schools." 393 U.S. at 507, 89 S.Ct. at 737. A public school is undoubtedly a "marketplace of ideas." Early involvement in social comment and debate is a good method for future generations of adults to learn intelligent involvement. But we cannot deny that Connecticut has authority to minimize or eliminate influences that would dilute or disrupt the effectiveness of the educational process as the state conceives it. The task of judging the actual effects of school policy statements and regulations is a delicate and difficult one. But, to the extent that the Board's policy statement here merely vests school officials under state law with authority which under *Tinker* they may constitutionally exercise, it is on its face unexceptionable.[4] Unless the policy, therefore, purports to delegate greater power to restrain the distribution of disruptive matter than *Tinker* allows, or unless it otherwise unreasonably burdens students' First Amendment activity, it is valid.

III.

The policy criteria by which school authorities may prevent students from distributing literature on school property departs in no significant respect from the similarly very general and broad instruction of *Tinker* itself. Although the policy does not specify that the foreseeable disruption be either "material" or "substantial" as *Tinker* requires, we assume that the Board would never contemplate the futile as well as unconstitutional suppression of matter that would create only an immaterial disturbance. Thus, the regulation tracks the present state of the authoritative constitutional law, and while we realize this does not end the matter it does save the regulation from the charge that it is on its face fatally overbroad, since the policy statement does not purport to authorize suppression of a significant class of protected activity. See *Ginsberg* v. *New York,* 390 U.S. 629, 643, 88 S.Ct. 1274, 1282, 20 L.Ed.2d 195 (1968) (statute construed as "virtually identical to the Supreme Court's most recent statement of the elements of obscenity" not overbroad or too vague).

Absence of overbreadth, of course, does not in itself absolve the policy statement of the plaintiffs' charge that it is also unduly vague. The phrase "invasion of the rights of others" is not a model of clarity or preciseness. But several factors present here lessen or remove the familiar dangers to First Amendment freedoms often associated with vague statutes. Thus, the statement does not attempt to authorize *punishment* of students who publish literature that under the policy may be censored by school officials. If it did, students would be left to guess at their peril the thrust of the policy in a specific case and the resultant chill on First Amendment activity might be intolerable. See *Keyishian* v. *Board of Regents,* 385 U.S. 589, 604, 87 S.Ct. 675, 17 L.Ed.2d 629 (1967). Also, because any ban that school authorities may impose would apply only to students *on school property,* the policy statement does not threaten to foreclose, e.g., from the publisher of a newspaper, a significant market or block of potential buyers should the publisher guess wrongly as to the kind of literature that a school principal will tolerate under particular circumstances. Cf. *Interstate Circuit, Inc.* v. *City of Dallas,* 390 U.S. 676, 88 S.Ct. 1298, 20 L.Ed.2d 225 (1968). The policy does not in any way interfere with students' freedom to disseminate and to receive material outside of school property; nor does it threaten to interfere with the predominate responsibility of *parents* for their children's welfare. The statement is, therefore, in many ways narrowly drawn to achieve its permissible purposes, and indeed may fairly be characterized as a regulation of speech, rather than a blanket prior restraint.[5]

In sum, we believe that the Board's policy statement is neither overbroad nor unconstitutionally vague, so far as it prescribes *criteria* by which school officials may prevent the distribution on secondary school property of written or printed matter. See *Sill* v. *Penna. State Univ.,*318 F.Supp. 608 (M.D.Pa. filed Sept. 25, 1970), (regulation forbidding activity that "unreasonably" interfered with school "operations" held sufficiently specific).

IV.

Since, however, the policy statement is in other ways constitutionally deficient, it would not be remiss for us to observe that greater specificity in the statement would be highly desirable. The Board would in no way shackle school administrators if it attempted to confront and resolve in some fashion, prior to court intervention, some of the difficult constitutional issues that will almost inevitably be raised when so broad a rule is applied to particular cases. For example, to what extent and under what circumstances does the Board intend to permit school authorities to suppress criticism of their own actions and policies? See Berkman, Students in Court: Free Speech & the Functions of Schooling in America, 40 Harv.Educ.Rev., 567, 589 (1970); cf. *New York Times Co.* v. *Sullivan,* 376 U.S. 254, 84 S.Ct. 710, 11 L.Ed.2d 686 (1964). Similarly, does the Board anticipate that school officials will take reasonable measures to minimize or forestall potential disorder and disruption that might otherwise be generated in reaction to the distribution of controversial or unpopular opinions before they resort to banishing the ideas from school grounds? See *Terminiello* v. *City of Chicago,* 337 U.S. 1, 69 S.Ct. 894, 93 L.Ed. 1131 (1949).[6] The Board might also undertake to describe the kinds of disruptions and distractions, and their degree, that it contemplates would typically justify censorship, as well as other distractions or disorders that it would consider do not justify suppression of students' attempts to distribute literature. At the same time it would be wise for the Board to consider the areas of school property where it would be appropriate to distribute approved material.

Refinements of the sort we mention would lessen the possibility that the policy statement under attack here because of its tendency to over-generalization, will be administered arbitrarily, erratically, or unfairly, see *Interstate Circuit, Inc.* v. *Dallas,* 390 U.S. 676, 685, 88 S.Ct. 1298, 20 L.Ed.2d 225 (1968). By grappling with some of the difficult issues suggested, the Board might also succeed in demonstrating its conscientious intent to formulate policy not only within the outer limits of constitutional permissibility, but also with a sensitivity to some of the teaching reflected in relevant constitutional doctrine and to the dangers lurking in improper and unconstitutional administration of a broad and general standard.

Finally, greater specificity might reduce the likelihood of future litigation and thus forestall the possibility that federal courts will be called upon again to intervene in the operation of Stamford's public schools. It is to everyone's advantage that decisions with respect to the operation of local schools be made by local officials. The greater the generosity of the Board in fostering—not merely tolerating—students' free exercise of their constitutional rights, the less likely it will be that local officials will find their rulings subjected to unwieldy constitutional litigation.

V.

Although the Board's regulation passes muster as authorizing prior restraints, we believe it is constitutionally defective in its lack of procedure for prior *submission* by students for school administration approval, of written material before "distribution." In *Freedman* v. *Maryland,* 380 U.S. 51, 85 S.Ct. 734, 13 L.Ed.2d 649 (1965), the Court instructed that strict procedural formalities must be observed whenever a state attempts to enforce a requirement that motion picture exhibitors submit a film to a state board of censors for clearance before the film is shown to the public. In order "to obviate the dangers of a censorship system" the state must:

(1) assume the burden of proving that a film is obscene in the constitutional sense and hence unprotected by the first amendment;
(2) secure a judicial determination of the film's obscenity before it may "impose a valid final restraint"; and
(3) reach a final decision whether to restrain the showing of the film "within a specified brief period." *Id.* at 58–59, 85 S.Ct. 734.

For the reasons we have already set forth, we do not regard the Board's policy as imposing nearly so onerous a "prior restraint" as was involved in *Freedman*. Also, we believe that it would be highly disruptive to the educational process if a secondary school principal were required to take a school newspaper editor to court every time the principal reasonably anticipated disruption and sought to restrain its cause. Thus, we will not require school officials to seek a judicial decree before they may enforce the Board's policy.[7] As for the burden of proof, *Tinker* as well as other federal cases, e. g., *Blackwell v. Issaquena County Board of Education*, 363 F.2d 749 (5th Cir. 1966), and a companion case cited with approval in *Tinker*, *Burnside v. Byars*, 363 F.2d 744 (5th Cir. 1966), establish that, if students choose to litigate, school authorities must demonstrate a reasonable basis for interference with student speech, and that courts will not rest content with officials' bare allegation that such a basis existed. We believe that this burden is sufficient to satisfy the intent of *Freedman* in the special context of a public secondary school. Of course, this standard is a matter for courts to enforce and need not be reflected in the policy statement.

We see no good reason, however, why the Board should not comply with *Freedman* to the extent of ensuring an expeditious review procedure. The policy as presently written is wholly deficient in this respect for it prescribes no period of time in which school officials must decide whether or not to permit distribution. To be valid, the regulation must prescribe a definite brief period within which review of submitted material will be completed.

The policy is also deficient in failing to specify to whom and how material may be submitted for clearance. Absent such specifications, students are unreasonably proscribed by the terms of the policy statement from distributing *any* written material on school property, since the statement leaves them ignorant of clearance procedures. Nor does it provide that the prohibition against distribution without prior approval is to be inoperative until each school has established a screening procedure.

Finally, we believe that the proscription against "distributing" written or printed material without prior consent is unconstitutionally vague. We assume that by "distributing" the Board intends something more than one student passing to a fellow student his copy of a general newspaper or magazine. Indeed, this assumption underpins most of our discussion concerning the constitutional validity of the policy statement, apart from the deficiencies we describe here. If students are to be required to secure prior approval before they may pass notes to each other in the hallways or exchange *Time*, *Newsweek* or other periodicals among themselves, then the resultant burden on speech might very likely outweigh the very remote possibility that such activities would ever cause disruption. We assume, therefore, that the Board contemplates that it will require prior submission only when there is to be a *substantial* distribution of written material, so that it can reasonably be anticipated that in a significant number of instances there would be a likelihood that the distribution would disrupt school operations. If the Board chooses to redraft its policy in light of what we have said in this opinion, it must make its intentions in this respect clear. Once it does, courts may better evaluate the potential "chill" of the policy on speech. The Board would be wise to be mindful of this danger zone.

For the reasons stated above, we affirm the declaratory judgment by the district court that the Board's policy statement is unenforceable. Because we disagree with the district court's conclusion that under all circumstances, any system for prior submission and restraint would be unconstitutional, the district court must modify its grant of injunctive relief so as to restrain only the enforcement of this particular policy. We therefore affirm and remand the case to the district court for entry of an appropriate judgment in accordance with this opinion.

NOTES

1. The problems raised by this case defy geometric solutions. The best one can hope for is to discern lines of analysis and advance formulations sufficient to bridge past decisions with new facts. One must be satisfied with such present solutions and cannot expect a clear view of the terrain beyond the periphery of the immediate case. It is a frustrating process which does not admit of safe analytic harbors.
2. *Tinker* upheld the right of public secondary school students to wear black arm bands to school in protest of the Vietnam War, a protest that the majority characterized as "a silent, passive, expression of opin-

ion, unaccompanied by any disorder or disturbance." 393 U.S. at 508, 89 S.Ct. at 737. *Tinker* has been characterized as adopting the view "that the process of education in a democracy must be democratic." Note, The Supreme Court, 1968 Term, 83 Harv.L.Rev. 7, 159 (1969).

3. E. g., *Butts* v. *Dallas Ind. School Dist.,* 436 F.2d 728 (filed Jan. 14, 1971, 5th Cir.); *Scoville* v. *Board of Educ.,* 425 F.2d 10, 14 (7th Cir. 1970) (en banc), cert. denied, 400 U.S. 826, 91 S.Ct. 51, 27 L.Ed.2d 55 (1970) (school must make "affirmative showing" that it could reasonably forecast "substantial disruption"); *Richards* v. *Thurston,* 424 F.2d 1281 (1st Cir. 1970); *Zucker* v. *Panitz,* 299 L.Ed.2d 102 (S.D.N.Y.1969).

4. This holding is in accord with the sensible observation in *Richards* v. *Thurston,* 424 F.2d 1281, 1282 (1st Cir. 1970), that the Constitution does not condition the exercise of power to prevent disruption of public schools upon the pre-existence of a rule specifically authorizing the particular action taken.

5. Because of such factors as the larger size of university campuses, and the tendency of students to spend a greater portion of their time there, the inhibitive effect of a similar policy statement might be greater on the campus of an institution of higher education than on the premises of a secondary school and the justifications for such a policy might be less compelling in view of the greater maturity of the students there.

6. See also *Feiner* v. *New York,* 340 U.S. 315, 71 S.Ct. 303, 95 L.Ed. 267 (1951); cf. *Bachellar* v. *Maryland,* 397 U.S. 564, 90 S.Ct. 1312, 25 L.Ed.2d 570 (1970); *Gregory* v. *City of Chicago,* 394 U.S. 111, 117, 89 S.Ct. 946, 22 L.Ed.2d 134 (1969) (Black, J. concurring); *Wright* v. *Georgia,* 373 U.S. 284, 83 S.Ct. 1240, 10 L.Ed.2d 349 (1963). The difficult constitutional problems raised by "the heckler's veto," Kalven, The Negro and the First Amendment 140–41 (1965), becomes particulary acute in a public school, where the threshold of disturbance which may justify official intervention is relatively low.

We do not imply by the suggestion in the text to which this footnote is appended, that school authorities must tolerate and indeed protect distribution on secondary school property of the kind of racial or religious slander involved in *Terminiello.* And although it is clear that by appropriate procedures authorities could ban material from school property that would be obscene in the constitutional sense if read by children, see *Ginsberg* v. *New York,* 390 U.S. 629, 88 S.Ct. 1274, 20 L.Ed.2d 195 (1968), that does not imply that the Constitution protects the distribution on secondary school property of all sexually oriented material. We only mean to recommend that school authorities address themselves to these delicate issues and resolve them adminstratively before federal courts are called upon to do so.

7. Nor do we find any basis for holding, as the district court suggested, that the school officials must in every instance conduct an adversary proceeding before they may act to prevent disruptions, although the throroughness of any official investigation may in a particular case influence a court's retrospective perception of the reliablity and rationality of officials' fear of disruption.

THE United States Court of Appeals, Seventh Circuit, decides against Wisconsin College officials who had prohibited the Wisconsin State University-Whitewater Campus newspaper from publishing editorial advertisements dealing with racial discrimination, Vietnam, and an announcement of a union meeting on safety regulations. In deciding that the refusal to accept the editorial advertisements was unconstitutional, the Court of Appeals stated that: "The substantive question is whether the defendants, having opened the campus newspaper to commercial and certain other types of advertising, could constitutionally reject plaintiffs' advertisements because of their editorial character." The Court argued that "decisions cited by the District Court support the proposition that a state public body which disseminates paid advertising of a commercial type may not reject other paid advertising on the basis that it is editorial in character. Other decisions condemn other facets of discrimination in affording the use of newspapers and other means of expression on public campuses."

Lee v. Board of Regents of State Colleges, 441 F.2d 1257 (1971)

FAIRCHILD, Circuit Judge.[1]

This is an appeal from a judgment, entered on motion for summary judgment, declaring that defendants have unlawfully deprived plaintiffs of freedom of speech by refusing to print in a university campus newspaper editorial advertisements submitted by plaintiffs. The opinion of the district court appears at 306 F.Supp. 1097 (1969), and we will avoid unnecessary repetition. We affirm.

1. *State action.* It is conceded that the campus newspaper is a state facility. Thus the appeal does not present the question of whether there is a constitutional right of access to press under private ownership.[2]

2. *The issue presented.* The substantive question is whether the defendants, having opened the campus newspaper to commercial and certain other types of advertising, could constitutionally reject plaintiffs' advertisements because of their editorial character. The case does not pose the question whether defendants could have excluded all advertising nor whether there are other conceivable limitations on advertising which could be properly imposed.

The student publications board had adopted the following policy:

"TYPES OF ADVERTISING ACCEPTED

"The ROYAL PURPLE will accept advertising which has as its main objective the advertising of

1. A COMMERCIAL PRODUCT.
2. A COMMERCIAL SERVICE.
3. A MEETING. The pitch of an advertisement of this type must clearly be 'come to the meeting'. The topic may be announced, but may not be the main feature of the ad.
4. A POLITICAL CANDIDATE whose name will appear on a local ballot. Political advertising must deal solely with the platform of the advertised person. Such copy cannot attack directly opponents or incumbents. Such advertising must contain the following: This advertisement authorized and paid for by (*name of person or organization.*)
5. A PUBLIC SERVICE.-Advertising of a public service nature will be accepted if it is general in nature, in good taste, and does not attack specific groups, institutions, products, or persons.

The ROYAL PURPLE has the right to refuse to publish any advertisement which it may deem objectionable."

Plaintiff Riley submitted an advertisement describing the purposes of a university employees' union and announcing a meeting on safety regulations. It was rejected under the policy because part of it dealt with the business of the meeting.

Plaintiff Scharmach's advertisement was entitled "An Appeal to Conscience." It was signed by nine ministers and proclaimed the immorality of discrimination on account of color or creed.

Plaintiff Lee submitted an advertisement to be signed by himself and stating as follows:

"'You shall love your neighbor as yourself.'
Matthew 19:19
This verse should mean something to us all who are concerned with race relations and the Vietnam War."

The rejection stated in part, "Your ad could possibly come under the public service ad, but it deals with political issues, and is therefore not a public service."

Decisions cited by the district court[3] support the proposition that a state public body which disseminates paid advertising of a commercial type may not reject other paid advertising on the basis that it is editorial in character. Other decisions condemn other facets of discrimination in affording the use of newspaper and other means of expression on public campuses.[4]

Defendants rely upon *Adderley* v. *Florida* (1966), 385 U.S. 39, 87 S.Ct. 242, 17 L.Ed.2d 149 for the proposition that the state "has power to preserve the property under its control for the use to which it is lawfully dedicated." (p. 47, 87 S.Ct. p. 247). *Adderley* dealt with jail grounds, and rejected an asserted right to trespass there in order to demonstrate against certain arrests. The case is not apposite. The refusal to permit a demonstration on jail premises was expressly found to have been nondiscriminatory.

Defendants point out that the campus newspaper is a facility of an educational institution and itself provides an academic exercise. They suggest that the advertising policy is a reasonable means of protecting the university from embarrassment and the staff from the difficulty of exercising judgment as to material which may be obscene, libelous, or subversive. In *Tinker*,[5] the Supreme Court, albeit in a somewhat different context, balanced the right of free expression against legitimate considerations of school administration. *Tinker* demonstrates how palpable a threat must be present to outweigh the right to expression. The Court said, in part, "But, in our system, undifferentiated fear or apprehension of disturbance is not enough to overcome the right to freedom of expression.

"In order for the State in the person of school officials to justify prohibition of a particular expression of opinion, it must be able to show that its action was caused by something more than a mere desire to avoid the discomfort and unpleasantness that always accompany an unpopular viewpoint. Certainly where there is no finding and no showing that engaging in the forbidden conduct would 'materially and substantially interfere with the requirements of appropriate discipline in the operation of the school,' the prohibition cannot be sustained."[6]

The problems which defendants foresee fall short of fulfilling the *Tinker* standard.

3. *Joinder of the Board of Regents.* The argument on behalf of many of the defendants is confined to the merits. The defendant Board of Regents argues, in addition, (1) that the action is not maintainable against it because if so maintained, it would be an action against the state, and (2) that there is no foundation for declaratory judgment against it because it played no part in formulating the challenged policy.

With respect to the first point, "It has been settled law since *Ex parte Young,* 209 U.S. 123, 28 S.Ct. 441, 52 L.Ed. 714 (1908), that suits against state and county officials to enjoin them from invading constitutional rights are not forbidden by the Eleventh Amendment." *Griffin* v. *County School Board* (1964), 377 U.S. 218, 228, 84 S.Ct. 1226, 1232, 12 L.Ed.2d 256. The facts that the board is a "body corporate"[7] rather than a natural person and that this action is one for declaratory judgment rather than injunction seem to us not to differentiate the situation.[8] For the purpose of 42 U.S.C. § 1983, the board is a "person" where declaratory relief is sought against it.[9]

With respect to the second point, we think that the board's undoubted power over the administration of the state universities, including policies like the one in issue,[10] makes it a proper party in an action for declaratory relief, brought against other defendants, subject to the board's control, who actually created and enforced the policy out of which the controversy arose.

The judgment is affirmed.

NOTES

1. The Honorable William J. Campbell, Senior District Judge, Northern District of Illinois, is sitting by designation.
2. See *Chicago Joint Bd., Amal. Clth. Wkrs.* v. *Chicago Tribune Co.* (7th Cir., 1970), 435 F.2d 470; Barron, "Access to the Press—A New First Amendment Right," 80 Harv.L.Rev. 1641 (1967); Barron, "An Emerging First Amendment Right of Access to the Media?" 37 Geo.Wash.L.Rev. 487 (1969).
3. 306 F.Supp. 1101.
4. *Healey* v. *James* (D.Conn., 1970), 311 F.Supp. 1275 (status as campus organization); *Antonelli* v. *Ham-

mond (D.Mass., 1970), 308 F.Supp. 1329 (censorship of articles in newspaper); *Brooks* v. *Auburn University* (M.D.Ala., 1969), 296 F.Supp. 188 (speaker on campus); *Smith* v. *University of Tennessee* (E.D.Tenn., 1969), 300 F.Supp. 777 (speaker on campus); *Danskin* v. *San Diego Unified School Dist.* (1946), 28 Cal.2d 536, 171 P.2d 885 (meeting in school auditorium).
5. *Tinker* v. *Des Moines, etc., School Dist.* (1969), 393 U.S. 503, 89 S.Ct. 433, 21 L.Ed.2d 731.
6. P. 509, 89 S.Ct. p. 738. See also *Scoville* v. *Board of Ed. of Joliet Tp. H.S. Dist.* 204, etc., Ill. (7th Cir., 1970), 425 F.2d 10, 13.
7. Sec. 37.01, Wis.Stats.
8. See *Barry Laboratories, Inc.* v. *Wis. State Bd. of Pharm.* (1965), 26 Wis.2d 505, 510, 132 N.W.2d 833.
9. *Schnell* v. *City of Chicago* (7th Cir., 1969), 407 F.2d 1084, 1086, Adams v. City of Park Ridge (7th Cir., 1961), 293 F.2d 585. See also *Penn* v. *Stumpf* (N.D.Cal.1970), 308 F.Supp. 1238, 1241.
10. Sec. 37.11, Wis. Stats.

THE United States Court of Appeals, Fourth Circuit, decides for a high school student who had been suspended for distributing an "underground" newspaper in violation of a school rule providing that "each pupil is specifically prohibited from distributing, while under school jurisdiction, any advertisements, pamphlets, printed material, written material, announcments or other paraphernalia without the express permission of the principal of the school." In deciding for the student and declaring the rule invalid, the Court of Appeals said: "What is lacking in the present regulation and what renders its attempt at prior restraint invalid, is the absence both of any criteria to be followed by the school authorities in determining whether to grant or deny permission, and of any procedural safeguards in the form of 'an expeditious review procedure' of the decision of the school authorities."

Quarterman v. *Byrd,* 453 F.2d 54 (1971)

Donald Russell, Circuit Judge:

At the time of the commencement of this action, the plaintiff was a tenth grade high school student at Pine Forest High School near Southern Pines, North Carolina.

Among the regulations of Pine Forest High School were the following, designated as General School Rules 7 and 8:

7. Each pupil is specifically prohibited from distributing, while under school jurisdiction, any advertisements, pamphlets, printed material, written material, announcements or other paraphernalia without the express permission of the principal of the school.

8. All students shall be subject to suspension or dismissal by the principal, who willfully and persistently violate the rules of the school, or who may be guilty of immoral or disreputable conduct, during school term or out of school term whether on school property or not, or who may be a menace to the school as by law provided.

Authority to punish under such rules was authorized under North Carolina General Statute, Sections 115–147.[1]

On November 19, 1970, the plaintiff violated Rule 7, as quoted *supra,* by distributing in school an "underground" newspaper. For such infraction, he was suspended for ten school days and placed on probation. Some two months later, on January 29, 1971, he again distributed without permission, in violation of the school rule, an "underground" paper in which one of the articles concluded in large capital letters with this statement:

"... WE HAVE TO BE PREPARED TO FIGHT IN THE HALLS AND IN THE CLASSROOMS, OUT IN THE STREETS BECAUSE THE SCHOOLS BELONG TO THE PEOPLE. IF WE HAVE TO— WE'LL BURN THE BUILDINGS OF OUR SCHOOLS DOWN TO SHOW THESE PIGS THAT WE WANT AN EDUCATION THAT WON'T BRAINWASH US INTO BEING RACIST. AND THAT WE WANT AN EDUCATION THAT WILL TEACH US TO KNOW THE REAL TRUTH ABOUT THINGS WE NEED TO KNOW, SO WE CAN BETTER SERVE THE PEOPLE!!!"

On account of this second violation, he was again suspended for ten school days.

At this point, the plaintiff, suing both individually and as a representative of a class, began this action, seeking both a declaratory judgment that Rule 7 was violative of his First Amendment rights and a temporary and permanent injunction against the enforcement of his suspension and any other punishment for his violation of such rule, as well as damages. Following the filing of this action, he applied to the District Court for temporary injunctive relief pending the dispositition of the cause. The District Court denied the application and proceeded to stay the action until there had been an exhaustion of State administrative and judicial remedies by the plaintiff. From this order, the plaintiff has appealed to this Court. Incident to such appeal, he applied to Honorable J. Braxton Craven, Jr., Circuit Judge, under Rule 8, for injunctive relief pending the appeal. Judge Craven granted such relief, but added:

"Provided, however, that nothing contained herein shall be construed to prevent school authorities from enforcing discipline and preventing disruption of classes and other school activities, and to implement such purposes school authorities may, if so advised, prevent distribution of printed material during classes and at other times and places where such distribution is reasonably thought to be disruptive of normal school activity."

We vacate the stay of proceedings entered by the District Court, grant declaratory judgment and sustain injunctive relief as against the application of Rule 7 as presently drafted.

I.

The contention that this action, primarily for a declaratory judgment of the unconstitutionality of the school rule, should be stayed pending exhaustion of State remedies is without merit. Were the issue simply a matter of dicretionary school discipline, we might, recognizing that "Judicial interposition in the operation of the public school system of the Nation raises problems requiring care and restraint"[2] appropriately defer to the "expertise" of the school authorities and remand the plaintiff to his administrative remedies within the school hierarchy. *Press* v. *Pasadena Independent School District* (D.C.Tex.1971) 326 F.Supp. 550, 565. Even if the issue were whether the content of the challenged publication justified a judgment of "disruptive potential" sufficient to remove First Amendment protection against prior restraint, we would be inclined to give great, though not final, weight to the opinion of the school authorities. This is so because it is not the policy of Federal Courts to "intervene in the resolution of conflicts which arise in the daily operation of the school systems and which do not directly and sharply implicate basic constitutional values." *Epperson* v. *Arkansas, supra* (393 U.S. at p. 104, 89 S.Ct. at p. 270). Actually, *Tinker* v. *Des Moines School Dist.* (1969) 393 U.S. 503, 507, 89 S.Ct. 733, 737, 21 L.Ed.2d 731, the leading case on student constitutional rights, "emphasized the need for affirming the comprehensive authority of the States and of school officials, consistent with fundamental constitutional safeguards, to prescribe and control conduct in the schools." And in prescribing general conduct within the school, the school authorities must "have a wide latitude of discretion, subject only to the restriction of reasonableness." *Davis* v. *Ann Arbor Public Schools* (D.C.Mich.1970) 313 F.Supp. 1217, 1226; *Barker* v. *Hardway* (D.C.W.Va.1968) 283 F.Supp. 228, 235, aff. 4 Cir., 399 F.2d 638, cert. den. 394 U.S. 905, 89 S.Ct. 1009, 22 L.Ed.2d 217. But the issue posed by the plaintiff in this case as to the validity of the rule is not a simple matter of school discipline; it is not related to any question of state law; it deals "directly" and "sharply" with a fundamental constitutional right under the First Amendment. That constitutional claim under the Federal constitution, as Judge Craven observed in his order granting injunctive relief pending appeal, is properly justiciable in the federal courts. School administrative procedures provide no satisfactory alternative for the resolution of such federal constitutional claim and the plaintiff's choice of a federal forum instead of the state forum in a suit filed under Section 1983, U.S.C., is to be respected. The District Court accordingly erred in staying this action and requiring an exhaustion of State remedies, preliminary to any right to vindicate federal constitutional claims in a federal court. Section 1983, 42 U.S.C.; *Monroe* v. *Pape* (1961) 365 U.S. 167, 183, 81 S.Ct. 473, 5 L.Ed.2d 492; *McNeese* v. *Board of Education* (1963) 373 U.S. 668, 671–674, 83 S.Ct. 1433, 10 L.Ed.2d 622; *Lewis* v. *Kugler* (3d Cir. 1971) 446 F.2d 1343, 1346.

II.

Though it might well be argued that the language in the publication distributed by the plaintiff on January 29, 1971, as quoted *supra,* was inflammatory and potentially disruptive,[3] the plaintiff was not disciplined because of the content of the publication but because he had violated the regulation prohibiting the distribution of printed material without permission.[4] We are, therefore, not called upon in this appeal to assess the content of the publication; we are concerned only at this point with the constitutional validity of the regulation, for violation of which the plaintiff was disciplined.[5]

III.

The regulation, assailed by plaintiff, is facially invalid. Its basic vice does not lie in the requirement of prior permission for the distribution of printed material, though such requirement is manifestly a form of prior restraint of censorship. Free speech under the First Amendment, though available to juveniles and high school students, as well as to adults, is not absolute and the extent of its application may properly take into consideration the age or maturity of those to whom it is addressed. Thus, publications may be protected when directed to adults but not when made available to minors,[6] or, as Justice Stewart emphasized it in his concurring opinion in *Tinker*, First Amendment rights of children are not "co-extensive with those of adults". Similarly, a difference may exist between the rights of free speech attaching to publications distributed in a secondary school and those in a college or university.[7] It is generally held that the constitutional right to free speech of public secondary school students may be modified or curtailed by school regulations "reasonably designed to adjust these rights to the needs of the school environment." *Antonelli* v. *Hammond* (D.C.Mass.1970) 308 F.Supp. 1329, 1336.[8] Specifically, school authorities may by appropriate regulation, exercise prior restraint upon publications distributed on school premises during school hours in those special circumstances where they can "reasonably 'forecast substantial disruption of or material interference with school activities'" on account of the distribution of such printed material.[9] If a reasonable basis for such a forecast exists, it is not necessary that the school stay its hand in exercising a power of prior restraint "until disruption actually occurred." *Butts* v. *Dallas Independent School District (5th Cir. 1971)* 436 F.2d 728, 731; *Norton* v. *Discipline Committee of East Tenn. State Univ., supra,* 419 F.2d at p. 199. The school authorities are not required to "wait until the potential (for disorder) is realized before acting." *LeClair* v. *O'Neil* (D.C.Mass.1969) 307 F.Supp. 621, 625, aff. 401 U.S. 984, 91 S.Ct. 1219, 28 L.Ed.2d 524. And if there are substantial facts which reasonably support a forecast of likely disruption, the judgment of the school authorities in denying permission and in exercising restraint will normally be sustained. *Butts* v. *Dallas Independent School District, supra.*[10]

What is lacking in the present regulation, and what renders its attempt at prior restraint invalid, is the absence both of any criteria to be followed by the school authorities in determining whether to grant or deny permission, and of any procedural safeguards in the form of "an expeditious review procedure" of the decision of the school authorities. The order of Judge Craven, granting the plaintiff relief pending appeal from the order of suspension, added in the paragraph already quoted, a guideline which follows broadly the ruling in *Tinker* in establishing a reasonable criterion for measuring the extent of the school's power of restraint. Such language is not as precise as that which might be required in a criminal statute; but no such exacting standard is necessary in formulating school regulations. *Estaban* v. *Central Missouri State College* (8th Cir. 1969) 415 F.2d 1077, 1089–1090, cert. den. 398 U.S. 965, 90 S.Ct. 2169, 26 L.Ed.2d 548. Even with the addition of such guideline, however, the regulation does not provide the procedural safeguards mandated by *Freedman* v. *Maryland* (1965) 380 U.S. 51, 85 S.Ct. 734, 13 L.Ed.2d 649, as modified to take into account what *Eisner, supra,* refers to as the practical problems involved in applying *Freedman* to the school environment. *Eisner,* which involved largely the same issue as is presented here, set forth the reasonable requirements for "an expeditious review procedure" that are practical as applied in connection with the operation of a public school and that will meet the basic requirements of *Freedman*.(440 F.2d at pp. 810–811) As we have said, the regulation involved in this action includes neither such limited procedural safeguards nor any guidelines for determining the right to publish or distribute and is accordingly constitutionally defective.

It follows that the plaintiff was entitled to declaratory judgment that, as presently framed, the regulation is invalid and its subsequent enforcement should have been enjoined.

IV.

The plaintiff, also, asks that his suspension be voided and expunged from his school record. Actually, the suspension was not enforced, since the order of Judge Craven restrained its imposition. The school year has now ended. The issue of the suspension itself has accordingly become moot.[11] Since the suspension was never enforced, it will not support an award of damages but it would seem proper, in these particular circumstances, to expunge it from the plaintiff's record.

Accordingly, the Order of the District Court is vacated and the cause is remanded to the District Court for the entry of relief in accordance with the views herein expressed.

NOTES

1. "G.S. § 115-147: *Power to suspend or dismiss pupils.*The principal of a school shall have authority to suspend or dismiss any pupil who wilfully and persistently violates the rules of the school or who may be guilty of immoral or disreputable conduct, or who may be a menace to the school: Provided, any suspension or dismissal in excess of 10 school days and any suspension or dismissal denying a pupil the right to attend school during the last 10 school days of the school year shall be subject to the approval of the county or city superintendent.... Every suspension or dismissal for cause shall be reported at once to the superintendent and to the attendance counselor, who shall investigate the cause and deal with the offender in accordance with rules governing the attendance of children in school."
2. *Epperson* v. *Arkansas* (1968) 393 U.S. 97, 104, 89 S.Ct. 266, 270, 21 L.Ed.2d 288.

3. Compare, *Norton* v. *Discipline Committee of East Tenn. State Univ.* (6th Cir.1969) 419 F.2d 195, 198, cert. den. 399 U.S. 906, 90 S.Ct. 2191, 26 L.Ed.2d 562, where language perhaps less inflammatory than that in this case was found to be "an open exhortation to the students to engage in disorderly and destructive activities", with *Scoville* v. *Board of Ed. of Joliet Tp. H. S. Dist.* 204, etc., Ill. (7th Cir. 1970) 425 F.2d 10, cert. den. 400 U.S. 826, 91 S.Ct. 51, 27 L.Ed.2d 55. It should be noted that, while the school rules were freely criticized in *Scoville,* there was no exhortation to violate such rules.

4. Freedom of the press extends to distribution as well as to writing or printing. *Talley* v. *California* (1960) 362 U.S. 60, 64, 80 S.Ct. 536, 4 L.Ed.2d 559; cf., *Breard* v. *Alexandra* (1951) 341 U.S. 622, 71 S.Ct. 920, 95 L.Ed. 1233.

5. Cf., *Riseman* v. *School Committee of City of Quincy* (1st Cir. 1971) 439 F.2d 148: "The denial (of the right of students to distribute) was not based on the nature of the materials sought to be distributed, but on a refusal to change the existing School Committee regulation, . . . ".

6. See *Prince* v. *Massachusetts* (1944) 321 U.S. 158, 170, 64 S.Ct. 438, 88 L.Ed. 645; *Ginsberg* v. *New York*(1968) 390 U.S. 629, 638, 88 S.Ct. 1274, 20 L.Ed.2d 195; *Tinker* v. *Des Moines School Dist. supra*(393 U.S. 503, 89 S.Ct. 733) concurring opinion of Justice Steward (p. 515, 89 S.Ct. 733), and dissenting opinion of Justice Black (p. 521, 89 S.Ct. p. 744), to the effect that high school pupils do not carry with them into the school "a complete right to freedom of speech and expression."

   See Emerson, Toward a General Theory of the First Amendment, 72 Yale L.J. 877, 938–9, (1963) cited with approval in *Ginsberg:*

   "School authorities . . . may impose more stringent regulations upon the constitutional rights of minors than upon those of adults. . . . the power of the state to control the conduct of children reaches beyond the scope of its authority over adults."

7. Trager, Freedom of the Press in College and High School, 35 Albany L.Rev. 161, 166 (1971); *Press* v. *Pasadena Independent School District* (D.C.Tex.1971) 326 F.Supp. 550, 565, note 9.

   See, also, *Schwartz* v. *Schuker*(D.C.N.Y.1969) 298 F.Supp. 238, 242:

   "A special note should be taken that the activities of high school students do not always fall within the same category as the conduct of college students, the former being in a much more adolescent and immature stage of life and less able to screen fact from propaganda."

   Note, Developments in the Law: Academic Freedom, 81 Harv.L.Rev. 1045, 1128–29:

   "With few exceptions—most notably certain programs conflicting with religious freedom—rules and disciplinary measures administered at elementary or secondary levels have not been thought to violate pupils' constitutional liberties; . . . ."

8. See, Haskell, Student Expression in the Public Schools: Tinker Distinguished, 59 The Georgetown L.Journal, 37, 57–8 (1970):

   "It seems reasonable that the constitutional limits on student expression in the schoolhouse may be different from those in the community at large, because there are different elements in balancing the private and public interests involved. The school environment is unique due to its physcially confining nature, the immaturity of its population and the special demands and needs of the educational purpose.

   "Obviously those limits to expression applicable to society generally are also applicable to the schoolhouse. Given the peculiar nature and purpose of the school environment, it seems that the school adminstrator should have the discretion to impose somewhat more restrictive limits where he deems it advisable or necessary. . . . Rigid constitutional constraints imposed by a judiciary untrained in the problems of operating public schools would have the effect of precluding the exercise of prudent judgment by those knowledgable and trained in public school administration."

   See, also dissenting opinion of Justice Harlan In *Tinker* (393 U.S. p. 526, 89 S.Ct. p. 747) that, in any attack on the school authority's discretion, the student must assume the burden of showing that a "particular school measure was motivated by other than legitimate school concerns—for example, a desire to prohibit the expression of an unpopular point of view, while permitting expression of the dominant opinion."

9. *Eisner* v. *Stamford Board Of Education* (2d Cir. 1971) 440 F.2d 803, 806–807; *Chaplinsky* v. *New Hampshire* (1942) 315 U.S. 568, 572, 62 S.Ct. 766, 86 L.Ed. 1031.

   A similar rule prevails where the printed material is obscene. *Close* v. *Lederle* (1st Cir. 1970) 424 F.2d 988, 990, cert. den., 400 U.S. 903, 91 S.Ct. 141, 27 L.Ed.2d 140; *Baker* v. *Downey City Board of Education* (D.C.Cal.1969) 307 F.Supp. 517, 526–527; but, cf., *Keefe* v. *Geanakos* (1st Cir. 1969) 418 F.2d 359; *Vought* v. *Van Buren Public Schools* (D.C.Mich.1969) 306 F.Supp. 1388, 1392.

   The American Civil Liberties Union, in its bulletin, Academic Freedom in the Secondary Schools (at 11–12) phrases the right of prior restraint, as applied to high school students, thus:

   "Neither the faculty advisors nor the prinicpal should prohibit the publication or distribution of material except when such publication or distribution would clearly endanger the health or safety of the students, or clearly and imminently threaten to disrupt the educational process, or might be of a libelous nature. Such judgment, however, should never be exercised because of disapproval or disagreement with the article in question."

   This statement is quoted in Abbott, The Student Press: Some First Impressions, 16 Wayne L.Rev. 1, 22 (1970).

   Cf., opinion of Justice Fortas in *Tinker,*where in summarizing his conclusions, he said:

   ". . . the record does not demonstrate any facts which might reasonably have led school authorities to forecast substantial disruption of or material interference with school activities, and no disturbances or disorders on the school premises in fact occurred." (393 U.S. at p. 514, 89 S.Ct. at p. 740).

   As a matter of fact, the defect in the District Court's decision in that case was in the judgment of the prevailing opinion that it "made no such finding".

10. See, Goldstein, The Scope and Sources of School Board Authority to Regulate Student Conduct and

Status: A Nonconsititutional Analysis, 117 U.Pa.L.Rev. 373, 429 (1969):

"Judicial review should be limited to a determination, whether, on the basis of this record as a whole, there is substantial evidence to support the school board's finding of a reasonable likelihood of harm."

See, also, Note, 52 Marquette L.Rev. 606, 611:

"Note that *Tinker* involved the reasonable anticipation of a level of disruption insufficient to warrant curtailment of speech.... The opinion goes no further than to imply that such anticipation need only be not unreasonable."

It has been suggested that Courts may well take note of the significant differences between symbolic speech, especially when directed towards a non-school matter, and the distribution of an underground newspaper in assessing the reasonableness of a judgment of likely school disruption. Thus, in Nahmod, Black Arm Bands and Underground Newspapers: Freedom of Speech in the Public Schools, 51 Chicago Bar Record, 144, 148–9 (1969), the author states:

"*Tinker* and *Burnside* [Burnside v. Byars, 5 Cir., 363 F.2d 744] involved worn symbols which were viewed by comparatively few students, while underground newspapers have a theoretically unlimited student readership and thereby a potentially more disruptive influence. In addition, *Tinker* and *Burnside* involved expressions of opinion on a non-school, albeit controversial, matter, while underground newspapers which engage in attacks on school administrators and their policies would seem to affect school discipline more directly."

11. A number of cases, concerned with the alarming rise in school disciplinary problems, have held that a high school student may be punished for gross disobedience of school rules and gross disrespect of school authorities, without regard to the constitutionality of the rule or the action of the school official. *Schwartz* v. *Schuker, supra,* 298 F.Supp. at p. 242; *Hatter* v. *Los Angeles City High School District* (D.C.Cal.1970) 310 F.Supp. 1309, 1311–1312: *Graham* v. *Houston Independent School District* (D.C.S.D.Tex.1970) 335 F.Supp. 1164 (opinion by Hon. Joe Ingraham, Circuit Judge, sitting by designation): cf., however, *Scoville* v. *Board of Ed. of Joliet Tp. H. S. Dist.* 204, etc., Ill., *supra* (425 F.2d 10; *Sullivan* v. *Houston Independent School District* (D.C.Tex. 1969) 307 F.Supp. 1328; and *Dickey* v. *Albama State Board of Education* (D.C.Ala.1967) 273 F.Supp. 613. All the cases are reviewed and the rule in *Schwartz* approved in Haskell, Student Expression in the Public Schools: Tinker Distinguished, 59 The Georgetown L. Journal 37 (1970). The *Schwartz* case, and those cases adopting its view, proceed on the theory that the student has a legal way to test the validity of a school regulation and there is accordingly no reason for him to disregard the school regulation or to flaunt school discipline. Recognizing the danger in insulating students from discipline for a flagrant violation of a school regulation, which has not been legally declared invalid, these cases are motivated by the real fear, expressed by Justice Black in his dissent in *Tinker,* that, under any other ruling, high school students "will be ready, able, and willing to defy their teachers on practically all orders." (393 U.S. at p. 525, 89 S.Ct. at p. 746.) It cannot be denied that to permit high school students to determine for themselves the validity of school rules, and to reward with impunity their impatience with school regulations—even those which later may be found improper—undermines school discipline and can interfere with the orderly operation of the school. Moreover, even though the school authorities might be enjoined from the exercise of a right of prior restraint over the distribution of printed material, it does not follow that the student might not be properly punished or disciplined on account of the actual distribution, if the material warrants a reasonable forecast of disruption in the school. See concurring opinion of Justice White in *New York Times Co.* v. *United States,* 403 U.S. 713, 91 S.Ct. 2140, 29 L.Ed.2d 822, filed June 30, 1971. In short, those who enjoy freedom from prior restraint "are answerable for any abuse thereof." Note, Freedom of the Press in College and High School, 35 Albany L.Rev. 161, 163 (1971).

THE United States Court of Appeals, Seventh Circuit, decides for high school students who had challenged the constitutionality of the Chicago Board of Education rule which read, in part: "No person shall be permitted . . . to distribute on the school premises any books, tracts, or other publications . . . unless the same shall have been approved by the General Superintendent of Schools." In deciding for the students who had been suspended for distributing their "underground" newspaper before and between classes and during lunch breaks, the Court said: "*Tinker* in no way suggests that students may be required to announce their intentions of engaging in certain conduct beforehand so school authorities may decide whether to prohibit the conduct. Such a concept of prior restraint is even more offensive when applied to the long-protected area of publication. . . . The *Tinker* forecast rule is properly a formula for determining when the requirements of school discipline justify *punishment* of students for exercise of their First Amendment rights. It is not a basis for establishing a system of censorship and licensing designed to *prevent* the exercise of First Amendment rights."

Fujishima v. *Bd. of Education,* 460 F.2d 1355 (1972)

SPRECHER, Circuit Judge.

This suit challenges the constitutionality of section 6–19 of the rules of the Chicago Board of Education:

No person shall be permitted . . . to distribute on the school premises any books, tracts, or other publications, . . . unless the same shall have been approved by the General Superintendent of Schools.

Plaintiffs are three high school students who were disciplined for violation of section 6–19. On behalf of themselves and of a class of all high school students in Chicago school districts, they sought declaratory and injunctive relief. They also asked for actual and exemplary damages.

Plaintiffs Burt Fujishima and Richard Peluso were seniors at Lane Technical High School. They were suspended for four and seven days respectively for distributing about 350 copies of the *The Cosmic Frog,* an "underground" newspaper they and another student published. The papers were distributed free both before and between classes and during lunch breaks.

Plaintiff Robert Balanoff, a sophomore at Bowen High School, was suspended for two days for giving another student an unsigned copy of a petition calling for "teach-ins" concerning the war in Vietnam. The exchange occurred in May of 1970 in a school corridor between classes.

In October 1970, Balanoff was suspended for five days for distributing leaflets about the war to 15 or 20 students. This distribution took place during a fire drill, while Balanoff and his classmates were in their assigned places across the street from the school.

Following filing of the complaint, plaintiffs filed motions for a temporary restraining order and preliminary injunction, for pretrial summary judgment on the declaratory-relief request and for permission to maintain the suit as a class action. Defendants filed a motion to dismiss on the grounds of lack of jurisdiction and failure to state a claim.

The court set a date for a hearing on the motion to dismiss, along with a schedule for briefs on that motion. At the beginning of the hearing, the district judge presented an oral opinion denying the motion to dismiss. He did not stop there. In apparent disregard of numerous of the Federal Rules of Civil Procedure,[1] the judge, without evidentiary hearing or oral argument, proceeded to rule on all the other pending motions.

He granted the motion for a preliminary injunction (which he made permanent) to the extent of ordering defendants to expunge the records of the Fujishima, Peluso and first Balanoff suspensions. He granted in part and denied in part plaintiffs' motion for summary judgment, but it is not clear either from his opinion or from the later colloquy with counsel just what he declared about the constitutionality of section 6–19. Specifically, we cannot tell whether he intended defendants to be able to enforce section 6–19. He also denied the class-action request and dismissed the case.

I

Plaintiffs appealed. Defendants' primary theory on the appeal is that section 6–19 is constitutionally permissible because it does not require approval of the *content* of a publication before it may be distributed. Unfortunately for defendants' theory, that is neither what the rule says nor how defendants have previously interpreted it. The superintendent must approve "the same," which refers back to "any books, tracts, or other publications." The superintendent cannot perform his duty under the rule without having the publication submitted to him. The principals believed the rule requires approval of the publication itself; the Fujishima and Peluso suspensions were for "distribution of unauthorized material in the school"; the Balanoff suspensions were for "distribution of unauthorized materials in the school building" and for "distributing unapproved literature in class during fire drill."

Because section 6–19 requires prior approval of publications, it is unconstitutional as a prior restraint in violation of the First Amendment. This conclusion is compelled by combining the holdings of *Near* v. *Minnesota ex rel. Olson,* 283 U.S. 697, 51 S.Ct. 625, 75 L.Ed. 1357 (1931), and *Tinker* v. Des Moines Independent Community School District, 393 U.S. 503, 89 S.Ct. 733, 21 L.Ed.2d 731 (1969). *Tinker* held that, absent a showing of material and substantial interference with the requirements of school discipline, schools may not restrain the full First-Amendment rights of their students. *Near* established one of those rights, freedom to distribute a publication without prior censorship.[2]

Other courts have held unconstitutional similar restraints on student distribution of underground newspapers and political literature.[3] In *Riseman* v. *School Committee,* 439 F.2d 148 (1st Cir. 1971), a rule directed against advertising and promoting on school grounds was used to deny permission to a student to distribute political literature. The First Circuit invalidated the rule as vague, overbroad and impermissible as a prior restraint. The court said the school might regulate the time, manner and place of distribution, but could not require advance approval of the content of the material.

The Fourth Circuit in *Quarterman* v. *Byrd,* 453 F.2d 54 (1971), enjoined the enforcement of a rule which required prior permission from the principal before distributing any material. The court in *Sullivan* v. *Houston Independent School District,* 333 F.Supp. 1149 (S.D.Tex.1971), refused to permit the school to give even a one-day review to the principal; the school could not justify imposition of any prior restraint on distribution of underground newspapers.

The district court in *Eisner* v. *Stamford Board of Education,* 314 F.Supp. 832 (D.Conn.1970), reached the same result in invalidating a rule which required prior approval.[4] On appeal the Second Circuit affirmed the invalidation, but modified the lower court's opinion so extensively as to obliterate it. 440 F.2d 803 (1971). The court allowed prior submission of publications if accompanied by elaborate procedural safeguards.[5]

We believe that the court erred in *Eisner* in interpreting *Tinker* to allow prior restraint of publication—long a constitutionally prohibited power—as a tool of school officials in "forecasting" substantial disruption of school activities. In proper context, Mr. Justice Fortas' use of the word "forecast" in *Tinker* means a prediction by school officials that existing conduct, such as the wearing of arm bands—if allowed to continue—will probably interfere with school discipline. 393 U.S. at 514, 89 S.Ct. 733. *Tinker* in no way suggests that students may be required to announce their intentions of engaging in certain conduct beforehand so school authorities may decide whether to prohibit the conduct. Such a concept of prior restraint is even more offensive when applied to the long-protected area of publication.

This interpretation of the *Tinker* forecast rule is supported by this court's opinion in *Scoville* v. *Board of Education,* 425 F.2d 10 (7th Cir.), cert. denied, 400 U.S. 826, 91 S.Ct. 51, 27 L.Ed.2d 55 (1970). There the court applied the rule to a decision made by school officials three days after publication and distribution of the newspaper. Even though *Grass High* contained articles critical of the school administration, this court found that the board could not reasonably have forecast substantial disruption and therefore could not expel the student authors.

The *Tinker* forecast rule is properly a formula for determining when the requirements of school discipline justify *punishment* of students for exercise of their First Amendment rights. It is not a basis for establishing a system of censorship and licensing designed to *prevent* the exercise of First Amendment rights.

Because we believe *Eisner* is unsound constitutional law, and because defendants in effect concede that they cannot require submission of publications before approval of distribution, we declare section 6–19 unconstitutional and remand the case for entry of an injunction against its enforcement.[6]

Such injunction will not prevent defendants from promulgating reasonable, specific regulations setting forth the time, manner and place in which distribution of written materials may occur. This does not mean, as defendants' brief suggests, that the board may require a student to obtain administrative approval of the time, manner and place of the particular distribution he proposes. The board has the burden of telling students when, how and where they may distribute materials. *See Sullivan* v. *Houston Independent School District,* 307 F.Supp. 1328, 1340 (S.D.Tex. 1969). The board may then punish students who violate those regulations. Of course, the board may also establish a rule punishing students who publish and distribute on school grounds obscene[7] or libelous literature.

II

Plaintiff Balanoff's second suspension remains on his record. He was punished under section 6–19[8] for distributing leaflets to classmates during a fire drill. Because the rule is unconstitutional, his suspension under it cannot stand.

Defendants argue that the justification for the suspension is "self-evident" from the record. All that appears in the record are the following allegations by plaintiffs:

At no time during the fire drill was there any disorder. The distribution of said leaflets did not disrupt classes; nor did it interfere with any other proper school activity, including the fire drill. At no time during the distribution was the Plaintiff asked to stop distributing the leaflets by any member of the Bowen faculty or administration.

Neither in the district court nor on appeal have defendants suggested that evidence exists to challenge those factual assertions.

The district court speculated that students might use a fire drill, or might even instigate one, to engage in disruptive activities. His error was similar to the district court's in *Scoville* v. *Board of Education,* 425 F.2d 10, 13–14 (7th Cir.), cert. denied, 400 U.S. 826, 91 S.Ct. 51, 27 L.Ed.2d 55 (1970). "No reasonable inference of [a showing that the action was taken on a reasonable forecast of a substantial disruption of school activity] can be drawn from the complaint. . . . "

The board might issue a rule prohibiting distribution of literature during a fire drill as a regulation of time and place, but it could not apply such a rule *ex post facto* to Balanoff.

The district court's order shall include a direction to expunge Balanoff's second suspension from his record.

There remains the question of the class suit. The district judge said: "Under this decision I find that there is no need for a class action and the motion for the establishment of such a class is thus denied." If the prerequisites and conditions of Fed.R.Civ.P. 23 are met, a court may not deny class status because there is not "need" for it.

Here the requirements of Rule 23(a) are satisfied because the number of Chicago high school students makes joinder impracticable, the question of law is common to the class, the claims of plaintiffs are typical of the class and plaintiffs have fairly and adequately protected the interests of the class. The action may be maintained under Rule 23(b)(2), which was intended to cover civil-rights cases. Notes of Advisory Committee on Rules. We note that a number of similar cases have been maintained as class actions. *Quarterman* v. *Byrd,* 453 F.2d 54 (4th Cir. 1971); *Sullivan* v. *Houston, Independent School District,* 307 F.Supp. 1328 (S.D.Tex. 1969), and 333 F.Supp. 1149 (S.D.Tex. 1971); *Zucker* v. *Panitz,* 299 F.Supp. 102 (S.D.N.Y.1969); *Snyder* v. *Board of Trustees,* 286 F.Supp. 927 (N.D.Ill. 1968). *See also Sprogis* v. *United Air Lines, Inc.,* 444 F.2d 1194, 1201–1202 (7th Cir.), cert. denied, 404 U.S. 991, 92 S.Ct. 536, 30 L.Ed.2d 543 (1971).

The district court's order denying class status is therefore reversed. On remand, the district court should order defendants to give notice of the final order to all class members under Rule 23(d)(2). The notice need not be given to students individually, but might be given through posted or intercom announcements.

The decision below, except for the portion granting injunctive and declaratory relief to plaintiffs, is reversed and the case remanded for entry of a judgment order consistent with this opinion.

NOTES

1. *E. g.,* Fed.R.Civ.P. 23 (see part III, *infra*); 56 (defendants had no opportunity to serve opposing affidavits to motion for summary judgment); 57 (defendants had no opportunity to respond to motion for declaratory judgment); 65 (no hearing was held before issuance of the injunction; the order granting the injunction was not specific, did not describe in detail the acts restrained and did not set forth reasons for issuance). The district judge also resolved a factual dispute against plaintiffs on the second Balanoff suspension without taking evidence.

2. For more recent Supreme Court cases on prior censorship, see *New York Times* v. *United States,* 403 U.S. 713, 91 S.Ct. 2140, 29 L.Ed.2d 822 (1971); *Organization for a Better Austin* v. *Keefe,* 402 U.S. 415, 91 S.Ct. 1575, 29 L.Ed.2d 1 (1971); *Freedman* v. *Maryland,* 380 U.S. 51, 85 S.Ct. 734, 13 L.Ed.2d 649 (1965); *Bantam Books, Inc.* v. *Sullivan,* 372 U.S. 58, 83 S.Ct. 631, 9 L.Ed.2d 584 (1963).
3. In harmony with the cases cited in the text are these analogous cases: *Antonelli* v. *Hammond,* 308 F.Supp. 1329 (D.Mass.1970) (board could not require prior submission of material to be printed in college newspaper): *Dickey* v. *Alabama State Board of Education,* 273 F.Supp. 613 (M.D.Ala.1967) (student editor could not be expelled for inserting "CENSORED" across blank columns where disapproved editorial was to have run); *Zucker* v. *Panitz,*299 F.Supp. 102 (S.D.N.Y.1969) (students could purchase ad in high school paper to express feelings against the war); *Brooks* v. *Auburn University,* 296 F.Supp. 188 (M.D.Ala.), aff'd, 412 F.2d 1171 (5th Cir. 1969), and *Snyder* v. *Board of Trustees,*286 F.Supp. 927 (N.D.Ill.1968) (banning certain speakers from appearing on campus was an unconstitutional prior restraint).
4. The rule gave the following guidelines for approval or disapproval:
   No material shall be distributed which, either by its content or by the manner of distribution itself, will interfere with the proper and orderly operation and discipline of the school, will cause violence or disorder, or will constitute an invasion of the rights of others.

   This section enabled the Second Circuit to surmise that the rule comported with the standards of *Tinker.* The court surely would not have been so lenient with a rule stating no guidelines for adminstrative decision, such as section 6–19.
5. The Fourth Circuit in *Quarterman* v. *Byrd, supra,* seems to follow *Eisner* in finding lack of criteria and procedural safeguards, rather than the impositon of a prior restraint, as the regulation's "basic vice." 453 F.2d at 59.
6. Plaintiffs omit damages from the "precise relief sought" in their brief. Our remand therefore does not include that issue.
7. Defendants here do not argue that *The Cosmic Frog* is obscene, but some school administrators have labeled as obscenity the sort of profanity and vulgarisms which appears in *The Cosmic Frog.* They are incorrect, because those words are not used to appeal to prurient sexual interests. *See Sullivan* v. *Houston Independent School District,* 333 F.Supp. 1149, 1162–1167 (S.D.Tex.1971).
8. Defendants argue that Balanoff was not suspended under section 6–19 because no section is specified in the suspension order and because the distribution did not occur "on school premises." Actually, all the suspensions were authorized by section 6–9, "for gross disobedience or misconduct." Section 6–19 was used solely to define the misconduct. Since his principal noted the reason for suspension as "distributing unapproved literature in class during fire drill," we believe he was using section 6–19 as the criterion for suspension.

THE United States Court of Appeals, Fifth Circuit, decides for high school seniors who had been suspended for distributing near school premises an "underground newspaper" they had authored and published during out-of-school hours and without using any materials or facilities owned or operated by the school system. In deciding for the students, the Court said: "When the *Burnside/Tinker* standards are applied to this case, it is beyond serious question that the activity punished here does not even approach the 'material and substantial' disruption that must accompany an exercise of expression, either in fact or in reasonable forecast. As a factual matter there were no disruptions of class; there were no disturbances of any sort, on or off campus, related to the distribution of the *Awakening*." In its concluding paragraph the Court declared: "Perhaps it would be well if those entrusted to administer the teaching of American history and government to our students began their efforts by practicing the document on which that history and government are based. Our eighteen-year-olds can now vote, serve on juries, and be drafted; yet the board fears the 'Awakening' of their intellects without reasoned concern for its effect upon school discipline. The First Amendment cannot tolerate such intolerance."

Shanley v. *Northeast Ind. School Dist.*, 462 F.2d 960 (1972)

GOLDBERG, Circuit Judge:

It should have come as a shock to the parents of five high school seniors in the Northeast Independent School District of San Antonio, Texas, that their elected school board had assumed suzerainty over their children before and after school, off school grounds, and with regard to their children's rights of expressing their thoughts. We trust that it will come as no shock whatsoever to the school board that their assumption of authority is an unconstitutional usurpation of the First Amendment.

Appellants, Mark S. Shanley, Clyde A Coe, Jr., William E. Jolly, John A. Alford, and John Graham, were seniors at MacArthur High School in the Northeast Independent School District of San Antonio. At least they were students there save for a period of three days during which they were suspended for violating a school board "policy." Each of the students here was considered a "good" or "excellent" student. All were in the process of applying for highly competitive slots in colleges or for scholarships. The three days of zeros that resulted from the suspensions substantially affected their grade averages at a critical time of their educational careers.

The occasion of the suspension was the publication and distribution of a so-called "underground" newspaper entitled *Awakening*. The newspaper was authored entirely by the students, during out of school hours, and without using any materials or facilities owned or operated by the school system. The students distributed the papers themselves during one afternoon after school hours and one morning before school hours. At all times distribution was carried on near but outside the school premises on the sidewalk of an adjoining street, separated from the school by a parking lot. The students neither distributed nor encouraged any distribution of the papers during school hours or on school property, although some of the newspapers did turn up there. There was absolutely no disruption of class that resulted from distribution of the newspaper, nor were there any disturbances whatsoever attributable to the distribution. It was acknowledged by all concerned with this case that the students who passed out the newspapers did so politely and in orderly fashion.

The *Awakening* contained absolutely no material that could remotely be considered libelous, obscene, or inflammatory. In fact, the content of this so-called "underground" paper is such that it could easily surface, flower-like, from its "underground" abode. As so-called "underground" newspapers go, this is probably one of the most vanilla-flavored ever to reach a federal court.

The five students were suspended by the principal for violation of school board "policy" 5114.2 which reads in pertinent part:

"Be it further resolved that *any* attempt to avoid the school's established procedure for administrative approval of activities such as the production for distribution and/or distribution of petitions or printed documents of *any* kind, sort, or type without the specific approval of the principal shall be cause for suspension and, if in the judgment of the principal, there is justification, for referral to the office of the Superintendent with a recommendation for expulsion. . . . "

Northeast Independent School District "policy" 5114.2 at 2–3, adopted Novemeber 20, 1969 [emphasis added].[1]

The students requested a hearing before the full school board, which was transcribed by a court reporter at the students' request and expense. Counsel for the students and the school board were present at the hearing. The students argued before the board that, after consulting with an attorney and a professor at a local law school, they had concluded that the regulation in question simply did not apply to conduct exercised entirely outside school hours and off school premises.[2]

The school board affirmed the suspensions one day later.

Objecting to the school board's bootstrap transmogrification into Super-Parent, the parents of the five affected students sought both temporary and permanent injunctive relief as next-friends in the federal courts, requesting that the school board be enjoined from entering the zeros into the students' permanent records and from prohibiting the distribution of the *Awakening* off campus and outside school hours. The district court denied all relief, dismissing the case on its own motion as "wholly without merit."[3] The district court also denied the students' request for an injunction pending appeal to this court, F.R.Civ.Pro. 62(c), and the students immediately appealed. On an emergency basis this court expedited the appeal and enjoined the school board from entering the zeros that resulted from the suspensions into the students' records and from refusing to afford the students a reasonable opportunity to complete and submit for academic credit the work that they had missed as a result of the suspensions, pending this appeal. F.R.App.Pro.8; F.R.Civ.Pro. 62(g).[4]

That courts should not interfere with the day-to-day operations of schools is a platitudinous but eminently sound maxim which this court has reaffirmed on many occasions. *See e.g., Burnside* v. *Byars,* 5 Cir. 1966, 363 F.2d 744; *Blackwell* v. *Issaquena County Board of Education, supra; Ferrell* v. *Dallas Independent School District,* 5 Cir. 1968, 392 F.2d 697, cert. denied, 393 U.S. 856, 89 S.Ct. 98, 21 L.Ed.2d 125; *Karr* v. *Schmidt,* 5 Cir. 1972 (en banc), 451 F.2d 1023. This court laid to rest more than a decade ago the notion that state authorities could subject students at public-supported educational institutions to whatever conditions the state wished. *Dixon* v. *Alabama State Board of Education,* 5 Cir. 1961, 294 F.2d 150, cert. denied, 368 U.S. 930, 82 S.Ct. 368, 7 L.Ed.2d 193. And of paramount importance is the constitutional imperative that school boards abide constitutional precepts:

"The Fourteenth Amendment, as now applied to the States, protects the citizen against the State itself and all of its creatures—Boards of Education not excepted."

West Virginia State Board of Education v. *Barnette,* 1943, 319 U.S. 624, 637, 63 S.Ct. 1178, 1185, 87 L.Ed. 1628, 1637.

The school board insists that "policy" 5114.2 is constitutional both "on its face" and "as applied" to the suspensions meted out under the circumstances of this case.

This case is anomalous in several respects, a sort of judicial believe-it-or-not. Essentially, the school board has submitted a constitutional fossil, exhumed and respired to stalk the First Amendment once again long after its substance had been laid to rest. Counsel for the school board insists vigorously that education is constitutionally embraced solely by the Tenth Amendment, leaving education entirely without the protective perimeters of the rest of the Constitution. We find this a rather quaint approach to the constitutional setting of education in light of *West Virginia State Board of Education* v. *Barnette, supra; Tinker* v. *Des Moines Independent Community School Dist.,* 1969, 393 U.S. 503, 89 S.Ct. 733, 21 L.Ed.2d 731; *Brown* v. *Board of Education of Topeka (Brown I),* 1954, 347 U.S. 483, 74 S.Ct. 686, 98 L.Ed. 873; *Brown* v. *Board of Education (Brown II),* 1955, *349 U.S. 294, 75 S.Ct. 753, 99 L.Ed. 1083; Bolling* v. *Sharpe,* 1954, 347 U.S. 497, 74 S.Ct. 693, 98 L.Ed. 884; *Cooper* v. *Aaron,* 1958, 358 U.S. 1, 78 S.Ct. 1401, 3 L.Ed.2d 5, 19; *Aaron* v. *Cooper,* 8 Cir. 1958, 261 F.2d 97; *Griffin* v. *Prince Edward County School Board,* 1964, 377 U.S. 218, 84 S.Ct. 1226, 12 L.Ed.2d 754, to cite only a few cases.[5] Even the educational progeny of *Plessy* v. *Ferguson,* 1896, 163 U.S. 537, 16 S.Ct. 1138, 41 L.Ed. 256, held that the manner in which a state operated its public school system *must* be subject to constitutional review. *See e.g., Missouri ex rel. Gaines* v. *Canada,* 1938, 305 U.S. 337, 59 S.Ct. 232, 83 L.Ed. 208; *Sweatt* v. *Painter,* 1950, 339 U.S. 629, 70 S.Ct. 848, 94 L.Ed. 1114; *McLaurin* v. *Oklahoma State Regents,* 1950, 339 U.S. 637, 70 S.Ct. 851, 94 L.Ed. 1149. The recent cases involving so-called "underground" newspapers or other modes of expression in high schools relate almost entirely to the circumstances under which a school board can constitutionally limit expression *during* class hours and *on* school premises. *See, e.g., Burnside* v. *Byars, surpa; Tinker* v. *Des Moines Independent Community School Dist., supra; Eisner* v. *Stamford Board of Education,* 2 Cir. 1971, 440 F.2d 803; *Scoville* v. *Board of Education of Joliet Twp.,* 7 Cir. 1970, 425 F.2d 10; *Riseman* v. *School Committee of Quincy,* 1 Cir. 1971, 439 F.2d 148. Our case involves the less difficult question of conduct that is removed from the school milieu in exercise and in effect. Since school boards have rarely asserted the breadth of authority that the Northeast School District "policy" attempts to assert here, the constitutional standards are not enirely embraced by precedent. It is clear, however, that the authority of the school board to balance school discipline against the First Amendment by forbidding or punishing off-campus activity cannot exceed its authority to forbid or punish on-campus activity. Therefore, we must first examine the authority of the school board to order the actions of students *on* school grounds and *within* school hours.

While a school is certainly a market-place for ideas, it is just as certainly not a market place. The educational process is thwarted by the milling, mooing, and haranguing, along with the aggressiveness that often accompanies a constitutionally-protected exchange of ideas on the street corner. There is, of course, a substantive difference between schools and the street corner in terms of weighing the sometimes competing interests of a completely free flow of any and all expression with the requirement that there be order and discipline. Thus, this court has endeavored to give "careful recognition to the differences between what are reasonable restraints in the classroom and what are reasonable restraints on the street corner." *Ferrell* v. *Dallas Independent School Dist.,* 392 F.2d at 704–705 (Godbold, J., specially concurring). Because high school students and teachers cannot easily disassociate themselves from expressions directed towards them on school property and during school hours, because disciplinary problems in such a populated and concentrated setting seriously sap the educational processes, and because high school teachers and administrators have the vital responsibility of compressing a variety of subjects and activities into a relatively confined period of time and space, the exercise of rights of expression in the high schools, whether by students or by others, is subject to reasonable constraints more restrictive than those constraints that can normally limit First Amendment freedoms.[6]

There is nothing unconstitutional per se in a requirement that students submit materials to the school administration prior to distribution. *See Eisner* v. *Stamford Board of Education, supra.* Given the necessity for discipline and orderly processes in the high schools, it is not at all unreasonable to require that materials destined for distribution to students be submitted to the school administration prior to distribution. As long as the regulation for prior approval does not operate to stifle the content of any student publication in an unconstitutional manner and is not unreasonably complex or onerous, the requirement of prior approval would more closely approximate simply a regulation of speech and not a prior restraint. Nor is there anything unconstitutional per se in a reasonable administrative ordering of the time, place, and manner of distributing materials on school premises and during school hours:

"In formulating regulations, including those pertaining to the discipline of school children, school officials have a wide latitude of discretion. But the school is always bound by the requirement that the rules and regulations must be reasonable. It is not for us to consider whether such rules are wise or expedient but merely whether they are a reasonable exercise of the power and discretion of the school authorities. . . . But, with all of this in mind, we must also emphasize that school officials cannot ignore expressions of feelings with which they do not wish to contend. They cannot infringe on their students' right to free and unrestricted expression as guaranteed to them under the First Amendment to the Constitution, *where the exercise of such rights in the school buildings and schoolrooms do not materially and substantially interfere with the requirements of appropriate discipline in the operation of the school."*
Burnside v. *Byars,* 363 F.2d at 748–749 [emphasis added], *cited with approval in Tinker* v. *Des Moines Independent Community School District, supra.*

When the constitutionality of a school regulation is questioned, it is settled law that the burden of justifying the regulation falls upon the school board. *Tinker* v. *Des Moines School District, supra; Burnside* v. *Byars, supra; Scoville* v. *Board of Education of Joliet Twp., supra.*[7] The test for curtailing in-school exercise of expression is whether or not the expression or its method of exercise "materially and substantially" interferes with the activities or discipline of the school. *See Burnside* v. *Byars, supra; Tinker* v. *Des Moines Independent Community School Dist., supra.* The purpose of any screening regulation, at least in theory, is to prevent disruption and not to stifle expression. Thus, the school board does not have a difficult burden to meet in order to justify the existence of a prior screening rule. *See, e g., Eisner* v. *Stamford Board of Education, supra.* However, the board cannot rely on *ipse dixit* to demonstrate the "material and substantial" interference with school discipline. Put another way, *Tinker* requires that presumably protected conduct by high school students cannot be prohibited by the school unless there are

"... facts which might reasonably have led school authorities to forecast substantial disruption of or material interference with school activities...."
Tinker v. *Des Moines Independent Community School Dist.,* 393 U.S. at 514, 89 S.Ct. at 740, 21 L.Ed.2d at 742.

Under the First Amendment and its decisional explication, we conclude that: (1) expression by high school students can be prohibited altogether if it materially and substantially interferes with school activities or with the rights of other students or teachers, or if the school administration can demonstrate reasonable cause to believe that the expression would engender such material and substantial interference; (2) expression by high school students cannot be prohibited solely because other students, teachers, administrators, or parents may disagree with its content; (3) efforts at expression by high school students may be subjected to prior screening under clear and reasonable regulations; and (4) expression by high school students may be limited in manner, place, or time by means of reasonable and equally-applied regulation.

I.

When the *Burnside/Tinker* standards are applied to this case, it is beyond serious question that the activity punished here does not even approach the "material and substantial" disruption that must accompany an exercise of expression, either in fact or in reasonable forecast. As a factual matter there were no disruptions of class; there were no disturbances of any sort, on or off campus, related to the distribution of the *Awakening. See Shanley* v. *Northeast Independent School Dist.,* W.D.Tex.1972, Case no. SA-72-CA-48 [February 2, 1972]. Disruption in fact is an important element for evaluating the reasonableness of a regulation screening or punishing student expression. In a companion case to *Burnside,* this court held that conduct presumptively-protected in *Burnside* itself was not protected by the First Amendment when it was accompanied by disorderly and raucous distribution. *Blackwell* v. *Issaquena County Board of Education, supra.* One week after *Tinker* the Supreme Court denied *certiorari* in a case that had involved rather violent and disruptive activity by some college students. The district court found that the students had exceeded their constitutional privileges of free expression, *Barker* v. *Hardway,* S.D.W.Va.1968, 283 F.Supp. 228, affirmed, *Barker* v. *Hardway,* 4 Cir. 1968, 399 F.2d 638. In the Supreme Court's denial of review, Mr. Justice Fortas, who wrote for the majority in *Tinker,* observed in concurrence that "the petitioners... engaged in an aggressive and violent demonstration, and not in peaceful nondisruptive expression," *Barker* v. *Hardway,* 1969, 394 U.S. 905, 89 S.Ct. 1009, 22 L.Ed.2d 217.

The "reasonable forecast" of disruption that might result from the exercise of expression is a more difficult standard to apply. It is not necessary that the school administration stay a reasonable exercise of restraint "until disruption actually occur[s]." *Butts* v. *Dallas Independent School Dist.,*5 Cir. 1971, 436 F.2d 728, 731. *Accord Norton* v. *Discipline Committee of East Tennessee State University,* 6 Cir. 1969, 419 F.2d 195, cert. denied, 399 U.S. 906, 90 S.Ct. 2191, 26 L.Ed.2d 562; *Quarterman* v. *Byrd,* 4 Cir. 1971, 453 F.2d 54. Nor does the Constitution require a specific rule regarding every permutation of student conduct before a school administration may act reasonably to prevent disruption. *See Eisner* v. *Stamford Board of Education, supra; Richards* v. *Thurston,* 1 Cir. 1967, 424 F.2d 1281. The Northeast school board has made our task of applying *Tinker's* "reasonable forecast" test somewhat easier here since, in substance, the board does *not* on appeal defend its suspensions on the basis of disruptions, either potential or actual. However, giving the board the benefit of every doubt in the instance of the application of one of its disciplinary rules, we note that there is some testimony in the record of the school board hearing that the school administration believed the contents of the *Awakening* to be potentially disruptive.[8] Perhaps this point was not pressed on appeal precisely because it is fraught with constitutional dangers. *See Near* v. *Minnesota ex rel. Olson,* 1931, 283 U.S. 697, 51 S.Ct. 625, 75 L.Ed. 1357. The *Awakening* contains no remarks that could remotely be considered obscene, libelous, or inflammatory, and protection has been afforded to publications much more hortatory than the one before this court. *See Quarterman* v. *Byrd, supra.* We do not here delimit the categories of materials for which a high school administration may exercise a reasonable prior restraint of content to only those materials obscene, libelous, or inflammatory, for we realize that specific problems will require individual and specific judgments. Therefore, in deference to the judgment of the school boards, we refer ad hoc resolution of these issues to the neutral corner of "reasonableness." We do conclude, however, that the school board's burden of demonstrating reasonableness becomes geometrically heavier as its decision begins to focus upon the content of materials that are not obscene, libelous, or inflammatory. The best that can be said for the adminstration's concern in this case is that two topics mentioned in the *Awakening* are "controversial" in the community. Yet it should be axiomatic at this point in our nation's history that in a democracy "controversy" is, as a matter of constitutional law, never sufficient in and of itself to stifle the views of any citizen:

> "The vitality of civil and political institutions in our society depends on free discussion. . . . [I]t is only through free debate and free exchange of ideas that government remains responsive to the will of the people and peaceful change is effected. The right to speak freely and to promote diversity of ideas and programs is therefore one of the chief distinctions that sets us apart from totalitarian regimes."

Terminiello v. *Chicago,* 1949, 337 U.S. 1, 4, 69 S.Ct. 894, 895, 93 L.Ed. 1131, 1134–1135; *see also* Brooks v. *Auburn Univ.*, M.D.Ala. 1969, 296 F.Supp. 188, aff'd, 5 Cir. 1969, 412 F.2d 1171.

The two "controversial" subjects in the *Awakening* are a statement advocating a review of the laws regarding marijuana and another statement proffering information on, among other things, birth control.[9] We find the allegedly outrageous and "controversial" nature of these two subjects rather peculiar. Encouragements to become informed of social issues are certainly not the "fighting words" of *Chaplinsky* v. *New Hampshire,* 1941, 315 U.S. 568, 62 S.Ct. 766, 86 L.Ed. 1031, words that inherently prompt only divisiveness and disruption. Indeed, the President's Commission on Marijuana has advocated precisely what the *Awakening* is said to advocate, only the Commission did so in much stronger terms. And the school librarian testified at the school board hearing that a large number of books and newspapers on file for all students to read deal with the subject of birth control. We might add that a casual glance at any public medium would assure even the most doubtful observer that the general subjects of marijuana and birth control are rather widely-discussed. It appears odd to us that an educational institution would boggle at "controversy" to such an extent that the mere representation that students should become informed of two widely-publicized, widely-discussed, and significant issues that face the citizenry should prompt the board to stifle the content of a student publication. Perhaps newer educational theories have become in vogue since our day, but our recollection of the learning process is that the purpose of education is to spread, not to stifle, ideas and views.

Ideas in their pure and pristine form, touching only the minds and hearts of school children, must be freed from despotic dispensation by all men, be they robed as academicians or judges or citizen members of a board of education.

One of the great concerns of our time is that our young people, disillusioned by our political processes, are disengaging from political participation. It is most important that our young become convinced that our Constitution is a living reality, not parchment preserved under glass.[10] Almost thirty years ago the Supreme Court noted that boards of education

> ". . . have, of course, important, delicate, and highly discretionary functions, but none that they may not perform within the limits of the Bill of Rights. That they are educating the young for citizenship is reason for scrupulous protection of Constitutional freedoms of the individual, if we are not to strangle the free mind at its source and teach youth to discount important principles of our government as mere platitudes."

West Virginia State Board of Education v. *Barnette,* 319 U.S. at 637, 63 S.Ct. at 1185, 87 L.Ed. at 1637.

It is incredible to us that in 1972 the First Amendment was deemed inapplicable under these circumstances to high school students living at the threshold of voting and dying for their country.

We have discussed potential disturbance a great deal, for in substance that is what school discipline is designed to prevent. However, we must emphasize in the context of this case that even reasonably forecast disruption is not *per se justification* for prior restraint or subsequent punishment of expression afforded to students by the First Amendment:

> "[U]ndifferentiated fear or apprehension of disturbance is not enough to overcome the right to freedom of expression. Any departure from absolute regimentation may cause trouble. Any variation from the majority's opinion may inspire fear. Any word spoken, in class, in the lunchroom or on the campus, that deviates from the views of another person may start an argument or cause a disturbance. But our Constitution says we must take this risk . . . ; and our history says that it is this sort of hazardous freedom—this kind of openness—that is the basis of our national strength and of the independence and vigor of Americans who grow up and live in this relatively permissive, often disputatious, society."

Tinker v. *Des Moines Independent Community School Dist.*, 393 U.S. at 508–509, 89 S.Ct. at 737, 21 L.Ed.2d at 739.[11]

Reasonable regulation of expression is constitutionally preferable to restraint:

> "[A] function of free speech under our system of government is to invite dispute. It may indeed best

serve its high purpose when it induces a condition of unrest, creates dissatisfaction with conditions as they are, or even stirs people to anger. Speech is often provocative and challenging. It may strike at prejudices and preconceptions and have profound unsettling effects as it presses for acceptance of an idea. That is why freedom of speech, though not absolute . . . is nevertheless protected against censorship or punishment, unless shown likely to produce a clear and present danger of a serious substantive evil that rises far above public inconvenience, annoyance, or unrest. [citing cases]. There is no room under our Constitution for a more restrictive view."

Terminiello v. *Chicago*, 337 U.S. at 4, 69 S.Ct. at 896, 93 L.Ed. at 1135; *see also Shelton* v. *Tucker,* 1960, 364 U.S. 479, 81 S.Ct. 247, 5 L.Ed.2d 231.

If the content of a student's expression could give rise to a disturbance from those who hold opposing views, then it is certainly within the power of the school administration to regulate the time, place, and manner of distribution with even greater latitude of discretion. And the administration should, of course, take all reasonable steps to control disturbances, however generated. We are simply taking note here of the fact that disturbances themselves can be wholly without reasonable or rational basis, and that those students who would reasonably exercise their freedom of expression should not be restrained or punishable at the threshold of their attempts at expression merely because a small, perhaps vocal or violent, group of students with differing views might or does create a disturbance.

We realize that each situation involving expression and discipline will create its own problems of reasonableness, and for that reason we do not endeavor here to erect any immovable rules, but only to sketch guidelines. We emphasize, however, that there must be demonstrable factors that would give rise to any reasonable forecast by the school administration of "substantial and material" disruption of school activities before expression may be constitutionally restrained. While this court has great respect for the intuitive abilities of administrators, such paramount freedoms as speech and expression cannot be stifled on the sole ground of intuition. Thus, while we do not wholly disparage the comment of the MacArthur High School assistant principal in this case that the "attitude" of the school could somehow have changed during the minicrisis that was assertedly engendered by the appearance of the *Awakening,* we feel certain that the school administration can appreciate the fact that we must question this viewpoint unless it is substantiated by some objective evidence to support a reasonable "forecast" of disruption or by actual disruption. There is simply no demonstrable evidence whatsoever that the circumstances surrounding the distribution of the *Awakening* amounted to or could reasonably have been forecast to amount to a "material and substantial" disruption of school activity or discipline.

Although the students urge the argument, we do not feel it necessary to hold that *any* attempt by a school district to regulate conduct that takes place off the school ground and outside school hours can never pass constitutional muster. *See* Wright, The Constitution on Campus, 22 Vand.L.Rev. 1027. This court has evaluated situations involving off-campus activity and has required a fair hearing in such instances, *Dixon* v. *Alabama State Board of Education, supra,* but we have never had occasion to discuss the constitutional propriety of applying a school regulation directly to off-campus conduct. *See Sullivan* v. *Houston Independent School Dist., supra.* We do note, however, that it is not at all unusual to allow the geographical location of the actor to determine the constitutional protection that should be afforded to his or her acts. For example, the now-proverbial "fire" might be constitutionally yelled on the street corner, but not within the theater; or a march down the middle of a street might be protected activity, while a march down the hallway of a building might not. By the same token, it is not at all unusual in our system that different authorites have responsibility only for their own bailiwicks. An offense against one authority that it perpetrated within the jurisdiction of another authority is usually punishable only by the authority in whose jurisdiction the offense took place. Thus, contrary to the district court's opinion, the width of a street might very well determine the breadth of the school board's authority. Students, as any other citizens, are subject to the civil and criminal laws of the community, state, and nation. A student acting entirely outside school property is potentially subject to the laws of disturbing the peace, inciting to riot, littering, and so forth, whether or not he is potentially subject to a school regulation that the school board wishes to extend to off-campus activity. In our case the distribution of the *Awakening* was entirely off-campus and was effected only before and after school hours. The distribution was orderly and polite, and no disruption actually occurred or was reasonably foreseeable under the circumstances. Thus, we hold here only that the exercise of disciplinary authority by the school board under the aegis of "policy" 5114.2 was unconstitutionally applied to prohibit and punish presumptively-protected First Amendment expression that took place entirely off-campus and without "substantial and material" disruption of school activities, either actual or reasonably-foreseeable. Therefore, the Northeast Independent School District is enjoined from entering any zeros upon the permanent records of these five students that resulted from the unlawful suspensions or from preventing the students from making up work missed during the suspensions. We decline to enjoin the school board from prohibiting distribution of the *Awakening* under any and all circumstances, and we see no need under the traditional bases of equitable remedies to issue a protective injunction against the board. As we have made clear in this opinion, the balancing of expression and discipline is an exercise in judgment for school administrations and school boards, subject only to the constitutional requirement of reasonableness under the circumstances. We decline to attempt to conjure and transcribe every possible permutation of circumstances regarding the distribution of the *Awakening*, and we have complete faith that the school board and the school administration will make every effort to abide by the Constitution.

II.

However, under the circumstances of this case and this appeal, we are compelled to proceed further with "policy" 5114.2. Recognizing the close distinction between "unconstitutional as applied" and "facially unconsitiutional as overbroad," we are nevertheless compelled to declare the regulation is question facially unconstitutional as both overbroad and vague, and also as a denial of procedural due process. We do so with great hesitation and regret. But we do so in the interests of the sound judicial administration of this case and of those cases that might reasonably arise under the "policy" in question. In this case, in fact, the school board does *not* base its primary arguments on appeal upon potential or actual disruption of schol activities. Rather, the board chooses to assert that the suspensions of these five students are valid simply because the students allegedly violated "policy" 5114.2. Especially if the regulation is the sole rationale for punishment, the regulation must have a rationale constitutionally sufficient on its face. See *Eisner* v. *Stamford Board of Education, supra*.

Counsel for the school board argues on appeal that the regulation should be upheld facially because it *could* be interpreted in a reasonable manner. Counsel then proceeds to advocate a school board interpretation that is thoroughly unreasonable. Passing over the fact that the school board in this appeal has relied to a remarkable degree upon the conditional verb "could," we simply note that it is the school board's own actions that demonstrate most convincingly that the regulation is both overbroad and vague, and, therefore, constitutionally infirm on its face. Put another way, it is the school board's response to the circumstances involved in the distribution of the *Awakening* that has convinced us that counsel for the students is correct in urging that a facial approach to "policy" 5114.2 is required of this court.

We conclude that the regulation is overbroad: (1) because it purports to establish a prior restraint on any and all exercise of expression by means of the written word on the part of high school students at any time and in any place and for any reason; and (2) because it contains no standards whatsoever by which principals might guide their administrative screenings of "petitions or printed documents of any kind, sort, or type."

There is absolutely no requirement in "policy" 5114.2 that the proscribed activity of attempting to publish or distribute "any printed document" relate in any way whatsoever to maintaining the orderly conduct of school activities. The regulation in question does not facially lend itself to any limitation in terms of intent, time, or geography to what should be its principal concern—the sound administration of the school. It is true, as the school board insists on appeal, that freedom of expression is not an absolute and that expression must, on occasion, be balanced against other constitutional considerations. However, in insisting that expression be "balanced" the school board neglects to suggest what the ballast on the other side of the constitutional scales should be. The Second Circuit in *Eisner* v. *Stamford Board of Education, supra*, confronted a regulation regarding prior restraints on student publications and implied that the regulation there might be constitutional on its face as a matter of overbreadth. But the regulation in *Eisner* was at least school-oriented, whereas "policy" 5114.2 is life-away-from-home regulatory:

"The policy [of *Eisner*] does not in any way interfere with students' freedom to disseminate and to receive material outside of school property; nor does it threaten to interfere with the predominate responsibility of *parents* for their children's welfare."

Eisner v. *Stamford Board of Education*, 440 F.2d at 808 [emphasis in text].

If there were some limiting language in the "policy," we would be very much inclined to pretermit this holding. Unfortunately there is no such limitation, and the school board's action here has confirmed our worst fears regarding the variations of interpretation that could pervert the regulation. When questioned at the school board hearing regarding the scope of the "policy," the assistant principal of MacArthur High School responded:

"I think that any student publication should be presented to us and since this is broad, I think it is left up to a Principal's good judgment. For approval, any student publication, as far as time and miles, or feet, or blocks, if this is what you are interpreting it is left up to the good judgment of the school administrator."

At the district court hearing the school superintendent generally agreed with this assessment of the scope of the policy. We repeat that we do not derogate the "good judgment of the school administrator" in any way whatsoever. But the Constitution can be no more loosely interpreted because the motivations behind its infringement may be benign. Because that part of "policy" 5114.2 that deals with the publication and distribution of materials, by its terms and by the announced administrative interpretations accorded it, sweeps protected activity wholly outside the school context along with proscribed activity, the "policy" is facially overbroad and unconstitutional to that extent. See Zwickler v. Koota, 1967, 389 U.S. 241, 88 S.Ct. 391, 19 L.Ed.2d 444; Hobbs v. Thompson, 5 Cir. 1971, 448 F.2d 456; see also NAACP v. Button, 1963, 371 U.S. 415, 83 S.Ct. 328, 9 L.Ed.2d 405.

The "policy" is also facially overbroad because there are no standards whatsoever by which a principal may accept or reject a student publication or distribution. It appears that some petitions or documents of a political nature, regarding a pending school bond election, were distributed at MacArthur High School with the blessing and even the encouragement of the administration and the school board. We have absolutely no way of discerning on what basis those documents were accepted while the *Awakening* was not, or why a student may pass around the *San Antonio Light,* which might have a number of informational or advocative stories on marijuana laws or on birth control, or on any other "controversial" subject, but not the *Awakening*. We do not doubt in any manner the existing and continuing good faith of the school administration and the school board in attempting to enforce discipline by means of "policy" 5114.2. But our constitutional system does not permit any school board or administrator, however well-intentioned, to be the unaccountable imperator of the lives of our children. We cannot withdraw from the Constitution to the extent that the intellectual training of school-aged minds utterly escapes First Amendment rights and responsibilities. The mere statement of the potential penumbral invasion contemplated by this "policy" shudders the conscience of those to whom the First Amendment is sacred. It can be negated by benevolent, though perhaps misguided, satraps of our schools. In order to remedy this element of overbreadth, the thrust of the "policy" in question must include guidelines stating clear and demonstrable criteria that school administrators should utilize to evaluate materials submitted to them for prior clearance and distribution. We have discussed earlier the problems involved in attempts to regulate content for content's sake, and we reemphasize it at this point only to encourage the school board to seek administrative resolution of these content problems before cases reach the federal courts. See Riseman v. School Committee of Quincy, supra.

In addition, we must conclude that the regulation in question is unconstitutionally vague because the blanket prohibition against "distributions" or "attempts to distribute" does not reflect any reasonable, constitutional standards of the First Amendment as applied to the orderly administration of high school activities. The language of "policy" 5114.2 regarding what is intended by "distribution" is such that reasonable men not only can differ and have differed, but *should* differ substantially as to its meaning. See Connally v. General Construction Co., 1926, 269 U.S. 385, 46 S.Ct. 126, 70 L.Ed. 322; see also Baggett v. Bullit, 1964, 377 U.S. 360, 84 S.Ct. 1316, 12 L.Ed.2d 377. There is no intimation, let alone a requirement, that any proscribed "distribution" must interfere in a material and substantial way with the administration of school activity and discipline. In fact, the assistant principal of MacArthur High school conceded under interrogation at the board hearing that one student handing *Time* magazine to another student without the permission of the principal was presumptively in violation of "policy" 5114.2, and the school superintendent agreed with that evaluation of the "policy" at the district court hearing. See Eisner v. Stamford Board of Education, supra, for discussion of a very similar vagueness problem. If the school board here can punish students on the strength of this blunderbuss regulation for passing out any printed matter, off school grounds, outside school hours, and without any disruptions whatsoever, then why cannot the school board also punish any student who hands a Bible to another student on a Saturday or Sunday morning, as long as it does so in good faith? We resist the temptation to answer. In order to remedy its vagueness, the policy in question must include guidelines stating the relationship between the prevention or curtailment of "distribution" and the prevention of material and substantial disruption of school activities that the "policy" seeks to remedy.

Finally, we must conclude that the regulation in question is unconstitutional as a matter of due process. There is no provision in "policy" 5114.2, nor, to our knowledge, in any other school regulation, allowing for appeal from the decision of the school principal not to permit distribution and specifying a time period during which the principal or the appellate board must make their decisions. The occasions calling for the exercise of various forms of protected speech are fleeting, and lack of clarity or a delay in implementation of screening regulations carry the inherent danger that the exercise of speech might be chilled altogether during the period of its importance. Imprecision and delay serve only to underscore the fact that the constitutional ideal can be thwarted in petty ways, a frustrating experience in a democracy. Any regulation that proposes to screen and to sift out publications distributable to high school students under a regulation purporting to prevent substantial and material school disruption must: (1) state clearly the means by which students are to submit proposed materials to the principal or school administration; (2) state a brief and reasonable period of time during which the principal or administration must make their decisions; (3) state clearly a reasonable appellate mechanism and its methodology; and (4) state a brief and reasonable time during which the appeal must be decided. See Freedman v. Maryland, 1965, 380 U.S. 51, 85 S.Ct. 734, 13 L.Ed.2d 649; see also Eisner v. Stamford Board of Education, supra; Stacy v. Williams, N.D. Miss.1969 (three-judge court), 306 F.Supp. 963. Because "policy" 5114.2 contains none of these procedural safeguards, and because we can find no other regulation in the record before us that contains such safeguards, "policy" 5114.2 must be declared unconstitutional on its face insofar as it purports to restrain expression without provision for timely administrative appeal.

Tinker's dam to school board absolutism does not leave dry the fields of school discipline. This court has gone a considerable distance with the school boards to uphold its disciplinary fiats where reasonable. *See, e.g., Blackwell* v. *Issaquena School Dist., supra; cf. Karr* v. *Schmidt, supra; Ferrell* v. *Dallas Independent School Dist., supra. Tinker* simply irrigates, rather than floods, the fields of school discipline. It sets canals and channels through which school discipline might flow with the least possible damage to the nation's priceless topsoil of the First Amendment. Perhaps it would be well if those entrusted to administer the teaching of American history and government to our students began their efforts by practicing the document on which that history and government are based. Our eighteen-year-olds can now vote, serve on juries, and be drafted; yet the board fears the "awakening" of their intellects without reasoned concern for its effect upon school discipline. The First Amendment cannot tolerate such intolerance. This case is therefore reversed for entry of an order not inconsistent with this opinion.

Reversed.

CLARK, Circuit Judge (specially concurring):

I concur in all of Judge Goldberg's opinion except that portion of Part II holding that due process requires that school authorities not only provide a prompt administrative decision-making process for regulation of student expression, but also that they must create an administrative appellate mechanism as a part of such review process.

Although I agree that if school authorities provide for administrative appeals, such appeals must be prompt in decision and reasonable in procedure, I do not agree that such administrative appeal procedures are constitutionally bound to exist.

NOTES

1. The entire text of "policy" 5114.2, including an appended Texas statute on "disruption," reads as follows:
   "Policies on Disruptive Activities and Unauthorized Publications
   In keeping with the policy of this district to maintain, at all times, a proper learning situation, the board of Trustees hereby establishes what will be known as Policies on Disruptive Activities and Unauthorized Publications.
   Whereas several non-school organizations have publicized their intent to involve students in school boycotts for the purpose of focusing attention on the various concerns of these individual organizations and
   Whereas any distraction on a school campus works against the achievement of educational objectives and against the best interests of the entire student body and faculty and
   Whereas any non-approved loss of instructional time endangers a school's ability to meet accreditation standards and jeopardizes the value of scholastic records of all students and
   Whereas there is in existence in the schools of the North East District a structure for student government which provides opportunity for constructive involvement of all students in discussion and expression of opinion on appropriate topics and
   Whereas students and their parents have access to communication with the administration in individual schools and with the Central Office administration and
   Whereas there exists in each of the schools of the North East District many varied opportunites for student participation in school organizations and
   Whereas the established curricular offerings of the North East District include opportunities for students to develop communicative skill in creative arts,
   Be it resolved that any student who participates in a boycott, sit-in, stand-in, walk-out, or other related form of unauthorized activity shall by this action be subject to suspension or expulsion and
   Be it further resolved that any attempt to avoid the school's established procedure for administrative approval of activities such as the production for distribution and/or the distribution of petitions or printed documents of any kind, sort, or type without the specific approval of the principal shall be cause for suspension and, if in the judgment of the principal there is justification, for referral to the Office of the Superintendent with a recommendation for expulsion and
   Be it further resolved that any staff member who initiates by his instruction or who supports by his position any student or any group of students who

are involved in disruptive activity shall be subject to disciplinary action by the Superintendent and the Board of Trustees.

In addition to the above policies those disruptive activities which are specified and defined in House Bill 141 of the 1969 Session of the Texas Legislature (as shown immediately following this paragraph) shall be cause in this school district for suspension or recommendation for expulsion as appropriate in the judgment of the principal of the school concerned.

PROHIBITING CERTAIN DISRUPTIVE ACTIVITIES IN PRIVATE OR PUBLIC SCHOOLS OR INSTITUTIONS OF HIGHER EDUCATION

'Section 1. No person or group of persons acting in concert may willfully engage in disruptive activity or disrupt a lawful assembly on the campus or property of any private or public school or institution of higher education or public vocational and technical school or institute.

'Sec. 2. (a) For the purposes of this act, "Disruptive activity" means:

'(1) obstructing or restraining the passage of persons in an exit, entrance, or hallway or any building without the authorization of the administration of the school;

'(2) seizing control of any building or portion of a building for the purpose of interfering with any administrative, educational, research, or other authorized activity;

'(3) preventing or attempting to prevent by force or violence or the threat of force or violence any lawful assembly authorized by the school administration;

'(4) disrupting by force or violence or the threat of force or violence a lawful assembly in progress; or

'(5) obstructing or restraining the passage of any person at an exit or entrance to said campus or property or preventing or attempting to prevent by force or violence or by threats thereof the ingress or egress of any person to or from said property or campus without the authorization of the administration of the school.

'(b) For the purposes of this Act, a lawful assembly is disrupted when any person in attendance is rendered incapable of participating in the assembly due to the use of force or violence or due to a reasonable fear that force or violence is likely to occur.

'Sec. 3. A person who violates any provision of this Act is guilty of a misdemeanor and upon conviction is punishable by a fine not to exceed $200 or by confinement in jail for not less than 10 days nor more than 6 months, or both.

'Sec. 4. Any person who is convicted the third time of violating this Act shall not thereafter be eligible to attend any school, college, or university receiving funds from the State of Texas for a period of two years from such third conviction.

'Sec. 5. Nothing herein shall be construed to infringe upon any right of free speech or expression guaranteed by the Constitutions of the United States or the State of Texas.'

Students and parents are advised that, in addition to the school administrative procedures, school officials, wherever deemed advisable, will initiate complaints with legal authorities against any person or persons who violate HB 141 or any of its terms."

2. Counsel for the school board insisted in his brief and during oral argument that the students here sought confrontation, desiring the attendant publicity. If that were true, the students would find themselves in a precarious position. It is not part of the learning process in high school to challenge regulations, however questionable, by confrontation and suit in federal court. School regulations are best left to be resolved at the local level, where the problems are more familiar to those involved and the procedures are more personal. The students are asking for relief that is equitable in nature, and, as in any equity suit, they must come with "clean hands." If there are administrative procedures to clarify or to challenge the questioned regulation, then those procedures should be tried first. *See Quarterman* v. *Byrd,* 4 Cir. 1971. 453 F.2d 54: Blackwell v. *Issaquena County Board of Education,* 5 Cir. 1966, 363 F.2d 749. However, we feel that counsel for the school board substantially misrepresented the students in this case. Despite substantial questioning by the board's counsel during the school board hearing regarding the suspensions, the students maintained convincingly that they honestly and reasonably interpreted the regulation as inapplicable to the course of conduct that they had followed. In addition, even if there might be some other internal administrative regulation that the students might have used to get an authoritative interpretation or to appeal any interpretation of "policy" 5114.2, and we have no such regulation in the appellate record, there is overwhelming testimony in the transcript of the school board hearing that no such mechanism was ever brought to the attention of the student body. The error of judgment by the students in engaging in their conduct without first consulting school authorities, if it were indeed an error in judgment, is much less objectionable than the concomitant error in judgment by the school board. While the students perhaps failed to recognize the intended scope of the regulation as actually applying to conduct exercised completely out of school and off school premises, the school board likewise failed to recognize even the bare existence of the First Amendment when it first drafted that part of "policy" 5114.2 which is involved in this appeal.

3. The district court's order reads as something of a hybrid: part dismissal, F.R.Civ.Pro. 12(b) (6), part summary judgment, F.R.Civ.Pro. 56(b), part "abstention," part equity, and part a denial of federal question jurisdiction, 28 U.S.C.A. § 1331.

4. With regard to high school discipline cases, one district court has hypothesized a distinction between "major" and "minor" penalties, the former subject to judicial review and the latter presumably too *de minimis* for application of constitutional standards. *Soglin* v. *Kauffman,* W.D.Wis.1968, 295 F.Supp. 978, aff'd., 7 Cir. 1969, 418 F.2d 163. While we intimate no view with regard to the overall propriety of this distinction, we merely observe that the "magnitude" of a penalty should be gauged by its effect upon the student and not simply meted out by formula. For example, a suspension of even one hour could be quite critical to an individual student if that hour encompassed a final examination that provided for no "make-up." We are convinced here that the three-day suspensions issued to these five high school seniors, who were in the process of applying to and interviewing for college admission and for scholarships, constitute a justiciable penalty under any "major"/"minor" dichotomy.

5. The district court apparently agreed with counsel for the school board. Although citing *Burnside* as applicable to

in the manner that the public school systems are operated by the respective sovereign States." *Shanley* v. *Northeast Independent School Dist.*, W.D.Tex.1972, Case No. SA-72-CA-48 [February 2, 1972]. We find this refusal unacceptable in light of the plethora of cases involving school systems. A trial court is sometimes confronted with the prospect of applying laws from a legislative body or a high court that do not fit four-square with its own interpretations. But proper application under those circumstances is, to our understanding, the single most important guiding principle of law and of orderly process well back into our Anglo-Saxon legal heritage.

6. For example, we doubt that a school board could not restrain the sort of inflammatory and vitriolic exhortation that was protected by the Supreme Court in *Terminiello* v. *Chicago*, 1949, 337 U.S. 1, 69 S.Ct. 894, 93 L.Ed. 1131, in the context of a speaking engagement before paying adults.

7. We see no reason to toy with *Tinker's* placement of that burden on the school board when the regulation is alleged to have been unconstitutionally applied rather than unconstitutional on its face: first, since it is the school board that asserts the right to curtail presumptively protected activity, the board should bear the burden of establishing why; and second, the school board presumably has the essential information that led it to conclude that the activity had to be curtailed.

8. One may also exceed his or her constitutional rights of expression by adopting a method of expression that materially and substantially interferes with the rights of others or with the conduct of school activities. *See, e. g., Blackwell* v. *Issaquena Board of Education, supra; Barker* v. *Hardway, supra; Tate* v. *Board of Education of Jonesboro*, 8 Cir. 1972, 453 F.2d 975. The more active the methodology of expression, the more inherent its potential interference. Although passing out newspapers is a more active mode of expression than the wearing of buttons, *see Burnside* v. *Byars, supra; Tinker* v. *Des Moines Independent Community School Dist., supra*, and therefore subject to greater disruptive potential, the *Tinker* rationalization of the First Amendment and high school discipline has been held applicable to various so-called active forms of expression, including the distribution of high school newspapers. *See, e. g., Eisner* v. *Stamford School Dist., supra; Scoville* v. *Joliet Twp. School Dist., supra; Sullivan* v. *Houston Independent School Dist., supra; Quarterman* v. *Byrd, supra.* All parties to this case agree that distribution of the *Awakening* was polite, orderly, and non-disruptive. None of the students tried to force papers on anyone; no one attempted to block ingress or egress to a building; students were, in fact, discouraged from taking the papers onto the school grounds. The distributors of the *Awakening* merely handed newspapers to those who wished to read them, nothing more. We find nothing whatsoever in the means of distribution followed by these students that is offensive to the rights of others or potentially disruptive in a material and substantial way to the conduct of school activities.

9. The assertedly objectionable parts of the *Awakening* read as follows:

"An estimated 23 million Americans have smoked marijuana including 43% of all college students. Under the existing laws all of them could go to jail. Smoking marijuana isn't the issue, unjust laws are.
NORMAL
(National Organization for the Reform of Marijuana Laws) For information write . . .
  NORMAL
  Washington, D. C.,
  2105 N Street Northwest."
  * * *
"For information & treatment of
  A. V.D.
  B. Birth Control
  C. Food & Nutrition
  D. General Medical Treatment
  E. Psychological Aid
  F. Drug Counseling
  G. Draft Counseling
San Antonio Free Clinic
  Call .... 733–0383."

10. The school administration also expressed concern at what it believed to be the "negative" attitude of the newspaper and at the criticism overt and covert, of the school administration. "Negativism" is, of course, entirely in the eye of the beholder, and presumably the school administration's eye became fixed upon the criticism by the students. As those to whom public and private criticism, of widely varying degrees of intention and rationality, has been directed, we can say with some pained assurance that "criticism," like "controversy," is not a bogey, at least not in a democracy. Of course, constructive criticism is far more helpful than any other sort of critique. But almost any effort to explain a different mode of operation or approach serves to illuminate the issue being questioned. If the criticism is irrational or ill-intentioned, then surely the American citizenry, even that of high school age, will have enough good sense to attach that much more credibility to the criticized actors and their actions. Without discussing any ramifications, since no discussion is compelled, suffice it to say that aversion to "criticism" is not a constitutionally reasonable justification for forbidding the exercise of First Amendment expression. The First Amendment's protection of speech and expression is part of the Bill of Rights precisely because those governed and regulated should have the right and even the responsibility of commenting upon the actions of their appointed or elected governors and regulators.

11. *But cf Karr* v. *Schmidt, supra*, where the majority concluded that the possibility that short-haired students might physically challenge long-haired students was an acceptable reason for a prior restraint upon the length of students' hair. *See Massie* v. *Henry*, 4 Cir. 1972, 455 F.2d 779, for a different treatment of the same argument. However, *Karr* was premised upon the holding of the majority that long hair was not in that instance a constitutionally-protected mode of expression within the contours of the First Amendment. No one seriously questions that a newspaper is not a presumptively-protected mode of expression within the First Amendment.

THE Court of Appeals of New York decides against taxpayers who sought to compel college officials "to suppress publication in student newspapers of articles grossly offensive to religion." In concluding that such censorship was unconstitutional, the Court said: "In the instant case, there is no showing that college officials originally intended or now intend to promote or inhibit religion by sponsoring the student newspapers. Indeed, the secular objectives furthered by the provision for these newspapers are several and obvious. Students who work on newspapers develop skills in journalism and management. The newspaper provides the campus community with the news and with a calendar of events. College officials, campus organizations, students, and alumni may communicate with other groups. The newspaper provides an opportunity for the exchange of intellectual ideas, not necessarily good ones. It serves as a neutral forum for debate of social and local issues of campus concern. A neutral forum by definition provides place or space for contention on controversial issues. If religious issues fall within that purview they may not be excluded as unmentionable, so long as the provider of the forum maintains its strict neutrality. In short, the purpose of sponsorship of student newspapers is neither advancement nor inhibition of religion, if there is in truth a neutral forum. . . . There is no showing that the articles attacking religion were systematic or continuing, or that articles and letters presenting counterattacks were excluded. . . . That the debate may at times be illiterate, distasteful, insulting, and even shocking, indeed by intention, does not change the original purpose of the college support. The grant of financial aid benefited the attacked as well as the attackers. Use of state moneys to support the newspapers does no more to establish a religion or inhibit it, than use of state moneys to build auditoriums, to provide police protection for speakers, or to subsidize distribution of literature, including religious proselyzing through the mails."

Panarella v. *Birenbaum,* 296 N.E.2d 238 (1973)

BREITEL, Judge.

These are consolidated proceedings under CPLR article 78 to compel the officials of two tax-supported public colleges to suppress publication in student newspapers of articles grossly offensive to religion. The articles attack particular organized religions in terms derogatory, profane, and blasphemous. In one of the articles, the vocabulary of common obscenity is used, although no party tenders any issue of obscenity. The newspapers are financed out of college funds and mandatory student fees.

The issue is whether student papers underwritten by the school, open to the expression of diverse opinions, which, at least on two occasions, have crossed over into the area of religion, may be prohibited from so doing on the ground that government's neutrality on religious issues is thereby violated.

Special Term 60 Misc.2d 95, 302 N.Y.S. 2d 427, had directed the college officials to regulate the content of the newspapers insofar as religious materials were concerned. The Appellate Division 37 A.D.

987, 327 N.Y.S.2d 755, reversed.

The order of the Appellate Division should be affirmed. Tax-supported colleges may provide financial assistance for a student newspaper publishing an occasional article attacking religious beliefs, so long as the nature of the attack is arguably within constitutionally protected publication. The colleges merely provided a neutral forum for debate, and did not evidence an intent to advance or destroy religious beliefs. Only if the colleges continued financial support to a newspaper systematically attacking religion over a period of time, without balance, might there be an attempt to "establish" a "secular religion". Absent such a showing, censorship by college officials of occasional articles touching on religious beliefs would violate freedom of the press.

Petitioners in the Panarella proceeding are a student at Staten Island Community College and his father. In the Mahoney proceeding, petitioners are four taxpaying students at Richmond College. Both colleges are components of the City University of New York. Both are financed in part by State and local funds, and are under the control of the Board of Higher Education of the City of New York.

The students at Staten Island Community College publish a student newspaper called *The Dolphin*.Sometime before April 16, 1969, an article appeared in the newspaper entitled, "The Catholic Church—
Cancer of Society". The article by a purportedly former Catholic is a vulgar and not too literate diatribe against the Catholic Church. The Church hierarchy is described as the ("holy Mafia"; the saints as "neurotic masochists"; and Catholic schools are termed "institutions of lunacy". The tone is unrelentingly disputatious and insulting.

Nine letters to the editor of the student publication appeared in response to this article. Eight took issue with the article's criticism of the Church, some insisting that the author was abusing the freedom of speech. One letter commented favorably on the article.

The student newspaper at Richmond College is *The Richmond Times*. During 1969, the newspaper printed an article entitled "From the Hart," evidently expressing a Black militant attitude toward Christianity. At best it may be described as a sexual allegory of the reaction of prejudiced whites against Jesus Christ reborn of a black mother. Its tone is "shockingly vile and offensive." The imagery borders on the obscene, and the language, as noted, is drawn from the vocabulary of obscenity.

The student newspapers are funded by mandatory student fees collected at the beginning of each semester. *The Richmond Times* displays the official seal of the City University of New York, and *The Dolphin*displays the seal of the Community College. The staffs of the publications are severally provided with an office on campus and a college telephone. Faculty members serve as advisors. Students are invited in student handbooks to participate in publishing the newspapers.

The petitioning students and taxpayers contend that permitting the publication of articles attacking religion in newspapers supported by public funds and identified with public institutions violates the establishment clause of the First Amendment. They contend that college newspapers, sponsored by public institutions, may not publish articles hostile to religion and disparaging to sacred religious beliefs. They argue that the freedom of expression has no relevance where the effect of the articles is to establish a "secular religion". Petitioners request that the colleges adopt and enforce regulations prohibiting derogatory references to religion.

Special Term found for the petitioners and directed the college officials to prevent publication of similar articles in the future. The court held there was a violation of the establishment clause, reasoning that "a government that underwrites attacks on religion is no longer neutral." The Appellate Division reversed and dismissed the petitions holding that the colleges had merely established a forum for the free expression of ideas, and that once having established such a forum, college officials may not "place limitations upon its use which infringe upon the rights of the students to free expression". Mr. Justice Munder, dissenting in the Richmond College case, found *The Richmond Times* article so offensive that it should be suppressed to prevent the State from subverting religion and to enforce decorum on the campus.

The establishment clause of the First Amendment has been interpreted to prevent the government from becoming an active participant in religious affairs. Thus, the Supreme Court has held invalid a system of release time for religious instruction conducted on public school premises (*McCollum* v. *Board of Educ.*,333 U.S. 203, 68 S.Ct. 461, 92 L.Ed. 649), a program of prayers and Bible-reading in the public schools (*Abington School Dist.* v. *Schempp,* 374 U.S. 203, 83 S.Ct. 1560, 10 L.Ed.2d 844; *Engel* v. *Vitale,*370 U.S. 421, 82 S.Ct. 1261, 8 L.Ed.2d 601), and programs of public school instruction favoring a religious view of life (*Epperson* v. *Arkansas,* 393 U.S. 97, 89 S.Ct. 266, 21 L.Ed.2d 228). On the other hand, the Supreme Court has sustained government programs and laws having secular objectives, despite incidental benefit or hindrance to religion. Thus, States have been permitted to enforce Sunday closing laws (*McGowan*v. *Maryland,* 366 U.S. 420, 81 S.Ct. 1101, 6 L.Ed.2d 393), to reimburse parents for the cost of transporting their children to parochial schools (*Everson* v. *Board of Educ.,*330 U.S. 1, 67 S.Ct. 504, 91 L.Ed. 711), and to provide textbooks for students in these schools (*Board of Educ.* v. *Allen,* 392 U.S. 236, 88 S.Ct. 1923, 20 L.Ed.2d 1060). (See, generally, P. G. Kauper, the Walz Decision: More on the Religion Clauses of the First Amendment, 69 Mich.L.Rev. 179, 180–181.)

The *Schempp* case (374 U.S. 203, 83 S.Ct. 1560, 10 L.Ed.2d 844, *supra*), involving prayers in public schools, provides a general standard for determining if government action violates the establishment clause: "The test may be stated as follows: what are the purpose and the primary effect of the enactment? If either is the advancement or inhibition of religion then the enactment exceeds the scope of legislative power as circumscribed by the Constitution. That is to say that to withstand the strictures of the Establishment Clause there must be a secular legislative purpose and a primary effect that neither advances nor inhibits religion." (374 U.S., at p. 222, 83 S.Ct., at p. 1571.) Similarly, in the *Epperson* case (393 U.S. 97, 89 S.Ct. 266, 21 L.Ed.2d 228, *supra*), where the court struck down an Arkansas statute making it unlawful for a teacher in a State-supported school to teach a theory of biological evolution, the court stated that government "may not be hostile to any religion or to the advocacy of no-religion; and it may not aid, foster, or promote one religion or religious theory against another or even against the militant opposite" (393 U.S., at P. 104, 89 S.Ct., at p. 270).

In the recent case of *Walz* v. *Tax Comm.,* 397 U.S. 664, 90 S.Ct. 1409, 25 L.Ed.2d 697, the court sustained property tax exemptions to religious organizations for properties used solely for religious worship. Chief Justice Burger's opinion for a 7–1 majority states that for those who wrote the religion clause of the First Amendment the "establishment" of religion connoted "sponsorship, financial support, and active involvement of the sovereign in religious activity" (397 U.S., at p. 668, 90 S.Ct., at p. 1411). As a definition, this language suggests a more restrictive view of establishment than some of the court's earlier utterances (*id.,* see Kauper, *op. cit., supra,* 69 Mich.L.Rev., at p. 197; Comment, The Supreme Court, 1969 Term, 84 Harv.L.Rev. 32, 129). As Chief Justice Burger elaborated: "The course of constitutional neutrality in this area cannot be an absolutely straight line; rigidity could well defeat the basic purpose of these provisions, which is to insure that no religion be sponsored or favored, none commanded, and none inhibited. The general principle deducible from the First Amendment and all that has been said by the Court is this: that we will not tolerate either governmentally established religion or governmental interference with religion. Short of those expressly proscribed governmental acts there is room for play in the joints productive of a benevolent neutrality which will permit religious exercise to exist without sponsorship and without interference." (397 U.S., at P. 669, 90 S.Ct., at p. 1412.)

In the instant case, there is no showing that college officials originally intended or now intend to promote or inhibit religion by sponsoring the student newspapers. Indeed, the secular objectives furthered by the provision for these newspapers are several and obvious. Students who work on newspapers develop skills in journalism and management. The newspaper provides the campus community with the news and with a calendar of events. College officials, campus organizations, students, and alumni may communicate with other groups. The newspaper provides an opportunity for the exchange of intellectual ideas, not necessarily good ones. It serves as a neutral forum for debate of social and local issues of campus concern. A neutral forum by definition provides place or space for contention on controversial issues. If religious issues fall within that purview they may not be excluded as unmentionable, so long as the provider of the forum maintains its strict neutrality. In short, the purpose of sponsorship of student newspaper is neither advancement nor inhibition of religion, if there is in truth a neutral forum.

There is no showing that the articles attacking religion were systematic or continuing, or that articles and letters presenting counterattacks were excluded. The record indicates that two articles were published, one in each paper, and one of these was answered by letters to the editor. That the debate may at times be illiterate, distasteful, insulting, and even shocking, indeed by intention, does not change the original purpose of the college support. The grant of financial aid benefited the attacked as well as the attackers. Use of State moneys to support the newspapers does no more to establish a religion or inhibit it, than use of State moneys to build auditoriums, to provide police protection for speakers, or to subsidize distribution of literature, including religious proselyzing, through the mails. The action of college officials may not be interpreted as an attempt to establish a "secular religion"; they simply have not spared religion, any more than love of country, from the attack of individuals expressing their own contentions.

Granting financial means to a newspaper occasionally publishing articles promoting or condemning religion may give rise to some, but yet a lesser, involvement than censoring articles having a religious subject, or terminating financial aid when religious attacks are published. The questions are "whether the involvement is excessive, and whether it is a continuing one calling for official and continuing surveillance leading to an impermissible degree of entanglement" (*Walz* v. *Tax Comm.*, 397 U.S. 667, 675, 90 S.Ct. 1414, *supra*). Control for the content of the newspaper would entail sustained and detailed review of religious material submitted for publication. The hazards that articles indirectly favorable to established religions may be allowed while hostile articles are suppressed, or the other way around, are hardly less under a system of review by college officials, than the hazards that articles of one persuasion or another may appear with undue frequency in an unfettered, subsidized press.

Indeed, on reflection it should be evident that exclusion of all religious material from a student newspaper, however balanced or neutrally supervised, could defeat a significant number or acceptable civilized purposes. Would such neutrality prohibit the listing of church and religious events, or even extended advertising of such events? Would it prohibit the publication of serious, well-written descriptions of religious practices and customs? Would indeed neutrality in religion prohibit the study—the critical study—of comparative religion and religious history? Or, even more troublesome, the study of religious controversy as a part of a course in secular history? It would be difficult, in the interest of preserving religion from attack to avoid excluding every passing reference to religion or religious event. Thus, the test is not the appearance of derogatory or critical material, but whether government, and government schools, maintain neutrality in the sense of permitting all sides of any religious controversy to be raised and never permit one side or another to be favored directly or indirectly. This is not to say that the problem for the schools and, therefore, for the courts is not a subtle one, and one that will not arise again to require decisions even more difficult than this one. This must be so if only because there is a collision here between two primary constitutional principles, contained indeed in the same First Amendment of the Federal Constitution (cf. N.Y. Const., art. I, §§ 3, 8). It would be a sad day when only in private colleges legitimate controversies engendered by religion could be the subject of study and discussion.

There remains only the suggestion by the dissenter at the Appellate Division that the *Richmond Times* article, described by him as "a vile, vulgar and lewd attack upon Christianity", should be suppressed to maintain an efficient school system. It suffices to say that neither petitioners nor college officials have urged that either of the articles be suppressed on this ground. Indeed, unless it can be shown that suppression is necessary to avoid material and substantial interference with the requirements of order and discipline in the operation of the college, publication is protected by freedom of the press (*Trujillo* v. *Love,* 322 F.Supp. 1266, 1270–1271 [D.Col.]; *Antonelli* v. *Hammond,* 308 F.Supp. 1329, 1336–1337 [D.Mass.]; *Dickey* v. *Alabama State Bd. of Educ.,* 273 F.Supp. 613, 617–618 [M.D.Ala.]; cf. *Tinker* v. *Des Moines School Dist.,* 393 U.S. 503, 511, 89 S.Ct. 733, 21 L.Ed.2d 731; *Burnside* v. *Byars,* 363 F.2d 744, 748–749 [5th Cir.]).

Nor is any issue presented that the schools have incompetently permitted newspapers of such poor quality and content to be purveyed that they are subject to administrative correction for that reason. Obviously, such an issue would not be available in a judicial proceeding of this kind.

Accordingly, the order of the Appellate Division should be affirmed, without costs.

FULD, C. J., and JASEN, GABRIELLI, JONES and WACHTLER, JJ., concur with BREITEL, J.

BURKE, J., dissents in part and votes to affirm as to Staten Island Community College and to reverse as to Richmond College on the dissenting opinion at the Appellate Division.

Order affirmed.

A United States District Court in New Hampshire declares unconstitutional the Portsmouth Board of Education's rule forbidding distribution of non-school sponsored written materials on school grounds. Also, the Court states that "if the school continues to provide a forum for outside speakers, it do so in a manner consistent with the constitutional principles herein specified." The Court concludes with its "order" which reads, in part: "1. The defendants are enjoined from enforcing the present rule relative to the distribution of non-school sponsored written materials. 2. All suspensions for the distribution of leaflets on school property and grounds are hereby voided, and it is ordered that defendants expunge the students' records of all such suspensions.... 9. The procedural requirements relative to suspensions and expulsions shall be made a part of the Student Handbook. 10. This opinion and order is to be posted on the school bulletin board in a prominent place, and copies of this opinion and order are to be made available to the students in the school library."

Vail v. Bd. of Education of Portsmouth School Dist., 354 F.Supp. 592 (1973)

BOWNES, District Judge.

This is a students civil rights class action brought pursuant to 42 U.S.C. § 1983 in which the plaintiffs seek declaratory relief under 28 U.S.C. § 2201 and 2202 and injunctive relief for the alleged deprivations, under color of State law, of rights of public school students secured by the First and Fourteenth Amendments to the United States Constitution. Jurisdiction is based on 28 U.S.C. § 1343(3, 4).

Three basic constitutional issues are raised:

First, does the Portsmouth School Board rule forbidding "the distribution of non-school sponsored written materials within Portsmouth schools and on school grounds for a distance of 200 feet from school entrances" violate the First and Fourteenth Amendments to the United States Consititution.

Second, does the Portsmouth High School policy concerning outside speakers violate the First and Fourteenth Amendments to the United States Constitution.

Third, does the Portsmouth School Board suspension procedure whereby students are suspended without a prior hearing violate the Due Process Clause of the Fourteenth Amendment.

This is a class action maintainable under F.R.Civ.P. 23(b)(2). Plaintiff Vail is a twelfth grade student and plaintiff Mayo is an eleventh grade student at Portsmouth High School, Portsmouth, New Hampshire. The class consists of all of those students similarly situated to the named plaintiffs.

The defendants, all of whom are sued in their official capacities, consist of the Board of Education of the Portsmouth School District and all of the members thereof and James J. Cusick, Superintendent of Schools.

Plaintiffs' motion for a preliminary injunction was denied on September 29, 1972. A hearing was held on February 1, 1973.

THE FACTS

The essential facts have been stipulated.

On November 12, 1969, the Board of Education of the Portsmouth School District adopted a rule forbidding "the distribution of non-school sponsored written materials within Portsmouth schools and on school grounds for a distance of 200 feet from school entrances." All of the students and the general public have been apprised of this rule. There have been in excess of eight suspensions of students for distributing leaflets without permission in violation of the rule.

Plaintiff Vail has been suspended three times for violating this rule. On June 2, 1970, plaintiff Vail and others were suspended from school for distributing written materials outside the front door of Portsmouth High School before the start of the school day, but while the school was open. On April 13, 1972, Vail was suspended from school for five days for "[d]istribution of leaflets on school property and/or grounds." On that same day, Larry Dukes was suspended from school for five days for "giving out leaflets on the school grounds Wednesday, April 12, without permission."

Rule 15 of the Discipline Code adopted by the Portsmouth Board of Education on August 25, 1970, reads in pertinent part as follows:

> Students who are defiant to school officials, including teachers, will be suspended for ten school days....

On several occasions, school officials have told Vail that the distribution of written materials on school grounds constituted "defiance."

Prior to the March, 1972 presidential primary, a number of presidential candidates spoke at the Portsmouth High School during the school day. During these talks, representatives of the candidates distributed leaflets, stickers, and buttons within the school contrary to the School Board rule.

In early November, 1971, an attorney representing plaintiffs Vail, Mayo, and other students met with the Superintendent of Schools to discuss the distribution of literature at the Portsmouth High School. Specifically, the students asked that they be allowed to distribute the *Strawberry Grenade*, a local Portsmouth, New Hampshire, publication. On November 16, 1971, Attorney Johnson requested that the Board of Education place the matter of distribution of literature on the agenda of its next meeting. On November 23, 1971, Johnson met with the Board of Education and presented the views of the students he represented as to the distribution of literature at the school. The Board denied the petition presented by Attorney Johnson requesting that his clients (students) be allowed to distribute the *Strawberry Grenade* in the Portsmouth schools because the rule of November 12, 1969, prohibited such distribution and because the specific publication in question (November 11, 1971, issue of the *Strawberry Grenade*) "has no redeeming educational, social, or cultural value; that its distribution could substantially disrupt normal educational activities; and that its distribution might incite lawless action."

In the period prior to the March, 1972 New Hampshire presidential primary, a number of presidential candidates spoke in the Portsmouth High School during the school day. The speakers included Edmund Muskie, George McGovern, Samuel Yorty, Vance Hartke, and Paul McCloskey. In addition, a representative of Paul McCloskey spoke on behalf of Mr. McCloskey.

Shortly thereafter, plaintiffs Vail and Mayo attempted to secure permission for Andrew Pulley, Vice-Presidential candidate of the Socialist Workers Party, to speak in the school. Over a period of several weeks, contacts were made with the school principal, the faculty advisor to the Junior World Council (a club), and a student member of the Junior World Council. These persons made no definitive statement regarding Mr. Pulley's speaking at the school. At the suggestion of the school principal, Vail and Mayo made an appointment with Superintendent Cusick to discuss the question of Mr. Pulley's speaking in the Portsmouth High School. A meeting was held on April 5, 1972, during which Superintendent Cusick inquired about Mr. Pulley's age and the views of the Socialist Workers Party. In a memorandum dated April 5, 1972, Mr. Cusick denied the students' request on the grounds that Mr. Pulley was not a bona fide candidate, since he was not eligible to serve as Vice-President because he had not attained the age of thirty-five as required by Article 2, Section 1, Clause 5, of the United States Constitution.

No written rules were given plaintiffs during their efforts to secure permission for Mr. Pulley to speak. After this action was filed, defendants produced, at plaintiffs' request, undated rules concerning political candidates. In a document entitled "Rules and Regulations Governing the Guest Speakers for the Social Studies Department and Junior World Council," it is stated that "[c]andidates seeking political office who are bona fide candidates are given equal time."

In 1971–72 there were four speakers at the High School in addition to the specified candidates, including a man who spoke about religion and representatives of the V.F.W. and American Legion who discussed patriotism. Vail testified that on January 19, 1973, he spoke to the Principal of Portsmouth High School with regard to the bringing of an anti-war speaker to the school. The principal suggested that a debate between a pro-war and an anti-war speaker might be arranged and told Vail to return with a concrete program for such a debate. Vail testified that no pro-war speaker could be located and that, therefore, the principal denied permission for any anti-war speaker to address the school.

The suspensions for periods up to five days that Vail and other students received for violations of the November 12, 1969, literature distribution rule were effected without any prior hearings. A suspended student receives a zero for school work missed and must have a form, entitled "No Make-up," signed by teachers upon returning to school. The daily absentee list designates by an "S" next to his or her name that a student is suspended. A copy of the notice letter informing parents of the suspension is placed in the student's permanent record file.

Other suspensions during the 1971–72 school year occurred for the following reasons: (1) "for stealing a wallet with money in it"; (2) "for making a derogatory remark about Mr. Bacon in front of the school in the presence of several students"; (3) "disruption of history class by excessive talking and disrespect for the teacher's authority"; and (4) "defiance and obscene language to a teacher."

DISTRIBUTION OF LITERATURE

It is well settled that First Amendment rights are available to both students and teachers in the school environment as well as elsewhere. The Supreme Court in *Tinker* v. *Des Moines School Dist.,* 393 U.S. 503, 506, 89 S.Ct. 733, 736, 21 L.Ed.2d 731 (1969), made this clear when it stated that neither "students [n]or teachers shed their constitutional rights to freedom of speech or expression at the schoolhouse gate." On the other hand, the Supreme Court in *Tinker, supra,* also emphasized "the need for affirming the comprehensive authority of the States and of school officials, consistent with fundamental constitutional safeguards, to prescribe and control conduct in the schools." At page 507, 89 S.Ct. at page 737. [Citations omitted.]

The Portsmouth School Board adopted a regulation on November 12, 1969, expressly forbidding "the distribution of non-school sponsored written material within Portsmouth schools and on school grounds for a distance of 200 feet from school entrances." Several students have been suspended from Portsmouth High School for distributing literature on school grounds in violation of this rule. What is presented by these facts is a direct collision between the students' exercise of their First Amendment rights and a rule of the school authorities.

When the constitutionality of a school regulation is questioned, the burden of justifying the regulation falls upon the school board. *Tinker* v. *Des Moines School Dist., supra; Burnside* v. *Byars,* 363 F.2d 744 (5th Cir. 1966). The test for curtailing in-school exercise of expression is whether or not the expression or its method of exercise "materially and substantially" interferes with the activities or discipline of the school. See *Burnside* v. *Byars, supra,* at 749; *Tinker* v. *Des Moines School Dist., supra,* at 509. And, of course, the authority of the school board to balance school discipline against the First Amendment by forbidding or punishing activity on school grounds cannot exceed its authority to forbid or punish in-school activity. See *Shanley* v. *Northeast Ind. Sch. Dist., Bexar County, Tex.,* 462 F.2d 960, 968 (5th Cir. 1972), reh. denied (1972). The sole purpose of any literature distribution regulation is to prevent disruption and not to stifle expression.

The regulation assailed by the plaintiffs is a blanket prohibition against the distribution of all non-school sponsored written materials. It does not reflect any reasonable, constitutional standards of the First Amendment as applied to the orderly administration of high school activities. There is no intimation, let alone a requirement, that any proscribed "distribution" must interfere in a "material and substantial" way with the administration of school activity and discipline or with the rights of other students. The rule in question does not facially lend itself to any limitation in terms of intent, time, place, and manner of distribution of literature. *Riseman* v. *School Committee of City of Quincy,* 439 F.2d 148 (1st Cir. 1971). The regulation does not reflect any effort on the part of the School Board to minimize the adverse effect of prior restraint. *Freedman* v. *Maryland,* 380 U.S. 51, 85 S.Ct. 734, 13 L.Ed.2d 649 (1965); *Riseman* v. *School Committee of City of Quincy, supra.*

I find that the rule is unconstitutional as overbroad and that it violates the First Amendment right of freedom of speech of the plaintiffs. This ruling does not prevent the defendants from promulgating reasonable, specific regulations setting forth the time, manner, and place in which distribution of written materials may occur. This does not mean, however, that the School Board may require a student to obtain administrative approval of the time, manner, and place of the particular distribution he proposes. Rather, the Board has the burden of telling students when, how, and where they may distribute materials, consistent with the basic premise that the only purpose of any restrictions on the distribution of literature is to promote the orderly administration of school activities by preventing disruption and not to stifle freedom of expression. For example, the Board may provide that all leafletting is to take place outside of the school building or in the student lounge and in such a manner that regular classroom and other school activities are not interfered with.

Because the rule is unconstitutional, the suspensions under it cannot stand. *Fujishima* v. *Board of Education,* 460 F.2d 1355, 1359 (7th Cir. 1972); *Quarterman* v. *Byrd,* 453 F.2d 54 (4th Cir. 1971). In the present case, there is no evidence and no finding can be made that the suspended plaintiffs were disciplined because of the content of the publications being distributed. The letter (Attachments 5 and 6 to the Stipulation of Facts) announcing the suspensions of plaintiffs Vail and Dukes indicate that the reason for the supensions was solely the "distribution of leaflets on school property and grounds."

Plaintiffs were denied permission to distribute the *Strawberry Grenade* in the Portsmouth schools not only because of the ban on the distribution of non-school sponsored literature, but also because the specific issue in question (November 11, 1971) was found to have "no redeeming educational, social, or cultural value; its distribution could substantially disrupt normal educational activities; and its distribution might incite lawless action."

Free speech under the First Amendment is not absolute, and the extent of its application may properly take into consideration the age or maturity of those to whom it is addressed. As Justice Stewart stated in his concurring opinion in *Tinker* v. *Des Moines School Dist., supra*, "the First Amendment rights of children are not co-extensive with those of adults." 393 U.S. at page 515, 89 S.Ct. at p. 741. It is generally held that the constitutional right to free speech of public secondary school students may be modified or curtailed by school regulations "reasonably designed to adjust these rights to the needs of the school environment." *Antonelli* v. *Hammond*, 308 F.Supp. 1329, 1336 (D.C.Mass.1970). Specifically, school authorities may exercise a reasonable prior restraint on the content of publications distributed on school premises during school hours only in those special circumstances where they can "reasonably 'forecast substantial disruption of or material interference with school activities'" on account of the distribution of such printed material. *Eisner* v. *Stamford Board of Education*, 440 F.2d 803, 806–807 (2nd Cir. 1971). A similar policy prevails where the printed material is obscene or libelous. See *Shanley* v. *Northeast Ind. Sch. Dist., Bexar County, Tex., supra*, at 970–971 of 462 F.2d.

I do not here delimit the categories of materials over which a high school administration may exercise a reasonable prior restraint of content, for I realize that specific problems will require individual and specific judgments. The *ad hoc* resolution of such issues, however, must be based on "reasonableness" and not upon the "undifferentiated fear or apprehension of disturbance," *Tinker* v. *Des Moines School Dist., supra*, 393 U.S. at 508, 89 S.Ct. at 737, nor upon dislike or disagreement with the views expressed in the written material.

The *Strawberry Grenade* is a periodical whose content may vary from issue to issue. Therefore, one cannot generalize about the periodical except to note that it is clearly not of high journalistic, literary, cultural, or educational standards. The sort of profanity and vulgarisms which appear in the November 11, 1971, issue of the *Strawberry Grenade*, however crude they may seem, do not compel a finding that the periodical is obscene. The words that appear in that issue are not used to appeal to prurient sexual interests, see *Sullivan* v. *Houston Indep. School Dist.*,333 F.Supp. 1149, 1162–1167 (S.D.Tex.1971), and fall without the prevailing legal definition of obscenity. See *Roth* v. *United States*, 354 U.S. 476, 77 S.Ct. 1304, 1 L.Ed.2d 1498 (1957), and *Cohen* v. *California*, 403 U.S. 15, 91 S.Ct. 1780, 29 L.Ed.2d 284 (1971), reh. denied, 404 U.S. 876, 92 S.Ct. 26, 30 L.Ed.2d 124 (1971).

The Portsmouth School Board found that the distribution of the November 11, 1971, issue of the *Strawberry Grenade* "*could* substantially disrupt normal educational activities" and "*might* incite lawless action." [Emphasis added.] The Board's "could" or "might" ruling does not comport with the controlling case law standards established in *Tinker*v. *Des Moines School Dist., supra.*

But, in our system, undifferentiated fear or apprehension of disturbance is not enough to overcome the right to freedom of expression. Any departure from absolute regimentation *may* cause trouble. Any variation from the majority's opinion *may*inspire fear. Any word spoken, in class, in the lunchroom, or on the campus, that deviates from the views of another person *may* start an argument or cause a disturbance. But our Constitution says we must take this risk, *Terminiello* v. *Chicago,*337 U.S. 1, 69 S.Ct. 894, 93 L.Ed. 1131 and our history says that it is this sort of hazardous freedom—this kind of openness—that is the basis of our national strength and of the independence and vigor of Americans who grow up and live in this relatively permissive, often disputatious, society.

In order for the State in the person of school officials to justify prohibition of a particular expression of opinion, it must be able to show that its action was caused by something more than a mere desire to avoid the discomfort and unpleasantness that always accompany an unpopular viewpoint. Certainly where there is no finding and no showing that engaging in the forbidden conduct *would*"materially and substantially interfere with the requirements of appropriate discipline in the operation of the school," the prohibition cannot be sustained. *Burnside* v. *Byars, supra*, 363 F.2d at 749.

* * *

On the contrary, the action of the school authorities appears to have been based upon an urgent wish to avoid the controversy *which might result* from the expression, even by the silent symbol of armbands, of opposition to this Nation's part in the conflagration in Vietnam. (393 U.S. at pp. 508–510, 89 S.Ct. at pp. 737, 738. Emphasis added, footnote omitted.)

Therefore, the absolute ban on the distribution of the *Strawberry Grenade* in the Portsmouth schools cannot withstand constitutional attack as it constitutes an unreasonable prior restraint of freedom of expression. This ruling is not to be interpreted as judicial acquiescence in the views espoused by the *Strawberry Grenade* nor as judicial license to distribute all future issues of the periodical on school grounds. School authorities may, by appropriate regulation, exercise prior restraint upon publications distributed on school premises during school hours only in those special circumstances where they can "reasonably 'forecast substantial disruption of or material interference with school activities'" on account of the distribution of such printed material. *Eisner* v. *Stamford Board of Education, supra,* at 806–807, of 440 F.2d. If a reasonable basis for such a forecast exists, it is not necessary that the school stay its hand in exercising a power of prior restraint "until disruption actually occurred." *Butts* v. *Dallas Ind. School Dist.,* 436 F.2d 728, 731 (5th Cir. 1971); *Norton* v. *Discipline Committee of East Tenn. State Univ.,* 419 F.2d 195, 198 (6th Cir. 1969), cert. denied, 399 U.S. 906, 90 S.Ct. 2191, 26 L.Ed.2d 562 (1970); *LeClair* v. *O'Neil,* 307 F.Supp. 621, 625 (D.C. Mass.1969), aff'd. 401 U.S. 984, 91 S.Ct. 1219, 28 L.Ed.2d 524 (1971). But there must be substantial facts which reasonably support a forecast of likely disruption. For example, if on the basis of substantial reliable information, the school authorities believe that a given publication is pornographic or advocates destruction of school property or urges "physical violence" against teachers or fellow students, then the school officials would be justified in prohibiting the distribution of such material on school premises during school hours.

OUTSIDE SPEAKERS

Although the speaker sought to be invited to the Portsmouth High School is not a plaintiff in this suit, the legal interests of the students who sought to invite Andrew Pulley and who would have made up part of the audience are sufficient to present a substantial legal controversy with the school authorities who denied permission for Pulley's appearance. *Smith* v. *University of Tennessee,* 300 F.Supp. 777, 780 (E.D.Tenn.1969); *Snyder* v. *Board of Trustees of University of Illinois,* 286 F.Supp. 927 (N.D.Ill.1968).

This particular issue involves the balancing of the rights of students protected by the First and Fourteenth Amendments of the United States Constitution and of the school officials to control and regulate public speaking on school property.

Freedom of speech encompasses the right to "receive information and ideas." *Stanley* v. *Georgia,* 394 U.S. 557, 564, 89 S.Ct. 1243, 22 L.Ed.2d 542 (1969); *Lamont* v. *Postmaster General,* 381 U.S. 301, 85 S.Ct. 1493, 14 L.Ed.2d 398 (1965). The First Amendment protection of free speech embraces the right to hear and, therefore, extends to listeners. *Lamont* v. *Postmaster General, supra; Brooks* v. *Auburn University,* 412 F.2d 1171 (5th Cir. 1969); *Martin* v. *City of Struthers,* 319 U.S. 141, 63 S.Ct. 862, 87 L.Ed. 1313 (1943).

The only speaker regulation in effect at the Portsmouth High School pertains to political candidates and reads as follows:

Candidates seeking political office who are bona fide candidates are given equal time.

Pulley was denied permission to speak because Superintendent Cusick was of the opinion that he was not a "bonafide" candidate.[1] The only standard in the regulation is that the potential speaker be a "bonafide candidate." While it may have been improper for the Superintendent to have made a determination as to who is a "bonafide candidate," the focus at this point (the election having passed) must be on the standards for non-candidates where there are apparently no rules.

While the school might bar all outside speakers, the interchange of ideas and beliefs that is fostered by providing a forum for outside speakers is healthy and beneficial to the entire educational process.

If the school provides a forum for outside speakers, as Portsmouth High School has done, it must do so in a manner consistent with constitutional principles. Access to the podium must be permitted without discrimination. It is not for the school to control the influence of a public forum by censoring the ideas, the proponents, or the audience. The right of the student to hear a speaker cannot be left to the discretion of school authorities on a pick and choose basis. Freedom of speech and assembly require that outside speakers be fairly selected and that equal time be given to opposing viewpoints.

The plaintiffs contend that there is persuasive evidence that school officials have discriminated against them in violation of the equal protection clause of the Fourteenth Amendment because of the refusal to allow Pulley to speak, because of the refusal to allow an anti-war speaker to address the school, and because of the allowance of proponents of religion and patriotism to speak. I am not convinced on the basis of this slim evidence that purposeful discrimination has occurred. The political candidate regulation purports to give equal time to opposing candidates. Furthermore, the Principal of Portsmouth High School indicated his evenhandedness by suggesting that if a debate between a pro-war and an anti-war speaker could be arranged, the school would provide a forum.

Because the election has passed, I am not constrained to order that Pulley be given an opportunity to address the students at Portsmouth High School. I do, however, order that if the school continues to provide a forum for outside speakers, it do so in a manner consistent with the constitutional principles herein specified.

SUSPENSION PROCEDURE

Plaintiffs also raise the constitutional issue of whether the Due Process Clause requires that a student be afforded notice and the opportunity for a hearing prior to his being suspended. Although the suspensions complained of are void because the rule that the plaintiffs violated and which was the basis for their suspension is unconstitutional, this due process issue is not moot and is properly before the court.

The Portsmouth High School Discipline Code does not provide for any hearing prior to suspension. Suspensions for up to ten days are authorized under the Code in some instances, i.e., defiance to school officials and threats and intimidation to fellow students.[2] It is uncontradicted that the plaintiffs were suspended without a hearing of periods up to five days.

The following statutory provisions contained in New Hampshire Revised Statutes Annotated are relevant:

189:1 *Days of School.* The school board of every district shall provide standard schools for at least one hundred and eighty days in each year., ...

189:1-a *Duty to Provide Education.* It shall be the duty of the school board to provide, at district expense, elementry and secondary education to all pupils under twenty-one years of age who reside in the district, provided that the board may exclude specific pupils for gross misconduct or for neglect or refusal to conform to the reasonable rules of the school, ...

189:15 *Regulations.* The school board may, unless otherwise provided by statute or state board regulations, prescribe regulations for the attendance upon, and for the management, classification and discipline of, the schools; . . . .

193:1 *Duty of Pupil* Every child between six and sixteen years of age shall attend [school] . . . .

193:13 *Suspension and Dismissal of Pupils.* The superintendent, or his representative as designated in writing, is authorized to suspend pupils from school for gross misconduct, providing that where there is a suspension lasting beyond five school days, the parent or guardian has the right to appeal any such suspension to the local board. Any suspension to continue beyond twenty school days must be approved by the local board. Any pupil may be dismissed from school by the local school board for gross misconduct or for neglect or refusal to conform to the reasonable rules of the school and said pupil shall not attend school until restored by the local board. Any dismissal must be subject to review if requested prior to the start of each school year and further, any parent or guardian has the right to appeal any such dismissal by the local board to the state board of education.

The requirements of procedural due process apply only to the deprivation of interests encompassed within the Fourteenth Amendment's protection of liberty and property. When protected interests are implicated, the right to some kind of prior hearing is paramount.[3] *Board of Regents of State Colleges et al.* v. *Roth,* 408 U.S. 564, 92 S.Ct. 270, 33 L.Ed.2d 548 (1972). But the range of interest protected by procedural due process is not infinite.

While the meaning of "liberty" guaranteed by the Fourteenth Amendment has not been defined with precise exactness, the term has received much judicial consideration, and some of the rights included within it have been defined and stated. Without doubt, it denotes the right of an individual "to acquire useful knowledge," *Meyer* v. *Nebraska,* 262 U.S. 390, 399, 43 S.Ct. 625, 67 L.Ed.2d 1042 (1923).

The precise nature of the private interest sought to be protected here is the right of students to remain in attendance at a public school in order to obtain an education. It requires no argument to demonstrate that education is vital, and, indeed, basic to civilized society. Society now recognizes that public elementary and secondary school education is a state-granted constitutional right. See NH RSA 189:1-a and 193:1.

Having concluded that the plaintiffs' interest is one that is protected by the Due Process Clause, the resolution of the issue in this case depends in large part on whether the student's interest in having a prior hearing outweighs the school's interest in swift and summary adjudication for disciplinary purposes. Minimum procedural requirements necessary to satisfy due process depend upon the circumstances and the interest of the parties involved. *Hobson* v. *Bailey,* 309 F.Supp. 1393, 1402 (W.D.Tenn.1970).

If a school is to function properly, it is necessary that rules governing the conduct of students, which do not rise to the level of criminality, but which are designed to regulate the relationship between the school authorities and the students based upon practical and ethical considerations, be formulated and promulgated. It is now established that adequate notice of the prohibited conduct must be provided. The Student Handbook in this case does list various offenses for which discipline may be imposed.

The point at which disciplinary actions becomes subject to constitutional scrutiny is when the action adversely affects the basic right of a student to an education. It is settled law that a school must afford some opportunity for a hearing when dealing with expulsions. See *Dixon* v. *Alabama State Board of Education,* 294 F.2d 150 (5 Cir. 1961); *Knight* v. *Board of Education of City of New York,* 48 F.R.D. 108, 111 (E.D.N.Y.1969); *Baker* v. *Downey City Board of Eduction,* 307 F.Supp. 517 (C.D.Calif.1969); *Vought* v. *Van Buren Public Schools,* 306 F.Supp. 1388 (E.D.Mich.1969). When the prospective discipline involved is a lengthy suspension, it is nearly equivalent in its adverse effect[4] upon the student as an expulsion and should, therefore, fall within the rule requiring a hearing. *Madera* v. *Board of Education of City of New York,* 386 F.2d 778, 784 (2nd Cir. 1967).

I am aware that if the temporary suspension of a high school student could not be accomplished without first preparing written specification of charges and giving notice of and holding a fair hearing, the discipline and ordered conduct of the educational program and the moral atmosphere required by good educational standards would be difficult to maintain. Therefore, it is only when punishment by a lengthy suspension is to be imposed that the constitutional right to due process requires written specification of charges, notice, and a full prior hearing.

I hold that due process requires at least an informal administrative consultation with a student before any suspension is imposed so that the student can know why he is being disciplined and so that the student can have the opportunity to persuade the school official that the suspension is not justified, e.g., that this is a situation of mistaken identity or that there is some other compelling reason not to take action. However, when a student is expelled or suspended for a period of more than five school days, minimal standards of procedural due process require the following:

1. The accused student and at least one of his parents or his guardian shall be furnished, either in person or by mail directed to the student's last known address, [a letter] with written notice of the charges and of the nature of the evidence against the accused student.
2. The accused student and at least one of his parents or his guardian shall be offered a formal hearing after sufficient time to prepare a defense or reply, at which hearing evidence in support of the charge shall be presented by school officials and the accused student or his parent or guardian shall have ample opportunity to present any defense or reply.
3. The decision of school officials to impose such discipline shall be based upon a dispassionate and fair consideration of substantial evidence that the accused student committed the acts for which suspension is to be imposed and that such acts are in fact a proper reason for such suspension.

These minimal due process requirements are in addition to the statutory rights of appeal contained in NH RSA 193:13.

ORDER

1. The defendants are enjoined from enforcing the present rule relative to the distribution of non-school sponsored written materials.
2. All suspensions for the distribution of leaflets on school property and grounds are hereby voided, and it is ordered that defendants expunge the students' records of all such suspensions.
3. Written notice of the expungement is to be provided to all students who are affected by this action.
4. Counsel for the parties shall jointly review defendants' suspension records from the date of the adoption of the November, 1969, rule to the present to identify any additional suspensions for violation of the distribution rule, and such suspensions shall be expunged and the students so notified.
5. Counsel shall have the right to inspect school records to see to it that there has been compliance with this court's order.
6. The defendants are further ordered to study the records of all students affected by the suspensions to determine the impact, if any, of the policies of awarding zeros and denying make-up work because of suspensions. The defendants shall report to this court, and to opposing counsel, not later than thirty days after the date of this court's order, on the results of this review. The report shall cover:
    (a) In general, the steps taken to comply with this paragraph;
    (b) The impact, if any, of each suspension on the affected students' grades; and
    (c) The feasibility, if and where an impact is shown, of adjusting grades and permanent school records.
7. The Portsmouth School Board is ordered to comply with the due process requirements set forth herein with regard to the suspension or expulsion of students from school.
8. Notice of the statutory provisions of NH RSA 193:13 shall be given to any student suspended for more than five days and to his parent or guardian.
9. The procedural requirements relative to sus-

pensions and expulsions shall be made a part of the Student Handbook.

10. This opinion and order is to be posted on the school bulletin board in a prominent place, and copies of this opinion and order are to be made available to the students in the school library.

The court will retain jurisdiction pending compliance with this court order.

NOTES

1. It is undisputed that Pulley was not eligible to serve as Vice-President in that he had not attained the age of thirty-five as required by Article 2, Section 1, Clause 5, of the United States Constitution.
2. See guidelines 15 and 16 for disciplinary action contained in the Portsmouth High School Student Handbook.
3. Before a person is deprived of a protected interest, he must be afforded opportunity for some kind of a hearing, "except for extraordinary situations where some valid governmental interest is at stake that justifies postponing the hearing until after the event." *Boddie* v. *Connecticut,* 401 U.S. 371, 379, 91 S.Ct. 780, 786, 28 L.Ed.2d 113 (1971). "While '[m]any controversies have raged about...the Due Process Clause,'... it is fundamental that except in emergency situations due process requires that when a State seeks to terminate [a protected] interest..., it must afford 'notice and opportunity for a hearing appropriate to the nature of the case' *before* the termination become effective." *Bell* v. *Burson,* 402 U.S. 535, 542, 91 S.Ct. 1586, 1591, 29 L.Ed.2d 90 (1971).
4. In addition to a suspended student receiving zeros for all work missed and being denied an opportunity to "make-up" the work, a copy of the notice of suspension is placed in the students' permanent record file. A lengthy or indefinite suspension may prevent the student from obtaining credit for a particular course or term and may well affect the grades received. In addition, the record of the suspension may jeopardize a student's future employment and educational opportunities as guidance counselors prepare student recommendations after having examined the student's permanent record file which contains the notice of suspension.

THE United States Court of Appeals, Fifth Circuit, decides against high school students who had been suspended from school for violating school regulations requiring "prior submission to the school principal of all publications, not sponsored by the school, which were to be distributed on the campus or off campus in a manner calculated to result in their presence on the campus." The Court argued that there was more at issue in this case than the students' non-compliance with the distribution regulations: "In our view . . . Paul's [one of the plaintiffs] conduct in the instant case outweighs his claim of First Amendment protection and gave school officials sufficient grounds for disciplining him . . . . Paul defied Mr. Cotton's request that he stop selling the newspapers, persisted in returning to the campus during the initial six-day suspension period, and twice shouted profanity at Mr. Cotton within the hearing of others. Paul's reappearance on the campus and continued sale of the newspapers on October 26 served only to exacerbate the situation. . . . Considering Paul's flagrant disregard of established school regulations, his open and repeated defiance of the principal's request and his resort to profane epithet, we cannot agree that the school authorities were powerless to discipline Paul simply because his actions did not materially and substantially disrupt school activities." The Court went out of its way to make clear what it was deciding: "We hasten to point out that by thus limiting our review of this case we do not invite school boards to promulgate patently unconstitutional regulations governing student distribution of off-campus literature. Nor, needless to say, do we encourage school authorities to use otherwise valid regulations as a pretext for disregarding the rights of students. Today, we merely recognize the right of school authorities to punish students for the flagrant disregard of established school regulations; we ask only that the student seeking equitable relief from allegedly unconstitutional actions by school officials come into Court with clean hands."

Sullivan v. *Houston Independent School Dist.*, 475 F.2d 1071 (1973)

THORNBERRY, Circuit Judge:

This case arises from the unauthorized distribution of an "underground" newspaper near a high school campus, and presents the now-familiar clash between claims of First Amendment protection on the one hand, and the interests of school boards in maintaining an atmosphere in the public schools conducive to learning, on the other. We vacate the supplemental grant of injunctive relief to plaintiff-appellee Paul Kitchen. In doing so, we hope to furnish guidelines that will prove helpful to all parties— students, school officials, and courts—in balancing the competing interests in this delicate and crucial area of the law.

The case is here on appeal from an order of the district court, 333 F.Supp. 1149, supplementing a 1969 permanent injunction. The facts giving rise to that first permanent injunction are set out at 307 F.Supp. 1328, and need not be recounted here. Suffice it to say that Dan Sullivan and another student at Sharpstown High School in Houston had been summarily expelled for distributing, free of charge, a publication of their own creation, *Pflashlyte*. This disciplinary action had been taken ostensibly as punishment for the boys' violation of an extremely vague regulation of the Houston Independent School District[1] and of the school principal's unwritten and unannounced interpretation of that regulation.[2] The boys filed suit in the court below seeking declaratory and injunctive relief under 42 U.S.C. § 1983. After issuing a comprehensive memorandum, Judge Woodrow Seals set out detailed requirements to be met by the School District in regulating student distribution of literature on or near the campus and in disciplining students for violations of school regulations.[3] The School District appealed from this order, but the appeal was dismissed on the District's own motion on May 21, 1970.

Rather than prosecute the appeal, the School District chose to formulate a new set of regulations. A biracial committee of students, school officials, parents, attorneys, and representatives of other interested groups held hearings and developed an extensive set of regulations dealing with various aspects of school discipline. The rules required prior submission to the school principal of all publications, not sponsored by the school, which were to be distributed on the campus or off campus in a manner calculated to result in their presence on the campus. The principal was given one working day to review the publication before general distribution. If, in the opinion of the principal and School District attorneys, the publication contained "libelous or obscene language or advocate[d] illegal action or disobedience to published rules on student conduct adopted by the Board of Trustees," then the principal could withhold his approval of the publication and it could not be distributed. The rule provided, however, that distribution could not be prohibited because the publication "contained the expression of any idea, popular or unpopular." Besides requiring prior submission, the regulation expressly permitted distribution before and after school hours on school premises, absolutely prohibited the sale of publications on school premises and the distribution of political campaign material or material consisting primarily of commercial advertising, and required that the publication contain the names of the contributors, editors, and publishers.

In addition to these provisions governing distribution of publications, the new regulations contained specific provisions governing suspension procedures. For violation of any published regulation of the School District governing student conduct, a student could be suspended for a reasonable time not exceeding three school days upon the giving of written notice to parents or guardian of the reasons for the suspension. If the suspension was to last for more than three school days or for an indefinite period, the student and his parents or guardian were entitled to written notice of the reasons for suspension and were to be offered a prompt hearing before the principal, at which they could produce witnesses and be assisted by counsel. The student was to be given the right to appeal the principal's decision to the assistant superintendent for a *de novo* hearing. The assistant superintendent could affirm the principal's decision if the *de novo* hearing produced substantial evidence supporting it, and the student could appeal the assistant superintendent's decision to the School Board. The School Board adopted the new regulations in February or March 1970, and copies were posted in each school building in the District. Several months later, the event occurred that forms the basis for the instant appeal.

Before classes started on the morning of October 20, 1970, Paul Kitchen, a junior student at Waltrip Senior High School, was standing near an entrance to the campus selling *Space City!*, an "underground" newspaper, to students as they entered the campus. Gordon Cotton, the Waltrip principal, purchased a copy and scanned its contents. On the second page he noticed a letter, captioned "High Skool is F... ed" and containing several other instances of coarse language. Mr. Cotton told Paul that he was selling the papers in violation of the prior submission rule, and asked him to stop. Paul continued selling the papers. At this point, Mr. Cotton determined to suspend Paul for his failure to comply with both the prior submission rule and Mr. Cotton's request that he stop selling the papers. Before Paul was sent home, Mr. Cotton notified both his parents by telephone that Paul was being suspended and told them the reasons for his decision. Mr. Cotton requested that both parents come to the school for a conference, but Mr. Kitchen replied that his job would prevent his attending a conference until six days later. A conference was agreed to be held on Ocotber 26, 1970, and it was agreed that Paul would remain on suspension until that date. As Paul was leaving Mr. Cotton's office after being informed that he was to be suspended, he slammed the door and shouted "I don't want to go to this goddamn school anyway" within the hearing of two of Mr. Cotton's female assistants.

During the period of Paul's agreed suspension between October 20 and October 26, he returned to the campus several times purportedly to talk with his teachers. Each time school officials told him to leave the campus because students were not allowed on school premises while under suspension. On the morning of October 26, the day on which the conference with Paul's parents was scheduled, Paul was again at the entrance to the campus selling *Space City!* to students on their way to school. Mr. Cotton showed Paul a copy of the prior submission rule, and told him that if he did not stop selling the papers he would call the police. In response, Paul shouted "the common Anglo-Saxon vulgarism for sexual intercourse" in apparent reference to Mr. Cotton. Paul was taken to the police station but was released without charges having been filed. Mr. Kitchen obtained legal counsel and failed to appear for the scheduled conference with Mr. Cotton. Later that day, Mr. Cotton notified Paul's parents in writing that he was suspending Paul for violating the prior submission rule and using profanity in the presence of his secretary, and informed them of the suspension procedures available to students and parents under the new regulations.

On October 29, 1970, Mr. Cotton conducted a hearing at which Paul was represented by counsel. Following the hearing Mr. Cotton suspended Paul for the remainder of the semester, on the basis of Paul's violation of the prior submission rule and his use of profanity toward Mr. Cotton. A *de novo* appellate hearing was conducted before the assistant superintendent on November 9, 1970. Paul appeared with his father and an attorney; an extensive evidentiary hearing was held during which witnesses were cross-examined and testimony was transcribed by a court reporter. The assistant superintendent affirmed Mr. Cotton's decision; and the transcript of the appellate hearing was reviewed by the Deputy Superintendent for Secondary Schools and the Superintendent for Instruction and Administration, who both affirmed the suspension.

On November 23, 1970, Paul and his father applied in the court below for an order holding the School District in contempt for violating the 1969 permanent injunction, and for supplementary injunctive relief and damages in aid of the injunction. On the following day the court entered an *ex parte* temporary restraining order directing that Paul be permitted to attend classes at Waltrip High School; without the consent of the School District, this temporary restraining order was extended for ten-day periods for a total of fifty-nine days. At the direction of the court, a four-hour hearing was held before the School Board, at which Paul and his father, represented by counsel, presented and cross-examined witnesses. The Board declined to entertain a facial challenge to the new regulations, ordered Paul suspended for an additional two weeks beginning January 4, 1971, and directed that he be placed on probation for the remainder of the school year.

Following a hearing, the court below chastised Paul for not challenging the new regulations by orderly means, found that he had been unlawfully suspended, ordered that he be allowed credit for school work missed during the suspension, and declined to hold the School Board in contempt or award damages or attorney fees because the defendants had acted in good faith. On October 7, 1971, the court issued a supplementary injunctive decree, clarifying and elaborating the terms of its original 1969 injunction. Both sides appeal, urging a myriad of contentions regarding the trial court's refusal to vacate the 1969 permanent injunction, the reasons for suspending Paul, the procedures used in his suspension, and the failure to award damages and attorney fees. The view we take of this case makes it necessary for us to address only a few of these contentions.

I

On appeal and in the court below, Paul Kitchen's position has been basically, that his selling the newspaper was an activity protected by the First Amendment. Pointing to the fact that sale of the newspaper created little, if any, disruption of normal school activities—let alone the "material and substantial" disruption required by *Tinker* v. *Des Moines Independent Community School District,* 393 U.S. 503, 89 S.Ct. 733, 21 L.Ed.2d 731 (1969), and its progeny—he argues that the prior submission rule was unconstitutionally applied to him. He claims further that the language in the newspaper was not constitutionally obscene and that therefore the school officials could not suppress it. In our view, however, Paul's conduct in the instant case outweighs his claim of First Amendment protection, and gave school officials sufficient grounds for disciplining him.

As the court below recognized when it rebuked Paul for failing to challenge the prior submission rule by "lawful" means, Paul's conduct can hardly be characterized as the pristine, passive acts of protest "akin to pure speech" involved in *Tinker, supra.* Rather, Paul defied Mr. Cotton's request that he stop selling the newspapers, persisted in returning to the campus during the initial six-day suspension period, and twice shouted profanity at Mr. Cotton within the hearing of others. Paul's reappearance on the campus and continued sale of the newspapers on October 26 served only to exacerbate the situation.

Moreover, Paul never once attempted to comply with the prior submission rule. Given the widespread publicity accorded the new rules, it taxes credulity to say that on October 20 Paul was unaware of the rule requiring prior submission; he most certainly knew about the rule after Mr. Cotton showed him a copy on October 26 before suspending him for a second time. Had Paul submitted the newspaper prior to distribution and had it been disapproved, then he could have promptly sought relief in the courts without having been first suspended from school. Having chosen to disregard established school policy regarding distribution of off-campus literature, Paul's opportunity for obtaining relief from the principal's decision was delayed by several months of administrative appellate hearings, during which his academic career suffered severely from continued suspension.

Considering Paul's flagrant disregard of established school regulations, his open and repeated defiance of the principal's request, and his resort to profane epithet, we cannot agree that the school authorities were powerless to discipline Paul simply because his actions did not materially and substantially disrupt school activities. In the years since *Tinker* was decided courts have refused to accord constitutional protection to the actions of students who blatantly and deliberately flout school regulations and defy school authorities. Thus, in *Schwartz v. Schuker,* E.D.N.Y.1969, 298 F.Supp. 238, a high school student disregarded several prior warnings of the principal not to distribute literature without prior permission. The court declined to reach the student's constitutional arguments and refused to grant him injunctive relief because he had failed to challenge the principal in an orderly manner. The same result was reached in *Graham v. Houston Independent School District,* S.D.Tex.1970, 335 F.Supp. 1164, where Judge Ingraham of this court, sitting as a district judge by designation, based his denial of injunctive relief on the student's disregard of established school regulations. *See also Duke v. North State Univ.,* 5th Cir. 1972, 469 F.2d 829; *Esteban v. Central Missouri State College,* 8th Cir. 1969, 415 F.2d 1077; *Quarterman v. Byrd,* 4th Cir. 1971, 453 F.2d 54, 60 n. 11. Finally, in *Healy v. James,* 408 U.S. 169, 92 S.Ct. 2338, 33 L.Ed.2d 266 (1972), the Court approved the principle that the open disregard of school regulations is a sufficient and independent ground for imposing discipline, when, citing *Esteban, supra,* it held that a student group's announced refusal to abide by campus regulations would be a proper reason for denying university recognition to the group. 92 S.Ct. at 2351–52.

It may be noted that the regulations in the instant case are the product of an extensive and good faith effort by the School District to formulate a valid code of student conduct. This court has recognized that there is nothing *per se* unreasonable about requiring a high school student to submit written material to school authorities prior to distribution. *Shanley v. Northeast Independent School Dist.,* 5th Cir. 1972, 462 F.2d 960.[4] And it cannot be seriously urged that this prior submission rule is unconstitutionally vague or overbroad; this court has recently upheld a statute cast in more general terms than is the rule in question here. *Pervis v. LaMarque Independent School Dist.,* 5th Cir. 1972, 466 F.2d 1054. Finally, it is undisputed that substantial evidence supported Paul's suspension. Accordingly, we limit our review of his suspension to the question whether the School District accorded him due process.

We hasten to point out that by thus limiting our review in this case we do not invite school boards to promulgate patently unconstitutional regulations governing student distribution of off-campus literature. Nor, needless to say, do we encourage school authorities to use otherwise valid regulations as a pretext for disregarding the rights of students. Today we merely recognize the right of school authorities to punish students for the flagrant disregard of established school regulations; we ask only that the student seeking equitable relief from allegedly unconstitutional actions by school officials come into court with clean hands.

II

As to the procedures used in his suspension, the thrust of Paul's attack is that the October 29 hearing before Mr. Cotton was not the "fair and dispassionate" hearing required by due process and by the original permanent injunction. Although this court has never adopted a rule that school administrative personnel involved in the initiation and investigation of charges are *per se* disqualified from conducting hearings related to those charges, *see Murray v. West Baton Rouge Parish School Bd.,* 5th Cir. 1973, 472 F.2d 438; *Duke, supra; Lance v. Thompson,* 5th Cir. 1970, 432 F.2d 767; *cf. Wasson v. Trowbridge,* 2nd Cir. 1967, 382 F.2d 807; *Jones v. State Bd. of Educ.,* M.D.Tenn.1969, 279 F.Supp. 190, aff'd, 6th Cir. 1969, 407 F.2d 834, cert. dism'd, 397 U.S. 31, 90 S.Ct. 779, 25 L.Ed.2d 27 (1970), we have uniformly recognized that the facts of a case may demonstrate that a school official's involvement in an incident is such as to preclude his affording the student an impartial hearing. *E. g. Murray, supra; cf Mayberry v. Pennsylvania,* 400 U.S. 455, 91 S.Ct. 499, 27 L.Ed.2d 532 (1971). In our view, Paul Kitchen made such a showing in the instant case. The incidents for which Paul was suspended were cast largely in terms of a personal confrontation with Mr. Cotton. On two occasions Paul used profanity toward him, and Paul's appearance on the campus on October 26 to resume sales of the newspaper was clearly a direct challenge to Mr. Cotton's earlier demand that Paul stop selling the newspaper. Under these circumstances it is difficult to imagine that Mr. Cotton could have given Paul an impartial hearing. Indeed, it is not surprising that Mr. Cotton's primary aim in conducting the October 29 hearing was not to hear Paul's side of the story but rather, as Mr. Cotton testified in the district court, to hear Paul apologize.

It is, however, well settled that a procedural defect in an initial hearing before school officials can be cured by subsequent hearings. *Murray, supra; Speake* v. *Grantham,* 5th Cir. 1971, 440 F.2d 1351, aff'g S.D.Miss.1970, 317 F.Supp. 1253.[5] In the instant case, Paul was afforded two extensive *de novo* appellate hearings at which he was represented by counsel and presented and cross-examined witnesses. In our view, the procedural fidelity that characterized these appellate hearings cured the procedural defect in the hearing before Mr. Cotton.

We believe that a further word is necessary with regard to the timing of Paul's hearings, although neither party raises the issue directly. The question whether, and under what circumstances, disciplinary action must be *preceded* by a hearing has recently been before this court on a number of occasions. *Black Students of North Fort Myers Jr.-Sr. High School* v. *Williams,* 5th Cir. 1972, 470 F.2d 957 [1972] (hearing required before imposition of up to ten days' suspension); *Pervis, supra* ("an even more basic tenet of due process is . . . that punishment cannot be imposed before a hearing is given"); *Dunn* v. *Tyler Independent School Dist.,* 5th Cir. 1972, 460 F.2d 137 (no hearing required for "minor" punishment such as three days' suspension); *Banks* v. *Bd. of Public Instruction,* S.D.Fla.1970, 314 F.Supp. 285 (3-Judge court), vacated for entry of single-judge order, 401 U.S. 988, 91 S.Ct. 1223, 28 L.Ed.2d 526 (1971), aff'd after remand, 5th Cir. 1971, 450 F.2d 1103 (no prior hearing required for suspension up to ten days). In this case, Paul was suspended initially for an agreed period of six days without having been given a prior hearing. The lack of a hearing, however, was due to the unusual requirements of Mr. Kitchen's work which prevented his attendance until six days after the suspension had been imposed. On October 26, Mr. Cotton again suspended Paul, this time indefinitely. No hearing was held until three days later. But it must be recalled that the October 26 hearing would have taken place and the second suspension might not have occurred if Paul had not returned to campus on October 26 and resumed selling the newspapers, an event that triggered Mr. Cotton's calling the police and Mr. Kitchen's refusal to attend the October 26 hearing. Under these circumstances, and considering Paul's part in the delay, we decline to hold that the lack of a prior hearing was a denial of due process. The hearing was held as soon as circumstances would permit.

All that remains is the question whether the court below abused its discretion in denying the School District's motion made pursuant to Rule 60(b), F.R.Civ.P., to vacate the original 1969 permanent injunction. The School District's position is that, by promulgating new regulations that literally comply with the conditions set out in the injunction, the 1969 judgment has been "satisfied," and there is no longer any need to keep the School District under threat of a contempt judgment for violating the injunction. Granting relief pursuant to Rule 60(b) is largely within the discretion of the trial court, *Elgin National Watch Co.* v. *Barrett,* 5th Cir. 1954, 213 F.2d 776, and we are unable to say that the court below abused that discretion in failing to vacate the injunction. The original injunction dealt not only with the promulgation of regulations, but also with their enforcement. The School District has failed to show that continuation of the 1969 injunction is unnecessary to insure that the rules will not be unconstitutionally applied to students in the future. Although the District cites extensive authority for the familiar proposition that school discipline is primarily a matter for school authorities, the treatment that we give the instant case recognizes the District's right to impose punishment for violation of its established regulations. We decline to disturb the trial court's choice not to vacate the 1969 permanent injunction.

With the exception of that part of the order denying the School District's motion to vacate the 1969 injunction, the supplemental injunction decree entered on July 6, 1971, and the supplementary permanent injunctive decree entered on October 7, 1971, are vacated with instructions that the suit be dismissed.

Vacated with instructions.

NOTES

1. That regulation read as follows:
   The school principal may make such rules and regulations that may be necessary in the administration of the school and in promoting its best interests. He may enforce obedience to any reasonable and lawful command.
2. The School District stipulated that
   the rule [quoted above] is construed by responsible officials of the Houston Independent School District to prohibit the type of publication and distribution engaged in by Michael Fischer and Dan Sullivan in February and March of 1969.
3. In a permanent injunction decree and declaratory judgment rendered on December 30, 1969, Judge Seals enjoined the School District from promulgating or enforcing any regulation dealing with the production or distribution of written materials by tenth, eleventh, and twelfth grade students, unless the regulation was in writing and students were given notice of the rule, and unless it met the following conditions:
   (1) The rule must be specific as to places and times where possession and distribution of published materials is prohibited.
   (2) The rule must be understandable to persons of the age and experience of covered students.

(3) The rule must not prohibit or inhibit conduct which is orderly, peaceful and reasonably quiet and which is not coercive of any other person's right to accept or reject any written material being distributed subject to the rule.

(4) The rule may prohibit such distribution at times and in places where normal classroom activity is being conducted. Such rule may not prohibit such distribution at other times and places unless such prohibition is necessary to prevent substantial and material interference with or delay of normal classroom activity or normal school function.... [There follow definitions of "normal classroom activity" and "normal school function."]

(5) The rule must not subject any covered student to the threat of discipline because of the reaction or the response of any other person to the written material, provided, however, that defendants and their successors in office may prohibit distribution of obscene material or of libelous material for which a cause of action may exist in some person."

In addition, the decree set out the following requirements that the district was to meet in imposing "substantial discipline" (i. e., suspension for more than three days, or for an indefinite period):

(1) The covered student and at least one of his parents or guardian shall be furnished, either in person or by mail directed to the student's last known address, with written notice of the charges and of the nature of the evidence against such covered student.

(2) The covered student and at least one of his parents or guardian shall be offered a formal hearing after sufficient time to prepare a defense or reply at which hearing evidence in support of the charge shall be presented by school officials and the affected covered student or his parent or guardian shall have ample opportunity to present any defense or reply.

(3) The decision of school officials to impose such discipline shall be based upon a dispassionate and fair consideration of substantial evidence that the covered students committed the acts for which discipline is to be imposed and that such acts are in fact a proper reason for such discipline.

4. *Both Shanley* and *Eisner v. Stamford Bd. of Educ.*, 2nd Cir. 1971, 440 F.2d 803, require that prior submission rules include procedures of prompt administrative review of a decision not to permit distribution. The regulations of the Houston Independent School District contain no such procedure for appellate review. However, since Paul never submitted the newspaper for prior approval in the first place and since he was given two extensive *de novo* appellate hearings in which he could have urged approval of the newspaper for distribution, this defect in the prior submission rule should not affect the result in the instant case.

5. We note that the facts of the instant case are distinguishable from those in *Pervis, supra,* where no hearing was held until three months after the students' summary suspension.

THE United States Court of Appeals, Fifth Circuit, decides against the University of Mississippi Chancellor and others who refused to allow publication and distribution of an issue of the student literary magazine, *Images,* because of objections to two stories which included "what must be termed some quite 'earthy' language. It appears to be the University's position that because of its connection with this magazine it has a right to prevent publication and distribution solely because it has determined that this language is inappropriate and in bad taste." In affirming "the decision of the District Court ordering the University of Mississippi not to interfere with the publication and distribution of this magazine," the Court of Appeals declared: "Since the University is relying primarily on a claim that these stories are too tasteless and inappropriate to be connected with the University, *merely* because of the words which appear in the stories, we find that justification particularly hard to accept as compelling because of the admitted facts we have set out above. There has been testimony by a literary expert that these stories have literary merit and that was also the collective judgment of the student editorial board. The University has not really attacked literary merit, but has instead focused its argument on the mere presence in the story of these words. Yet these words appear and are more or less forced upon any student who takes certain courses at the university. It does not seem necessary to get into a discussion of whether or not the stories of this author have as much literary merit as a novel by James Joyce. That is irrelevant to the consideration of the issue as it has been framed by the University itself. We do not see how the University can draw a line, based on the grounds it asserts, between these short stories, which are intended only for those persons, mostly students and under five hundred in number, who pay one dollar for the issue, and a novel which students are required to buy and read in order to receive course credit. . . .

As a final word, we can only reiterate that speech cannot be stifled by the state merely because it would perhaps draw adverse reaction from the majority of people, be they politicians or ordinary citizens, and newspapers. To come forth with such a rule would be to virtually read the First Amendment out of the constitution and, thus, cost this nation one of its strongest tenets."

Bazaar v. *Fortune,* 476 F.2d 570 (1973)

Lewis R. MORGAN, Circuit Judge:
This appeal grows out of a confrontation between students and officials at the University of Mississippi over the content of a certain issue of the student literary publication *Images.* The District Court for the Northern District of Mississippi entered a temporary restraining order prohibiting the University from interfering with the publication and distribution of this magazine. This court, to avoid publication which would moot the serious legal issue involved,

issued a stay of that temporary restraining order pending review of the case on the merits. After careful consideration, we affirm the decision of the district court ordering the University of Mississippi not to interfere with the publication and distribution of this magazine.

I.

The magazine in question, *Images,* is a University chartered and recognized student publication at the University of Mississippi. Since its conception in 1969, *Images* has published several issues on a more or less irregular basis. The magazine was designed for presentation of student-written and student-edited literary compositions.

The relationship of the University of Mississippi to this student publication has been gleaned by this court after careful examination of the record. Interdepartmental communications between officials of the University establish that *Images* was to be a student literary journal published with the advice of the English department. The publication was to be reproduced at the University's central duplicating facility, with an anticipated press run of 500 copies. The 1969 costs for this service was set at approximately $300.00. From the outset it was understood by all that the amounts collected from sales of the magazine would be used to offset, hopefully *in toto,* this printing cost. Student editors and faculty members would, of course, contribute their time and effort without remuneration. There was a further provision that in the event the sales of the magazine fell short of recouping the total publication cost, the English department would underwrite any loss from its current activities budget. There is also evidence that the magazine, at least for this past academic year, received a $400.00 grant from the Associated Student Body Activities Fund, which is, in turn, collected from student fees.

In actual operation, the magazine was staffed and run by students with editorial advice from an English department appointed adviser, Dr. Evans Harrington, Professor of English at the University. The magazine was closely connected with a course in creative writing maintained as a regular portion of the English department's curriculum and taught by Professor Harrington. It was intended that the core of student materials for publication in *Images* come from student efforts in this creative writing course with the possible use of other student submitted materials. The magazine was apparently not designed for widespread circulation, but rather was to be limited to approximately 500 copies per issue and to be offered for sale primarily to students at the University through University bookstore facilities.[1]

II.

Until the issue of *Images* set for publication in the spring of 1972, there had apparently been no conflict between University officials and the magazine's editorial board and no attempts of censorship or control by the University's hierarchy.[2] After the spring issue had been edited into final form and sent to central duplicating, however, a dispute arose. The superintendent of the University's printing facilities informed Chancellor Porter Fortune that the University should take a close look at the stories to be published. The Chancellor then acted to hold up binding and distribution of the spring issue. He formed a committee consisting of the deans of the various University departments which was to determine if the material in the magazine was suitable for publication. It is not very clear in the record what types of hearings or evaluation this committee gave the magazine. There are allegations that it consistently refused to receive statements from the students or from their adviser, Professor Harrington. This panel of deans decided that publication would be "inappropriate", apparently basing its decision on matters of "taste". The University then refused to finish binding the journal or allow its distribution.

The reluctance of the University to allow the publication and distribution of this magazine centers on two short stories which are contained in the issue.[3] Both stories were originally written by a student in the creative writing course for presentation and criticism by the class. The themes of the two stories are interracial love and black pride. The author of the stories is an 18-year-old regularly-enrolled black student at the University of Mississippi.[4] In framing its objections to the stories, the University was careful to disclaim any unhappiness with the presented themes. Rather, the University based its entire objection to both stories solely upon the grounds of the inclusion therein of what must be termed some quite "earthy" language. It appears to be the University's position that because of its connection with this magazine it has the right to prevent publication and distribution solely because it has determined that this language is inappropriate and in bad taste.

III.

It is necessary to have a clear grasp of the nature of the stories, their characters, and the manner in which the language found objectionable by the University is used. The objectionable portions consist of what are commonly known as "four-letter words," often colloquially referred to as "obscenities." They include use of "that four-letter word" generally felt to be the most offensive in polite conversation. While the University does not specify which words it most objects to, we assume that this epithet and its derivatives are high on the list. We feel that it is imperative, however, to stress the manner in which these words are used and the alleged literary justification for their use.

The protagonist of each story is a black male growing up in and confronted by a basically white society. Each of the two "heroes" is suggestive of a latter-day, black Holden Caulfield,[5] struggling to find himself in the world. As what could be termed a natural and necessary phase of character development, the "heroes" of these stories occasionally talk and think in a vernacular which is definitely not suited for parlor conversation.

It must be realized that these characters are young blacks who often express themselves by using somewhat crude epithets of the street. The language, while admittedly unacceptable in some quarters, is readily recognized as commonplace in various strata of society, both black and white. The tendency to use such language would seem more prevalent among young males in less-favored social groups of all races. In short, it could well be considered strained and artificial for these characters to speak and think in proper prep school diction.

We also note that the language is not used in a manner which would be termed "pandering". The words are not used in a sexual sense nor are there vulgar passages describing such activities. Throughout the work, the "offensive" words are usually used as modifiers strictly included for their effect and to convey a mood. They are not used in any literal sense. While some may feel that they are used a bit too often, this is a difficult matter to judge and rests largely with individual taste. Certainly, it seems an unsuitable standard for governmental censorship.

Thus, the sole question presented in this case is whether or not a university, under these circumstances, may prevent publication and distribution of a student publication solely on grounds of "taste" and "appropriateness" merely because certain words appear therein, no matter in what context and for what reasons the words are used.

IV.

It is well established that not all rights to freedom of speech and the press are lost by those who attend state-supported colleges and universities. *Tinker* v. *Des Moines Independent Community School District,* 393 U.S. 503, 89 S.Ct. 733, 21 L.Ed.2d 731 (1969); *Healy* v. *James,* 408 U.S. 169, 92 S.Ct. 2338, 33 L.Ed.2d 266 (1972). In this case it has become incumbent on the University of Mississippi to justify the censorship it has sought to exercise herein. Despite several rather ingenious arguments put forth by the University, we feel their efforts have failed. We find it necessary to address only two specific issues in this opinion. First, does the University here have the status of a private publisher with the right to choose what it will or will not publish. Secondly, if this special status cannot be afforded the University, has the University demonstrated sufficient "special circumstances" to justify censorship.

The University as Publisher

The facts before us in this case do not establish the University's claim that it here stands in the shoes of a private publisher. The evidence shows that the University's financial connection with this endeavor was somewhat tenuous. There was no special appropriation for this magazine. Rather, as envisioned from the outset, it was intended to be self-supporting, with the University supplying printing facilities, more or less on open account, with the costs for such services to be repaid from sale proceeds. The English department, it is true, agreed to underwrite any loss out of current funds, but this was expected to be irregular, small, and indeed hopefully never necessary. Furthermore, part of the financing for this current year came as a separate grant from the student activity funds of the Associated Student Body. As to considerations other than monetary, the University points to the fact that this publication will bear a statement saying that it is published by students at the University with the advice of the English department. We do not feel that this simple statement, even if joined with the somewhat speculative financial connection, is enough to equate the University with a private publisher and endow it with absolute arbitrary powers to decide what can be printed.

Moreover, there is a more basic reason why the University cannot be accorded the omnipotent position it seeks. The University here is clearly an arm of the state and this single fact will always distinguish it from the purely private publisher as far as censorship rights are concerned. It seems a well-established rule that once a University recognizes a student activity which has elements of free expression, it can act to censor that expression only if it acts consistent with First Amendment constitutional guarantees. As was stated in *American Civil Liberties Union of Virginia* v. *Radford College,* 315 F.Supp. 893 (W.D.Va., 1970):

> There have been a number of cases in the last several years involving Constitutional challenges on first amendment grounds to the actions of college administrators. A perusal of these cases

makes clear a recurring theme that once a public school makes an activity available to its students, faculty, or even the general public, it must operate the activity in accord with first amendment principles. . . . Neither can a state university support a campus newspaper and then try to restrict arbitrarily what it may publish, even if only to require that material be submitted to a faculty board to determine whether it complies with "responsible freedom of the press". Id. at 896–897.

Antonelli v. *Hammond,* 308 F.Supp. 1329 (Mass.1970), involved issues strikingly similar to the ones present in this case. Students at Fitchburg State College, a state-supported institution of high learning in Massachusetts, published, with University support, a campus newspaper, *The Cycle.* In that case, the student newspaper published a story, "Black Moochie", written by Eldridge Cleaver. The paper's usual printer, whose daughter was a student at the college, read the article prior to printing and objected strenuously to its content. He brought this matter to the attention of the President of the University who held up this issue of *The Cycle.* The primary reason for objection to the article given by the University was that it contained "obscene" language. In addition to preventing publication of this issue of *The Cycle,* the President of the University set up an advisory board which would have to give its prior approval to all articles and materials intended for publication in the newspaper.[6]

The court in *Antonelli* expressly considered the claim of the University that it had the power to censor because it paid the funds for publication of *The Cycle:*

> We are well beyond the belief that any manner of state regulation is permissible simply because it involves an activity which is part of the university structure and is financed with funds controlled by the administration. The state is not necessarily the unrestrained master of what it creates and fosters. Thus in cases concerning school-supported publications or the use of school facilities, the courts have refused to recognize as permissible any regulations infringing free speech when not shown to be necessarily related to the maintenance of order and discipline within the educational process. See, e.g. *Dickey* v. *Alabama State Board of Education,* 1967, N.D.Ala., 273 F.Supp. 613; *Snyder* v. *Board of Trustees of University of Illinois,* 1968, N.D.Ill., 286 F.Supp. 927; *Brooks* v. *Auburn University,* 1969, N.D.Ala., 296 F.Supp. 188; *Zucker* v. *Panitz,* 1969, S.D.N.Y., 299 F.Supp. 102; *Smith* v. *University of Tennessee,*1969, E.D.Tenn., 300 F.Supp. 777; *Close*v. *Lederle,* 1969, D.Mass., 303 F.Supp. 1109. Id. at 1337.

The principles enunciated in these two cases have been derived from a long line of legal opinions dealing with the struggle between college students and university administrators over matters involving freedom of speech and expression. The cases involving student publications are quite similar to, and owe much of their rationale to, those cases which have been characterized as "open forum" cases. This circuit has recognized the strong constitutional guarantees where an attempt was made by a university to prevent an invited speaker from giving an address by simply refusing to pay for his appearance. *Brooks* v. *Auburn University,* 5 Cir. 1969, 412 F.2d 1171.

The University has apparently conceded that the above rule is indeed the governing standard. The University, however, seeks to distinguish this literary publication, *Images,* from a campus newspaper or campus annual. The counsel for the University admitted at oral argument that it was the University's position that they could not censor either the campus newspaper, *The Daily Mississippian,* or the campus annual, *The Ole Miss.* In light of this frank admission, we are somewhat at a loss to see the distinction between the magazine *Images* and either of these publications. Both the newspaper and annual are paid for through University administered funds. In fact, it is our understanding that both these other publications, while paid for by students, are in reality financed by a non-waivable fee which is paid by every student as part of his regular tuition fees at the time of his enrollment for the current term. Both of those publications are clearly, on their face, identified with the University.

The University attempts a distinction by pointing out that here *Images* was to be published with the "advice" of the English department, although it does not show any evidence that the other publications are not similarly subject to "advice." They go so far as to suggest that this means it will be identified as speaking for the English department and thus the University. We do not feel this factor is very relevant. The advice contemplated was directed at helping the students in choosing material of literary merit for publication and, indeed, in this case the material objected to was approved by the English department's appointed adviser for the magazine, who testified in this case on behalf of the student editors, author and magazine. Thus, we see no difference between this and other University publications which the University concedes, quite correctly in our opinion, that it cannot censor except within constitutional limitations. The literary magazine, *Images,* is certainly within the broad class of publications to which the board rule enunciated in *Antonelli* was designed to apply.

Special Circumstances

Having disposed of any claim by the University that it has an arbitrary power because of its relationship with *Images* to censor its content, we now turn to the issue of whether the censorship imposed in this case was justified under the rationale of "special circumstances" permitting the state to circumscribe certain activity which would otherwise fall within the generally protected area. We are convinced that no such special circumstances exist in this case.

There has been no claim that publications of this magazine containing these short stories would or could lead to any significant disruption on the University campus. Basically, the special circumstances which the University seeks to have this court recognize consist of matters of taste and the right of the University to prevent activities which it would feel would lead to criticism of it from outside sources. There was also, at one time, a claim by the University that publishing these articles might subject it to state prosecution under the state obscenity laws.

The University apparently never attempted to show that the materials herein were legally obscene and it appears now that they have dropped this contention altogether on appeal. The court is satisfied that these stories as written do not meet the standard of legal obscenity. We do not, however, automatically say that the University is in all cases forbidden from interference in First Amendment cases unless it can show that a legal definition of obscenity is satisfied. We simply do not have to reach that issue in the disposition of this case. Assuming arguendo that the University does indeed have a power to impose some restrictions on language which does not measure up to legal obscenity, we do not feel that the language objected to in this case, used as it is, would give sufficient grounds for interference. This analysis will also be sufficient to dismiss the "taste" and "appropriateness" arguments of the University.

We have previously pointed out the nature of the words involved in these short stories and the manner in which they are used by the author. We feel that we are past the point in this country today where the mere use of any single word in a public arena can be immediately branded as so tasteless or inappropriate that its use is subject to unbridled censorship or restriction by government authority. The short stories involved in this case, as noted contain the word which has historically been viewed as the "worst" obscenity. With regard to this very four-letter word, the Supreme Court has stated that:

> While the particular four-letter word being litigated here is perhaps more distasteful than most of its genre, it is nevertheless often true that one man's vulgarity is another's lyric. Indeed, we think

it is largely because government officials cannot make principled distinctions in this area that the Constitution leaves matters of taste and style so largely to the individual. *Cohen v. California,* 403 U.S. 15, 25, 91 S.Ct. 1780, 1788, 29 L.Ed.2d 284 (1971).

In that same opinion, the Court noted another factor which is relevant in this case. The Court refused to sanction the view that the Constitution, while solicitous of the cognitive content of individual speech, has little or no regard for that emotive function which, practically speaking, may often be the more important element of the overall message sought to be communicated.

* * *

Finally, and in the same vein, we cannot indulge in the facile assumption that one can forbid particular words without also running a substantial risk of suppressing ideas in the process. Indeed, governments might soon seize upon the censorship of particular words as a convenient guise for banning the expression of unpopular views. We have been able, as noted above, to discern little social benefit that might result from running the risk of opening the door to such grave results. Id. at 26, 91 S.Ct. at 1788.

As we have previously noted in this opinion, much of the literary justification for the use of these words in the short stories rests on the emotive feeling and mood they are designed to create. They bear both on the development of the central characters and also may be read to serve as part of the comment which this author intends to make to his reader through these stories.[7] Thus, we feel it would be extremely difficult to censor these words merely for their presence in the story because of their possible relation to the themes which the author strives to present.

Furthermore, we cannot help but take note that these words have been recognized as not that unusual when found in connection with college students and use on college campuses.[8] In fact, at the hearing below, one of the witnesses, a student at the University of Mississippi, stated that he had heard all of the words contained in these short stories spoken on campus by University of Mississippi students, and that, indeed, he believed he had heard them spoken by faculty members. The University also admits that commercial publications are sold on the University campus which contain these words and other words which it would classify as "distasteful". For instance, the evidence establishes that the magazine *Playboy* is sold on campus at various bookstore facilities. Furthermore, the University admits that the *Kudzu,* an "underground" newspaper which admittedly contains "ragged" language similar to that found objectionable in these stories, had been previously sold without interference on the University campus. The only attempted distinction by the University is that here they are more connected with this magazine since it is published by students and with the advice of the English department. As noted, we do not feel that that mere distinction waives all constitutional privileges of the students involved.

Finally, the court feels that it is extremely significant that the University admits that works in its library and, indeed, works that are assigned to students as required reading for courses contain the same words, used in much the same way, as are found in these stories to which the University now objects. It is also admitted that these same words objected to by the University here appear frequently in well-respected literature, especially that of the twentieth century. These words are often found in the works of such accepted literary figures as J. D. Salinger,[9] James Baldwin,[10] Norman Mailer,[11] Bernard Malamud,[12] and Truman Capote,[13] to name a few. Similar language is also abundant in many recent best-sellers, including *Love Story, The Godfather, Portnoy's Complaint, The Adventurers,* and *Valley of the Dolls.* Even the works of William Faulkner, an author indelibly associated with Oxford and the University of Mississippi, contain a high number of "obscenities" much like the words under attack here. Thus, here the University is seeking to restrain the use of certain words which it acknowledges are often used in literary compositions and words which are found in the books it offers for student reading through its library.

Finally, we note that the testimony established that the University goes so far as to prescribe as required reading at least one work which includes most, if not all, of the words found in these short stories. It also contains the word to which the University, we would surmise, most strenuously objects. Professor Harrington testified that as part of his course in the twentieth century novel, he assigned as required reading the recognized literary masterpiece *Ulysses,* written by James Joyce. We note that once, years ago, that work was also subject to attempts at censorship by governmental authorities in this country. See *United States of America* v. *One Book Called "Ulysses",* 5 F.Supp. 182 (S.D.N.Y., 1933), aff'd. *United States* v. *One Book Entitled Ulysses by James Joyce,* 2 Cir. 1934, 72 F.2d 705. Anyone familiar with the soliloquy of Molly Bloom will recall that her statement includes many of the same words found objectionable here. Thus, students who take this course in modern novels are *required* to read at least one work which includes the same or very similar words to the ones here condemned. This, indeed, begins to become a strange double standard.

Since the University is relying primarily on a claim that these stories are too tasteless and inappropriate to be connected with the University, *merely* because of the words which appear in the stories, we find that justification particularly hard to accept as compelling because of the admitted facts we have set out above. There has been testimony by a literary expert that these stories have literary merit and that was also the collective judgment of the student editorial board. The University has not really attacked literary merit, but has instead focused its argument on the mere presence in the story of these words. Yet these words appear and are more or less forced upon any student who takes certain courses at the University. It does not seem necessary to get into a discussion of whether or not the stories of this author have as much literary merit as a novel by James Joyce. That is irrelevant to the consideration of the isuse as it has been framed by the University itself. We do not see how the University can draw a line, based on the grounds it asserts, between these short stories, which are intended only for those persons, mostly students and under five hundred in number, who pay one dollar for the issue, and a novel which students are required to buy and read in order to receive course credit. While the anomaly present in this factual situation is not really necessary for the legal opinion we render in this case,[14] we think it should be pointed out because it illustrates the folly in making matters of free speech and word usage turn on a state's interpretation.[15] As far as the words are concerned, the words themselves, their mere presence can be no less offensive because they appear in a recognized literary triumph rather than in the first attempts by one who could be characterized a budding young author, out to "forge in the smithy of [his] soul the uncreated conscience of [his] race."[16]

Finally, the University attempts to invoke the special consideration that publication of this story, as long as it acknowledged any recognized connection with the University of Mississippi, would endanger the current public confidence and good will which the University of Mississippi now enjoys. See *Duke* v. *North Texas State University,* 5 Cir. 1972, 469 F.2d 829. While we recognize that such considerations can go into the determination of whether a given interference with freedom of speech is justified, we feel it is also very clear that use of such a rationale should be handled gingerly and applied only in what can be characterized as most extreme cases.[17]

We do not read *Duke* as saying that a university has the right to restrict any activity involving free speech or expression merely because it might cause adverse reaction in the newspapers or because some segment of the state's population might be unhappy with the university's actions. *Duke* was itself a very close case, and we feel it should be read restrictively to apply only where the actions involved are quite extreme in light of the educational purposes of a university. We see no such factors here.

As a final word, we can only reiterate that speech cannot be stifled by the state merely because it would perhaps draw an adverse reaction from the majority of people, be they politicans or ordinary citizens, and newspapers. To come forth with such a rule would be to virtually read the First Amendment out of the Constitution and, thus, cost this nation one of its strongest tenets. It would be unthinkable to say that the University of Mississippi could censor and forbid publication of an article in its law school journal on the grounds that the article concerned some sensitive issue, such as forced busing or abortion, which, because of the resolution reached in the article, the University determined would create an overwhelmingly adverse reaction among members of the bar and the public. The First Amendment simply took the power to make such judgment out of the hands of the state.

The University alleges that it here is acting to preserve what it considers an acceptable level of decency in this publication. That statement, however, illustrates the core issue of this problem—what level of "decency" and who should decide when it has been reached. As previously noted, the use of the language is, at the very least, arguably justified in a literary context. It is not used suggestively nor does it approach pandering. The words are not being forced on an unwilling audience through public display. There is no chance of violent disruption from their use. The nature of the language is no longer really that unusual in current literature, films, and conversation—especially among the young. The trend to its use, both in spoken and written arts, while not to be commended, certainly must be recognized. "An acceptable level of decency" is obviously not a static proposition nor one easily determined. One needs only look around to see that things considered horribly "indecent" a few years ago are quite commonplace today. It is for this reason that, where modes of expression are involved, the First Amendment casts a heavy burden on any governmental body which seeks to censor on the grounds of "public decency". As the Supreme Court stated in *Cohen* v. *California, supra:*

> Against this perception of the constitutional policies involved, we discern certain more particularized considerations that peculiarly call for reversal of this conviction. First the principle contended for by the State seems inherently boundless. How is one to distinguish this from any other offensive word? Surely the State has no right to cleanse public debate to the point where it is grammatically palatable to the most squeamish among us. Yet no readily ascertainable general principle exists for stopping short of that result were we to affirm the judgment below. 403 U.S. 15 at 25, 91 S.Ct. 1780, at 1788.

Thus, we conclude here that the University has not shown sufficient special circumstances to justify the interference it is attempting to impose on the full exercise of First Amendment freedoms. As previously noted, we do not in this opinion mean to say that no language or conduct short of legal obscenity can be regulated by a college or university when a student literary publication is involved. We do not have to reach that issue here. We are satisfied that on the facts of this case the University has not demonstrated that the language used in parts of these stories is so unusual, so condemnatory, that the requisite special circumstances have been achieved.

In closing, we must take note of the historical role of the University in expressing opinions which may well not make favor with the majority of society and in serving in the vanguard in the fight for freedom of expression and opinion. As the United States Supreme Court has recently reaffirmed:

> The precedents of this Court leave no room for the view that, because of the acknowledged need for order, First Amendment protections should apply with less force on college campuses than in the community at large. Quite to the contrary, "[t]he vigilant protection of constitutional freedoms is nowhere more vital than in the community of American schools". *Shelton* v. *Tucker,* 364 U.S. 479, 487 [81 S.Ct. 247, 5 L.Ed.2d 231] (1960). The college classroom with its surrounding environs is peculiarly the "market place of ideas" and we break no new constitutional ground in reaffirming this Nation's dedication to safeguarding academic freedom. *Keyishian* v. *Board of Regents,* 385 U.S. 589, 603 [87 S.Ct. 675, 17 L.Ed.2d 629] (1967); *Sweezy* v. *New Hampshire,* 354 U.S. 234, 249–250 [77 S.Ct. 1203, 1211, 1 L.Ed.2d 1311] (plurality opinion of Mr. Chief Justice Warren), 262 [77 S.Ct. 1217] (1957)
>
> (Mr. Justice Frankfurter's concurring opinion). *Healy* v. *James,* 408 U.S. 169, 92 S.Ct. 2338, 2346, 33 L.Ed.2d 266, 279 (1972).

Therefore, we feel it is incumbent on this court to deny the University the power to restrict what must be recognized as a legitimate manner of expression on the basis of the justifications it seeks to assert in this case.

From our careful consideration of this case, we note with some sadness an undercurrent which permeates this whole controversy. We see no real spirit of compromise or accommodation on the part of either side. Throughout the record in this case we sense an air of confrontation, derived both from the actions of the students and the administration. The students are accused of deliberately taunting the University, throwing down a gauntlet which they knew the University must accept. For its part, there are numerous allegations, generally admitted, that the University and its chosen committee repeatedly refused to hear the students or their advisers, and to consider their points of view. It would seem to this court that perhaps a greater spirit of accommodation could have avoided the necessity of a costly and time-consuming resort to the federal courts. Perhaps some mutual editing could have removed much of the offensiveness which the University objected to. Perhaps the well-known practice of initial letters followed by blanks or dashes could have conveyed the meaning without unduly upsetting the University officials or the author. Perhaps a stated disclaimer as to content on the part of the University would have been sufficient.[18] But from the record before us, neither side really made an attempt at compromise. This is an unfortunate situation, especially where the conflict is between a university and its students and between censorship and expression.

For the reasons stated in this opinion, we hold that the district court was correct in granting the order restraining the University from further interference with the printing of the magazine *Images* and that order is hereby

Affirmed.

NOTES

1. There was evidence that there was a mailing list of about 25 subscribers with the rest of the magazines to be sold on campus. It was admitted that commercial success was not an aim of the publication.
2. Evidence at the hearing below established that the University had no rules or regulations on the content of student publications, and that the University had never in the past attempted to prevent publication of a student periodical.
3. In addition to these stories, the issue contained several poems and illustrations.
4. Although only eighteen, the author was classified as a first semester junior.
5. Salinger, J. D., *The Catcher in the Rye.*
6. The only viable difference between the *Antonelli* case and the one at bar is related to this advisory board. We feel that difference is not relevant to the legal issues involved. One other factual difference which bears on the legal issue is that in *Antonelli* the article and issue of *The Cycle* in dispute was, indeed, published by another printer at the expense of private individuals and then distributed on the campus. Here the restraints imposed by the University have continued to hold publication of this issue of *Images* in abeyance.
7. Professor Harrington, author of one novel and several shorter works of fiction, testified as to literary merit and style at the hearing below.
8. We note that at least one Circuit Court of Appeals has suggested that one of the objectionable terms present in the stories, literally referring to an incestuous son but more commonly used as an abusive epithet, is not that unusual or condemnatory when it reaches the tender young ears of high school seniors. Judge Bailey Aldrich, writing for the First Circuit in Keefe V. Geannakos, 1969, 418 F.2d 359, addressed a situation involving the possible punishment of a high school teacher who read an article to a senior class which repeatedly used the epithet referred to above. In speaking directly to the school board's alleged fear of adverse parental reaction, the learned jurist stated:

   With regard to the word itself, we cannot think that it is unknown to many students in the last year of high school, and we might well take judicial notice of its use by young radicals and protesters from coast to coast. No doubt its use genuinely offends the parents of some of the students—therein, in part, lay its relevancy to the article.

   Hence, the question in this case is whether a teacher may, for demonstrated educational purposes, quote a "dirty" word currently used in order to give special offense, or whether the shock is too great for high school seniors to stand. If the answer were that the students must be protected from such exposure, we would fear for their future. We do not question the good faith of the defendants in believing that some parents have been offended. With the greatest of respect to such parents, their sensibilities are not the full measure of what is proper education. [Footnotes omitted]. Id. at 361–362.
9. See, e. g., *The Catcher in the Rye.*
10. See, e.g., *Another Country.*
11. See, e.g., *Prisoner of Sex.*
12. See, e.g., *The Tenants.*
13. See, e.g., *In Cold Blood.*
14. Again we refer to the opinion of Judge Aldrich in *Keefe v. Geanakos, supra,* note 8, for in that case he was confronted with a situation where the high school library contained at least five separate works by five separate authors which contained the word used in class by the teacher under attack. We can only restate his salient comment:

    Such inconsistency on the part of the school has been regarded as fatal. [Citation omitted]. We, too, would probably so regard it. At the same time, we prefer not to place our decision on this ground alone, lest our doing so diminish our principal holding, or lead to a bowdlerization of the school library. 418 F.2d at 362–363.
15. As to literary merit, Professor Harrington testified for plaintiffs that he felt the stories had literary merit. Chancellor Fortune did not address literary merit directly but did state that he felt any literary merit was offset by the use of the objectionable language.
16. See Joyce, James, *A Portrait of the Artist as a Young Man,* Viking Press, Ellmann ed., 1964, page 253.
17. For instance, we find the *Duke* case easily distinguishable. First, we were there dealing with somewhat different principles of law since it involved an employer-employee relationship. Furthermore, that case

involved quite vitriolic and vulgar personal attacks on the administration of the university made by a teacher who had not yet achieved tenure. They were certainly not made in the relatively sterile context of a literary composition. The statements and the way they were presented were, in the opinion of the court, enough to cast considerable doubt on whether the person making those statements could effectively continue as an instructor, working with an administration she had so crudely attacked. Finally, the procedural devices present in the *Duke* case, at least as the procedures followed have been outlined to us, are significantly different from those in this case.

18. Under questioning at the hearing Chancellor Fortune did testify that he felt such a statement would not have been enough for the university.

THE United States Court of Appeals, Fourth Circuit, decides for college students who had challenged the withdrawal of financial support from the North Carolina Central University student newspaper *Campus Echo,* the withdrawal of support based on the contention of university officials that the newspaper's "segregationist editorial policy and racially discriminatory practices violate the Fourteenth Amendment and the Civil Rights Act of 1964." In deciding for the students, the Court of Appeals distinguished between unprotected speech and the expression involved in this case: "Students, like all other citizens, are forbidden advocacy which 'is directed to inciting or producing imminent lawless action and is likely to incite or produce such action.' See *Brandenburg* v. *Ohio.* . . . *Tinker* v. *Des Moines Ind. Community School Dist* . . . expressly limits the free and unrestricted expression of opinion in schools to instances where it does not 'materially and substantially interfere with the requirements of appropriate discipline in the operation of the school.' We previously considered these limitations in *Quarterman* v. *Byrd.* . . . In his brief President Whiting acknowledges that there does not appear to have been any danger of physical violence or disruption at the University because of the publication of the *Echo*. The record, of course, does disclose that the paper's message of racial devisiveness and antagonism was distasteful to the president, and it may well have offended other members of the University community. However, no white faculty members or students complained that the paper's editorial policy incited anybody at the University to harass or interfere with them. The case, therefore, does not present a situation that *Brandenburg, Tinker,* and *Quarterman* recognize as justifying restriction of free expression."

Joyner v. *Whiting,* 477 F.2d 456 (1973)

BUTZNER, Circuit Judge:

Johnnie Edward Joyner, editor of the *Campus Echo,* the official student newspaper of North Carolina Central University, and Harvey Lee White, president of the university's student government association, appeal from an order of the district court, which (a) denied their application for declaratory and injunctive relief to secure reinstatement of financial support for the *Echo,* and (b) permanently enjoined Albert N. Whiting, president of the university, and his successors in office, from granting future financial support to any campus newspaper. *Joyner* v. *Whiting,* 341 F.Supp. 1244 (M.D.N.C.1972). Joyner and White assert that the decree violates the First and Fourteenth Amendments. President Whiting urges affirmance on the ground that the paper's segregationist editorial policy and racially discriminatory practices violate the Fourteenth Amendment and the Civil Rights Act of 1964. We reverse because the president's irrevocable withdrawal of financial support from the *Echo* and the court's decree reinforcing this action abridge the freedom of the press in violation of the First Amendment.

I

EDITORIAL COMMENT

The first issue of the *Echo* under Joyner's editorship published a banner headline on the front page that asked, "Is NCCU Still a Black School," and an article entitled, "Look and You Shall See," which stated in part:

"There is a rapidly growing white population on our campus.

* * *

"We want to know why they are here. How many are here? Why more and more come every year (by the hundreds)?

* * *

"But I think that the reason we will be taken over so quickly and so easily is our fault.

"Black students on this campus have never made it clear to those people that we are indeed separate from them, in so many ways, and wish to remain so. And until we assume the role of a strong, proud people we will continue to be co-opted. Until we chose to make this clear, by any means necessary, the same thing will continue to happen. . . .

"I maintain that we must pick up the cry of Frantz Fanan who has said, 'Each generation must discover its mission, fulfill it or betray it.' And the words of H. Rap Brown, 'I do what I must out of the love for my people. My will is to fight. Resistance is not enough. Aggression is the order of the day.' And more over that we take nothing from the oppressor, but only in turn get that which is ours.

"Now will you tell me, whose institution is NCCU? Theirs? Or ours?"

In addition, the paper contained a survey of student opinion which reflected strong opposition to the admission of white students.

President Whiting responded with the following letter to Joyner:

"In my view the September 16 issue of the Campus Echo does not meet standard journalistic criteria nor does it represent fairly the full spectrum of views on this campus. Because of this, I am writing to advise that funds for the publication of additional issues will be withheld until agreement can be reached regarding the standards to which further publications will adhere.

"If consensus cannot be established then this University will not sponsor a campus newspaper. That portion of remaining funds collected or allocated to the Campus Echo budget will accrue to the credit of all contributing students for this school year."[1]

Despite a meeting to resolve the differences, no agreement could be reached. The president's counsel then advised him that because North Carolina Central University is a state institution he could not constitutionally refuse to financially support the newspaper if his refusal was contingent on the paper's meeting journalistic standards or other subjective criteria. Accordingly, acting on advice of counsel, the president irrevocably terminated the paper's financial support and refunded to each student the pro rata share of the activities fee previously allocated to the *Echo*. The president took no action to bar Joyner, or any other student, from publishing and circulating a privately funded newspaper on the campus. Indeed, several issues of the *Echo* were published without the university's financial support, but it became apparent that the paper could not survive unless it received its usual subsidy from the student activities fees.

Fortunately, we travel through well charted waters to determine whether the permanent denial of financial support to the newspaper because of its editorial policy abridged the freedom of the press. The First Amendment is fully applicable to the states, *Gitlow* v. *New York*, 268 U.S. 652, 666, 45 S.Ct. 625, 69 L.Ed. 1138 (1925); *Stromberg* v. *California*, 283 U.S. 359, 368, 51 S.Ct. 532, 75 L.Ed. 1117 (1931), and precedent establishes "that state colleges and universities are not enclaves immune from [its] sweep." A college, acting "as the instrumentality of the State, may not restrict speech . . . simply because it finds the views expressed by any group to be abhorrent." *Healy* v. *James*, 408 U.S. 169, 180, 187, 92 S.Ct. 2338, 2345, 2349, 33 L.Ed.2d 266 (1972); *see* Wright, The Constitution on the Campus, 22 Vand.L.Rev. 1027, 1037 (1969). It may well be that a college need not establish a campus newspaper, or, if a paper has been established, the college may permanently discontinue publication for reasons wholy unrelated to the First Amendment. But if a college has a student newspaper, its publication cannot be suppressed because college officials dislike its editorial comment. *Panarella* v. *Birenbaum*, 37 A.D.2d 987, 327 N.Y.S.2d 755, 757 (1971); *cf. Danskin* v. *San Diego Unified School Dist.*, 28 Cal.2d 536, 171 P.2d 885, 892 (1946).[2] This rule is but a simple extension of the precept that freedom of expression may not be infringed by denying a privilege. *Sherbert* v. *Verner*, 374 U.S. 398, 404, 83 S.Ct. 1790, 10 L.Ed.2d 965 (1963).

The principles reaffirmed in *Healy* have been extensively applied to strike down every form of censorship of student publications at state-supported institutions. Censorship of constitutionally protected expression cannot be imposed by suspending the editors,[3] suppressing circulation,[4] requiring imprimatur of controversial articles,[5] excising repugnant material,[6] withdrawing financial support,[7] or asserting any other form of censorial oversight based on the institution's power of the purse.[8]

But the freedom of the press enjoyed by students is not absolute or unfettered. Students, like all other citizens, are forbidden advocacy which "is directed to inciting or producing imminent lawless action and is likely to incite or produce such action." *See Brandenburg* v. *Ohio,* 395 U.S. 444, 447, 89 S.Ct. 1827, 1829, 23 L.Ed.2d 430 (1969). *Tinker* v. *Des Moines Ind. Community School Dist.,* 393 U.S. 503, 513, 89 S.Ct. 733, 740, 21 L.Ed.2d 731 (1969), expressly limits the free and unrestricted expression of opinion in schools to instances where it does not "materially and substantially interfere with the requirements of appropriate discipline in the operation of the school." We previously considered these limitations in *Quarterman* v. *Byrd,* 453 F.2d 54, 58 (4th Cir.1971):

> "Specifically, school authorities may by appropriate regulation, exercise prior restraint upon publications distributed on school premises during school hours in those special circumstances where they can 'reasonbly "forecast substantial disruption of or material interference with school activities" ' on account of the distribution of such printed material."

In his brief President Whiting acknowledges that there does not appear to have been any danger of physcial violence or disruption at the university because of the publication of the *Echo.* The record, of course, does disclose that the paper's message of racial devisiveness and antagonism was distasteful to the president, and it may well have offended other members of the university community. However, no white faculty members or students complained that the paper's editorial policy incited anybody at the university to harass or interfere with them. The case, therefore, does not present a situation that *Brandenburg, Tinker,* and *Quarterman* recognize as justifying restriction of free expression.

As a foundation for its decree, the district court fashioned a unique exception to the well-established body of law dealing with censorship of college newspapers. Describing the *Echo* as a state agency, the court upheld the termination of its funding by the university on the ground that the Fourteenth Amendment and Civil Rights Act of 1964 bar a state agency from spending state funds to discourage racial integration of the university "by a program of harassment, discourtesy, and indicia of unwelcome."

Censorship of the paper cannot be sustained on the court's theory. The record contains no proof that the editorial policy of the paper incited harassment, violence, or interference with white students and faculty. At the most, the editorial comments advocated racial segregation contrary to the Fourteenth Amendment and the Civil Rights Act of 1964. The court's rationale disregards the distinction between the First Amendment's clause prohibiting the establishment of religion and its clause protecting freedom of the press. Neither federal nor state governments may expend funds to establish a religion. The First Amendment, however, contains no similar ban against speech or press. Both governments may spend money to publish the positions they take on controversial subjects. The speeches and publications that originate in government offices attest to the diversity of views that are freely expounded. But under the rule that President Whiting urges us to affirm, no state official could use his office to criticize, as the editor of the *Echo* did, government policy on race relations with which he disagrees. We need not decide whether the *Echo* is a state agency; it is enough to say that even if it were, it would not be prohibited from expressing its hostility to racial integration. The Fourteenth Amendment and the Civil Rights Act proscribe state action that denies the equal protection of the laws, not state advocacy. To be sure, the line between action and advocacy may sometimes be difficult to draw, but it is clear that nothing written in the *Echo* crossed it.

A college newspaper's freedom from censorship does not necessarily imply that its facilities are the editor's private domain. When a college paper receives a subsidy from the state, there are strong arguments for insisting that its columns be open to the expression of contrary views and that its publication enhance, not inhibit, free speech. *Cf. Red Lion Broadcasting Co., Inc.* v. *FCC,* 395 U.S. 367, 390 89 S.Ct. 1794, 23 L.Ed.2d 371 (1969). However, this case provides no occasion for formulating a principle akin to the fairness doctrine for the college press. The record does not disclose that Joyner rejected any articles that were opposed to his editorial policy, and President Whiting does not claim the paper refused to publish his pro-integration plea.

The president, emphasizing that the students are still free to publish and circulate a newspaper on the campus without university support, protests that the denial of financial support cannot be considered censorship because it is permanent. Permanency, he suggests, does not link the ebb and flow of funds with disapproval or approval of editorial policy. Absent this correlation, he claims, there is no censorship. But this argument overlooks the fact that one of the reasons for the president's withdrawal of funds was his displeasure with the paper's editorial policy. The abridgement of freedom of the press is nonetheless real because it is permanent. Freedom of the press cannot be preserved, as Mr. Justice Frankfurter noted, by prohibitions calculated "to burn the house to roast the pig." *Butler* v. *Michigan,* 352 U.S. 380, 383, 77 S.Ct. 524, 526, 1 L.Ed.2d 412 (1957). The president has failed to carry the "heavy burden of showing justification for the imposition of" a prior restraint on expression. *Organization for a Better Austin* v. *Keefe,* 402 U.S. 415, 419, 91 S.Ct. 1575, 29 L.Ed.2d 1 (1971). He has proved only that he considers the paper's editorial comment to be abhorrent, contrary to the university's policy, and inconsistant with constitutional and statutory guarantees of equality. This is plainly insufficient. *Healy* v. *James,* 408 U.S. 169, 187, 92 S.Ct. 2338, 33 L.Ed.2d 266 (1972); *cf. Brandenburg* v. *Ohio,* 395 U.S. 444, 449, 89 S.Ct. 1827, 23 L.Ed.2d 430 (1969).

Similarly, the district court's permanent injunction against the university's funding of the paper cannot stand. The court's grant of the injunction was intended to protect the student press by eliminating the enducement of future financial support "as a possible method for censorship." But the proper remedy against censorship is restraint of the censor, not suppression of the press. A court, no less than the executive and the legislature, must defer to the First Amendment. Twice in the history of the nation the Supreme Court has reviewed injunctions that imposed prior restraints on the publication of newspapers, and twice the Court has held the restraints to be unconstitutional. *New York Times Co.* v. *United States,* 403 U.S. 713, 91 S.Ct. 2140, 29 L.Ed.2d 822 (1971); *Near* v. *Minnesota,* 283 U.S. 697, 51 S.Ct. 625, 75 L.Ed. 1357 (1931). In both instances the proof was insufficient to overcome the presumption of unconstitutionality under which prior restraint of expression labors. Because this case is marked by the same defect, the injunction must be dissolved.

II

DISCRIMINATORY PRACTICES

Early in September of 1971, Joyner, who had been elected editor the previous spring, told the *Echo's* faculty advisor that the paper would be black- oriented and that neither whites nor foreigners would be allowed to serve as staff members. The first edition of the paper under Joyner's editorship, published later in the month, contained a notice that the paper would not carry advertising for white merchants.

The president asserts that the *Echo* is an agency of the state, and that continued financial support of the paper despite its discriminatory practices would violate the equal protection clause of the Fourteenth Amendment and Title VI of the Civil Rights Act of 1964. In contrast, the Board of Governors of the University of North Carolina[9] takes the position that the *Echo* is not an agency of the state, but it justifies the president's withholding of funds as a permissible means of enforcing a valid campus regulation proscribing racial discrimination.

We need not choose between these theories. Under both of them, the president was justified in prohibiting racial discrimination in staffing the newspaper and accepting advertising. The equal protection clause forbids racial discrimination in extracurricular activities of a state-supported institution. *United States* v. *Jefferson County Bd. of Educ.,* 372 F.2d 836, 899 (5th Cir. 1966), cert. denied, 389 U.S. 840, 88 S.Ct. 67, 19 L.Ed.2d 103 (1967), and freedom of the press furnishes no shield for discrimination in advertising. *United States* v. *Hunter,* 459 F.2d 205, 211 (4th Cir.), cert. denied, 409 U.S. 934, 93 S.Ct. 235, 34 L.Ed.2d 189 (1972); *cf. Lee* v. *Board of Regents,* 441 F.2d 1257 (7th Cir. 1971). Even if the *Echo* is not, strictly speaking, an agency of North Carolina, the president was not powerless to act. Campus organizations claiming First Amendment rights must comply with valid campus regulations, *Healy* v. *James,* 408 U.S. 169, 191, 92 S.Ct. 2338, 33 L.Ed.2d 266 (1972), and the state, acting through the president, possesses adequate power to promulgate and enforce rules prohibiting discrimination. *Railway Mail Ass'n* v. *Corsi,* 326 U.S. 88, 65 S.Ct. 1483, 89 L.Ed. 2072 (1945).

It does not follow, however, that the appropriate remedy for the paper's racial discrimination was the permanent cessation of financial support. During a meeting with the president after suspension of financing, Joyner disavowed his black only staff policy. Moreover, the second issue of the *Echo* carried a notice repudiating its statement that it would not accept any more business from white advertisers. Henceforth, the notice said, the *Echo* will "only accept ads from white businesses that employ on an equal opportunity basis."

We cannot accept the contention pressed by Joyner and the Board of Governors that the issues of discrimination in staffing and advertising are now moot. Neither the president nor the district court were required to give credence to the disavowal of the discriminatory practices, and, as the president points out, the paper is still free to take ads from black businesses which are not equal opportunity employers. Therefore, on remand, the president should be afforded an opportunity to amend his pleadings to apply for relief against discriminatory practices in staffing and advertising. If he does, the district court should determine whether "there exists some cognizable danger of recurrent violation." *United State* v. *W. T. Grant Co.,* 345 U.S. 629, 633, 73 S.Ct. 894, 898, 94 L.Ed. 1303 (1953). If the court finds that this danger exists, it may enjoin these discriminatory practices.

The permanent withdrawal of funds, however, is not an appropriate remedy. While the state may suppress speech when it is thoroughly enmeshed with unlawful conduct, *Milk Wagon Drivers' Union* v. *Meadowmoor Dairies, Inc.,* 312 U.S. 287, 61 S.Ct. 552, 85 L.Ed. 836 (1941), this record fails to disclose that the discriminatory staffing and advertising policies are inextricably related to the news and editorial content of the paper. To comply with the First Amendment, the remedy must be narrowly drawn to rectify only the discrimination in staffing and advertising. *Cf. Youngdahl v. Rainfair, Inc.,* 355 US. 131, 78 S.CT. 206, 2 L.Ed.2d 151 (1957).

III

Two other matters require but brief comment. The parties have argued about the right of a student to resist having a part of his student activities fee allocated to the *Echo. Cf. International Ass'n of Machinists v. Street,* 367 U.S. 740, 81 S.Ct. 1784, 6 L.Ed.2d 1141 (1961). This issue is speculative. No student has protested that he was compelled to subscribe to the paper. We, therefore, express no opinion concerning this aspect of the case.

The second issue which we do not reach is the contention that the students have been denied the equal protection of the laws because eleven other state supported universities in North Carolina sponsor college newspapers. In view of our disposition of the case, we find it unnecessary to consider this alternative ground for relief.

The judgment of the district court is reversed, and the injunction which it entered is dissolved. This case is remanded for the entry of a declaratory judgment consistent with this opinion. In the exercise of its sound discretion, the district court may grant or withhold injunctive relief. *See Antonelli v. Hammond,* 308 F.Supp. 1329, 1338 (D.Mass.1970).

FIELD, Circuit Judge (dissenting in part):

The high regard I have for my brothers of the majority makes me somewhat hesitant to dissent, but I simply do not see this case as they apparently do. No one would now question that the constitutional freedoms of speech and press guaranteed by the First Amendment protect the students of our colleges and universities from unreasonable administrative interference, and the school authorities may not restrict the students' freedom of speech merely because they find the views expressed to be abhorrent. *Healy v. James,* 408 U.S. 169, 92 S.Ct. 2338, 33 L.Ed.2d 266 (1972), and the related authorities in this area cited by the majority solidly support this principle.[1] However, as pointed out by Professor Van Alstyne in his *amicus* brief, the issue in this case does not involve the more familiar form of abridgment by restriction of expression of opinion by the students as individuals either on or off the campus of NCCU,[2] nor does it present the case where financial support of the college newspaper was temporarily withheld for the purpose of inducing editorial policies acceptable to the administration. *Cf. Antonelli v. Hammond,* 308 F.Supp. 1329 (D.C.Mass.1970).

The issue as I see it is whether President Whiting had the right if not, indeed, the duty to terminate the University's subsidy of the *Echo* when he had reasonable grounds to believe that the newspaper was engaged in conduct which was violative of the Constitution and laws of the United States and which, under the circumstances, jeopardized the University's participation in the various federal funding programs necessary to its operation. I submit that President Whiting's decision on this basis to irrevocably discontinue the subsidy to avoid future involvement in the terms of the school's possible responsibility for the editorial content of the *Echo,* coupled with the express disavowal on his part that the subsidy might be renewed in the event the newspaper would accede to acceptable "journalistic standards" or other subjective criteria, violated no First Amendment rights of the plaintiffs,[3] and that the conclusion of the district court on the primary issue in this case was correct.

Referring to the action of the district judge in upholding the termination of the subsidy on the theory that the racist editorial policy of Joyner was violative of the Fourteenth Amendment and the Civil Rights Act of 1964, the majority suggests that he "fashioned a unique exception to the well established body of law dealing with censorship of college newspapers" which cannot be sustained. In all deference, I suggest that there was nothing unique about the rationale of the district court's decision and that it finds solid support in law and in fact.

For almost two decades since *Brown v. Board of Education,* 347 U.S. 483, 74 S.Ct. 686, 98 L.Ed. 873 (1954), the school authorities of this country have been "clearly charged with the affirmative duty to take whatever steps might be necessary to convert to a unitary system in which racial discrimination would be eliminated root and branch." *Green v. County School Board,* 391 U.S. 430 (1968) at 437–438, 88 S.Ct. 1689 at 1694, 20 L.Ed.2d 716 It is an understatement to say that the transition from segregated schools to a non-racial system of public education has not been a simple task, and this is especially true for an educator in the position of President Whiting confronted with the delicate responsibility of converting a previously all black university into an integrated educational facility.

The constitutional responsibility to eliminate racial discrimination articulated by the courts has received substantial support from the Congress of the United States, and the national policy against support for segregated education emerged in provisions adopted by the Congress in the Civil Rights Act of 1964. Title VI, Section 601 of the Act, 42 U.S.C. § 2000d, provides that "[n]o person in the United States shall, on the ground of race, color, or national origin, be exluded from participation in, be denied the benefits of, or be subjected to discrimination under any program or activity receiving Federal financial assistance." Section 602 of the Act, 42 U.S.C. § 2000d–1 directs each federal agency administering programs of financial assistance to take action by rule, regulation or order to effectuate the principles of Section 601, and to effect compliance with those requirements under this section an agency is authorized to terminate or refuse to grant assistance under a program to any recipient as to whom there has been a finding of a failure to comply with such requirements.

It is in the context of this background that President Whiting's action should properly be appraised. The majority states that Joyner's message of racial divisiveness and hostility was distasteful to Whiting. This may well be true, but the record clearly shows that the reason for the termination of the subsidy was not President Whiting's personal displeasure with the editorial policy of the *Echo* but his fear, based upon the advice of the Attorney General of North Carolina, that continued support of the student newspaper could be construed as "state action" in the context of the various civil rights acts passed by the Congress as well as the Federal Constitution. Whiting's apprehension that continued subsidization might jeopardize the University's federal funding was well founded for the federal agencies have not hesitated to act pursuant to Section 602 of the Civil Rights Act and terminate federal assistance where the authorities of a state have failed to take affirmative action to eliminate discrimination in its schools. *State of Georgia* v. *Mitchell,* 450 F.2d 1317 (C.A.D.C.1971); *see also, Green* v. *Connally,* 330 F.Supp. 1150 (D.C.D.C.1971), aff'd per curiam sub nom., *Coit et al.* v. *Green et al.,* 404 U.S. 997, 92 S.Ct. 564, 30 L.Ed.2d 550 (1971).

Unquestionably the activities of the *Echo,* subsidized as it was by the University, constituted "state action" in the area of civil rights, *Lee* v. *Board of Regents of State Colleges,* 441 F.2d 1257 (7 Cir. 1971); *Zucker* v. *Panitz,* 299 F.Supp. 102 (S.D.N.Y.1969); *Panarella* v. *Birenbaum,* 37 A.D.2d 987, 327 N.Y.S.2d 755 (1971), and if its editorial content was violative of Federal Constitutional or statutory proscriptions, the responsibility necessarily would fall squarely on NCCU. It should be borne in mind that we are not dealing here with a "letter to the editor" nor a casual news article or student poll. What we have before us is the lead editorial in the first issue of the subsidized house organ of NCCU greeting the matriculating students with a clear and violent statement of policy which the district court found to be designed to discourage racial integration of the University "by a program of harrassment, discourtesy and indicia of unwelcome." The majority disposes of this finding, however, with the observation that the record fails to show that the editorial policy incited harassment, violence or interference with white students. Conceding that the editorial advocated racial segregation contrary to the Fourteenth Amendment and the Civil Rights Act of 1964, my brothers would countenance it on the ground that it was not proscribed "state action" but was acceptable "state advocacy." I must confess I find the import of this statement somewhat obscure and, assuredly, of questionable validity on the issue before us.[4]

In *Smith* v. *St. Tammany Parish School Board,* 316 F.Supp. 1174 (D.C.E.D.La.1970), aff'd, 448 F.2d 414 (5 Cir. 1971), the district court ordered all Confederate flags as well as other symbols of racism removed from the schools with this observation at page 1176:

"In this connection, the principal of the Covington High School understands today's symbolism of the Confederate battle flag as well as he understands the symbolism of a Black Panther or a Black Power flag. But none of these flags are constitutionally permissible in a unitary school system where both white and black students attend school together. At the moment, the Covington principal insists on the display of the Confederate battle flag; but the display of the flag is an affront to every Negro student in the school, just as the display of the Black Panther flag would be an affront to every white student in a school whose principal was a Negro. The retention of Confederate flags in a unitary school system is no way to eliminate racial discrimination 'root and branch' from the system."

I respectfully suggest that Mr. Joyner's editorial policy was at least as much of an affront to the white minority of NCCU as the Confederate flag was to the black students of St. Tammany Parish. Whether we label it "advocacy" or "action," the *Echo's* editorial policy was violative of the Fourteenth Amendment and the Civil Rights Act of 1964, and President Whiting acted reasonably and responsibly in irrevocably terminating the subsidy and removing the imprimatur of the University from Joyner's racist views.[5]

I, of course, am in agreement with the views expressed by the majority relative to the discriminatory staffing and advertising policies of the *Echo* under Joyner's leadership. I also agree that the district court's permanent injunction against the future funding of any newspaper at NCCU was improper. While this action of the court was designed to eliminate the possiblity of the use of such support in the future "as a possible method of censorship," such an anticipatory measure was neither necessary nor appropriate in the disposition of this case. Accordingly, I would affirm the court below in its denial of declaratory and injunctive relief to the plaintiffs, and remand the case with directions to dissolve the permanent injunction against possible future funding.

NOTES

1. The president also circulated the following memorandum to all members of the university community:

   "By now I am certain that most of you have read the September 16 issue of the *Campus Echo*. Because of the very pronounced critical position taken in this paper regarding integration in the University Community, I feel it my duty as President to indicate clearly and unequivocally what the official policy of the Institution is and will continue to be in accordance with the present law of the land and the State of North Carolina. North Carolina Central University has always been opposed to any policies and practices which deprive any individual of a right or a privilege because of race, color, creed, or national origin. It will not extend recognition to or knowingly affiliate with and condone any group, organization, or association, espousing policies which discriminate on such bases.

   "Because of historical circumstances issuing out of the shameful segregated past this institution is and will continue to be in the forseeable future predominantly Black or Negro (whichever word one chooses to use here is a matter of personal choice). It has had a prideful and heroic educational tradition and in its various forms, from the date of its founding, has contributed significantly and effectively to the development and well-being of those who have had the good fortune to attend. Because of relatively recent social changes, integration on all college and university campuses and, as a matter of fact, in all legitimate schools has become more visible. This is no longer a reversible trend and it is sheer folly to think otherwise. Presently, at North Carolina Central University we have an array of ethnic and racial types but in actuality only a statistically insignificant number of non-Negroes. This notwithstanding, the point that I wish to make is that as a State-Supported Institution especially, but also in terms of what is morally and legally right, this institution is not a 'Black University' and does not intend to become one.

   "To those who find this assertion and this fact uncomfortable and/or intolerable I wish to make it perfectly clear that they must, while here, operate within the framework of the University policies regarding this. If this is not possible, then my advice is to seek enrollment and/or employment in institutions where such attitudes are acceptable.

   "In line with this point of view, I am herewith announcing that all funds for the publication of the *Campus Echo* have been temporarily suspended until consensus can be established regarding the journalistic standards to which this paper will adhere and its role on this campus. If consensus cannot be developed, then the university will no longer sponsor a campus newspaper and that proportion of funds collected and allocated to the budget of the *Campus Echo* will accrue to the credit of all contributing students for this school year."

2. In *Danskin*, Mr. Justice Traynor dealt with the validity of a school board rule requiring persons seeking use of a school auditorium for meetings to take an oath renouncing the overthrow of the government by force or unlawful means. In holding that such a requirement violated the First Amendment, he wrote:

   "It is true that the state need not open the doors of a school building as a forum and may at any time choose to close them. Once it opens the doors, however, it cannot demand tickets of admission in the form of convictions and affiliations that it deems acceptable." 171 P.2d at 892.

3. *Scoville* v. *Board of Educ. of Joliet Tp. H. S. Dist.* 204, 425 F.2d 10 (7th Cir.), cert. denied, 400 U.S. 826, 91 S.Ct. 51, 27 L.Ed.2d 55 (1970); *Sullivan* v. *Houston Ind. School Dist.*, 307 F.Supp. 1328 (S.D.Tex.1969); *Dickey* v. *Alabama State Bd. of Educ.*, 273 F.Supp. 613 (M.D.Ala.1967).

4. *Channing Club* v. *Board of Regents*, 317 F.Supp. 688 (N.D.Tex.1970).

5. *Quarterman* v. *Byrd*, 453 F.2d 54 (4th Cir. 1971); *Eisner* v. *Stamford Bd. of Educ.*, 440 F.2d 803 (2d Cir. 1971); *Trujillo* v. *Love*, 322 F.Supp. 1266 (D.Colo.1971); *Panarella* v. *Birenbaum*, 37 A.D.2d 987, 327 N.Y.S.2d 755 (1971).

6. *Korn* v. *Elkins*, 317 F.Supp. 138 (D.Md.1970); *Zucker* v *Panitz*, 299 F.Supp. 103 (S.D.N.Y.1969).

7. *Korn* v. *Elkins*, 317 F.Supp. 138 (D.Md.1970); *Antonelli* v. *Hammond*, 308 F. Supp. 1329 (D.Mass.1970).

8. *Trujillo* v. *Love*, 322 F.Supp. 1266 (D.Colo.1971); *Korn* v. *Elkins*, 317 F.Supp. 138 (D.Md.1970); *Antonelli* v. *Hammond*, 308 F.Supp. 1329 (D.Mass.1970); *Dickey* v. *Alabama State Bd. of Educ.*, 273 F.Supp. 613 (M.D.Ala.1967); *Panarella* v. *Birenbaum*, 37 A.D.2d 987, 327 N.Y.S.2d 755 (1971); *see* Developments in the Law-Academic Freedom, 81 Harv.L.Rev. 1045, 1130 (1968): "[S]tate financial support alone is not enough to prevent application of the First Amendment to student newspapers."

9. The Board is the governing body of the University of North Carolina system, which includes North Carolina Central University. It filed a brief *amicus curiae*.

DISSENTING (IN PART) OPINION NOTES

1. The majority apparently recognizes, however, that a university has no constitutional responsibility to establish a campus newspaper. See *Dickey* v. *Alabama State Board of Education*, 273 F.Supp. 613, 618 (M.D. Ala.1967); Cf. *Danskin* v. *San Diego Unified School District*, 28 Cal.2d 53, 171 P.2d 885, 892 (1946).

2. Neither Joyner nor anyone else was subjected to suspension, expulsion, or any other reprisal; nor as stated by the majority, was there any attempt by President Whiting to suppress the publication or circulation of any privately funded newspaper on the campus. These factors are sufficient to distinguish this case from practically all of the authorities cited by the majority.

3. It should be noted that in a post-subsidy issue of the *Echo*, Joyner wrote an article relative to the institution of this litigation in the district court which carried the

utterly tasteless and offensive headline *"So, We took his ass to court."* Demonstrating commendable restraint and respect for Joyner's First Amendment rights of expression, President Whiting took no punitive or repressive action against either Joyner or the publication.

4. The nub of the present controversy becomes more readily apparent if we reverse the circumstances. Suppose that incident to a program of integration, the advent of black students on the campus of a previously all white state-supported university in North Carolina or elsewhere had been greeted by a similar message in the subsidized university newspaper denouncing the admission of blacks to the institution. I submit that this court or any court would have had little difficulty in finding such "advocacy" to be state action which was violative of the law of the land.

5. Even should it be assumed *arguendo* that the Echo's editorial policy was not violative of the law, the record clearly supports the conclusion that Presdient Whiting acted in the reasonble belief that Joyner's conduct was illegal and, under these circumstances, termination of the subsidy could well be sustained under the rationale of *Sellers* v. *Regents of University of California,* 432 F.2d 493 (9 Cir. 1970).

THE United States Court of Appeals, Fourth Circuit, decides for high school students who had challenged the constitutionality of school regulations involving prior restraint on the distribution of non-school literature. In deciding that the school regulations were unconstitutional, the Court declared: "By way of summary, we hold that the Montgomery County [Maryland] prior restraint regulation is unconstitutional and that its enforcement must be enjoined. Our decision rests upon these propositions of law: (A) Secondary school children are within the protection of the First Amendment, although their rights are not coextensive with those of adults. (B) Secondary school authorities may exercise reasonable prior restraint upon the exercise of students' First Amendment rights. (C) Such prior restraints must contain precise criteria sufficiently spelling out what is forbidden so that a reasonably intelligent student will know what he may write and what he may not write. (D) A prior restraint system, even though precisely defining what may not be written, is nevertheless invalid unless it provides for: (1) A definition of 'distribution' and its application to different kinds of material; (2) prompt approval or disapproval of what is submitted; (3) specification of the effect of failure to act promptly; and, (4) an adequate and prompt appeals procedure."

Baughman v. *Freienmuth,* 478 F.2d 1345 (1973)

CRAVEN, Circuit Judge:

This is another freedom of speech case in the high school context. We are asked to extend our decision in *Quarterman* v. *Byrd,* 453 F.2d 54 (4th Cir. 1971) to prohibit *any* prior restraint based on content from being exercised by school officials over written material to be distributed on school grounds. We decline to do so. However, the application of *Quarterman* to this case requires that the decision of the district court be vacated insofar as it fails to grant the plaintiffs the complete relief to which they are entitled.

I.

The plaintiffs, parents on behalf of their children in the Montgomery County school system, brought this action seeking injunctive and declaratory relief against the Montgomery County Board of Education, its members and officers, and against the Maryland State Board of Education. The complaint attacked certain regulations (contained in a policy statement re-issued September 20, 1971) as an unlawful prior restraint on the distribution of non-school sponsored literature in violation of the First Amendment.

Distribution of a pamphlet criticizing the prior restraint regulations resulted in a warning letter from the principal and subsequently the commencement of this litigation. As in *Quarterman,* we need not assess the content of the pamphlet; we are concerned only with the constitutional validity of the September 20, 1971, regulations and the scope of further relief to which plaintiffs are entitled.

The challenged regulations of the board provide in relevant part:

Under the following procedures, student publications produced without school sponsorship may be distributed in schools:

* * *

4) A copy must be given to the principal for his review. (He may require that the copy be given to him up to three school days prior to its general distribution.) If, in the opinion of the principal, the publica-

tion contains libelous or obscene language, advocates illegal actions, or is grossly insulting to any group or individual, the principal shall notify the sponsors of the publication that its distribution must stop forthwith or may not be initiated, and state his reasons therefor. The principal may wish to establish a publications review board composed of staff, students, and parents to advise him in such matters. Students may distribute or display on designated bulletin boards materials from sources outside the school subject to the same procedures that govern student publications. . . .

The district court 343 F.Supp. 487, held: (1) that the regulation was invalid in restraining material which "advocates illegal actions, or is grossly insulting," and in failing to require the principal to act promptly; (2) that provisions for a review of the principal's action were gratuitous and unnecessary; and (3) that the prior restraint of libelous and obscene material was valid even though those terms are not otherwise defined. We affirm in part and reverse in part.

II.

The regulation complained of reaches the activity of pamphleteering which has often been recognized by the Supreme Court as a form of communication protected by the First Amendment. *Organization for a Better Austin* v. *Keefe,* 402 U.S. 415, 419, 91 S.Ct. 1575, 29 L.Ed.2d 1 (1971). It does not deal with such expression in neutral terms of time, place, and manner of distribution.[1] Rather it is a rule imposing prior restraint on expression because of "its message, its ideas, its subject matter, or its content"—a power of restraint denied government by the First Amendment in public areas including state college campuses.[2] *Police Dep't of the City of Chicago* v. *Mosley,* 408 U.S. 92, 95, 92 S.Ct. 2286, 33 L.Ed.2d 212 (1972).

In the secondary school setting First Amendment rights are not coextensive with those of adults and while such rules of prior restraint may be valid, they nevertheless come to this court with a presumption against their constitutionality. *Tinker* v. *Des Moines Community School Dist.,* 393 U.S. 503, 513, 89 S.Ct. 733, 21 L.Ed.2d 731 (1969); *see University of So. Miss. Chapter of the Miss. Civil Liberties Union* v. *University of So. Miss.,* 452 F.2d 564, 566 (5th Cir. 1971). To overcome this presumption, school regulations must come within the constitutional limits defined in *Quarterman.*

It is generally held that the constitutional right to free speech of public secondary school students may be modified or curtailed by school regulations "reasonably designed to adjust these rights to the needs of the school environment.". . . Specifically, school authorities may by appropriate regulation, exercise prior restraint upon publications distributed on school premises during school hours in those special circumstances where they can "reasonably 'forecast substantial disruption of or material interference with school activities'" on account of the distribution of such printed material . . . .

What is lacking in the present regulation, and what renders its attempt at prior restraint invalid, is the absence both of any criteria to be followed by the school authorities in determining whether to grant or deny permission, and of any procedural safeguards in the form of "an expeditious review procedure" of the decision of the school authorities. 453 F.2d at 58–59.

The present regulation, like the one in *Quarterman,* is impermissible. It lacks the procedural safeguard of a specified and reasonably short period of time in which the principal must act. Moreover, the regulation fails to provide for the contingency of the principal's failure to act within a specified brief time, *i.e.,* whether upon such failure the material then could be distributed. *See Freedman* v. *Maryland,* 380 U.S. 51, 59, 85 S.Ct. 734, 13 L.Ed.2d 649 (1965). It is not our province to suggest a time limit, but we caution that whatever period is allowed, the regulation may not lawfully be used to choke off spontaneous expression in reaction to events of great public importance and impact. *See Wright,* at 1044. Furthermore, as pointed out in *Quarterman,* "'An expeditious review procedure' of the decision of the school authorities" is required. 453 F.2d at 59. The present regulation lacks these procedural safeguards and is, therefore, an unreasonable restriction on the First Amendment rights of school children. *See Burnside* v. *Byars,* 363 F.2d 744, 747–748 (5th Cir. 1966).

Moreover, the proscription against "distribution" is unconstitutionally vague. With respect to some communicative material there may be no prior restraint unless there is "a *substantial* distribution of written material, so that it can reasonably be anticipated that in a significant number of instances there would be a likelihood that the distribution would disrupt school operations." *Eisner* v. *Stamford Bd. of Education,* 440 F.2d at 803, 811. With respect to other types of material, *e.g.,* pornography, one copy, indeed, the *only* copy may be the subject of what is legitimate prior restraint if what is forbidden is precisely defined.[3] The prohibition of material which "advocates illegal actions, or is grossly insulting to any group or individual" seems to belong in the first category and thus goes beyond the permissible standard (for that type of material) of forecasting substantial disruption. *See Tinker* v. *Des Moines Com-*

munity School Dist., 393 U.S. 503, 514, 89 S.Ct. 733, 21 L.Ed.2d 731 (1969).

III.

While the district court found the regulation invalid, the court nevertheless found "that the Montgomery County Rule, insofar as it allows the imposition of a prior restraint upon obscene or libelous material, is valid." We agree that material which is, in the constitutional sense, unprivileged libel or obscenity if read by children[4] can be banned from school property by school authorities. *See Eisner* v. *Stamford Bd. of Educ.,* 440 F.2d 803, 809 n. 6 (2d Cir. 1971). If there were no contemplated prior restraint but instead merely post-publication sanction, the problem of vagueness would not be intolerable. Put affirmatively, we think that a regulation imposing prior restraint must be much more precise than a regulation imposing post-publication sanctions. As Mr. Justice Marshall said in *Interstate Circuit, Inc.* v. *Dallas,* 390 U.S. 676, 88 S.Ct. 1298, 20 L.Ed.2d 225 (1968): "The vice of vagueness is particularly pronounced where expression is sought to be subjected to licensing." 390 U.S. at 683, 88 S.Ct. at 1303. He quoted Chief Judge Fuld with approval: "It is . . . essential that legislation aimed at protecting children from allegedly harmful expression—no less than legislation enacted with respect to adults—be clearly drawn and that the standards adopted be reasonably precise so that those who are governed by the law and those that administer it will understand its meaning and application." 390 U.S. at 689, 88 S. Ct. at 1306.

To do otherwise is to leave administrators "adrift upon a boundless sea. . . ." *Jospeh Burstyn, Inc.* v. *Wilson,* 343 U.S. 495, 504, 72 S.Ct. 777, 96 L.Ed. 1098 (1952).

In *Bantam Books, Inc.* v. *Sullivan,* 372 U.S. 58, 83 S.Ct. 631, 9 L.Ed.2d 584 (1963), the Court spoke critically of a system of prior restraint comparing it unfavorably with post-publication criminal sanctions:

> In thus obviating the need to employ criminal sanctions, the State has at the same time eliminated the safeguards of the criminal process. Criminal sanctions may be applied only after a determination of obscenity has been made in a criminal trial hedged about with the procedural safeguards of the criminal process. The Commission's practice is in striking contrast, in that it provides no safeguards whatever against the suppression of nonobscene, and therefore constitutionally protected, matter. It is a form of regulation that creates hazards to protected freedoms markedly greater than those that attend reliance upon the criminal law.

> What Rhode Island has done, in fact, has been to subject the distribution of publications to a system of prior administrative restraints, since the Commission is not a judicial body and its decisions to list particular publications as objectionable do not follow judicial determinations that such publications may lawfully be banned. Any system of prior restraints of expression comes to this Court bearing a heavy presumption against its constitutional validity. See *Near* v. *Minnesota,* 283 U.S. 697 [, 51 S.Ct. 625, 75 L.Ed. 1357] (1931); *Lovell* v. *Griffin,* 303 U.S. 444, 451 [, 58 S.Ct. 666, 668, 82 L.Ed. 949] (1938); *Schneider* v. *State,* 308 U.S. 147, 164 [, 60 S.Ct. 146, 152, 84 L.Ed. 155] (1939); *Cantwell* v. *Connecticut,* 310 U.S. 296, 306 [, 60 S.Ct. 900, 904, 84 L.Ed. 1213] (1940); *Niemotko* v. *Maryland,* 340 U.S. 268, 273 [, 71 S.Ct. 325, 328, 95 L.Ed. 267] (1951); *Kunz* v. *New York,* 340 U.S. 290, 293 [, 71 S.Ct. 312, 314, 95 L.Ed. 280] (1951); *Staub* v. *Baxley,* 355 U.S. 313, 321 [, 78 S.Ct. 277, 281, 2 L.Ed.2d 302] (1958). We have tolerated such a system only where it operated under judicial superintendance and assured an almost immediate judicial determination of the validity of the restraint. *Kingsley Books, Inc.* v. *Brown,* 354 U. S. 436 [, 77 S.Ct. 1325, 1 L.Ed.2d 1469] (1957).

372 U.S. at 69–71, 83 S.Ct. at 639.

In short, we think letting students write first and be judged later is far less inhibiting than vice versa. For that reason vagueness that is intolerable in a prior restraint context may be permissible as part of a post-publication sanction. As stated by Justice Harlan:

> One danger of a censorship system is that the public may never be aware of what an administrative agent refuses to permit to be published or distributed. A penal sanction assures both that some overt thing has been done by the accused and that the penalty is imposed for an activity that is not concealed from the public.

A Quantity of Books v. *Kansas,* 378 U.S. 205, 223, 84 S.Ct. 1723, 1732, 12 L.Ed.2d 809 (1964) (dissenting opinion).

Thus a regulation requiring prior submission of material for approval *before* distribution must contain narrow, objective, and reasonable standards by which the material will be judged. *See Quarterman,* 453 F.2d at 59. Such a standard is required in order that those charged with enforcing the regulation are not given impermissible power to judge the material on an *ad hoc* and subjective basis and that forbidden activity be clearly delineated so as not to inhibit basic First Amendment freedoms. *See Grayned* v. *City of Rockford,* 408 U.S. 104, 109, 92 S.Ct. 2294, 33 L.Ed.2d 222 (1972).

The use of terms of art such as "libelous" and "obscene" are not sufficiently precise and understandable by high school students and administrators untutored in the law to be acceptable criteria. Indeed, such terms are troublesome to lawyers and judges. None other than a Justice of the Supreme Court has confessed that obscenity "may be indefinable."[5] *Jacobellis* v. *Ohio,* 378 U.S. 184, 197, 84 S.Ct. 1676, 12 L.Ed.2d 793 (1964) (Stewart J., concurring). "Libelous" is another legal term of art which is quite difficult to apply to a given set of words. Moreover, that words *are* libelous is not the end of the inquiry: libel is often privileged. *New York Times Co.* v. *Sullivan,* 376 U.S. 254, 84 S.Ct. 710, 11 L.Ed.2d 686 (1964).

Thus, while school authorities may ban obscenity and unprivileged libelous material there is an intolerable danger, in the context of prior restraint, that under the guise of such vague labels they may unconstitutionally choke off criticism, either of themselves, or of school policies, which they find disrespectful, tasteless, or offensive. That they may not do.[6]

By way of summary, we hold that the Montgomery County prior restraint regulation is unconstitutional and that its enforcement must be enjoined. Our decision rests upon these propositions of law:

(a) Secondary school children are within the protection of the First Amendment, although their rights are not coextensive with those of adults.

(b) Secondary school authorities may exercise reasonable prior restraint upon the exercise of students' First Amendment rights.

(c) Such prior restraints must contain precise criteria sufficiently spelling out what is forbidden so that a reasonably intelligent student will know what he may write and what he may not write.

(d) A prior restraint system, even though precisely defining what may not be written, is nevertheless invalid unless it provides for:

    (1) A definition of "Distribution" and its application to different kinds of material;

    (2) Prompt approval or disapproval of what is submitted;

    (3) Specification of the effect of failure to act promptly; and,

    (4) An adequate and prompt appeals procedure.

For the reasons stated, we reverse with regard to the denial of declaratory and injunctive relief and remand for further proceedings.

Reversed in part.
Affirmed in part.
Remanded.

NOTES

1. To the extent that a prior submission rule is to control the time, place, and manner of distribution, it is valid. "Just as in the community at large, reasonable regulations with respect to the time, the place, and the manner in which student groups conduct their speech-related activities must be respected." *Healy* v. *James,* 408 U.S. 169, 192–193, 92 S.Ct. 2338, 2352, 33 L.Ed.2d 266 (1972); *Jones* v. *Board of Regents,* 436 F.2d 618, 620 (9th Cir. 1970), *See* Wright, The Constitution on the Campus, 22 Vand.L.Rev. 1027, 1044 (1969).

2. *Healy* v. *James,* 408 U.S. 169, 180, 92 S.Ct. 2338, 33 L.Ed.2d 266 (1972); *Papish* v. *University of Mo. Bd. of Curators,* 410 U.S. 667, 93 S.Ct. 1197, 35 L.Ed.2d 618 (1973).

3. The illustrations in Sec. 1851 of the proposed revisions of the federal criminal code seem to be a careful attempt to describe what is meant by Mr. Justice Stewart's phrase "hard core pornography". Selections from President's Version of Revised Federal Criminal Code § 1851, 13 Crim.L.W. 3005, 3016 (April 11, 1973).

4. *See Ginsberg* v. *New York,* 390 U.S. 629, 88 S.Ct. 1274, 20 L.Ed.2d 195 (1968).

5. It is instructive that the President's current proposed revision of the federal criminal code undertakes detailed explicit illustrations of "obscene material". Section 1851, *supra,* note 4.

6. *Scoville* v. *Board of Educ.* 425 F.2d 10, 14 (7th Cir.), cert. denied, 400 U.S. 826, 91 S.Ct. 51, 27 L.Ed.2d 55 (1970). *See also Pickering* v. *Board of Educ.,* 391 U.S. 563, 573–574, 88 S.Ct. 1731, 20 L.Ed.2d 811 (1968); *Eisner,* 440 F.2d at 809.

THE United States Supreme Court decides, 6–3, for a University of Missouri School of Journalism student who had been expelled for distributing on campus a newspaper "containing forms of indecent speech." In deciding for the student, the Court said: "This case was decided [by the lower court] several days before we handed down *Healy* v. *James* . . . [the Court decided for Students for a Democratic Society (SDS) which had been denied university recognition], in which, while recognizing a state university's undoubted prerogative to enforce reasonable rules governing student conduct, we reaffirmed that 'state colleges and universities are not enclaves immune from the sweep of the First Amendment. . . . We think *Healy* makes it clear that the mere dissemination of ideas—no matter how offensive to good taste—on a state university campus may not be shut off in the name alone of 'conventions of decency.' Other recent precedents of this Court make it equally clear that neither the political cartoon nor the headline story involved in this case can be labeled as constitutionally obscene or otherwise unprotected. . . . There is language in the opinions below which suggests that the University's action here could be viewed as an exercise of its legitimate authority to enforce reasonable regulations as to the time, place, and manner of speech and its dissemination. While we have repeatedly approved such regulatory authority . . . , the facts set forth in the opinions below show clearly that petitioner was dismissed because of the disapproved *content* of the newspaper rather than the time, place, or manner of its distribution."

Papish v. *Universtiy of Missouri Curators*, 410 U.S. 667 (1973)

PER CURIAM.

Petitioner, a graduate student in the University of Missouri School of Journalism, was expelled for distributing on campus a newspaper "containing forms of indecent speech"[1] in violation of a bylaw of the Board of Curators. The newspaper, the *Free Press Underground*, had been sold on this state university campus for more than four years pursuant to an authorization obtained from the University Business Office. The particular newspaper issue in question was found to be unacceptable for two reasons. First, on the front cover the publishers had reproduced a political cartoon previously printed in another newspaper depicting policemen raping the Statue of Liberty and the Goddess of Justice. The caption under the cartoon read: " . . . With Liberty and Justice for All." Secondly, the issue contained an article entitled "M-----f----- Acquitted," which discussed the trial and acquittal on an assault charge of a New York City youth who was a member of an organization known as "Up Against the Wall, M-----f-----."

Following a hearing, the Student Conduct Committee found that petitioner had violated paragraph B of Art. V of the General Standards of Student Conduct which requires students "to observe generally accepted standards of conduct" and specifically prohibits "indecent conduct or speech."[2] Her expulsion, after affirmance first by the Chancellor of the University and then by its Board of Curators, was made effective in the middle of the spring semester. Although she was then permitted to remain on campus until the end of the semester, she was not given credit for the one course in which she made a passing grade.[3]

After exhausting her administrative review alter-

108 FREEDOM TO PUBLISH

natives within the University, petitioner brought an action for declaratory and injunctive relief pursuant to 42 U.S.C. § 1983 in the United States District Court for the Western District of Missouri. She claimed that her expulsion was improperly premised on activities protected by the First Amendment. The District Court denied relief. 331 F.Supp. 1321, and the Court of Appeals affirmed, one judge dissenting. 464 F.2d 136. Rehearing *en banc* was denied by an equally divided vote of all the judges in the Eighth Circuit.

The District Court's opinion rests, in part,[4] on the conclusion that the banned issue of the newspaper was obscene. The Court of Appeals found it unnecessary to decide that question. Instead, assuming that the newspaper was not obscene and that its distribution in the community at large would be protected by the First Amendment, the court held that on a university campus "freedom of expression" could properly be "subordinated to other interests such as, for example, the conventions of decency in the use and display of language and pictures." *Id.*, at 145. The court concluded that "[t]he Constitution does not compel the University ... [to allow] such publications as the one in litigation to be publicly sold or distributed on its open campus." *Ibid.*

This case was decided several days before we handed down *Healy* v. *James*, 408 U.S. 169 (172), in which, while recognizing a state university's undoubted prerogative to enforce reasonable rules governing student conduct, we reaffirmed that "state colleges and universities are not enclaves immune from the sweep of the First Amendment." *Id.*, at 180. See *Tinker* v. *Des Moines Independent School District*, 393 U.S. 503 (1969). We think *Healy* makes it clear that the mere dissemination of ideas—no matter how offensive to good taste—on a state university campus may not be shut off in the name alone of "conventions of decency." Other recent precedents of this Court make it equally clear that neither the political cartoon nor the headline story involved in this case can be labeled as constitutionally obscene or otherwise unprotected. *E.g., Kois* v. *Wisconsin*, 408 U.S. 229 (1972); *Gooding* v. *Wilson*, 405 U.S. 518 (1972); *Cohen* v. *California*, 403 U.S. 15 (1971).[5] There is language in the opinions below which suggests that the University's action here could be viewed as an exercise of its legitimate authority to enforce reasonable regulations as to the time, place, and manner of speech and its dissemination. While we have repeatedly approved such regulatory authority, *e.g.*, 408 U.S., at 192–193, the facts set forth in the opinions below show clearly that petitioner was dismissed because of the disapproved *content* of the newspaper rather than the time, place, or manner of its distribution.[6]

Since the First Amendment leaves no room for the operation of a dual standard in the academic community with respect to the content of speech, and because the state University's action here cannot be justified as a non-discriminatory application of reasonable rules governing conduct, the judgments of the courts below must be reversed. Accordingly the petition for a writ of certiorari is granted, the case is remanded to the District Court, and that court is instructed to order the University to restore to petitioner any course credits she earned for the semester in question and, unless she is barred from reinstatement for valid academic reasons, to reinstate her as a student in the graduate program.

Reversed and remanded.

Mr. Chief Justice BURGER, dissenting.

I join the dissent of Justice REHNQUIST which follows and add a few observations.

The present case is clearly distinguishable from the Court's prior holdings in *Cohen, Gooding,* and *Rosenfeld,* as erroneous as those holdings are.* *Cohen, Gooding,* and *Rosenfeld* dealt with prosecutions under criminal statutes which allowed the imposition of severe penalties. Unlike such traditional First Amendment cases, we deal here with rules which govern conduct on the campus of a university.

In theory, at least, a university is not merely an arena for the discussion of ideas by students and faculty; it is also an institution where individuals learn to express themselves in acceptable, civil terms. We provide that environment to the end that students may learn the self-restraint necessary to the functioning of a civilized society and understand the need for those external restraints to which we must all submit if group existence is to be tolerable.

I find it a curious—even bizarre—extension of *Cohen, Gooding,* and *Rosenfeld* to say that a university is impotent to deal with conduct such as that of the petitioner. Students are, of course, free to criticize the university, its faculty, or the Government in vigorous, or even harsh, terms. But it is not unreasonable or violative of the Constitution to subject to disciplinary action those individuals who distribute publications which are at the same time obscene and infantile. To preclude a university or college from regulating the distribution of such obscene materials does not protect the values inherent in the First Amendment; rather, it demeans those values. The anomaly of the Court's holding today is suggested by its use of the now familiar "code" abbreviation for the petitioner's foul language.

The judgment of the Court of Appeals was eminently correct. It should be affirmed.

Mr. Justice REHNQUIST, with whom The Chief

Justice and Mr. Justice BLACKMUN join, dissenting.

We held in *Healy* v. *James,* 408 U.S. 169, 180 (1972), that "state colleges and universities are not enclaves immune from the sweep of the First Amendment." But that general proposition does not decide the concrete case now before us. *Healy* held that the public university there involved had not afforded adequate notice and hearing of the action it proposed to take with respect to the students involved. Here the Court of Appeals found, and that finding is not questioned in the Court's opinion, that "the issue arises in the context of a student dismissal, after service of written charges and after a full and fair hearing, for violation of a University rule of conduct." 464 F.2d 136, 138.

Both because I do not believe proper exercise of our jurisdiction warrants summary reversal in a case dependent in part on assessment of the record and not squarely governed by one of our decisions, and because I have serious reservations about the result reached by the Court, I dissent from the summary disposition of this case.

I

Petitioner Papish has for many years been a graduate student at the University of Missouri. Judge Stephenson, writing for the Court of Appeals in this case, summarized her record in these words:

"Miss Papish's academic record reveals that she was in no rush to complete the requirements for her graduate degree in Journalism. She possesses a 1958 academic degree from the University of Connecticut; she was admitted to graduate school at the University of Missouri in September in 1963; and although she attended school through the fall, winter, and summer semesters, she was, after 6 years of work, making little, if any, significant progress toward the achievement of her stated academic objective. At the time of her dismissal, Miss Papish was enrolled in a one-hour course entitled 'Research Journalism' and in a three-hour course entitled 'Ceramics 4.' In the semester immediately preceding her dismissal, she was enrolled only in 'Ceramics 3.'" 464 F.2d, at 138 n. 2.

Whatever may have been her lack of ability or motivation in the academic area, petitioner had been active on other fronts. In the words of the Court of Appeals:

"3. On November 1, 1967, the Faculty Committee on Student Conduct, after notice of charges and hearing, placed Miss Papish on disciplinary probation for the remainder of her student status at the University. The basis for her probation was her violation of the general standard of student conduct.... This action arose out of events which took place on October 14, 1967 at a time when the University was hosting high school seniors and their parents for the purpose of acquainting them with its educational programs and other aspects of campus life. She specifically was charged, *inter alia,*with openly distributing, on University grounds, without the permission of appropriate University personnel, two non-University publications of the Students for Democratic Society (SDS). It was alleged in the notice of charges, and apparently established at the ensuing hearing, that one of these publications, the *New Left Notes,* contained 'pornographic, indecent and obscene words. "f---," "bulls---," and "sh--s."' The notice of charges also recites that the other publication, *The CIA at College: Into Twilight and Back,* contained 'a pornographic and indecent picture depicting two rats apparently fornicating on its cover....'

"4. Some two weeks prior to the incident causing her dismissal, Miss Papish was placed on academic probation because of prolonged submarginal academic progress. It was a condition of this probation that she pursue satisfactory work on her thesis, and that such work be evidenced by the completion and presentation of several completed chapters to her thesis advisor by the end of the semester. By letter dated January 31, 1969, Miss Papish was notified that her failure to comply with this special condition within the time specified would result in the termination of her candidacy for a graduate degree." *Id.,* at 138–139, nn. 3, 4.

It was in the light of this background that respondents finally expelled petitioner for the incident described in the Court's opinion. The Court fails to note, however, two findings made by the District Court with respect to the circumstances under which petitioner hawked her newspaper near the memorial tower of the University:

"The Memorial Tower is the central unit of integrated structures dedicated to the memory of those students who died in the Armed Services in World Wars I and II. Other adjacent units include the Student Union and a Non-Sectarian chapel for prayer and meditation. Through the Memorial Arch pass parents of students, guests of the University, students, including many persons under 18 years of age and high school students." 331 F.Supp. 1321, 1325 n. 4.

"The plaintiff knowingly and intentionally participated in distributing the publication to provoke a confrontation with the authorities by pandering the publication with crude, puerile, vulgar obscenities." *Id.,* at 1325.

II

I continue to adhere to the dissenting views

expressed in *Rosenfeld* v. *New Jersey,* 408 U.S. 901 (1972), that the public use of the word "M-----f-----" is "lewd and obscene" as those terms were used by the Court in *Chaplinsky* v. *New Hampshire,* 315 U.S. 568 (1942). There the Court said:

> "There are certain well-defined and narrowly limited classes of speech, the prevention and punishment of which have never been thought to raise any Constitutional problem. These include the lewd and obscene, the profane, the libelous, and the insulting or "fighting" words—those which by their very utterance inflict injury or tend to incite an immediate breach of the peace. It has been well observed that such utterances are no essential part of any exposition of ideas, and are of such slight social value as a step to truth that any benefit that may be derived from them is clearly outweighed by the social interest in order and morality." *Id.,* at 571–572.

But even were I convinced of the correctness of the Court's disposition of *Rosenfeld,* I would not think it should control the outcome of this case. It simply does not follow under any of our decisions or from the language of the First Amendment itself that because petitioner could not be criminally prosecuted by the Missouri state courts for the conduct in question, she may not therefore be expelled from the University of Missouri for the same conduct. A state university is an establishment for the purpose of educating the State's young people, supported by the tax revenues of the State's citizens. The notion that the officials lawfully charged with the governance of the university have so little control over the environment for which they are responsible that they may not prevent the public distribution of a newspaper on campus which contained the language described in the Court's opinion is quite unacceptable to me, and I would suspect would have been equally unacceptable to the Framers of the First Amendment. This is indeed a case where the observation of a unanimous Court in *Chaplinsky* that "such utterances are no essential part of any exposition of ideas, and are of such slight social value as a step to truth that any benefit that may be derived from them is clearly outweighed by the social interest in order and morality" applies with compelling force.

III

The Court cautions that "disenchantment with Miss Papish's performance, understandable as it may have been, is no justification for denial of constitutional rights." Quite so. But a wooden insistence on equating, for constitutional purposes, the authority of the State to criminally punish with its authority to exercise even a modicum of control over the university which it operates, serves neither the Constitution nor public education well. There is reason to think that the "disenchantment" of which the Court speaks may, after this decision, become widespread among taxpayers and legislators. The system of tax-supported public universities which has grown up in this country is one of its truly great accomplishments; if they are to continue to grow and thrive to serve an expanding population, they must have something more than the grudging support of taxpayers and legislators. But one can scarcely blame the latter if, told by the Court that their only function is to supply tax money for the operation of the university, the "disenchantment" may reach such a point that they doubt the game is worth the candle.

COURT'S OPINION NOTES

1. This charge was contained in a letter from the University's Dean of Students, which is reprinted in the Court of Appeals' opinion. 464 F.2d 136, 139 (CA8 1972).
2. In pertinent part, the By-Law states:
   "Students enrolling in the University assume an obligation and are expected by the University to conduct themselves in a manner compatible with the University's functions and missions as an educational institution. For that purpose students are required to observe generally accepted standards of conduct.... [I]ndecent conduct or speech ... are examples of conduct which would contravene this standard...." 464 F.2d, at 138.
3. Miss Papish, a 32-year-old graduate student, was admitted to the graduate school of the University in September 1963. Five and one-half years later, when the episode under consideration occurred, she was still pursuing her graduate degree. She was on "academic probation" because of "prolonged submarginal academic progress," and since November 1, 1967, she also had been on disciplinary probation for disseminating SDS literature found at a university hearing to have contained "pornographic, indecent and obscene words." This dissemination had occurred at a time when the University was host to high school seniors and their parents. 464 F.2d, at 139 nn. 3 and 4. But disenchantment with Miss Papish's performance, understandable as it may have been, is no justification for denial of constitutional rights.
4. Prefatorily, the District Court held that petitioner, who was a nonresident of Missouri, was powerless to complain of her dismissal because she enjoyed no "federally protected or other right to attend a state university of a state of which she is not a domiciled resident." 331 F.Supp. 1321, 1326. The Court of Appeals, because it affirmed on a different ground, deemed it "unnecessary to comment" upon this rationale. 464 F.2d, at 141 n. 9. The District Court's reasoning is directly inconsistent with a long line of controlling decisions of this Court. See *Perry* v. *Sindermann,* 408 U.S. 593, 596–598 (1972), and the cases cited therein.
5. Under the authority of *Gooding* and *Cohen,* we have reversed or vacated and remanded a number of cases

involving the same expletive used in this newspaper headline.*Cason* v. *City of Columbus,* 409 U.S. 1053 (1972); *Rosenfeld* v. *New Jersey,* 408 U.S. 901 (1972); *Lewis* v. *City of New Orleans,* 408 U.S. 913 (1972); *Brown* v. *Oklahoma,* 408 U.S. 914 (1972). Cf. *Keefe* v. *Geanakos,* 418 F.2d 359, 361 and n. 7 (CA1 1969).

6. It is true, as Mr. Justice REHNQUIST's dissent indicates, that the District Court emphasized that the newspaper was distributed near the University's memorial tower and concluded that petitioner was engaged in "pandering." The opinion makes clear, however, that the reference to "pandering" was addressed to the content of the newspaper and to the organization on the front page of the cartoon and the headline, rather than to the manner in which the newspaper was disseminated. 331 F.Supp., at 1325, 1328, 1329, 1330, 1332. As the Court of Appeals opinion states, "[t]he facts are not in dispute." 464 F.2d. at 138. The charge against petitioner was quite unrelated to either the place or manner of distribution. The Dean's charge stated that the "forms of speech" contained in the newspaper were "improper on the University campus." *Id.,* at 139.

Moreover, the majority below quoted without disapproval petitioner's verified affidavit stating that "no disruption of the University's functions occurred in connection with the distribution." *Id.,* at 139–140. Likewise, both the dissenting opinion in the Court of Appeals and the District Court opinion refer to this same uncontroverted fact. *Id.,* at 145; 331 F. Supp., at 1328. Thus, in the absence of any disruption of campus order or interference with the rights of others, the sole issue was whether a state university could proscribe this form of expression.

JUSTICE BURGER'S OPINION NOTE

**Cohen v. *California,* 403 U.S. 15, 27 (1971) (BLACKMUN, J., with whom BURGER, C J., and BLACK, J., join, dissenting); *Gooding* v. *Wilson,* 405 U.S. 518, 528 (1972) (BURGER, C. J., dissenting), 534 (BLACKMUN, J., dissenting); *Rosenfeld* v. *New Jersey,* 408 U.S. 901, 902 (1972) (BURGER, C. J., dissenting), 903 (POWELL, J., dissenting), 909 (REHNQUIST, J., dissenting).

THE United States Court of Appeals, Fifth Circuit, decides for high school students who challenged the Indianapolis School Board's suppression of an unofficial student newspaper, the students arguing that the suppression of their newspaper constituted a violation of their First and Fourteenth amendment rights. In deciding that the Indianapolis school regulations on distribution of literature was too vague and unconstitutionally overbroad and concluding that the suppression of the high school newspaper was unjustified, the Court of Appeals declared: "The only possible question is whether the Board's educational responsibilities justify its preventing the use by students in these circumstances of words considered coarse or indecent. Clearly a university cannot constitutionally regulate expression on that ground. . . . Although there is a difference in maturity and sophistication between students at a university and at a high school, we conclude that the occasional presence of earthy words in the *Corn Cob Curtain* can not be found to be likely to cause substantial disruption of school activity or materially to impair the accomplishment of educational objectives."

Jacobs v. *Board of School Commissioners,* 490 F.2d 601 (1973)

FAIRCHILD, Circuit Judge.

Defendants are officials of the Indianapolis school system. They appeal from a judgment enjoining the enforcement of certain rules governing the distribution by students of communicative written materials within the Indianapolis public school buildings and upon the grounds of such buildings. The named plaintiffs were or had been high school students when the action was started. They challenged defendants' suppression of an unofficial student newspaper, entitled the *Corn Cob Curtain,* in the publication and distribution of which plaintiffs had participated. The relevant rules of the Board were amended while the action was pending. The decision and judgment appealed from are reported, *Jacobs* v. *Board of School Com'rs of City of Indianapolis,* 349 F.Supp. 605 (S.D.Ind., 1972).

1. Refusal to appoint a guardian ad litem.

Plaintiffs were minors, represented by counsel. They alleged that activities of defendants violated their First and Fourteenth Amendment rights. They sued on behalf of themselves and all other high school students under defendants' jurisdiction. They primarily sought injunctive relief except that they also prayed for $150 compensatory damages and nominal or other punitive damages. Except for the prayer for damages in modest amount, plaintiffs won.

The district court denied defendants' petition for appointment of a guardian ad litem. Under the present circumstances, it is doubtful that defendants have a sufficient interest to raise this point on appeal. There is little reason to suppose that defendants would be exposed to any risk as a result of a claim that plaintiffs or class members are not bound by the judgment because there was no personal representative, next friend, or guardian ad litem. In *Roberts* v. *Ohio Casualty Insurance Company,* 256 F.2d 35 (5th Cir., 1958), relied on by defendants, and where a judgment was reversed for failure to appoint, it was the unrepresented minor who sought reversal. Nevertheless, defendants argue that the judgment should be reversed on this ground.

Rule 17(c), F.R.Civ.P., provides in part: "The court shall appoint a guardian ad litem for an infant or incompetent person not otherwise represented in an action or shall make such other order as it deems proper for the protection of the infant or incompetent person."

Defendants apparently concede that neither the appointment of a guardian ad litem nor a protective order in lieu thereof is mandatory, and neither is required if the court considers the matter and makes a judicial determination that the infant is protected without a guardian. *Roberts, supra,* p. 39. *See Till* v. *Hartford Accident & Indemnity Co.,* 124 F.2d 405, 408 (10th Cir., 1941); *Westcott* v. *United States Fidelity & Guaranty Co.,* 158 F.2d 20, 22 (4th Cir., 1946).

Here the question was argued and considered. We do not agree with defendants that the court's emphasis, in its oral ruling, on the fact that constitutional issues were presented, and that substantial monetary recovery was not sought, demonstrates a failure to decide the appropriate question. Moreover, there is nothing in the record which indicates that the minors were represented inadequately or that any party was prejudiced by the absence of a guardian ad litem. *See Till* and *Westcott supra,* and *Rutland* v. *Sikes,* 203 F.Supp. 276 (E.D. S.C.,1962), aff'd on other grounds, 311 F.2d 538 (4 Cir.), cert. denied 374 U.S. 830, 83 S.Ct. 1871, 10 L.Ed.2d 1053.

2. The Constitutionality of the Board's Regulations.

During the 1971–1972 public school term, five issues of the *Corn Cob Curtain* were published. They contained letters, articles about politics, education, student affairs, religion, and American history, music, movie, and book reviews, poetry, and cartoons. The first four issues were distributed in Indianapolis high schools. At the time the fifth issue was ready for distribution, school authorities notified the student population that school board rules prohibit sales or solicitations on school grounds without the express prior approval of the General Superintendent. After conferring with various school officials, the named plaintiffs were informed that the *Corn Cob Curtain* could no longer be distributed because it contained obscene materials. Appellees refrained from distributing the fifth issue pending resolution of these issues in the courts.

At the time of the above events, Sections 11.05 and 11.06 of the Board's rules prohibited the sale or distribution of literature in the public schools without express prior approval of the General Superintendent. After the district judge stated his belief that these rules were unconstitutional prior restraints under *Fujishima* v. *Board of Education,* 460 F.2d 1355 (7th Cir., 1972), the defendants amended the rules to their present form. The district court held that the amended rules were unconstitutional.

The amended rules involved are set forth at 349 F.Supp. 607–609. Rule 11.05 consists of a series of numbered items or paragraphs, designated in the district court judgment as provisos. We adopt that term, and proceed to consider the arguments made by defendants with respect to them.

(a) Amended Rule 11.05, Proviso 1.1.1.3.

Reading provisos 1.1.1. and 1.1.1.3 together, they provide:

"No student shall distribute in any school any literature that is . . . either by its content or by the manner of distribution itself, productive of, or likely to produce a significant disruption of the normal educational processes, functions or purposes in any of the Indianapolis schools, or injury to others."

The district court held that this rule was both vague and overbroad. We agree.

It is well established that a criminal statute is void for vagueness if its prohibitions are not clearly defined. *Grayned* v. *City of Rockford,* 408 U.S. 104, 108, 92 S.Ct. 2294, 33 L.Ed.2d 222 (1972), *United States* v. *Dellinger,* 472 F.2d 340, 355 (7th cir., 1972), cert. denied 410 U.S. 970, 93 S.Ct. 1443, 35 L.Ed.2d 706. Vague laws are constitutionally offensive for several reasons:

"First, because we assume that man is free to steer between lawful and unlawful conduct, we insist that laws give the person of ordinary intelligence a reasonable opportunity to know what is prohibited, so that he may act accordingly. Vague laws may trap the innocent by not providing fair warning. Second, if arbitrary and discriminatory enforcement is to be prevented, laws must provide explicit standards for those who apply them. A vague law impermissibly delegates basic policy matters to policemen, judges, and juries for resolution on an *ad hoc* and subjective basis, with the attendant dangers of arbitrary and discriminatory application. Third, but related, where a vague statute 'abut[s] upon sensitive areas of basic First Amendment freedoms,' it 'operates to inhibit the exercise of [those] freedoms.' Uncertain meanings inevitably lead citizens to '"steer far wider of the unlawful zone"... than if the boundaries of the forbidden areas were clearly marked.'" *Grayned, supra,* 408 U.S. at 108–109, 92 S.Ct. at 2299, footnotes omitted.

Here, there is no criminal statute before us. Nonetheless, a student who violates amended Rule 11.05 is subject to suspension or expulsion or other disciplinary action. Proviso 1.61. We conclude that the penalties for violation are sufficiently grievous to mandate careful scrutiny for vagueness. *See generally Baggett* v. *Bullit,* 377 U.S. 360, 374, 84 S.Ct. 1316, 12 L.Ed.2d 377 (1964). We note the substantial danger of inadequate warnings to students, of arbitrary enforcement by teachers and principals, and of inhibition of full exercise of students' First Amendment rights.

We think that proviso 1.1.1.3 is vague in defining the consequences which will make a distribution of literature unlawful. Those consequences are articulated as "a significant disruption of the normal educational processes, functions, or purposes in any of the Indianapolis schools, or injury to others." Is decorum in the lunchroom a "normal educational... purpose"? If an article sparks strident discussion there, is the latter a "disruption"? When does disruption become "significant"? The phrase "injury to others" is also vague. Does it mean only physical harm? Does it include hurt feelings and impairment of reputation by derogatory criticism, short of defamation, since libelous material is already covered by proviso 1.1.1.2?

Defendants argue unpersuasively that proviso 1.1.1.3 is not over-vague because of its similarity to the text of the standard by which the Supreme Court tested a precise regulation against wearing armbands in *Tinker* v. *Des Moines School Dist.*, 393 U.S. 503, 514, 89 S.Ct. 733, 21 L.Ed.2d 731.[1] It does not at all follow that the phrasing of a constitutional standard by which to decide whether a regulation infringes upon rights protected by the First Amendment is sufficiently specific in a regulation to convey notice to students or people in general of what is prohibited.[2]

Proviso 1.1.1.3 is also unconstitutionally overbroad. In *United States* v. *Dellinger, supra,* 472 F.2d at 357, this court stated: "The doctrine of overbreadth applies when a statute lends itself to a substantial number of impermissible applications, such that it is capable of deterring protected conduct, when the area affected by the challenged law substantially involves First Amendment interests, and when there is not a valid construction which avoids abridgement of First Amendment interests." (footnotes omitted). These factors are present here.

The overbreadth stems both from the vagueness described above and from the inclusiveness of the phrase "productive of, or likely to produce" in the proviso. Expression may lead to disorder under many circumstances where the expression is not thereby deprived of First Amendment protection. See *Braxton* v. *Municipal Court*, 10 Cal.3d 138, 109 Cal. Rptr. 897, 514 P.2d 697 (1973). We do not read *Tinker* as authorizing suppression of speech in a school building in every such circumstance where the speech does not have a sufficiently close relationship with action to be treated as action. See *Dellinger, supra,* 472 F.2d at 360.

Where the boundaries between prohibited and permissible conduct are ambiguous, we can not presume that the curtailment of free expression is minimized. *NAACP* v. *Button*, 371 U.S. 415, 432, 83 S.Ct. 328, 9 L.Ed.2d 405 (1963); *United States* v. *Dellinger, supra,* 472 F.2d at 356–357. Instead the plaintiffs are permitted to attack the regulation by suggesting impermissible applications without demonstrating that their own conduct "could not be regulated by a statute drawn with the requisite narrow specificity." *Dombrowski* v. *Pfister*, 380 U.S. 479, 486, 85 S.Ct. 1116, 1121, 14 L.Ed.2d 22 (1965). See *Gooding* v. *Wilson*, 405 U.S. 518, 521, 92 S.Ct. 1103, 31 L.Ed.2d 408 (1972). Proviso 1.1.1.3 at least threatens a penalty for a student who distributed a controversial pamphlet in a lunchroom resulting in robust arguments or who distributed a newspaper including derogatory but not defamatory remarks about a teacher. Absent extraordinary circumstances, the school authorities could not reasonably forecast substantial disruption of or material interference with school discipline or activities arising from such incidents. See *Tinker, supra.* Finally, we note that this court lacks jurisdiction to place an authoritative limiting construction upon this state regulation in contrast with the power of federal courts with respect to interpretation of federal statutes or regulations. *United States* v. *37 Photographs, 402 U.S. 363, 369, 91 S.Ct. 1400, 28 L.Ed.2d 822 (1971), cert. denied 403 U.S. 924, 91 S.Ct. 2221, 28 L.Ed.2d 702.*

(b) Amended rule 11.05, Proviso 1.1.1.4.

Reading provisos 1.1.1 and 1.1.1.4 together, they provide: "No student shall distribute in any school any literature that is... not written by a student, teacher, or other school employees; provided, however, that advertisements which are not in conflict with other provisions herein, and are reasonably and necessarily connected to the student publication itself shall be permitted."

We have no doubt that this rule abridges First Amendment rights of plaintiffs, although not for the reason assigned by the district court. Whether the student distribution of literature be viewed as individual speech or as press publication, we think that authorship by a non-school person of the material distributed is not germane to any of the constitutional standards which must be met before conduct which is also expression can be prohibited.

Defendants suggest that student distribution of materials written by non-students and outside organizations tends to produce disorder and interference with school functions, and cite the example that "stores would undoubtedly pay students to distribute flyers advertising their products." Assuming, however, some area of possible validity, the rule is overbroad. It would prohibit use of materials written by individuals from all sorts of walks of life whose views might be thought by the students to be worthy of circulation. "Predictions about imminent disruption... involve judgments appropriately made on an individualized basis, not by means of broad classifications, especially those based on subject matter." *Police Department of Chicago* v. *Mosley*, 408 U.S. 92, 100, 92 S.Ct. 2286, 2293, 33 L.Ed.2d 212 (1972).

(c) Amended Rule 11.05, Proviso 1.3.1.6

Literature not proscribed under 1.1.1, 1.1.1.1 to 1.1.1.4, is referred to as 'distributable literature.' (Proviso 1.1.2). Reading provisos 1.3.1 and 1.3.1.6 together, they provide:

"No distributable literature shall be distributed by any student in any school . . . unless the name of every person or organization that shall have participated in the publication is plainly written in the distributable literature itself."

In *Talley* v. *California,* 362 U.S. 60, 80 S.Ct. 536, 4 L.Ed.2d 559 (1960), the Surpeme Court held invalid a city ordinance prohibiting the distribution of handbills in any place unless the handbills disclosed the names and addresses of the persons who printed, wrote, manufactured and distributed the handbills. Noting the historical importance of anonymous publications as a vehicle for criticizing oppressive practices and laws, the Court held that the broad prohibition of the ordinance violated the First Amendment. *Tally, supra,* 63–65, 80 S.Ct. 536.[3]

Anonymous student publications perform similarly within the school community; without anonymity, fear of reprisal may deter peaceful discussion of controversial but important school rules and policies. Although the rule leaves students free to distribute anonymous literature beyond the school house gate, the question here, as in *Tinker,* is whether the state has demonstrated a sufficent justification for this prohibition within the school community, where students and teachers spend a significant portion of their time. See *Tinker, supra,* 393 U.S. 506, 89 S.Ct. 733. Defendants contend that the names of persons who have "participated in the publication" of literature must be provided so that those responsible for the publication of libelous or obscene articles can be held accountable. However, here as in *Talley,* the requirement is not limited to material as to which such justification might be urged. Indeed, if the regulation be read literally, 1.3.1.6 applies only to literature the content of which is acceptable. School authorities could not reasonably forecast that the distribution of any type of anonymous literature within the schools would substantially disrupt or materially interfere with school activities or discipline. See *Tinker, supra,* 514, 89 S.Ct. 733.

(d) *Amended Rule 11.05, Proviso 1.3.1.5 and Rule 11.06.*

Reading 1.3.1 and 1.3.1.5 together, they provide: "No distributable literature shall be distributed by any student in any school . . . in immediate exchange for money or any other thing of value . . . whether the transaction is characterized as a sale of the distributable literature, as a contribution to finance the publication or distribution of the distributable literature, or as any other transaction whereunder money or any other thing of value (or a promise of either) immediately passes to or for the direct or indirect benefit of the student who is distributing the distributable literature. . . ." Amended Rule 11.06 provides that: "No person, including students and organizations or corporations, other than the school corporation acting through its designated agents, or organizations of parents and teachers or students whose sole use of funds is for the benefit of the particular school in which they are organized or in attendance, may sell merchandise or material, collect money, or solicit funds or contributions from the students for any cause or commercial activity within any school or on its campus."

Plaintiffs suggest that these rules were adopted to accomplish indirectly that which can not be accomplished directly: the blanket prohibition of the distribution of the *Corn Cob Curtain* and other similar student newspapers. Plaintiffs alleged the dependence of the paper upon contributions of money for survival. It can readily be observed that a ban upon the receipt of contributions on school grounds would create financial difficulties in raising the $120 to $150 necessary to publish each edition of the *Corn Cob Curtain.* In *Grosjean* v. *American Press Company,* 297 U.S. 233, 56 S.Ct. 444, 80 L.Ed. 660 (1935), the Supreme Court considered the constitutionality of a Louisiana tax upon the advertising revenue of newspapers with a circulation of more than 20,000 copies per week. After finding that the effect of the tax might be to destroy both the advertising and circulation of the newspapers and noting with suspicion the form of the tax, the Court concluded that the tax was a "deliberate and calculated device . . . to limit the circulation of information to which the public is entitled," in violation of the First Amendment. *Grosjean, supra,* 244, 250, 56 S.Ct. 444, 449.

Assuming, however, that the rules are not a "deliberate and calculated device" to suppress the student newspaper, it becomes necessary to analyze the justification offered by defendants. They assert the legitimacy of an interest in preventing the use of school premises "for non-school purposes— particularly commercial activities." Rule 11.06 is a general prohibition against sales of materials and solicitation of funds except for the benefit of the school. If there were any question of its intended applicability to sales by student of their unofficial newspaper, proviso 1.3.1.5 makes specific application.

We have little question of the legitimacy of the interest of the school authorities in limiting or prohibiting commercial activity on school premises by persons not connected with the school, either acting directly or through students as agents. But because students have First Amendment rights within the school, as recognized in *Tinker,* we think that the propriety of regulation of their conduct involving the exercise of protected rights must be independently justified. It is not enough to say that such activity by students is similar to commercial activity by others.

Sale of the newspaper, or other communicative material within a school, is conduct mixing both speech and nonspeech elements. In order to determine whether a "sufficiently important governmental interest in regulating the non-speech element can justify incidental limitations on First Amendment freedoms," we must consider whether the regulation "is within the constitutional power of the Government; if it furthers an important or substantial governmental interest; if the governmental interest is unrelated to the suppression of free expression; and if the incidental restriction on alleged First Amendment freedoms is no greater than is essential to the furtherance of that interest." *United States* v. *O'Brien,* 391 U.S. 367, 377, 88 S.Ct. 1673, 1679, 20 L.Ed.2d 672 (1968), reh. denied 393 U.S. 900, 98 S.Ct. 63, 21 L.Ed.2d 188.

Ultimately, defendants rely on the proposition that "Commercial activities are time-consuming unnecessary distractions and are inherently disruptive of the function, order and decorum of the school."

Provisos 1.3.1.2, .3 and .4 already regulate the place and manner of distribution so as to avoid interference with others and littering. They have not been challenged here. It has not been established, in our opinion, that regulation of the place, time, and manner of distribution can not adequately serve the interests of maintaining good order and an educational atmosphere without forbidding sale and to that extent restricting the First Amendment rights of plaintiffs.

(e) Amended Rule 11.05, proviso 1.3.1.1.

Reading provisos 1.31 and 1.3.1.1. together, they provide: No distributable literature shall be distributed by any student in any school . . . while classes are being conducted in the school in which the distribution is to be made."

It is well established that the right to use public places for expressive activity is not absolute and that "reasonable 'time, place and manner' regulations [which] may be necessary to further significant governmental interests" are constitutionally permissible. *Grayned* v. *City of Rockford,* 408 U.S. 104, 115, 92 S.Ct. 2294, 33 L.Ed.2d 222 (1972), and cases cited therein. The question here is whether the Board could reasonably forecast that the distribution of student newspapers anywhere within a school at any time while any class was being conducted would materially disrupt or interfere with school activities and discipline. See *Grayned* v. *City of Rockford, supra* at 118, 92 S.Ct. at 2294. In determining whether "the manner of expression is basically incompatible with the normal activity of a particular place at a particular time, . . . we must weigh heavily the fact that communication is involved [and] the regulation must be narrowly tailored to further the State's legitimate interest." *Grayned* v. *City of Rockford, supra* at 116-117, 92 S.Ct. at 2304.

We are hampered in evaluating proviso 1.3.1.1 by the paucity of evidence in the record with respect to arrangements and schedules of classes in the Indianapolis secondary schools. Nonetheless, it does appear that there are periods in the morning, around noon, and in the late afternoon when although some classes are in session, substantial numbers of students are on the premises, are not involved in classroom activity, and are barred by proviso 1.3.1.1 from distributing and indirectly from receiving student newspapers. We conclude that the defendants have not satisfied their burden of demonstrating that the regulation banning distribution at all these times is narrowly drawn to further the state's legitimate interest in preventing material disruptions of classwork. See *Tinker, supra* 513, 89 S.Ct. 733.

3. Defendants' claim concerning obscenity and profanity.

Defendants' original answer averred, among other things, that plaintiff's publication are obscene, indecent, vulgar, and profane. While the action was pending, the rules were amended so that when Rule 11.05, provisos 1.1.1 and 1.1.1.1, are read together, they provide: "No student shall distribute in any school any literature that is . . . obscene as to minors. . . ."

This district court did not directly decide defendants' claim that the existing issues of *Corn Cob Curtain* were obscene. Presumably the court deemed the proviso valid, for the decision indicates that the appropriate inquiry concerning obscenity would be whether future issues of the paper would be obscene as to minors. The decision, 349 F.Supp. at 610, set forth the then controlling *Roth-Memoirs* definition of obscenity, the concept of variable obscenity permitting a less exacting standard where material is directed at children, and other limitations to be regarded in making the determination.

Necessarily we observe that proviso 1.1.1.1 lacks the specific definition of sexual conduct the description of which is prohibited as now required for a valid law under *Miller* v. *California,* 413 U.S. 15, 26, 93 S.Ct. 2607, 2616, 37 L.Ed.2d 419 (1973).

In any event, a substantial portion of defendants' brief is devoted to what it terms the most crucial issue, "whether school authorities may constitutionally and legitimately prevent and/or punish the use of defamatory, obscene and indecent language in the school house which is contrary to the moral standards of the community."

In the first place, the issues of the *Corn Cob Curtain* in the record are very far from obscene in the legal sense. A few earthy words relating to bodily functions and sexual intercourse are used in the copies of the newspaper in the record. Usually they appear as expletives or at some similar level. One cartoon depicts a sequence of incidents in a bathroom. This material amounts only to a very small part of the newspapers, which are tabloid size, containing eight or twelve pages. These issues contain no material which is in any significant way erotic, sexually explicit, or which could plausibly be said to appeal to the prurient interest of adult or minor. *See Cohen* v. *California,* 403 U.S. 15, 20, 91 S.Ct. 1780, 29 L.Ed.2d 284 (1971).

In *Miller, supra,* the Supreme Court limited the scope of the obscenity exception to First Amendment protection to "works which depict or describe sexual conduct" and "which, taken as a whole, appeal to the prurient interest in sex, which portray, sexual conduct in a patently offensive way, and which, taken as a whole, do not have serious literary, artistic, political or scientific value." Clearly the newspaper issues in the record do not even approach fulfillment of this definition.

Nor need we speculate about the exact effect of *Miller* on the variable obscenity concept exemplified by *Ginsberg* v. *New York,* 390 U.S. 629, 88 S.Ct. 1274, 20 L.Ed.2d 195 (1968). Making the widest conceivable allowances for differences between adults and high school students with respect to perception, maturity, or sensitivity, the material pointed to by defendants could not be said to fulfill the *Miller* definition of obscenity.

It is well established that a distinction must be drawn between obscene materials and non-obscene materials containing profanity. *Cohen* v. *California,* 403 U.S. 15, 20, 91 S.Ct. 1780, 29 L.Ed.2d 284 (1971); *Fujishima* v. *Board of Education,* 460 F.2d 1355, 1359 n. 7 (7th Cir., 1972) The only possible question is whether the Board's educational responsibilities justify its preventing the use by students in these circumstances of words considered coarse or indecent. Clearly a university can not constitutionally regulate expression on that ground. *Papish* v. *University of Missouri Curators,* 410 U.S. 667, 93 S.Ct. 1197, 35 L.Ed.2d 618 (1973). Although there is a difference in maturity and sophistication between students at a university and at a high school, we conclude that the occasional presence of earthy words in the *Corn Cob Curtain* can not be found to be likely to cause substantial disruption of school activity or materially to impair the accomplishment of educational objectives. *Scoville* v. *Board of Ed. of Joliet T.P.H.S. Dist.* 204, Etc., Ill., 425 F.2d 10, 13 (7th Cir., 1970).

The injunction is broad enough to cover enforcement of the particular rules at all schools under the jurisdiction of defendants. At oral argument, plaintiffs conceded that their case was limited to the application of the rules in high schools. We therefore had no occasion to decide whether or not age difference and the like would lead to a different ruling concerning elementary schools. Should defendants apply to the district court to limit the injunction to high schools, nothing in this decision forecloses the consideration of the application on its merits.

The judgment appealed from is affirmed.

CHRISTENSEN, Senior District Judge (concurring in part and dissenting in part):

I am in general agreement with the majority opinion as it relates to the guardian ad litem problem and the invalidity of Provisos 1.1.1.4, 1.3.1.6, 1.3.1.5 and 1.3.1.1 of Rule 11.05, and rule 11.06 of the appellant board.

I dissent, however, from those parts of the opinion holding that Rule 11.05, Proviso 1.1.1.3, is invalid for vagueness and overbreadth* and that certain language used in the *Corn Cob Curtain* was not "obscene to minors" in the high school context and thus in contravention of Amended Rule 11.05, Proviso 1.1.1.1.

And I find myself in disagreemnt with the conclusion "that the occasional presence of earthy words in the *Corn Cob Curtain* cannot be found to be likely to cause substantial disruption of school activity or materially to impair the accomplishment of educational objectives". The euphemisms employed to describe contents of the publication do not fully indicate the type of language and imagery that are given rein; whether constituting the predominant part, or merely an inescapably dominating part of any particular issue, it seems clear that expressions are used which in a high school, not to mention an elementary school would materially impair the accomplishment of educational objectives.

More likely obscene in these contexts are certain *Corn Cob* expressions than those involved in *Papish* v. *University of Missouri Curators,* 410 U.S. 667, 93 S.Ct. 1197, 35 L.Ed.2d 618 (1973), would be in the setting of a university. Hence, it may not be presumptuous to suppose that when a situation is evaluated corresponding to the one we have before us the majority of that court may be inclined to accept an extrapolation of the views expressed in the dissent of the Chief Justice to the effect that preclusion of the regulation of such material by school authorities would not protect values inherent in the First Amendment but would demean them (410 U.S. at p. 672, 93 S.Ct. 1197), and those of Mr. Justice Rehnquist, with whom the Chief Justice and Mr. Justice Blackmun joined, that "insistence on equating, for constitutional purposes, the authority of the State to criminally punish with its authority to exercise even a modicum of control over the university [high school or elementary school] which it operates serves neither the Constitution nor public education well." (410 U.S. at p. 677, 93 S.Ct. at p. 1202.)

That at oral argument "plaintiffs conceded that their case was limited to the application of the rules in high schools" does not seem to me a sufficient reason for our failure to hold as to elementary schools of all places that the trial court's decision involved error. Apellees should not be permitted to waive the contentions of appellants, who have argued here both overbreadth and invalidity of the injunction. To the extent hereinabove indicated, I am of the opinion that appellants are right on both scores. And to that limited extent it appears to me that until now this court, as well as the Supreme Court, has not committed itself to an irreconcilable view.

NOTES

1. In *Tinker,* the Supreme Court held that a state may restrain students from fully exercising their First Amendment rights only if it is demonstrated that the school authorities reasonably forecast substantial disruption of or material interference with school activities or discipline. *Tinker, supra* 393 U.S. at 514, 89 S.Ct. 733.
2. *E. g., Miller* v. *California,* 413 U.S. 15, 26, 93 S.Ct. 2607, 2616, 37 L.Ed.2d 419 (1973).
3. We note that in the recent case of *Branzburg* v. *Hayes,* 408 U.S. 665, 680 ff, 92 S.Ct. 2646, 33 L.Ed.2d 626 (1972), the Supreme Court carefully distinguished the question of whether a newspaper reporter must respond to a grand jury subpoena from the question of whether the press could be required to publish or indiscriminately disclose all its sources.

JUDGE CHRISTENSEN'S OPINION NOTE

*No determinative difference is perceived between this rule and its rewording which the trial court thought "more apt to be constitutionally acceptable." 349 F.Supp. at pp. 611–612.

A United States District Court in New York decides against school officials who had seized a sex information supplement placed in the Farmingdale High School student newspaper; the principal "ordered the seizure of 700 undistributed copies of the newspaper. He also ordered that there be no further distribution of the newspaper and supplement." In declaring that the school officials' seizure of the supplement and the refusal to allow its distribution was an unconstitutional infringement on the students' rights, the District Court said: "In this Court's opinion, it is extremely unlikely that distribution of the supplement will cause material and substantial interference with schoolwork and discipline. Accordingly, the Court finds that seizure of the supplement and refusal to allow distribution were not reasonably necessary to avoid material and substantial interference with schoolwork or discipline." In response to the school officials' argument that "seizure was reasonable because publication of the supplement constituted an unauthorized intrusion into an area of secondary school curriculum," the District Court declared: "In this Court's view, publication of the newspaper and supplement is an extracurricular activity rather than part of the curriculum. This view is buttressed by the fact that no academic credit is given for serving as a member of the newspaper staff."

Bayer v. *Kinzler,* 383 F.Supp. 1164 (1974)

MEMORANDUM and ORDER

COSTANTINO, District Judge.

This is an action on behalf of two minors by their parents and natural guardians against the Superintendent of Schools of the Union Free School District No. 22, the principal of Farmingdale High School, and the Board of Education of the Union Free School District No. 22. Defendants were ordered to show cause why an order should not issue (1) requiring defendants to permit plaintiffs to distribute and receive copies of the October 25, 1974 school newspaper and accompanying sex information supplement; (2) requiring the defendants to return to the student editors the seized copies of the newspaper and supplement; (3) declaring that the defendants' prohibition against distribution is an unconstitutional infringement of plaintiffs' First Amendment rights; (4) granting plaintiffs compensatory and punitive damages in the amount of $500.00 and (5) awarding plaintiffs the costs of this action.

The facts of the case are as follows: The October 25, 1974 issue of the Farmingdale High School student newspaper contains a sex information supplement. One plaintiff is an editor of the newspaper. A second plaintiff is a student who states that she wishes to receive the supplement. The four page supplement is primarily composed of articles dealing with contraception and abortion. The articles are serious in tone and obviously intended to convey information rather than appeal to prurient interests. It is conceded that articles are not obscene. On October 25, 1974, defendant principal ordered the seizure of 700 undistributed copies of the newspaper. He also ordered that there be no further distribution of the newspaper and supplement. Defendants have expressed, however, a willingness to release the newspapers without the supplements. This proposal is not satisfactory to plaintiffs.

In *Tinker* v. *Des Moines School District,* 393 U.S. 503, 89 S.Ct. 733, 21 L.Ed.2d 731 (1969), the Court held that a school regulation prohibiting expression of a particular opinion is impermissible under the

First and Fourteenth Amendments without evidence that the regulation is "necessary to avoid material and substantial interference with schoolwork or discipline," 393 U.S. at 511, 89 S.Ct. at 739. Although *Tinker* is factually distinguishable because it involved expression of an opinion rather than publication of factual information (which is primarily involved here), the test seems equally valid in this case. The newspaper staff's attempt to educate their fellow students by means of a number of thoughtfully written articles seems at least equally deserving of protection under the First and Fourteenth Amendments as the symbolic wearing of an armband, the protected activity in *Tinker*.

In this court's opinion, it is extremely unlikely that distribution of the supplement will cause material and substantial interference with schoolwork and discipline. Accordingly, the court finds that seizure of the supplement and refusal to allow distribution were not reasonably necessary to avoid material and substantial interference with schoolwork or discipline.

Relying on *Eisner* v. *Stamford Board of Education*, 440 F.2d 803 (2d Cir. 1971), defendants claim that there is no violation of the First Amendment where the action taken has a reasonable basis. Assuming that this is the proper standard, none of the reasons given by defendants provide a reasonable basis for their actions. There is no merit, for example, to defendants' argument, based on *Schenck* v. *United States*, 249 U.S. 47, 52, 39 S.Ct. 247, 63 L.Ed. 470 (1919), that the actions were reasonable because distribution presents a "clear and present danger" that will bring about substantial evils that the state has a right to prevent. In this court's view, no clear and present danger is presented by distribution. It is ironic that defendants view the dissemination of knowledge here as presenting a "danger" which will bring about "evils." It is relevant to note that in *Russo* v. *Central School District No. 1*, 469 F.2d 623, 633 (2d Cir. 1972), cert. denied, 411 U.S. 932, 93 S.Ct. 1899, 36 L.Ed.2d 391 (1973), the court in dictum recognized that tenth graders were sufficiently mature that a teacher's symbolic act in failing to lead the flag salute would not have a "destructive effect" on her students. The court noted, "Young men and women at this stage of development are approaching an age when they form their own judgments," 469 F.2d at 633. The court also noted that knowledge of controversial political viewpoints was not "something to be dreaded," 469 F.2d at 633. Responsible presentation of information about birth control to high school students is not to be dreaded.

Defendants contend that their actions have a reasonable basis because distribution abridges the First Amendment right of parents to freedom of religion. Defendants claim that distribution violates the principle that "the State shall compel no child to learn principles clearly contrary to the basic tenets of his religious faith" (Defendants' Memorandum at 5). This argument is invalid in a number of ways. For one, no student is compelled to read the school newspaper.

Defendants also assert that seizure was reasonable because publication of the supplement constituted an unauthorized intrusion into an area of secondary school curriculum. In this court's view, publication of the newspaper and supplement is an extracurricular activity rather than part of the curriculum. This view is buttressed by the fact that no academic credit is given for serving as a member of the newspaper staff.

Even assuming that the newspaper is part of the "curriculum," defendants' "intrusion" theory does not furnish a reasonable basis for interference with student speech. The invalidity of defendants' theory is demonstrated by examining the impact it would have in the factual context of *Tinker*. Social studies surely is part of the school curriculum. Under defendants' theory, the petitioners in *Tinker* might well not be permitted to wear armbands to protest the Vietnam war since their symbolic protest dealt with an area of the curriculum. Moreover, if defendants' theory is adopted, the presence of articles in the school newspaper dealing with political topics will make the newspaper subject to seizure in the future. Such a result is inconsistent with the right of high school students to free expression, subject to well-defined and relatively narrow limitations, *cf. Eisner*, 440 F.2d at 810 and *Katz* v. *McAulay*, 438 F.2d 1058, 1060 (2d Cir. 1971).

For the foregoing reasons, pursuant to 28 U.S.C. § 2201, this court declares that seizure and prohibition of distribution of the newspaper and supplement infringed plaintiffs' First and Fourteenth Amendment rights. Defendants are enjoined from preventing distribution of the seized copies of the newspaper and supplement. Since the Court finds no basis for awarding damages, plaintiffs' demand for damages is denied. In addition, plaintiffs' demand for the costs of this action is denied. So ordered.

T̲HE United States Court of Appeals, Fourth Circuit, decides that the Baltimore County Board of Education's statement of students' "rights and responsibilities" contained a student publications rule which violated the First and Fourteenth Amendments." A crucial flaw exists in the rule, said the Court, "since it gives no guidance whatsoever as to what amounts to a 'substantial disruption of or material interference with' school activities; and equally fatal, it fails to detail the criteria by which an administrator might reasonably predict the occurrence of such a disruption.... In addition, we note that the definition of 'libelous' material contained in rule 5130.1(c) fails to apply the standard of *New York Times* v. *Sullivan* . . . and its progeny. On its face, therefore, the Board's regulations are void for vagueness and overbreadth. In addition, we notice that there are other flaws which must be corrected if rule 5130.1 is to pass constitutional muster." While recognizing that "it is not the policy of Federal Courts to intervene in the resolution of conflicts which arise in the daily operation of the school systems," the Court declared: "Nevertheless, we cannot remain silent when we truly believe that the regulations as presently written will raise more problems than they will solve. We have both compassion and understanding of the difficulties facing school administrators, but we cannot permit those conditions to suppress the First Amendment rights of individual students."

Nitzberg v. *Parks,* 525 F.2d 378 (1975)

Mr. Justice CLARK.

This civil rights action under 42 U.S.C. § 1983 was brought in United States District Court after school officials of the Woodlawn Senior High School in Baltimore Co., Maryland, ordered two private student newspapers to cease publication in November of 1973. Appellants, the student publishers of the newspapers and their parents, alleged that Rule No. 5130–1—the Baltimore County Board of Education's statement of "Students' Rights and Responsbilities"—violated the First and Fourteenth Amendments insofar as it authorized prior restraint of "non-school literature."

The case proceeded on stipulated facts, none of which are relevant to our resolution of this matter.[1] The sole question is whether on its face Rule 5130–1 as presently stated meets the constitutional standards set forth in this Circuit's precedents, *Quarterman* v. *Byrd,* 453 F.2d 54 (1971), and *Baughman* v. *Freienmuth,* 478 F.2d 1345 (1973). We hold that it does not.[2]

After the filing of this suit in December of 1973, the Baltimore County school board reexamined its original regulations governing on-campus distribution of non-school sponsored literature and produced a second version on January 24, 1974. The district court, however, found the new rules vague and overbroad and, in an opinion filed February 25, 1974, gave the Board two weeks to meet constitutional standards. On March 26, 1974, the district court reviewed the Board's third version, again found them wanting, and enjoined the Board from enforcing the rules. On May 17, 1974, the court continued the injunction and ordered revision of the fourth version. The board again redrafted its rules, and on May 30, 1974, the district court approved the regulations and dissolved the injunction. This appeal followed.

Rule 5130.1(b) contains the Board's present policies regarding student publications and states in relevant part:

Literature may be distributed and posted by the student of the subject school in designated areas on school property as long as it is not obscene or libelous (as defined below) and as long as the distribution of said literature does not reasonably lead the principal to forecast substantial disruption of or material interference with school activities.

If a student desires to post or make a distribution of free literature which is not officially recognized as a school publication, the student shall submit such non-school material to the principal for review and prior approval. In exercising this right of prior restraint, principals shall follow the procedures specified in this policy. The principal shall render a decision and notify the student within two (2) pupil days of such submission. If the decision is in the negative, the principal shall state his reasons to the student in writing. During this period of review, any supply of the material may be retained by the student or may be left with the principal for safekeeping. Distribution of such material during the review and appeal period, or following a negative decision, shall be sufficient grounds for confiscation of such material and suspension of the student by the principal. If the student is dissatisfied with the decision of the principal with respect to the distribution of a non-school publication, the student may appeal this decision to the appropriate area assistant superintendent who shall render a decision, stating his reasons in writing, within three (3) pupil days of such appeal. If an administrator fails to act within the time periods specified in this paragraph, the student(s) who submitted the literature for review may distribute same. (Appeal from a decision of an assistant superintendent is to the superintendent of schools and thence to the Board of Education at the time of its next regularly scheduled meeting.)

The accompanying definitions of "libel or libelous material", "obscene or obscenity", and "distribution" are set forth in the margin.[3] Appellants contend that these regulations, detailed though they may seem, remain unconstitutionally vague and overbroad. We begin by restating the law of this Circuit in regard to such claims.

The controlling constitutional principles in student publication cases for this Circuit have been set forth by Judge Russell in *Quarterman* v. *Byrd,* 453 F.2d 54 (4th Cir. 1971), as follows:

Free speech under the First Amendment, though available to juveniles and high school students, as well as to adults, is not absolute.... [A]s Justice Stewart emphasized in his concurring opinion in *Tinker* v. *Des Moines School Dist.,* 393 U.S. 503, 515, 89 S.Ct. 733, 21 L.Ed.2d 731 (1969)], First Amendment rights of children are not "co-extensive with those of adults". Similarly, a difference may exist between the rights of free speech attaching to publications distributed in a secondary school and those in a college or university. It is generally held that the constitutional right to free speech of public secondary school students may be modified or curtailed by school regulations "reasonably designed to adjust those rights to the needs of the school environment."... Specifically, school authorities may by appropriate regulation, exercise prior restraint upon publications distributed on school premises during school hours in those special circumstances where they can "reasonably 'forecast substantial disruption of or material interference with school activities'" on account of the distribution of such printed material. [453 F.2d at 57–58 (footnotes omitted)].

Subsequently, in *Baughman* v. *Freienmuth,* 478 F.2d 1345 (4th Cir. 1973), Judge Craven re-emphasized the necessity of "narrow, objective, and reasonable standards" as the essential element in any scheme which required prior submission of material for approval before distribution and summarized the constitutional requirements as follows:

(a) Secondary school children are within the protection of the First Amendment, although their rights are not coextensive with those of adults.

(b) Secondary school authorities may exercise reasonable prior restraint upon the exercise of students' First Amendment rights.

(c) Such prior restraints must contain precise criteria sufficiently spelling out what is forbidden so that a reasonably intelligent student will know what he may write and what he may not write.

(d) A prior restraint system, even though precisely defining what may not be written, is nevertheless invalid unless it provides for:

(1) A definition of "Distribution" and its application to different kinds of material;

(2) Prompt approval or dispproval of what is submitted;

(3) Specification of the effect of failure to act promptly; and,

(4) An adequate and prompt appeals procedure.

[478 F.2d at 1351.]

Accord Eisner v. *Stamford Board of Education,* 440 F.2d 803 (2d Cir. 1971) (Kaufman, J.).

It is clear that Rule 5130.1(b) was intended to come within the exception to the ban on prior restraints suggested in *Tinker* v. *Des Moines School District,* 393 U.S. 503, 89 S.Ct. 733, 21 L.Ed.2d 731 (1969). There the court appeared to recognize the right of school administrators to block the distribution of literature which would substantially disrupt school work and discipline. Despite the protest of commentators, see Note, "Prior Restraints in Public High Schools," 82 Yale L.J. 1325 (1973), the Circuits which have dealt with the issue—with the exception of the Seventh—have accepted this interpretation of *Tinker*. See *Riseman* v. *School Committe of Quincy,* 439 F.2d 148 (1st Cir. 1971); *Eisner* v. *Stamford Board of Education,* 440 F.2d 803 (2d Cir. 1971); *Quarterman* v. *Byrd,* 453 F.2d 54 (4th Cir. 1971); *Shanley* v. *Northeast Ind. Sch. Dist., Bexar County, Tx.,* 462 F.2d 960 (5th Cir. 1972); *contra Fujishima* v. *Board of Education,* 460 F.2d 1355 (7th Cir. 1972). Applying this test, we find the challenged regulation to be improperly drawn in several respects.

The central paragraph in rule 5130.-1(b) states that:

> Literature may be distributed and posted by the student of the subject school in designated areas on school property as long as it is not obscene or libelous (as defined below) and as long as the distribution of said literature does not reasonably lead the principal to forecast substantial disruption of or material interference with school activities.

A crucial flaw exists in this directive since it gives no guidance whatsoever as to what amounts to a "substantial disruption of or material interference with" school activities; and, equally fatal, it fails to detail the criteria by which an administrator might reasonably predict the occurrence of such a disruption. Though the language comes directly from the opinion in *Tinker*, we agree with Judge Fairchild's remark in *Jacobs* v. *Board of School Commissioners,* 490 F.2d 601 (7th Cir. 1973), vacated as moot, 420 U.S. 128, 95 S.Ct. 848, 43 L.Ed.2d 74 (1975), that:

> It does not at all follow that the phrasing of a constitutional standard by which to decide whether a regulation infringes upon rights protected by the First Amendment is sufficiently specific in a regulation to convey notice to students or people in general of what is prohibited. [490 F.2d at 605 (footnote omitted).]

In addition, we note that the definition of "libelous" material contained in rule 5130.1(c) fails to apply the standard of *New York Times* v. *Sullivan*, 376 U.S. 254, 84 S.Ct. 710, 11 L.Ed.2d 686 (1964), and its progeny. On its face, therefore, the Board's regulations are void for vagueness and overbreadth. In addition, we notice that there are other flaws which must be corrected, if Rule 5130.1 is to pass constitutional muster.[4]

In *Baughman*, this Circuit made it quite plain that a prior restraint procedure, to be valid, must provide prompt and adequate review. Here, the procedures to be followed by the school administration are unclear. A principal must render a decision on a proposed publication within two "pupil days"; and the assistant superintendent who reviews the principal's decision must render his decision within three "pupil days". Nowhere is the term "pupil days" defined. More importantly, no time limit whatever is specified for an appeal from the assistant superintendent's decision to the superintendent, and ultimate review by the school board is permitted only "at the time of its next regularly scheduled meeting." Such protracted steps in the appeals procedure are obviously incompatible with the quick disposition so necessary in free speech cases.

We also believe that the nature of the review itself has been left too vague. The regulations call for the student desiring to distribute literature to "submit" the material to the principal. One would expect that such a submission would include the right of the student to appear and present his case, yet such a right is not specifically acknowledged at any point in the review process. Since the regulations specify that "Distribution of [non-school] material during the review and appeal period, or following a negative decision, shall be sufficient grounds for confiscation of such material and suspension of the student by the principal," elementary due process requires confrontation and a hearing of some type before a step as drastic as suspension is taken.[5] As the Supreme Court recently said in *Goss* v. *Lopez*, 419 U.S. 565, 95 S.Ct. 729, 42 L.Ed.2d 725 (1975):

> [I]t would be a strange disciplinary system in an educational institution if no communication was sought by the disciplinarian with the student in an effort to inform him of his defalcation and to let him tell his side of the story in order to make sure that an injustice is not done....
>
> We do not believe that school authorities must be totally free from notice and hearing requirements if their schools are to operate with acceptable efficiency.... [D]ue process requires, in connection with a suspension of ten days or less, that the student be given oral or written notice of the charges against him and, if he denies them, an explanation of the evidence the authorities have and an opportunity to present his side of the story. [419 U.S. at 580, 95 S.Ct. at 739].

This is the third time that this circuit has been confronted with the free speech aspects of secondary public school regulations and found it necessary to intervene in the conduct of such matters by the local school authorities. We deplore this, as was said in the first case "because it is not the policy of Federal Courts to 'intervene in the resolution of conflicts which arise in the daily operation of the school systems and which do not directly and sharply implicate basic constitutional values.'" *Quarterman* v. *Byrd, supra,* 453 F.2d at 56. Moreover, the Surpeme Court itself has "repeatedly emphasized the need for affirming the comprehensive authority of the States and of school officials, consistent with fundamental constitutional safeguards, to prescribe and control conduct in the schools." *Tinker* v. *Des Moines School Dist., supra,* 393 U.S. at 507, 89 S.Ct. at 737. Nevertheless, we cannot remain silent when we truly believe that the regulations as presently written will raise more problems than they will solve. We have both compassion and understanding of the difficulties facing school administrators, but we cannot permit those conditions to suppress the First Amendment rights of individual students.

Nor will any intolerable burden result from our decision. Indeed, it may ameliorate the relationship between the student and the disciplinarian and lead them to empathize with each other. As Judge Kaufman remarked in *Eisner, supra:*

> The Board would in no way shackle school administrators if it attempted to confront and resolve in some fashion, prior to court intervention, some of the constitutional issues that will almost inevitably be raised when so broad a rule is applied to particular cases. [440 F.2d at 809].

It would be salutary of the Board to require the disciplinarian to afford the student or students involved in a non-school publication, for example, an opportunity to have a fair give-and-take confrontation with the administrator before the latter rules on the distribution of such student publications. At such an informal meeting, the whole problem might be aired; hard feelings dissipated; distrust overcome; and mutual confidence established. At the least the affected student would have a better opinion of the disciplinary process.

As an alternative to the present scheme, the matter might be turned over to a Student-Faculty Relations Committee of the sort envisioned in Rule 5130.-1(b),[6] and the disruption and bitterness generated by an unpopular refusal of the administrator to allow circulation of a student publication might thus be alleviated. Through such a joint effort, final answers may be found for the many difficult questions precipitated by prior restraint of student publications. For example, such a committee might decide: (1) where on school property it would be appropriate to distribute approved material; (2) the type of material that might cause distractions and disruptions among the students; and (3) the question of how serious a "disruption" must be before prior restraint would be justified. Such a course would lessen the possibility of arbitrary action and unfair treatment which, in turn, we think, would improve teacher-student relations.

The judgment of the trial court is reversed and appropriate action in implementation of this opinion, including injunctive relief when necessary, is directed to the end that the regulations adopted by the Board be in keeping with the requirements hereof.

It is so ordered.

BRYAN, Senior Circuit Judge (concurring):

I have had considerable difficulty with this case because of the problems logically arising in the conflict between the effectuation of the school authorities' bona fide aim and the restrictions of the First Amendment. In ordering four rewrites of the School Board's regulations, District Judge Northrop scrupulously endeavored to avoid a trespass upon student rights. I concur in the present opinion of the Court because it provides a clear and explicit chart by which the District Court and the Board may achieve their object and yet not trample upon the students' First Amendment privileges.

NOTES

1. One of the papers, *The Woodlawn Lampoon,* for example, was banned from the high school because of an article about cheerleaders which apparently described them as "sex objects". School administrators called the article "obscene" and "demeaning" to the school, and threatened to suspend the students if they put out another issue. While we see no connection between the phrase "sex objects" and obscenity (or, for that matter, demeaning behavior), we need not here undertake an assessment of the content of this newspaper or its companion, *Today's World,* since the present controversy involves only the facial constitutionality of the school board's regulations.

2. The Supreme Court's recent decison in *Board of School Commissioners* v. *Jacobs,* 420 U.S. 128, 95 S.Ct. 848, 43 L.Ed.2d 74 (1975), presents no impediment to our consideration of this case. In *Jacobs,* the Court dismissed a complaint alleging an almost identical constitutional violation because the pending case had become moot as a result of the graduation of the named plaintiffs and their failure to have had a class action properly certified under Fed.R.Civ.P. 23. Here, though no effort was made to certify a class, it is stipulated by the parties that Richard Smith, one of the named plaintiffs, is currently a junior at Woodlawn Senior High School and is expected to be in attendance for another full school year. A live case or controversy therefore exists.

3. 1. Libel or libelous material—
The First Amendment of the Constitution of the United States protects the right of free expression by an individual, either in writing or in speech, on all matters of public or general concern about a person, without regard to whether such person is famous or anonymous, in whom the community and press have a legitimate and substantial interest because of who he is or what he has done. However, a written or oral statement about such a person which is made with "actual malice," that is, with knowledge that it was false or with reckless disregard of whether it was false or which was made with a high degree of awareness of its probable falsity, is subject to sanction and is not protected by the First Amendment of the Constitution.
A statement is libelous and not protected by the First

Amendment if it is made with "actual malice" and if it tends to expose one to public hatred, shame, obloquy, contumely, odium, contempt, ridicule, aversion, ostracism, degradation, or disgrace, or if it induces an evil opinion of one in the minds of right-thinking persons, or if it causes one to be shunned and avoided in society.

2. Obscene or obscenity—

The average person, applying contemporary community standards would find that it, taken as a whole, appeals to prurient interest;

It depicts or describes, in a patently offensive way, sexual conduct currently defined by Maryland law [27 Anno. Code of Md. §§ 416, 417];

Taken as a whole, it lacks serious literary, artistic, political or scientific value.

The Supreme Court has set forth the following examples of what types of materials can be prohibited as obscene:

> "(a) Patently offensive representations of descriptions of ultimate sexual acts, normal or perverted, actual or simulated.
> (b) Patently offensive representation or descriptions of masturbation, excretory functions, and lewd exhibition of the genitals." (*Miller* v. *California* [413 U.S. 15 at 25], 93 S.Ct. [2607] at 2615 [,37 L.Ed.2d 419]) These examples are adopted herewith as part of this policy.

3. Distribution—

A substantial dissemination of literature in any form which is thus made generally available to students. This includes the posting of literature in areas of a school which are generally frequented by students. The principal will require submission of literature for prior review when there is to be such a substantial distribution of literature, so that it can be reasonably anticipated that in a significant number of instances there would be a likelihood that the distribution would disrupt school operations, or in order to determine whether such material is libelous or obscene as defined in this policy.

4. For example, the regulation curiously appears to require the prior approval only of "free" student literature which is not officially recognized as a student publication. We can perceive no constitutional basis for distinguishing between commercial literature and "free" literature. Also, we find no clear purpose in the inclusion of Maryland's criminal statutes on obscenity in sections (d), (e), and (f) of rule 5130.1. Finally, we have some doubts about the adequacy of the publication provision of rule 5130.1(b), since it merely requires that "a copy of this policy shall be made available to all students in a readily accessible and announced location in each school building." We believe that a more effective notice would be attained through inclusion in official publications of the school or circulated to students in the same manner as other official materials, circulars, or bulletins.

5. We also note that to punish, *ipsa dixit,* a student who publishes literature which may have suffered improper prior restraint, places the student on his own peril and the resulting chill on First Amendment activity would be intolerable.

6. Rule 5130.1(b) provides:

    In each secondary school, and in each elementary school for the students who have demonstrated the maturity needed to participate effectively, a Student-Faculty Relations Committee should be established consisting of an equal number of faculty and students chosen by their respective groups for the purpose of receiving recommendations and discussing concerns. The President of the Student Council shall be a member of this committee, with all other students in the school eligible for membership. The method of selection and number shall be determined by the Student Council of each school.

T HE United States Court of Appeals, Fifth Circuit, decides against an off-campus homosexual group which had sought to compel the Mississippi State University student newspaper to publish a paid advertisement, rejected by the newspaper editor, announcing the availability of a "Gay Center" offering "counseling, legal aid and a library of homosexual literature." In deciding against the Mississippi Gay Alliance, the Court of Appeals concluded: "The editor of *The Reflector* had a right to take the position that the newspaper would not be involved, even peripherally, with this off-campus homosexually-related activity."

Judge Goldberg dissents, arguing, among other things, that the Mississippi Gay Alliance had a right to access to the advertising columns of *The Reflector:* "Whatever the scope of the minimum access requirements of free speech, a narrower doctrine is well established in Supreme Court precedent—when the State has provided a public forum through which speakers might have access to listeners, the State cannot discriminate among potential speakers on the basis of the content of their message. The notion that there must be equality of access to public forums is compelled not only by speech and associational rights, but also by the full force of the equal protection clause. . . . The State, of course, has considerable discretion in reasonably regulating the time, place and manner in which speech may be made from various public forums. What the State cannot do is to provide a forum through which some members of the public are able effectively to communicate their message to a certain audience while other members of the public are prohibited from utilizing the forum because of the content of their proposed message."

Mississippi Gay Alliance v. *Goudelock,* 536 F.2d 1073 (1976)

Before GEWIN, COLEMAN, and GOLDBERG, Circuit Judges.
COLEMAN, Circuit Judge.
This is not the ordinarily encountered First Amendment case in which a university student newspaper seeks to set aside an order directing it *not* to publish something which it wishes to publish.

To the contrary, it is a case in which a nebulous group, the Mississippi Gay Alliance, representing itself to be an association "basically comprised of homosexuals", seeks judicial compulsion against a student newspaper requiring publication of an advertisement which that paper does not want to publish.

The District Court refused to command publication. We affirm.

On August 16, 1973, a female, the self-styled chairwoman of the Mississippi Gay Alliance, presented a proposed paid advertisement to *The Reflector,* the student newspaper at Mississippi State University.

The proposed advertisement read as follows:

"Gay Center — open 6:00 to 9:00 Monday, Wednesday, and Friday nights.
"We offer — counselling, *legal aid* and a library of homosexual literature. (Emphasis added).
"Write to — The Mississippi Gay Alliance
P.O.Box 1328
Mississippi State University,
Ms. 39762."

The editor of the student newspaper refused to

accept the tendered paid advertisement.

On February 8, 1974, the same person presented an announcement to be printed in the "briefs" section of *The Reflector*. This, too, was rejected. The content of that announcement does not appear in the record.

Whereupon, suit was filed against the editor and others, alleging that the refusal to print the paid advertisement and announcement deprived the Gay Alliance of its First Amendment rights and praying that the defendants be ordered to print the rejected material. The suit also sought an order requiring defendants to print future advertisements and announcements tendered by the Gay Alliance. Actual and punitive damages were also demanded.

The parties agreed to stipulations, which might be summarized as follows:
1. The named plaintiffs are not MSU students nor is the MGA a recognized student organization.
2. No member of the MGA was enrolled as an MSU student.
   [This second stipulation was, at plaintiff's request, modified by court order in December, 1974, after the district court's ruling was issued. The new stipulation apparently says that some members of the MGA were MSU students. This modification did not affect the ruling of the district court].
3. The MSU student body elected Bill Goudelock as editor of *The Reflector*.
4. Funds supporting *The Reflector* are derived at least in part from a nonwaivable fee charged to students at MSU.
5. [University officials] Giles, Meyer, and Dudley did not give Goudelock any instructions not to accept the proffered material.

The trial court reviewed these facts, and determined that there were four issues in the case: (1) whether plaintiffs had standing to sue; (2) whether plaintiffs' unclean hands precluded the possibility of the court granting them the equitable relief they sought; (3) whether there was state action on the part of the defendant to support his § 1983 action; and (4) whether the First Amendment protection that covers a student newspaper meant that plaintiffs had no cause of action against Goudelock.

Deciding nothing with reference to the first two points, the District Court found, on the complaint and the stipulated facts, that there was no *indication* that any University official or faculty member had anything to do with the rejection of the advertisement or the announcement; that there was a complete lack of control over the student newspaper on the part of University officials.

The Court concluded that the rejection of the advertisement "does not constitute state action in any sense of the term".

Relying on *Bazaar* v. *Fortune,* 5 Cir., 1973, 476 F.2d 570, affirmed as modified, 489 F.2d 225 (en banc) and *Miami Herald Publishing Company* v. *Tornillo,* 1974, 418 U.S. 241, 94 S.Ct. 2831, 41 L.Ed.2d 730, it was held that in the absence of state action the student newspaper editor could "accept or reject such material as he saw fit".

While it is true that the student newspaper is supported, in part, by activity fees collected by the University, the students elect the editor. The complaint did not allege and the stipulations did not assert that University officials supervise or control what is to be published or not published in the newspaper.

As a matter of fact, in the context of the matter before us, this Court has held that the University authorities could not have ordered the newspaper not to publish the Gay Alliance advertisement, had it chosen to do so, see *Bazarr* v. *Fortune, supra.*

In *Miami Herald Publishing Company* v. *Tornillo, supra,* the Supreme Court flatly declared:

"The choice of material to go into a newspaper... constitute[s] the exercise of editorial control and judgment. It has yet to be demonstrated how governmental regulation of this crucial process can be exercised consistent with First Amendment guarantees of a free press as they have evolved to this time."

Since there is not the slightest whisper that the University authorities had anything to do with the rejection of this material offered by this off-campus cell of homosexuals, since such officials could not lawfully have done so, and since the record really suggests nothing but discretion exercised by an editor chosen by the student body, we think the First Amendment interdicts judicial interference with the editorial decision.

There are special reasons for holding that there was no abuse of discretion by the editor of *The Reflector.*

Hutchinson's Mississippi Code of 1848 included the following provision:

"Unnatural Intercourse; Punishment.

"Every person who shall be convicted of the detestable and abominable crime against nature, committed with mankind or a beast, shall be punished by imprisonment in the penitentiary for a term of not more than ten years."[1]

The exact language of this provision has been retained in the Code revisions of 1857, 1871, 1880, 1892, 1906, 1917, 1930, 1942, and 1972.[2]

The Mississippi statute condemns any intercourse which is unnatural, detestable and abominable, including acts committed per anus or per os, *State* v. *Davis,* 223 Miss. 862, 79 So.2d 452 (1955). This is not surprising. The very title of the statute shows it to have been directed against "Unnatural Intercourse".

The statute is not unconstitutional, *State* v. *Mays,* 329 So.2d 65 (Miss.1976).[3]

The editor of *The Reflector* had a right to take the position that the newspaper would not be involved, even peripherally, with this off-campus homosexually-related activity.[4]

The judgment of the District Court is Affirmed.
GOLDBERG, Circuit Judge (dissenting):
I respectfully dissent.

I understand the trial court and the majority of this panel to hold that the lack of direct involvement by university officials and the free expression rights of student editors combine to preclude any possible right of access to the *Reflector* on the part of the MGA. I disagree with that holding and, on the allegations, would find a narrowly circumscribed right of access which might extend to the MGA in this case.

The majority opinion here can be read as also deciding, in an alternative holding, that the advertisement tendered by the MGA was undeserving of any First Amendment protection which might otherwise exist, because the ad might have "involved" the newspaper "with ... off-campus homosexually related activity." This latter holding, if indeed it is that, is clearly and absolutely wrong.

A proper disposition of this case requires that we balance the rights of speakers and hearers of "protected" speech against special considerations supporting student control over student publications. In order that my position on the narrow but important First Amendment issues in this case might be fully understood, I find it necessary at this juncture to summarize briefly the course of this litigation. After reviewing the background, I will discuss what I consider to be an easy issue—whether the MGA advertisement is "protected" speech. Finally, I will attempt to explain why I would reconcile the competing First Amendment interests in a different fashion than did the trial court.

I. FACTS AND PROCEDURAL BACKGROUND

In August, 1973, the Mississippi Gay Alliance (MGA),[1] through one of its officers, submitted the following paid advertisement to be placed in the *Reflector,* the student newspaper at Mississippi State University (MSU):

"Gay Center — open 6:00 to 9:00 Monday, Wednesday and Friday nights.
"We offer — counselling, legal aid and a library of homosexual literature.
"Write to — The Mississippi Gay Alliance
P.O. Box 1328
Mississippi State University,
Ms. 39762."

Bill Goudelock, then the student editor of the paper, refused to accept the tendered advertisement. According to the plaintiffs' allegations, the *Reflector* at that time printed paid and unpaid advertisements of commercial, political, social, religious and informative natures.

In Febrary, 1974, the MGA presented an announcement (the contents of which are not in the record) to the *Reflector,* asking that it be placed in the "Briefs" section, wherein the paper regularly ran announcements of campus and local organizations free of charge. This was never printed. In March, 1974, the MGA and individual members of the MGA filed the instant suit, seeking to compel publication of their ads, and to obtain declaratory relief and damages. In addition to Goudelock the following were named as defendants: Henry F. Meyers, Faculty Adviser to the student paper; Sam Dudley, chairman of the MSU commmunications department; and William L. Giles, President of MSU. After limited discovery by both sides, the three MSU defendants moved to dismiss on the grounds that plaintiffs lacked standing to sue, had acted in bad faith, and had unclean hands.

At a hearing on this motion, the trial court proposed a set of stipulated facts. After some negotiation, the parties agreed to the stipulations which are summarized in the majority opinion. As indicated in that opinion, the district court did not decide the issues of standing[2] and unclean hands.[3] Rather, the trial court dismissed the action on the grounds now adopted by the panel here.

In determining the appropriate standard of review in this case, it should be noted that the exact nature of the procedural disposition by the lower court is uncertain. The ruling seems to say that no cause of action was stated, which would indicate dismissal under Fed.R.Civ.P. 12(b)6. On the other hand, the trial court's reliance on the stipulated facts suggests that the motion to dismiss was being treated as one for summary judgment (Rule 56 via Rule 12).

The MGA argues that if the latter analysis is accurate, the trial court erred in failing to follow the procedures set out in Rule 12 for converting the motion—the nonmoving party must be given a "reasonable opportunity to present all material made pertinent to such a motion by Rule 56." If the district court's view of the law is correct, however, the plaintiffs in effect had their "reasonable opportunity"—no material they could have presented could have changed the legal effect of the stipulated facts.

I think that it would be most appropriate to treat the disposition below as a summary judgment. The major issues before this court could then be stated as follows: 1) does there exist in any circumstances a Constitutional right of access to the advertising and announcement sections of student newspapers at state universities? 2) If so, are there any factual questions in this case which, if resolved in favor of the plaintiffs, could lead to the conclusion that the plaintiffs were within the scope of such a right? If both questions are answered affirmatively, then summary judgment was improper, and, *a fortiori,* disposition under Rule 12(b)(6) would have been improper.

Before discussing those major issues, however, I will address the issue raised for the first time in the majority's apparent alternative holding—whether the MGA ad is "protected" speech.

II. PROTECTED SPEECH

As I have indicated, the majority's discussion of "special reasons" justifying the student editor's refusal to accept his ad can be read as an implicit holding that the MGA ad was "unprotected" speech for First Amendment purposes. Such a holding obviously would be fallacious. If other local groups had a right of access to the *Reflector,* that right could not be denied the MGA in respect to the advertisement at issue here. The ad directly solicits nothing approaching criminal activity, and the publication of the ad would not involve the *Reflector,* "even peripherally," in the proscribed activities discussed in the majority opinion.

The advertisement simply sought to notify persons who were homosexuals, who were interested in the subject of homosexuality or who had problems relating to homosexuality that certain services were available to them at a "gay center." No statute, in Mississippi or in any relevant jurisdiction, makes criminal the status of being a homosexual.[4] Indeed, no statute could do that and survive Constitutional challenge. *See Robinson* v. *California,* 1962, 370 U.S. 660, 82 S.Ct. 1417, 8 L.Ed.2d 758. On the face of it, none of the services listed in the advertisement could conceivably be characterized as illegal. The suggestion of Judge Coleman that the criminal taint in the ad is demonstrated by the offer of "legal aid" implies a presumption of illegality whenever lawyers are involved[5]—surely the level of respect for the profession has not reached this nadir.

Thus, the exception whereby statements which propose illegal transactions are rendered valueless for First Amendment purposes cannot be applied to this advertisement.[6] Neither could the advertisement even arguably be characterized as "unprotected" speech on any other ground. It is not "directed to inciting or producing imminent lawless action."[7] The ad could occasion no substantial disruption of classroom activity,[8] nor could it be construed as an "intolerable" invasion of a "substantial" privacy interest.[9] No basis exists for suggesting that the ad is libelous,[10] obscene[11] or "fighting words."[12] In short, nothing in the record contradicts the following statement of the trial court:

> It is certainly true that this ad tendered by Anne DeBary appears quite innocuous on its face. It certainly would not be such matter that might be regarded as obscene, or, in the eyes of many people, offensive.[13]

The ad carried an informative statement with regard to a matter of social concern, and, as seen, its contents trigger none of the recognized exceptions to freedom of speech.

Thus, this is not an "unnatural intercourse" case, and there exist no "special reasons" related to the content of the ad which would justify its discriminatory rejection in the face of a general right of nondiscriminatory access. I turn, then, to the difficult First Amendment questions actually presented in this case.

III. A CONSTITUTIONAL RIGHT OF ACCESS

The MGA's argument that it had a right of access to the advertising columns of the *Reflector* is based on the notion that when the state provides a communication forum generally open to the public, the state may not discriminatorily forbid the use of the forum by certain individuals because of the content of their proposed messages. After discussing the contours of this "public forum" doctrine as it might be applied to a state newspaper, I will address two separate questions which the trial court and the majority have commingled: 1) should the *Reflector* be viewed as a state newspaper?; 2) assuming that the *Reflector* engages in state action, do the free expression rights guaranteed to student editors preclude any right of access on the part of outside groups? As will be seen, I conclude that on the basis of the allegations the advertising and announcement sections of the *Reflector* can be seen as a public forum to which the MGA might have a right of nondiscriminatory access.

A. *Equal Access: State Newspapers as Public Forums.*

There is authority for the proposition that the First Amendment's guarantee of free speech carries with it some requirement that the state provide "minimum access"—that is, that the state accommodate speakers' attempts to obtain access to listeners.[14] Freedom of association, as well as freedom of speech, supports such a requirement in some situations.[15]

Whatever the scope of the minimum access requirements of free speech, a narrower doctrine is well established in Supreme Court precedent—when the state has provided a public forum through which speakers might have access to listeners, the state cannot discriminate among potential speakers on the basis of the content of their message.[16] The notion that there must be equality of access to public forums is compelled not only by speech and associational rights, but also by the full force of the equal protection clause.

The Supreme Court expounded on equal access in *Police Dep't of Chicago* v. *Mosley,* 1972, 408 U.S. 92, 95–96, 92 S.Ct. 2286, 2290, 33 L.Ed.2d 212:

> ... [A]bove all else, the First Amendment means that government has no power to restrict expression because of its message, its ideas, its subject matter, or its content.... To permit the continued building of our politics and culture, and to assure self-fulfillment for each individual, our people are guaranteed the right to express any thought, free from government censorship. The essence of this forbidden censorship is content control. Any restriction on expressive activity because of its content would completely undercut the "profound national commitment to the principle that debate on public issues should be uninhibited, robust, and wide-open."...
>
> Necessarily, then, under the Equal Protection Clause, not to mention the First Amendment itself, government may not grant the use of a forum to people whose views it finds acceptable, but deny use to those wishing to express less favored or more controversial views. And it may not select which issues are worth discussing or debating in public facilities. There is an "equality of status in the field of ideas," and government must afford all points of view an equal opportunity to be heard. Once a forum is opened up to assembly or speaking by some groups, government may not prohibit others from assembling or speaking on the basis of what they intend to say. Selective exclusions from a public forum may not be based on content alone and may not be justified by reference to content alone. [Citations and footnote omitted.]

The state, of course has considerable discretion in reasonably regulating the time, place and manner in which speech may be made from various public forums.[17] What the state cannot do is to provide a forum through which some members of the public are able effectively to communicate their message to a certain audience while other members of the public are prohibited from utilizing the forum because of the content of their proposed messages.[18]

I take it to be quite clear, for example, that a city, having established a "speaker's corner" in a public park from which almost anyone might speak about almost anything, could not constitutionally prohibit speeches dealing non-obscenely with the topic of homosexuality.[19]

Taking the hypothetical a step closer to the instant case, we might posit a newspaper paid for and published by the state—call it the "Open Forum"—in which all citizens are invited to express their views on any issue, subject only to reasonable space limitations and a small fee to help offset printing costs. Could the "Open Forum" refuse to print a tendered statement on the ground that it expressed a political view contrary to that of the Governor, or on no stated ground at all? Surely not. Conceivably, the state could place many non-content-oriented restrictions on the form of the messages, but the state could not refuse tendered statements otherwise similar in form to those regularly accepted solely because the proffered ads were disagreeable in content.[20]

The conclusion I reach with regard to the "Open Forum" hypothetical finds support in the case law. In a case with striking similarities to the one before us, the Seventh Circuit held that a state university's campus newspaper which was open to commercial and some political and service advertisements could not constitutionally reject, because of editorial content, advertisements describing the purposes of a university employees' union, an advertisement proclaiming the immorality of racial discrimination, or advertisements pertaining to race relations and the Vietnam War. *Lee* v. *Board of Regents,* 7 Cir. 1971, 441 F.2d 1257, *aff'g,* 306 F.Supp. 1097. Indeed, the only potentially important distinction between *Lee* and the instant case is that in *Lee,* it was "conceded that the campus newspaper is a state facility." 441 F.2d at 1258. The rules under which the tendered advertisements were rejected had been promulgated by a faculty-student committee. 306 F.Supp. at 1099.

In *Zucker* v. *Panitz,* S.D.N.Y.1969, 299 F.Supp. 102, the district court reviewed a claim by high school students seeking to publish in the high school newspaper paid advertisements opposing the Vietnam War. The court found that the newspaper was "a forum for the dissemination of ideas," noting that other articles on the war and the draft had been published in the paper and that the paper was open to the free expression of ideas in news and editorial columns and in letters to the editor. Relying on *Tinker* v. *Des Moines Indep. Comm'ty School Dist.,* 1969, 393 U.S. 503, 503 S.Ct. 733, 21 L.Ed.2d 731, the district court enjoined the school officials from interfering with the right of students in the high school to place advertisements in the school newspaper.

In *Radical Lawyers Caucus* v. *Pool,* W.D. Tex.1970, 324 F.Supp. 268, Judge Roberts held that the Texas Bar Journal, conceded to be an agency of the state of Texas, was prohibited by the First and Fourteenth Amendments from refusing to accept an advertisement publicizing an upcoming meeting of the plaintiff organization. The court disposed of the defendant's argument that the Journal be permitted to refuse "political and editorial" advertising so that it might "maintain its neutrality in controversial matters," by pointing to position-taking political statements that had appeared in the Journal. *Id.* at 270.

A "state" newspaper could not constitutionally refuse advertisements advocating one side of a public issue while accepting advertisements advocating the other side. No less offensive to the First and Fourteenth Admendments should be a case in which advertisements dealing with public issues are generally accepted, but advertisements on certain public issues are selectively and arbitrarily excluded.[21]

Were the *Reflector* clearly a paper run by and for the state, then, the allegations of the MGA (unaltered by the stipulated facts) that the paper regularly accepted paid and unpaid messages and announcements from other local groups would be sufficient to raise a genuine issue of material fact. If the allegations were true, the state would have denied the MGA equal access to a public forum.

On the other hand, if the *Reflector* were purely a private newspaper, there presumably would exist no such right of access. The editor of a private newspaper is constitutionally protected in a decision not to publish a political reply advertisement, even in the face of a state right to reply statute. See *Miami Herald Publishing Co. v. Tornillo,* 1974, 418 U.S. 241, 94 S.Ct. 2831, 41 L.Ed.2d 730. Clearly, then, a federal court would have no power, under statutes requiring "state action," to prohibit a nonstate newspaper from exercising selective content discrimination in its publication of advertisements.[22]

The first question thus becomes whether the *Reflector* can be characterized as the state. Even if, under traditional analysis, "state action" is found, the court must proceed to the further question of whether the newspaper is, at least in part, a public forum. That question will require a review of special considerations relating to student newspapers, and a balancing of competing First Amendment interests.

B. State Action.

As indicated above, *Lee* and *Zucker* were not difficult cases with regard to the question of state action. It was clear in both that officials, not students, exercised ultimate responsiblity for the censorship decision. Indeed, the student editors in *Zucker* were plaintiffs, seeking to compel publications of the advertisements. Although the students in *Lee* may have supported the official rules and the specific decision not to publish, it was conceded that the censorship was the product of state action. In this case, by contrast, the university officials argue that they do not and indeed could not countermand specific editorial decisions of the student editor of the *Reflector,* and thus that the "state action" required to trigger the public forum doctrine is lacking. The trial court and the majority here have agreed with this argument.

The absence of affirmative involvement by university officials in the decision to refuse the MGA ad should not end state action inquiry. Were direct, active involvement by state officials to become a prerequisite for a state action finding, *Burton* v. *Wilmington Parking Authority,* 1961, 365 U.S. 715, 81 S.Ct. 856, 6 L.Ed.2d 45, and *Marsh* v. *Alabama,* 1946, 326 U.S. 501, 66 S.Ct. 276, 90 L.Ed. 265, would have to be overruled, and cases like *Hudgens* v. *N.L.R.B.,* 1976, 424 U.S. 507, 96 S.Ct. 1029, 47 L.Ed.2d 196; *Moose Lodge No. 107* v. *Irvis,* 1972, 407 U.S. 163, 92 S.Ct. 1965, 32 L.Ed.2d 627, and *Golden* v. *Biscayne Bay Yacht Club,* 5 Cir. 1976, 530 F.2d 16 (en banc) would be very easy cases. State action, of course, is not so simple. A number of factors must be examined to determine if the action challenged as detrimental to individual rights should be considered to be state action for fourteenth amendment purposes. As Judge Coleman emphasized in *Golden,* the ultimate question is whether the facts establish "significant state involvement" in what otherwise may appear to be private activity. 530 F.2d at 19.

To my mind, the allegations of the MGA, if shown to be true, would establish that actions taken by the *Reflector,* as it deals with and appears to members of the public, should be considered to be state action. The complaint in this action set forth the following allegation:

> The *Reflector* is the official newspaper of MSU, a state supported and controlled institution of higher learning. The major portion of the *Reflector's* financing comes from the Student Activity Fund which is collected by MSU and disbursed to the *Reflector.* The *Reflector* is printed on MSU facilities and it is an organ of MSU.

The stipulations included the fact that funds supporting the *Reflector* were derived from a non-waivable fee charged to students at MSU.

The *Reflector's* funding is thus derived from what is in effect a tax charged by the state to the students.[23] The allegations suggest that the imprimatur of the state is clearly stamped on the paper. In these circumstances, I have little doubt that this court would review a decision by the students to exclude blacks from participation on the newspaper staff as a decision imbued with state action.[24] To my mind, the pure "state action" question should be the same in the First Amendment context. *Cf. Golden, supra,* 530 F.2d at 19.

Having concluded, on the issue of "state action," that appellants are deserving of at least a remand,[25] I turn to what I consider the most significant question in this case: does the Constitution permit student editors of an official publication at a state university to pursue a general policy of accepting from local groups advertisements dealing with matters of public interest, but at the same time to exclude, because of its content, a certain advertisement proffered by a similarly situated group?

C. *A Right to Edit.*

Clearly, student editors of a campus newspaper are protected by their own First Amendment rights.[26] As the cases discussed below demonstrate, these rights include in some contexts the right to refuse to print as well as the right to print. The district court seems to have determined that these rights extend to provide complete student autonomy over all sections of the newspaper. Relying on this Circuit's decision in *Bazaar* v. *Fortune*,[27] and the Fourth Circuit's opinion in *Joyner* v. *Whiting*,[28] the trial judge concluded that student editor of the *Reflector* was protected in his decision to reject the MGA advertisement by the same protections which, in *Tornillo*, shielded the Miami Herald's decision not to run a reply to its editorial.

Bazaar held that, on the facts before it, state university officials could not censor the contents of a student literary magazine. The court rejected the defendants' argument that, because the magazine was published with the advice of the university's English department, the magazine would be identified as speaking for the university, which gave the defendants a right to censor. Neither was censorship justified on the ground that four-letter words used in the objected-to stories made them "too tasteless and inappropriate" to be connected with the university. Our *en banc* court modified *Bazaar* only by making explicit the university's right to print a disclaimer of official responsibility with the stories. 489 F.2d 225.[29]

Joyner held that a state university's withdrawal of financial support from the official newspaper, in response to the newspaper's segregationist editorial policy, abridged the freedom of press rights of the students. 477 F.2d at 460–62.[30]

These cases do not suggest that the *Reflector* should be thought of as something other than a state newspaper—indeed, they suggest the contrary. The rationale of *Bazaar* is expressly grounded on the "open forum" cases discussed in the preceding section. 476 F.2d at 575. Although *Joyner* invokes "freedom of the press", the result in that case is certainly consistent with public forum notions, and the *Joyner* court also relies on the open forum cases cited above. 477 F.2d at 460. *Bazaar* and *Joyner* indicate that state school officials, having provided a forum for free expression by students, cannot censor the content of the messages that the students seek to disseminate. That rule, on its face, would not be inconsistent with a requirement that the columns of the state-sponsored paper be open to anyone with anything to say. The *Joyner* court seemed to recognize this possibility:

When a college paper receives a subsidy from the state, there are strong arguments for insisting that its columns be open to the expression of contrary views and that its publication enhance, not inhibit, free speech.

477 F.2d at 462.

In my opinion, however, a requirement of wide-open access to the pages of a student newspaper would sweep much too broadly. To the extent that the right of student editors to free expression is to be protected, that right must include the right to edit. With limited space for news and editorial columns, and with attribution on the masthead as "editors," students operating a student paper must necessarily exercise some discretion in choosing what to publish and what not to publish. This is most clear, perhaps, when the materials to be edited are generated solely by the student staff, but the "right to edit" (based in part on the necessity for editing) would logically extend to articles or columns submitted by outside sources.

This principle is supported by *Joyner's* reliance on a "freedom of the press" rationale, and by the Third Circuit's decision in *Avins* v. *Rutgers, State University of New Jersey,* 3 Cir. 1967, 385 F.2d 151, *cert. denied,* 1968, 390 U.S. 920, 88 S.Ct. 855, 19 L.Ed.2d 982. *Rutgers* upheld the right of the student editors of a state university law review to reject a tendered article. The court stressed the impossibility and undesirability of a requirement that student editors publish every article submitted, and held that "the acceptance or rejection of articles submitted for publication in a law school law review necessarily involves the exercise of editorial judgment." 385 F.2d at 153. Both *Joyner* and *Rutgers* assumed without deciding that state action existed, but, nevertheless, *Joyner* held that the school officials could not censor the paper, and *Rutgers* held that an outside author could demand no right of access to the space allotted to outside articles.

I fully support the result in the *Rutgers* case and the implication it bears for a general right to edit on the part of students editors of state-supported publications. The question thus becomes one of competing First Amendment interests, and the search must be for a reconciliation between the interests, on the one hand, of student autonomy in control over the contents of the newspaper, and, on the other, of nondiscriminatory public access to a communication forum sponsored by the state.

D. *A Reconciliation of Competing Interests.*

I think that the two interests discussed above can be accommodated through a doctrine which permits student editors of state newspapers unfettered discretion over what might be termed the "editorial product" of the newspaper, yet requires that when the newspaper devotes space to unedited advertisements or announcements from individuals outside the newspaper staff, access to such space must be made available to other similarly situated individuals on a nondiscriminatory basis.

I use "editorial product" to comprehend the news and editorial columns of the paper, and other sections that by tradition and popular perception would be subject to editorial input from the operators of a newspaper. Guest columns and letters to the editor, although closer to the borderline because of the authorship, probably would be included in this "editorial product" notion.[31]

As to the sections of the newspaper which would be subject to the requirement of nondiscriminatory access, I take the two sections of the *Reflector* at issue in this suit to be paradigmatic. According to the allegations of the MGA, the sections of the *Reflector* to which access was sought were regularly available to local organizations for announcements and messages of social, political and informative natures.[32] Also, the student editors apparently do not purport to exercise editorial responsibility over the issues raised by or the content of these paid advertisements and unpaid announcements. No one would be likely to confuse statements appearing in them as officially endorsed by the students or the school.[33] Were there any problems in this regard, clear disclaimers as to the source of the messages easily could be added.[34]

I want to emphasize that the right of equal access I would invoke could, for the purposes of this case, be carefully circumscribed.[35] For example, the newspaper could perhaps provide access only to students or other members of the university community and not be guilty of content discrimination.[36] Perhaps access could even be restricted to local community businesses and groups.[37] The possibility of various source restrictions need not be reached in this case, however. The allegations of the plaintiffs suggest that other local groups, similarly situated to the MGA, were allowed access to the advertising and "briefs" sections of the paper. If that is true, impermissible content discrimination will have been shown—the "state" cannot accept advertisements from some local groups and refuse those from others because of their content.

Conceivably, other limitations on the envisioned right of equal access could arise in response to logistics and cost. A state newspaper which had provided a public forum for the publication of any message from anyone could in one week receive thousands of proposed messages on the same subject. It may not be feasible to print them all.[38] A word-per-message limitation might be useful, but situations still might exist in which there were simply too many similar messages to print. If the "public forum" is to remain that, some content-neutral means of selection would become necessary—*e.g.*, requiring payment of a reasonable fee,[39] printing the first however many submissions, or selecting statements at random. Again, we need not reach these questions to decide this case. There is no indication that any other advertisements, or announcements in the "briefs" section, had ever been refused by the newspaper, or that any consideration of space limitations was relevant in the decision to exclude the MGA ad.

I mention these possible limitations on the right of equal access to a state student newspaper to illustrate how narrowly a decision in the instant case could be written, and how careful a court should be in delineating the scope of such a right. These factors are closely related, of course, to the notion that time, place and manner restrictions are permissible "provided that they are justified without reference to the content of the regulated speech, that they serve a significant governmental interest, and that in so doing they leave open ample alternative channels for communication of the information." *Virginia State Bd. of Pharmacy* v. *Virginia Citizens Consumer Council,* 1976,—U.S.—,—, 96 S.Ct. 1817, 1830, 48 L.Ed.2d 346. The best way for the regulating agency to demonstrate that its restrictions are not based on content is through the formulation of specific rules governing what will and will not be published. When no rules guide the decision to exclude a controversial message from what otherwise appears to be a public forum, the courts are properly very skeptical of any proffered justification for the exclusion.[40]

CONCLUSIONS

I think it must be plain by now that I consider this a most difficult area of conflicting First Amendment interests. It should also be plain that I am convinced that the majority has reached an erroneous conclusion, and has failed adequately to consider the difficult issues actually presented in the case. As I have indicated, I would hold that there exits in some situations a right to nondiscriminatory access to the advertising and announcement sections of state-supported newspapers. I would remand this case to the district court for findings on state action (the nature of the funding, and the extent to which the *Reflector* can fairly be characterized as the official newspaper of MSU), on the other types of advertisements and announcements carried by the *Reflector* and on the practice followed by the student editors in rejecting advertisements.[41]

One reason for extreme caution in suggesting the sort of rules I have envisioned in my dissent is the danger that the state may provide "nondiscriminatory" access by providing no access, at least through the student newspapers under consideration here. While that danger counsels sensitivity in insuring that the requirements placed on the student newspapers are reasonable, I do not think that it should deter the courts from requiring the equality of access which the First Amendment has properly been read to guarantee. I am not so cynical as to suppose that state school officials and student editors of state school publications would uniformly choose to permit no outside views to be expressed in their publications rather than to permit, in a designated section of the publication, a free and open discussion of public issues.

The accommodation of competing interests which I have tried to sketch in this opinion may seem, on the surface, to lead to anomalous distinctions, especially from the perspective of university officials. Students may not be censored in their decision to publish, nor countermanded in their fashioning of an "editorial product." Yet student editors may themselves be treated, in effect, as agents of the state in their dealings with the public. On close consideration, I feel, these lines are not anomalous.

Bazaar and the other cases discussed above placed in student hands the right to be free of official censorship and, by implication, the right to edit. Neither *Bazaar* nor any other case, however, equips student editors of a state publication with the scyth of the censor to be used arbitrarily in cutting a few out of many submissions from the public. Although a bright line (*e. g.*, student editors of state publications have all the rights of private editors) might be easier to draw, I believe that when each side of the balance is weighted with important constitutional interests the court cannot abdicate its calligraphic responsibility to draw careful lines reflecting the optimum accommodation of rights.

The key to the reconciliation here is an emphasis in each situation on the powerful interests of speakers and listeners in free expression. In each context—officials attempting to censor students, and students attempting selectively to censor certain messages from the public on the basis of content—the court must balance the competing interests, but always with its thumb on the side of full and open discussion of public issues.[42]

For the reasons stated, I DISSENT.

NOTES

1. Chapter 64, Art. 12, Title 7(20).
2. The current statute is Section 97–29–59, Mississippi Code of 1972. For mention of the significance to be attached to the ancient origin of a similar statute in Virginia, see *Doe* v. *Commonwealth*, 403 F.Supp. 1199, 1202, 1203 (E.D.Va., 1975), Affirmed,—U.S.—, 96 S.Ct. 1489, 47 L.Ed.2d 751 (1976), [44 U.S.L.W. 3543].
3. The Mississippi Supreme Court relied on the decision of the Supreme Court of the United States in *Rose* v. *Locke*, 423 U.S. 48, 96 S.Ct. 243, 46 L.Ed.2d 185 (1975). In *Rose*, a Tennessee statute prohibited "Crimes against nature, either with mankind or any beast". The Supreme Court, reversing the Sixth Circuit, held that interpreting the Tennessee statute to include cunnilingus did not render it unconstitutional. It cited, 96 S.Ct. at 245, *State* v. *Crawford*, 478 S.W.2d 314 (Mo. 1972), which held that crime against nature embraces within its terms acts of sodomy, bestiality, buggery, fellatio, and cunnilingus.
4. One may not be prosecuted for being a homosexual, but he may be prosecuted for the commission of homosexual acts. Taking into consideration the laws of Mississippi on the subject, speaking as only one member of the panel, Judge Coleman is of the opinion that *no* newspaper in the State may be required to advertise solicitations for homosexual contacts, any more than a paper could be expected to advertise solicitations for contacts with prostitutes. The advertisement tendered by the Gay Alliance offered *legal aid*. Such an offer is open to various interpretations, one of which is that criminal activity is contemplated, necessitating the aid of counsel.

DISSENTING OPINION NOTES

1. The complaint described the MGA as follows: The MGA is an association located in Starkville, Mississippi. Some of its members attend Mississippi State University. The purpose of the MGA is to provide a forum where ideas may be discussed, information disseminated, and members freely associate between themselves and their friends. The MGA membership is composed primarily of homosexuals.
2. The trial court considered standing to be an issue but pretermitted it to reach the substantive issues. In their brief, the MSU defendants-appellees argue standing at length, urging that because the MSU officials caused plaintiffs no direct injury, *i.e.*, because the officials were passive, plaintiffs do not have standing to sue these officials. This argument is unpersuasive. Plaintiffs have alleged a distinct injury (their ad was rejected) and have alleged a causal relationship between the action of Goudelock, the acquiescence of the MSU officials, and that injury. The most recent cases seem to treat standing as a preliminary determination looking to objective factors: Has plaintiff alleged 1) an injury which sets him apart from other interested citizens, and 2) some degree of responsibility on the part of the defendant for that injury? The purpose of this exercise is simply

to assure the court that it will have a sincere contest—an actual "case or controversy"—and will not be called upon to render advisory opinions. *See generally Korioth v. Briscoe,* 5 Cir. 1975, 523 F.2d 1271. Plaintiffs' allegations here are sufficient to support their standing—whether they have stated a cause of action is another question.

3. Although the trial judge explicitly avoided reaching the issue, he did quote at length from letters written by plaintiff DeBary, and indicated a concern with the cleanliness *vel non* of the plaintiffs' hands. In one letter DeBary stated, *inter alia,* "the ad is really unimportant. It is being used as a tool to begin 'legal freedom' for gays in Mississippi." In another communication, DeBary stated, "we deliberately created a lawsuit for publicity and power. Really absurd, if you were one of the very few who knew the real story. The officers of the MGA were, at best, only three people."

   As a general rule, the determination of whether the "unclean hands" maxim should be applied to bar relief in a specific case is left in the first instance to the trial court. *See, e. g., United States v. Second Nat'l Bank of Miami,* 5 Cir. 1974, 502 F.2d 535; *Wolf v. Frank,* 5 Cir. 1973, 477 F.2d 467, *cert. denied,* 414 U.S. 975, 94 S.Ct. 287, 38 L.Ed.2d 218. Although it would thus be appropriate to leave this question to the trial court on remand, I feel constrained to note that the situation before us seems an unlikely one for the applicability of this equitable defense.

   Claimants in equity who practice fraud, deceit, or the like, even if not to a degree suffcient to be held criminally or civilly liable, may in some situations properly be denied equitable relief. *See generally Munchak v. Cunningham,* 4 Cir. 1972, 457 F.2d 721; *Washington Capitols Basketball Club, Inc. v. Barry,* 9 Cir. 1969, 419 F.2d 472.

   In this case, however, the evidence shows only that DeBary hoped to get some publicity from the suit and that she did not consider the nominal issue—whether the *Reflector* had the right to refuse her ad—as the overriding concern. No cases have been cited in which a claimant has been held to have "unclean hands" simply because she hoped that her suit would publicize a cause. I expect that much civil rights litigation might have been thwarted had such a rule been applied. The law is full of "test" cases which have determined important constitutional matters in seemingly minor disputes. I seriously doubt that the DeBary letters could justify a refusal to grant equitable relief on the basis of unclean hands.

4. *Doe v. Commonwealth,* E.D.Va.1975, 403 F.Supp. 1199 *aff'd,* 1976,——U.S.——, 96 S.Ct. 1489, 47 L.Ed.2d 751, and *Rose v. Locke,* 1975, 423 U.S. 48, 96 S.Ct. 243, 46 L.Ed.2d 185, relied on by the majority, dealt of course with proscribed acts (*Rose,* in fact, dealt with heterosexual acts). *Cf. Gay Students Organization v. Bonner,* 1 Cir. 1974, 509 F.2d 652; *Toward a Gayer Bicentennial Committee v. Rhode Island Bicentennial Foundation,* D.R.I.1976, 417 F.Supp. 632 [44 L.W. 2577, June 9, 1976]. *But cf. Gay Lib v. University of Missouri,* W.D.Mo. 1976,——F.Supp.—— [45 L.W. 2051, June 29, 1976].

5. *See* note 4 of the majority opinion.

6. *Compare Pittsburgh Press Co. v. Pittsburgh Comm'n on Human Relations,* 1973, 413 U.S. 376, 384–86, 93 S.Ct. 2553, 37 L.Ed.2d 669 *and United States v. Hunter,* 4 Cir. 1972, 459 F.2d 205, *cert.denied,* 409 U.S. 934, 93 S.Ct. 235, 34 L.Ed.2d 189 *with Bigelow v. Virginia,* 1975, 421 U.S. 809, 95 S.Ct. 2222, 44 L.Ed.2d 600 *and Virginia State Bd. of Pharmacy v. Virginia Citizens Consumer Counsel,* 1976,——U.S.——, 96 S.Ct. 1817, 48 L.Ed.2d 346.

   Had the tendered ad expressly solicited "unnatural intercourse," or had the editor of the *Reflector* grounded his refusal to publish the ad on his knowledge that the "library of homosexual literature" contained obscene materials, I might well reach a different conclusion. Plainly, neither of these situations has been shown to exist in the case before us, so I remain convinced that the tendered advertisement should be accorded full First Amendment protection.

7. *Brandenburg v. Ohio,* 1969, 395 U.S. 444, 447, 89 S.Ct. 1827, 1829, 23 L.Ed.2d 430 (per curiam):

   [T]he constitutional guarantees of free speech and free press do not permit a State to forbid or proscribe advocacy of the use of force or of law violation except where such advocacy is directed to inciting or producing imminent lawless action and is likely to incite or produce such action.

   For an argument that the *Brandenburg* test should be applied to cases involving noncriminal sanctions, see Comment "Brandenburg: A Test for All Seasons?" 43 *U.Chi.L.Rev.*151, 165–91 (1975).

8. *Tinker v. Des Moines Indep. School Dist.,*1969, 393 U.S. 503, 513, 89 S.Ct. 733, 740, 21 L.Ed.2d 731, suggests that student conduct in a high school that "materially disrupts classwork or involves substantial disorder or invasion of the rights of others is, of course, not immunized by the constitutional guarantee of freedom of speech." Compare *Blackwell v. Issaquena Co. Bd. of Educ.,* 5 Cir. 1966, 363 F.2d 749 with *Burnside v. Byars,* 5 Cir. 1966, 363 F.2d 744, 749.

   The tradition of academic freedom and the greater maturity of students on a college campus suggest that courts should be particularly solicitous of First Amendment rights in such a setting. The Supreme Court has made it clear, for example, that "the mere dissemination of ideas—no matter how offensive to good taste—on a state university campus may not be shut off in the name alone of 'conventions of decency.' " *Papish v. Board of Curators of University of Missouri,* 1973, 410 U.S. 667, 670, 93 S.Ct. 1197, 1199, 35 L.Ed.2d 618; *see also Healy v. James,* 1972, 408 U.S. 169, 92 S.Ct. 2338, 33 L.Ed.2d 266. *But see Gay Lib v. University of Missouri,* W.D.Mo.1976, 416 F.Supp. 1350 [45 L.W. 2021, 1976] (a case which, in my opinion, cannot be reconciled with *Healy*).

9. *See Erznoznik v. City of Jacksonville,* 1975, 422 U.S. 205, 95 S.Ct. 2268, 45 L.Ed.2d 125; *Cohen v. California,* 1971, 403 U.S. 15, 91 S.Ct. 1780, 29 L.Ed.2d 284. Justice Stewart's description of the motion pictures at issue in *Young v. American Mini Theatres,* 1976,—— U.S. ——,——, 96 S.Ct. 2440, 49 L.Ed.2d 310 [44 U.S.L.W. 4999, 1976 (dissenting opinion), is obviously applicable to the MGA ad:

   The kind of expression at issue here is no doubt objectionable to some, but that fact does not diminish its protected status any more than did the particular content of the "offensive" expression in *Erznoznik* . . . (display of nudity on a drive-in movie screen); *Lewis v. City of New Orleans,* 415 U.S. 130 [94 S.Ct. 970, 39 L.Ed.2d 214] (utterance of vulgar epithet); *Hess v. Indiania,* 414 U.S. 105 [94 S.Ct. 326, 38 L.Ed.2d 303] (utterance of vulgar remark);

136 FREEDOM TO PUBLISH

10. *Papish* ... (indecent remarks in campus newspaper); *Cohen* ... (wearing of clothing inscribed with a vulgar remark); *Brandenburg* ... (utterance of racial slurs); or *Kingsley Pictures Corp* v. *Regents,* 360 U.S. 684 [79 S.Ct. 1362, 3 L.Ed.2d 1512] (alluring portrayal of adultery as proper behavior).
10. "[T]here is no Constitutional value in false statements of fact." *Gertz* v. *Robert Welch, Inc.,* 1974, 418 U.S. 323, 340, 94 S.Ct. 2997, 3007, 41 L.Ed.2d 789; 805; *cf. New York Times* v. *Sullivan,* 1964, 376 U.S. 254, 84 S.Ct. 710, 11 L.Ed.2d 686.
11. *See Miller* v. *California,* 1973, 413 U.S. 15, 93 S.Ct. 2607, 37 L.Ed.2d 419; *Roth* v. *United States,* 1957, 354 U.S. 476, 77 S.Ct. 1304, 1 L.Ed.2d 1498. *Cf. Young* v. *American Mini Theatres, Inc.,*——U.S.——, 96 S.Ct. 2440, 49 L.Ed.2d 310 [44 U.S.L.W. 4999, 1976], discussed *infra* at note [44]; *Ginsberg* v. *New York,* 1968, 390 U.S. 629, 88 S.Ct. 1274, 20 L.Ed.2d 195 (upholding conviction for selling to minor magazines which were concededly not "obscene" if shown to adults).
12. Communications "which by their very utterance inflict injury" are Constitutionally unprotected. *Chaplinsky* v. *New Hampshire,* 1942, 315 U.S. 568, 572, 62 S.Ct. 766, 769, 86 L.Ed. 1031.
13. I assume that the majority implicitly has held this finding by the trial court to be clearly erroneous.
14. *See* Kalven, "The Concept of the Public Forum: *Cox* v. *Louisiana,*" 1965 *Sup.Ct.Rev.* 1; Note, "The Public Forum: Minimum Access, Equal Access, and the First Amendment," 28 *Stan.L.Rev.* 117 (1975). For an example of a court's adoption and use of the minimum access view in the context of a nontraditional public forum, see *Albany Welfare Rights Organization* v. *Wyman,* 2 Cir. 1974, 493 F.2d 1319, *cert. denied,* 1976, 419 U.S. 838, 95 S.Ct. 66, 42 L.Ed.2d 64 (absolute ban on leafleting in welfare office waiting room was unconstitutional abridgment of free speech).
15. There is right of the listener to protected speech that, in this case, coincides with the associational rights of some students. MGA asserts that some of its members are MSU students, and the amended stipulation apparently supports this. There may be other MSU students who are interested in attending MGA meetings or using MGA facilities. These and other readers of the *Reflector* have been denied information that may have been necessary or important to the full exercise of their First Amendment rights freely to associate with others. It is not sufficient to suggest that other means of communicating the existence of their organization or the time and place of their meetings remain with the MGA, for the *Reflector* may be the cheapest, easiest, and most effective means of communicating with a specific audience. Particularly on a matter as personal as sexual preference, the reader may wish to preserve his or her anonymity, and his or her receipt of a widely distributed school paper may serve this need better than, say, attendance at an MGA speech on campus.

    The guarantee to those interested in homosexuality of the right freely to associate with one another would be a hollow promise indeed unless they are also assured of equal, nondiscriminatory access to information relevant to their concerns. "[T]he central First Amendment concern remains the need to maintain free access of the public to the expression." *Young* v. *American Mini Theaters, Inc.,* 1976,——U.S.——, ——, 96 S.Ct. 2440, 2455, 49 L.Ed.2d 310 [44 U.S.L.W. 4999, 5007, 1976] (Powell, J., concurring). "[T]his Court has referred to a First Amendment right to 'receive information and ideas,' ... [F]reedom of speech 'necessarily protects the right to receive.'" *Virginia State Bd. of Pharmacy* v. *Virginia Citizens Consumer Council, Inc.* 1976,——U.S.——, ——, 96 S.Ct. 1817, 1823, 48 L.Ed.2d 346, 355.

16. *See Police Dept. of Chicago* v. *Mosley,* 1972, 408 U.S. 92, 92 S.Ct. 2286, 33 L.Ed.2d 212, and cases there cited; *Southeastern Promotions, Ltd.* v. *City of West Palm Beach,* 5 Cir. 1972, 457 F.2d 1016. *See also* Karst, "Equality as a Central Principle in the First Amendment," 43 *U.Chi.L.Rev.* 20 (1975); Kalven, *supra* note 14; Stone, "Fora Americana: Speech in Public Places," 1974 *Sup.Ct.Rev.* 233; Note, *supra* note 14. First amendment protections, of course, are fully applicable against the states through the due process clause of the Fourteenth Amendment. *See, e.g., Bigelow* v. *Virginia,* 1975, 421 U.S. 809, 811, 95 S.Ct. 2222, 44 L.Ed.2d 600.
17. *See, e. g., Grayned* v. *City of Rockford,* 1972, 408 U.S. 104, 116, 92 S.Ct. 2294, 2303, 33 L.Ed.2d 222, 232; *Kovacs* v. *Cooper,* 1949, 336 U.S. 77, 85–87, 69 S.Ct. 448, 452–454, 93 L.Ed. 513, 521–522.
18. The result in *Lehman* v. *City of Shaker Heights,* 1974, 418 U.S. 298, 94 S.Ct. 2714, 41 L.Ed.2d 770, seems to indicate a departure from the principle stated in text in that the Court there upheld a city transit system's refusal to permit political advertising within its vehicles, despite the acceptance of commercial ads by the transit system. A plurality opinion, for various reasons related to a city's operation of a bus system, tested the ordinance under a weak "rational relationship" standard. Justice Douglas' critical fifth vote, however, was placed solely on a concern for the "captive audience" in the city vehicles and he vehemently rejected any justification for the city's policy based on the content of the advertising messages. *Id.* at 304–309, 94 S.Ct. at 2717–20, 41 L.Ed. at 777–780.

    The author of the *Lehman* plurality opinion (Justice Blackman) apparently now regards the case as having turned on the captive audience concern. *See Southeastern Promotions, Ltd.* v. *Conrad,* 1975, 420 U.S. 546, 555, 95 S.Ct. 1239, 1245, 43 L.Ed.2d 448. Indeed, speaking for a majority of the Court, Justice Blackmun has approved the *Lehman* dissenters' rejection of any simplistic distinction between commercial and political advertising for purposes of the First Amendment. *See Virginia State Bd. of Pharmacy* v. *Virginia Citizens Consumer Council,* 1976,——U.S.——, —— n. 16, 96 S.Ct. 1817, 1824 n.16, 48 L.Ed.2d 346, 356 n.16.

    Nothing in the case before us suggests any "captive audience" problem.

19. This seems axiomatic from *Mosley*. (The implication of the "special reasons" portion of the majority opinion in this case is that the statement of law in the text is far from being "quite clear." With respect, I can only submit again that I think the majority is clearly wrong.)

    Part III of the plurality opinion in *Young* v. *American Mini Theatres, Inc.,* 1976,——U.S.——, ——, 96 S.Ct. 2440, 49 L.Ed.2d 310 [44 U.S.L.W. 4999, 1976] suggests that *Mosley's* statement on the prohibition of content discrimination should be read only in light of *Mosley's* facts (involving an ordinance permitting labor picketing near a school but forbidding picketing on other issues). Justice Powell's fifth vote, however, was needed for the result in *Young*(upholding a zoning ordinance regulating locations of purveyors of "adult" but non-obscene materials), and he explicitly disapproved of Part III of the plurality opinion. Id. at ——, n.1, 96 S.Ct. 2440 [44 U.S.L.W. at 5006 n.1]. The four dissenters apparently would read *Mosley* for all it seems to say. *Id.*——U.S. at ——& n.2, 96 S.Ct. 2440 [44 U.S.L.W. at 5009 & n.2]. In these circumstances, I believe that for "equal access" purposes *Young* should be read as limited to the municipal zoning concerns expressed in Justice Powell's concurrence. " ... [T]his situation is not analogous to cases involving expression in public forums or to those involving individual expression or, indeed, to any other prior case...." Id. at ——, 96 S.Ct. at 2455 [44 U.S.L.W. at 5007] (Powell, J., concurring).

20. I will discuss in text *infra* the types of restrictions which might be permissable.

21. The Supreme Court has never passed on a claim of equal access to a state publication. The suggestion that the Court would recognize the rights found in *Lee, Zucker* and *Radical Lawyers* is not undermined by, and indeed receives implicit support from, *Columbia Broadcasting System* v. *Democratic National Committee,* 1973, 412 U.S. 94, 93 S.Ct. 2080, 36 L.Ed.2d 772. This complex case prompted six opinions, and its result—network broadcasters are not required to accept paid political advertising—must be seen as resting at least in part on a feeling that the private broadcasters were not the government for First Amendment purposes.

Arguably, the Court alternatively reached the same result, 5–4, even under the assumption that the broadcasters were engaged in governmental action. This latter holding, I think, must be seen as narrowly limited to the unique characteristics of the regulated broadcast industry. *See Red Lion Broadcasting Co.*v. *FCC, 1969, 395 U.S. 367, 89 S.Ct. 1794, 23 L.Ed.2d 371;* Note, "The Supreme Court, 1972 Term," 87 Harv.L.Rev. 57, 175 (1973). Compare *Red Lion* with *Tornillo, supra* note 13. See also *Mink* v. *Radio Station WHAR,* 1976 [FCC No. 76–529, 44 L.W. 2584, June 8, 1976].

Several statements by individual Justices in *CBS* seem to indicate that if governmental action were found, full rights of equal access should apply. For example, the Chief Justice stated:

Were we to read the First Amendment to spell out governmental action in the circumstances presented here, few licensee decisions on the content of broadcasts or the processes of editorial evaluation would escape constitutional scrutiny.

412 U.S. at 120, 93 S.Ct. at 2095, 36 L.Ed.2d at 793.

Justice Douglas rejected the notion that the broadcasters engaged in governmental action. He speculated on the effect of a contrary finding as follows:

If these cases involved [the Corporation for Public Broadcasting], we would have a situation comparable to that in which the United States owns and manages a prestigious newspaper like the New York Times, Washington Post, and Sacramento Bee. The Government as owner and manager would not, as I see it, be free to pick and choose such news items as it desired. For by the First Amendment it may not censor or enact or enforce any other "law" abridging freedom of the press. Politics, ideological slants, rightist or leftist tendencies could play no part in its design of programs ... More specifically, the programs tendered by the respondents in the present cases could not then be turned down.

Id. at 149–50, 93 S.Ct. at 2109–10, 36 L.Ed.2d at 810.

As will be seen in my later discussion of the scope of the right to access, the scope of the right envisioned by Justice Douglas is broader than that which I would find in relation to student publications.

Justice Brennan, joined by Justice Marshall, dissented in *CBS.* They felt that broadcast licensees satisfied state-action criteria, and thus they would have applied the public forum doctrine:

... [T]here can be no doubt that the broadcast frequencies allotted to the various radio and television licensees constitute appropriate "forums" for the discussion of controversial issues of public importance. Indeed, unlike the streets, parks, public libraries and other "forums" that we have held to be appropriate for the exercise of First Amendment rights, the broadcast media are dedicated *specifically* to communication. And, since the expression of ideas—whether political, commercial, musical or otherwise—is the exclusive purpose of the broadcast spectrum, it seems clear that the adoption of a limited scheme of editorial advertising would in no sense divert that spectrum from its intended use.

Id. at 194–95, 93 S.Ct. at 2132–33, 36 L.Ed.2d at 836.

22. *Cf. Pittsburgh Press Co.* v. *Pittsburgh Comm'n on Human Relations,* 1973, 413 U.S. 376, 391, 93 S.Ct. 2553, 2562, 37 L.Ed.2d 669, 680:

[W]e affirm unequivocally the protection afforded to editorial judgment and to the free expression of views on these and other issues, however controversial.

23. For a consideration of the relationship between the fund supporting a student newspaper and the state in a very different context (the Eleventh Amendment), see *Schiff* v. *Williams,* 5 Cir. 1975, 519 F.2d 257. *Cf. Smith* v. *Doehler Metal Furniture Co.,* 1943, 195 Miss. 538, 15 So.2d 421; *Coleman* v. *Whipple,* 1941, 191 Miss. 287, 2 So.2d 566.

24. *See* Karst, *supra* note 16, at 46–47 & n. 137. *Cf. Joyner* v. *Whiting,* 4 Cir. 1972, 477 F.2d 456, 462–63 (question discussed but not decided); *Zucker* v. *Panitz,*S.D.N.Y.1969, 299 F.Supp. 102, 105 n. 4:

Different policy considerations govern whether a privately owned newspaper has affirmative duty to grant access to its pages, and whether a school newspaper has such a duty. For instance, there would be involved the thorny issue of finding state action, a problem which does not exist regarding a school newspaper.

25. The argument might be made that the stipulated funding arrangement in itself is enough upon which to base a state action finding. Appellants ask only for a remand on this issue, however. If facts were found on remand to establish public perception of the *Reflector* as the official campus newspaper, the state action determination could be made with more confidence.

26. "It can hardly be argued that either students or teachers shed their constitutional rights to freedom of speech or expression at the schoolhouse gate." *Tinker*v. *Des Moines Indep. School Dist.,* 1969 393 U.S. 503, 506, 89 S.Ct. 733, 736, 21 L.Ed.2d 731, 737.

27. 1973, 476 F.2d 570, aff'd. as modified,1974, 489 F.2d 225 (en banc).
28. 1973, 477 F.2d 456.
29. The dissent from the *en banc* court's decision stressed the narrowness of the issues presented in *Bazaar*— whether the university must appear to have sponsored the offending publication. The dissent also noted that the university had admitted that it could not censor the student newspaper. 489 F.2d at 226–28. *Cf. Schiff* v. *Williams,* 5 Cir. 1975, 519 F.2d 257, 263 (Gee, J., specially concurring) (the *Bazaar* panel's view of the law was "scarcely unprecedented.")
30. The college involved in *Joyner* was predominantly black, the student newspaper staff was all black, and the offending editorials were "black power" in tone.
31. The location in the newspaper of guest columns and letters to the editor, as well as the perception that more of each may be submitted than editors care to print, supports an assumption that the editors at least choose what issues are to be discussed, if not what statements are to be made. Again, I do not consider whether a demand for "minimum access" might be strengthened by a student newspaper's regular acceptance of letters to the editor.
32. In deciding whether a public facility should be considered to be a public forum, we have used the following standard:
    > The crucial query is whether or not the particular public facility involved in this litigation constitutes an appropriate place for the exercise of First Amendment rights. In order to answer this issue we consider the following factors relevant:
    > "does the character of the place, the pattern of usual activity, the nature of its essential purpose and the population who take advantage of the general invitation extended make it an appropriate place for communication of views on issues of political and social significance."

    Wolin v. *Port of New York Authority,* 2 Cir. 1968, 392 F.2d 83, 89, cert. denied, 393 U.S. 940, 89 S.Ct. 290, 21 L.Ed.2d 275.
    Southeastern Promotions, Ltd. v. *City of West Palm Beach,* 5 Cir. 1972, 457 F.2d 1016, 1019.
33. This case could perhaps be analogized to the situation of a large bulletin board centrally located in the student union building. Suppose school officials have left control of the board to a student group selected by other students. Suppose these students then determine that the major portion of the board is to be given over to thematic displays on selected topics of student interest, to be designed by the elected student group each week. Suppose further that the remainder of the board is to be used by anyone wishing to present a message of any kind to students generally. Perhaps the MGA could not require that it be allowed to present a display in the major portion of the board, but I doubt that the MGA could constitutionally be prohibited from posting an announcement on the "open forum" section of the bulletin board.
34. *Cf. Bazaar* v. *Fortune,* 5 Cir. 1974, 489 F.2d 225 (en banc).
35. An important modification on any right of access is the notion that certain categories of speech are constitutionally valueless, and thus may be legitimately suppressed on the basis of content. This "two-level" theory of speech has been subject to much criticism, *see, e. g.,* Karst, *supra* note 16, at 31 ("The two-level theory is radically inconsistent with the principle of equal liberty of expression."); Kalven, "The Metaphysics of the Law of Obscenity," 1960 *Sup.Ct.Rev.* 1, 19, but the recent Supreme Court opinions cited in notes 6 through 12 indicate that the two-level theory is still with us. As demonstrated at the outset of this opinion, the MGA ad could not possibly be placed in any of the unprotected groups.
36. *See* Comment, "The Public School as Public Forum," 54 *Tex.L.Rev.* 90, 118–19 (1975). The state cannot, of course, arbitrarily discriminate in the recognition and access rights given to various student groups. *See Healy* v. *James,*1972, 408 U.S. 169, 92 S.Ct. 2338, 33 L.Ed.2d 266; *Gay Students Organization* v. *Bonner,* 1 Cir. 1974, 509 F.2d 652. *But see Gay Lib* v. *University of Missouri,* W.D.Mo.1976, 1350 F.Supp. 416 [45 L.W. 2021, June 29, 1976].
37. *Cf. Markham Advertising Co.* v. *State,* 1968, 73 Wash.2d 405, 439 P.2d 248, *appeal dismissed for want of a substantial federal question,* 1969, 393 U.S. 316, 89 S.Ct. 553, 21 L.Ed.2d 512 (state statute may permit highway billboards to advertise businesses located in the neighborhood but not elsewhere).

    Even broadly drawn and superficially content-neutral source restrictions may produce unjustifiable content discrimination. If the Radical Lawyer's Caucus can demand and acquire access to the State Bar Journal, why cannot the Radical Doctor's Caucus do the same?

    For a discussion of a "limited public forum" (limited according to general subject matter),*see Toward a Gayer Bicentennial Committee* v. *Rhode Island Bicentennial Foundation,* D.R.I. 1976, 417 F.Supp. 632 [44 L.W. 2577, June 9, 1976].
38. *See* A. Meiklejohn, Free Speech and Its Relation to Self-Government 25 (1948) ("What is essential is not that everyone shall speak, but that everything worth saying shall be said."); Karst, *supra* note 16, at 39–41 (criticizing Meiklejohn's position).
39. The scope of any "reasonable fee" restriction need not be closely marked in this case. The MGA has alleged in effect that the *Reflector* provided both a paid and an unpaid public forum. If both in its paid advertising and its free announcements the *Reflector* regularly published submissions from groups similar in form to the MGA, the MGA's claim might well be upheld as to both sections of the paper.

    One danger in such a limitation on the right of access, of course, is that if the fee is too high, the right becomes one available only to the wealthy. This was a concern expressed in the Chief Justice's opinion in *CBS,* discussed in note 21, *supra.*
40. *See Southeastern Promotions,* Ltd. v. *Conrad,* 1975, 420 U.S. 546, 95 S.Ct. 1239, 43 L.Ed.2d 448; *Southeastern Promotion, Ltd.* v. *City of West Palm Beach,* 5 Cir. 1972, 457 F.2d 1016. Of course, explicit regulations may reveal that the state is clearly engaged in content discrimination, but, in any event, judicial review will have been facilitated. *See Erznoznik* v. *City of Jacksonville,* 1975, 422 U.S. 205, 95 S.Ct. 2268, 45 L.Ed.2d 125; *Police Dep't of Chicago* v. *Mosley,* 1972, 408 U.S. 92, 92 S.Ct. 2286, 33 L.Ed.2d 212. *But see Young* v. *American Mini Theaters, Inc.,* 1976, ——U.S.——, 96 S.Ct. 2440, 49 L.Ed.2d 310 [44 U.S.L.W. 4999 1976].
41. One other aspect of this case, closely related to the

"state action" issue discussed above, would be troubling on remand. Bill Goudelock, the former studenteditor of the *Reflector* and named defendant, has moved on to other endeavors. The plaintiffs have not attempted to substitute the successor editors as defendants in their official capacity. Arguably, then, the MSU officials are the only defendants against whom effective relief could be ordered. Are school officials to be ordered to keep hands off any decision made by student editors of student publications *except* when the decision is to refuse to publish some (but not all) advertisements from local groups, and in the excepted case are the officials to be ordered to compel the publication of all such ads? The result is not untenable, but it does sound a little strange. *Cf. Lee* v. *Board of Regents,* 7 Cir. 1971, 441 F.2d 1257. Declaratory relief would presumably be available against all defendants.

42. *See* Klaven *supra* note 14.

BOTH a United States District Court in Virginia and the United States Court of Appeals, Fourth Circuit, decide for high school students who had brought action against school officials who had prohibited the publication in the school newspaper of an article entitled "Sexually Active Students Fail to Use Contraception." The short, three paragraph Court of Appeals' opinion ends with the following sentence: "Because we conclude that the District Court's findings are substantially supported by both the evidence and the law, we affirm for the reasons stated in its opinion." Gambino v. *Fairfax City School Bd.*, 564 F.2d 157 (1977)] Since the Court of Appeals affirmed "for the reasons stated in" the District Court's opinion and since the arguments are not as fully developed in the Court of Appeals' opinion as in the District Court's, the latter is reprinted here. In deciding for the students, the District Court declared: "Having determined that *The Farm News* is entitled to the First Amendment protection afforded a public forum, that the circumstances at Hayfield [Secondary School] do not justify application of the 'captive audience' theory, and that publication of the proposed article cannot be suppressed solely because its subject matter does not accord with the School Board's notion of appropriate course content, the Court finds that the application of the regulations under which the defendants acted in this instance was constitutionally invalid."

Gambino v. *Fairfax Cty. Sch. Bd.*, 429 F.Supp. 731 (1977)

MEMORANDUM OPINION AND ORDER

Albert V. Bryan, Jr., District Judge.

This action was brought pursuant to 42 U.S.C. § 1983 and 28 U.S.C. § 1343 to enjoin the defendant from prohibiting the publication of an article entitled "Sexually Active Students Fail to Use Contraception" in *The Farm News,* a newspaper published in the Hayfield Secondary School (Hayfield). Stipulations of Fact have been filed and the issues were briefed and orally argued to the Court on February 15, 1977. Both parties commendably have resolved any factual dispute (with one possible exception discussed below) and agree that there are no material facts not covered by the Stipulations which the Court adopts as its findings of fact.

Hayfield is governed by the Fairfax County School Board (the School Board), an agency of the Commonwealth of Virginia. On August 11, 1976 the School Board issued notice 6130 which prohibited the schools from offering sex education until a decision was reached on a proposed program (Stipulations of Fact, Appendix 4). The article in question here was submitted for publication on November 22, 1976, while the School Board's notice was in effect. Pursuant to a prior agreement regarding potentially controversial material, this article was submitted to the principal, Doris Torrice, for review. Perceiving that portions of the submission containing information on contraceptives, apparently viewed apart from those portions incorporating results obtained from a canvass of Hayfield student attitudes toward birth control, violated notice 6130, she ordered plaintiffs not to publish it as written. Although plaintiffs were given the option of publishing the article with the objectionable passages excised, they chose to insist on printing all or none of the piece.

Ms. Torrice's decision was reviewed and upheld by the Advisory Board on Student Expression based upon a reading of Section 2, Chapter II of Policy 2330.1, Responsibilities and Rights—Secondary School Students (RR–SSS) (Stipulations of Fact,

Appendices 4 and 8). The relevant language of that provision of RR–SSS is as follows:

> The student activity program is an integral part of the total educational offering for Fairfax Public Schools. As such, it is subject to the same administrative controls as other educational programs. . . . All student activities . . . shall meet the following guidelines: . . . B. Student activites shall relate generally to the school program and not interfere with school operation.

The Farm News, being a school publication, is a student activity.

The action of the Advisory Board was sustained by the Division Superintendent of the Fairfax County Public Schools and by the School Board. A few days before hearing plaintiffs' appeal, the School Board adopted Regulation 6131 approving a sex education program but specifically proscribing birth control as a subject of that program (Stipulations of Fact, Appendix 6(B)).

As noted above, *The Farm News* is a student activity. Some staff members are enrolled in Journalism and receive academic credit for their work on the paper (Stipulations of Fact, Appendix 1). Other staff members work on the paper as an extracurricular activity. The paper is written and edited in the school during school hours and at the homes of the participants. Revenues are generated from advertising, allocations by the School Board, sales of individual issues, and student subscriptions. This latter source involves a tie-in with the school yearbook, i.e., no student may receive the yearbook unless he also subscribes to the newspaper. In the year 1975–76 (which the Court treats as typical) those sources yielded the following amounts:

Advertising	$ 783.48
School Board allocation	1,000.00
Individual sales	148.58
Subscription	1,852.00

Additionally, the faculty advisor provided to supervise the paper was paid a salary supplement of $1,225.00. Copies of the newspaper usually are distributed to student subscribers in homeroom.

As the Court views it, this case turns upon one issue—whether *The Farm News* is a publication protected by the First Amendment. The authority of the School Board to determine course content in the school curriculum is not questioned. Nor is there any contention that the content of the article would fall outside the limits of First Amendment freedom if the newspaper otherwise is protected. In fact, upon an actual reading of the article, the Court is surprised at its innocuousness and that it could spawn the controversy at hand.[1] Nevertheless, the defendants have perceived sufficient danger in the publication to warrant judicial resolution of the problem. Defendants also recognize that if the newspaper is found to be a First Amendment forum the regulations pursuant to which this suppression was undertaken are open to serious question under the principles established in *Nitzberg* v. *Parks,* 525 F.2d 378 (4th Cir. 1975); *Baughman* v. *Freienmuth,* 478 F.2d 1345 (4th Cir. 1973); and *Quarterman* v. *Byrd,* 453 F.2d 54 (4th Cir. 1971).

The defendants rely on the contention that *The Farm News* is not a public forum entitled to First Amendment protection. They argue that the newspaper is essentially an "in-house" organ of the school system, or alternatively that the students in Hayfield are a "captive audience," rendering the publication subject to reasonable regulation.

While the state may have a particular proprietary interest in a publication that legitimately precludes it from being a vehicle for First Amendment expression, it may not foreclose constitutional scrutiny by mere labelling. *Cf. Trujillo* v. *Love,* 322 F.Supp. 1266 (D.Colo.1971). Once a publication is determined to be in substance a free speech forum, constitutional protections attach and the state may restrict the content of that instrument only in accordance with First Amendment dictates.

The extent of state involvement in providing funding and facilities for *The Farm News* does not determine whether First Amendment rights are applicable. The language of *Antonelli* v. *Hammond,* in 308 F.Supp. 1329 (D.Mass.1970), is persuasive.

> We are well beyond the belief that any manner of state regulation is permissible simply because it involves an activity which is a part of the university structure and is financed with funds controlled by the administration. The state is not necessarily the unrestrained master of what it creates and fosters.

Id. at 1337; *accord, Bazaar* v. *Fortune,* 476 F.2d 570, 574–75 (5th Cir.), *modified en banc,* 5 Cir., 489 F.2d 225 (1973) (per curiam), *cert. denied,* 416 U.S. 995, 94 S.Ct. 2409, 40 L.Ed.2d 774 (1974). *See Joyner* v. *Whiting,* 477 F.2d 456, 460 (4th Cir. 1973).

The defendants urge that this principle is inapposite because the cited decisions have arisen out of the college environment. They point out, and the Court does not dispute, that the "First Amendment rights of children are not 'co-extensive with those of adults.'" *Quarterman, supra* 453 F.2d at 58, *quoting Tinker* v. *Des Moines Ind. Comm. Sch. Dist.,* 393 U.S. 503, 515, 89 S.Ct. 733, 21 L.Ed.2d 731 (1969) (Stewart, J., concurring). *Cf. Ginsberg* v. *New York,* 390 U.S. 629, 88 S.Ct. 1274, 20 L.Ed.2d 195 (1968). Further, the defendants assert the illogic of applying the First Amendment to a high school newspaper, conjuring up visions of irresponsible and uncontrollable publication.

There are, however, two distinctions that invalidate these objections. While the scope of constitutional freedom may vary with the nature of the environment and the maturity of the individuals affected, the considerations governing the applicability of First Amendment analysis in the first instance do not change. Either the First Amendment is operative, or it is not. And if it is applicable, only then does the distinction between the *extent* to which speech is protected in colleges and in high schools become significant.[2]

Defendants' fears of irresponsible journalism are met first by the fact that no evidence of it has surfaced in the past or in the article here in question, nor has there been any demonstrated likelihood of it in the future. More significantly, defendants have failed to appreciate the very real distinction between what a private citizen and the state constitutionally may do with regard to limiting otherwise protected speech. *See Bazaar, supra* 476 F.2d at 574. The First Amendment mandate is directed toward state action, not private. As no contention has been made that the student editorial board of *The Farm News* acts as an agent of the state, the argument that the newspaper is powerless to control the content of its own publication is without merit. Irresponsible journalism may occur at some point in the future, but speculation is not a proper consideration in the decision of the case presently before the Court.

Turning to the substantive question of whether *The Farm News* was established as a vehicle for expression, the Court finds, based upon the language in the RR–SSS concerning publications (Stipulations of Fact, Appendix 8 at 11–12) and upon review of articles published in the past by the newspaper without objection (Stipulations of Fact, Appendix 1(A)) that this instrument was conceived, established, and operated as a conduit for student expression on a wide variety of topics. It falls clearly within the parameters of the First Amendment.

The defendants have suggested, however, that the circumstances under which the newspaper is produced require an application of the "captive audience" principle most recently employed by the Supreme Court in Lehman v. *City of Shaker Heights,* 418 U.S. 298, 94 S.Ct. 2714, 41 L.Ed.2d 770 (1974). There the Court focused upon the lack of free choice which effectively compelled the users of the city transit system to receive the messages displayed on the system's vehicles, and determined that no public forum existed. Reliance was placed upon *Packer Corp.* v. *Utah,* 285 U.S. 105, 52 S.Ct. 273, 76 L.Ed. 643 (1932), where Justice Brandeis observed that communication of this sort is "constantly before the eyes of observers on the streets and in street cars to be seen without the exercise of choice or volition on their part." *Id.* at 110, 52 S.Ct. at 274. But Justice Brandeis also distinguished "the case of newspapers and magazines [where] there must be some seeking by the one who is to see and read the advertisement." *Id.* From that standpoint, defendants' application of the "captive audience" concept appears untenable.

The defendants have asserted, however, that the subscription tie-in with the yearbook, the distribution in home rooms, the official status of the newspaper, and peer pressure, coupled with mandatory attendance all combine to compel the student body's exposure to the contents of *The Farm News*. The Court is not persuaded that these circumstances establish the kind of captive audience that concerned the *Lehman* court. No substantive distinction can be drawn between the relative lack of choice in exposure to the communication in this case and that in *Tinker.* If anything, the students of Hayfield are less captive because they must act affirmatively to pick up the newspaper. In *Tinker* the non-protesting students were required to avert their eyes to avoid the message.

Katz v. *McAulay,* 438 F.2d 1058 (2d Cir. 1971), *cert. denied,* 405 U.S. 933, 92 S.Ct. 930, 30 L.Ed.2d 809 (1972), which the defendants cite as an application of the captive audience principle to the high school milieu, is not to the contrary. There the court was considering an interlocutory appeal from a denial of a prelimary injunction. The rules under which the school authorities acted appeared sufficiently precise to render plaintiffs' probability of success short of the threshold beyond which denial of a preliminary injunction becomes an abuse of discretion. The significance of the captive nature of the student audience to the Court was its tendency to amplify conduct to a level of material and substantial disruption. The Court did not hold, nor could it have held consistent with *Tinker,* that First Amendment rights in the school were extinguished by the mere fact of compulsory attendance.

Finally defendants argue that to allow the students to publish this article would permit them to override the decision of the School Board not to include birth control in the sex education curriculum. As noted above, the Court does not question the authority of the School Board to prescribe course content. Further, while even under principles of liberal construction a considerable effort is required to find the questioned portions of the article instructional, the Court assumes that the article does contain information which, if it appeared in material used in a sex education course, would contravene the School Board's policy.

A corollary of the finding that *The Farm News* was established as a vehicle for First Amendment expression and not as an official publication is that the newspaper cannot be construed objectively as an integral part of the curriculum offered at Hayfield. *Cf. Bayer v. Kinzler*, 383 F.Supp. 1164 (E.D.N.Y.1974), *aff'd. without opinion*, 515 F.2d 504 (2d Cir. 1975). Rather, it occupies a position more akin to the school library where more extensive and explicit information on birth control philosophy and methodology is available. (Stipulations of Fact, Appendix 7). In either place, the material is not suppressible by reason of its objectionability to the sensibilities of the School Board or its constituents. *See Minarcini v. Strongsville City School Dist., 541 F.2d 577 (6th Cir. 1976); Joyner, supra.* Therefore, because the newspaper is not in reality a part of the curriculum of the school, and because it is entitled to First Amendment protection, the power of the School Board to regulate course content will not support its action in this case.

Having determined that *The Farm News* is entitled to the First Amendment protection afforded a public forum, that the circumstances at Hayfield do not justify application of the "captive audience" theory, and that publication of the proposed article cannot be suppressed solely because its subject matter does not accord with the School Board's notion of appropriate course content, the Court finds that the application of the regulations under which the defendants acted in this instance was constitutionally invalid. The RR–SSS lacks the detailed criteria required by the line of Fourth Circuit decisions defining the permissible regulation of protected speech in high schools: *Quarterman, Baughman,* and *Nitzberg, supra.* The Court declines, however, to declare the regulations facially invalid and limits its holding solely to the application of those regulations to prohibit publication in *The Farm News* of any portion of the article "Sexually Active Students Fail to Use Contraception."

Accordingly the plaintiffs are entitled to an injunction prohibiting the defendants, or those acting in concert with them, from banning the publication in *The Farm News* of those portions of the article which were found objectionable.

The Court further finds that the plaintiffs are the prevailing party within the meaning of the Civil Rights Attorney's Fees Awards Act of 1976, Pub.L.No.94–559 (Oct. 19, 1976), and are entitled to an award of reasonable attorney's fees.

Plaintiffs should prepare a decree awarding the injunction mentioned above. The decree also should award the plaintiffs their costs including attorney's fees. If the amount of the latter cannot be agreed upon, the Court will fix those fees. The decree should be presented for entry after submission to counsel for the defendants for approval as to form. In the event of any disagreement as to form or as to the amount of attorney's fees, these matters should be noticed promptly for hearing.

It is so ordered.

NOTES

1. A controversy which, given the normal curiosity and ingenuity of youth, has assured that copies of the offending article now have been secured by many if not most of the students sought to be protected.
2. While it was stipulated that Hayfield's enrollment includes grades seven through twelve, there was some uncertainty between the parties at argument as to the lower grades' access to the paper. From the representations of plaintiff's counsel which were not contested by defendants, it appears that the newspaper is not distributed to the seventh and eighth grades in homeroom; that the tie-in with the yearbook is not imposed at that level; that students in these lower grades may purchase individual copies of *The Farm News;* that there is no prohibition against transmittal of copies to younger students by older; and that the seventh and eighth grades are physically isolated in the school building (with areas of common use including the library). These circumstances indicate that restriction of formal distribution of *The Farm News* to those students would not be impracticable.

The youth of the audience is not determinative of the existence *vel non* of First Amendment protection, however. The immaturity of readers may necessitate limiting constitutional freedom, but any such limitation would require an examination of the content of the matter to be published and a balancing of the impact of that content against the state's interest measured by reference to constitutionally valid standards. As the defendants here stake their position on the inapplicability of the First Amendment, the Court does not need to define the boundaries of its protection in terms of the content of this article except insofar as the regulatory scheme may or may not be adequate to support the defendants' action. Consistent with their contention, the defendants introduced no evidence that the information in the article would be harmful to students in any of the age groups at Hayfield.

A United States District Court in Virginia decides against school officials who had suspended a high school student after he continued distributing, over the objection of the principal, an "underground" newspaper at Washington Lee High School in Arlington, Virginia. In enjoining the school officials from disciplining the student, the District Court declared: "The United States Court of Appeals for the Fourth Circuit has addressed the issue of free press in a high school setting on several occasions. In general, school regulations which act as a prior restraint on the distribution of student literature are constitutionally permissible *only* where the substantive justifications for such restraint are precisely defined and the procedures for making these determinations and the review of any decision to restrain distribution are adequate.... In this case, both the substantive standards and procedural safeguards are facially inadequate." The school regulations pertaining to the distribtion of literature at the high school, said the Court, did not "pass the constitutional muster" and were "infected with blatant constitutional defects of both a substantive and procedural nature."

Liebner v. *Sharbaugh,* 429 F.Supp. 744 (1977)

MEMORANDUM

MERHIGE, District Judge.

Plaintiff, a minor who sues by his next friend, is a student at Washington Lee High School, Arlington, Virginia who brings this action under 42 U.S.C. § 1983 to challenge the constitutionality of certain school regulations pertaining to the distribution of literature in the high school. Plaintiff seeks declaratory, monetary and injunctive relief. The defendants include the principal of Washington Lee High School, the Superintendent of Schools for Arlington County, Virginia, and the individual members of the School Board of that County. The matter comes before the Court on the plaintiff's motion for a temporary restraining order. Counsel have argued their respective positions and the matter is ripe for determination.

The sworn complaint and affidavits submitted by the parties reflect the following: The plaintiff is a junior at Washington Lee High School, a public school in Arlington County, Virginia. On October 17, 1976, the plaintiff published and sold (during free periods outside the classroom) the first issue of an "underground" newspaper titled the *Green Orange*. Pursuant to school policy, plaintiff submitted the newspaper to the school principal for his approval. The principal, Dr. Sharbaugh, orally forbade further distribution of the publication and ordered the confiscation of all distributed issues. The second issue of the paper was circulated in early November of 1976. Dr. Sharbaugh told the plaintiff to discontinue distribution of the newspaper upon threat of suspension. On Friday, November 5, the plaintiff sold an issue of the paper at a school football game. The following Monday the plaintiff was suspended. In the notification letter sent to the parents of the plaintiff, Dr. Sharbaugh gave the following reasons for the suspension: (1) the newspaper was distributed without receiving prior approval as required by the Student Responsibility and Rights Policy of Arlington County; (2) the publication did not identify the author as required by the school rules: and (3) the newspaper was of questionable taste, decency, and journalistic standards. On protesting the lack of a hearing prior to being suspended, the plaintiff was advised that the two oral warnings given by Dr. Sharbaugh constituted whatever "hearing" due process might mandate. On the condition that the plaintiff agree to refrain from distributing the paper, he was readmitted to school on November 15, 1976.

Counsel for the plaintiff has described the *Green Orange* as "a showcase of bad taste." Affidavits submitted by the defendant Sharbaugh and two students at Washington Lee High School attest that in their opinions, the content of the paper might offend certain segments of the student population—particularly racial minorities—and lead to acts of physical confrontation.

The plaintiff presently petitions the Court to enjoin the defendants from prohibiting the distribution of the *Green Orange* by threats of disciplinary measures. At the heart of this controversy are the substantive rules and procedures pertaining to distribution of student publications on campus. A student desiring to distribute written material must submit a copy of the text to the school principal at least one school day prior to the day of intended distribution. The material itself "should conform to journalistic standards of accuracy, taste, and decency maintained by the newspapers of general circulation in Arlington; it shall not contain obscenity, incitements to crime, material in violation of law or lawful regulation, or libelous material."[1] Should a principal refuse to permit the distribution of the submitted material, the student may appeal to the Director of School and Community Activities. The Director must reply to the appeal within one week. An adverse decision by the Director may be appealed to the Superintendent of Schools who must act within one week of receiving any such appeal. A complainant may ultimately have the decision reviewed by the School Board at its then next regular meeting. The student may submit additional materials for the consideration of the School Board but no speakers will be heard on the matter unless the Board so directs.[2]

In considering whether to grant a temporary restraining order, the Court must take into account the threat of immediate irreparable harm to the plaintiff should injunctive relief be denied; the injury to other parties should the injunction issue; the probabilities that the plaintiff will succeed on the merits; any interest of the public. *Cf. Conservation Council of North Carolina v. Costanzo*, 505 F.2d 498, 507 (4th Cir. 1974); *Long v. Robinson*, 432 F.2d 977, 979 (4th Cir. 1970).

The pleadings and affidavits submitted to date indicate to the Court's satisfaction that the plaintiff is likely to prevail on the merits of this controversy. The United States Court of Appeals for the Fourth Circuit has addressed the issue of free press in a high school setting on several occasions. In general, school regulations which act as a prior restraint on the distribution of student literature are constitutionally permissible *only* where the substantive justifications for such restraint are precisely defined and the procedures for making these determinations and the review of any decision to restrain distribution are adequate. *Nitzberg v. Parks*, 525 F.2d 378 (4th Cir. 1975); *Baughman v. Freienmuth*, 478 F.2d 1345 (4th Cir. 1973); *Quarterman v. Byrd*, 453 F.2d 54 (4th Cir. 1971). In this case, both the substantive standards and procedural safeguards are facially inadequate. Student publications must conform to the "journalistic standards of accuracy, taste, and decency maintained by the newspapers of general circulation in Arlington..." This 'standard' represents a monument to vagueness. There are no guidelines or criteria by which such levels of accuracy, taste and decency may be ascertained by either the author of literature or the reviewing principal. Indeed, this is the type of vagueness which led to the invalidation of the regulations litigated in *Quarterman v. Byrd, supra*, and *Baughman v. Freienmuth, supra*. Proscriptions against distributing obscene or libelous material do not define those terms. This, too, renders the regulation unconstitutionally vague. *See Baughman v. Freienmuth, supra*, 478 F.2d at 1348. Similarly defective are the bans against the distribution of material "in violation of law or lawful regulation" or for "incitements to crime." As noted in *Nitzberg v. Parks, supra*, 525 F.2d at 383, the directives must (1) provide sufficient guidance to students as to what may be distributed with impunity; and (2) detail the criteria by which an adminsitrator may reasonably determine whether these directives have been violated. As noted by Circuit Judge Craven, "a Regulation imposing prior restraint must be *much more precise* than a regulation imposing post-publication sanctions." *Baughman v. Freienmuth, supra*, 478 F.2d at 1349 (emphasis added). That the regulation in issue fails to meet this standard is pointedly illustrated by that portion of same which authorizes prior restraint in instances of "blatant obscenity, incitement to crime, *etc.*" (emphasis added).

Procedures contemplated under the regulations are also constitutionally defective. Several weeks may pass between the time a student submits literature for approval and the time final action is taken, if necessary, by the School Board. There is no time limit specified within which a principal must render a decision as to whether a submitted piece of literature may be distributed. An appeal of a principal's decision adverse to the student may take as much as two weeks before being considered at the then next regular meeting of the School Board. A virtually identical procedure was struck down in *Nitzberg v. Parks, supra*, 525 F.2d at 383–385. It must also be noted that at no point in the administrative process is a student guaranteed an opportunity to orally present his or her side of the issue. Such a procedure is constitutionally suspect where, as here, the distribution of material without prior approval can result in the suspension of the student. *See Nitzberg* v. *Parks, supra,* 525 F.2d at 384. *Cf. Goss* v. *Lopez,* 419 U.S. 565, 95 S.Ct. 729, 42 L.Ed.2d 725 (1975).

In short, the regulation in controversy is infected with blatant constitutional defects of both a substantive and procedural nature. The affidavits submitted by the defendants pertain to the potential disruptive impact of the distribution of the *Green Orange* would have had on Washington Lee High School in the fall of 1976. These affidavits are necessarily speculative as the potential disruption was diffused by the suppression of the newspaper. The Court must, in deciding whether to grant injunctive relief, look to the future rather than the past. Accordingly, the threat of disruption as of October-November of 1976 is of little relevance to the issue at hand. The possibility of disrupting school activities is, of course, a significant consideration. Before activity protected by the First Amendment[3] can be repressed on this basis, however, both the criteria for determining the likelihood of disruption and the process for rendering such a determination must be adequate. *Quarterman* v. *Byrd, supra.* A blanket conclusion does not pass the constitutional muster.

Having concluded that the regulations in question are facially constitutionally defective, the Court must now consider whether irreparable harm will result from the failure to issue a restraining order. The plaintiff could not represent to the Court that he would attempt to publish his paper within the then next ten days. While this mitigates his claim of immediacy, the inquiry does not stop here. As succinctly stated by Mr. Justice Clark, "that to punish, *ipsa dixit* a student who published literature which may have suffered improper prior restraint, places the student on his own peril and *the resulting chill on First Amendment activity would be intolerable." Nitzberg* v. *Parks, supra,* 525 F.2d at 384 n.5 (emphasis supplied). This Court concludes that the chilling effect of the regulations in issue constitute immediate and irreparable harm.

The issuing of a restraining order, although an interference with school policy, will not unduly burden school officials. *See Nitzberg* v. *Parks, supra,* 525 F.2d at 384. Any burdens which do arise are necessary because "we cannot permit those conditions to suppress the First Amendment rights of individual students." *Nitzberg* v. *Parks, supra,* 525 F.2d at 384. The Court's observation in this regard indicates that the public interest, indeed, is advanced by the protection and not the repression of First Amendment activity.

An appropriate order will issue.

NOTES

1. Section IIIC. Student Responsibilities and Rights, Arlington Public Schools, Arlington, Virginia provides:
C. In secondary schools the right of student groups to freedom of press, such as by posters, pamphleting, distributing newspapers or newsletters cannot be abridged, censored, or subject to prior restraint, except as provided herein. Regulations may provide for the time, location and manner of distributing such materials. These publications should conform to journalistic standards of accuracy, taste, and decency maintained by the newspapers of general circulation in Arlington; they shall not contain obscenity, incitements to crime, material in violation of law or lawful regulation, or libelous material. Any student or student group intending to distribute written material shall submit a copy of the text of such material to the school principal as soon as the text of such material is available, but in no case less than one school day prior to the day of intended distribution, without permission of the principal. Except when blatant obscenity, incitement to crime, etc., clearly justifies prior restraint, violations may be the subject of only subsequent disciplinary action. Any such material produced by a student shall bear the name of at least one student, who shall be responsible for its contents. But others directly and knowingly contributing to violation of limitations set forth above shall likewise be held answerable.

2. The grievance procedure is set forth in Section IVA of the Student Responsibilities and Rights, Arlington Public Schools, Arlington, Virginia as follows:
Any member of the school community (students, faculty, administrators and parents who may also speak and act on behalf of their children) who has been aggrieved by any action or failure to take action on the part of school personnel which is or was violative of the provisions set forth in this statement may, within ten days of the events giving rise to the complaint, complain in writing to the director of school and community activities.

Such complaint should set forth briefly but specifically the facts complained of and point out the language in this statement that is alleged to be controlling. The director receiving such a complaint shall reply in writing within one week, giving his decision on the complaint, which shall contain a summary of the facts on which the decision is based. If facts other than those set forth in the complaint are relied upon by the director, the decision shall set forth the source and reasons for reliability of those additional facts.

If the complainant remains unsatisfied, he may, within 5 days of receipt of the decision, appeal to the Superintendent of Schools by giving the director of school and community activities a written notice he wishes to appeal to the Superintendent.

The director of school and community activities will forthwith forward all papers on the matter to the Superintendent of Schools. The complainant may send to the Superintendent any additional written materials he thinks applicable.

The Superintendent will reply in writing within

one week, and the same way as is required by the director of school and community activities.

If the complainant desires to appeal the decision of the Superintendent to the School Board, he may do so within five days of the Superintendent's decision by giving the Superintendent written notice of his desire to appeal. The Superintendent shall forward copies of all papers on the matter to the School Board as one of the administrative items to be considered by the School Board at its next regular meeting. The complainant may submit such additional materials to the School Board as he desires, but no speakers will be heard on the matter unless the Board so directs.

3. The fact that the prior restraint goes to distribution rather than publication is of no consequence. *Quarterman* v. *Byrd,* 453 F.2d 54, 57 n.4 (4th Cir. 1971). Similarly, it is of no consequence that the publication was being sold rather than freely distributed. *Nitzberg* v. *Parks,* 525 F.2d 378, 383 n.4 (4th Cir. 1975).

THE United States Court of Appeals, Second Circuit, decides for school officials who had prohibited high school students from taking a survey of the sexual attitudes of students at Stuyvesant High School in New York City with the intent of publishing the results of the survey in the student publication "The Stuyvesant Voice." Writing for the majority, Judge Lumbard said: "The First Amendment right to express one's views does not include the right to importune others to respond to questions when there is reason to believe that such importuning may result in harmful consequences. Consequently where school authorities have reason to believe that harmful consequences might result to students, while they are on the school premises, from solicitation of answers to questions, then prohibition of such solicitation is not a violation of any Constitutional rights of those who seek to solicit. In sum, we conclude that the record established a substantial basis for defendants' belief that distribtuion of the questionnaire would result in significant emotional harm to a number of students throughout the Stuyvesant population."

In his dissenting opinion, Judge Mansfield declared: "Even accepting arguendo the majority's thesis to the effect that other students' rights include the right to be free of any emotional stress, defendants have failed to sustain their burden of showing that the First Amendment values in the present case are outweighed by the risk of psychological harm. The right of a newspaper to conduct a survey on a controversial topic and to publish the results represents the very quintessence of activity protected by the First Amendment. In a school environment, moreover, there is a positive value in the students' exercise of responsibilities associated with the publication of a newspaper, which gives them a greater appreciation for the true meaning and value of the Bill of Rights than they might otherwise possess."

Trachtman v. *Anker,* 563 F.2d 512 (1977)

LUMBARD, Circuit Judge:

These are cross appeals from a judgment of the Southern District, Constance Baker Motley, Judge, entered on December 16, 1976, which enjoined defendants from restraining plaintiffs' attempts to distribute a sex questionnaire to eleventh and twelfth-grade students at Stuyvesant High School in New York City and to publish the results in the student publication, *The Stuyvesant Voice.* Plaintiffs Jeff Trachtman, then a senior student at Stuyvesant and editor-in-chief of the *Voice,*[1] and his father, Gilbert M. Trachtman, appeal from so much of the court's decision that allows defendants to prohibit distribution of the questionnaire to ninth and tenth-grade students at Stuyvesant. Defendants, Chancellor of the New York City Public Schools and officials of the New York City school system, contend that the district court erred in holding that their prohibition of the distribution of the questionnaire to any students at Stuyvesant violated the First Amendment. We conclude that defendants' actions in prohibiting the proposed sexual survey did not violate any constitutional right of the plaintiffs; accordingly, the order of the district court is reversed insofar as it restrains defendants from prohibiting distribution of the questionnaire to eleventh and twelfth-grade students at

Stuyvesant.

This controversy began when Jeff Trachtman and Robert Marks, a staff member of the *Voice,* submitted a plan to survey the sexual attitudes of Stuyvesant students and publish the results in the *Voice* to the school's principal, defendant Fabricante. Initially, the plan contemplated oral interviews of a "cross section" of the student population to be conducted by a group of student researchers. Mr. Fabricante denied the students permission to conduct the survey and, on December 4, 1975, Marks wrote to defendant Gelernter, Administrator of Student Affairs, seeking approval of the project. Gelernter responded by letter, dated December 17, 1975, stating that the proposed survey could not be conducted.

The students sought review of Gelernter's decision by Chancellor Anker. By this time the focus of the proposed survey had shifted from oral interviews to a questionnaire. Thus, in their letter to Anker, dated December 24, 1975, Trachtman and Marks submitted for review a questionnaire consisting of twenty-five questions, which, they advised, was to be used as a means for obtaining information for an article on "Sexuality in Stuyvesant" to appear in the *Voice.* The questions, which the district court described as "requiring rather personal and frank information about the student's sexual attitudes, preferences, knowledge and experience," covered such topics as pre-marital sex, contraception, homosexuality, masturbation and the extent of students' "sexual experience." The questionnaire included a proposed cover letter which described the nature and purpose of the survey; it stressed the importance of honest and open answers but advised the student that, "[y]ou are not required to answer any of the questions and if you feel particularly uncomfortable—don't push yourself.

The students sought permission to distribute the questionnaire on school grounds on a random basis. The answers were to be returned anonymously and were to be kept "confidential." The students were to tabulate the results and publish them in an article in the *Voice,* which would also attempt to interpret the results.

Having received no reply from Chancellor Anker, on January 13, 1976 Marks and Trachtman wrote to Harold Siegel, Secretary of the Board of Education, and requested approval of their plan. Siegel responded in a letter dated February 27, 1976, to which he attached the decision of the Board. The decision advised the students that the survey could not be conducted stating, "Freedom of the press must be affirmed; however no inquiry should invade the rights of other persons." The decision indicated that the type of survey proposed could be conducted by professional researchers, with the consent of the students' parents. The decision noted that "[m]atters dealing with sexuality could have serious consequences for the well being of the individual," and pointed out that the students lacked the requisite expertise to conduct such a survey and that the survey proposed made no provision for parental consent and did not guarantee the anonymity of those who answered.

Mr. Siegel responded to a request for reconsideration by indicating that the Board believed that many students would be harmed if confronted with the questions propounded by the questionnaire.

Plaintiffs commenced this action on August 26, 1976, seeking declaratory and injunctive relief under 42 U.S.C. § 1983, on the ground that the defendants' actions in prohibiting the dissemination of the questionnaire and publication of its results violated the First Amendment.

At a hearing on plaintiffs' motion for a preliminary injunction on September 23, 1976, the court decided to consolidate the motion with trial on merits. See Fed.R.Civ.P. 65(a)(2). Thereafter, the parties agreed that the court should decide the issues on the basis of affidavits. Accordingly, the district court's decision was based upon the briefs, and affidavits of the parties and their expert witnesses.

Judge Motley found that permission to distribute the questionnaire could be denied consistently with the First Amendment only if defendants could prove that "there is a strong possibility the distribution of the questionnaire would result in significant psychological harm to members of Stuyvesant High School." She found that the "thrust" of defendants' evidence was that many high school students were only beginning to develop sexual identities and that the questionnaire would force emotionally immature individuals to confront difficult issues prematurely and become "quite apprehensive or even unstable as result of answering this questionnaire." The court found this argument convincing with respect to thirteen and fourteen year old students; however, as to older students, the court found the claims of potential emotional damage unconvincing and concluded that the psychological and educational benefits to be gained from distribution of the questionnaire to this group of students outweighed any potential harm. Accordingly, the court held that defendants could not prohibit the students from distributing the questionnaire to eleventh and twelfth-grade students and from publishing the results in the *Voice.* The court also found that certain safeguards should guide distribution of the questionnaire and ordered that the students and school officials should negotiate a plan to implement distribution and to provide for "both confidential and public discussion groups for students who would like to talk with school personnel after the distribution of the survey and publication of the results in the *Voice*."

On appeal both parties agree that the defendants' restraint of the students' efforts to collect and disseminate information and ideas involves rights protected by the First Amendment. See *Tinker* v. *Des Moines Independent Community School District*, 393 U.S. 503, 89 S.Ct. 733, 21 L.Ed.2d 731 (1969); cf. *Kleindienst* v. *Mandel*, 408 U.S. 753, 762–63, 92 S.Ct. 2576, 33 L.Ed.2d 683 (1972). Essentially, resolution of the issues here turns upon a narrow question: What was it necessary for the defendants to prove to justify the prohibition of the distribution of the questionnaire and did the defendants meet this burden of proof?

Our inquiry must begin with *Tinker*, where the Supreme Court stated:

> The principal use to which the schools are dedicated is to accommodate students during prescribed hours for the purpose of certain types of activities. Among those activities is personal intercommunication among the students. This is not only an inevitable part of the process of attending school; it is also an important part of the educational process. A student's rights, therefore, do not embrace merely the classroom hours. When he is in the cafeteria, or on the playing field, or on the campus during the authorized hours, he may express his opinions, even on controversial subjects..., if he does so without "materially and substantially interfer[ing] with the requirements of appropriate discipline in the operation of the school" and without colliding with the rights of others. But conduct by the student, in class or out of it, which for any reason—whether it stems from time, place, or type of behavior—materially disrupts classwork or involves substantial disorder or invasion of the rights of others is, of course, not immunized by the constitutional guarantee of freedom of speech.

393 U.S. at 512–13, 89 S.Ct. at 739–40 (citations and footnotes omitted).

Essentially, the defendants' position is that the students here seek not only to communicate an idea but to utilize school facilities to solicit a response that will invade the rights of other students by subjecting them to psychological pressures which may engender significant emotional harm.[2] Plaintiffs do not question defendants' authority to protect the physical and psychological well being of students while they are on school grounds, see, e. g., *Ginsberg* v. *New York*, 390 U.S. 629, 640–41, 88 S.Ct. 1274, 20 L.Ed.2d 195 (1968); *Prince* v. *Massachusetts*, 321 U.S. 158, 165 64 S.Ct. 438, 88 L.Ed. 645 (1944); *Kampmeier* v. *Nyquist*,553 F.2d 296 (2d Cir. 1977); rather, they contend that defendants have not made a sufficient showing to justify infringment of the students' rights to speech and expression.[3]

In interpreting the standard laid down in *Tinker*,this court has held that in order to justify restraints on secondary school publications, which are to be distributed within the confines of school property, school officials must bear the burden of demonstrating "a reasonable basis for interference with student speech, and ... courts will not rest content with officials bare allegation that such a basis existed." *Eisner* v. *Stamford Board of Education*, 440 F.2d 803, 810 (2d Cir. 1971).[4] At the same time, it is clear that school authorities need not wait for a potential harm to occur before taking protective action. See *Tinker* v. *Des Moines Independent Community School District*,supra, 393 U.S. at 514, 89 S.Ct. 733; *Russo* v. *Central School District No. 1, Towns of Rush*, 469 F.2d 623, 632 (2d Cir. 1972), cert. denied, 411 U.S. 932, 93 S.Ct. 1899, 36 L.Ed.2d 391 (1973); *Quarterman* v. *Byrd*,453 F.2d 54, 58–59 (4th Cir. 1971). Although this case involves a situation where the potential disruption is psychological rather than physical, *Tinker* and its progeny hold that the burden is on the school officials to demonstrate that there was reasonable cause to believe that distribution of the questionnaire would have caused significant psychological harm to some of the Stuyvesant students.[5]

In support of their argument that students confronted with the questionnaire could suffer serious emotional harm, defendants submitted affidavits from four experts in the fields of psychology and psychiatry. Florence Halpern, professor of psychology at the New York University School of Medicine, stated that many adolescents are anxious about the "whole area of sex" and that attempts to answer the questionnaire by such students "would be very likely" to create anxiety and feelings of self-doubt; further, she stated that there were almost certainly some students with a "brittle" sexual adjustment and that for "such adolescents, the questionnaire might well be the force that pushes them into a panic state or even a psychosis." She concluded that distribution of the questionnaire was a "potentially dangerous" act that was "likely to result in serious injury to at least some of the students."

Dr. Aaron H. Esman, chief psychiatrist at the Jewish Board of Guardians (an organization providing mental health treatment to emotionally disturbed children) and an associate in psychiatry at the Columbia University College of Physicians and Surgeons, indicated that a number of the questions (particularly those dealing with homosexuality, masturbation, and "sexual experience") were "highly inappropriate," particularly for children ages twelve through fourteen; such questions, in Dr. Esman's opinion, were likely to arouse considerable anxiety and tension," which "might well lead to serious emotional difficulties."

Vera S. Paster, a psychologist and assistant director of the Bureau of Child Guidance (the mental health agency for the New York City school system) asserted that there were a "large number" of high school students who would need help dealing with the anxiety reactions caused by confronting the questionnaire and that the proposed methodology of the survey would make it impossible to provide "back up support or protection" for such students.

Dr. Ingram Cohen, chief school psychiatrist of the Bureau of Child Guidance, indicated that there are wide discrepancies in the physical and psychological developement of adolescent students, even among students of the same age. Dr. Cohen also pointed out that the survey made no provision for assistance to students who reacted adversely to it and concluded that it had a sufficient potential for harm to justify prohibiting its dissemination.

The record shows that the curriculum at Stuyvesant includes various courses on sex and sexuality and that professionally supervised peer-group discussions are sponsored by the school. The defendants have consistently treated the topic of sexuality as an important part of students' lives, which requires special treatment because of its sensitive nature. Thus, the school system has provided several courses on the physical and emotional aspects of sex; such courses are taught by teachers with special qualifications and adminstrative materials emphasize the sensitive nature of the topic.[6] Further, the Board has consistently taken the position that even professional researchers may not conduct "sexual surveys" of students without meeting certain specific requirements.[7]

Plaintiffs offered statements from five experts, including Gilbert Trachtman, who is a professor of educational psychology at New York University. Plaintiffs' experts questioned the possibility that any emotional harm could be caused by students' attempts to answer the questionnaire, pointed out that the survey might be of substantial benefit to many students, and expressed the opinion that "squelching" the survey could have deleterious effects. They indicated that the topics covered in the questionnaire are of normal interest to adolescents and are common subjects of conversation; further, some of these experts emphasized that students in Manhattan are bombarded with sexually explicit materials and that it was highly unlikely that any student could be harmed by answering the questionnaire. It is noteworthy, however, that at least two of plaintiffs' experts, one of whom was Gilbert Trachtman, recognized that there was some possibility that some students would suffer emotional damage as a result of answering the questionnaire.[8]

The district court evidently found that there was a "strong possibility" that distribution of the questionnaire would result in significant psychological harm to ninth and tenth-grade students at Stuyvesant. The court did not find that there was no possibility of harm to eleventh and twelfth-grade students; rather, it concluded that any harm was outweighed by psychological and educational benefits to be gained from the questionnaire's distribution. This observation is substantiated by the fact that the court ordered the parties to provide for "confidential and public discussion groups" for students who wished to talk with school personnel after the survey; apparently, this was in response to defendants' contention that the survey as proposed failed to make any provision for counseling students who were disturbed by the questionnaire.

In determining the constitutionality of restrictions on student expression such as are involved here, it is not the function of the courts to reevaluate the wisdom of the actions of state officials charged with protection with the health and welfare of public school students. The inquiry of the district court should have been limited to determining whether defendants had demonstrated a substantial basis for their conclusion that distribution of the questionnaire would result in significant harm to some Stuyvesant students. In this regard, we must keep in mind the repeated emphasis of the Surpeme Court that,

> Judicial interposition in the operation of the public school system of the Nation raises problems requiring care and restraint.... By and large, public education in our Nation is committed to the control of state and local authorities.

Goss v. *Lopez,* 419 U.S. 565, 578, 95 S.Ct. 729, 738, 42 L.Ed.2d 725 (1975), quoting *Epperson* v. *Arkansas,* 393 U.S. 97, 104, 89 S.Ct. 266, 21 L.Ed.2d 228 (1968). See *Ingraham* v. *Wright,* 430 U.S. 651, 680, 97 S.Ct. 1401, 51 L.Ed.2d (1977); *Tinker* v. *Des Moines Independent Community School District, supra,* 393 U.S. at 507, 89 S.Ct. 733; *Buck* v. *Board of Education of the City of New York,* 553 F.2d 315, 320 (2d Cir. 1977).

We believe that the school authorities did not act unreasonably in deciding that the proposed questionnaire should not be distributed because of the probability that it would result in psychological harm to some students. The district court found this to be so with respect to ninth and tenth-grade students. We see no reason why the conclusion of the defendants that this was also true of eleventh and twelfth-grade students was not within their competence. Although pyschological diagnoses of the type involved here are by their nature difficult of precision, cf. *Cruz* v. *Ward,*

558 F.2d 659, 662 (2d Cir. 1977), we do not think defendants' inability to predict with certainty that a certain number of students in all grades would be harmed should mean that defendants are without power to protect students against a foreseen harm. We believe that the school authorities are sufficiently experienced and knowledgeable concerning these matters, which have been entrusted to them by the community; a federal court ought not impose its own views in such matters where there is a rational basis for the decisions and actions of the school authorities. See *Eisner* v. *Stamford Board of Education,* supra, 440 F.2d 810; *Butts* v. *Dallas Independent School District,* 436 F.2d 728, 732 (5th Cir. 1971). Their action here is not so much a curtailment of any First Amendment rights; it is principally a measure to protect the students committed to their care, who are compelled by law to attend the school, from peer contacts and pressures which may result in emotional disturbance to some of those students whose responses are sought. The First Amendment right to express one's views does not include the right to importune others to respond to questions when there is reasons to believe that such importuning may result in harmful consequences.[9] Consequently where school authorities have reason to believe that harmful consequences might result to students, while they are on the school premises, from solicitation of answers to questions, then prohibition of such solicitation is not a violation of any constitutional rights of those who seek to solicit.

In sum, we conclude that the record established a substantial basis for defendants' belief that distribution of the questionnaire would result in significant emotional harm to a number of students throughout the Stuyvesant population. Accordingly, the judgement is reversed insofar as it restrains defendants from prohibiting distribution of the questionnaire to 11th- and 12th-grade students at Stuyvesant and the case is remanded with instructions to dismiss the complaint.

GURFEIN, Circuit Judge, concurring:

In view of Judge Mansfield's dissent, I would simply add to Judge Lumbards' persuasive opinion the following comments.

First, while the passing out of the several questionnaires might not provoke a breach of the peace, a blow to the psyche may do more permanent damage than a blow to the chin. "Invasion of the rights of others is, of course, not immunized by the constitutional guarantee of freedom of speech." *Tinker* v. *Des Moines School dist.,* 393 U.S. 503, 513, 89 S.Ct. 733, 740, 21 L.Ed.2d 731 (1969).

Second, whether such a traumatic effect can be foreseen is the subject of dispute among recognized psychiatrists, as Judge Mansfield notes, I think such dispute is better resolved by professional educators than by federal judges even when they find the credentials of plaintiffs' experts "more impressive". This is not a case where there is no evidence to support the school officials.

Lastly, this is not a case involving "distribution of sexual material in school." It is, as Judge Lumbard states, a case that involves individual responses to various aspects of sex from the point of view of personal history, a matter different from the simple dissemination of reading matter dealing with sex, which the majority opinion does not purport to ban. *See* footnote 2. That deserves further emphasis in response to the dissenting opinion, lest the majority decision serve as an unintended precedent in derogation of First Amendment right.

MANSFIELD, Circuit Judge, dissenting.

With due respect I must dissent for the reason that in my view the defendants have completely failed to sustain their burden of showing that they are justified in depriving plaintiffs of their First Amendment right to engage in constitutionally protected freedom of expression by distributing to students the questionnaire regarding sex attitudes.

There is no suggestion of any danger that the questionnaire would disrupt school activities or lead to a breach of the peace, which are the type of "substantive evils" that might justify a prior restraint, *see Schenck* v. *United States,* 249 U.S. 47, 52, 39 S.Ct. 247, 63 L.Ed. 470 (1919). Instead the majority, relying upon dicta in *Tinker* v. *Des Moines School District,* 393 U.S. 503, 508, 513, 89 S.Ct. 733, 737, 740, 21 L.Ed.2d 731 (1969), to the effect that school authorities may prohibit speech "that intrudes upon ... the rights of other students," or "involves ... an invasion of the rights of others" would include in these amorphous terms the dissemination to others of non-disruptive, non-defamatory and non-obscene material because it might cause some kind of "psychological" harm to an undefined number of students. With this I disagree. It represents an entirely too vague and nebulous extension of the concept of "rights" to support the drastic type of censorship and prior restraint sought by the defendants.

As we said in *Eisner* v. *Stamford Board of Education,* 440 F.2d 803, 808 (2d Cir. 1971), "The phrase 'invasion of the rights of others' is not a model of clarity or preciseness." The *Tinker* test makes sense as a standard designed to insure that school officials will be permitted, even at the expense of some freedom of expression, to maintain order on the school premises, particularly in the classroom, and it has been construed by ouselves and other circuits as permitting an abridgement of free speech toward that end. *See Eisner* v. *Stamford Board of Education, supra; Katz* v. *McAulay,* 438 F.2d 1058 (2d Cir. 1971), *cert. denied,* 405 U.S. 933, 92 930, 30 L.Ed.2d 809 (1972); *James* v. *Board of Education,* 461 F.2d 566 (2d Cir.), *cert. denied,* 409 U.S. 1042, 93 S.Ct. 529, 34 L.Ed.2d 491 (1972); *Quarterman* v. *Byrd,* 453 F.2d 54 (4th Cir. 1971); *Nitzberg* v. *Parks,* 525 F.2d 378 (4th Cir. 1975); *Burnside* v. *Byars,* 363 F.2d 744 (5th Cir. 1968); *Butts* v. *Dallas Independent School Dist.,* 436 F.2d 728 (5th Cir. 1971); *Scoville* v. *Board of Education,* 425 F.2d 10 (7th Cir.), *cert. denied,* 400 U.S. 826, 91 S.Ct. 51, 27 L.Ed.2d 55 (1970). Where physical disruption or violence is threatened, some inroads on free expression are tolerable because the interests of students and school officials are relatively specific and lend themselves to concrete evaluation. But a general undifferentiated fear of emotional disturbance on the part of some student readers strikes me as too nebulous and as posing too dangerous a potential for unjustifiable destruction of constitutionally protected free speech rights to support a prior restraint. A public school's premises are the very "marketplace of ideas" where personal intercommunication between students, in or out of the classroom, is "an important part of the educational process" even though some students may experience a degree of mental trauma in that process, *Tinker* v. *Des Moines School Dist.,* 393 U.S. at 512, 89 S.Ct. at 740. If school officials are permitted to ban a questionnaire of the type here at issue because of possible "psychologial" harm, they could prohibit the dissemination of a broad range of other articles on school premises on the same theory, even though the publications were readily available elsewhere and the information in them was instructive. Within the last few years, for instance, the *New York Times,* which represents that it publishes "All the News That's Fit to Print," has published numerous articles on the very matters that are the subject of plaintiffs' questionnaire, including items regarding the number of pregnant girls in public schools, the operation by New York City of a separate school for pregnant schoolgirls attended by up to 2,000 students annually, sexual activity among American teenagers, and the results of a nationwide study of adolescent sexuality.[1] Under the majority's decision, distribution of these items among students would be prohibited as posing a psychological danger to some. The possibilities for harmful censorship under the guise of "protecting" the rights of students against emotional strain are sufficiently numerous to be frightening.

Even accepting arguendo the majority's thesis to the effect that other students' rights include the right to be free of any emotional stress, defendants have failed to sustain their burden of showing that the First Amendment values in the present case are outweighed by the risk of psychological harm. The right of a newspaper to conduct a survey on a controversial topic and to publish the results represents the very quintessence of activity protected by the First Amendment. In a school environment, moreover, there is a positive value in the students' exercise of responsibilities associated with the publication of a newspaper, which gives them a greater appreciation for the true meaning and value of the Bill of Rights than they might otherwise possess.

The majority's holding that the values inherent in these basic rights are outweighed by the potential psychological harm which the questionnaire might cause to some students is based on conclusory and speculative opinions of a few psychologists, which are expressed in short affidavits, hypothetical rather than supported by any factual bases, untested by cross-examination, and flatly controverted by contrary affidavit opinions of other experts who possess equal if not superior qualifications as psychologists. All of the affidavits submitted by defendants, moreover, assume that a student possessed of fragile sensibilities would not only read the questionnaire but make an intensive effort to answer it, notwithstanding the statement on its face that "The survey is random and completely confidential.—You are not required to answer any of the questions and if you feel particularly uncomfortable—don't push yourself."[2] Some of the defendants' affidavits appear to be concerned principally with an issue not before the court—the methodology used by the questionnaire and its invalidity from a scientific statistical viewpoint,—rather than its psychological impact on students.

The conclusory and factually unsupported nature of the affidavit opinions relied on by the majority may be gathered from a brief summary of their contents. A 1½ page affidavit of Ingram Cohen, Chief School Psychiatrist of the Bureau of Child Guidance of the defendant Board of Education, offers his view that "a" student "may become anxious or even depressed" when he is asked for a judgment about himself and has doubts concerning sexual orientation, and that the "administration" of the questionnaire to immature high school youths, "still in the throes of resolving personal identity," would be sufficiently "provocative" to be "potentially harmful and arouse concern." The two page affidavit of Vera S. Paster, Assistant Director of the same Bureau, states that dissemination of the questionnaire "constitutes a potentially harmful exposure to some students" because, in attempting to answer it they would experience an "up-churning of anxiety, conflict, self-doubt and other symptoms of stress" arising out of "conflicts about their own sexuality issues." Defendant's official in charge of evaluating research, Dr. Anthony J. Polemeni, who "was asked to apply professionally accepted research standards to [the] proposed research study," states that it does not meet such standards because it "presented significant possibility of violating the privacy of students and having harmful consequences to... students." In reviewing the questionnaire at issue, his standard was that "one does not undertake a non-critical survey which may, even remotely, create psychological trauma for even one person." In my view this is error. The standard should not be the effect of the questionnaire upon one or even a few exceptionally immature and impressionable students but its effect on the average. *Cf. Roth* v. *United States,* 354 U.S. 476, 489, 77 S.Ct. 1304, 1 L.Ed.2d 1498 (1957); *Butler* v. *Michigan,* 352 U.S. 380, 383–84, 77 S.Ct. 524, 1 L.Ed.2d 412 (1957).

Defendant also presented two affidavits from person outside its own staff. One is Aaron H. Esman, Chief Psychiatrist at the Jewish Board of Guardians, which provides mental health services to emotionally disturbed children, a Director of Psychiatric Training at Madeleine Borg Child Guidance Institute, and Associate in Psychiatry at Columbia. He states that the survey may arouse "considerable anxiety and tension in a significant number of students" because of "bald" questions about sex. He concludes that while "it might be possible to devise a valid study of the sexual beliefs and attitudes ... [It] is my view that this survey is poorly designed, unlikely to yield valid, verifiable or useful information and is potentially dangerous to the group for whom it was intended." Finally, Florence Halpern, a Clinical Professor at New York University School of Medicine and a former project director at HEW in charge of developing mental health guidelines for certain programs, states that "emotional and psychological harm is likely to occur and the chance of this happening is far greater than the possibility that no children will be injured." She continues: "Reading the questionnaire and thinking of answers to many of the queries would be very likely to stir up questions, doubts, fantasies and anxiety, resulting in impaired school performance because of sexual preoccupation, sleeplessness, heightened feelings of self-doubt, depression, and in some instances, even more disturbing reactions." For some students, she concludes, "the questionnaire might well be the force that pushes them into a panic state or even a psychosis."

The foregoing affidavits are flatly controverted by five eminently well-qualified experts who have worked extensively in the field of school psychology. Dr. Adam Munz, Chief Psychologist at St. Luke's Hospital, Assistant Professor of Clinical Psychiatry at Columbia University, consultant to the Columbia University Health Services (where he actively works with students) and to the Cathedral School of St. John the Divine, swears in part:

"I have had the opportunity to peruse the material presented in connection with the 'Sexuality in Stuyvesant' questionnaire, including the questionnaire itself and the various affidavits submitted by all concerned with said questionnaire.

I would like to state, by way of a summary of my opinion in this matter, that in the more than 25 years of active experience as a clinical psychologist I have *never* encountered a situation in which a child, adolescent, or adult has been adversely affected by a questionnaire!—the statement that 'in some cases confrontation of this sort might lead to serious emotional difficulties' is totally unfounded and speculative.

The realities of life, the rawness of the world around us to which these youngsters are exposed daily on their way to and from school, are undoubtedly far more eroding of their development than a questionnaire could ever be." (Appendix, p. 148)

A detailed nine-page affidavit was furnished by plaintiff Gilbert M. Trachtman, professor of educational psychology, director of a school psychology program and of the NYU children's consultation service, president of the School Psychology Educators Council of New York State, past-president of the Nassau County Psychological Association and of the School Division of New York Psychological Association and a consultant to numerous public and private schools. He swore in part:

"3. I have objectively reviewed the questionnaire proposed for the article on 'Sexuality in Stuyvesant'. I emphasize that it is not only relevant and germane to the interests and concerns of the students in the 13–18 year age range, but can affirm from personal and professional experience that every question listed [in the questionnaire] touches upon topics frequently occurring in day to day conversations among students in this age group and no question could be unexpected, arcane or upsetting to students who associate in any manner with their peers, whose discussions will perforce include adversions to sexual issues.

4. The administration of Stuyvesant High School has, in the past, offered rap groups on sexuality to its students and encouraged participation in these open-ended, face to face verbal discussions. While these groups may have been led by trained teachers, they nevertheless exposed students to a degree of peer pressure and verbal confrontation far in excess of any impact created by a voluntary and anonymous written questionnaire. This statement in no way constitutes a criticism of peer rap groups, which are to be applauded, but is meant to place in proper perspective the mild impact of the projected questionnaire, which is

considerably less invasive of personal privacy and much less likely to arouse anxiety.

5. For those youngsters who have already discussed sexual matters freely with peers, the questionnaire will have little or no impact. Those youngsters who have not participated freely in such discussion are quite likely to be reserved, shy or already anxious about sexual matters and therefore unwilling to share information and attitudes with peers. Such youngsters are likely to be less informed, to have less access to current relevant peer group norms and attitudes and to be anxious about themselves on the basis of misinformation, distortion or fantasy. For such youngsters the questionnaire may serve as an outlet for private communication, and reassurance that others are concerned about similar matters, and the projected article based on this questionnaire may well serve a valuable educational purpose in reducing fantasy and distortion and relieving anxiety.

6. Youngsters of this age, living and travelling in an urban environment are constantly bombarded by sexually-laden stimuli, The media— advertising, newspaper reports, TV drama, film, theatre— are constantly dealing with homosexuality, unisexuality, bisexuality, premarital sex and all of the other topics covered in this questionnaire. Walking to and from school, youngsters meet prostitutes, are handed advertisements for massage parlors, and witness homosexual courtships. The defendants seem to assert that some of the questions in this questionnaire may arouse undue anxiety in some youngsters who are less well defended or whose personality adjustment is somewhat precarious. I would suggest that any youngster sufficiently fragile to suffer serious anxiety or depression upon reading questions which (s)he may ignore with impunity or respond to anonymously, is a youngster too fragile to have survived the trip from home to school. There is absolutely no evidence that the impact of this questionnaire will even remotely approximate the impact of all the sexually laden environmental stimuli already imposed upon these youngsters....

9. The environment in the context in which the questionnaire at issue will be used, is an urban (New York City) high school in 1976. A school, as noted, situated in a city which bombards its inhabitants with sexual stimuli. Sexual stimuli, which include all topics covered in the proposed survey and extending quite beyond it. Indeed, recent research, 'Adolescent Sexuality in Contemporary America', Sorensen, R. C., 1973, N.Y.: World Publishing Co., indicates that sexual behavior is on the upswing among adolescents and that young people are increasingly explicit about sex.

The proposed survey is not only projected within this environmental context but, in turn, is an additional component within the environment. It is pertinent, therefore, to note the relevant characteristics of the questionnaire, and the manner of distrubtion of the proposed survey:

(1) It is voluntary; (2) it requires a written (and therefore private) communication, rather than a verbal (and public) communication; (3) it is anonymous; (4) a proposed cover letter outlines all of the above and further encourages the volunteer respondents to ignore any specific questions which make them uncomfortable." (Appendix, pp. 93–95, 96–97).

Harry B. Gilbert, Professor of Education at Fordham and Coordinator of the Urban School Psychology Program, was from 1955 to 1966 in charge of the examination for licensing of all school psychiatrists, psychologists, and guidance personnel for defendant, and prior to that served a supervisor of psychologists at defendant's Bureau of Child Guidance. He stated, among other things:

"I see the survey project and questionnaire here at issue as a classic example of adolescents reaching out for information and relief of concern in an area of great developmental moment to them. Adolescents are most interested in their newly developed sexual abilities and their inability to achieve expression of their interest and desires. Quite appropriately, there are legitimate reasons why sexual expression is difficult to achieve for young adolescents. But society makes the problem even more difficult by its failure to explore the extent of sexual knowledge, attitudes, practices and concerns among teenagers and to make provision for the sharing of such findings among teenagers in order to allow alleviation of anxiety that is prevalent ...

5. The danger that some students might be exposed to anxiety arousal exists. But it is so minute compared with the enormous benefit to be derived from students learning that their concerns are common and developmentally normal. Moreover, this would provide opportunity for genuine information to be shared and not leave sexual information to be gained solely from furtive peer whisperings or pornographic literature which does abound.

6. An effect of squelching this student proposal can only serve to drive sexual feelings further underground and to provide adolescents with a cause to do battle with authority figures who treat students as children, not budding adults." (Appendix, pp. 102, 103)

Professor Max Siegel (A104), President of the

Division of Clinical Psychology of the American Psychological Association, past-president of the New York State Psychological Association and program head of the Graduate Program of School Psychology at Brooklyn College, states in part:

> "Given that the questionnaire is voluntary and anonymous so that a student may choose not to participate without embarrassment [sic] or concern for peer pressure, there seems to be no basis for any expectation of emotional harm to individual students.
>
> Indeed, I would conclude that the questionnaire and the resultant article may prove a valuable service and fill an important need for the students of Stuyvesant High School, providing them as it does with normative and demographic information which can play a valuable role in providing reality based contexts for discussion in areas of sexuality. Most adolescents discuss sexual issues frequently, and those who do not enter such discussions frequently are nevertheless quite likely to obsess and ruminate privately about these same issues, but with less facts and less information about their fellow students, and with consequent possibilities of more fantasy and more distortion, and, as a consequence, irrational anxiety. It is much more likely that collection and dissemination of relevant facts and attitudes from peers will prove to be constructive and useful than in any way harmful." (Appendix, pp. 105–106)

Victor B. Elkin (A107), director of the National Institute of Mental Health Project—Psychology in the schools, and for 20 years director of psychological services for the Long Beach City School District, swears:

> "As a result of my 25 years of direct service to public school children, I have become sensitive and aware of the need to appropriately respect and effectively relate to the children in our schools. Not only do I not find this questionnaire objectionable or dangerous, but actually I find it to have positive mental health implications. In today's day and age, with sexuality ramptantly [sic] used in advertising, entertainment, in literature, the questions presented in this questionnaire are actually benign.
>
> 4. For many young boys or girls of high school age, such a questionnaire could serve as a positive impetus for facing and coming to grips with many issues regarding their own personal thoughts and feelings about themselves, within a sexual context. Very much like the cliché, that it is healthier for the child to learn about sexuality from a parent rather that 'in the street,' it is although healthier for a child to learn about or become in touch with his or her own thoughts and feelings, and even anxieties from a questionnaire which might stimulate thinking, rather than from headlines and various magazines, newspapers, or the screaming announcements of theater marquees." (Appendix, pp. 108, 109)

If the issues before us were to be decided on the credentials and independence of the experts offered by both sides, plaintiffs would probably have the edge. Without denigrating the standing of defendants' experts, the credentials and experience of plaintiffs' experts are more impressive. Moreover, four of the five experts offered by the plaintiffs (Munz, Gilbert, Siegel and Berger) are independent, whereas a majority of the defendants' psychologists (Cohen, Paster, and Polemeni) are employed by the defendants. More important, however, is the failure of the defendants, who have the burden, to provide any factual foundation for the conclusions voiced by them and their experts. In this day and age, when children in New York City are literally bombarded with explicit sex materials on public newsstands on the way to and from school, when they are encouraged openly and frankly to discuss sex topics and problems in "rap sessions" sponsored by their schools (which, unlike the questionnaire at issue are face-to-face and not anonymous), when the children actually do discuss sex with their peers at school, when the number of teenage pregnancies in New York City's public high schools such as Stuyvesant is so high that the city has operated a special high school for pregnant high school girls attended by up to 2,000 pregnant teenagers annually, when adolescent sexuality is openly discussed in New York newspapers, I believe the defendants have failed completely to demonstrate any reasonable likelihood that the questionnaire poses any substantial harm to any appreciable number of high school students.

The picture drawn by the defendants of high school freshman and sophomores (to say nothing of juniors and seniors) as fragile, budding egos flushed with the delicate rose of sexual naivety, is so unreal and out of touch with contemporary facts of life as to lead one to wonder whether there has been a communications breakdown between them and the next generation. Yet the defendants' sponsorship of "rap sessions" among students to discuss these very matters indicates not only an awareness of the high school student's knowledge and insight into sex matters but a strange inconsistency with the defendants' attitude toward the questionnaire. If face-to-face, non-anonymous discussions between students of the very matters that are the subject of the questionnaire causes no psychological harm to those involved, I cannot believe that an anonymous questionnaire, which states right on its face that the recipient need not answer it but is free to throw it away, would do so, I can only conclude that the defendants are more concerned about the structure and methodolgy of the questionnaire than about its alleged psychological impact.

Other courts, when faced with substantially the same problem, have not hesitated to find that distribtuion of sexual material in school to students is protected by the First Amendment and that school authorities failed to sustain their heavy burden of demonstrating that prohibition of such distribution was reasonably necessary to guard against harm to the students' rights. *See, e.g., Shanley* v. *Northeast Independent School Dist.,* 462 F.2d 960 (5th Cir. 1972) (school newspaper article discussing birth control). Indeed, in *Bayer* v. *Kinzler,* 383 F.Supp. 1164 (E.D.N.Y.), *aff'd,* 515 F.2d 504 (2d Cir. 1974), we affirmed a district court decision finding that the distribution of a sex information supplement to a school newspaper was constitutionally protected. I fail to find any significant legal distinction between these holdings and the present case.

I do agree with the majority that Judge Motley's Solomonic judgment, which would cut the baby in half by permitting distribution of the questionnaire to juniors and seniors while denying it to freshmen and sophomores, cannot stand, in view of the failure of the record to reveal any substantial evidentiary basis for the distinction other than the surmise that the younger students would be more vulnerable to possible psychological trauma than the older ones. However, for the reason stated, the defendants have failed to sustain their burden as to either group.

Accordingly I would affirm the district court's holding that the questionnaire may be distributed to juniors and seniors, reverse its holding that the questionnaire may not be distributed to freshmen and sophomores and direct the court to retain jurisdiction for the purpose of resolving any dispute that might arise with respect to distribution of any resulting school newspaper article that might be written.

NOTES

1. We note that the senior class at Stuyvesant was scheduled to graduate on June 22, 1977 and, thus, Jeff Trachtman may no longer be a member of the student body. However, assuming Trachtman has graduated, we do not think that the case has thereby become moot. See, e.g., *DeFunis* v. *Odegaard,* 416 U.S. 312, 94 S.Ct. 1704, 40 L.Ed.2d 164 (1974). In bringing this suit Trachtman was acting not only as a student but in a representational capacity as editor-in-chief of *The Stuyvesant Voice.* Thus, plaintiffs' complaint states that Trachtman is the editor-in-chief of the *Voice* and that the proposed survey was prepared by members of the *Voice* staff in preparation for an article to appear in a March 1976 issue of the *Voice.* The record indicates that the questionnaire at issue and the proposed article were approved by the entire editorial board of the *Voice.* The complaint requests relief on behalf of "plaintiffs and other [sic] similarly situated" and asks that the defendants be enjoined from prohibiting the publication and intepretation of the results of the questionnaire in the *Voice.* Further, Judge Motley specifically noted that in seeking permission to conduct the survey Trachtman was acting "in his capacity as editor-in-chief of . . . the *Voice.*"

    Although the compaint did not formally so assert, Trachtman was litigating in a representational capactiy. Cf. *Richardson* v. *Ramirez, 418 U.S. 24, 36–40, 94 S.Ct. 2655, 41 L.Ed.2d 551 (1974).* Plaintiffs seek to vindicate not only Trachtman's rights as an individual student, but the right of the *Voice* and its staff to conduct the survey. Accordingly, we think the fact that Trachtman may no longer be a student at Stuyvesant does not moot the case as we have no doubt that there is a proper adversary relationship here to assure proper presentation of the issues (plaintiffs are represented by an attorney affiliated with the New York Civil Liberties Union), See *Franks* v. *Bowman Transportation Co.,* 424 U.S. 747, 752–57, 96 S.Ct. 1251, 47 L.Ed.2d 444 (1976), and plaintiffs may be considered as acting on behalf of a student association and its members who have a continuing stake in this litigation. Cf. *Hunt* v. *Washington State Apple Advertising Commission,*——U.S.——, ——, 97 S.Ct. 2434, 53 L.Ed.2d 383 (1977).

2. Plaintiffs desire to use Stuyvesant students as research subjects distinguishes this case from such cases as *Shanley* v. *Northeast Independent School,* 462 F.2d 960 (5th Cir. 1972) and *Bayer* v. *Kinzler,* 383 F.Supp. 1164 (E.D.N.Y.1974), aff'd, 515 F.2d 504 (2d Cir. 1975), which held that school officials could not restrain the distribution of school newspapers containing information about birth control. The questionnaire does not seek to convey information but to obtain it in a manner that school officials contend may result in psychological damage. The fact that some students may read the proposed cover letter and decide not to answer the questionnaire does not diminish the legitimate concern of school officials for those students who decide to answer it.

    Further, we cannot ignore the fact that plaintiffs intend to present a report on "Sexuality in Stuyvesant," which will attempt to interpret the results of the questionnaire and make conclusions based thereon. We think the school officials may legitimately be concerned that the proposed article will attempt to make "scientific" conclusions about the sexual habits of Stuyvesant students that may be misleading.

3. Plaintiffs do not challenge the procedure by which the Board's decision was reached and this case does not involve any administrative regulation placing a per se ban on all student surveys. Compare *Eisner* v. *Stamford Board of Education,* 440 F.2d 803 (2d Cir. 1971). It is clear that defendants have not tried to suppress all forms of student expression on sex-related matters. Indeed, the curriculum at Stuyvesant includes both formal courses on sex education and peer-group dis-

cussion sessions. See discussion, infra. Further, the record shows that defendants would not have attempted to prevent distribution of the questionnaire off school grounds. In addition, this entire controversy has been reported in an article in the school newspaper, which included one of the questions in the questionnaire. See Record, affidavit of Sanford Gelernter, exhibit K. Thus, this case involves restriction of only one among many methods of communication between students on sex-related matters, which the Supreme Court has noted, "is not without significance to First Amendment analysis, since laws regulating the time, place or manner of speech stand on a different footing than laws prohibiting speech altogether." *Linmark Associates, Inc.* v. *Township of Willingboro,* 431 U.S. 85, 93, 97 S.Ct. 1614, 1618, 52 L.Ed.2d 155 (1977).

4. Similarly, in *Katz* v. *McAuley,* 438 F.2d 1058 (2d Cir. 1971), cert. denied, 405 U.S. 933, 92 S.Ct. 930, 30 L.Ed.2d 809 (1972), we upheld the denial of a preliminary injunction against high school officials' refusal to allow the distribution of leaflets soliciting funds for a political cause on public school grounds noting that, "The Board's regulation appears to be reasonable and proper and has a rational relationship to the orderly operation of the school system." *Id.* at 1061. See *Tinker* v. *Des Moines Independent Community School District,* supra, 393 U.S. at 513, 89 S.Ct. 733. *Nitzberg* v. *Parks,* 525 F.2d 378, 382–83 (4th Cir. 1975); *Butts* v. *Dallas Independent School District,* 436 F.2d 728, 732 (5th Cir. 1971); *Scoville* v. *Board of Education, Joilet Township,* 425 F.2d 10, 13–15 (7th Cir.), cert. denied, 400 U.S. 826, 91 S.Ct. 51, 27 L.Ed.2d 55 (1970). See also, *Presidents Council, District 25* v. *Community School Board No. 25,* 457 F.2d 289 (2d Cir.), cert. denied, 409 U.S. 998, 93 S.Ct. 308, 34 L.Ed.2d 260 (1972).

5. Although *Tinker* provides that "undifferentiated fear or apprehension" of a distrubance is not sufficient cause to justify interference with students' freedom of speech, 393 U.S. at 508, 89 S.Ct. 733, school authorities need only demonstrate that the basis of their belief in a potential disruption is reasonable and not based upon speculation. See *Eisner* v. *Stamford Board of Education,* supra, 440 F.2d at 810; note 3, supra.

6. For example, the Board of Education has promulgated "Guidelines for Implementation of Family Living/Sex Education Programs." The guidelines provide that teachers desiring to teach such courses must have special training and "all teachers must possess sensitivities about adolescents and sex, their parents, the value system of families, and have a sense of propriety in their classroom behavior."

7. Thus, the Board guidelines, see note 6, supra, which were promulgated in May, 1974, provide, "Teachers, college students, agencies shall neither administer nor participate in surveys eliciting responses about personal sexual behavior from students. Such sex-behavior inventories, as all other health-related surveys, must receive approval from the Board of Education through its Coordinating Council on School Health."

The Board has also promulgated a handbook for research applicants, which provides for certain requirements and safeguards before research involving student subjects may be conducted. The district court rejected the argument that the survey could not go forward because it did not comply with the handbook, which the court found did not apply to student projects, and this issue has not been raised on appeal. However, defendants point out that the handbook and other administrative regulations demonstrate the Board's concern in protecting the well being of students.

8. See affidavits of Gilbert Trachtman and Harry B. Gilbert. See also affidavit of Max Siegel.

9. We find no merit in plaintiffs argument that defendants' concern is for only a minority of students and amounts to a "heckler's veto." See *Eisner* v. *Stamford Board of Education,* supra, 440 F.2d at 809 n.6. The issue here is not to what extent school authorities are obligated to protect the dissemination of unpopular views. There is a clear distinction between the speaker's right not to be shouted down and the listener's right to be protected against the importunities of those who seek answers to questions.

Further, we cannot ignore that the district court not only restrained defendants from prohibiting the survey but ordered them to take steps to oversee the distribution of the questionnaire and provide counseling for those students who were disturbed by it; in effect, defendants were told to expend time and money to provide "safeguards" for a survey they insisted could not be made safe. The student's right to speech and expression simply does not extend so far.

DISSENTING OPINION NOTES

1. A few recent New York Times articles or editorials pertaining to the subject are summarized in its index: *E. g.,* New York Times, March 21, 1976, at p. 29, col. 1; *id.,* Oct. 16, 1976, at p. 27, col. 2; *id.,* June 28, 1974, at P. 17, col. 4.

2. I would have no objection to our conditioning distribution of the questionnaire upon the same or similar language being printed in bold type and given an even more prominent position either on the face of the letter covering the questionnaire or on the questionnaire itself.

T̲ʜᴇ Supreme Judicial Court of Massachusetts decides against two Massachusetts Institute of Technology students who had been convicted of violating the state statute providing in part: "Whoever willfully interrupts or disturbs a school or other assembly of people met for a lawful purpose shall be punished by imprisonment for not more than one month or by a fine of not more than fifty dollars . . . ." In deciding against the students who had entered Massachusetts Institute of Technology classrooms while classes were in progress and had attempted to address the students and distribute leaflets, the Court declared: "The statute does not prohibit expressive conduct or speech that is compatible with the free flow of ideas essential to the learning process. It merely insulates the schools from activity that so significantly disrupts their functioning as to impair the accomplishment of their educational goals. No constitutional protection extends to conduct, whether it be expressive or otherwise, that materially obstructs the operation of the schools."

Commonwealth v. *Bohmer,* 372 N.E.2d 1381 (1978)

QUIRICO, Justice.

This case is before us on a bill of exceptions challenging the defendants' conviction of willfully interrupting or disturbing a school in violation of G.L. c. 272, § 40.[1] The defendants question the constitutionality of the statute, both on its face and as applied, and challenge certain of the trial judge's evidentiary rulings, his instructions to the jury, and his exclusion of the brother of one of the defendants from the court room. We hold that there was no error, and we affirm.

The evidence most favorable to the prosecution is summarized. The convictions arose out of two incidents at the Massachusetts Institute of Technology (MIT). On January 16, 1970, the defendant Peter Bohmer entered the classroom of MIT Professor John Wulff, while class was in progress, apparently in order to make an announcement. Bohmer attempted to address the students but Wulff cut him off and ordered him out of the room. George Katsiaficas[2] then entered and attempted to distribute leaflets, and Bohmer again began speaking. Wulff demanded that both of them leave. When Bohmer attempted a third time to speak, Wulff again ordered him to be silent and called on members of the class for help. Two students responded and ushered the defendants out of the classroom.

Later the same day the defendants entered another MIT classroom while a class was being conducted. The teacher, professor Edwin Bransome, asked the defendants if he could help them. Bohmer stated that he wished to address the class. Bransome refused, but Bohmer nevertheless began to speak. Bransome then made an attempt to lead Bohmer out the door. Words were exchanged, Bohmer telling Bransome to "take your hands off me," and Bohmer requested that the professor allow the class to decide for itself whether the defendants should be allowed to speak. Bransome also refused this request, and led both Bohmer and Katsiaficas out of the room. When the door was closed on Katsiaficas's foot an exchange of name calling ensued. Both incidents lasted approximately five minutes, and class resumed after each one.[3]

Criminal complaints were filed by Professors Wulff and Bransome against the two defendants, charging each with willfully interrupting and disturbing a school in violation of G.L. c. 272, § 40. After appealing a District Court conviction, the defendants were convicted by a jury in the Superior Court.[4] They appealed the conviction, and we ordered direct appellate review. G.L. c. 211A, § 10(A).

1. The defendants first contend that G.L. c. 272, § 40, is void for vagueness,[5] and that their conviction

under it is therefore a denial of their right to due process of law under the Fourteenth Amendment to the Constitution of the United States.

Due process requires that a criminal statute be sufficiently clear to give notice of the conduct that it prohibits. A "statute which either forbids or requires the doing of an act in terms so vague that men of common intelligence must necessarily guess at its meaning and differ as to its application, violates the first essential of due process of law." *Connally* v. *General Constr. Co.,* 269 U.S. 385, 391, 46 S.Ct. 126, 127, 70 L.Ed. 322 (1926). *Commonwealth* v. *Carpenter,* 325 Mass. 519, 521, 91 N.E.2d 666 (1950). Due process requirements also mandate that no statute have such a standardless sweep that arbitrary and dicriminatory enforcement by the police and the courts is permitted. *Commonwealth* v. *A Juvenile,* 368 Mass. 580, 595 n.15[a], 334 N.E.2d 617, 627, n. 15 (1975). *Grayned* v. *Rockford,* 408 U.S. 104, 108–109, 92 S.Ct. 2294, 33 L.Ed.2d 222 (1972). "It would certainly be dangerous if the legislature could set a net large enough to catch all possible offenders, and leave it to the courts to step inside and say who could be rightfully detained, and who should be set at large." *Smith* v. *Goguen,* 415 U.S. 566, 573 n.9, 94 S.Ct. 1242, 1247, 39 L.Ed.2d 605 (1974), quoting from *United States* v. *Reese,* 92 U.S. 214, 221, 23 L.Ed. 563 (1875).

However, since words are the elements that constitute a statute, mathematical precison in the definition of legislative enactments is not required. *Grayned, supra,* 408 U.S. at 110, 92 S.Ct. 2294. A statute is satisfactory so long as it clearly indicates what it prohibits as a whole. *Id.* "A law is not vague, however, if it requires a person to conform his conduct to an imprecise but comprehensible normative standard so that men of common intelligence will know its meaning." *Commonwealth* v. *Orlando,*——Mass.—— ,——[b], 359 N.E.2d 310 (1977). Uncertainty as to whether marginal offenses are included within the coverage of a statute does not render it unconstitutional if its scope is substantially clear. *Commonwealth* v. *Jarrett,* 359 Mass. 491, 496–497, 269 N.E.2d 657 (1971). *United States Civil Serv. Comm'n* v. *National Ass'n of Letter Carriers,* 413 U.S. 548, 579, 93 S.Ct. 2880, 37 L.Ed.2d 796 (1973).

We conclude that G.L. c. 272, § 40, is sufficiently definite to satisfy the notice requirements of the due process clause.[6] The statute proscribes only such activity as actually creates an interruption or disturbance of the normal functioning of a school. Because of the limited scope of the statute's application, viz., to disturbances in schools or other public meetings, the degree of interruption necessary to constitute a violation is easily measured by its impact on, and incompatibility with, the functioning of such institutions. *Grayned, supra* at 112, 92 S.Ct. 2294. Additionally, the statute requires that the acts which cause the disturbance be willfully done. We believe that these limitations on the scope of the statute provide a person of common intelligence with sufficient notice of what the law prohibits; due process requirements are therefore satisfied.[7]

2. The defendants also attack the school disturbance statute on overbreadth grounds, contending that it is invalid on its face because it punishes activities that are constitutionally protected.

Generally a litigant is not allowed to challenge the application of a statute to himself on the basis that it might be unconstitutional as it applies to others. *Commonwealth* v. *LaBella,* 364 Mass. 550, 553, 306 N.E.2d 813 (1974). *Broadrick* v. *Oklahoma,* 413 U.S. 601, 610, 93 S.Ct. 2908, 37 L.Ed.2d 830 (1973). However an exception to this traditional rule of standing has been recognized in certain limited circumstances where a case arises under the First Amendment. *United States* v. *National Dairy Prods. Corp.,* 372 U.S. 29, 36, 83 S.Ct. 594, 9 L.Ed.2d 561 (1963). This exception is based on an overriding interest in preventing any "chill" on the exercise of First Amendment rights. *Id.* As a result of the exception, a criminal defendant may, in certain circumstances, attack a statute on its face because it prohibits conduct protected by the First Amendment even though his own conduct is clearly not so protected. *Dombrowksi* v. *Pfister,* 380 U.S. 479, 486, 85 S.Ct. 1116, 14 L.Ed.2d 22 (1965). Such a facial overbreadth attack is allowed where the statute challenged is incapable of being construed so as to limit its application to unprotected activity, and where it presents a real and substantial deterrent to protected expression. *Young* v. *American Mini Theatres, Inc.,* 427 U.S. 50, 60, 96 S.Ct. 2440, 49 L.Ed.2d 310 (1976). *Erznoznik* v. *Jacksonville,* 422 U.S. 205, 216, 95 S.Ct. 2268, 45 L.Ed.2d 125 (1975). Because we conclude that G.L. c. 272, § 40, does not substantially deter the exercise of First Amendment rights, we reject the overbreadth challenge made by the defendants in this case.

The free speech clause of the First Amendment protects expressive speech or conduct from governmental regulation. This protection is not, however, absolute, since "reasonable 'time, place and manner' regulations may be necessary to further significant governmental interests, and are permitted." *Grayned, supra,* 408 U.S. at 115, 92 S.Ct. at 2303. Whether such regulations are reasonable depends on "whether the manner of expression is basically incompatible with the normal activity of a particular place at a particular time." *Grayned, supra* at 116, 92 S.Ct. at 2303.

The regulation of expressive conduct within the

special characteristics of the school environment is an issue of particular sensitivity. First Amendment rights must be zealously guarded in our schools in order to promote the free exchange of ideas that is central to the development of this country's younger citizens. *Keyishian* v. *Regents of Univ. of the State of N.Y.*, 385 U.S. 589, 603, 87 S.Ct. 675, 17 L.Ed.2d 629 (1967). *Shelton* v. *Tucker*, 364 U.S. 479, 487, 81 S.Ct. 247, 5 L.Ed.2d 231 (1960). "The vigilant protection of constitutional freedoms is nowhere more vital than in the community of American schools." *Shelton* v. *Tucker, supra*, at 487, 81 S.Ct. at 251. It is also of importance, however, to preserve a measure of order in our schools so that an atmosphere favorable to education can be maintained. See *Grayned, supra,* 408 U.S. at 119, 92 S.Ct. 2294.

The problem presented by these competing factors has recently been considered by the Supreme Court of the United States in *Tinker* v. *Des Moines Independent Community School Dist.*, 393 U.S. 503, 89 S.Ct. 733, 21 L.Ed.2d 731 (1969), and *Grayned* v. *Rockford, supra*. In the *Tinker* case, public school children in Des Moines, Iowa, were suspended from classes because they wore black armbands in protest against the United States participation in the war in Vietnam. The protesting students did not engage in any conduct that was "actually or potentially disruptive," *Tinker, supra* at 505, 89 S.Ct. 733, or that materially or substantially interfered with school discipline or the rights of others. *Id.* at 512–514, 89 S.Ct. 733. As a result the Court held that their activity was protected by the First Amendment and could not be regulated by school authorities. *Id.* The same standard of review was applied in the *Grayned* case, where the Court upheld against an overbreadth attack an ordinance that made it a crime for anyone, while on grounds adjacent to a school building, to "willfully make or assist in the making of any noise or diversion which disturbs or tends to disturb the peace or good order of [a] school session or class thereof . . ." *Grayned, supra,* 408 U.S. at 107–108, 92 S.Ct. at 2298. The Court concluded that this ordinance, notwithstanding the fact that it had not been construed by the State courts, *Grayned, supra* at 109–110, 92 S.Ct. 2294, met the test established in *Tinker*. It stated that the ordinance was "narrowly tailored to further Rockford's compelling interest in having an undisrupted school session conducive to the students' learning, and does not necessarily interfere with First Amendment rights." *Id.* at 119, 92 S.Ct. at 2305.

We conclude that the school disturbance statute challenged here, similar to that questioned in *Grayned*, does not extend its prohibitions to activity protected by the First Amendment and is constitutional. The statute does not prohibit expressive conduct or speech that is compatible with the free flow of ideas essential to the learning process. It merely insulates the schools from activity that so significantly disrupts their functioning as to impair the accomplishment of their educational goals. No constitutional protection extends to conduct, whether it be expressive or otherwise, that materially obstructs the operation of the schools.

3. The defendants also argue as ground for reversal that the instructions to the jury were in error because they allowed a conviction on the basis of constitutionally protected activity. This argument fails because there is a lack of significant evidence of expressive speech or conduct on the part of the defendants. If a jury instruction defines as criminal both activity that is protected by the First Amendment and activity that is unprotected, and evidence of both classes of conduct has been presented to the jury, an ensuing conviction would have to be set aside because of the possibility that it rested on an unconstitutional ground. *Bachellar* v. *Maryland*, 397 U.S. 564, 571, 90 S.Ct. 1312, 25 L.Ed.2d 570 (1970). That, however, is not the situation in the present case. There was no evidence before the jury in this case that the interruption resulted from speech or conduct that was expressive and thus subject to First Amendment protection. This was not a situation where the disturbance was caused by the speech of the defendant, see, e.g., *Terminiello* v. *Chicago*, 337 U.S. 1, 69 S.Ct. 894, 93 L.Ed. 1131 (1949), or by conduct that conveyed a message, see, e.g., *Tinker, supra*. Rather, the evidence here indicates that the disruption was caused by the defendants' intrusion into the two classrooms and their resistance to efforts to silence and remove them. Neither party contended that the minimal speech involved was the basis for the prosecution, and we do not feel that it played a significant enough part in the incidents alleged to warrant a limiting instruction from the judge.[8] See *Commonwealth* v. *Richards*, 369 Mass.——, ——[c], 340 N.E.2d 892 (1976). The fact that some speech occurred does not bring the otherwise unprotected conduct of the defendants within the ambit of the First Amendment. *Id.* Therefore, regardless of any overbreadth in the jury instruction, the absence of evidence of expressive conduct on which the jury might have rested their decision precludes a reversal on this basis.

For the same reasons we reject the claim that the application of the statute to the defendant's activity violates the First Amendment. The disturbances charged here resulted from nonexpressive conduct, and thus no constitutional violation exists.

4. The defendants next argue their exceptions to certain evidentiary rulings. They challenge the exclusion of (a) their own testimony to the effect that they did not intend to cause a disturbance, (b) the

testimony of a MIT professor that, on the same day as the incidents charged, they had left his classroom quietly after having been refused permission to address the class, and (c) the testimony of a second MIT professor that classroom announcements at MIT were not an unusual occurrence. This excluded evidence was offered to show that the defendants did not possess a specific intent to disturb the school proceedings. The willfulness requirement of G.L. c. 272, § 40, demands, however, only that the acts of the defendants be willfully performed; so long as the acts were intentional and not due to accident or inadvertence, the requirement is satisfied. *Commonwealth* v. *Porter*, 1 Gray 476, 480 (1854). The possession of a specific intent to cause a disturbance is not an element of the crime.[9] Therefore, the evidence, all of which was offered for its relevance to the issue of the specific intent of the defendants, was properly excluded. See *Kramer* v. *John Hancock Mut. Life Ins. Co*, 336 Mass. 465, 467, 146 N.E.2d 357 (1957).

5. It is also argued by the defendants that there were several errors in the judge's charge.

They contend, first, that the instructions incorrectly defined the willfulness necessary for a violation of G.L. c. 272, § 40. Although the charge might properly have been more thorough in this regard, we conclude that it was adequate, in light of the evidence presented to the jury.[10] For the reasons already discussed above,[11] we reject the defendants' contention that the jury should have been instructed to return a guilty verdict only if they found that the defendants had a specific intent to disturb the classes.

We also reject the defendants' argument that the judge improperly instructed the jury that MIT was a school within the meaning of G.L. c. 272, § 40. This court, in *Commonwealth* v. *Porter*, 1 Gray 476 (1854), stated that disturbances within colleges were covered by the statute. *Id.* at 477. We see no reason to depart from that position now.

It is next argued that the judge erred in informing the jury that the defendants had been convicted of these same charges, in a District Court, prior to their *de novo* appeal.[12] The defendants assert that the presumption of innocence to which they were entitled was seriously prejudiced by this instruction. Although we have reservations about the wisdom of giving the jury this information (see *Ludwig* v. *Massachusetts*, 427 U.S. 618, 637, 96 S.Ct. 2781, 49 L.Ed.2d 732 [1976] ([Stevens, J., dissenting]) in the context of the instruction considered as a whole the mention of the convictions was not error. Cf. *Andres* v. *United States*, 333 U.S. 740, 744–745, 68 S.Ct. 880, 92 L.Ed. 1055 (1948). The judge correctly informed the jury that the defendants are to be presumed innocent until evidence is introduced to the contrary, and that no weight should be given to the District Court convictions. We have held that such an instruction was sufficient in the somewhat analogous situation where the jury were informed of the grand jury's conclusion of probable guilt by indicting a defendant. *Commonwealth* v. *Powers*, 294 Mass. 59, 63–64, 200 N.E. 562 (1936); See *Commonwealth* v. *Madeiros*, 255 Mass. 304, 316, 151 N.E. 297 (1926). We have stated many times that the presumption of innocence requires no more than a statement to the jurors that a District Court finding of guilty is not to be considered against the accused. E.g., *Commonwealth* v. *Devlin*, 335 Mass. 555, 569, 141 N.E.2d 269 (1957); *Commonwealth* v. *Madeiros, supra,* 255 Mass. at 316, 151 N.E. 297; *Commonwealth* v. *DeFrancesco*, 248 Mass. 9, 13, 142 N.E. 749 (1924); see *Commonwealth* v. *Boyd,* 367 Mass. 169, 187, 189, 326 N.E.2d 320 (1975). This exception is therefore overruled.

The defendants also claim error in that part of the jury instruction that described the guilt of joint actors. The language of this part of the charge was somewhat confusing, but we think that it was sufficient when read in light of another portion of the instruction which limits conviction to the situation where the jury find "that that particular defendant did willfully interrupt or disturb a classroom." "The sufficiency and correctness of instructions to a jury are to be determined by consideration of the charge as a whole, and not on the basis of fragments lifted from context and then subjected to scrutiny as though each fragment had to stand or fall on its own without the aid of the remainder of the charge." *Commonwealth* v. *Whooley,* 362 Mass. 313, 319, 284 N.E.2d 914, 918 (1972). *Commonwealth* v. *McInerney,*——Mass.——, ——[d], 365 N.E.2d 815. *Commonwealth* v. *Aronson,*330 Mass. 453, 457, 115 N.E.2d 362 (1953).

6. The defendants contend finally that their right to a public trial was violated by the exclusion of Bohmer's brother from the court room during part of the proceeding. It has been the universal practice of our courts to provide open trials, unless a statute demands otherwise. *Commonwealth* v. *Blondin,* 324 Mass. 564, 569 571, 87 N.E.2d 455 (1949), cert. denied, 339 U.S. 984, 70 S.Ct. 1004, 94 L.Ed. 1387 (1950). *Ottoway Newspapers, Inc.* v. *Appeals Court,* ——Mass.——, ——[e], 362 N.E.2d 1189 (1977). We have recently held that the public trial guaranty of the Sixth Amendment to the Constitution of the United States is applicable to the courts of the Commonwealth under the Fourteenth Amendment. *Commonwealth* v. *Marshall, 356 Mass. 432, 435, 253 N.E.2d 333 (1969).* This guaranty, the importance of which cannot be overstated, exists primarily to prevent the courts from becoming instruments of persecution. *In re Oliver,* 333 U.S. 257, 270, 68 S.Ct. 499, 92 L.Ed. 682 (1948). "The knowledge that every criminal trial is subject to contemporaneous review in

the forum of public opinion is an effective restraint on possible abuse of judicial power." *Id.*[13]

This right to a public trial is not, however, absolute and inflexible. We have recognized the power of a judge to exclude spectators from trials involving particularly sordid sexual offenses. *Commonwealth* v. *Blondin,* 324 Mass. 564, 570–573, 70 S.Ct. 1004, 94 L.Ed. 1387 (1949). The judge must also have the power to maintain order in court proceedings so that the administration of the criminal law will be fair and just. See *Illinois* v. *Allen,* 397 U.S. 337, 343, 90 S.Ct. 1057, 25 L.Ed.2d 353 (1970). As a corollary to this power a judge has the authority to exclude spectators whose presence intimidates the witnesses, see *United States ex. rel. Laws* v. *Yeager,* 448 F.2d 74, 79–81 (3d Cir. 1971), cert. denied, 405 U.S. 976, 92 S.Ct. 1201, 31 L.Ed.2d 251 (1972), or who conduct themselves in a manner that disrupts the order and decorum of the proceeding. See *United States ex rel. Orlando* v. *Fay,* 350 F.2d 967, 970–971 (2d Cir. 1965), cert. denied sub nom. *Orlando* v. *Follette,* 384 U.S. 1008, 86 S.Ct. 1961, 16 L.Ed.2d 1021 (1966); *United States* v. *Kobli,* 172 F.2d 919, 922 (3d Cir. 1949); *State* v. *Genese,* 102 N.J.L. 134, 142, 130 A. 642 (1925); 6 J. Wigmore, Evidence § 1835 at 443 (Chadbourn rev.1976).

The record before us indicates that the removal of Bohmer's brother was preceded by laughing and snickering in the court room The judge warned the spectators that exclusion from the court room would result if the noise continued. There is no claim that the brother was removed for any reason other than that he was causing a disturbance. The significant interest of a defendant in having relatives and friends present at his trial, *Marshall, supra* at 434–435, may be outweighed by the need to exclude spectators who disrupt the proceedings. We find no abuse of the judge's discretion on the facts presented here.

7. Having considered all of the exceptions raised by the defendants before this court, we find no error.

Exceptions overruled.

NOTES

1. The statute, which as originally enacted was entitled "An Act to prevent disturbances of schools and public meetings," St.1849, c. 59, provides in part: "Whoever willfully interrupts or disturbs a school or other assembly of people met for a lawful purpose shall be punished by imprisonment for not more than one month or by a fine of not more than fifty dollars . . . ." G.L. c. 272, § 40, as appearing in St.1969, c. 463, § 1.
2. It appears from the record that at the time of these events both Bohmer and Katsiaficas were MIT students.
3. Witnesses for the defense testifed that neither defendant spoke after entering the classrooms until spoken to by the professor, and that neither physically resisted the effort to remove them from the rooms. Evidence was also introduced that the events in the Wulff classroom took from one to two and one-half minutes, while those in the class of Professor Bransome took one and one-half minutes.
4. The District Court judge sentenced both defendants to one month in a house of correction on each complaint, the sentences to run concurrently. After their conviction in the Superior Court, they were again sentenced to one month on each complaint. The judge in the Superior Court, however, ordered that the sentences run consecutively.
5. The defendants characterize their claim as a facial attack on the statute. However, in the context of a vagueness challenge, the defendants have no standing to assert the rights of others. *Young* v. *American Mini Theatres, Inc.,* 427 U.S. 50, 59, 96 S.Ct. 2440, 49 L.Ed.2d 310 (1976). *Broadrick* v. *Oklahoma,* 413 U.S. 601, 608, 93 S.Ct. 2908, 37 L.Ed.2d 830 (1973). They may properly contend that the statute contains no standards and thus, as applied to them, does not provide sufficient notice to satisfy due process requirements. See *Smith* v. *Goguen,* 415 U.S. 566, 577–578, 94 S.Ct. 1242, 39 L.Ed.2d 605 (1974); *Coates* v. *Cincinnati,* 402 U.S. 611, 614, 91 S.Ct. 1686, 29 L.Ed.2d 214 (1971). Where, however, a statute clearly proscribes some conduct, but is vague as to its reach over other acts, a defendant charged with conduct that falls into the first category, a so called hard-core violator, is not entitled to raise a vagueness challenge. *Smith, supra.* If the claimed vagueness of a statute, in addition to providing due process notice problems, also threatens rights protected by the First Amendment to the Constitution of the United States, then an overbreadth challenge may be proper. Only in the context of an overbreadth challenge may a party assert the rights of others. See *Broadrick* v. *Oklahoma, supra* at 607–615, 91 S.Ct. 1686, 29 L.Ed.2d 214.
   a. Mass.Adv.Sh. (1975) 2766, 2788–2789 n.15.
   b. Mass.Adv.Sh. (1977) 84, 87.
6. The statute has been previously construed by this court only once, in the case of *Commonwealth* v. *Porter,* 1 Gray 476 (1854), but that opinion has little bearing on the issues presented here.
7. Questions similar to those raised here were recently passed on by the Supreme Court of the United States in *Grayned* v. *Rockford,* 408 U.S. 104, 92 S.Ct. 2294, 33 L.Ed.2d 222 (1972). In that case the defendants were convicted under a statute that provided in part: "[N]o person, while on public or private grounds adjacent to any building in which a school or any class thereof is in session, shall willfully make or assist in the making of any noise or diversion which disturbs or tends to disturb the peace or good order of such school session or class therof . . . ." *Id.* at 107–108, 92 S.Ct. at 2298. The Court rejected a vagueness challenge to the statute, holding that the necessity of willful conduct, as well as of a significant disturbance of school activity, provided sufficent definition to satisfy due process requirements. *Id.* at 111–114, 92 S.Ct. 2294.
8. The evidence indicated that the defendants never said anything fully in Professor Wulff's classroom, except to ask if they could request the class's opinion as to

whether they should be allowed to speak. It appears that Katsiaficas also handed out one leaflet. In the Bransome classroom Bohmer asked if he could talk to the class about a particualr matter, and asked that the class be allowed to decide. He also told Bransome to remove his hands from his, Bohmer's, arm when the professor tried to remove the defendants from the room. Some name-calling occurred when Katsiaficas's foot was shut in the door.

c. Mass.Adv.Sh. (1976) 47, 55.

9. Of the States that have decided this question, Alabama and Arkansas have held that the specific intent to disturb is not an element of the crime, see *Salter* v. *State,* 99 Ala. 207, 208–209, 13 So. 535 (1892); *West* v. *State,* 105 Ark. 175, 179, 150 S.W. 695 (1912); while North Carolina appears to hold to the contrary. *State* v. *Wiggins,* 272 N.C. 147, 154, 158 S.E.2d 37 (1967), cert. denied, 390 U.S. 1028, 88 S.Ct. 1418, 20 L.Ed.2d 285 (1968).

10. The entire instruction on willfullness consisted of the following: "So if you find in any one of the complaints that you have before you that that particular defendant did willfully interrupt or disturb a classroom of either Professor Wulff or Professor Bransome, then it is your duty to find him guilty as charged. If you find, of course, by the same token that they did not willfully interrupt or disturb the class in said MIT, then, of course, you must find them not guilty.

Now, a person can be guilty even though there is no evidence that he says, 'I am willfully interrupting or disturbing this class.' He does not say that. But a person is presumed to intend the natural consequences of his act."

Since the evidence in this case contained no basis for a finding that the actions of the defendants were accidental, the instruction was sufficient.

11. *See supra* at 326–327.

12. The jury were instructed in part: "The fact that these people here, these defendants, were brought before a District Court Judge who found them guilty as charged; the fact that they appealed that conviction to a jury of 12; the fact that they are defendants in this action, the law says that you are to draw no inferences of guilt based on just those things but rather you are to decide the guilt or innocence of these defendants based on the evidence that you have heard in this case; and also based on any reasonable inferences that you care to draw with regard to the facts that you find to be so in this case." The judge also charged the jury separately on the presumption of innocence.

d. Mass.Adv.Sh. (1977) 1619, 1635.

e. Mass.Adv.Sh. (1977) 973, 980.

13. Other reasons for holding trials in the view of the public exist. Witnesses are encouraged to be more truthful, and other people with relevant information, as yet unknown to the parties, become aware of the proceedings and make themselves available to testify. Additionally, the openness of trials allows spectators to learn about the operation of the judicial system and acquire confidence in its remedies. 6 J. Wigmore, Evidence § 1834 at 435–438 (Chadbourn rev.1976).

A United States District Court in New York decides for school officials who had prohibited the distribution of a high school newspaper, which was to be distributed on the last day of classes and containing two letters objected to by the principal. One letter contained language described by the principal as "vulgar," "obscene," and "fighting words." Another letter contained inaccurate and derogatory information about a named student's academic and activities record. While the District Court pointed out that the language objected to by the principal was not obscene and did not constitute fighting words, it also argued that the principal had a "rational basis grounded in fact for his conclusion that publication would create a substantial risk of disruption of school activities." As to the letter criticizing and attacking a student, the Court said: "Based upon his prompt investigation, personal knowledge of the student, and the virtually certain irreparable harm which would result from the letter, defendant Andrews [the principal] had a rational and substantial basis for preventing its publication." In response to the the argument presented by the students who challenged the censorship that the student attacked in the letter was vice-president of the student government and was thus a "public figure," the Court declared: "For the law to place a high school member of the student government organization in the same withering spotlight of the press as it does our publicly elected officials, would serve neither the policies of the First Amendment nor the democratic principles it seeks to further."

Frasca v. *Andrews*, 463 F. Supp. 1043 (1979)

MEMORANDUM AND ORDER

George C. Pratt, District Judge.

INTRODUCTION

When plaintiffs commenced this action they moved by order to show cause for a preliminary injunction preventing defendants from barring distribution of one issue of a high school newspaper on the ground that defendants' actions in seizing the newspaper violated the First and Fourteenth Amendments. Declaratory relief, class action certification, and damages are also sought. Jurisdiction stems from 42 U.S.C. § 1983 and 28 U.S.C. §§ 1343, 2201. Oral argument was heard on plaintiffs' motion for a preliminary injunction on August 24, 1978. Because the essential facts are not in dispute, the action may be disposed of without an evidentiary hearing, and the trial on the merits is deemed to be advanced and consolidated with the preliminary injunction proceedings. FRCP 65(a)(2).

PARTIES

Plaintiffs Renee Frasca and Joan Falcetta are, respectively, the former Editor-in-Chief and present Assistant Editor of the *Chieftain,* the official student newspaper of Sewanhaka High School, which is located in Floral Park, Nassau County, New York. The school contains grades 9-12 and has approximately 1,500 students, ranging in age from 13 to 21 years. The *Chieftain's* editorial board and staff consists of 25 students.

Defendants in this action are: Robert Andrews, the building principal of Sewanhaka High School; W.

Wallace Purdy, the district principal; and the Board of Education of Sewanhaka Central High School District.

FACTS

Copies of the June 1978 issue of the *Chieftain* were returned to the school from the printer on the evening of June 14, 1978 and placed in the home room mail boxes in the school office for distribution on the following day, June 15, 1978, the last day of the school year. The next morning, the newspaper staff discovered that all copies of the June 1978 issue had been seized by the building principal, defendant Andrews, who prohibited their distribution. The bases for the seizure and the focal points of this suit were two letters printed in the paper and designated in the court documents as Exhibits "A" and "B".

Exhibit "A" appeared on page 8 of the *Chieftain* and read as follows:

Sports editor,

We, the Lacrosse players of Sewanhaka would like to know why you do not have any sports articles in the Chieftain. We would like a formal apology in public or else we will kick your greasy ass.

[signed] Pissed Off
S.H.S. Lacrosse Team

The editor's response, printed immediately below, read:

We would like to reply by saying that the articles were stolen. We would also like to say that you hotheaded, egotistical, "Pissed Off" jocks of the Lacrosse team do not deserve an apology for anything. You should be giving one.

The Editors

Exhibit "B", which appeared on page 2, criticized the conduct of a particular student who was then vice-president of the student government. The student will be referred to as "John" in this decision, as in the court papers, to protect him from further unnecessary embarrassment. The letter stated, *inter alia*, that John "has been a total failure in performing his duties" and is a "total disgrace to the school", that he had been suspended from school, that he did not maintain a high academic average, that he attended only a few of the many student council meetings, and that he had changed his report card grades "by typing over the letters on the computer terminal". It also stated that John had been given one major responsibility, to head the Interclub Council, but that the council "completely died" because John "never showed up for his own meetings". Although Exhibit "B" begins "as a group ... we feel ...", the paper does not identify either the author or the "group".

The *Chieftain* is an extra-curricular activity funded entirely by the local school district, which provides space, utilities, supplies, desks, typewriters, and printing. The paper is staffed solely by students, who primarily determine the content, management, and control of the newspaper. The district has no written policies, guidelines, or rules pertaining to the *Chieftain*'s content, or to possible prior review, restraint, or censorship by the faculty or administration. Nevertheless, defendants regard the newspaper as being under the jurisdiction and direction of the English Department's chairperson, and ultimately under the supervision and control of the Board of Education, administered through the district principal and the building principal. They consider the student editors and staff to be subject to supervision "in a manner consistent with sound educational practice".

Although the faculty advisor was generally familiar with the content of each issue of the *Chieftain* before it went to press, he denies ever having exercised a "prerogative of censorship" and states that it was not his practice to review the final draft of the paper before it went to press. Apparently, the absence of written regulations, policies and guidelines is intended to provide the staff with an atmosphere of free inquiry and expression.

The controversial June 1978 issue of the *Chieftain* was an "extra additional issue" for the end of the school year. While there is a factual dispute about whether the faculty advisor was given an opportunity to review the paper's content prior to publication, that factual issue is not material. It is undisputed that prior to press time the faculty advisor did not actually see Exhibits "A" and "B" or, indeed, any of the material in the paper.

Defendant Andrews first read the June 1978 issue on the morning of June 15, after copies had been placed in the homeroom mailboxes for distribution to the students. Andrews' personal acquaintance with members of the lacrosse team caused him to doubt "very much whether the team as a whole, or for that matter, even a majority of the team members would concur in and write such a letter". As to Exhibit "B", Andrews knew of his own knowledge that John was an excellent student, a senior, and that this was the last issue of the paper for the year. He recognized that John had no opportunity to defend himself and that, true or false, the letter would have a "devastating impact" upon him. Because he doubted the truth, both of the signature on Exhibit "A" and of the content of Exhibit "B", Andrews had all the papers removed from the mailboxes, thereby preventing their distribution, and immediately commenced an investigation.

With respect to Exhibit "A", purportedly a letter from the "SHS Lacrosse team", Andrews called in five members of the team, including two of the three captains. None had any knowledge of the contents of the letter or of who had written it. Neither did the team's coaches know of the letter's contents or origin. Later investigation by an assistant coach disclosed that one member of the team had written the letter during his lunch hour, with three other team members present. No one else on the 25 man team had knowledge of the letter prior to or at the time it was written. As of June 15, the day the paper was to have been distributed, only four other players, and none of the team captains, knew of the letter.

Andrews' initial doubts about the letter focused on the falsity of representing it as a product of the entire lacrosse team. In his affidavit he also notes his concern that the "fighting words" of the letter might "easily trigger a physical as well as verbal confrontation between the lacrosse teams on the one hand, (we have three, freshman, JV and Varsity), and the staff of the *Chieftain* on the other". He expresses concern, too, over the "obscene" and vulgar language of Exhibit "A".

Andrews' investigation of Exhibit "B" was more extensive. He first spoke with the faculty director of student activities and learned that John had attended not "a few", but 75% of the student council meetings, and contrary to Exhibit "B", not only attended meetings of the Interclub Council but "tried his best to get the club functioning". John's records revealed that he ranked 101 out of a junior class of 557, and had no failing marks on his report card. Andrews knew that John had received an award from the senior high school Science Fair and was one of ten finalists for an Otis Elevator scholarship. Based on his investigation, Andrews determined that the content of Exhibit "B" was substantially false, and that if distributed on the last day of the school year with no offsetting response and no realistic opportunity to reply, great harm could be done to John and his reputation. Andrews was also concerned about possible libel liability of the school district, himself, and the staff members of the *Chieftain*, and about a possible violation of federal law by publishing information about a school suspension in a school newspaper.

Andrews spoke to the plaintiffs individually. Frasca indicated to him that she knew who had actually written the lacrosse team letter, but she "evaded" the question as to whether the letter had been authored by the team as a whole. With respect to Exhibit "B", Frasca told Andrews that she had reliable information that the letter's contents were true. Frasca's affidavit states that based on a discussion with the author as to his sources of information, and based on certain alleged eyewitnesses to the misconduct charged "we [were] convinced of its truth".

In their brief, plaintiffs argue that Exhibit "B" is true and offer to prove its truth at a hearing. No factual support has been presented, however, to rebut the specific falsities pinpointed by defendants' affidavits. Exhibit "B" purports to be from a "group", yet in describing its preparation, Frasca refers only to a single individual as "the letter's author" with whose consent she had revised the letter. While she claims to have spoken to individuals who claimed to be eyewitnesses to the misconduct alleged in the letter, she does not identify them, nor does she present any of their supporting affidavits. Moreover, plaintiff Falcetta told Andrews that John did not change his grade, but that someone else did.

As a result of his investigation, Andrews concluded that Exhibit "A" was false in that it was not authorized by the "SHS Lacrosse team", that certain words in the letter were obscene and vulgar and that, if published, the letter might provoke a physical as well as verbal confrontation between the lacrosse teams and the staff of the *Chieftain*. With respect to Exhibit "B", Andrews concluded that several of its statements were false and, in his opinion, libelous, that its publication would have a devastating impact on John, and that there would be no reasonable opportunity to reply. He ordered that the copies of the paper which had previously been removed from the homeroom mailboxes be destroyed, thereby preventing their distribution to the students. This suit followed.

ISSUES

The parties agree that a high school newspaper is generally protected by the First Amendment. They disagree as to whether the June 1978 *Chieftain* enjoyed that protection. Plaintiffs argue that none of the recognized justifications for limiting first amendment rights apply here. They argue that Exhibit "A" was not "obscene", that it did not contain "fighting words", and that there was no reasonable basis on which Andrews could have concluded that distribution of Exhibit "A" would cause substantial, material, disruption of school activities.

Plaintiffs further argue that Exhibit "B" was not libelous, that its publication did not violate federal privacy laws, and that its publication could not be banned simply because it was anonymous. Further, plaintiffs argue that libel principles could not be applied to Exhibit "B" since it dealt with the vice-president of the student government who was a "public figure" within the meaning of *New York Times v. Sullivan,* 376 U.S. 254, 84 S.Ct. 710, 11 L.Ed.2d 686 (1964), and that there is no suggestion of malice. Finally, plaintiffs argue that without written policies, guidelines, or regulations, defendants had no power whatsoever to prevent distribution of the *Chieftain*.

Defendants stress that the incidents here arose in a special educational environment and, therefore, must be viewed in that context. They argue that Andrews' actions in prohibiting distribution of the *Chieftain,* were justified under constitutional principles, because Exhibit "A" was obscene and inflammatory, because Andrews had a reasonable expectation that Exhibit "A" would cause substantial disruption of, or material interference with, school activities and the rights of others, and because Exhibit "B" was libelous and contained confidential student information whose publication would violate family, educational, and privacy rights which are protected under 20 U.S.C. § 1232g. More generally, defendants argue that they have not only the right, but the duty, to restrain publication of obscene, libelous, inflammatory, or substantially disruptive materials proposed to be included in the school paper, that they may do so even in the absence of written policies, guidelines, or regulations, and that under the circumstances here, there was a rational basis for Andrews' decision to restrain publication. Finally, defendants argue that their good faith, under the circumstances, precludes any award of punitive damages or attorneys fees.

DISCUSSION

An appropriate starting point for analysis is the Supreme Court's decision in *Tinker* v. *Des Moines Independent Community School District,* 393 U.S. 503, 89 S.Ct. 733, 21 L.Ed.2d 731 (1969), a case involving an official ban on the wearing of black arm bands by public school students while on school premises. The court there held that such a prohibition of expression in the schools is impermissible under the First and Fourteenth Amendments unless there is evidence that it is "necessary to avoid material and substantial interference with schoolwork or discipline...." *Id.* at 511, 89 S.Ct. at 739. The Court went on to state that

> ... conduct by the student in class or out of it, which for any reason—whether it stems from time, place, or type of behavior—materially disrupts classwork or involves substantial disorder or invasion of the rights of other is, of course, not immunized by the constitutional guarantee of freedom of speech. *Id.* at 513, 89 S.Ct. at 740.

The court added that prohibition or regulation of expression by students in schools would not be impermissible where school officials can "demonstrate any facts which might reasonably [lead] school authorities to forecast substantial disruption of or material interference with school activities...." *Id.* at 514, 89 S.Ct. at 740.

Although *Tinker* might be distinguished on its facts because it involved an expression of an opinion rather than restraint of a student publication, its test of "material and substantial" disruption has been utilized by many courts, including those in this circuit, in cases involving student publications. See, *e.g., Trachtman* v. *Anker,* 563 F.2d 512 (CA2 1977); *Eisner* v. *Stamford Board of Education,* 440 F.2d 803 (CA2 1971); *Bayer* v. *Kinzler,* 383 F.Supp. 1164 (E.D.N.Y.1974 aff'd 515 F.2d 504 (CA2 1975); *Baughman* v. *Freienmuth,* 478 F.2d 1345 (CA4 1973); *Quarterman* v. *Byrd,* 453F.2d 54 (CA4 1971); *Shanley* v. *Northeast Independent School District, Bexar County, Texas,* 462 F.2d 960 (CA5 1972); *Scoville* v. *Board of Education of Joliet,* 425 F.2d 10 (CA7 1970); *Gambino* v. *Fairfax County School Board,* 429 F.Supp. 731 (E.D.Va. 1977) *aff'd* 564 F.2d 157(CA4 1977); *Pliscou* v. *Holtville Unified School District,* 411 F.Supp. 842 (S.D.Cal.1976).

Applying the *Tinker* standard, the Second Circuit has held that:

> ... in order to justify restraints on secondary school publications, which are to be distributed within the confines of school property, school officials must bear the burden of demonstrating "a reasonable basis for interference with student speech, and ... courts will not rest content with officials bare allegation that such a basis existed." *Eisner* v. *Stamford Board of Education,* 440 F.2d 803, 810 (2d Cir. 1971). At the same time, it is clear that school authorities need not wait for a potential harm to occur before taking protective action. *Trachtman* v. *Anker, supra,* 563 F.2d at 517.

Trachtman involved the attempted distribution of a sex questionnaire to high school students and planned publication of the results in a student newspaper. Affirming the district court's decision that the school officials had properly barred distribution of the questionnaire, the Second Circuit held that "the school authorities did not act unreasonably in deciding that the proposed questionnaire should not be distributed because of the probability that it would result in psychological harm to some students." *Id.* at 519. The court also said that:

> In determining the constitutionality of restrictions on student expression such as are involved here, it is not the function of the courts to reevaluate the wisdom of the actions of state officials charged with protecting the health and welfare of public school students. The inquiry of the district court should ... [be] limited to determining whether defendants had demonstrated a substantial basis for their conclusion that distribution of the questionnaire would result in significant harm to some ... students. *Id.*

Before evaluating the circumstances of this case in light of the foregoing principles, we must consider plaintiff's categorical argument that absent written policies, guidelines, or regulations, defendants had no power whatsoever to exercise any prior restraint over publication of the *Chieftain*. All of the cases cited by plaintiff in support of this argument, *Eisner* v. *Stamford Board of Education*, 440 F.2d 803 (CA2 1971); *Shanley* v. *Northeast Independent School District*, 462 F.2d 960 (CA5 1972); *Baughman* v. *Freienmuth*, 478 F.2d 1345 (CA2 1973); *Quarterman* v. *Byrd*, 453 F.2d 54 (CA4 1971), dealt with "underground" newspapers which, unlike the *Chieftain,* were not sponsored by the school district, not represented as a school newspaper, not financed in any way by public funds, and not in any way supervised by faculty members.

More significantly, each of those cases involved an attack upon a written school policy which required advance permission to distribute the underground newspaper. True, each case required that certain procedural standards be met in administering a program of review in advance of distribution, but none of them held that in the absence of a written policy, distribution of a school sponsored paper can not be prevented. Even assuming that the same protection must be accorded to a school newspaper as to an "underground" publication, the power of school officials in a proper case to prevent distribution within the school of material which is libelous, obscene, disruptive of school activities, or likely to create substantial disorder, or which invades the rights of others, does not disappear merely because the school board has failed to adopt written policies requiring review in advance of distribution. Written policies and guidelines undoubtedly have a pedagogical value; they probably help to avoid problems such as have arisen in this case, by offering to students a clearer indication of what is permitted and what is proscribed. In addition, when a prior restraint is actually imposed they enhance a sense of fairness and provide an opportunity for discussion, negotiation, and compromise in order to accommodate competing interests. All of that may be desirable, but is not required by the constitution.

In determining whether a school official's suppression of a particular newspaper is reasonable, all the circumstances must be evaluated, including whether or not written guidelines have been established for such action. Absent such guidelines, suppression of publication by school officials must, of course, be scrutinized more carefully than if the issue were presented to the court after guideline procedures had been pursued. To be consistent with the first amendment drastic post-publication suppression, particularly, as here, on the last day of school, should be permitted only when clearly justified.

Not all of the justifications offered by defendants can be accepted. Andrews' view that Exhibit "A" was obscene and vulgar is only half right, since terms such as "ass" and "pissed off", while certainly vulgar, fall far short, in this day and age, of the constitutional standard of obscenity. Nor does the court view the content of Exhibit "A" as rising to the level of "fighting words" within the meaning of *Chaplinsky* v. *New Hampshire*, 315 U.S. 568, 62 S.Ct. 766, 86 L.Ed. 1031 (1942).

In connection with Exhibit "B", the court finds no merit in defendants' reliance upon the so-called "Buckley amendment" part of which, 20 U.S.C. § 1232g, prevents disclosure by a school district of certain information about students which is deemed to be confidential. Although some of the information in Exhibit "B" would fall within the scope of the Buckley amendment if the source of that information had been school records, the prohibitions of the amendment cannot be deemed to extend to information which is derived from a source independent of school records. Even though a school suspension is listed in protected records, as in the present case, the suspension would also be known by members of the school community through conversation and personal contact. Congress could not have constitutionally prohibited comment on, or discussion of, facts about a student which were learned independently of his school records.

The other justifications offered by defendants, however, have greater merit. Although it might be argued that any disruption of school activities caused by publication of a newspaper on the last day before a two month summer holiday could not be "substantial" by reason of the short period of time in which its effect would be felt, the court does not interpret *Tinker* to require that "substantial disorder" be expected to continue for any particular length of time.

Three school officials expressed concern over the possibility that one or more of the school's lacrosse players might have taken literally the threat of violence expressed in Exhibit "A". Defendant Andrews, the building principal, referred to the possibility that:

> an impressionable 14 year old member of the freshman Lacrosse team [might] take the letter as a license to hunt up the sports editor for the stated purpose of the letter. Andrews' Aff. ¶ 11.

Assistant lacrosse coach Flatley stated that

> In my opinion, such a letter could create an inharmonious relationship between the students engaged in the publication of the *Chieftain* on the one hand and the members of the lacrosse teams on the other, and could easily generate into a physically disruptive and verbally abusive situation within the school between the two factions without serving any public or educational benefit to anyone.

Flatley Aff. ¶ 7.

The *Chieftain's* faculty advisor, George Doolittle, an English teacher of 27 years' experience, said that:

some members of the student body could and would take this letter literally and the letter foreseeably could provoke a confrontation between athletes on one hand, and the staff members of *The Chieftain* on the other. This letter could very well culminate in a physical confrontation between members of the two groups. Doolittle Aff. ¶ 110.

Mr. Doolittle, in addition, offered the insight that some members of the lacrosse team might well object to having had an offensive letter such as Exhibit "A" falsely attributed to them.

In light of such opinions, offered by professionals having extensive experience with students of comparable age and maturity, and having specific acquaintance with members of the editorial staff and lacrosse teams, the court is satisfied that defendant Andrews had a rational basis grounded in fact for his conclusion that publication would create a substantial risk of disruption of school activities.

As stated by the Second Circuit in *Trachtman:*

...we do not think defendants' inability to predict with certainty that a certain number of students in all grades would be harmed should mean that defendants are without power to protect students against a foreseen harm. We believe that the school authorities are sufficiently experienced and knowledgeable concerning these matters, which have been entrusted to them by the community; a federal court ought not to impose its own views in such matters where there is a rational basis for the decisions and actions of the school authorities. See *Eisner* v. *Stamford Board of Education, supra,* 440 F.2d 810; *Butts* v. *Dallas Independent School District,* 436 F.2d 728, 732 (5th Cir. 1971). *Trachtman* v. *Anker, supra,* at 519.

In opposition, plaintiffs argue that the staff of the *Chieftain* had already seen the letter purporting to be from the "SHS Lacrosse Team" and that no arguments or violence had ensued. The argument ignores, however, the obvious facts that the lacrosse team (a) had not yet seen the letter, (b) had not seen the published reply of "the editors", and (c) might well be viewed as more likely to express their feelings physically than would less athletic staff members of the *Chieftain.*

An additional factor highlighted by Doolittle's affidavit is the potential impact of this falsely attributed epistle on non-assenting team members. To have authored such a document bespeaks to many not only crudity and bad taste, but an immature preoccupation with violence as a solution to relatively trivial disputes. Thus, for non-assenting team members Exhibit "A" created an unfair potential of harm to personal relationships and individual reputations, whose impact would only be aggravated by the lack of any meaningful opportunity to disclaim or explain the letter to the same audience who would have received it initially.

The remaining problem, Exhibit "B", focuses upon the defendant Andrews' reasoned and supported conviction that its content was substantially false, would have a devastating impact on John, and would leave John without any reasonable opportunity to respond, correct, or explain. Based upon his prompt investigation, personal knowledge of the student, and the virtually certain irreparable harm which would result from the letter, defendant Andrews had a rational and substantial basis for preventing its publication.

Plaintiffs have asserted in conclusory fashion that the content of the letter is true, and they seek now to prove its truth on the theory that truth is a complete defense to any claim of libel. A factual hearing into the truth or falsity of the statements would, of course, involve further unnecessary exposure of John to the publicity already generated by these plaintiffs. That fact alone, however, if necessary to a determination of the issues here, would not deter the court. But, even assuming that the statements contained in Exhibit "B" were to found true after a trial, all such a finding would establish would be that Andrews had erred when, under the time pressure of the day and with inadequate information supplied to him by plaintiffs, he determined that there was a reasonable and substantial basis to conclude that the letter's content was not only damaging, but false.

Since the disputes which arise in the day-to-day operations of our public schools cannot as a general rule be resolved by federal district judges, who necessarily must view them after the fact, from a remote point of view, and without direct responsibility for the immediate and practical consequences of the determinations, the rule has been wisely established that decisions of school officials will be sustained, even in a First Amendment context, when, on the facts before them at the time of the conduct which is challenged, there was a substantial and reasonable basis for the action taken. *Trachtman* v. *Anker, supra.* Because there was such a basis to support Andrews' determination here, there is no basis for court intervention.

Plaintiff's final argument with respect to the libel implications of Exhibit "B" focuses upon John's position as vice-president of the student government. From this, plaintiffs argue that John was a "public figure" within the meaning of *New York Times* v. *Sullivan, supra,* and that since there is no suggestion of malice, there could be no libel. As important as an unrestrained press may be to the furtherance of our democratic government and society, the "public figure" exception to libel liability ought not to be extended to the level of a high school newspaper editor's comments about a fellow student. Significant here is the educational function, not only of the school newspaper, but also of the student government and every other activity carried on in the school. Part of the educational process is to learn in a protected environment where one's mistakes do not have damaging or irrevocable consequences. For the law to place a high school member of the student government organization in the same withering spotlight of the press as it does our publicly elected officials, would serve neither the policies of the First Amendment nor the democratic principles it seeks to further.

Even if the *New York Times* v. *Sullivan* principle were to be applied here, thereby insulating the individual defendants, the school district, and the editorial staff from a possible damage judgment for publishing Exhibit "B", Andrews' suppression of the article under the circumstances that faced him on June 15, 1978, knowing the harm that would be done without any reasonable opportunity to mitigate or correct it if wrong, was a rational, reasonable decision made on the basis of substantial evidence before him at the time.

Accordingly, plaintiffs' motion for a preliminary injunction is denied, and the complaint is dismissed.

So Ordered.

A United States District Court in Georgia decides against school officials who had on various occasions censored the high school newspaper because it contained materials which school officials deemed inaccurate, in poor taste and possibly libelous. After rejecting the school officials' arguments attempting to justify the several censorship episodes, the Court concluded with an "order" which declared that the school officials be preliminarily restrained and enjoined from:

A. Prohibiting or interfering with the distribution of the September 27, 1979 edition of *The McEachern Arrowhead* containing any of the following material:

(1) The occasional use of the word "damn."

(2) The paragraph describing the attitudes of new teachers at McEachern high school toward homosexual teachers. . . . .

(3) The article explaining why the September 27 edition of the *Arrowhead* was not distributed as scheduled. . . . The "Order" also prohibited school officials from engaging in prior restraint of the *Arrowhead;* it was further ordered that the *Arrowhead* be reinstated as the newspaper of the high school and that the plaintiff [Charles Reineke] be immediately reinstated as co-editor-in-chief of the newspaper.

Reineke v. *Cobb County School Dist.*, 484 F.Supp. 1252 (1980)

MEMORANDUM AND ORDER

TIDWELL, District Judge.

This is an action for injunctive relief and a declaratory judgment brought on behalf of the plaintiff, Charles E. Reineke, by his father as next friend, seeking to enjoin the defendants from engaging in certain alleged acts of censorship and control over *The McEachern Arrowhead* (hereinafter, "the *Arrowhead*" or "the newspaper"). The *Arrowhead* was a monthly newspaper written, edited, and published by certain students at McEachern High School. Its publication has currently been suspended. The plaintiff was the co-editor-in-chief. The newspaper was printed at a private printing company and was sold on the campus of McEachern High. Some financial support was provided by the high school, but most funding was derived from advertising and sales of individual copies. The student editors and staff of the *Arrowhead* were enrolled in a journalism class at McEachern for which they received academic credit. The teacher of the journalism class served as the faculty advisor to the newspaper.

McEachern High School is a public high school within the Cobb County School District and receives public funds for its operation. The Cobb School District is a political subdivision of the State of Georgia, controlled and governed by the Cobb County School Board. Defendant Hatcher is the principal of McEachern High School and is an employee of the Cobb County School Board. Defendant Protteau is a faculty member of McEachern High School whose duties for the 1979-80 school year included teaching the journalism class and serving as the faculty advisor for *The McEachern Arrowhead*.

This action seeks a mandatory injunction ordering the defendants to reinstate publication of the newspaper, to allow the plaintiff to publish certain material in the *Arrowhead,* and to allow distribution on the McEachern High School Campus of those copies of the *Arrowhead* containing such material. The matter is presently before the court on the plaintiff's motion for a preliminary injunction and the defendants' affidavits submitted in opposition to the motion for preliminary injunction.

FACTS

The parties have submitted numerous briefs and affidavits in support of their respective positions. Basically, four acts of censorship have been alleged. After the September 27, 1979 edition of the *Arrowhead* was returned from the printer, it was distributed to the journalism class that was responsible for publishing the newspaper. At this time, the plaintiff noticed that several changes had been made to the issue. In an article entitled "New Teachers at McEachern", a paragraph dealing with the new teachers' general attitudes toward homosexual teachers had been deleted. In addition, the word "darn" had been substituted for the word "damn" in a quote attributed to a local radio personality. These changes were admittedly made by the faculty advisor while the September 27 edition was still at the printer, and constitute the first act of censorship alleged by the plaintiff.

On the following morning, the students began selling the newspaper. Shortly thereafter, the principal ordered the distribution stopped, and requested the return of all copies that had already been sold. The principal had several objections to the content of the September edition of the *Arrowhead*. He thought that photographs had been used from other publications without permission, authority, or waiver of copyright; that an article entitled "Vietnam Syndrome" was in poor taste and possibly libelous; that an article regarding ticket prices to high school football games contained erroneous statistics; that an article concerning the student body president was a personal attack upon that student; that an article entitled "Advertising Metamorphoris" [sic], which quoted the 1960 segregationist stance of a current member of the Cobb County Board of Education, would adversely affect racial relationships at the high school; and that a purported letter to the editor signed "D. Newburn" would be falsely attributed to the student chaplain, Danny Newburn, and would cause a disruption of school activities. The principal also noted that there were a number of technical defects in the newspaper in grammar and spelling. The confiscation of the September 27 edition in its entirety is the second act of censorship alleged by the plaintiff.

Several weeks thereafter, the second issue of the *Arrowhead* for the 1979-80 school year was published and distributed as scheduled. However, two articles in this October edition were deleted by the faculty advisor while the newspaper was at the printer. One was a story about the high school football team, written by the team's manager, who also served as the student sports editor. The faculty advisor objected to this article on the ground that it constituted inappropriate editorializing on the sports page. The other story that was deleted concerned the confiscation of the September issue. These actions by the faculty advisor constitute the third alleged act of censorship.

By letter dated October 30, 1979, an attorney retained by the plaintiff contacted the school principal and advised him that the aforementioned actions constituted censorship of the school newspaper in violation of his client's First Amendment rights. Subsequently, the principal suspended further publication of the *Arrowhead,* pending termination of the threatened litigation. A literary magazine was substituted as an alternative means of student expression. This suspension of publication constitutes the fourth act of alleged censorship.

DISCUSSION

I.

The court will first address the plaintiff's motion to strike three affidavits which have been submitted by the defendants in this action: the Affidavit of Students; the Affidavit of Staff; and the Affidavit of Linda Charles. The plaintiff has objected to these affidavits on the grounds that the affiants, not having read the newspaper articles in question, do not have personal knowledge of the subject matter of their testimony, thereby violating Rule 602, Federal Rules of Evidence; that the affidavits are inadmissible opinion evidence by non-experts; and that the affidavits are unreliable on their face.

The affidavits in question state that the affiants have "learned" of the contents of the controversial articles in the September issue of the *Arrowhead,* thus indicating that they have personal knowledge of their contents. Moreover, the affidavits of the students and staff state, in part, that the publication of these articles "did materially disrupt class work, involved substantial disorder and invasion of rights of others", and this assertion does not involve the expression of an opinion. (The plaintiff has conceded that a teacher, such as Linda Charles, may qualify as an expert for the purpose of rendering opinion evidence in this type of case. The court agrees.) Finally, the plaintiff's third argument goes to the weight, and not the admissibility, of the affidavits. Accordingly, the plaintiff's motion to strike the aforementioned affidavits is hereby overruled and denied.

II.

A logical starting point when discussing student First Amendment rights is the landmark case of *Tinker* v. *Des Moines Independent Community School District,* 393 U.S. 503, 89 S.Ct. 733, 21 L.Ed.2d 731

(1969), which concerned a public school policy forbidding the wearing of black armbands by students in protest of the Vietnam war. While affirming the comprehensive authority of school officials to prescribe and control conduct in the nation's schools, the Supreme Court emphasized that neither students nor teachers "shed their constitutional rights to freedom of speech or expression at the schoolhouse gate." 393 U.S. at 506, 89 S.Ct. at 736. The Court held that a prohibition of expression in a school setting such as that involved in *Tinker* was impermissible under the First and Fourteenth Amendments, unless there was evidence that it was "necessary to avoid material and substantial interference with schoolwork or discipline. . . ." 393 U.S. at 511, 89 S.Ct. at 739. In formulating this standard, the Supreme Court embraced the reasoning of the Fifth Circuit in *Burnside v. Byars*, 363 F.2d 744 (5th Cir. 1966). In that case, the Court of Appeals had reversed the denial of a preliminary injunction which had been sought to prevent high school authorities from enforcing a regulation prohibiting students from wearing civil rights "freedom buttons." The Fifth Amendment held that school officials could not infringe on students' First Amendment rights unless the exercise of such rights "materially and substantially interfere[d] with the requirements of appropriate discipline in the operation of the school." 363 F.2d at 749. The Supreme Court in *Tinker* approved the *Burnside* holding, but further cautioned that

. . . conduct by the student, in class or out of it, which for any reason—whether it stems from time, place, or type of behavior—materially disrupts classwork or involves substantial disorder or invasion of the rights of others is, of course, not immunized by the constitutional guarantee of freedom of speech. 393 U.S. at 513, 89 S.Ct. at 740.

The *Tinker* standard of material and substantial disruption has been applied by numerous courts, including those in this circuit, in cases involving student publications. See cases cited in *Frasca v. Andrews*, 463 F.Supp. 1043, 1049 (E.D.N.Y.1979). In *Shanley v. Northeast Independent School District, Bexar County, Texas*, 462 F.2d 960 (5th Cir. 1972), the Fifth Circuit Court of Appeals summarized the decisional implications of *Tinker* and its progeny as follows:

. . . (1) expression by high school students can be prohibited altogether if it materially and substantially interferes with school activities or with the rights of other students or teachers, or if the school administration can demonstrate reasonable cause to believe that the expression would engender such material and substantial interference; (2) expression by high school students cannot be prohibited solely because other students, teachers, administrators, or parents may disagree with its content; (3) efforts at expression by high school students may be subjected to prior screening under clear and reasonable and equally-applied regulations. 462 F.2d at 970.

There is a "heavy burden" on the defendants to justify their actions where they constitute a prior restraint. *See Healy* v. *James,* 408 U.S. 169, 184, 92 S.Ct. 2338, 2347, 33 L.Ed2d 266 (1972); *Shanley, supra,* 462 F.2d at 969. The primary issue is whether the school officials can demonstrate reasonable cause to believe that the prohibited expression would have engendered material and substantial interference with school activities or with the rights of others. It is clear that school administrators need not await the occurrence of actual disruption before exercising reasonable restraint over a student publication. *Butts v. Dallas Independent School District,* 436 F.2d 728, 731 (5th Cir. 1971). However, mere "undifferentiated fear or apprehension of disturbance is not enough to overcome the right to freedom of expression." *Tinker, supra,* 393 U.S. at 508, 89 S.Ct. at 737. As the Fifth Circuit stated in *Butts, supra:*

. . . [W]e do not agree that the precedential value of the *Tinker* decision is nullified whenever a school system is confronted with disruptive activities or the possibility of them. Rather we believe that the Supreme Court has declared a constitutional right which school authorities must nurture and protect, not extinguish, unless they find the circumstances allow them no practical alternative. As to the existence of such circumstances, they are the judges, and if within the range where reasonable minds may differ, their decisions will govern. But there must be some inquiry, *and establishment of substantial fact,* to buttress the determination. 436 F.2d at 732 (emphasis added).

III.

Turning to the circumstances of the case at bar, the defendants have attempted to justify the first act of alleged censorship on several grounds. The faculty advisor claims that the printer had recommended the elimination of one or more paragraphs of the story, "New Teachers at McEachern", in order to improve the appearance of the page. The faculty advisor deleted the paragraph concerning new teachers' attitudes about homosexual teachers (which is reprinted as Appendix "A" to this Order), since he felt that it "did not fit in with the rest of the story and because the writer, Jennifer Dehart, had also felt that it did not fit." Protteau Affidavit, ¶ 10.

The faculty advisor was also responsible for substituting the word "darn" for the word "damn" in another article about a local radio personality. The faculty advisor maintains that he took this action in view of Cobb County School Board regulations that prohibit the use on campus of obscenities or vulgar language. He also felt that it would have caused a disruption among conservative and religious students and their parents.

The court finds that these justifications, even though made in good faith, fail to satisfy the legal standards expressed in *Tinker* and *Shanley, supra.* To allow the faculty advisor to excise possibly controversial material in the name of improving an article's appearance would too easily allow a circumvention of the *Shanley* rule that student expression may not be prohibited solely because of disagreement with its content. It is also inconceivable that the use of the word "damn" one time in the newspaper would have caused material and substantial interference with school activities. The actions of the faculty advisor cannot be sustained.

IV.

The most serious allegation of censorship concerns the confiscation of the entire September edition of the *Arrowhead*. The defendants have sought to justify their actions in this regard on numerous grounds. The school principal expressed concern that the use of photographs from other publications without permission might have exposed the school to a suit for copyright infringement. Although this may have been a sufficient reason to delay distribution of the *Arrowhead* for a few days until competent legal advice was obtained on the matter, the court cannot conclude that it justified a total suppression of the newspaper.

The principal also felt that an article entitled "Vietnam Syndrome" might be libelous. Although the article may be in poor taste, it clearly does not rise to the level of actionable libel under the standard set forth in *New York Times Co. v. Sullivan,* 376 U.S. 254, 84 S.Ct. 710, 11 L.Ed.2d 686 (1963). Again, had the principal merely delayed distribution of the *Arrowhead* while legal counsel was consulted, there would be no objection to his conduct. However, total suppression of the newspaper was not justified.

The principal also noted that an article regarding ticket prices to McEachern High football games contained statistics which were in error. In addition, the Chairman of the English Department pointed out a number of technical defects in the newspaper in grammar and spelling. These reasons are clearly insufficient to permit the school administration to infringe upon students' free speech, for these faults are not the sort which would lead to a significant disruption of the educational process. *See Schiff* v. *Williams,* 519 F.2d 257 (5th Cir. 1975).

The defendants have most closely approached the legal standard which justifies the prohibition of student expression in their assertion that the publication of certain articles in the September edition would have resulted in a substantial disturbance and disruption of student activities at McEachern High. One such article was entitled "Council Activities," and the defendants have alleged that it would have caused a substantial disturbance because it was critical of the student body president. They have also alleged that the article was a personal attack on that student, and thus constituted an "invasion of the rights of others" which has no constitutional protection under *Tinker, supra,* 393 U.S. at 513, 89 S.Ct. at 740.

The court is unable to discern any reason why the publication of this article would have led to a substantial interference with educational activities. It is the court's conclusion, after considering all of the evidence before it, that the article's appearance would have, at most, provoked discussion and comment among the students at McEachern. Perhaps some students would have found the statements which the plaintiff made at the Student Council meeting and which were reported in the article to be controversial. But as was stated in *Shanley, supra,* 462 F.2d at 971, "it should be axiomatic at this point in our nation's history that in a democracy 'controversy' is, as a matter of constitutional law, never sufficient in and of itself to stifle the views of any citizen. . . . " It may also be true that the majority of students would have supported the opposing views of the student body president (which were also reported in the article), since he had been overwhelmingly elected by a 95% vote of the students. Be that as it may, it has been stated that in the context of student publications, "speech cannot be stifled by the state merely because it would perhaps draw an adverse reaction from the majority of people. . . " *Bazaar* v. *Fortune,* 476 F.2d 570, 579, *rehearing en banc,* 489 F.2d 225 (5th Cir. 1973).

Nor is the court able to comprehend the manner in which the article in question constitutes a personal attack upon the student body president. Although the story reports a dispute which occurred at a Student Council meeting with regard to the powers of the officers to assess dues, it does not vilify or ridicule the president, nor does it in any way attack his reputation or character. As such, the article is quite different in nature from the material involved in *Frasca* v. *Andrews,* 463 F.Supp. 1043 (E.D.N.Y.1979), which the defendants have cited in support of their position. In *Frasca,* the post-publication seizure of a high school newspaper was upheld, in part, on the ground that it contained an unsigned letter criticizing the vice-president of the student government. The letter stated, *inter alia,* that the student in question had "been a total failure in performing his duties" and was a "total disgrace to the school", that he did not maintain a high academic average, that he attended only a few of many student council meetings, and that he had changed his report card grades "by typing over the letters on the computer terminal." 463 F.Supp. at 1046. There is nothing in the "Council Activities" article presently before the court that even remotely resembles the type of personal attack found in the *Frasca* letter. Moreover, in the New York case, the newspaper was to have been distributed on the last day of the school year, thus allowing no opportunity for rebuttal on the part of the student who was the subject of the letter. Under those circumstances, it could well be said that based upon "the virtually certain irreparable harm which would result from the letter, . . . [there was] a rational and substantial basis for preventing its publication." *Frasca, supra,* 463 F.Supp. at 1052. Such was not the case here.

The defendants also objected to a fictitious "Letters" column, and were particularly concerned with a letter attributed to "D. Newburn" from "McEachern, GA", which reads, in full, as follows:

I've been hearing a lot about a School Spirit. I don't know about everyone else, but I'm scared to death about spirits. Shoudn't we call an Exorcist or something?

The student chaplain at McEachern High School is named Danny Newburn. Because the McEachern student body is generally religious and conservative, the principal felt that this letter would cause a disturbance and disruption if published. The court concludes, however, that the principal's good faith belief amounted to no more than an "undifferentiated fear or apprehension of disturbance," which *Tinker, supra,* instructs us "is not enough to overcome the right to freedom of expression." 393 U.S. at 508, 89 S.Ct. at 737. In the absence of additional, compelling evidence, it was unreasonable to equate the possibility of controversy or adverse reaction with a substantial likelihood of disruption. Moreover, the letter itself seems innocuous enough. If the student chaplain had felt that his rights had been invaded in any way by its content, then a less restrictive solution would have been to require a retraction or an apology to be printed in the following issue.

The final allegation by the defendants concerning the September issue is that the article entitled "Advertising Metamorphoris" [*sic*] would have adversely affected racial relations at McEachern High School and caused a substantial disruption of student activities due to increased racial tensions. The article quotes a 1960 political advertisement from the *Marietta Daily Journal* which states "W. O. Smitha will provide leadership to keep our schools on a segregated basis. He knows it to be in the best interest to educate the white children apart from the colored." The court concludes that there was no reasonable basis to forecast that the publication of this material would cause a significant and material disruption at McEachern High. By all accounts, racial relations at the high school are good. The principal termed them "very good," while another of defendants' affiants, a black teacher, thinks they are "excellent." Hatcher Affidavit, ¶ 10; Charles Affidavit, ¶ 5. Of the seventeen hundred students at McEachern, only approximately 100 are black. Yet the student body president, who is black, was overwhelmingly elected by a 95% vote of the entire student body. (Thus the case at bar is distinguishable from *Augustus* v. *School Board of Escambia County,* 507 F.2d 152 (5th Cir. 1975), cited by the defendants in their briefs, where some restrictions on student First Amendment rights were upheld against the background of continuing violence and racial unrest at a Florida high school.) There is no reason to believe that the article in question will destroy this harmonious atmosphere. In addition, suppression of the September *Arrowhead* was not justified on the ground that this material was potentially libelous, for the same reasons heretofore expressed regarding the "Vietnam Syndrome" article.

V.

The third act of alleged censorship concerns the deletion of two articles from the October 16 issue of the newspaper, which was distributed to the student body as scheduled. The faculty advisor admittedly removed an article on the football team "because it was not in a proper journalistic form for publication on the sports page." Protteau Affidavit, ¶ 24. Although the text of the proposed article is not before the court, the stated justification for its removal again too closely resembles censorship of content in the guise of correcting technical defects, a practice which has been disapproved as violative of freedom of expression. *See Schiff, supra.* The other article that was removed is set out as Appendix "B" to this Order and concerns the confiscation of the first issue of the *Arrowhead.* The faculty advisor states that he removed this article "because the story had received extensive coverage in the Atlanta and Marietta newspapers and because reporting on it would have reopened all the antagonism, disturbance, and interference with school activities caused and threatened by the issue when it was shown to the [journalism] class and selected students." Protteau Affidavit, ¶ 25. The court has read the article in question and finds that it is straightforward news reporting of an incident which would be of no small importance to the faculty and students at McEachern High. The court concludes that there was no reasonable basis for the faculty advisor to predict that a substantial disruption of school activities would be caused by its publication.

VI.

The fourth act of alleged censorship occurred when the principal decided to discontinue the newspaper because litigation had been threatened. A literary magazine was substituted instead. The court fails to understand how the plaintiff's actions in resorting to the courts in an attempt to vindicate his First Amendment rights would justify a further abridgement of those rights by the school authorities. The principal has also alleged that the *Arrowhead* was financially insolvent and unable to meet its bills due to insufficient advertising revenues. However, it appears that the major cause of the loss of advertising revenue was the confiscation of the September issue, since ads that had been previously sold had to be run in the October issue at no charge. The defendants cannot justify their suspension of the newspaper on the basis of a financial crisis for which they, themselves, were responsible. The defendants have also claimed that no additional school funds are available for the *Arrowhead*. This is no defense. If necessary, the funding must be provided by the defendants from sources otherwise available. As was stated in *Joyner v. Whiting*, 477 F.2d 456 (4th Cir. 1973):

> The principles reaffirmed in *Healy v. James, supra* have been extensively applied to strike down every form of censorship of student publications at state-supported institutions. Censorship of constitutionally protected expression cannot be imposed by suspending the editors, suppressing circulation, requiring imprimatur of controversial articles, excising repugnant material, withdrawing financial support, or asserting any other form of censorial oversight based on the institution's power of the purse.

477 F.2d at 460 (footnotes omitted).

The *Arrowhead*'s current financial status does not preclude the relief sought in the present case.

VII.

Additional arguments made by the defendants are also unpersuasive. Although the evidence shows that the distribution of the September issue of the *Arrowhead* to the journalism class responsible for its publication resulted in discussion and comment, and some controversy, this was not necessarily contrary to the educational process in that class. It is clear that class activities were not substantially disrupted, for the students accomplished their intended task of readying the newspaper for distribution the following day. Apparently, some students raised questions about why their articles were not published, why a certain individual's name was not included on the masthead, whether certain articles had been substituted for others, and whether one story's by-line was correct. These were primarily journalistic concerns regarding the manner in which the newspaper had been compiled, and such problems could have been settled within the framework of the journalism class itself. It was unreasonable for the defendants to base a forecast of material and substantial disruption among the student body as a whole upon a controversy which occurred among the newspaper staff concerning journalistic matters.

REQUIREMENTS FOR A PRELIMINARY INJUNCTION

In order to be entitled to a preliminary injunction, the plaintiff must be able to show the following: (1) a substantial likelihood that he will prevail on the merits; (2) a substantial threat that he will suffer irreparable injury if the injunction is not granted; (3) that the threatened injury to him outweighs the potential harm that the injunction may inflict on the defendants; and (4) that the public interest will not be harmed by granting the injunction. *Hillsboro News Co. v. Tampa*, 544 F.2d 860 (5th Cir. 1977).

Before examining these factors, the court notes that the defendants have raised the equitable defense of plaintiff's unclean hands, relying on *Sullivan v. Houston Independent School District*, 475 F.2d 1071 (5th Cir. 1973). The defendants claim that the plaintiff personally dominated the newspaper, arbitrarily rejected articles prepared by other students, failed to run or altered advertisements, and was rude and disrespectful to the faculty advisor. After considering the evidence, the court declines to accept all of the defendants' contentions in this regard. In any event, the defendants' allegations fall far short of the situation described in *Sullivan, supra*, 475 F.2d at 1076, where the Fifth Circuit held that a student's "flagrant disregard of established school regulations, his open and repeated defiance of the principal's request [to cease selling a certain underground newspaper], and his resort to profane epithet" precluded equitable relief. By way of contrast, the plaintiff in the present case has sought to challenge the defendants' actions in an orderly manner by resorting to the courts, and the most serious example of disrespectfulness that the defendants have cited was the plaintiff's telling the faculty advisor that he was "crazy" to want to change the *Arrowhead*'s printer. Without condoning such behavior, the court concludes that the plaintiff is not precluded from obtaining equitable relief on the basis of unclean hands.

Based on the foregoing analysis and a consideration of all the evidence before it, the court finds that the plaintiff has shown a strong likelihood of prevailing on the merits in this action. Moreover, the plaintiff, who was appointed as co-editor-in-chief of the *Arrowhead* for the 1979-80 school year, is suffering irreparable harm in being deprived of his editorial position. The newspaper was intended to be a learning experience for those students interested in journalism. This educational opportunity has been suspended. In addition, the students are being denied the right to disseminate and receive the information that would have been published in the newspaper. Under these circumstances, the court concludes that irreparable injury has been adequately demonstrated.

The court also finds that the benefits to the plaintiff arising from the issuance of a preliminary injunction are not outweighed by the harm to the other parties, since it is apparent that the defendants will not suffer any harm if the material in question is published and distributed. Finally, the public interest will not be harmed by granting the injunction. On the contrary, the vindication of First Amendment rights is in the public interest. This is especially true in the present situation, since "[t]he vigilant protection of constitutional freedoms is nowhere more vital than in the community of American schools." *Shelton v. Tucker*, 364 U.S. 479, 487, 81 S.Ct. 247, 251, 5 L.Ed.2d 231 (1960). For all of the foregoing reasons, the court concludes that a preliminary injunction should issue.

ORDER

It is hereby ordered that the defendants, individually and in their official capacities, and their officers, agents, servants, employees, and those persons in active concert or participation with them who receive actual notice of this Order by personal service or otherwise (hereinafter collectively referred to as "Defendants and their agents"), be preliminarily restrained and enjoined from:

A. Prohibiting or interfering with the distribution of the September 27, 1979 edition of *The McEachern Arrowhead* or any material contained therein:

B. Prohibiting or interfering with the publication and distribution of an issue or issues of *The McEachern Arrowhead* containing any of the following material:

(1) the occasional use of the word "damn";

(2) the paragraph describing the attitudes of new teachers at McEachern High School toward homosexual teachers, which is attached as Appendix "A" to this Order:

(3) the article explaining why the September 27 edition of the *Arrowhead* was not distributed as scheduled, which article is attached as Appendix "B" to this Order:

C. Engaging in prior restraint of the *Arrowhead* by any means including but not limited to cutting off funds from or terminating the existence of the *Arrowhead,* censoring material in or from an issue of the *Arrowhead,* prohibiting or interfering with the distribution of an issue of the *Arrowhead,* or ordering any editor or staff member not to publish material in an issue of the *Arrowhead,* unless the material censored by one of the above described means or otherwise is one of the following:

(1) Obscene as to minors aged fourteen through eighteen, as defined in accordance with applicable legal standards;

(2) Libelous, as defined in accordance with applicable legal standards; or

(3) Material which Defendants and their agents could reasonably forecast would cause substantial disruption of or material interference with school activities or material interference with the rights of other students or faculty, and which disruption and interference cannot be controlled or prevented by means other than censoring the material;

D. Denying any rights or privileges to the Plaintiff because of the activity of the Plaintiff in connection with this litigation; or disciplining the Plaintiff for any action taken by the Plaintiff prior to the date of this Order in connection with publication of the *Arrowhead,* unless the Plaintiff is first afforded a proper hearing.

It is further ordered that the Defendants and their agents:

E. Immediately release, for purpose of sale and distribution, all copies of the September 27, 1979 edition of the *Arrowhead* in their possession, custody, or control, except that Defendants and their agents may retain no more than twenty (20) copies of the September edition;

F. Immediately reinstate the *Arrowhead* as the newspaper of McEachern High School;

G. Immediately reinstate the Plaintiff as co-editor-in-chief of the *Arrowhead;*

H. Effective March 10, 1980, at the beginning of the next school quarter, reinstate the journalism class having as class members the editors and staff of the *Arrowhead* and having as one of the class activities the monthly publication of the *Arrowhead.*

The court points out that no procedures are presently in effect at McEachern High School which would provide guidelines with respect to the prior screening of student expression. While expressing no opinion as to whether the promulgation of publication policy regulations should be undertaken by the school authorities, the court notes that none exist at the present time.

This Order shall remain in force and effect until further Order by this court or until June, 1981, whichever is earlier.

APPENDIX "A"

How do these teachers feel about homosexual teachers? The reaction varies. "I would not want my children to have a homosexual teacher, homosexuality goes against my religion." "Sexuality is private, unless it interferes with teaching." "Homosexuals should be able to teach without prejudice, but not impress their sexual views."

APPENDIX "B"
Confiscation of Issue One

Issue One of the *Arrowhead* for this year was printed, but the copies of the newspaper were confiscated by Principal T. J. Hatcher on the date scheduled for publication.

In a meeting with *Arrowhead* Editors, Hatcher said that he principally objected to an article quoting a school board member's segregationist stance in a 1960 election. He also objected to the overall "negative attitude" of the paper.

The incident received considerable newspaper attention and articles appeared in the *Cobb Extra,*, the *Atlanta Journal* and *The Marietta Daily Journal,* and editorials by Lewis Grizzard and Richard Matthews were in the *Atlanta Journal* and *Constitution,* respectively, favoring the editors of the *Arrowhead.*

THE United States Court of Appeals, Fourth Circuit, decides against high school students who had brought suit against school officials who banned an underground newspaper being distributed on school grounds. The principal, applying a school guideline providing for halting the distribution of a publication if it encouraged "actions which endanger the health and safety of students," prohibited the distribution of *Joint Effort* because, among other things, it contained an advertisement for drug paraphernalia. The Court argued that the guideline applied by the principal was not unconstitutional on its face. The Court held that "the regulation which allows the principal to halt the distribution of materials that encourage 'actions which endanger the health or safety of students' is not violative of the First Amendment. The school officials thus acted within their constitutional authority in halting and banning the further distribution of the *Joint Effort* on school property."

Williams v. *Spencer,* 622 F.2d 1200 (1980)

WIDENER, Circuit Judge:

Gregory J. Williams and Mark I. Gutstein, students at the time of filing this action at Springbrook High School within the Montgomery County, Maryland school district, brought suit seeking declaratory and injunctive relief, damages, and attorneys' fees against the Montgomery County Board of Education, the superintendent of schools, an area assistant superintendent, a school principal, and a building monitor. They claimed an alleged interference with their First Amendment rights, and sought an order enjoining the school authorities from restraining on school property the distribution of their non-school sponsored publication, the *Joint Effort,* Issue 2, and from enforcing the Publication Guidelines of Montgomery County. From a judgment in favor of the defendants, plaintiffs appeal. We affirm.

During the 1976-77 school term, the plaintiffs published and distributed the first issue of the *Joint Effort,* a self-styled underground newspaper designed as an alternative for student expression. This issue was distributed on school grounds with the express permission of the principal.

Following the success of that first issue, the plaintiffs published a second issue of the paper the following school year. The second issue contained various literary contributions, cartoons, and advertisements.

The plaintiffs printed approximately 350 copies of the *Joint Effort,* and acquired advance approval of the school officials for the distribution of the paper on February 17, 1978. The plaintiffs were not, however, required to seek prepublication or predistribution approval of the contents of the publication. In fact, the school officials were not even aware of the contents of the publication prior to the commencement of distribution.

Ten to twenty minutes after the sale of the paper began, the building monitor, Mr. Austin Patterson, halted the sale of the paper, confiscated the remaining copies, and took them to the school principal, Dr. Thomas P. Marshall. Patterson was the subject of a cartoon on the back cover of the paper that depicted him in cowboy clothing and speaking in dialect.[1] The students had distributed approximately eighty copies of the paper before the distribution was halted.

Marshall upheld Patterson's seizure of the paper and banned any further distribution of Issue 2 on school property. The principal did, however, return the confiscated papers to the plaintiffs at the conclusion of the same day on which the papers were confiscated. The ban on distribution applied only to distribution on school property.

As required by the Student Rights and Responsibilities Policy (S.R.R.P.) § IVC-2(d);[2] the school principal, within two school days of halting distribution, stated in writing his reasons for the action.³ In his letter, Marshall stated:

1. A copy of the "Joint Effort" was reviewed and the publication was found to be in violation of Section 4C, titled "Publications." The specific violation is under C-2(c)(2). A member of the staff was depicted in derogatory terms with clear indications of racial overtones.

2. A second violation occurs in the promotion of drug paraphernalia. This is a violation of Section 2-C(c)(5), which prohibits the distribution of material which encourages actions which endanger the health and safety of students.

The first reason referred to the cartoon depicting the building monitor in western clothing. The second reason for halting the distribution of the *Joint Effort* referred to an advertisement for the Earthworks Headshop, a store that specializes in the sale of drug paraphernalia. The advertisement primarily promoted the sale of a waterpipe used to smoke marijuana and hashish.⁴ The ad also advertised paraphernalia used in connection with cocaine.

Following the principal's decision to ban any further distribution of that issue of the *Joint Effort*, the students followed the appeals procedure provided for in S.R.R.P. § XIII—Due Process—Appeal of the Decision of the Principal. The students first appealed to the area assistant superintendent, Dr. George B. Thomas, and obtained an informal hearing on March 15, 1978. In an undated memorandum, but issued apparently within the five school days called for in S.R.R.P. § XIIIC-3(c), Thomas upheld the decision of the principal.

The students then appealed to the superintendent of schools, Dr. Charles M. Bernardo, who rendered his decision in writing on April 14, 1978, also within the time limit provided for in S.R.R.P. § XIII. Bernardo supported the decision of the principal and upheld the ban on further distribution on school property of that issue of the *Joint Effort*. The superintendent expressly noted that the ban did not apply to any future issue of the publication that did not violate the guidelines.⁵

Following their unsuccessful adminstrative appeals, the students filed this suit against members of the school board, the superintendent, the area assistant superintendent, the principal, and the building monitor. The plaintiffs claimed that the seizure and continued restraint against distribution of the *Joint Effort* violated their First Amendment rights, and that the school system's regulatory scheme was facially invalid. The students sought damages for the restraint on distribution of the *Joint Effort*, and declaratory relief and an injunction to prohibit the school officials from further preventing its distribution. Additionally, the plaintiffs sought to enjoin the enforcement of the publication guidelines of Montgomery County.

Regarding the alleged First Amendment violation from the prohibition against distribution, the district court considered only whether the presence of the advertisement for the head shop provided the school with the right to halt the distribution of the *Joint Effort*, and held that the school was justified in halting and prohibiting further distribution of the paper.⁶ As to the alleged facial invalidity of the guidelines, the court held that the health and safety regulation was not so vague as to violate First Amendment standards, and that the time involved in the school administrative appeal procedure was not unconstitutional.

As to the plaintiffs' charges of facial invalidity regarding certain other regulations,⁷ the district court held that the plaintiffs lacked standing to challenge them because the regulations were not directly involved in halting the distribution of the *Joint Effort*, and thus the plaintiffs suffered no personal injury because of them. We affirm because the plaintiffs have failed to show that they were injured by the operation of the regulation. *Ashwander v. T. V. A.*, 297 U.S. 288, 341, 347, 56 S.Ct. 466, 480, 483, 80 L.Ed. 688 (Mr. Justice Brandeis concurring).

The record indicates that the plaintiffs will have now graduated from Springbrook High School. Thus, we treat as moot the claims for injunctive relief for the case presents no question that is capable of repetition, yet evades review. *Indianapolis School Commissioners v. Jacobs*, 420 U.S. 128, 95 S.Ct. 848, 43 L.Ed.2d 74 (1975); *DeFunis v. Odegaard*, 416 U.S. 312, 94 S.Ct. 1704, 40 L.Ed.2d 164 (1974). We do not decide the claims for declaratory relief because the merits of the health and safety regulation are decided in connection with the claim for damages. This is not a case, for example, in which declaratory relief may be proper, but equitable relief withheld for equitable reasons.

Because the plaintiffs sought compensatory damages for the cost of promoting the publication, and also exemplary damages, we must determine whether the school officials violated the plaintiffs' First Amendment rights when the copies of the *Joint Effort* were seized and distribution on school property prohibited. The question is whether the publication guidelines involved in the stoppage of distribution and subsequent administrative appeal violate the First Amendment.

While secondary school students do not "shed their constitutional rights to freedom of speech or expression at the schoolhouse gate," *Tinker v. Des Moines Independent Community School District*, 393 U.S. 503, 506, 89 S.Ct. 733, 736, 21 L.Ed.2d 731

(1969), neither are their First Amendment rights necessarily "co-extensive with those of adults." Id. at 515, 89 S.Ct. at 741. (Justice Stewart concurring). "It is generally held that the constitutional right to free speech of public secondary school students may be modified or curtailed by school regulations 'reasonably designed to adjust these rights to the needs of the school environment.'" *Quarterman* v. *Byrd,* 453 F.2d 54, 58 (4th Cir. 1971).

In this case, S.R.R.P. § IVC-2(c) provides in pertinent part: "Distribution may be halted, and disciplinary action taken by the principal after the distribution has begun, if the publication: ... (5) Encourages actions which endanger the health or safety of students." The school principal, under this regulation, halted and prohibited further distribution of the student publication that contained an advertisement for drug paraphernalia.

Plaintiffs challenge this regulation as being impermissibly vague and thus violative of the First Amendment. We disagree. In *Baughman* v. *Freienmuth,* 478 F.2d 1345, 1351 (4th Cir. 1973), we held that a prior restraint regulation "must contain precise criteria sufficiently spelling out what is forbidden so that a reasonably intelligent student will know what he may write and what he may not write." We find no merit to the argument that a reasonably intelligent high school student would not know that an advertisement promoting the sale of drug paraphernalia encourages actions that endanger the health or safety of students. The district court took judicial notice of the problem of drugs in today's society and their danger to the health and safety of those who use them. We find no error in that determination by the district court. Because of the infinite variety of materials that might be found to encourage actions which endanger the health or safety of students, we conclude that the regulation describes as explicitly as is required the type of material of which the principal may halt distribution. See *Arnett* v. *Kennedy,* 416 U.S. 134, 161, 94 S.Ct. 1633, 1647, 40 L.Ed.2d 15 (1974), holding valid against a vagueness claim removal for "such cause as may promote the efficiency of the service." The First Amendment rights of the students must yield to the superior interest of the school in seeing that materials that encourage actions which endanger the health or safety of students are not distributed on school property. Because the only type of material regulated by the guideline is material that must yield to the school's superior interest, we think the guideline does not prohibit constitutionally protected conduct of the students. Thus, the guideline is not unconstitutional on its face.

Nor can it be disputed that an advertisement encouraging the use of drugs encourages actions which in fact endanger the health or safety of students. The district court took judicial notice of this, and we agree with that determination. Indeed, the plaintiffs themselves as much as concede that drug use is a harmful activity endangering health and safety.

We also find no merit to the argument of plaintiffs that the school officials had to demonstrate that the material would substantially disrupt school activities. We note that the Supreme Court in *Tinker* v. *Des Moines Independent Community School District,* 393 U.S. 503, 509, 89 S.Ct. 733, 737, 21 L.Ed.2d 731 (1969), and this court in *Quarterman, Baughman,* and *Nitzberg* v. *Parks,* 525 F.2d 378, 382-83 (4th Cir. 1971), indicated that "school authorities may by appropriate regulation, exercise prior restraint upon publications distributed on school premises during school hours in those special circumstances where they can 'reasonably "forecast substantial disruption..."' on account of such printed material." *Quarterman* v. *Byrd,* 453 F.2d at 58 (footnote omitted). Such disruption, however, is merely one justification for school authorities to restrain the distribution of a publication; nowhere has it been held to be the sole justification.

Nor is the present case in conflict with prior Fourth Circuit cases dealing with high school publications. The nature of the restraint in this case is far less burdensome than was true in *Quarterman, Baughman,* and *Nitzberg.* In those cases, the relevant regulations required that the publication be submitted to the principal *prior* to distribution, whereas here the students were not required to acquire approval before beginning distribution of the paper. Indeed, those cases could be read to apply only to those situations where prior approval from the appropriate school official is required before distribution may occur. See *Baughman,* 478 F.2d at 1350. In the case at hand, only after the publication was partially distributed did the school authorities even become aware of the contents of the paper. Additionally, the applicable regulations in *Quarterman, Baughman,* and *Nitzberg* failed to meet minimum constitutional requirements. In *Quarterman,* for example, the regulation failed to provide any standard at all for the determination of what materials could be distributed on school grounds. Such is not the case here. Finally, we think the fact that the advertisement was purely commercial is an additional reason for upholding the prohibition against distributing the *Joint Effort* on school property. Commercial speech, although protected by the First Amendment, is not entitled to the same degree of protection as other types of speech. See, e.g., *Bates* v. *State Bar of Arizona,* 433 U.S. 350, 363, 380-82, 97 S.Ct. 2691, 2692, 2707-2708, 53 L.Ed.2d 810 (1977). This case is quite different from one, for example, in which a school prohibits the distribution of a publication containing an article of some literary value that may examine drugs and drug use. The printed material in issue here was paid for by a store seeking to profit from its encouragement of the use of drugs. In *Quarterman, Baughman,* and *Nitzberg,* none of the disputed materials involved commercial advertisements.

We hold therefore that the regulation which allows the principal to halt the distribution of materials that encourage "actions which endanger the health or safety of students" is not violative of the First Amendment. The school officials thus acted within their constitutional authority in halting and banning the further distribution of the *Joint Effort* on school property.

Plaintiffs also claim that the appeals procedure provided for in S.R.R.P. fails to meet minimum constitutional guarantees, alleging that the length of the appeal in this instance was excessive. We find no merit to that contention.

S.R.R.P. § IVC-2(d) provides that if the principal decides to halt distribution of a non-school sponsored publication, he shall state his reasons in writing within two school days and provide the students with a copy of his reasons. S.R.R.P. § XIII—Due Process—Appeal of the Decision of the Principal, sets out the procedure to be followed for an appeal from the principal's decision. The aggrieved student may, within ten school days, appeal the decision to the area assistant superintendent who must issue a written decision within ten school days after receiving the appeal. If the student requests an informal hearing, the hearing must be held within ten school days, and the assistant superintendent then must render his decision within five school days of the hearing. The student may then appeal an adverse decision to the superintendent of schools who must render his decision in writing within five school days. The guidelines do not provide for an appeal to the School Board. The record in this case indicates that only eight weeks, including holidays, elapsed from the time the distribution was first halted until the superintendent rendered his decision.

We hold that the appeals procedure provided for meets the requirement of this court that there be an "adequate and prompt appeals procedure." *Quarterman,* 453 F.2d at 59; *Baughman,* 478 F.2d at 1349; *Nitzberg,* 525 F.2d at 383. First, the time limits are on their face quite reasonable, two days for the principal to state reasons, and ten days for the area assistant superintendent (five if after a hearing), and five days for the superintendent to decide. Ten day limits to appeal decisions of the principal and assistant superintendent discourage delay. Nor was the duration of the administrative appeal in this case unduly long. There is no indication that there was any undue delay in handing down the various decisions required. Also, the record does not disclose what portion of the eight week period was expended by plaintiffs in exercising various appeals. And we again emphasize that the students were not required to submit a copy of the publication for prior approval, and they were free to distribute the papers off school property the same day distribution on school property was halted, thus lessening the impact from the duration of the administrative appeals process.[8] Therefore, we find no infirmity in the length of the appeals process.

In deciding this case, although there was no prior restraint in the sense of previous approval of content of the printed matter, we have, to give the plaintiffs the benefit of the doubt, considered that the regulations complained of come with a presumption of invalidity, *Baughman,* p. 1348, although, without deciding the question, it may be doubtful that such heavy burden should exist on the facts of this case. In all events, we are of the opinion any such burden to establish validity as may exist has been successfully borne by defendants.

Were injunctive relief all that plaintiffs prayed for, we would remand for the dismissal of those claims as moot. *Jacobs,* 420 U.S. p. 130, 95 S.Ct. p. 850. Because we decide the substantive merits of the controversy, however, without considering the availability of injunctive relief because the question is moot, and, of course, not deciding that question, we simply affirm the order of the district court appealed from which entered judgment for the defendants.

Affirmed.

NOTES

1. The cartoon shows Patterson dressed as a sheriff in western style clothing. He holds a smoking pistol and the caption reads: "DON' SMOKE DAT EVIL WEED, I'LL BUST YO ASS!"
2. S.R.R.P. § IVC-2(d) provides:
    If the distribution is halted, the principal shall state his/her reasons in writing within two school days, providing a copy to the students making the distribution and a copy to the area assistant superintendent. Such a decision may be appealed.
3. The principal's letter, dated February 27, 1978, was provided to the students within two school days. School was closed for vacation the week following the distribution halt.
4. Additionally, in about one-half of the 350 papers printed for distribution was inserted a piece of cigarette rolling paper. Our word assassin is derived from hashish, Webster's Third New International Dictionary (1971) p. 150.

Marijuana, hashish, and cocaine are all controlled substances under both Maryland and federal law. See Md.Code Art. §§ 277, 279, 286, 287; 21 U.S.C. §§ 802, 812, 841, 844, 845.

5. The review by the superintendent is the final step provided for by S.R.R.P. The superintendent, in his letter to the students, however, indicated that they could request a hearing before the School Board, which would decide whether to grant the request. The students did not avail themselves of this offer.

6. Because of its reliance on the health or safety regulation, the district court did not determine whether the prohibition in S.R.R.P. § IVC-2(c)(2) against the distribution of a publication containing libelous material allowed the school to halt distribution because of the cartoon. Our affirmance of the district court on the health or safety ground makes it unnecessary to consider that rule allowing the school to halt the distribution of libelous material.

7. Plaintiffs also challenged the constitutionality of other aspects of the publication guidelines, on the ground that they were facially invalid. These included (1) the absence of a provision for the principal's failure to explain his reason for halting distribution, within the time required by the rules; (2) the absence of a written requirement of a hearing before the principal; (3) the absence of a time limit for noting an administrative appeal from the superintendent to the school board; (4) the prohibition on distribution of anonymously sponsored publications; and the meaning or definition or lack thereof for the terms (5) "school days"; (6) "distribution"; and (7) "substantial disruption." As we note in the text, plaintiffs concede that these portions of the publication guidelines were not directly involved in the halt of distribution of the *Joint Effort*.

8. Plaintiffs rely upon *Leibner* v. *Sharbaugh*, 429 F.Supp. 744 (E.D.Va.1977), as authority for the proposition that the duration of the appeals procedure in this case was excessive. In that case, however, as in *Nitzberg*, 525 F.2d at 383-85, the students were required to submit to the principal a copy of the publication prior to beginning distribution, and no time limit was set within which the principal was required to render a decision. In the case at hand, the principal's halt of distribution is in effect a decision, and he then has only two school days in which to explain his decision. If our decision may be considered to be contrary to *Leibner*, we decline to follow that case.

THE United States Court of Appeals, Ninth Circuit, decides against a probationary journalism teacher who was not rehired after the two year probationary period, the teacher alleging "that his employment as a high school journalism teacher was terminated wrongfully as a result of constitutionally protected action he took as his school's newspaper advisor." In deciding against the teacher, the Court stated: "When considering a public employer's motivation for dismissing an employee, the trier of fact must examine the various proffered reasons and determine whether constitutionally protected activities played a substantial role in the decision.... In the present case, the District Court made the factual finding that First Amendment considerations did not motivate the decision not to rehire the appellant. Accordingly, we must affirm unless this determination is clearly erroneous.... The record in the present case fully supports the lower court's finding that the school board's actions were properly motivated. The evidence in the record demonstrates that Nicholson failed to follow several rules governing school bookkeeping duties and declined, on several occasions, to require his students to follow school rules. Moreover, Nicholson repeatedly disobeyed orders of his immediate supervisor regarding the student newspaper—a fact that concededly led to the deterioration of an important school relationship."

Nicholson v. *Board of Education*, 682 F.2d 858 (1982)

SPENCER WILLIAMS, District Judge:

This appeal results from an action filed by plaintiff and appellant Don Patrick Nicholson in which he alleged that his employment as a high school journalism teacher was terminated wrongfully as a result of constitutionally protected action he took as his school's newspaper advisor. The United States District Court for the Central District of California rendered judgment for the defendants on the ground that Nicholson had failed to establish that his rights under the first amendment were infringed. We agree and therefore affirm.

I. FACTS

Appellant, Don Patrick Nicholson, was employed as a probationary teacher of journalism at Torrance High School from September 1968 until termination of his employment in May 1970. During the course of his two years of employment, which included service as the advisor to the school-sponsored newspaper, Nicholson became involved in a series of disputes with school officials regarding publication of certain articles. These articles concerned a number of controversial subjects including a feature story on minority unrest in a local community, an article on police-student relations and a critical commentary on the school's treatment of the Fifth Amendment rights of students.

In light of the sensitive nature of these articles, the school's principal, Dr. Ahee, informed Nicholson that articles on these limited subjects must be submitted to him before publication to ensure their accuracy. in addition, Dr. Ahee made it clear that he wanted students in the journalism class to adhere to the general ethical standards enunciated by the Rotary International, of which the principal was a member. The standards consisted of the "Four-Way Test" that evaluated expression based on its truth, fairness, good will and benefit.

On several occasions, Nicholson refused to comply with his supervisor's instructions regarding pre-publication review of student-written articles. When articles were presented for review, Dr. Ahee often expressed his disapproval but never denied publication or censored the submitted piece.

At the end of his two year probationary period, Nicholson was informed by the school district that he would not be recommended for reemployment. Appellant sought a hearing before a state administrative officer as provided by California Education Code § 44949(c).

At the hearing on Nicholson's claim, it became clear that the school district had acted on several independent grounds when it refused to grant him tenure. Appellant had a history of failure to comply with record keeping requirements. During his two years at Torrance High School, Nicholson failed to return an interest survey regarding his employment, he failed to complete a required check-out list of materials and he did not submit an identification for school property which resulted in the loss of twenty-eight textbooks.

On other occasions, Nicholson permitted his students to violate school rules and regulations. Appellant often permitted his students to leave class early or even to leave campus entirely in violation of school policies. On one occasion, Nicholson allowed his students to attend a taped television interview in direct violation of the principal's instructions. Another time, appellant permitted a survey to be circulated without prior approval from the administration as was required by school district regulations. After school officials informed him of the violation, Nicholson permitted the survey to continue and published the results in the student newspaper.

Appellant was given a five day hearing in June 1970 at which time he argued that his first amendment rights had been violated. At the conclusion of the proceedings, the hearing officer rendered a decision that the dismissal was justifed on several independent grounds including insubordination, failure to obey school rules and failure to cooperate with school officials in his capacity as journalism teacher.

Three years later, Nicholson filed the instant lawsuit contending *inter alia* that the defendants' refusal to renew his teaching contract was based on actions protected by the first and fourteenth amendments[1]

The court below tried the case on the factual record from the administrative hearing pursuant to stipulation. The court found that the plaintiff failed to carry his burden of showing that the defendants had violated his rights of free expression and subsequently filed Findings of Fact and Conclusions of Law from which the plaintiff appealed.

II. QUESTIONS PRESENTED

On appeal, the questions presented are whether the trial court's conclusion that the school district's decision was not premised on an impermissible motive is erroneous, whether appellant has a personal first amendment right to encourage publication of controversial articles in the high school newspaper and whether the district court's findings of fact are sufficiently comprehensive so as to allow for meaningful review.

III. DISCUSSION

A decision not to rehire an individual is improper if it is made by reason of that person's exercise of constitutionally protected rights. *Mt. Healthy City School Dist. Bd. of Educ.* v. *Doyle,* 429 U.S.274, 283-84, 97 S.Ct. 568, 574, 50 L.Ed.2d 471 (1977). In cases such as the instant one where the dismissal was based on several grounds, only some of which relate to activity allegedly protected by the Constitution, the plaintiff has the initial burden to show that the press-related activities were constitutionally protected and that these activities played a substantial role in the nonrenewal decision. If the plaintiff meets this burden, the defendant must then demonstrate by a preponderance of the evidence that it would have reached the same decision in the absence of the protected conduct. *Id.* at 287, 97 S.Ct. at 576.

A. *Students' First Amendment Rights*

The first question presented by this appeal is whether newspaper writers for a high school publication, and vis-a-vis their faculty advisor,[2] have a constitutional right to be free from pre-publication review by the school principal. The district court found that the defendants had no impermissible motive in seeking to terminate plaintiff's employment and therefore necessarily concluded that the rights of the high school students had not been infringed. This court agrees and affirms the trial court's conclusion that the principal's actions did not violate constitutionally protected rights.

It is now well-established that secondary students do not "shed their constitutional rights to freedom of speech or expression at the schoolhouse gate." *Tinker* v. *Des Moines Indep. Community School Dist.,* 393 U.S. 503, 506, 89 S.Ct. 733, 736, 21 L.Ed.2d 731 (1969). However, these rights are not coextensive with those of adults and may be modified or curtailed by school policies that are reasonably designed to adjust those rights to the needs of the school environment. *See Williams* v. *Spencer,* 622 F.2d 1200, 1205 (4th Cir. 1980).

Writers on a high school newspaper do not have an

unfettered constitutional right to be free from pre-publication review. In fact, the special characteristics of the high school environment, particularly one involving students in a journalism class that produces a school newspaper, call for supervision and review by school faculty and administrators. Under the precise circumstances of this case administrative review of a small number of sensitive articles for accuracy rather than for possible censorship or official imprimatur does not implicate first amendment rights.[3]

In the high school setting, school officials and teachers must be accorded wide latitude over decisions affecting the manner in which they educate students.[4] The role of the judiciary in the supervision of public education, therefore, is limited and arises only where the resolution of conflicts in school administration clearly involves constitutional values. *Epperson* v. *Arkansas,* 393 U.S. 97, 104, 89 S.Ct. 266, 270, 21 L.Ed.2d 228 (1968); Diamond, *The First Amendment and Public Schools: The Case Against Judicial Intervention,* 59 Tex.L. Rev. 477 (1981).

In the present case, the school possessed a substantial educational interest in teaching young, student writers journalistic skills which stressed accuracy and fairness. While appellant properly stressed the value of a *free* press, the school principal also was acting within appropriate bounds when he emphasized the concomitant need for a *responsible* press. When Dr. Ahee informed appellant and his journalism class that certain articles in the school-sponsored newspaper must be reviewed for accuracy,[5] he properly exercised his supervisorial authority to read those occasional articles about subjects so sensitive that it would be derelict to accord untrained, adolescent writers absolute freedom from pre-publication review for accuracy.

Accordingly, the lower court properly recognized that the principal's conduct was substantially related to the educational process and that the appellant had not been denied rights guaranteed by the first and fourteenth amendments.

B. *Motivating Factors Behind Dismissal*

When considering a public employer's motivation for dismissing an employee, the trier of fact must examine the various proffered reasons and determine whether constitutionally protected activities played a substantial role in the decision. *Mt. Healthy City School Dist. Bd. of Educ.* v. *Doyle,* 429 U.S. 274, 283-84, 97 S.Ct. 568, 574, 50 L.Ed.2d 471 (1977). In the present case, the district court made the factual finding that first amendment considerations did not motivate the decision not to rehire the appellant. Accordingly, we must affirm unless this determination is clearly erroneous. Fed.R.Civ.P. 52(a)[6]

The record in the present case fully supports the lower court's finding that the school board's actions were properly motivated. The evidence in the record demonstrates that Nicholson failed to follow several rules governing school bookkeeping duties and declined, on several occasions, to require his students to follow school rules. Moreover, Nicholson repeatedly disobeyed orders of his immediate supervisor regarding the student newspaper—a fact that concededly led to the deterioration of an important school relationship. *See Simard* v. *Board of Educ.,* 473 F.2d 988, 996 (2d Cir. 1973).

While courts must be vigilant in protecting employees from dismissals based on their participation in constitutionally protected activities, this protection does not extend to employees who legitimately are not reappointed. *Mabey* v. *Reagan,* 537 F.2d 1036, 1045 (9th Cir. 1976). The decision to terminate a probationary teacher's employment is based on many subjective factors, the application of which must be left, in the first instance, to the discretion of local school officials. *Id.* at 1044-45.

Notwithstanding the special consideration that must be given to pretextual reasons which may conceal an actual motive to terminate an instructor for exercising first amendment rights, the decision as to an employer's true motivation plainly is one reserved to the trier of fact. In this case, the district court's finding on this factual question was not clearly erroneous.

C. *Appellant's Personal First Amendment Rights*

Appellant contends that he had a personal right to encourage publication of controversial articles in the high school newspaper and that his discharge for failure to submit articles on sensitive topics to school officials was improper.[7] The district court disagreed and found that the defendants did not suppress Nicholson's freedom of expression. We agree and affirm the district court's conclusion.

The question whether a school teacher's speech is constitutionally protected expression requires balancing "the interests of the teacher as a citizen, in commenting upon matters of public concern and the interest of the State, as an employer, in promoting the efficiency of the public services it performs through its employees." *Pickering* v. *Board of Educ.,* 391 U.S. 563, 568, 88 S.Ct. 1731, 1734, 20 L.Ed.2d 811 (1968).

In *Pickering,* the Supreme Court identified several factors to consider in striking a balance between the competing interests. Pickering was a teacher who was dismissed for writing and publishing in a newspaper a letter criticizing certain actions taken by the local board of education. In holding that Pickering could not be dismissed because of the statements he made, the Court observed that

[t]he statements are in no way directed towards

any person with whom appellant would normally be in contact in the course of his daily work as a teacher. Thus no question of maintaining either discipline by immediate superiors or harmony among coworkers is presented here. Appellant's employment relationships with the Board and, to a somewhat lesser extent, with the superintendent are not the kind of close working relationships for which it can persuasively be claimed that personal loyalty and confidence are necessary to their proper functioning.

Id. at 569-70, 88 S.Ct. at 1735.

The Court also noted that a teacher's expression might not be entitled to protection if it impeded the teacher's proper performance of his daily duties in the classroom or interfered with the regular operation of the school generally. Id. at 572-73, 88 S.Ct. at 1736-1737.

Application of the Pickering factors to the present case amply supports the district court's finding that Nicholson's own first amendment rights were not infringed.[8] Unlike the activity at issue in the Pickering case, the conduct for which appellant seeks protection did involve questions of supervisorial discipline, loyalty and harmony among coworkers. First, appellant concedes that his working relationship with the school principal deteriorated when he refused to comply with instructions regarding the school newspaper.[9] The effectiveness of this close working relationship was further undermined when appellant openly defied the wishes of Dr. Ahee when he allowed his students to attend a taped television interview. Finally, the school board properly concluded that its interests were threatened when appellant conducted and published the student newspaper's survey in direct violation of established administrative policy. See Mt. Healthy City School Dist. Bd. of Educ. v. Doyle, 429 U.S. 274, 284, 97 S.Ct. 568, 574, 50 L.Ed.2d 471 (1977).

Furthermore, several of the articles which appellant failed to submit to the principal concerned other members on the school's faculty who were extremely anxious to ensure accurate and fair reporting due to the sensitive nature of the subject matter being discussed. When these articles were published, several containing inaccuracies and misimpressions, Nicholson's coworkers became angry and dissatisfied with the school newspaper and its advisor. As such, the potential for further personality conflicts within the faculty was sure to have a detrimental effect on intra-school harmony. See Lefcourt v. Legal Aid Society, 312 F.Supp. 1105, 1112-13 (S.D.N.Y. 1970), aff'd, 445 F.2d 1150 (2d Cir. 1971).

Therefore, the trial court properly concluded that the school board did not violate appellant's rights of free expression under the circumstances of this case.

D. *District Court's Findings*

Finally, appellant argues in the alternative that the district court's order does not provide a basis for determining whether the court properly rejected his constitutional challenge. Specifically, appellant contends that the lower court's findings misallocated the burden of proof and failed to indicate what the court thought motivated the defendant and why it was permissible.[10]

The test in this circuit as to the adequacy of findings of fact is whether they are explicit enough on the ultimate issues to give the appellate court a clear understanding of the basis of the decision and to enable it to determine the grounds on which the trial court reached its decision. *South-Western Publishing Co.* v. *Simons,* 651 F.2d 653, 655 (9th Cir. 1981), cert. denied,—U.S.—, 102 S.Ct. 1714, 72 L.Ed.2d 136 (1982); 5A J. Moore, Moore's Federal Practice ¶ 52.06[1] (2d ed. 1980).

Nicholson is correct that the lower court's Finding No. 7 implied a misallocation of the burden of proof announced in the *Mt. Healthy* decision. In fact, a plaintiff need not prove that his dismissal was based *solely* upon his constitutionally protected activities, only that these activities constituted "a substantial factor" in the nonrenewal decision. *Mt. Healthy,* 429 U.S. at 287, 97 S.Ct. at 576.

Notwithstanding the error contained in Finding No. 7, the district court's order must be affirmed first because it still states a basis that supports the judgment. Under the *Mt. Healthy* rule, the plaintiff bears the additional and independent burden to show that the press-related activities were constitutionally protected. With respect to this dispositive question, the lower court found that Nicholson "failed to establish that defendants acted to suppress plaintiff's freedom of expression." The trial court further concluded that the plaintiff had "not been denied rights guaranteed by the First and Fourteenth Amendment of the United States Constitution . . ." (Conclusion of Law No. 2, Record p. 58). Accordingly, the trial court clearly found that the plaintiff failed to discharge his evidentiary burden on this issue.

Second, the lower court cited our decision in *Mabey* v. *Reagan,* 537 F.2d 1036 (9th Cir. 1976) and concluded that the defendants had no impermissible motive in seeking to terminate plaintiff's employment, i.e. one based on constitutionally protected activity. The district court necessarily found, therefore, that the defendants' true motives were proper. This finding is fully supported by the evidence. (See discussion, *supra,* at p. 864.[11])

IV. CONCLUSION

The district court properly found that the defendants did not infringe either Nicholson's or his students' constitutional rights. Additionally, the findings of the district court are sufficiently comprehensive and pertinent to dispositive issues as to form a basis for its decision.

The judgment of the district court is affirmed.

NOTES

1. The appellees did not argue the defense of the statute of limitations in the lower court or in their brief on this appeal. See Smith v. Cremins, 308 F.2d 187, 189 (9th Cir. 1962). As such, the statute of limitations defense, if there was any, has been waived because it was not raised in the court below. United States v. Krasn, 614 F.2d 1229, 1236 (9th Cir. 1980).
2. Appellees do not address the contention raised by the appellant that a high school journalism teacher has standing to assert the first amendment rights of his students. However, since Nicholson alleges that he has directly suffered "injury in fact" and he certainly is in a position to assert the rights of his students just as effectively as they would themselves, he may challenge the school official's actions as applied to his students. Craig v. Boren, 429 U.S. 190, 193, 97 S.Ct. 451, 454, 50 L.Ed.2d 397 (1976).
3. This court is not faced with a situation where school officials prohibited or censored a student publication. Since scholastic newspapers fall within the ambit of the first amendment, outright prohibition or censorship would require a strong showing on the part of the school administrators that publication of the forbidden materials would "materially and substantially interfere with the requirements of appropriate discipline in the operation of the school." Tinker v. Des Moines Indep. Community School Dist., 393 U.S. 503, 509, 89 S.Ct. 733, 737, 21 L.Ed.2d 731 (1969). See also Thomas v. Board of Educ., 607 F.2d 1043 (2d Cir. 1979), cert. denied, 444 U.S. 1081, 100 S.Ct. 1034, 62 L.Ed.2d 765 (1980); Quarterman v. Byrd, 453 F.2d 54 (4th Cir. 1971); Reineke v. Cobb County School Dist., 484 F.Supp. 1252 (N.D.Ga.1980); Trager, *Freedom of the Press in College and High Schools,* 35 Albany L. Rev. 161 (1971); Cal.Ed. Code § 48916.
4. Different considerations govern application of the first amendment on the college campus and at lower level educational institutions. The activities of high school students, for example, may be more stringently reviewed than the conduct of college students, as the former are "in a much more adolescent and immature stage of life and less able to screen fact from propaganda." Schwartz v. Schuker, 298 F.Supp. 238, 242 (E.D.N.Y.1969); Wright, *The Constitution on the Campus,* 22 Vand.L.Rev. 1052, 1053 (1969).
5. Dr. Ahee also explained the so-called "Four-Way Test" to appellant and his classes. However, the record reveals that the principal did not impose this test as an absolute standard for review nor did the students feel compelled to implement it as an official directive.
6. The "clearly erroneous" standard applies to findings of fact even when the trial court relies, as it did in this case, solely on a written record. United States v. Mountain States Constr. Co., 588 F.2d 259, 264 n.5 (9th Cir. 1978).
7. Nicholson also argues that the school board could not discharge him for refusing to comply with a directive that would violate the first amendment rights of his students. See, e.g., Bertot v. School Dist. No. 1, 522 F.2d 1171, 1183 (10th Cir. 1975). However, the right to refrain from actions that would infringe another's constitutional rights is derivative and depends on the validity of the other party's claim. Here the requested action would not have violated the first amendment rights of Nicholson's students. (See discussion *supra* at pp. 862-864.) Therefore any derivative rights based thereon must fail.
8. Our decisions have indicated that this court itself is required to review the record and weigh the *Pickering* factors because this is a question of law. Bernasconi v. Tempe Elementary School Dist. No. 3, 548 F.2d 857, 862 (9th Cir.) cert. denied, 434 U.S. 825, 98 S.Ct. 72, 54 L.Ed.2d 82(1977). See also Boehm v. Foster, 670 F. 2d 111, 113 (9th Cir. 1982) (expression which seriously undermines effectiveness of close working relationship is not constitutionally protected speech).
9. Appellant is, of course, correct when he asserts that if the deterioration in the working relationship resulted from imposition of requirements that Dr. Ahee was constitutionally forbidden to impose, the strained relationship could not be considered as a factor supporting the state's interests. In the present case, however, the school principal's restrictions were not unlawful. (See discussion *supra* at pp. 862 864.)
10. The trial court made the following relevant findings of fact:

    (7) Plaintiff, in this action pursued in Federal Court, has failed to establish that his dismissal from defendant school district was based solely upon his actions as a faculty advisor to the school newspaper.
    (8) Plaintiff has failed to establish that defendants acted to suppress plaintiff's freedom of expression.
    (9) Plaintiff has failed to establish that defendants had any impermissible motive in seeking to terminate plaintiff's employment in defendant school district.

    (Record p. 57.)
11. An appellate court may affirm on the basis of any evidence in the record that supports the trial court's judgment. The failure to include express findings on all relevant facts "does not require remand if a complete understanding of the issues may be had without the aid of separate findings." Swanson v. Levy, 509 F.2d 859, 861 (9th Cir. 1975); see also South-Western Publishing Co. v. Simons, 651 F.2d 653, 652 n.2 (9th Cir. 1981); cert. denied,—U.S.—, 102 S.Ct. 1714, 72 L.Ed.2d 136 (1982).

A United States District Court in Maine decides against school officials who had refused to publish "in the 1984 Brunswick High School Yearbook a quotation which the plaintiff [a senior] had previously selected for inclusion in the Yearbook. The quotation selected for publication by the plaintiff from the January 24, 1983 issue of *Time* magazine, reads as follows: 'The executioner will pull this lever four times. Each time 2000 volts will course through your body, making your eyeballs first bulge, then burst, and then broiling your brains. . . . ' " In its discussion of the student's right to place the quotation next to her yearbook picture, the Court said: "In the legitimate exercise of her right of free speech, this plaintiff has the option to convey her conviction by the use of the most graphic language, even, if she so chooses, by language so physiologically stark that others may believe her to 'be a jerk.' Government has no legitimate nor compelling interest in preserving this lone woman from that fate if her own utterances shall visit it upon her. Rather, the First Amendment declares that the highest interest of the people is best served if government is required to stay its hand and permit her, and millions like her, to take upon their personal risk the ability of their ideas and convictions to survive and propagate in the marketplace of ideas. . . . The public interest may be thought to be best served if schools and teachers practice the historical orthodoxies of our political freedom while they preach the temporally transitory orthodoxies of 'taste.' They may legitimately, and should, seek to inculcate the latter, but they may not, in the effort to do so, transgress upon the former. In the final analysis, under our constitution individual liberty of expression must be accorded its day even at the expense of the promotion of aesthetic sophistication."

Stanton v. *Brunswick School Dept.,* 577 F.Supp. 1560 (1984)

GENE CARTER, District Judge.

I. PROCEDURAL BACKGROUND AND FACTS

This is a civil action in which the Plaintiff seeks injunctive relief and damages for the Defendants' refusal to publish in the 1984 Brunswick High School Yearbook a quotation which the Plaintiff had previously selected for inclusion in the yearbook. The quotation selected for publication by the Plaintiff from the January 24, 1983, issue of *Time* magazine, reads as follows:

> The executioner will pull this lever four times. Each time 2000 volts will course through your body, making your eyeballs first bulge, then burst, and then broiling your brains. . . .

It is contended by Plaintiff that representatives of the Defendant Brunswick School Board, which is charged under state law (20 M.R.S.A. § 1011) to exercise overall responsibility for the operation of the Brunswick School Department, have, acting pursuant to their legal authority, refused to permit the inclusion of the selected quotation in the 1984 Brunswick High School Yearbook. Plaintiff brings her cause of action pursuant to the First Amendment of the United States Constitution, 42 U.S.C. § 1983, and 28 U.S.C. § 1343(3).

Plaintiff filed a motion with the original complaint seeking entry of a temporary restraining order "requiring defendants to forward to the publisher her yearbook information form; and to otherwise insure that, pending trial on the merits, Plaintiff's quotation will appear in the 1984 school yearbook." The Court having declined to act on said motion *ex parte,* and notice having been given to the Defendants and a hearing held, the Court treats the motion as one for a preliminary injunction pursuant to Fed.R.Civ.P. 65(a). *Dilworth* v. *Riner,* 343 F.2d 226, 229 (5th Cir.1965).

The allegations in the original complaint[1] set forth the following facts in support of the application for relief. For the last ten years, approximately, the Defendants have published the High School Yearbook at the conclusion of each school year. Complaint, at ¶ 14. The yearbook has contained a section in which pictures of all of the members of the senior class appear together with biographical information about each student and a short quotation selected for inclusion by each student. *Id.* In years prior to 1984, it is alleged, there has existed no articulated policy, either written or oral, regulating the contents of the quotations selected by students for inclusion in the yearbook. Id. at ¶ 5. In the last several years student quotations have appeared in the yearbook encouraging the use of unlawful drugs and alcohol, and student quotations also have appeared in the yearbook from various "rock and roll" artists, some of whom speak in negative terms about traditional American values and promulgate statements which glorify sexual activity. *Id.* at ¶ 6. In addition, quotations reflect the views of such diverse individuals as John F. Kennedy and Bertolt Brecht. *Id.* Plaintiff claims that this utilization of the annual high school yearbook constitutes that publication, for First Amendment purposes, "a public forum." *Id.* at ¶ 7.

On or about November 1, 1983, Brunswick High School senior students were required to turn in information forms providing to the yearbook staff the biographical information to be included in the yearbook, as well as the individual student's selected quotation. *Id.* at ¶ 10. The Plaintiff returned such an information form. *Id.* The Plaintiff's designated quotation was indicated on the information form. Plaintiff chose this quotation "because she wanted to draw people's attention to the horror of both murder and what she believed to be, on occasion, an appropriate punishment for it." *Id.* at ¶ 11. Plaintiff was thereafter requested in meetings with two faculty members, Sharon Bumgardner and Nancy Moore, to change her selected quotation. *Id.* at ¶ 12. Plaintiff indicated that she did not wish to do so. She then met with the Defendant Millett, the principal of the high school, who also attempted to persuade her to change her quotation. Again, she declined to do so. Defendant Millett then indicated to her that the quotation would not be used and could not be published in the yearbook. *Id.* The reason for the rejection of the quotation for publication given by the faculty members and the Defendant Millett was "that the quotation was too graphic and was unacceptable for public consumption. . . . [T]he quotation could not be printed because it would be 'disruptive to the community.' " *Id.* at ¶ 13. In answer to her inquiry, Plaintiff was informed that the yearbook was published by the school "and the school could decide what goes in and what doesn't." *Id.* at ¶ 14. Defendants continue to refuse to accept the Plaintiff's designated quotation for publication in the 1984 edition of the yearbook. *Id.* at ¶ 15.

The Plaintiff asserts that these actions of the Defendants have been conducted "under color of state law." *Id.* at ¶ 16. Additionally, it is asserted that for some of the allegedly wrongful conduct of the Defendants "plaintiff has no adequate remedy at law." *Id.* at ¶ 17. The yearbooks will not actually be distributed until April or May of 1984, but the immediacy of publishing deadlines is asserted to be a cause for the granting of immediate relief. *Id.* at ¶ 18. Such relief is claimed to be necessary in order to secure the publication of the Plaintiff's designated quotation in the event that this Court shall determine under the Fourteenth Amendment and 42 U.S.C. § 1983 that Plaintiff may not be denied the opportunity to have the designated quotation published in the yearbook. *Id.*

The Defendants have submitted a number of affidavits in opposition to the granting of temporary injunctive relief. The first of these is that of Audrey Harlow, a senior at Brunswick High School, who serves as editor-in-chief for the 1984 Brunswick High School Yearbook. In that position she exercises overall responsibility for publication of the yearbook in conjunction with other editors, staff, and two faculty advisors. She confirms the information provided in the Plaintiff's complaint as to categories of information that are published in the senior section of the yearbook. She states that after receiving the information forms from the seniors, those forms were reviewed by Mrs. Bumgardner, one of the faculty advisors, and herself. She also asserts that "it is the policy of the yearbook staff that the materials published in the yearbook be tasteful and appropriate for all students and people in the community in 1984 and in future years." Harlow affidavit ¶ 5. The activity form filled out by the Plaintiff was initially reviewed by Mrs. Bumgardner, who sought Ms. Harlow's judgment as to whether "the quote selected by [the Plaintiff] should be accepted for inclusion in the yearbook." *Id.* at ¶ 6. Ms. Harlow states: "After reading the quote, I felt strongly and still feel strongly that the wording of the quote is not appropriate for the yearbook and agreed that it should not be approved. I would approve a statement either for or against the concept of capital punishment, if the wording were appropriate for the yearbook." *Id.* at ¶ 6.

Defendants have also submitted an affidavit of Sandra Bumgardner in which she states that she is one of two faculty advisors for the 1984 Brunswick High School Yearbook, with duties which "include reviewing of material to be published, assisting the editors in insuring that publishing deadlines are met, and helping with typing." Mrs. Bumgardner indicates that she was advised by J. Guy Levesque, a faculty advisor for prior yearbooks, and Defendant Millett, the principal of Brunswick High School, "that in prior years a policy has been established and followed that excluded material which involved alcohol, sex or drugs or was distasteful or inappropriate for a Brunswick High School Yearbook." Bumgardner affidavit at ¶ 3. She states that she subsequently explained this policy to the senior section editors of the 1984 yearbook staff and indicated that this same policy would govern material for the 1984 yearbook. Those senior section editors agreed that Emily Moll "would speak to the senior class assembly on September 13, 1983, and set forth these guidelines for completion of the activity sheets." *Id.* at ¶ 3. Mrs. Bumgardner's affidavit further states that the information sheets were distributed to seniors on Monday, September 26, 1983.

Although the deadline for return of the sheets was October 14, 1983, some of the sheets were not returned until the end of October or early November. Upon their return she states that she reviewed the information sheets initially "to insure that they were properly completed and were acceptable to the yearbook." *Id.* at ¶ 6. Mrs. Bumgardner also states that upon review of the Plaintiff's information sheet, "I concluded that the quote which she requested was inappropriate since it was in poor taste." *Id.* at ¶ 7. She thereafter spoke with Plaintiff and suggested that the selected quotation be changed or that Plaintiff provide a substitute for it. Upon Plaintiff's refusal to accept that suggestion, Mrs. Bumgardner reviewed the designated quote with the other faculty advisor and with Ms. Harlow, the editor-in-chief of the yearbook, and with one Stephanie Smith, the senior section editor. She states that all of them agreed that the quote "was inappropriate and should not be included in the yearbook." *Id.* Mrs. Bumgardner then took the matter up with the assistant principal, Mr. Fairbrother, who also agreed that "the quote was inappropriate." *Id.* On November 3, 1983, she told the Plaintiff that it was the conclusion of the yearbook staff that the designated quotation "should not be in the yearbook." *Id.* at ¶ 8. She indicates that "the yearbook staff and I did not object to a statement relating to capital punishment but rather objected to the particular language used." *Id.* It also appears from this affidavit that the material for the senior section of the yearbook has been submitted to the publisher and that the editors have received proofs from the publisher for review. As matters now stand, all of the material indicated in the Plaintiff's information sheet will appear in the yearbook next to her picture except for the designated quote.

Defendants have also submitted the affidavit of Emily L. Moll, a senior at Brunswick High School who serves as the arts editor and layout editor for the 1984 yearbook. She states that this position "entails a variety of duties, including review of formats, design placement (along with other members of the staff), and participation in decisions of what is appropriate material to represent the student yearbook, student body and the administration." Moll affidavit at ¶ 2. Ms. Moll states that she spoke in front of the entire senior class of Brunswick High School at a senior assembly and explained the filling out of the information sheets, including the selected quotation to be printed next to the individual senior student's picture. She describes a pertinent part of her presentation as follows:

> To the best of my knowledge and recollection, this is what I verbally stated to the senior class on September 23, 1983; "No words or phrases about alcohol, sex, drugs or implying anything about those things or ideas are acceptable to the 1984 Brunswick High School Yearbook. Good taste, common sense and decorum should be exercised by the student body in choosing their quote for what goes next to their picture." I remember further saying: "Don't be jerks, use your common sense. Don't submit anything to the yearbook staff for publication that is seemingly distasteful or inappropriate or that you won't want your kids to read fifteen years from now. We will just have to return it for revision, so please save us all the unneeded effort. Let's have the best yearbook ever and thank you."

Id. at ¶ 5. The affidavit demonstrates Ms. Moll's continued objection to the inclusion of the Plaintiff's designated quotation in the 1984 yearbook "since it is distasteful and not appropriate for a yearbook." *Id* at ¶ 6. Ms. Moll says that she suggested to the Plaintiff that "she modify the language without changing the expression of her view on capital punishment" and suggested alternative sources of similar quotations. *Id.* at ¶ 6.

The affidavit of the Defendant Millett, principal of Brunswick High School, is also part of the record. In it he states that on November 7, 1983, Plaintiff "came to my office to appeal a decision by the yearbook staff regarding her activity sheet." Millett affidavit at ¶ 2. He states that he denied the appeal but advised

Plaintiff that "she could appeal my decision to the superintendent." *Id.* Millett thereafter had conversations with the Plaintiff's father, William A. Stanton, and with an attorney for the Plaintiff. Both men indicated that the Plaintiff did not wish to utilize an appeal process which Millett had described to them in those conversations. Thereafter, on December 12, 1983, a meeting was scheduled between the Plaintiff, her parents, their counsel, and the Defendant Millett and Defendant's counsel. Defendant's counsel was unable to attend the meeting but the meeting went forward under the direction of Daniel A. Calderwood, the superintendent of schools. It is simply asserted that as a result of that meeting, "the dispute was not resolved." *Id.* at ¶ 5.

Mr. Millett asserts that school records reflect that the Plaintiff was present at school on September 23, 1983, the date of the senior assembly described in the Moll affidavit. He also indicates that he has discussed publishing deadlines with the publisher of the yearbook. As Millett understands the situation:

[T]he proofs of the senior section which have been received by the yearbook staff should be returned as soon as possible. The senior section will then normally be printed, thus assuring a shipping date of no later than June 1, 1984. However, if return of the proofs is delayed until approximately January 20, 1984, or if changes are made prior to that time, the publishing and shipping schedules would not be altered. Changes to the proofs subsequent to January 20, 1984, but prior to February 20, 1984, could result in either extension of the shipping date or an additional charge of up to $1,000 to maintain the original shipping date. Changes to the proof subsequent to February 20, 1984, could result in both an additional charge of up to $2,000 and extension of the shipping date." *Id.* at ¶ 8.

Finally, Defendants have submitted the affidavit of Daniel A. Calderwood, superintendent of schools in Brunswick, Maine, which deals with the factual predicate for Defendants' defense of Plaintiff's alleged failure to exhaust administrative remedies.

On January 6, 1984, Defendants filed their answer to the Plaintiff's complaint, which sets out general and specific admissions and denials of the allegations of substantive facts set forth in the original complaint, thus generating the substantive factual issues in this litigation. In addition, the answer asserts the following affirmative defenses to the Plaintiff's claim for relief: (1) failure to state a claim upon which relief can be granted; (2) lack of jurisdiction in this Court as a result of Plaintiff's failure to name the proper parties; (3) lack of this Court's jurisdiction because the named defendant, Defendant Brunswick School Department, is not a suable entity under Maine law;[2] (4) lack of this Court's jurisdiction under 28 U.S.C. § 1343 because of the absence of any "state action" in this case; and (5) lack of jurisdiction in this Court due to the failure of the Plaintiff to exhaust her available administrative remedies.

Since the filing of the documents of the Defendant referred to hereinabove, Plaintiff's counsel has filed a reply brief accompanied by a supplemental affidavit of the Plaintiff. In that affidavit, the Plaintiff states that she attended the senior assembly at which Ms. Moll spoke and describes her recollection of it in the following language:

It lasted for approximately 40 minutes and was devoted almost exclusively to a presentation by a gentleman whose name I do not know about a magazine subscription drive. The purpose of the subscription drive, which was to take place in Brunswick, was to, among other things, raise money for the senior class because members of the senior class would be selling the subscriptions to Brunswick businesses. At the end of the period, for no more than five minutes, Ms. Moll made some remarks about the yearbook. I remember that she said, 'Don't be jerks, use your common sense. [Don't submit anything] you don't want your kids to read fifteen years from now. We will just have to return it for revision so please save us all the unneeded effort. Let's have the best yearbook ever and thank you.' I have no recollection of her saying anything else to which she refers in her affidavit.

Plaintiff's supplemental affidavit at ¶ 3. Plaintiff further states that at the time the information sheets were passed out, "we were given no instructions, either oral or written, about the contents of the sheet." *Id.* at ¶ 4. The affidavit also contains assertions that Plaintiff is generally familiar with the contents of student quotations and other similar student material utilized in prior editions of the Brunswick High School Yearbook. She states: "My interest in the questions of crime and punishment began when I read *In Cold Blood* by Truman Capote in my sophomore year in high school. We discussed that book at home and in particular talked about whether capital punishment was a suitable punishment for the defendants who had committed such a horrible crime." *Id.* ¶ 7. She further states:

The reason I chose the quotation I selected was to possibly provoke some of my classmates to think a little more deeply than if I had written a standard butterfly quote. I wanted to make them aware of the realities that exist in today's world. The issue isn't that of capital punishment alone, but of those realities of which [sic] people prefer to avoid. It is important to think about these things because we are seniors and we are going to be on our own very soon." *Id.* at ¶ 8.

II. JUSTICIABILITY

Original jurisdiction of the Plaintiff's action pursuant to 42 U.S.C. § 1983 is conferred upon this Court by 28 U.S.C. § 1343(3). The complaint sufficiently alleges state action that subjects the Plaintiff to an actual deprivation of civil rights which are guaranteed by the First and Fourteenth Amendments to the Constitution of the United States. The controversy of which the complaint seeks resolution is ripe for the exercise of Article III judicial power arising under the Civil Rights Act and the First and Fourteenth Amendments. Venue is properly laid in the District of Maine where all Defendants reside and the action arises. 28 U.S.C. § 1391(b). There is no requirement of federal court abstention presented by this matter since there are no unsettled questions of state law requiring clarification by the courts of the State of Maine. *See Railroad Commission of Texas* v. *Pullman Co.,* 312 U.S. 496, 61 S.Ct. 643, 85 L.Ed. 971 (1941). Likewise, there are no pending or required state judicial or administrative proceedings warranting abstention. *See Younger* v. *Harris,* 401 U.S. 37, 91 S.Ct. 746, 27 L.Ed.2d 669 (1971); *Rizzo* v. *Goode,* 423 U.S. 362, 96 S.Ct. 598, 46 L.Ed.2d 561 (1976).

III. PRELIMINARY INJUNCTIVE RELIEF

As previously noted, the Court treats the pending motion for a temporary restraining order as a motion for preliminary injunction in view of the fact that notice and opportunity for hearing have been afforded to the Defendants with respect to the issues raised by the Plaintiff's claim of entitlement to temporary injunctive relief pending further proceedings and a determination of those issues on the merits. *Supra,* at 1561. Plaintiff must satisfy four essential requirements in order to prevail on a claim for temporary injunctive relief. This Court has had occasion in the past to set out succinctly those requirements in *UV Industries, Inc.* v. *Posner,* 466 F.Supp. 1251, (D.Me.1979) (per Gignoux, J.):

> It is well settled law that, in the ordinary case, a plaintiff must satisfy four criteria in order to be entitled to a preliminary injunction. The Court must find: (1) that the plaintiff will suffer irreparable injury if the injunction is not granted; (2) that such injury outweighs any harm which the granting of injunctive relief would inflict on the defendant; (3) that plaintiff has exhibited a likelihood of success on the merits; and (4) that the public interest will not be adversely affected by the granting of the injunction.

Id. at 1255; *see also Women's Community Health Center, Inc.* v. *Cohen,* 477 F.Supp. 542, 544 (D.Me.1979) (per Gignoux, J.)

This formulation of these criteria has been approved by the United States Court of Appeals for the First Circuit. *Planned Parenthood League* v. *Bellotti,* 641 F.2d 1006, 1009 (1st Cir.1981) (quoting *Women's Community Health Center, Inc.*); *Keefe* v. *Geanakos,* 418 F.2d 359 (1st Cir.1969); *Automatic Radio Manufacturing Co. Inc.* v. *Ford Motor Co.,* 390 F.2d 113 (1st Cir.1968) *cert. den.,* 391 U.S. 914, 88 S.Ct. 1807, 20 L.Ed.2d 653 (1968). This Court has only recently indicated the continuing applicability of these requirements to requests for temporary injunctive relief. *Sheck* v. *Baileyville School Committee,* 530 F.Supp. 679 (D.Me.1982) (per Cyr, J.).

Further, it is well established law that the Court is to bear constantly in mind that an "[i]njunction is an equitable remedy which should not be lightly indulged in, but used sparingly and only in a clear and plain case." *Plain Dealer Publishing Co.* v. *Cleveland Type. Union #53,* 520 F.2d 1220, 1230 (6th Cir.1975), *cert. den.* 428 U.S. 909, 96 S.Ct. 3221, 49 L.Ed.2d 1217 (1977). The Court's hesitation to utilize so drastic an aspect of its prerogative should be heightened where the relief requested is only temporary in nature. *Kass* v. *Arden-Mayfair, Inc.,* 431 F.Supp. 1037, 1047 (C.D.Cal.1977).

Moreover, the Court should only sparingly exercise its authority to issue an interlocutory injunction which requires a defendant to take affirmative action. *Jones* v. *Snead,* 431 F.2d 1115 (8th Cir. 1970). The purpose of preliminary injunctive relief is to preserve the *status quo* until a final adjudication can be had upon the merits. *Toledo, A.A. to N.M. Ry. Co.* v. *Pennsylvania Co.,* 54 F. 730 (C.C.N.D. Ohio 1893). In framing the terms of a preliminary injunction the Court is to go no further than is necessary to preserve the litigating posture of the moving party and must avoid any unnecessary encroachment upon that of the adverse party.

Indeed, the Court cannot seriously consider equitable relief as drastic as that proposed by Plaintiff which would effectively act as a final determination of the issue. It is clear that "[a]ny denial of plaintiff's rights pending a determination on the merits would work an irretrievable loss of constitutionally-guaranteed liberties for which no adequate remedy exists at law." *Sheck,* 530 F.Supp. at 684 (emphasis in original). The injunction proposed by Plaintiff, however, would cause a similarly irretrievable loss to Defendants if they must publish Plaintiff's quotation before the case is decided on the merits and their position ultimately prevails. A temporary injunction which simply prevents the Defendants from authorizing final printing and publication of the yearbook until resolution of this controversy will adequately protect Plaintiff's rights without foreclosing the possibility of relief for Defendants. This narrower remedy accords with the conservative mode described above as appropriate for the consideration of preliminary injunctions. The Court will, therefore, apply the traditional analysis to this more limited remedy.

(1) *Irreparable Injury*

Plaintiff in this case founds her claims on alleged deprivations of her First and Fourteenth Amendment rights resulting from the Defendant's denial to her of the opportunity to have her selected quotation published in the 1984 yearbook. "It is well established that the loss of First Amendment freedoms constitutes irreparable injury. *Maceira* v. *Pagan,* 649 F.2d 8, 18 (1st Cir.1981) (citing *Elrod* v. *Burns,* 427 U.S. 347, 373, 96 S.Ct. 2673, 2689, 49 L.Ed.2d 547 (1976)); *Sheck,* 530 F.Supp. at 684; *see also Keefe* v. *Geanakos,* 418 F.2d 359 (1st Cir.1969). Plaintiff's claim that she stands at risk of being denied the exercise of her right of free expression of her ideas, secured by the First Amendment, constitutes a colorable showing, rising above a "chilling effect," *see Maceira,* at 18, of a denial of her constitutionally-secured prerogatives. Money damages will not suffice to redress such a deprivation of Plaintiff's one-time opportunity to have her ideas published in the yearbook, which opportunity has been made available to her classmates. Such would be the case even if there were no legal impediments to the recovery of damages in this action. *See Harlow* v. *Fitzgerald,* 457 U.S. 800, 102 S.Ct. 2727, 73 L.Ed.2d 396 (1982).

(2) *Weighing the Competing Harms to Plaintiff and Defendants*

In balancing the hardships that might be occasioned by the Court's action (or inaction), it is clear that failure of the Court to enter any injunctive relief would cause Plaintiff irreparable harm. The temporary injunction postponing publication until after final resolution of this case would prevent this harm while causing only minor difficulties for Defendants.

The affidavits of the Defendants establish only that printing and publication schedules have been established. It is not demonstrated that any harm rising above the level of inconvenience and the incurring of modest additional publishing costs, much less any irreparable harm, will result from delay of those printing and publication schedules. While it is asserted that such delay may occasion increased expense in the form of publication costs, it is not shown that these Defendants will bear those costs. Even if it were so shown, those charges would hardly constitute irreparable injury by comparison to the harm that would be done to the Plaintiff's constitutionally-protected First Amendment rights by presently scheduled publication of the yearbook without the inclusion of her designated quotation. Further, offsetting the significance of the possibility of delay resulting from the granting of interim injunctive relief, is the fact that given the limited scope of the injunctive relief considered by the Court, *supra,* at 1567, the school authorities will not be prevented from or inhibited in proceeding as scheduled with the preparation of all aspects of the yearbook except the one page of the senior section on which Plaintiff's photograph and allied data will appear. Finally, it is not shown that there is any irreparable harm which will result *to these Defendants* in the event that the ultimate outcome of such delay should be that no 1984 yearbook is published.

It is clear, on balance, that the protection of the Plaintiff's constitutionally-based interests predominate on the present factual calculus, and that an adequate showing has been made that the Plaintiff's potential injury, in the absence of temporary injunctive relief, will outweigh any harm which the granting of an appropriately-framed injunction would inflict on these Defendants.

3. *Plaintiff's Likelihood of Success on the Merits*

Plaintiff here asserts a claim which challenges the right to *initiate* expression. In this respect the case differs from *Sheck,* 530 F.Supp. 679, 685–6, with respect to the primacy of the value of the conduct which is claimed to be protected by the First Amendment right of free speech. In *Sheck,* this Court recognized a qualitative distinction, for analytical purposes, between official conduct which restricts a student's "right to receive information and ideas, *the indispensible reciprocal of any meaningful right of expression,"* id. at 685 (emphasis in original), and the right to initiate expression. In the present case there is no question that the alleged conduct of the Defendants is claimed to prevent the publication of a quotation expressing the Plaintiff's idea in a claimed public forum. As such, the claim is indisputably that the official conduct infringes upon her First Amendment right *to initiate* expression. *Id.* That right is clearly and expressly granted to her by the First Amendment and it is not necessary for analytical purposes, as it was in *Sheck, supra,* to establish the meaningfulness of the Plaintiff's claimed right. We deal here with the right of expression itself in its most direct exercise.

In assessing whether Plaintiff is likely to succeed with her claim that the school authorities have infringed her right to initiate expression, it is necessary to consider the specific issues raised by the pleading posture of this case. These are:

(a) Whether Plaintiff is required to exhaust available administrative remedies before seeking relief in this Court under Section 1983;
(b) Whether the yearbook is a public forum for the expression of ideas;
(c) Whether the alleged restriction of the Plaintiff's First Amendment right of free speech was accomplished under color of state law;
(d) Whether the content of the standard actually applied to reject for publication the Plaintiff's designated quotation meets constitutional requirements as a basis for restricting the First Amendment right of free speech;[3]

(a) *Exhaustion of State Remedies*

The Defendants contend that the Plaintiff may not pursue this action under § 1983 without first exhausting administrative remedies available in the form of an appeal of the decision of the principal of the high school to the Brunswick School Board. This contention is not well founded. The United States Supreme Court, in a long series of decisions beginning in 1963, has rejected the argument that a § 1983 action must be dismissed where the plaintiff has not exhausted state administrative remedies. *McNeese* v. *Board of Education,* 373 U.S. 668, 83 S.Ct. 1433, 10 L.Ed.2d 622 (1963); *see also Gibson* v. *Berryhill,* 411 U.S. 564, 93 S.Ct. 1689, 36 L.Ed.2d 488 (1973); *Carter* v. *Stanton,* 405 U.S. 669, 92 S.Ct. 1232, 31 L.Ed.2d 569(1972); *Wilwording* v. *Swenson,* 404 U.S. 249, 92 S.Ct. 407, 30 L.Ed.2d 418 (1971); *Houghton* v. *Shafer,* 392 U.S. 639, 640, 88 S.Ct. 2119, 2120, 20 L.Ed.2d 1319 (1968); *King* v. *Smith,* 392 U.S. 309, 312, n. 4, 88 S.Ct. 2128, 2131, n. 4, 20 L.Ed.2d 1118 (1968); *Damico* v. *California,* 389 U.S. 416, 88 S.Ct. 526, 19 L.Ed.2d 647 (1967); *cf. Steffel* v. *Thompson,* 415 U.S. 452, 472-3, 94 S.Ct. 1209, 1222-3, 39 L.Ed.2d 505 (1974). This line of decisions has been recently capped by the United States Supreme Court's decision in *Patsy* v. *Florida Board of Regents,* 457 U.S. 496, 102 S.Ct. 2557, 73 L.Ed.2d 172 (1982). There, the Court, after a general review of the legislative history of § 1983 found that

> [t]his legislative history supports the conclusion that our prior decisions, holding that exhaustion of state administrative remedies is not a prerequisite to an action under § 1983, did not misperceive the statutory intent: it seems fair to infer that the 1871 Congress did not intend that an individual be compelled in every case to exhaust state administrative remedies before filing an action under § 1 of the Civil Rights Act.
> *Id.,* at 507, 102 S.Ct. at 2563.

After additionally considering various policy considerations which were there argued to support the imposition by judicial decision of a requirement of exhaustion of administrative remedies, the Court stated: "[W]e conclude that exhaustion of state administrative remedies should not be required as a prerequisite to bringing an action pursuant to § 1983." *Id.* at 516, 102 S.Ct. at 2568. The foregoing authorities make clear that this Plaintiff need not exhaust administrative remedies available within the Brunswick School Department before seeking to vindicate her First Amendment rights under § 1983. A substantial likelihood exists, therefore, that the Plaintiff will prevail on this issue when this case is finally determined.

(b) *The Yearbook as a "Public Forum"*

The next issue raised by Plaintiff's claim is whether or not the yearbook is a public forum for the expression of ideas. The Court notes that Plaintiff alleged in the original complaint that:

> For the last ten years, or thereabouts, the defendant School Department has published a high school yearbook at the conclusion of each and every school year. That yearbook has contained a section in which appear the pictures of all of the members of the senior class as well as biographical information about each such student *and a short quotation selected for inclusion by the students.*

Complaint, at ¶ 4 (emphasis added). By their answer, the Defendants admitted the allegations of paragraph 4 of the complaint. Answer, at ¶ 4. Defendants' affidavit of Ms. Harlow states:

> The senior section of the yearbook consists of individual photographs of seniors. They are allowed to submit information on an activity sheet relating to nickname, *a quote,* activities, likes, dislikes, and future goals. This information is then reviewed and edited by the yearbook staff including faculty advisors for accuracy, appropriateness, punctuation, and length.

Harlow affidavit at ¶ 3 (emphasis added).
Attached to the affidavit of Mr. Millett, the principal of the high school, as Exhibit D, is a copy of the 1983 Brunswick High School Yearbook. An examination of that exhibit demonstrates beyond any doubt that in the 1983 yearbook each picture of a senior student is accompanied by a quotation reflecting the student's philosophical, social, ethical or other personal views of life. None of the affidavits submitted by Defendants controvert to any extent the factual proposition that in past years the Brunswick High School Yearbook has been permitted, as a matter of fact, to serve the

purpose of affording a forum in which senior students may express their personal views, opinions, and ideas through the selection of quoted material. Those affidavits also make it clear that that practice is intended to be continued in the preparation of the 1984 Brunswick High School Yearbook.

The present record of this case, therefore, contains a forceful showing that, completely apart from the question of whether or not the school authorities could be *required* to provide a vehicle for the expression and transmission of personally-held views on matters of importance to senior students, the Brunswick High School Yearbook has now been so utilized for a period of years under the *aegis* of those representatives of the school department who are charged with preparing and publishing the yearbook. The record shows an intent to continue this practice in the 1984 yearbook. Those representatives of the school system, acting within the scope of their authority, as that is displayed on the present record, have created of the Brunswick High School Yearbook a *de facto* public forum for the expression of senior students' personal ideas. At trial on the merits of this proceeding, further evidence may be adduced upon this issue. However, the present record amply demonstrates a substantial likelihood that the Plaintiff will prevail in establishing the "public forum" status of the 1984 Brunswick High School Yearbook.

(c) *Action "Under Color of State Law"*

Defendants contend that Plaintiff has not demonstrated that Defendants rejection of her designated quotation for publication was done "under color of state law" as required by 42 U.S.C. § 1983. *See Parratt v. Taylor,* 451 U.S. 527, 101 S.Ct. 1908, 68 L.Ed.2d 420 (1981). The Defendants base this contention on the premise that "[t]o date, the responsible governmental entity—the Brunswick School Board—has taken no action at all; it has not yet even had the opportunity to do so." Defendant's Memorandum of Law, at 14.

Defendants' argument too rigidly restricts the scope of the "under color of state law" requirement of § 1983. That requirement does not mandate for its satisfaction action by the governmental authority ultimately responsible for activity authorized by law. That requirement is satisfied as well by a showing that the acts complained of are performed by any person who acts pursuant to authority conferred upon that person, or derived by the person from others, pursuant to state law.

The record here reflects that the preparation and publication of the high school yearbook is an integral part of the general program of secondary education provided under the auspices of the Brunswick School Board, which is charged by Maine law with overseeing the education of Brunswick's citizens. That program involves the participation of students who act under the supervision of assigned faculty members of the high school. The operations of the editorial board are subject to the review and oversight of not only the assigned faculty members, but that of the assistant principal, principal, and, ultimately, of the superintendent of schools. Although initially student editors rejected Plaintiff's designated quotation, at least one faculty advisor participated in and ultimately ratified that decision. Both the high school principal and the assistant principal subsequently concurred in that decision and the reason given for it. The superintendent of schools participated in efforts to "resolve" the issue and has done nothing to change or overturn the decision reached by school employees at any lower level of the administrative chain of command.

Nothing in the record suggests that the oversight and review activities of the Brunswick school officials mentioned above have been conducted in any way other than in the course and scope of their activity and duties as agents of the school board. Their actions are patently taken for purposes of implementing the educational programs and policies of Brunswick as they are formulated by the school board pursuant to 20 M.R.S.A. § 1011. Those officials are clearly the agents of the board and their acts are thus sanctioned by law. Their acts are, by elemental rules of law, the acts of the school board itself. Plaintiff, therefore, has shown a substantial likelihood of prevailing at trial on the question of whether Defendants acted "under color of state law" in rejecting the Plaintiff's designated quotation.

(d) *The Constitutional Adequacy of the Defendants' Publication Standard*

We must now consider the constitutional legitimacy of the standards that were applied by the editorial board and the school authorities to restrict Plaintiff's right of free expression. It is to be noted preliminarily that issues may exist at trial as to whether there was in fact any established standard for such purposes. If so, further questions may arise as to the specific content of the standard, and, perhaps, whether the content of any such standard was ever communicated to the Plaintiff. The Court's present inquiry is limited, however, to a determination of the likelihood of Plaintiff's success on the merits. Such a determination is predictive in nature, and the Court in making it is constrained by the contents of the record now before the Court. It is not necessary to make any factual prediction concerning the standard, however, because the present record shows that the standard actually applied, in any formulation supported by the record, cannot pass constitutional muster. No possible formulation of the standard provides criteria that are sufficiently objective and specific to distinguish publishable material from that which is not publishable.

We must recognize at the inception of this inquiry that:

> The constitutional right of free expression is powerful medicine in a society as diverse and populous as ours. It is designed and intended to remove governmental restraints from the arena of public discussion, putting the decision as to what views shall be voiced largely into the hands of each of us, in the hope that use of such freedom will ultimately produce a more capable citizenry and more perfect polity and in the belief that no other approach would comport with the premise of individual dignity and choice upon which our political system rests.

Cohen v. *California,* 403 U.S. 15, 24, 91 S.Ct. 1780, 1787, 29 L.Ed.2d 284 (1971); *see Whitney* v. *California*, 274 U.S. 357, 47 S.Ct. 641, 71 L.Ed. 1095 (1927) (Brandeis, J., concurring).

Because of the paramount significance which our basic political doctrine extends to free expression as a vehicle for the fostering of that premise, free public expression may not be subjected to governmentally sponsored censorship by vague, subjective or non-discrete standards. Public officials may not exercise untrammeled discretion in regulating the content of public speech. *Smith* v. *Goguen,* 415 U.S. 566, 573, 94 S.Ct. 1242, 1247, 39 L.Ed.2d 605 (1974); *see Police Department* v. *Mosley,* 408 U.S. 92, 92 S.Ct. 2286, 33 L.Ed.2d 212 (1972). Free public expression cannot be burdened with governmental predictions or assessments of what a discrete populace will think about good or bad "taste." "The social value of the conceptual and emotive content of censored expression is not to be sacrificed to arbitrary official standards of vocabular taste without constitutional recourse." *Sheck,* 530 F.Supp. at 687. As Justice Harlan aptly stated in *Cohen* v. *California:*

> Surely the State has no right to cleanse public debate to the point where it is grammatically palatable to the most squeamish among us. Yet no readily ascertainable general principle exists for stopping short of that result.... [I]ndeed, we think it is largely because governmental officials cannot make principled distinctions in this area that the Constitution leaves matters of taste and style so largely to the individual.... [M]uch linguistic expression serves a dual communicative function: it conveys not only ideas capable of relatively precise, detached explication, but otherwise inexpressable emotions as well. In fact, words are often chosen as much for their emotive as their cognitive force. We cannot sanction the view that the Constitution, while solicitous of the cognitive content of individual speech, has little or no regard for that emotive function which, practically speaking, may often be the more important element of the overall message sought to be communicated.

Cohen, 403 U.S. at 25-6, 91 S.Ct. at 1788-89.

Here the Plaintiff asserts that she feels strongly about the issues of murder and capital punishment. She selected her designated quotation to "provoke some of my classmates to think a little more deeply than if I had written a standard butterfly quote." Plaintiff's supplemental affidavit, at ¶ 8. She seeks to convey her message, in part at least, through the "shock effect" of graphic prose. She seeks to utilize the "emotive function" of language. Yet, it is precisely because the chosen language serves that function well that the quotation has been rejected because, it is said, it is "inappropriate."

Giving to the people the right of individual expression free from unwarranted governmental interference must ultimately be seen as a calculated, historical gamble to which, through the vehicle of the Constitution, the Founding Fathers have committed this nation and its people so long as the Constitution shall endure. Mr. Justice Black saw accurately their assessment of the risks inherent in that gamble:

> Since the earliest days, philosophers have dreamed of a country where the mind and spirit of man would be free; where there would be no limits to inquiry; where men would be free to explore the unknown and to challenge the most deeply rooted beliefs and principles. Our First Amendment was a bold effort to adopt this principle—to establish a country with no legal restrictions of any kind upon the subjects people could investigate, discuss, and deny. The Framers knew, better perhaps than we do today, the risks they were taking. They knew that free speech might be the friend of change and revolution. But they also knew that it is always the deadliest enemy of tyranny. With this knowledge they still believed that the ultimate happiness and security of a nation lies in its ability to explore, to change, to grow and ceaselessly to adapt itself to new knowledge born of inquiry free from any kind of governmental control over the mind and spirit of man. Loyalty comes from love of good government, not fear of a bad one.

Black, *The Bill of Rights,* 35 N.Y.U.L.Rev. 865, 880-1 (1960).

We need not shrink from the hazards of a free people saying without restraint what they believe. We have a sufficient security in the Framers' profound conviction that the decency and sound judgment of an *informed* citizenry will, in good time, winnow the rash statement from the reasonable one, reject the foolish proposal for the principled one, discern the zealot from the diplomat, and distinguish the demagogue from the democrat. That conviction is our substitute for the more immediately attainable safety provided by government control, in the name of "taste" and "appropriateness," of what we as individuals may say and write. It sustains our rule that the exercise of official discretion in proscribing certain content of public speech must reflect a specific and considered judgment restricting speech only in terms of a particular time and place for the achievement of a discernible and reasonable public goal, *see Grayned* v. *City of Rockford,* 408 U.S. 104, 121, 92 S.Ct. 2294, 2306, 33 L.Ed.2d 222 (1972), and that the government is constrained to the use of reasonably precise and ascertainable standards in implementing any regulation of free expression. *Keyishian* v. *Board of Regents,* 385 U.S. 589, 603-4, 87 S.Ct. 675, 683-4, 17 L.Ed.2d 629 (1967).[4]

The Defendants' regulation of Plaintiff's speech in this case is based upon the imposition of a standard that is shown, by the existing record, to be phrased in various terms.[5] Plaintiff's designated quotation was not rejected for publication because it "involved alcohol, sex or drugs" or views that implied "anything about those things." Moll affidavit at ¶ 5. The record makes clear that the quotation was rejected because it was "not appropriate for the yearbook," Harlow affidavit at ¶ 6, "inappropriate since it was in poor taste," Bumgardner affidavit at ¶7,[6] and "distasteful and not appropriate for a yearbook," Moll affidavit at ¶ 6. The principal, Mr. Millett, *denied an appeal from those decisions* of the editorial staff of the yearbook and its faculty advisors with no indication that any additional ground for rejection was considered by him.

Rejection of Plaintiff's designated quotation on the basis of a standard of "poor taste" or "appropriateness" either to the yearbook or to some narrow segment of public opinion, such as Brunswick High School seniors, or to a wider segment, such as the populace of Brunswick, fixes no discrete, objective limits to the determination of what may or may not be published therein. That test must always be, by such standards, completely subjective in at least two respects; what the official making the decision as to publishability thinks to be "tasteful" or "appropriate" *and* what that official believes others may think to be so.

The vagueness and uncertainty of the standard is geometrically increased when it is prospectively applied, as was done here, through a period of future years. If the intellectual and ideological ferment of the last four decades of the American social experience teaches anything, it teaches us that whatever may be the accepted meaning of "good taste" on any given day, the content of that meaning does not rigidly abide through time. The passage from the acceptability in the public forum of the content of the *Esquire* magazine of the 1940s to that of *Hustler* in the 1980s is not an historical accident. It is, rather, an historical proof that the open expression of individual views and tastes, the exposure of the public to new and challenging ideas, and the promotion of a continually widening exposure of the society to new information is effective to shape the public consensus. These are all processes which underlie and are intended to be secured by the First Amendment. To deny the reality of their contribution to our well-being is to deny alike the value of the eloquence and courage of a General Washington addressing his troops at Valley Forge, a President Kennedy inspiring the nation at his Inaugural, or of a Martin Luther King bespeaking the conscience of the nation from the steps of the Lincoln Memorial. These historical phenomena take their driving force from the dynamic effect of free expression by a free people. The sense of vigor which they bring to the direction of the affairs of the Republic may not be suppressed by government intervention in the name of "good taste" and "appropriateness."

The criteria shown by the existing record to have been actually applied here as a basis for the rejection for publication of the Plaintiff's designated quotation failed to address adequately any of the constitutional requirements. They do not, therefore, pass constituional muster as criteria sufficient in content to limit the Plaintiff's right to free expression of her ideas in a public forum. If these criteria are ultimately shown to be all that was applied to deny Plaintiff her First Amendment right, she will clearly prevail at trial on this aspect of her claim.

4. *The Public Interest*

Justice Frankfurter framed lucidly the pertinent calculus when he said that the right of free expression "means not only informed and responsible criticism but the freedom to speak foolishly and without moderation." *Baumgartner* v. *United States,* 322 U.S. 665, 674, 64 S.Ct. 1240, 1245, 88 L.Ed. 1525 (1944). In the legitimate exercise of her right of free speech, this Plaintiff has the option to convey her conviction by the use of the most graphic language, even, if she so chooses, by language so physiologically stark that others may believe her to "be a jerk."[7]

Government has no legitimate nor compelling interest in preserving this lone woman from that fate if her own utterances shall visit it upon her. Rather, the First Amendment declares that the highest interest of the people is best served if government is required to stay its hand and permit her, and millions like her, to take upon their personal risk the ability of their ideas and convictions to survive and propagate in the marketplace of ideas. It is a matter of little moment, in the larger sense, whether she fails in that endeavor; it is of vital moment that she and her idea not be denied, by the instrumentalities of the political establishment, the *opportunity to succeed* in that marketplace. It is, indeed, of paramount importance to the public interest that she have that opportunity. *See Sheck,* 530 F.Supp. at 693. "The vigilant protection of constitutional freedoms is nowhere more vital than in the community of American schools." *Shelton* v. *Tucker,* 364 U.S. 479, 487, 81 S.Ct. 247, 251, 5 L.Ed.2d 231 (1960).

The public interest may be thought to be best served if schools and teachers practice the historical orthodoxies of our political freedom while they preach the temporally transitory orthodoxies of "taste." They may legitimately, and should, seek to inculcate the latter, but they may not, in the effort to do so, transgress upon the former. In the final analysis, under our Constitution, individual liberty of expression must be accorded its day even at the expense of the promotion of aesthetic sophistication. *See Keyishian,* 385 U.S. at 603, 87 S.Ct. at 683.

In light of the careful limitation of the scope of the Court's preliminary injunction, no countervailing public interest is damaged by the injunction. The Court requires the Defendants to do nothing save to hold their hand with respect to *final* publication until the rights of both parties to this litigation may be finally adjudicated. The Defendants are no more entitled to commit the preclusive act of final publication in advance of that adjudication *without* Plaintiff's designated quotation than is the Plaintiff entitled to have the Court require, in advance thereof, an equally preclusive publication *with* the quotation. The injunction will not interfere in any other respect with the activities of the school authorities in preparing the yearbook against the day of a publication when this Court will have performed its constitutional function. Thus will be avoided "any irreparable loss of important individual liberties during the interim before the parties can be fully heard on the merits." *Sheck,* 530 F.Supp. at 679. Yet, any significant intrusion upon the public policy that the Court not "intervene in the resolution of conflicts which arise in the daily operation of school systems ... which do not directly and sharply implicate basic constitutional values," *Epperson* v. *Arkansas,* 393 U.S. 97, 104, 89 S.Ct. 266, 270, 21 L.Ed.2d 228 (1968), is minimized. The limited interim injunctive relief here granted serves the public interest in all respects.

5. *Conclusion*

The Court concludes that the Plaintiff has made a strong showing of entitlement to preliminary injunctive relief preventing final publication of the 1984 Brunswick High School Yearbook until a final adjudication on the merits of this action. *See Planned Parenthood* v. *Bellotti,* 641 F.2d 1006, 1009 (1st Cir.1981). A preliminary injunction shall issue forthwith in the form and substance of Appendix "A" attached hereto.

So Ordered.

APPENDIX "A"

PRELIMINARY INJUNCTION

Plaintiff's motion for a Temporary Restraining Order having come on for hearing and argument on January 11, 1984, and notice and hearing thereon having been ordered by the Court, and the motion now being considered by the Court as one for a Preliminary Injunction, and the Court having this date separately made its findings of fact and conclusions of law in its Findings of Fact, Conclusions of Law, Opinion and Order of this date,

It is hereby ordered, that the Defendant Gerald Millett and all others acting in concert with him, be, and are hereby, enjoined from authorizing, allowing, causing or permitting, pursuant to any authorization, permission or order therefore previously given or to be given after this date, any final printing, publication, or distribution of a 1984 Brunswick High School Yearbook prior to this Court's final adjudication of the merits of the above-entitled matter, the content of which shall exclude therefrom the Plaintiff's designated quotation, viz:

> "The executioner will pull this lever four times. Each time 2000 volts will course through your body, making your eyeballs first bulge, then burst, and then broiling your brains ..."

from the Senior Section thereof next to the photograph and biographical data previously submitted by Plaintiff and approved for publication therein by the yearbook editorial staff and said Gerald Millett.

Nothing contained in this Preliminary Injunction shall preclude the interim preparation, including printing, of other material to be included in said 1984 Brunswick High School Yearbook in accordance with existing or other schedules of the editorial staff.

NOTES

1. "Defendants' conduct violates Plaintiff's right to have access to a public forum for the assertion of her views, whether those views are political or not." Complaint, at

¶ 19.

2. The Plaintiff's initial Verified Complaint, accompanied by a motion for a temporary restraining order, was filed with the Court on December 21, 1983. That complaint named as Defendants the Brunswick School Department and Gerald Millett, the high school principal. After the application for interlocutory injunctive relief was scheduled for hearing by the Court, Defendants filed, on January 6, 1984, their answer, which set out, *inter alia,* as affirmative defenses that: (1) the complaint failed to name the proper parties; and (2) the Brunswick School Department is not a suable entity. Plaintiff filed on January 10, 1984, an Amended Complaint, which names as Defendants the Brunswick School Department, The Brunswick School Board, Daniel Calderwood, the superintendent of schools, and Gerald Millett, the high school principal. The Amended Complaint is not verified as required by Fed.R.Civ.P. 65(b)(1). Defendants have not yet filed a responsive pleading to the amended complaint.

At the hearing, Defendants objected to the Court's consideration of the content of the Amended Complaint because, pursuant to Fed.R.Civ.P. 15(a), the amendment is untimely and can be granted only by leave of Court, "which leave shall be freely given when justice so requires." *Id.* The Court granted such leave on January 11, 1984. The Amended Complaint realleges without significant change or addition the substantive factual allegations of the original Verified Complaint. The only significant change made by the latter pleading is to add as additional Defendants the Brunswick School Department and Daniel Calderwood, the Brunswick Superintendent of Schools. Though the pleading was served upon counsel for the original Defendants, the record reflects no proof of service upon, nor any acceptance of service by, these new Defendants. For present purposes, therefore, they are not yet subject to the jurisdiction of the Court. In addition, the Amended Complaint is not verified. Accordingly, its contents may not be considered by the Court in granting interlocutory injunctive relief. Fed.R.Civ.P. 65(b)(1). For that reason, Plaintiff's request for interlocutory injunctive relief is considered solely on the basis of the substantive factual allegations of the initial Verified Complaint.

The Court need not adjudicate at this juncture the viability of the "proper party" and "suable entity" affirmative defenses since the Court unquestionably has jurisdiction over the high school principal, Mr. Millett, as a party defendant. The record clearly shows that he is the principal of the high school. The Court may grant effective interlocutory injunctive relief in this proceeding by an injunction directed against him and all others acting in concert with him. Defendants' counsel represented at oral argument that any injunction issued by the Court against Mr. Millett would be accorded legal effect by the Defendants.

3. Defendants also raise as a defense that a temporary injunction cannot require them to violate the rights of *Time* magazine under the Copyright Law, 17 U.S.C. § 106, *et seq.,* by publishing without permission copyrighted material from the magazine. The issue is not immediately generated for decision in these proceedings since this Court's preliminary injunction will not require Defendants to publish anything. The issue must be considered, however, in a predictive context in determining whether Plaintiff has demonstrated a "substantial likelihood of success on the merits."

Plaintiff does not dispute that her designated quotation is copyrighted material. She does assert that its proposed use in the 1984 yearbook will not be an infringement of *Time* magazine's copyright under the "fair use" doctrine authorized by 17 U.S.C. § 107. That statutory provision excepts from the category of infringement, "the fair use of a copyrighted work ... for purposes such as ... comment ..." *Id.* The statute then prescribes four criteria to be applied to determine if a particular use qualifies as an excepted "fair use" under § 107.

The Court has considered the use proposed here in the light of the statutory criteria. In view of the nature and substantiality of the use (e.g., publication of a two-line segment out of a six-page magazine article in a noncompeting high school yearbook to convey an ethical conviction); the nature of the copyrighted work (e.g., an internationally-circulated weekly news magazine); and the total lack of any economic effect upon the commercial value of the copyright, the Court is completely satisfied that such an issue at trial would be resolved in favor of a determination that publication of Plaintiff's designated quotation in the 1984 yearbook was within the "fair use" exception of § 107. *See Triangle Publications* v. *Knight-Ridder Newspapers,* 626 F.2d 1171, 1177 (5th Cir.1980).

4. The need for ascertainable and specific standards is dictated by at least three purposes: (1) to apprise the citizen who seeks to speak of what he may, in a specific circumstance, properly aspire to express; (2) to provide to responsible officials criteria that are objective and discrete in order that they may respond fairly to the legitimate interests of the citizen; and, finally (3) to provide to the courts, where they are called upon to do so, some factually-based and meaningful basis upon which they may adjudicate controversies arising out of conflict between the constitutionally-based rights and interests of the citizen and the rationally-based needs of society at large and of the government.

5. The standard, in one formulation, *allows* publication of material that is "tactful and appropriate for all students and the community in 1984 and in future years." Harlow affidavit at ¶ 5. In another formulation it *proscribes* material "which involved alcohol, sex or drugs, or was distasteful or inappropriate for a Brunswick High School Yearbook." Bumgardner affidavit at ¶ 3. By still another version, it enjoins students to exercise "[g]ood taste, common sense and decorum" in selecting a designated quotation. Moll affidavit at ¶ 5. The students were told not to "submit anything ... that is *seemingly distasteful* or inappropriate or that you won't want your kids to read fifteen years from now." *Id.*(emphasis added).

6. Assistant Principal Fairbrother agreed with Mrs. Bumgardner that "the quote was inappropriate." Bumgardner affidavit at ¶ 7.

7. *See* Moll affidavit at ¶ 5; Plaintiff's supplemental affidavit, at ¶ 3.

THE United States Court of Appeals, Ninth Circuit, decides against the governing board of Grossmont Union High School District (California) which had rejected an anti-draft advertisement that the San Diego Committee Against Registration and the Draft (CARD) wanted to place in several of the school district's student newspapers. In deciding that the banning of the advertisement was a violation of the First Amendment, the Court stated: "CARD's advertisement comes within the boundaries of the limited public forum the Board has created. Having established a limited public forum the Board cannot, absent a compelling governmental interest, exclude speech otherwise within the boundaries of the forum.... In particular, the Board cannot allow the presentation of one side of an issue, but prohibit the presentation of the other side.... Here, the Board permitted mixed political and commercial speech advocating military service, but attempted to bar the same type of speech opposing such service. The Board has failed to advance a compelling governmental interest justifying its conduct. Accordingly, the Board violated the First Amendment when it excluded CARD's advertisements from the newspapers." The Court concluded: "The Board has failed to advance any reasonable grounds for excluding CARD's advertisement from the newspapers. Accordingly, even if we assume that the newspapers are a nonpublic forum, that is, the type of forum which receives the least protection under the First Amendment, we must conclude that the Board violated the guarantees of that amendment when it prevented the publication of CARD's advertisement."

San Diego Committee v. *Governing Bd.*, 790 F.2d 1471 (1986)

REINHARDT, Circuit Judge:

I. BACKGROUND

The San Diego Committee Against Registration and the Draft (CARD) appeals the district court's denial of its request for a preliminary injunction enjoining the Governing Board of Grossmont Union High School District (the Board) from enforcing certain policies, rules and regulations, pursuant to which the Board has rejected an anti-draft advertisement submitted by CARD for placement in a number of the district's student newspapers.[1]

CARD is a non-profit organization located in San Diego County, California that is actively involved in counseling young men on alternatives to compulsory military service. CARD's membership consists of both students and non-students. The Board is the governing body of the Grossmont Union School District and retains ultimate responsibility for the adoption and enforcement of polices, rules and regulations relating to administration of the district's schools, including policies affecting the student newspapers.

In October, 1982, CARD sought to purchase advertising space from five student newspapers published by high schools within the district. According to CARD, its advertisement was directed toward providing information and counseling to male students regarding alternatives to military service. CARD's requests were referred to faculty advisors for review and subsequently submitted to the principals of the five high schools. The principals, in turn, requested Robert Pyle, Superintendent of the school district, to issue a policy guideline.

On November 8, 1982, Bob King, Acting Assistant Superintendent, issued a directive instructing all principals to reject CARD's requests on the ground that publication of the advertisements would contribute to the solicitation of illegal acts by the district's students.[2] On January 17, 1983, CARD filed an administrative claim with the Board in which it sought reversal of the Superintendent's decision. This claim was rejected on February 3, 1983.

On March 16, 1983, CARD brought suit against the Board pursuant to 42 U.S.C. § 1983 (1982), alleging that the Board's actions and policies had deprived CARD of its rights under the First and Fourteenth Amendments. CARD sought, *inter alia,* to enjoin the Board from enforcing those policies, rules and regulations that had resulted in the rejection of CARD's advertisements. CARD argued, as it does here, that because the Board permitted military service advertising, including various military recruitment advertisements, to be published in the five high school newspapers, it could not constitutionally exclude CARD's proffered advertisement.

The district court found that "[t]he student newspapers in the Grossmont High School District are limited in nature as a public forum." The district court also found that the military service advertisements that had appeared in the student newspaper were "non-political and offer[ed] vocational opportunities to the students." Finally, the district court found that the Grossmont Union High School District policies permitting publication of political speech by students only and restricting newspaper access by non-students to commercial speech were "reasonable in light of the purpose of school publications." The district court concluded that CARD had failed to show either probable success on the merits of its claim or that it had raised a question that was sufficiently serious to warrant issuance of a preliminary injunction. In this appeal, CARD contends that the district court erred in concluding that it had failed to meet the higher standard—the probability of success on the merits. We agree, although we do not intend to suggest that meeting the lower standard—the raising of a serious question—would not have been sufficient to warrant the relief sought.[3]

II. JURISDICTION

As a threshold matter, we address the Board's contention that we lack jurisdiction to hear this appeal as a result of CARD's failure to file its formal notice of appeal within the period of time prescribed by Fed.R.App.P. 4(a). In relevant part, Rule 4(a) provides that

> [i]n a civil case in which an appeal is permitted by law as of right . . . the notice of appeal . . . shall be filed with the clerk of the district court within 30 days after the date of entry of the judgment or order appealed from. . . .[4]

The provisions of Rule 4(a) are both mandatory and jurisdictional. *Browder v. Director, Illinois Department of Corrections,* 434 U.S. 257, 264, 98 S.Ct. 556, 560, 54 L.Ed.2d 521 (1978).

The district court entered an order denying CARD's request for a preliminary injunction on June 14, 1983. On June 24, 1983 rather than filing a notice of appeal pursuant to Rule 4(a), as it should have, CARD filed a motion for permission to appeal the order under Fed.R.App.P. 5(a). The latter rule provides that a district judge may certify an appeal from an order not otherwise appealable. The district court denied this motion on July 11, 1983. On July 19, 1983, CARD filed a Rule 4(a) notice of appeal.

Because CARD's formal Rule 4(a) notice of appeal was not filed within the period of time required by the rule, its appeal is timely only if we construe its Rule 5(a) motion as a notice of appeal. Fed.R.App. 3(c) requires us to construe CARD's Rule 5(a) motion in that manner. Rule 3(c) provides that "[a]n appeal shall not be dismissed for informality of form or title of the notice of appeal." Pursuant to this rule, we are required to broadly construe the notice of appeal provisions of Rule 4(a). *See Cel-A-Pak v. California Agricultural Labor Relations Board,* 680 F.2d 664, 667 (9th Cir.), *cert. denied,* 459 U.S. 1071, 103 S.Ct. 491, 74 L.Ed.2d 633 (1982) (Rule 3(c) mandates liberality in determining compliance with Rule 4(a)). Moreover, we have discretion, where the interests of substantive justice require it, to disregard irregularities in the form or procedure for filing a notice of appeal. *Id.*

In *Cel-A-Pak,* we recognized that documents not formally denominated notices of appeal have nevertheless been treated as such "as long as they clearly evince the party's intent to appeal and provide notice to both the opposing party and the court." *Id.*(citations omitted). *See also Cobb v. Lewis,* 488 F.2d 41, 44 (5th Cir.1974). Here, CARD's Rule 5(a) motion, filed ten days after entry of the district court's order, provided clear notice to both the court and the Board that CARD intended to appeal the order. Accordingly, we construe this motion as a Rule 4(a) notice of appeal which we find to have been timely filed.[5]

III. THE PUBLIC FORUM DOCTRINE AND THE FIRST AMENDMENT

CARD contends, in essence, that because others' advertisements relating to military service were published in several Grossmont high school newspapers, the Board could not exclude CARD's advertisement, particularly since CARD's advertisement presented an opposing viewpoint to the position taken in the previous ads.

The values embodied in the First Amendment require the state, under certain circumstances, to provide members of the public with access to its facilities for purposes of speech. Certain state facilities, which may be appropriately used for communication, enjoy special constitutional status as "public forums." *See generally Cornelius* v. *NAACP Legal Defense & Educational Fund,*—U.S.—, 105 S.Ct. 3439, 87 L.Ed.2d 567 (1985); *Perry Education Association* v. *Perry Local Educators' Association,* 460 U.S. 37, 103 S.Ct. 948, 74 L.Ed.2d 794 (1983). In these public forums, the First Amendment narrowly circumscribes the government's power to exclude or regulate speech. Of course, a state's mere ownership or control of a facility does not, in itself, guarantee access under the First Amendment. *United States Postal Service* v. *Council of Greenburgh Civic Associations,* 453 U.S. 114, 129-30, 101 S.Ct. 2676, 2685, 69 L.Ed.2d 517 (1981). Similarly, merely permitting public access to a government facility does not necessarily open it for use as a public forum. *Greer* v. *Spock,* 424 U.S. 828, 836, 96 S.Ct. 1211, 1216, 47 L.Ed.2d 505 (1976). However, even with respect to nonpublic forums, the state may not act unreasonably. *Cornelius,* 105 S.Ct. at 3448.

In *Perry* and *Cornelius,* the Supreme Court identified three types of forums to which the public's right of access varies, as does the type of limitations the state may impose upon the right. The Court first focused on "places which by long tradition or by government fiat have been devoted to assembly and debate," such as streets and parks, where "the rights of the state to limit expressive activity are sharply circumscribed." *Perry,* 460 U.S. at 45, 103 S.Ct. at 954; *accord Cornelius,* 105 S.Ct. at 3449. The Court stated that

> [i]n these quintessential public forums, the government may not prohibit all communicative activity. For the state to enforce a content-based exclusion it must show that its regulation is necessary to serve a compelling state interest and that it is narrowly drawn to achieve that end. The state may also enforce regulations of the time, place and manner of expression which are content-neutral, are narrowly tailored to serve a significant government interest, and leave open ample alternative channels of communication.

Perry, 460 U.S. at 45, 103 S.Ct. at 955 (citations omitted); *accord Cornelius,* 105 S.Ct. at 3448-49.

The second type of public forum on which the Court focused consists of "public property which the State has opened for use by the public as a place for expressive activity." *Perry,* 460 U.S. at 45, 103 S.Ct. at 955; *accord Cornelius* 105 S.Ct. at 3449. The courts have come to call this type of public forum a "limited public forum" or a "public forum by designation." In such a forum, "[t]he Constitution forbids a state to enforce certain exclusions from a forum generally open to the public even if it was not required to create the forum in the first place." *Perry,* 460 U.S. at 45, 103 S.Ct. at 955; *accord Cornelius,* 105 S.Ct. at 3449. A limited public forum may, depending on its nature and the nature of the state's actions, be open to the general public for the discussion of all topics, or there may be limitations on the groups allowed to use the forums or the topics that can be discussed. Thus, a limited public forum may be open to certain groups for the discussion of any topic, *Perry,* 460 U.S. at 46 n. 7, 103 S.Ct. at 955 n. 7 (citing *Widmar* v. *Vincent,* 454 U.S. 263, 102 S.Ct. 269, 70 L.Ed.2d 440 (1981)), or to the entire public for the discussion of certain topics, *Perry,* 460 U.S. at 46 n. 7, 103 S.Ct. at 955 n. 7 (citing *City of Madison Joint School District* v.*Wisconsin Employment Relations Comm'n,* 429 U.S. 167, 97 S.Ct. 421, 50 L.Ed.2d 376 (1976)), or some combination of the two.

Once the state has created a limited public forum, its ability to impose further constraints on the type of speech permitted in that forum is quite restricted:

> [a]lthough a State is not required to indefinitely retain the open character of the facility, as long as it does so it is bound by the same standards as apply in a traditional public forum. Reasonable time, place and manner regulations are permissible, and a content-based prohibition must be narrowly drawn to effectuate a compelling state interest.

Perry, 460 U.S. at 46, 103 S.Ct. at 955 (citations omitted).

"Thus the identical broad free speech rights attach to the first and second types of public forums," *Cinevision Corp.* v. *City of Burbank,* 745 F.2d 560, 569 (9th Cir.1984), *cert. denied,*—U.S.—, 105 S.Ct. 2115, 85 L.Ed.2d 480 (1985); *accord Cornelius,* 105 S.Ct. at 3448, although in the latter type of forums those broad rights apply only within the particular boundaries of the specific forum that has been established.

The third type of forum is "[p]ublic property... which is not by tradition or designation a forum for public communication," *Cinevision,* 745 F.2d at 569 n. 8 (quoting *Perry,* 460 U.S. at 46, 103 S.Ct. at 955), such as a military base or jail. The Court recognized that this type of forum is governed by standards different from those applicable to the first two. The Court stated that

> [i]n addition to time, place and manner regulations, the state may reserve the forum for its intended purposes, communicative or otherwise, as long as the regulation on speech is *reasonable.*

Perry, 460 U.S. at 46, 103 S.Ct. at 955 (emphasis added); *accord Cornelius,* 105 S.Ct. at 3448. "The existence of reasonable grounds for limiting access to a nonpublic forum, however, will not save a regulation that is in reality a facade for viewpoint-based discrimination." *Cornelius,* 105 S.Ct. at 3454.

IV. SCHOOL NEWSPAPERS AS A LIMITED PUBLIC FORUM

The Board first contends that the school newspapers fall into the third category of forums, nonpublic forums. We disagree, and hold that the newspapers fall into the second category, limited public forums. In deciding whether a particular forum is a limited public forum or a nonpublic forum, we must determine what type of forum the government intended to create. *Cornelius,* 105 S.Ct. at 3449. The government's intent is evidenced by "[its] policy and practice . . . [as well as] the nature of the property and its compatibility with expressive activity." *Id.*

In the case before us, the evidence clearly indicates an intent to create a limited public forum. Newspapers, including the Board's, are devoted entirely to expressive activity. Everything that appears in a newspaper is speech, whether commercial, political, artistic, or some other type. It is difficult to think of any other kind of property that is more compatible with expressive activity. In addition, the admitted policy and practice of the Board is to allow a particular group—the students—to discuss any topic in the newspapers, subject only to certain conditions not relevant to the issues before us. Thus, under the test enumerated in *Cornelius,* the Board's newspapers, like most other school papers, constitute, at a minimum, a limited public forum of the type found in *Widmar. See supra* pp. 1475-76.

The Board also allows non-students to use the forum it has created in the newspapers. The Board's admitted policy and practice is to allow members of the general public to avail themselves of the forum as long as their speech consists of advertisements offering goods, services, or vocational opportunities to students. Because the newspapers are open to the entire public for the discussion of these limited topics, the Board has also created a limited public forum of the type found in *City of Madison. See supra* pp. 1475-76.[6]

As a result, the dispute between the Board and CARD reduces itself to a debate over the precise limitations on the topics that may be discussed by non-students in the limited public forum the Board has created. The Board argues that it permits non-students to engage only in non-political commercial speech in the newspapers. It claims that the military service advertisements were non-political, but that CARD's ad is not. The district court, agreed with the Board and found that the military service advertisements published in the newspapers (1) offered vocational or career opportunities to students and (2) were non-political.

We agree with the first part of the district court's finding but disagree with the second. The advertisements regarding military service career opportunities are different from most career ads in several important respects. First, most career ads are commercial in nature. They involve the advertiser's "economic interests." *Central Hudson Gas & Electric Co. v. Public Service Commission,* 447 U.S. 557, 561, 100 S.Ct. 2343, 2348, 65 L.Ed.2d 341 (1980). The "commercial speech" doctrine "rests heavily on the 'common sense' distinction between speech proposing a commercial transaction and other varieties of speech." *Zauderer v. Office of Disciplinary Counsel,*—U.S.—, 105 S.Ct. 2265, 2275, 85 L.Ed.2d 652 (1985) (quoting *Ohralik v. Ohio State Bar Ass'n,* 436 U.S. 447, 455-56, 98 S.Ct. 1912, 1918-19, 56 L.Ed.2d 444 (1978)). Here, the government's interest in promoting military service is not an economic one; it is essentially political or governmental. Nor is any commercial transaction being proposed.

Second, it has long been recognized that the subject of military service is controversial and political in nature. There has been opposition to military service, both compulsory and voluntary, throughout our nation's history. *See, e.g., United States v. Seeger,* 380 U.S. 163, 85 S.Ct. 850, 13 L.Ed.2d 733 (1965) (discussing history of conscientious objection). Opposition to compulsory service—the draft—is often simply a manifestation of a more deeply rooted opposition to military service in any form. *See, e.g., Wayte v. United States,*—U.S.—, 105 S.Ct. 1524, 84 L.Ed.2d 547 (1985); *Welsh v. United States,* 398 U.S. 333, 90 S.Ct. 1792, 26 L.Ed.2d 308 (1970); *Sicurella v. United States,* 348 U.S. 385, 75 S.Ct. 403, 99 L.Ed. 436 (1955). The controversy over military service led to student protests in the late 1960's and early 1970's. Many of our nation's finest universities and colleges barred military recruiters from their campuses and terminated the Reserve Officer Training Corps program they had previously offered. For other manifestations of the controversy over voluntary and involuntary military service, *see, e.g., In re Summers,* 325 U.S. 561, 65 S.Ct. 1307, 89 L.Ed. 1795 (1945) (attorney could properly be denied admission to state bar because of his opposition to military service); *United States v. Schwimmer,* 279 U.S. 644, 49 S.Ct. 448, 73 L.Ed. 889 (1929) (alien could properly be denied citizenship due to opposition to military service); *United States v. Macintosh,* 283 U.S. 605, 51 S.Ct. 570, 75 L.Ed. 1302 (1931) (same); *United States v. Bland,* 283 U.S. 636, 51 S.Ct. 569, 75 L.Ed. 1319 (1931) (same); *Girouard v. United States,* 328 U.S. 61, 66 S.Ct. 826, 90 L.Ed. 1084 (1946) (overruling *Schwimmer, Macintosh,* and *Bland).*

One need not agree with those opposed to military

service in order to recognize the fact that there is indeed a well-established and continuing controversy surrounding the subject. The ads sponsored by the military advanced the position taken by the proponents of one side to that political dispute. Accordingly, the district court erred when it found that the military recruitment advertisements were nonpolitical.[7]

Thus, the Board has allowed certain members of the public—various military recruiters—to use its newspapers to engage in speech that is not essentially commercial in nature but that combines elements of political and commercial speech. As a result, the Board's *actual* policy and practice leads, under *Cornelius*, to the conclusion that the Board has established the school newspapers as a limited public forum in which students can discuss any topic, and in which non-students can engage in commercial speech generally and in speech which is both political and commercial with respect to at least one important and highly controversial topic—military service. Because the Board on a number of occasions permitted the publication of advertisements advocating military service, there can be no question but that the Board intended to open the newspapers for advertisements on this topic—at least by one side to the debate.

CARD's advertisement comes within the boundaries of the limited public forum the Board has created. Having established a limited public forum, the Board cannot, absent a compelling governmental interest, exclude speech otherwise within the boundaries of the forum. *See supra* pp. 1475-1476. In particular, the Board cannot allow the presentation of one side of an issue, but prohibit the presentation of the other side. *City of Madison*, 429 U.S. at 175-76, 97 S.Ct. at 426-27. Here, the Board permitted mixed political and commercial speech advocating military service, but attempted to bar the same type of speech opposing such service.[8] The Board has failed to advance a compelling governmental interest justifying its conduct. Accordingly, the Board violated the First Amendment when it excluded CARD's advertisements from the newspapers.[9]

V. NONPUBLIC FORUMS

In the alternative, we hold that even if the Board is correct in its assertion that the school newspapers are a nonpublic forum, its conduct still violated the First Amendment because its refusal to accept CARD's ads was unreasonable and constitutes viewpoint-based discrimination.

A. *Reasonableness Test*

1. *Generally*

The Board claims that its exclusion of CARD from the newspapers was reasonable and therefore constitutional, and offers three arguments in support of this conclusion. First, the Board claims that pursuant to the District's Publications Code, the Board may, in its discretion, restrict publication of ads proffered by nonstudent entities to non-political advertisements offering goods, services or vocational opportunities to students. Second, the Board urges that its refusal of CARD's advertisement was lawful because publication of the ad would have amounted to advocacy of an illegal act. Third, the Board claims, relying principally on its Publications Code, that because publication of CARD's advertisement would have necessarily reduced the space available to students to express themselves, the rejection of the ad was lawful.

2. *Political Nature of the Ads*

We have already demonstrated the fallacy in the Board's first argument. As discussed above, p. 1477, the military recruitment advertisements were of a mixed political and commercial character. CARD's ad pertained to the same topic, and like the recruitment ads, offered goods, services, or vocational opportunities to students. *See supra* note 8. Because CARD's ad dealt with the same politically controversial topic as previously-published ads, the political character of the ad did not provide a reasonable basis for excluding it from the newspapers.

3. *The Threat of Illegal Conduct*

The Board urges the prospect of illegal conduct as a reason not to publish CARD's advertisement. In the Board's view, its publication would amount to advocacy of non-registration—an illegal act.

We agree, of course, that the Board has a strong interest in promoting law abiding conduct among its students. But we are unable to conclude that its prohibiting the publication of CARD's advertisement serves this interest. The Board bases its argument on the fact that the organization has styled itself "The Committee Against Registration and the Draft." The Board further contends that the advertisement, when viewed in its entirety, advocates non-registration.

That the organization's name implies opposition to a particular law is not, in our view, sufficient to support a conclusion that the organization advocates unlawful conduct. Moreover, there is nothing in the text of the advertisement suggesting that CARD encourages non-registration. *See supra,* note 1. In fact, the record discloses that according to Superintendent Pyle the Board had no evidence that the purpose of the advertisement was to stop students from registering, and that the Board had derived such intent solely from a reading of the organization's name.

It is true that a state may act to prohibit individuals from advocating violations of the law when such advocacy is directed toward inciting or producing imminent lawless action and is likely to accomplish that objective. *See Brandenberg* v. *Ohio,* 395 U.S. 444, 447, 89 S.Ct. 1827, 1829, 23 L.Ed.2d 430 (1969). "But, in our system, undifferentiated fear or apprehension of disturbance is not enough to overcome the right to freedom of expression." *Tinker* v. *Des Moines Independent Community School District,* 393 U.S. 503, 508, 89 S.Ct. 733, 737, 21 L.Ed.2d 731 (1969). Mere speculation on the part of the state that individuals might at some time engage in illegal activity is insufficient to justify regulation. *Gay Students Organization* v. *Bonner,* 509 F.2d 652, 662 (1st Cir.1974).

The Board's conclusion that publication of CARD's advertisement would result in unlawful conduct was, at best, speculative. The record is devoid of any evidence that CARD advocated illegal conduct or that publication of the advertisement was likely to give rise to such conduct. To the contrary, the record indicates that CARD, through its advertisement, sought to apprise eligible students of legitimate and lawful alternatives to the draft, such as the availability of student deferments. Accordingly, we conclude that the Board's fear of illegal advocacy did not provide a reasonable basis for excluding CARD from the newspapers.

4. *Reduction of Opportunities*

Finally, the Board contends that its refusal to publish CARD's advertisement is justified by its interest, reflected in its Publications Code, in providing its students with a forum for free expression. The Board claims that excluding material written or sponsored by outsiders such as CARD from its student newspapers increases the students' opportunities to express themselves in print. We acknowledge, and the parties do not dispute, that the Board may, in light of various practical constraints, prohibit or impose limits on the amount of material from non-students that may be published in student newspapers. However, any such restriction may not be arbitrary or unreasonable. *See Cornelius.* The Board has offered no valid reason that distinguishes the reduction in student opportunities for freedom of expression due to publication of the recruitment ads from the reduction that would occur from publication of CARD's advertisement; nor does the Board suggest that there is any objective system for limiting the number of ads or choosing among ads concerning the same general subject or relating to the same type of service or vocation. The differentiation in treatment between CARD's ad and the military's was thus arbitrary and as a result impermissible. Accordingly, we hold that the Board's policy on student self-expression did not provide a reasonable basis for excluding CARD from its newspapers.

5. *Conclusion*

The Board has failed to advance any reasonable grounds for excluding CARD's advertisement from the newspapers.[10] Accordingly, even if we assume that the newspapers are a nonpublic forum, that is, the type of forum which receives the least protection under the First Amendment, we must conclude that the Board violated the guarantees of that amendment when it prevented the publication of CARD's advertisement. *See Cornelius,* 105 S.Ct. at 3448.[11]

B. *Viewpoint-Based Discrimination*

Furthermore, it appears that the Board was engaging in viewpoint-based discrimination. By allowing the publication of the military recruitment advertisements, the Board allowed the presentation of one side of a highly controversial issue. The Board provided a forum to those who advocate military service. The Board then refused, without a valid reason, to allow those who oppose military service to use the same forum. The only reasonable inference is that the Board was engaging in viewpoint discrimination. As the Supreme Court has stated, "[t]o permit one side of a debatable public question to have a monopoly in expressing its views ... is the antithesis of constitutional guarantees." *City of Madison,* 429 U.S. at 175-76, 97 S.Ct. at 426-27. In other words, "the First Amendment means that the government has no power to restrict expression because of its message, its ideas, its subject matter, or its content." *Bolger* v. *Youngs Drug Products Corp.,* 463 U.S. 60, 65, 103 S.Ct. 2875, 2879, 77 L.Ed.2d 469 (1983) (quoting *Police Department of Chicago* v. *Mosley,* 408 U.S. 92, 95, 92 S.Ct. 2286, 2289-90, 33 L.Ed.2d 212 (1972)). Viewpoint-based discrimination is not permitted even in a non-public forum. *Cornelius,* 105 S.Ct. at 3554. Accordingly, the Board's viewpoint discrimination provides a second ground for holding that even if the school newspapers do not constitute a public forum, the Board violated the First Amendment in excluding CARD's advertisement.

VI. CONCLUSION

Because CARD has shown a substantial likelihood that it will prevail on the merits of its claim, we conclude that the district court abused its discretion in denying CARD's request for a preliminary injunction. We remand the matter and, pending trial on the merits, instruct the district court to enter a preliminary injunction in favor of CARD.

Reversed and remanded.

WALLACE, Circuit Judge, dissenting:

I first address a preliminary problem with the majority disposition. I believe the majority is far too generous in considering a document which does not purport to be a notice of appeal as complying with Fed.R.App.P. 4(a). I cannot distinguish *Selph* v. *Council of the City of Los Angeles,* 593 F.2d 881 (9th Cir.1979), from this case and, therefore, conclude we have no jurisdiction to hear this appeal.

If this were the only vice of the majority disposition, my separate opinion would be brief. But the majority has run afoul of Supreme Court precedent on a fundamental issue. Last Term, in *Cornelius* v. *NAACP Legal Defense & Educational Fund, Inc.,*—U.S.—, 105 S.Ct. 3439, 87 L.Ed.2d 567 (1985) (*Cornelius*), the Court presented its most thorough elaboration of the public forum doctrine. *See id.* at 3446-55. Unfortunately, the majority misreads or disregards *Cornelius* and manufactures an analysis that is patently inconsistent with the analysis of the Court.

I

In *Cornelius,* the Court addressed a claim that the federal government violated the first amendment by excluding legal defense and political advocacy organizations from participation in the Combined Federal Campaign (the campaign), a charity drive conducted in the federal workplace. An executive order limited participation in the campaign to "voluntary, charitable, health and welfare agencies that provide or support direct health and welfare services to individuals or their families" and specifically excluded organizations that seek to influence election or public policy through political activity, lobbying, or litigation. *Id.* at 3445-46, *quoting* Exec. Order No. 12404 § 1(b), 3 C.F.R. 151 (1984). After acknowledging that charitable solicitation of funds is a form of protected speech, *id.* at 3447-48, the Court turned to examine the status of the campaign under the public forum doctrine. Following *Perry Education Association* v. *Perry Local Educator's Association,* 460 U.S. 37, 45-46, 103 S.Ct. 948, 954-55, 74 L.Ed.2d 794 (1983) (*Perry*), the Court recognized three categories of fora: (1) the traditional public forum; (2) the public forum created by government designation, which includes the "limited public forum"; and (3) the nonpublic forum. 105 S.Ct. at 3449.

The Court determined that the campaign was a nonpublic forum, rather than a public forum created by government designation. The key to distinguishing between these two categories, the Court ruled, is the *government's intent:*

> The government does not create a public forum by inaction or by permitting limited discourse, but only by intentionally opening a non-traditional forum for public discourse. Accordingly, the Court has looked to the policy and practice of the government to ascertain whether it intended to designate a place not traditionally open to assembly and debate as a public forum.

Id. (citation omitted).

Thus, the Court observed, the internal mail system in *Perry* was a nonpublic forum since "school board policy did not grant general access to the school mail system." *Id.* at 3450; *see Perry,* 460 U.S. at 47, 103 S.Ct. at 956 (forum is nonpublic if there is no policy or practice of "indiscriminate use by the general public"). Similarly, the advertising space on city transit buses in *Lehman* v. *City of Shaker Heights,* 418 U.S. 298, 94 S.Ct. 2714, 41 L.Ed.2d 770 (1974), was a nonpublic forum because the city's policy of allowing only commercial and not political advertisements showed that it intended to limit access. *Cornelius,* 105 S.Ct. at 3450.

Applying this intent test, the Court explicitly rejected the contention that the campaign was a limited public forum open to all charitable organizations. The Court stated that the government's policy and practice of limiting access to the campaign precluded the conclusion that the campaign had been purposefully designated for public use. The Court also observed that the nature of the government property involved is relevant to determining intent and that the government has the right to control access to the workplace to avoid disruption. Consequently, the selective access granted to certain charitable organizations did not convert the campaign into a public forum. *Id.* at 3450-51.

Because the campaign was a nonpublic forum, the Court subjected its restrictions to limited scrutiny: "Control over access to a nonpublic forum can be based on subject matter and speaker identity so long as the distinctions drawn are reasonable in light of the purpose served by the forum and are viewpoint neutral." *Id.* at 3451; *see Perry,* 460 U.S. at 46, 49, 103 S.Ct. at 954, 957. The Court found the restrictions on access reasonable since they were intended to avoid "the appearance of political favoritism" and to limit disruption of the forum. *Cornelius,* 105 S.Ct. at 3453-54. The Court remanded the case, however, because the lower courts had not made a finding on whether the restrictions were "in reality a facade for viewpoint-based discrimination." *Id.* at 3454-55.

The proper application of *Cornelius* is well illustrated by *Student Coalition for Peace* v. *Lower Merion School District Board of School Directors*, 776 F.2d 431 (3rd Cir.1985) (*Student Coalition*). In *Student Coalition*, the Third Circuit encountered a fact situation closely analogous to this case. Indeed, the few differences that exist make ours an even stronger case for the application of *Cornelius*. Student Coalition for Peace (SCP), a nonschool-sponsored student organization dedicated to the cause of world peace through nuclear disarmament, requested permission to use Arnold Field, an athletic field on school premises, for a Peace Fair. The field had been regularly used for nonschool-sponsored community events, including annual Memorial Day services honoring the nation's war dead. The field was also used regularly without permission by members of the community for recreational purposes. The school board denied the student group permission to use the field for the Peace Fair on the ground that the field was not available for political events. The student group brought suit, claiming that the public forum doctrine required that it be granted use of the field. *Id.* at 433-34.

The Third Circuit, adhering closely to the guidance provided by the Supreme Court in *Cornelius,* determined that the field was a nonpublic forum:

> We do not think that the evidence in this case shows an intent by appellees [(the school board and other school officials)] to create a public forum at Arnold Field. The Board's policy requires each nonschool sponsored organization, such as SCP, to obtain permission to use the Field.... SCP has not met its burden of showing that such permission was in fact granted as a matter of course. Thus, neither the written policy nor the actual practice of appellees manifests an intent to designate Arnold Field as a public forum.

Id. at 430.

The court then concluded that limiting the field to non-political events was reasonable in light of the "desire to avoid potentially disruptive political controversy and to maintain the appearance of neutrality." *Id.* at 437. Significantly, the court recognized that while other activities permitted on the field

> may have an implicit political message, that message is plainly subsidiary to other aspects of the event, and could thus pose less of a threat either of disruption or of the appearance of favoritism. The Board is not required to delineate with absolute clarity the distinction between the political and the nonpolitical, as long as the line it does draw is reasonable and not a subterfuge for viewpoint discrimination. In particular, the Board could reasonably conclude that Memorial Day services do not create the same risk of partisan controversy as the Peace Fair.

Id.

Accepting the district court's finding of no viewpoint discrimination, the court denied SCP's first amendment claim. *Id.* at 437-38.

II.

The majority concludes that the appearance of vocational military advertisements in the five student newspapers published by high schools governed by the Board created limited public fora from which CARD's advertisement could not be excluded. I believe that the majority, while purporting to apply *Cornelius*, ignores its teachings.

As I read *Cornelius*, the Board's acceptance of the vocational military advertisements in the five high school newspapers did not create limited public fora from which CARD's advertisement could not be excluded. The fora that we must address consist of the advertising spaces in the five papers. *See Cornelius,* 105 S.Ct. at 3449 (defining forum according to access sought by speaker). These fora are public only if the Board has purposefully designated them for public discourse. *See id.; see also Calash* v. *City of Bridgeport,* 788 F.2d 80, 83 (2d Cir.1986) ("not every possible vehicle for communication is a public forum"). "[S]elective access, unsupported by evidence of a purposeful designation for public use, does not create a public forum." *Cornelius,* 105 S.Ct. at 3451.

I see no indication that the Board intended to designate the advertising spaces in the five high school newspapers as public fora. As in *Perry, Lehman,* and *Cornelius,* the Board's policy and practice do not demonstrate an intention to grant general access to the newspapers' advertising space. On the contrary, the Board's policy states, in part, that "paid advertisements by nonstudents... shall not be published except... [i]nsofar as the publication staff and adviser in their sole discretion determine that the publication of such material will further the publication's primary purposes sufficiently to warrant publications...." Further, as a matter of practice, the Board developed criteria limiting access to the advertising space.

The nature of the government property involved in this case bolsters the conclusion that the Board did not intend to designate the newspapers' advertising spaces as public fora. I believe that the advertising spaces in the five high school newspapers exist not to promote the expressive activity of nonstudents but rather to teach students journalistic management skills and to help finance the publication of the newspapers. *See Nicholson* v. *Board of Education*

Torrance Unified School District, 682 F.2d 858, 863-64 (9th Cir.1982) (*Nicholson*). This enterprise is inconsistent with an intent to designate the advertising space as a public forum. *See Cornelius,* 105 S.Ct. at 3450 (discussing *Lehman*). Moreover, our obligation to apply first amendment rights "in light of the special characteristics of the school environment," *Tinker* v. *Des Moines Independent Community School District,* 393 U.S. 503, 506, 89 S.Ct. 733, 736, 21 L.Ed.2d 731 (1969), requires that we accept "school policies that are reasonably designed to adjust those rights to the needs of the school environment." *Nicholson,* 682 F.2d at 863. The Board has the right to control access to the newspapers' advertising spaces in order to avoid disruption of the educational process. *See Cornelius,* 105 S.Ct. at 3451; *Student Coalition,* 776 F.2d at 436-37. *Cornelius* therefore requires the conclusion that the newspapers' advertising spaces are nonpublic fora.

The majority's contrary conclusion rests on its mistaken belief that if speech admitted in a forum relates to a "controversial and political" issue, the government has created a limited public forum that encompasses the issue. *See* maj. op. at 1477-1478. That the majority's test conflicts with the Supreme Court's government test in *Cornelius* is evident from applying the majority's test to the issues addressed in *Cornelius* and *Student Coalition.* If the majority's term "controversial and political" has any discernible fixed meaning, it surely encompasses the provision of health and welfare services (*Cornelius*) and the subject of war and peace (*Student Coalition*). Since charitable organizations soliciting in the campaign in *Cornelius* engage in speech on a controversial and political issue, an evenhanded application of the majority's test would determine that the campaign is a limited public forum from which legal defense and political advocacy organizations could not be excluded—a conclusion expressly rejected by the Supreme Court in *Cornelius.* Similarly, the majority's test would determine that the Memorial Day services in *Student Coalition* converted the field into a limited public forum from which SCP could not be excluded—a conclusion expressly rejected by the Third Circuit faithfully adhering to *Cornelius.*[1]

III

Restrictions on access to a nonpublic forum need only be reasonable in light of the purpose served by the forum and be not viewpoint-based. *Cornelius,* 105 S.Ct. at 3451. The majority states that even if the fora at issue are nonpublic, the Board's refusal to accept CARD's advertisement violated the first amendment because it was unreasonable and viewpoint-based. I believe that this dicta is ill-considered. I would find the Board's restrictions reasonable; I would, however, remand for a determination whether the Board's rejection of CARD's advertisement was viewpoint-based.

I believe that the Board's exclusion of political advertisements is reasonably designed to avoid disruption.[2] *See id.* at 3453-54; *Student Coalition,* 776 F.2d at 437. While I understand the majority's view that vocational military advertisements may have political implications, I agree with the Third Circuit that the Board is obligated merely to draw a reasonable line between the political and the nonpolitical. *See Student Coalition,* 776 F.2d at 437; *see also Lehman,* 418 U.S. 298, 94 S.Ct. 2714, 41 L.Ed.2d 770 (upholding municipal policy that prohibited political advertising in city transit vehicles but allowed commercial advertising). Rather than following this line of reasoning, the majority instead incorporates by reference the discussion that it developed in the context of its limited public forum discussion. *See* maj. op. at 1479. It thus appears that the majority has improperly blended together the different standards of review applicable to restrictions on public and nonpublic forums.

It follows from the above discussion that I cannot agree with the majority that the only reasonable inference is that the Board's refusal of the CARD advertisement constituted viewpoint-based discrimination. None of the district court's findings, however, explicitly addresses whether the Board's rejection of CARD's advertisement was an attempt to suppress CARD's point of view. The district court found that CARD's advertisement was rejected because it was a political advertisement from a non-student source and because it was believed to advocate an illegal act. While these findings strongly suggest no viewpoint discrimination, it would be better if there were a specific finding on this issue. I would therefore remand to the district court for a determination of this issue.

IV

Thus, I conclude that the Supreme Court's recent pronouncement in *Cornelius* forecloses the contention that the Board's acceptance of the vocational military advertisements created a limited public forum from which CARD's advertisement could not be excluded. Instead, the forum is nonpublic, and the Board's restrictions are reasonable. Only if the Board sought to suppress CARD's point of view—an issue that should be determined on remand—have CARD's first amendment rights been violated. I cannot join the majority in instructing the district court to enter a preliminary injunction in favor of CARD because, on the present record, CARD has not shown a probability that it would succeed on the merits of its First Amendment claim.

NOTES

1. The advertisement depicted a ghost-like figure, stating "Don't Let The Draft Blow You Away!" The following statements appeared below the figure:
Know Your Rights!
Know Your Choices!
If the draft starts tomorrow, you could be in boot camp 11 days later.
Call or Write:
Committee Against
Registration and the Draft
735-7518, 283-6878
P.O. Box 15195
San Diego, CA 92115
2. In this appeal the Board advances several reasons for its refusal to permit publication of CARD's advertisement. CARD did not argue in the district court, nor does it argue here, that the Board is limited to relying on the reason Mr. King gave in rejecting CARD's ad. Accordingly, we do not consider whether, in responding to a First Amendment claim, the government may seek to justify its actions on grounds other than those relied upon at the time it acted. Instead, we assume for purposes of this case that it may.
3. Although it sometimes appears that there are two separate tests for the grant of a preliminary injunction, in fact there is only one, best described as a continuum in which the required showing of harm varies inversely with the required showing of meritoriousness. *See Benda v. Grand Lodge of the International Association of Machinists,* 584 F.2d 308, 314-15 (9th Cir.1978). The case before us turns on free speech rights under the First Amendment. The Supreme Court has noted that "[t]he loss of First Amendment freedoms, for even minimal periods of time, unquestionably constitutes irreparable injury.... The timeliness of political speech is particularly important." *Elrod* v. *Burns,* 427 U.S. 347, 373-74, 96 S.Ct. 2673, 2689-90, 49 L.Ed.2d 547 (1976) (plurality opinion) (citing *Carroll* v. *Princess Anne,* 393 U.S. 175, 89 S.Ct. 347, 21 L.Ed.2d 325 (1968)). *See also C.B.S.* v. *United States District Court,* 729 F.2d 1174, 1177 (9th Cir.1983) (mandamus petition: harm to First Amendment rights). Thus, given the type of serious harm claimed, CARD would still be entitled to an injunction even if it had made a lesser showing of meritoriousness than it actually did.
4. Appeals from a district court's interlocutory order "granting,... refusing or dissolving injunctions" are permitted by law as of right. 28 U.S.C. § 1292(a).
5. We find this case clearly distinguishable from *Selph* v. *Council of the City of Los Angeles,* 593 F.2d 881 (9th Cir.1979), in which this court rejected appellant's contention that its motion to extend the period of time in which to appeal should be construed as a notice of appeal. In *Selph,* the motion for an extension had been made 40 days after the entry of judgment. Thus, even if the court had construed appellant's motion for an extension of time as a notice of appeal, the motion would not have been timely. The court therefore rejected appellant's contention, concluding that "this Court has no authority under Rule 4(a) to extend the [30-day period of] time for filing a notice of appeal." *Id.* at 883. Here, appellant's Rule 5(a) motion was made 10 days after entry of judgment, and thus within the period of time provided under Rule 4(a). Unlike the court in *Selph,* we are not being asked to extend the 30-day time limit imposed by Rule 4(a). Accordingly, we do not find *Selph* to be of any relevance here.
6. The Board's reliance on *Perry Education Ass'n* v. *Perry Local Educators' Ass'n,* 460 U.S. 37, 103 S.Ct. 948, 74 L.Ed.2d 794 (1983) is misplaced. At issue in *Perry* was the validity of a collective bargaining agreement between the school district and the teachers' exclusive bargaining representatives which provided the bargaining representative with exclusive access to teacher mailboxes, thereby excluding the petitioner, a rival union. The Court observed that the school had not held the mail distribution system open to the general public. Rather, the school had, with few exceptions, restricted its use to official business: the communication of school-related matters to teachers. Thus, use of the system by an organization affiliated with the school—such as the recognized teachers' union—did not render the system a limited public forum. Here, unlike *Perry,* the Board has provided outside entities with access to its newspapers.
7. One of the district newspapers, the *Foothill Echoes* of Grossmont High, also ran an ad sponsored by the Selective Service System Registration Information Bureau which read as follows:
A Reminder from
SELECTIVE SERVICE
If you are a male citizen
or alien residing in the U.S., you
must register with Selective Service
within 30 days of your 18th
birthday.
If you were born in 1960, 61,
62 or 63 you should already
have registered. If you have not,
you should do so as soon as possible.
You may register at any
U.S. Post Office
Selective Service System
Registration Information Bureau
Washington, D.C. 20435
This ad also relates to a political and controversial question, but we cannot rest our holding on it here because, while CARD is seeking an injunction against all five of the student newspapers, the ad appeared in only one.
8. The advertisement at issue offers counseling services regarding involuntary military service. The ad also takes a position on the desirability of military service. Thus, the anti-military service ad is of a mixed political and commercial character in the same way or to the same extent that the pro-military service ads are. We do not mean to imply, however, that an advertisement opposing military service but not offering goods, services, or vocational opportunities would fall outside the boundaries of the limited public forum that has been created. The issue whether, having opened a forum for mixed political and commercial speech on a particular topic, the state may bar a response that constitutes pure political speech is not before us and we do not reach that question.
9. The dissent argues that our holding that the newspapers are limited public forums is inconsistent with *Student Coalition for Peace* v. *Lower Merion School District,*776 F.2d 431 (3rd Cir.1985). We do not agree. In *Student Coalition,* the Third Circuit held that a

school athletic field's traditional classification as a nonpublic forum remained appropriate despite the occasional use of the field for other purposes. The court noted that access to the field for non-athletic purposes was highly restricted and was not granted as a matter of course. As discussed above, the facts of the case before us are entirely different. We see little similarity—in their fundamental purposes—between a school baseball diamond and a school newspaper.

10. Our dissenting colleague argues that the Board could reasonably exclude CARD from the newspapers on the ground that publication of the advertisement would cause disruption in the schools. The Board did not advance that reason before this court, and thus it would not be proper for us to consider it. Furthermore, there is nothing in the record to suggest that the ad, if published, would have disrupted the schools. Finally, and most important, the Supreme Court has made it clear that "in our system, undifferentiated fear or apprehension of disturbance is not enough to overcome the right to freedom of expression" in the schools. *Tinker* v. *Des Moines Independent Community School District,* 393 U.S. 503, 508, 89 S.Ct. 733, 737, 21 L.Ed.2d 731 (1969). The dissent cites *Cornelius* in support of its conclusion, but in *Cornelius* the claims of possible disruption were well-documented in the record. 105 S.Ct. at 3453-54. Thus, the dissent is unable to advance a valid reason in support of the Board's actions.

11. The dissent argues that our holding that the Board's restrictions are not reasonable is contrary to those of *Cornelius* and *Student Coalition for Peace* v. *Lower Merion School District,* 776 F.2d 431 (3rd Cir.1985). We disagree. In *Cornelius,* the Supreme Court held that the government could reasonably exclude all "political" charities from participation in a federal charity drive in order to prevent disruption of the workplace and to maintain an appearance of neutrality. In the case before us, the Board has not excluded all politically controversial ads, there is no claim of disruption, and the Board's publication of only one side of a highly controversial issue has destroyed any appearance of neutrality. Thus, *Cornelius* is perfectly consistent with our holding here.

In *Student Coalition,* the Third Circuit held that a school district could properly exclude a "peace fair" from school grounds, even though it had in the past permitted memorial services for war dead, as well as certain activities for disabled and mentally retarded children, to take place on those grounds. The court held that the school board could reasonably conclude that the "peace fair" would be highly political and controversial, and that the memorial services and other charitable events were not. Similarly, the court found that any political implications relating to activities benefitting the disabled and mentally retarded were minimal at most. This is consistent with the Supreme Court's view of the federal charity drive in *Cornelius.* Thus, the Third Circuit held, no prior political activities had been conducted on the school grounds and, in order to avoid permitting the use of school facilities for political purposes, the school district could properly exclude the "peace fair." The court stated that the school board was "not required to delineate with absolute clarity the distinction between the political and the nonpolitical, as long as the line [drawn] is reasonable and not a subterfuge for viewpoint discrimination." 776 F.2d at 437.

The school board's line-drawing in *Student Coalition* was more than reasonable. A memorial service, like a charity drive or activities for the disabled and mentally retarded, is normally not political or controversial; even persons who oppose war are willing to mourn those who have died in our nation's service. While it is true that in unique circumstances a particular memorial service for war dead may be political and controversial, *viz* the visit of President Reagan to Bitburg where members of the Nazi S.S. are interred, *Student Coalition* did not involve services that were political or controversial in any respect.

In the case before us, the Board's actions cannot be described as reasonable. The fact that absolute clarity in line-drawing is not required does not mean that all line-drawing is per se permissible. The Board has permitted the newspapers to carry politically controversial ads. Therefore, as discussed above, it cannot exclude other ads merely because their content is political.

DISSENTING OPINION NOTES

1. The majority makes no effort to explain how its holding that a limited public forum has been created is reconcilable with *Cornelius.* Moreover, the majority's efforts to reconcile its holding with *Student Coalition* are entirely unconvincing. The majority's statement that the school grounds in *Student Coalition* were nonpublic because access to them was "highly restricted," maj. op. at 1478 n. 9, is untenable. The Third Circuit specifically noted that "Arnold Field has been regularly used for nonschool sponsored community events ... and is also used regularly without permission by members of the community for jogging, bicycle riding, picnics, and similar activities." *Student Coalition,* 776 F.2d at 433-34. Again, contrary to the majority's suggestion that the Memorial Day services were not "political or controversial in any respect," maj. op. at 1480 n. 11, the Third Circuit acknowledged that the services posed some "risk of partisan controversy." *Student Coalition,* 776 F.2d at 437.

2. The majority' refusal to accept this justification, see maj. op. at nn. 10-11, is flawed in several respects. First, irrespective of whether the Board has argued that publication of CARD's advertisements would cause disruption in the schools, the Board has acted pursuant to a policy that it argues was developed and implemented to limit disruption. Second, the majority's suggestion that disruption must already have occurred in order to be legitimately considered is flatly contrary to *Cornelius,* 105 S.Ct. at 3453 ("the Government need not wait until havoc is wreaked to restrict access to a nonpublic forum"), *Perry,* 460 U.S. at 52 n. 12, 103 S.Ct. at 959 n. 12 (proof of past disturbances not required to justify the denial of access to a nonpublic forum on grounds of potential disruption), and *Student Coalition,* 776 F.2d at 437 (same). The majority's further suggestion that the possibility of disruption must be well-documented in the record, *see* maj. op. at n. 10, is equally in conflict with Supreme Court precedent. *See Perry,* 460 U.S. at 52 n. 12, 103 S.Ct. at 959 n. 12.

THE United States Supreme Court, in a 5-3 decision, concludes that school authorities had not violated high school students' First Amendment rights when the principal deleted two pages of articles from a May 13, 1983 issue of *Spectrum,* the Hazelwood East High School (Missouri) student newspaper. In deciding against the staff members of the newspaper, the Court said: "School officials did not evince either 'by policy or by practice,'... any intent to open the pages of *Spectrum* to 'indiscriminate use,'... by its student reporters and editors, or by the student body generally. Instead, they 'reserve[d] the forum for its intended purpos[e],'... as a supervised learning experience for journalism students. Accordingly, school officials were entitled to regulate the contents of *Spectrum* in any reasonable manner.... It is this standard, rather than our decision in *Tinker,* that governs this case." The Court concluded that "the standard articulated in *Tinker* for determining when a school may punish student expression need not also be the standard for determining when a school may refuse to lend its name and resources to the dissemination of student expression. Instead, we hold that educators do not offend the First Amendment by exercising editorial control over the style and content of student speech in school-sponsored expressive activities so long as their actions are reasonably related to legitimate pedagogical concerns."

In his strongly worded dissenting opinion, Justice Brennan rejects the majority's "excuses" for granting more censorship powers to school authorities: "Even if we were writing on a clean slate, I would reject the Court's rationale for abandoning *Tinker* in this case. The Court offers no more than an obscure tangle of three excuses to afford educators 'greater control' over school-sponsored speech than the *Tinker* test would permit: the public educator's prerogative to control curriculum; the pedagogical interest in shielding the high school audience from objectionable viewpoints and sensitive topics; and the school's need to dissociate itself from student expression.... None of the excuses, once disentangled, supports the distinction that the court draws. *Tinker* fully addresses the first concern; the second is illegitimate; and the third is readily achievable through less oppressive means."

Hazelwood School Dist. v. *Kuhlmeier,* 108 S.Ct. 562 (1988)

Justice WHITE delivered the opinion of the Court.

This case concerns the extent to which educators may exercise editorial control over the contents of a high school newspaper produced as part of the school's journalism curriculum.

I

Petitioners are the Hazelwood School District in St. Louis County, Missouri; various school officials; Robert Eugene Reynolds, the principal of Hazelwood

East High School, and Howard Emerson, a teacher in the school district. Respondents are three former Hazelwood East students who were staff members of *Spectrum,* the school newspaper. They contend that school officials violated their First Amendment rights by deleting two pages of articles from the May 13, 1983, issue of *Spectrum.*

Spectrum was written and edited by the Journalism II class at Hazelwood East. The newspaper was published every three weeks or so during the 1982-1983 school year. More than 4,500 copies of the newspaper were distributed during that year to students, school personnel, and members of the community.

The Board of Education allocated funds from its annual budget for the printing of *Spectrum.* These funds were supplemented by proceeds from sales of the newspaper. The printing expenses during the 1982-1983 school year totaled $4,668.50; revenue from sales was $1,166.84. The other costs associated with the newspaper—such as supplies, textbooks, and a portion of the journalism teacher's salary—were borne entirely by the Board.

The Journalism II course was taught by Robert Stergos for most of the 1982-1983 academic year. Stergos left Hazelwood East to take a job in private industry on April 29, 1983, when the May 13 edition of *Spectrum* was nearing completion, and petitioner Emerson took his place as newspaper adviser for the remaining weeks of the term.

The practice at Hazelwood East during the spring 1983 semester was for the journalism teacher to submit page proofs of each *Spectrum* issue to Principal Reynolds for his review prior to publication. On May 10, Emerson delivered the proofs of the May 13 edition to Reynolds, who objected to two of the articles scheduled to appear in that edition. One of the stories described three Hazelwood East students' experiences with pregnancy; the other discussed the impact of divorce on students at the school.

Reynolds was concerned that, although the pregnancy story used false names "to keep the identity of these girls a secret," the pregnant students still might be identifiable from the text. He also believed that the article's references to sexual activity and birth control were inappropriate for some of the younger students at the school. In addition, Reynolds was concerned that a student identified by name in the divorce story had complained that her father "wasn't spending enough time with my mom, my sister and I" prior to the divorce, "was always out of town on business or out late playing cards with the guys," and "always argued about everything" with her mother. App. to Pet. for Cert. 38. Reynolds believed that the student's parents should have been given an opportunity to respond to these remarks or to consent to their publication. He was unaware that Emerson had deleted the student's name from the final version of the article.

Reynolds believed that there was no time to make the necessary changes in the stories before the scheduled press run and that the newspaper would not appear before the end of the school year if printing were delayed to any significant extent. He concluded that his only options under the circumstances were to publish a four-page newspaper instead of the planned six-page newspaper, eliminating the two pages on which the offending stories appeared, or to publish no newspaper at all. Accordingly, he directed Emerson to withhold from publication the two pages containing the stories on pregnancy and divorce.[1] He informed his superiors of the decision, and they concurred.

Respondents subsequently commenced this action in the United States District Court for the Eastern District of Missouri seeking a declaration that their First Amendment rights had been violated, injunctive relief, and monetary damages. After a bench trial, the District Court denied an injunction, holding that no First Amendment violation had occurred. 607 F.Supp. 1450 (1985).

The District Court concluded that school officials may impose restraints on students' speech in activities that are "'an integral part of the school's educational function'"—including the publication of a school-sponsored newspaper by a journalism class—so long as their decision has "'a substantial and reasonable basis.'" *Id.,* at 1466 (quoting *Frasca* v. *Andrews,* 463 F.Supp. 1043, 1052 (EDNY 1979)). The court found that Principal Reynolds' concern that the pregnant students' anonymity would be lost and their privacy invaded was "legitimate and reasonable," given "the small number of pregnant students at Hazelwood East and several identifying characteristics that were disclosed in the article." 607 F.Supp., at 1466. The court held that Reynolds' action was also justified "to avoid the impression that [the school] endorses the sexual norms of the subjects" and to shield younger students from exposure to unsuitable material. *Ibid.* The deletion of the article on divorce was seen by the court as a reasonable response to the invasion of privacy concerns raised by the named student's remarks. Because the article did not indicate that the student's parents had been offered an opportunity to respond to her allegations, said the court, there was cause for "serious doubt that the article complied with the rules of fairness which are standard in the field of journalism and which were covered in the textbook used in the Journalism II class." *Id.,* at 1467. Furthermore, the court concluded that Reynolds was justified in deleting two full pages of the newspaper, instead of deleting only the pregnancy and divorce stories or requiring that those stories be modified to address his concerns, based on his "reasonable belief that he had to make an immediate decision and that there was no time to make modifications to the articles in question." *Id.*, at 1466.

The Court of Appeals for the Eighth Circuit reversed. 795 F.2d 1368 (1986). The court held at outset that *Spectrum* was not only "a part of the school adopted curriculum," *Id.*, at 1373, but also a public forum, because the newspaper was "intended to be and operated as a conduit for student viewpoint." *Id.*, at 1372. The court then concluded that *Spectrum's* status as a public forum precluded school officials from censoring its contents except when "'necessary to avoid material and substantial interference with school work or discipline... or the rights of others.'" *Id.*, at 1374 (quoting *Tinker v. Des Moines Independent Community School Dist.*, 393 U.S. 503, 511, 89 S.Ct. 733, 739, 21 L.Ed.2d 731 (1969)).

The Court of Appeals found "no evidence in the record that the principal could have reasonably forecast that the censored articles or any materials in the censored articles would have materially disrupted classwork or given rise to substantial disorder in the school." 795 F.2d, at 1375. School officials were entitled to censor the articles on the ground that they invaded the rights of others, according to the court, only if publication of the articles could have resulted in tort liability to the school. The court concluded that no tort action for libel or invasion of privacy could have been maintained against the school by the subjects of the two articles or by their families. Accordingly, the court held that school officials had violated respondents' First Amendment rights by deleting the two pages of the newspaper.

We granted certiorari, 479 U.S.—, 107 S.Ct. 926, 93 L.Ed.2d 978 (1987), and we now reverse.

II

Students in the public schools do not "shed their constitutional rights to freedom of speech or expression at the schoolhouse gate." *Tinker, supra*, 393 U.S., at 506, 89 S.Ct., at 736. They cannot be punished merely for expressing their personal views on the school premises—whether "in the cafeteria, or on the playing field, or on the campus during the authorized hours," *Id.*, at 512-513, 89 S.Ct., at 739-740—unless school authorities have reason to believe that such expression will "substantially interfere with the work of the school or impinge upon the rights of other students." *Id.*, at 509, 89 S.Ct., at 738.

We have nonetheless recognized that the First Amendment rights of students in the public schools "are not automatically coextensive with the rights of adults in other settings," *Bethel School District No. 403 v. Fraser*, 478 U.S.—, —, 106 S.Ct. 3159, 3164, 92 L.Ed.2d 549 (1986), and must be "applied in light of the special characteristics of the school environment." *Tinker, supra*, 393 U.S., at 506, 89 S.Ct., at 736; cf. *New Jersey v. T.L.O.*, 469 U.S. 325, 341-343, 105 S.Ct. 733, 743-744, 83 L.Ed.2d 720 (1985). A school need not tolerate student speech that is inconsistent with its "basic educational mission," *Fraser, supra*, 478 U.S., at —, 106 S.Ct., at 3166, even though the government could not censor similar speech outside the school. Accordingly, we held in *Fraser* that a student could be disciplined for having delivered a speech that was "sexually explicit" but not legally obscene at an official school assembly, because the school was entitled to "disassociate itself" from the speech in a manner that would demonstrate to others that such vulgarity is "wholly inconsistent with the 'fundamental values' of public school education." *Ibid*. We thus recognized that "[t]he determination of what manner of speech in the classroom or in school assembly is inappropriate properly rests with the school board," *Id.*, at —, 106 S.Ct., at 3165, rather than with the federal courts. It is in this context that respondents' First Amendment claims must be considered.

A

We deal first with the question whether *Spectrum* may appropriately be characterized as a forum for public expression. The public schools do not possess all of the attributes of streets, parks, and other traditional public forums that "time out of mind, have been used for purposes of assembly, communicating thoughts between citizens, and discussing public questions." *Hague v. CIO*, 307 U.S. 496, 515, 59 S.Ct. 954, 964, 83 L.Ed. 1423 (1939). Cf. *Widmar v. Vincent*, 454 U.S. 263, 267-268, n. 5, 102 S.Ct. 269, 273, n. 5, 70 L.Ed.2d 440 (1981). Hence, school facilities may be deemed to be public forums only if school authorities have "by policy or by practice" opened those facilities "for indiscriminate use by the general public," *Perry Education Assn. v. Perry Local Educators' Assn.*, 460 U.S. 37, 47, 103 S.Ct. 948, 956, 74 L.Ed.2d 794 (1983), or by some segment of the public, such as student organizations. *Id.*, at 46, n. 7, 103 S.Ct., at 955, n. 7 (citing *Widmar v. Vincent*). If the facilities have instead been reserved for other intended purposes, "communicative or otherwise," then no public forum has been created, and school officials may impose reasonable restrictions on the speech of students, teachers, and other members of the school community. *Ibid*. "The government does not create a public forum by inaction or by permitting limited discourse, but only by intentionally opening a nontraditional forum for public discourse." *Cornelius* v. *NAACP Legal Defense & Educational Fund, Inc.,* 473 U.S. 788, 802, 105 S.Ct. 3439, 3449, 87 L.Ed.2d 567 (1985).

The policy of school officials toward *Spectrum* was reflected in Hazelwood School Board Policy 348.51 and the Hazelwood East Curriculum Guide. Board Policy 348.51 provided that "[s]chool sponsored publications are developed within the adopted curriculum and its educational implications in regular classroom activities." App. 22. The Hazelwood East Curriculum Guide described the Journalism II course as a "laboratory situation in which the students publish the school newspaper applying skills they have learned in Journalism I." *Id.,* at 11. The lessons that were to be learned from the Journalism II course, according to the Curriculum Guide, included development of journalistic skills under deadline pressure, "the legal, moral, and ethical restrictions imposed upon journalists within the school community," and "responsibility and acceptance of criticism for articles of opinion." *Ibid.* Journalism II was taught by a faculty member during regular class hours. Students received grades and academic credit for their performance in the course.

School officials did not deviate in practice from their policy that production of Spectrum was to be part of the educational curriculum and a "regular classroom activit[y]." The District Court found that Robert Stergos, the journalism teacher during most of the 1982-1983 school year, "both had the authority to exercise and in fact exercised a great deal of control over *Spectrum.*" 607 F.Supp., at 1453. For example, Stergos selected the editors of the newspaper, scheduled publication dates, decided the number of pages for each issue, assigned story ideas to class members, advised students on the development of their stories, reviewed the use of quotations, edited stories, selected and edited the letters to the editor, and dealt with the printing company. Many of these decisions were made without consultation with the Journalism II students. The District Court thus found it "clear that Mr. Stergos was the final authority with respect to almost every aspect of the production and publication of *Spectrum,* including its content." *Ibid.* Moreover, after each *Spectrum* issue had been finally approved by Stergos or his successor, the issue still had to be reviewed by Principal Reynolds prior to publication. Respondents' assertion that they had believed that they could publish "practically anything" in *Spectrum* was therefore dismissed by the District Court as simply "not credible." *Id.,* at 1456. These factual findings are amply supported by the record, and were not rejected as clearly erroneous by the Court of Appeals.

The evidence relied upon by the Court of Appeals in finding *Spectrum* to be a public forum, see 795 F.2d, at 1372-1373, is equivocal at best. For example, Board Policy 348.51, which stated in part that "[s]chool sponsored student publications will not restrict free expression or diverse viewpoints within the rules of responsible journalism," also stated that such publications were "developed within the adopted curriculum and its educational implications." App. 22. One might reasonably infer from the full text of Policy 348.51 that school officials retained ultimate control over what constituted "responsible journalism" in a school-sponsored newspaper. Although the Statement of Policy published in the September 14, 1982, issue of *Spectrum* declared that "*Spectrum,* as a student-press publication, accepts all rights implied by the First Amendment," this statement, understood in the context of the paper's role in the school's curriculum, suggests at most that the administration will not interfere with the students' exercise of those First Amendment rights that attend the publication of a school-sponsored newspaper. It does not reflect an intent to expand those rights by converting a curricular newspaper into a public forum.[2] Finally, that students were permitted to exercise some authority over the contents of *Spectrum* was fully consistent with the Curriculum Guide objective of teaching the Journalism II students "leadership responsibilities as issue and page editors." App. 11. A decision to teach leadership skills in the context of a classroom activity hardly implies a decision to relinquish school control over that activity. In sum, the evidence relied upon by the Court of Appeals fails to demonstrate the "clear intent to create a public forum," *Cornelius,* 473 U.S., at 802, 105 S.Ct., at 3449-3450, that existed in cases in which we found public forums to have been created. See *id.*at 802-803, 105 S.Ct., at 3449-3450 (citing *Widmar*v. *Vincent,* 454 U.S., at 267, 102 S.Ct., at 273; *Madison School District* v. *Wisconsin Employment Relations Comm'n,* 429 U.S. 167, 174, n. 6, 97 S.Ct. 421, 426, n. 6, 50 L.Ed.2d 376 (1976); *Southeastern Promotions, Ltd.* v. *Conrad,* 420 U.S. 546, 555, 95 S.Ct. 1239, 1245, 43 L.Ed.2d 448 (1975)). School officials did not evince either "by policy or by practice," *Perry Education Assn.,* 460 U.S., at 47, 103 S.Ct., at 956, any intent to open the pages of *Spectrum*to "indiscriminate use," *Ibid.,* by its student reporters and editors, or by the student body generally. Instead, they "reserve[d] the forum for its intended purpos[e]," *Id.,* at 46, 103 S.Ct., at 955, as a supervised learning experience for journalism students. Accordingly, school officials were entitled to regulate the contents of *Spectrum* in any reasonable manner. *Ibid.* It is this standard, rather than our decision in *Tinker,* that governs this case.

B

The question whether the First Amendment requires a school to tolerate particular student speech—the question that we addressed in *Tinker*—is different from the question whether the First Amendment requires a school affirmatively to promote particular student speech. The former question addresses educators' ability to silence a student's personal expression that happens to occur on the school premises. The latter question concerns educators' authority over school-sponsored publications, theatrical productions, and other expressive activities that students, parents, and members of the public might reasonably perceive to bear the imprimatur of the school. These activities may fairly be characterized as part of the school curriculum, whether or not they occur in a traditional classroom setting, so long as they are supervised by faculty members and designed to impart particular knowledge or skills to student participants and audiences.[3]

Educators are entitled to exercise greater control over this second form of student expression to assure that participants learn whatever lessons the activity is designed to teach, that readers or listeners are not exposed to material that may be inappropriate for their level of maturity, and that the views of the individual speaker are not erroneously attributed to the school. Hence, a school may in its capacity as publisher of a school newspaper or producer of a school play "disassociate itself," *Fraser*, 478 U.S. at —, 106 S.Ct., at 3166, not only from speech that would "substantially interfere with [its] work . . . or impinge upon the rights of other students," *Tinker*, 393 U.S., at 509, 89 S.Ct., at 738, but also from speech that is, for example, ungrammatical, poorly written, inadequately researched, biased or prejudiced, vulgar or profane, or unsuitable for immature audiences.[4] A school must be able to set high standards for the student speech that is disseminated under its auspices—standards that may be higher than those demanded by some newspaper publishers or theatrical producers in the "real" world—and may refuse to disseminate student speech that does not meet those standards. In addition, a school must be able to take into account the emotional maturity of the intended audience in determining whether to disseminate student speech on potentially sensitive topics, which might range from the existence of Santa Claus in an elementary school setting to the particulars of teenage sexual activity in a high school setting. A school must also retain the authority to refuse to sponsor student speech that might reasonably be perceived to advocate drug or alcohol use, irresponsible sex, or conduct otherwise inconsistent with "the shared values of a civilized social order," *Fraser, supra,* 478 U.S. at —, 106 S.Ct., at 3165, or to associate the school with any position other than neutrality on matters of political controversy. Otherwise, the schools would be unduly constrained from fulfilling their role as "a principal instrument in awakening the child to cultural values, in preparing him for later professional training, and in helping him to adjust normally to his environment." *Brown v. Board of Education,* 347 U.S. 483, 493, 74 S.Ct. 686, 691, 98 L.Ed. 873 (1954).

Accordingly, we conclude that the standard articulated in *Tinker* for determining when a school may punish student expression need not also be the standard for determining when a school may refuse to lend its name and resources to the dissemination of student expression.[5] Instead, we hold that educators do not offend the First Amendment by exercising editorial control over the style and content of student speech in school-sponsored expressive activities so long as their actions are reasonably related to legitimate pedagogical concerns.[6]

This standard is consistent with our oft-expressed view that the education of the Nation's youth is primarily the responsibility of parents, teachers, and state and local school officials, and not of federal judges. See, *e.g., Board of Education of Hendrick Hudson Central School Dist. v. Rowley,* 458 U.S. 176, 208, 102 S.Ct. 3034, 3051, 73 L.Ed.2d 690 (1982); *Wood v. Strickland,* 420 U.S. 308, 326, 95 S.Ct. 992, 1003, 43 L.Ed.2d 214 (1975); *Epperson v. Arkansas,* 393 U.S. 97, 104, 89 S.Ct. 266, 270, 21 L.Ed.2d 228 (1968). It is only when the decision to censor a school-sponsored publication, theatrical production, or other vehicle of student expression has no valid educational purpose that the First Amendment is so "directly and sharply implicate[d]," *Ibid.,* as to require judicial intervention to protect students' constitutional rights.[7]

III

We also conclude that Principal Reynolds acted reasonably in requiring the deletion from the May 13 issue of *Spectrum* of the pregnancy article, the divorce article, and the remaining articles that were to appear on the same pages of the newspaper.

The initial paragraph of the pregnancy article declared that "[a]ll names have been changed to keep the identity of these girls a secret." The principal concluded that the students' anonymity was not adequately protected, however, given the other identifying information in the article and the small number of pregnant students at the school. Indeed, a teacher at the school credibly testified that she could positively identify at least one of the girls and possibly all three. It is likely that many students at Hazelwood East would have been at least as successful in identifying the girls. Reynolds therefore could reasonably have feared that the article violated whatever pledge of anonymity had been given to the pregnant students. In addition, he could reasonably have been concerned that the article was not sufficiently sensitive to the privacy interests of the students' boyfriends and parents, who were discussed in the article but who were given no opportunity to consent to this publication or to offer a response. The article did not contain graphic accounts of sexual activity. The girls did comment in the article, however, concerning their sexual histories and their use or nonuse of birth control. It was not unreasonable for the principal to have concluded that such frank talk was inappropriate in a school-sponsored publication distributed to 14-year-old freshmen and presumably taken home to be read by students' even younger brothers and sisters.

The student who was quoted by name in the version of the divorce article seen by Principal Reynolds made comments sharply critical of her father. The principal could reasonably have concluded that an individual publicly identified as an inattentive parent—indeed, as one who chose "playing cards with the guys" over home and family—was entitled to an opportunity to defend himself as a matter of journalistic fairness. These concerns were shared by both of *Spectrum*'s faculty advisers for the 1982-1983 school year, who testified that they would not have allowed the article to be printed without deletion of the student's name.[8]

Principal Reynolds testified credibly at trial that, at the time that he reviewed the proofs of the May 13 issue during an extended telephone conversation with Emerson, he believed that there was no time to make any changes in the articles, and that the newspaper had to be printed immediately or not at all. It is true that Reynolds did not verify whether the necessary modifications could still have been made in the articles, and that Emerson did not volunteer the information that printing could be delayed until the changes were made. We nonetheless agree with the District Court that the decision to excise the two pages containing the problematic articles was reasonable given the particular circumstances of this case. These circumstances included the very recent replacement of Stergos by Emerson, who may not have been entirely familiar with *Spectrum* editorial and production procedures, and the pressure felt by Reynolds to make an immediate decision so that students would not be deprived of the newspaper altogether.

In sum, we cannot reject as unreasonable Principal Reynolds' conclusion that neither the pregnancy article nor the divorce article was suitable for publication in *Spectrum*. Reynolds could reasonably have concluded that the students who had written and edited these articles had not sufficiently mastered those portions of the Journalism II curriculum that pertained to the treatment of controversial issues and personal attacks, the need to protect the privacy of individuals whose most intimate concerns are to be revealed in the newspaper, and "the legal, moral, and ethical restrictions imposed upon journalists within [a] school community" that includes adolescent subjects and readers. Finally, we conclude that the principal's decision to delete two pages of *Spectrum*, rather than to delete only the offending articles or to require that they be modified, was reasonable under the circumstances as he understood them. Accordingly, no violation of First Amendment rights occurred.[9]

The judgment of the Court of Appeals for the Eighth Circuit is therefore

Reversed.

Justice BRENNAN, with whom Justice MARSHALL and Justice BLACKMUN join, dissenting.

When the young men and women of Hazelwood East High School registered for Journalism II, they expected a civics lesson. *Spectrum*, the newspaper they were to publish, "was not just a class exercise in which students learned to prepare papers and hone writing skills, it was a . . . forum established to give students an opportunity to express their views while gaining an appreciation of their rights and responsibilities under the First Amendment to the United States Constitution. . . ." 795 F.2d 1368, 1373 (CA8 1986). "[A]t the beginning of each school year," *Id.*, at 1372, the student journalists published a Statement of Policy—tacitly approved each year by school authorities—announcing their expectation that "*Spectrum*, as a student-press publication, accepts all rights implied by the First Amendment. . . . Only speech that 'materially and substantially interferes with the requirements of appropriate discipline' can be found unacceptable and therefore prohibited." App. 26 (quoting *Tinker* v. *Des Moines Independent Community School Dist.*, 393 U.S. 503, 513, 89 S.Ct. 733, 740, 21 L.Ed.2d 731 (1969)).[1] The school board itself affirmatively guaranteed the students of Journalism II an atmosphere conducive to fostering such an appreciation and exercising the full panoply of rights associated with a free student press. "School sponsored student publications," it vowed, "will not restrict free expression or diverse viewpoints within the rules of responsible journalism." App. 22 (Board Policy § 348.51).

This case arose when the Hazelwood East administration breached its own promise, dashing its students' expectations. The school principal, without prior consultation or explanation, excised six articles—comprising two full pages—of the May 13, 1983, issue of *Spectrum*. He did so not because any of the articles would "materially and substantially interfere with the requirements of appropriate discipline," but simply because he considered two of the six "inappropriate, personal, sensitive, and unsuitable" for student consumption. 795 F.2d, at 1371.

In my view the principal broke more than just a promise. He violated the First Amendment's prohibitions against censorship of any student expression that neither disrupts classwork nor invades the rights of others, and against any censorship that is not narrowly tailored to serve its purpose.

I

Public education serves vital national interests in preparing the Nation's youth for life in our increasingly complex society and for the duties of citizenship in our democratic Republic. See *Brown* v. *Board of Education,* 347 U.S. 483, 493, 74 S.Ct. 686, 691, 98 L.Ed. 873 (1954). The public school conveys to our young the information and tools required not merely to survive in, but to contribute to, civilized society. It also inculcates in tomorrow's leaders the "fundamental values necessary to the maintenance of a democratic political system. . . ." *Ambach* v. *Norwick,* 441 U.S. 68, 77, 99 S.Ct. 1589, 1595, 60 L.Ed.2d 49 (1979). All the while, the public educator nurtures students' social and moral development by transmitting to them an official dogma of "'community values.'" *Board of Education* v. *Pico,* 457 U.S. 853, 864, 102 S.Ct. 2799, 2806, 73 L.Ed.2d 435 (1982) (plurality opinion) (citation omitted).

The public educator's task is weighty and delicate indeed. It demands particularized and supremely subjective choices among diverse curricula, moral values, and political stances to teach or inculcate in students, and among various methodologies for doing so. Accordingly, we have traditionally reserved the "daily operation of school systems" to the States and their local school boards. *Epperson* v. *Arkansas,* 393 U.S. 97, 104, 89 S.Ct. 266, 270, 21 L.Ed.2d 228 (1968); see *Board of Education* v. *Pico, supra,* 457 U.S., at 863-864, 102 S.Ct., at 2806. We have not, however, hesitated to intervene where their decisions run afoul of the Constitution. See *e.g., Edwards* v. *Aguillard,* 482 U.S.—, 107 S.Ct. 2573, 96 L.Ed.2d 510 (1987) (striking state statute that forbade teaching of evolution in public school unless accompanied by instruction on theory of "creation science"); *Board of Education* v. *Pico, supra,*(school board may not remove books from library shelves merely because it disapproves of ideas they express); *Epperson* v. *Arkansas, supra* (striking state-law prohibition against teaching Darwinian theory of evolution in public school); *West Virginia Board of Education* v. *Barnette,*319 U.S. 624, 63 S.Ct. 1178, 87 L.Ed. 1628 (1943) (public school may not compel student to salute flag); *Meyer* v. *Nebraska,* 262 U.S. 390, 43 S.Ct. 625, 67 L.Ed. 1042 (1923) (state law prohibiting the teaching of foreign languages in public or private schools is unconstitutional).

Free student expression undoubtedly sometimes interferes with the effectiveness of the school's pedagogical functions. Some brands of student expression do so by directly preventing the school from pursuing its pedagogical mission: The young polemic who stands on a soapbox during calculus class to deliver an eloquent political diatribe interferes with the legitimate teaching of calculus. And the student who delivers a lewd endorsement of a student-government candidate might so extremely distract an impressionable high school audience as to interfere with the orderly operation of the school. See *Bethel School Dist. No. 403* v. *Fraser,* 478 U.S.—, 106 S. Ct. 3159, 92 L.Ed.2d 549 (1986). Other student speech, however, frustrates the school's legitimate pedagogical purposes merely by expressing a message that conflicts with the school's, without directly interfering with the school's expression of its message: A student who responds to a political science teacher's question with the retort, "Socialism is good," subverts the school's inculcation of the message that capitalism is better. Even the maverick who sits in class passively sporting a symbol of protest against a government policy, cf. *Tinker* v. *Des Moines Independent School Dist.,* 393 U.S. 503, 89 S.Ct. 733, 21 L.Ed.2d 731 (1969), or the gossip who sits in the student commons swapping stories of sexual escapade could readily muddle a clear official message condoning the government policy or condemning teenage sex. Likewise, the student newspaper that, like *Spectrum,* conveys a moral position at odds with the school's official stance might subvert the administration's legitimate inculcation of its own perception of community values.

If mere incompatibility with the school's pedagogical message were a constitutionally sufficient justification for the suppression of student speech, school officials could censor each of the students or student organizations in the foregoing hypotheticals, converting our public schools into "enclaves of totalitarianism," *Id.,* at 511, 89 S.Ct., at 739, that "strangle the free mind at its source," *West Virginia State Board of Education* v. *Barnette, supra,* 319 U.S., at 637, 63 S.Ct., at 1185. The First Amendment permits no such blanket censorship authority. While the "constitutional rights of students in public school are not automatically coextensive with the rights of adults in other settings," *Fraser, supra,* 478 U.S., at —, 106 S.Ct., at 3164, students in the public schools do not "shed their constitutional rights to freedom of speech or expression at the schoolhouse gate," *Tinker, supra,*

393 U.S., at 506, 89 S.Ct., at 736. Just as the public on the street corner must, in the interest of fostering "enlightened opinion," *Cantwell* v. *Connecticut,* 310 U.S. 296, 310, 60 S.Ct. 900, 906, 84 L.Ed. 1213 (1940), tolerate speech that "tempt[s] [the listener] to throw [the speaker] off the street," *Id.,* at 309, 60 S.Ct., at 906, public educators must accommodate some student expression even if it offends them or offers views or values that contradict those the school wishes to inculcate.

In *Tinker,* this Court struck the balance. We held that official censorship of student expression—there the suspension of several students until they removed their armbands protesting the Vietnam War—is unconstitutional unless the speech "materially disrupts classwork or involves substantial disorder or invasion of the rights of others. . . ." *Tinker,* 393 U.S., at 513, 89 S.Ct., at 740. School officials may not suppress "silent, passive expression of opinion, unaccompanied by any disorder or disturbance on the part of" the speaker. *Id.,* at 508, 89 S.Ct., at 737. The "mere desire to avoid the discomfort and unpleasantness that always accompany an unpopular viewpoint," *Id.,* at 509, 89 S.Ct., at 738, or an unsavory subject, *Fraser, supra,* 478 U.S., at —, 106 S.Ct., at 3167-3168 (BRENNAN., J., concurring in judgment), does not justify official suppression of student speech in the high school.

This Court applied the *Tinker* test just a Term ago in *Fraser, supra,* upholding an official decision to discipline a student for delivering a lewd speech in support of a student-government candidate. The Court today casts no doubt on *Tinker*'s vitality. Instead it erects a taxonomy of school censorship, concluding that *Tinker* applies to one category and not another. On the one hand is censorship "to silence a student's personal expression that happens to occur on the school premises." *Ante,* at 569. On the other hand is censorship of expression that arises in the context of "school-sponsored . . . expressive activities that students, parents, and members of the public might reasonably perceive to bear the imprimatur of the school." *Ibid.*

The Court does not, for it cannot, purport to discern from our precedents the distinction it creates. One could, I suppose, readily characterize the Tinkers' symbolic speech as "personal expression that happens to [have] occur[red] on school premises," although *Tinker* did not even hint that the personal nature of the speech was of any (much less dispositive) relevance. But that same description could not by any stretch of the imagination fit Fraser's speech. He did not just "happen" to deliver his lewd speech to an ad hoc gathering on the playground. As the second paragraph of *Fraser* evinces, if ever a forum for student expression was "school-sponsored," Fraser's was:

"Fraser . . . delivered a speech nominating a fellow student for student elective office. Approximately 600 high school students . . . attended the assembly. Students were required to attend the assembly or to report to study hall. The assembly was part of a *school-sponsored* educational program in self-government." *Fraser,* 478 U.S., at —, 106 S.Ct., at 3162 (emphasis added).

Yet, from the first sentence of its analysis, see *Id.,* at —, 106 S.Ct., at —, *Fraser* faithfully applied *Tinker.*

Nor has this Court ever intimated a distinction between personal and school-sponsored speech in any other context. Particularly telling is this Court's heavy reliance on *Tinker* in two cases of First Amendment infringement on state college campuses. See *Papish* v. *University of Missouri Board of Curators,* 410 U.S. 667, 671, n. 6, 93 S.Ct. 1197, 1199, n. 6, 35 L.Ed.2d 618 (1973) (*per curiam*); *Healy* v. *James,*408 U.S. 169, 180, 189, and n. 18, 191, 92 S.Ct. 2338, 2345, 2350, and n. 18, 2351, 33 L.Ed.2d 266 (1972). One involved the expulsion of a student for lewd expression in a newspaper that she sold on campus pursuant to university authorization, see *Papish, supra,* 410 U.S., at 667-668, 93 S.Ct., at 1197–1198, and the other involved the denial of university recognition and concomitant benefits to a political student organization, see *Healy, supra,* 408 U.S., at 174, 176, 181-182, 92 S.Ct., at 2342, 2343, 2346-2347. Tracking *Tinker*'s analysis, the Court found each act of suppression unconstitutional. In neither case did this Court suggest the distinction, which the Court today finds dispositive, between school-sponsored and incidental student expression.

II

Even if we were writing on a clean slate, I would reject the Court's rationale for abandoning *Tinker* in this case. The Court offers no more than an obscure tangle of three excuses to afford educators "greater control" over school-sponsored speech than the *Tinker* test would permit: the public educator's prerogative to control curriculum; the pedagogical interest in shielding the high school audience from objectionable viewpoints and sensitive topics; and the school's need to dissociate itself from student expression. *Ante,* at 569-570. None of the excuses, once disentangled, supports the distinction that the Court draws. *Tinker* fully addresses the first concern; the second is illegitimate; and the third is readily achievable through less oppressive means.

A

The Court is certainly correct that the First Amendment permits educators "to assure that participants learn whatever lessons the activity is designed to teach...." *Ante,* at 570. That is, however, the essence of the *Tinker* test, not an excuse to abandon it. Under *Tinker,* school officials may censor only such student speech as would "materially disrup[t]" a legitimate curricular function. Manifestly, student speech is more likely to disrupt a curricular function when it arises in the context of a curricular activity—one that "is designed to teach" something—than when it arises in the context of a noncurricular activity. Thus, under *Tinker,* the school may constitutionally punish the budding political orator if he disrupts calculus class but not if he holds his tongue for the cafeteria. See *Consolidated Edison Co.* v. *Public Service Comm'n,* 447 U.S. 530, 544-545, 100 S.Ct. 2326, 2337, 65 L.Ed.2d 319 (1980) (STEVENS, J., concurring in judgment). That is not because some more stringent standard applies in the curricular context. (After all, this Court applied the same standard whether the Tinkers wore their armbands to the "classroom" or the "cafeteria." 393 U.S., at 512, 89 S.Ct., at 740.) It is because student speech in the noncurricular context is less likely to disrupt materially any legitimate pedagogical purpose.

I fully agree with the Court that the First Amendment should afford an educator the prerogative not to sponsor the publication of a newspaper article that is "ungrammatical, poorly written, inadequately researched, biased or prejudiced," or that falls short of the "high standards for ... student speech that is disseminated under [the school's] auspices...." *Ante,* at 570. But we need not abandon *Tinker* to reach that conclusion; we need only apply it. The enumerated criteria reflect the skills that the curricular newspaper "is designed to teach." The educator may, under *Tinker,* constitutionally "censor" poor grammar, writing, or research because to reward such expression would "materially disrup[t]" the newspaper's curricular purpose.

The same cannot be said of official censorship designed to shield the *audience* or dissociate the *sponsor* from the expression. Censorship so motivated might well serve (although, as I demonstrate *infra,* at ——, cannot legitimately serve) some other school purpose. But it in no way furthers the curricular purposes of a student *newspaper,* unless one believes that the purpose of the school newspaper is to teach students that the press ought never report bad news, express unpopular views, or print a thought that might upset its sponsors. Unsurprisingly, Hazelwood East claims no such pedagogical purpose.

The Court relies on bits of testimony to portray the principal's conduct as a pedagogical lesson to Journalism II students who "had not sufficiently mastered those portions of the ... curriculum that pertained to the treatment of controversial issues and personal attacks, the need to protect the privacy of individuals ..., and 'the legal, moral, and ethical restrictions imposed upon journalists....' " *Ante,* at 572. In that regard, the Court attempts to justify censorship of the article on teenage pregnancy on the basis of the principal's judgment that (1) "the [pregnant] students' anonymity was not adequately protected," despite the article's use of aliases; and (2) the judgment "that the article was not sufficiently sensitive to the privacy interests of the students' boyfriends and parents...." *Ante,* at 571. Similarly, the Court finds in the principal's decision to censor the divorce article a journalistic lesson that the author should have given the father of one student an "opportunity to defend himself" against her charge that (in the Court's words) he "chose 'playing cards with the guys' over home and family...." *Ante,* at 572.

But the principal never consulted the students before censoring their work. "[T]hey learned of the deletions when the paper was released...." 795 F.2d, at 1371. Further, he explained the deletions only in the broadest of generalities. In one meeting called at the behest of seven protesting *Spectrum* staff members (presumably a fraction of the full class), he characterized the articles as " 'too sensitive' for 'our immature audience of readers,' " 607 F.Supp. 1450, 1459 (ED Mo.1985), and in a later meeting he deemed them simply "inappropriate, personal, sensitive and unsuitable for the newspaper," *ibid.* The Court's supposition that the principal intended (or the protesters understood) those generalities as a lesson on the nuances of journalistic responsibility is utterly incredible. If he did, a fact that neither the District Court nor the Court of Appeals found, the lesson was lost on all but the psychic *Spectrum* staffer.

B

The Court's second excuse for deviating from precedent is the school's interest in shielding an impressionable high school audience from material whose substance is "unsuitable for immature audiences." *Ante,* at 570 (footnote omitted). Specifically, the majority decrees that we must afford educators authority to shield high school students from exposure to "potentially sensitive topics" (like "the particulars of teenage sexual activity") or unacceptable social viewpoints (like the advocacy of "irresponsible se[x] or conduct otherwise inconsistent with 'the shared values of a civilized social order' ") through school-sponsored student activities. *Id.,* at 570 (citation omitted).

Tinker teaches us that the state educator's undeniable, and undeniably vital, mandate to inculcate moral and political values is not a general warrant to act as "thought police" stifling discussion of all but state-approved topics and advocacy of all but the official position. See also *Epperson* v. *Arkansas,* 393 U.S. 97, 89 S.Ct. 266, 21 L.Ed.2d 228 (1968); *Meyer* v. *Nebraska,* 262 U.S. 390, 43 S.Ct. 625, 67 L.Ed. 1042 (1923). Otherwise educators could transform students into "closed-circuit recipients of only that which the State chooses to communicate," *Tinker,* 393 U.S., at 511, 89 S.Ct., at 739, and cast a perverse and impermissible "pall of orthodoxy over the classroom," *Keyishian* v. *Board of Regents,* 385 U.S. 589, 603, 87 S.Ct. 675, 683, 17 L.Ed.2d 629 (1967). Thus, the State cannot constitutionally prohibit its high school students from recounting in the locker room "the particulars of [their] teenage sexual activity," nor even from advocating "irresponsible se[x]" or other presumed abominations of "the shared values of a civilized social order." Even in its capacity as educator the State may not assume an Orwellian "guardianship of the public mind," *Thomas* v. *Collins,* 323 U.S. 516, 545, 65 S.Ct. 315, 329, 89 L.Ed. 430 (1945) (Jackson, J., concurring).

The mere fact of school sponsorship does not, as the Court suggests, license such thought control in the high school, whether through school suppression of disfavored viewpoints or through official assessment of topic sensitivity.[2] The former would constitute unabashed and unconstitutional viewpoint discrimination, see *Board of Education* v. *Pico,* 457 U.S., at 878-879, 102 S.Ct., at 2813-2814 (Blackmun, J., concurring in part and concurring in judgment), as well as an impermissible infringement of the students' "'right to receive information and ideas,'" *id.,* at 867, 102 S.Ct., at 2808 (plurality opinion) (citations omitted); see *First National Bank* v. *Bellotti,* 435 U.S. 765, 783, 98 S.Ct. 1407, 1419, 55 L.Ed.2d 707 (1978).[3] Just as a school board may not purge its state-funded library of all books that "'offen[d] [its] social, political and moral tastes,'" 457 U.S. at 858-859, 102 S.Ct., at 2804 (plurality opinion) (citation omitted), school officials may not, out of like motivation, discriminatorily excise objectionable ideas from a student publication. The State's prerogative to dissolve the student newspaper entirely (or to limit its subject matter) no more entitles it to dictate which viewpoints students may express on its pages, than the State's prerogative to close down the schoolhouse entitles it to prohibit the nondisruptive expression of antiwar sentiment within its gates.

Official censorship of student speech on the ground that it addresses "potentially sensitive topics" is, for related reasons, equally impermissible. I would not begrudge an educator the authority to limit the substantive scope of a school-sponsored publication to a certain, objectively definable topic, such as literary criticism, school sports, or an overview of the school year. Unlike those determinate limitations, "potential topic sensitivity" is a vaporous nonstandard—like "'public welfare, peace, safety, health, decency, good order, morals or convenience,'" *Shuttlesworth* v. *Birmingham,* 394 U.S. 147, 150, 89 S.Ct. 935, 938, 22 L.Ed.2d 162 (1969), or "'general welfare of citizens,'" *Staub* v. *Baxley,* 355 U.S. 313, 322, 78 S.Ct. 277, 282, 2 L.Ed.2d 302 (1958)—that invites manipulation to achieve ends that cannot permissibly be achieved through blatant viewpoint discrimination and chills student speech to which school officials might not object. In part because of those dangers, this Court has consistently condemned any scheme allowing a state official boundless discretion in licensing speech from a particular forum. See, *e.g., Shuttlesworth* v. *Birmingham, supra,* 394 U.S., at 150-151, and n. 2, 89 S.Ct., at 938-939, and n. 2; *Cox* v. *Louisiana,* 379 U.S. 536, 557-558, 85 S.Ct. 453, 465-466, 13 L.Ed.2d 471 (1965); *Staub* v. *Baxley, supra,* 355 U.S., at 322-324, 78 S.Ct., at 282-283.

The case before us aptly illustrated how readily school officials (and courts) can camouflage viewpoint discrimination as the "mere" protection of students from sensitive topics. Among the grounds that the Court advances to uphold the principal's censorship of one of the articles was the potential sensitivity of "teenage sexual activity." *Ante,* at 570. Yet the District Court specifically found that the principal "did not, as a matter of principle, oppose discussion of said topi[c] in *Spectrum.*" 607 F.Supp., at 1467. That much is also clear from the same principal's approval of "the squeal law" article on the same page, dealing forthrightly with "teenage sexuality," "the use of contraceptives by teenagers," and "teenage pregnancy," App. 4-5. If topic sensitivity were the true basis of the principal's decision, the two articles should have been equally objectionable. It is much more likely that the objectionable article was objectionable because of the viewpoint it expressed: It might have been read (as the majority apparently does) to advocate "irresponsible sex." See *ante,* at 570.

C

The sole concomitant of school sponsorship that might conceivably justify the distinction that the Court draws between sponsored and nonsponsored student expression is the risk "that the views of the individual speaker [might be] erroneously attributed to the school." *Ante,* at 570. Of course, the risk of erroneous attribution inheres in any student expression, including "personal expression" that, like the Tinkers' armbands, "happens to occur on the school premises," *Ante,* at 569. Nevertheless, the majority is certainly correct that indicia of school sponsorship increase the likelihood of such attribution, and that state educators may therefore have a legitimate interest in dissociating themselves from student speech.

But "'[e]ven though the governmental purpose be legitimate and substantial, that purpose cannot be pursued by means that broadly stifle fundamental personal liberties when the end can be more narrowly achieved.'" *Keyishian* v. *Board of Regents,* 385 U.S., at 602, 87 S.Ct., at 683 (quoting *Shelton* v. *Tucker,* 364 U.S. 479, 488, 81 S.Ct. 247, 252, 5 L.Ed.2d 231 (1960)). Dissociative means short of censorship are available to the school. It could, for example, require the student activity to publish a disclaimer, such as the "Statement of Policy" that *Spectrum* published each school year announcing that "[a]ll . . . editorials appearing in this newspaper reflect the opinions of the *Spectrum* staff, which are not necessarily shared by the administrators or faculty of Hazelwood East," App. 26; or it could simply issue its own response clarifying the official position on the matter and explaining why the student position is wrong. Yet, without so much as acknowledging the less oppressive alternatives, the Court approves of brutal censorship.

III

Since the censorship served no legitimate pedagogical purpose, it cannot by any stretch of the imagination have been designed to prevent "materia[l] disrup[tion of] classwork," *Tinker,* 393 U.S., at 513, 89 S.Ct., at 740. Nor did the censorship fall within the category that *Tinker* described as necessary to prevent student expression from "inva[ding] the rights of others," *Ibid.* If that term is to have any content, it must be limited to rights that are protected by law. "Any yardstick less exacting than [that] could result in school officials curtailing speech at the slightest fear of disturbance," 795 F.2d, at 1376, a prospect that would be completely at odds with this Court's pronouncement that the "undifferentiated fear or apprehension of disturbance is not enough [even in the public-school context] to overcome the right to freedom of expression." *Tinker, supra,* 393 U.S., at 508, 89 S.Ct., at 737. And, as the Court of Appeals correctly reasoned, whatever journalistic impropriety these articles may have contained, they could not conceivably be tortious, much less criminal. See 795 F.2d, at 1375-1376.

Finally, even if the majority were correct that the principal could constitutionally have censored the objectionable material, I would emphatically object to the brutal manner in which he did so. Where "[t]he separation of legitimate from illegitimate speech calls for more sensitive tools" *Speiser* v. *Randall,* 357 U.S. 513, 525, 78 S.Ct. 1332, 1342, 2 L.Ed.2d 1460 (1958); see *Keyishian* v. *Board of Regents, supra,* 385 U.S., at 602, 87 S.Ct., at 683, the principal used a paper shredder. He objected to some material in two articles, but excised six entire articles. He did not so much as inquire into obvious alternatives, such as precise deletions or additions (one of which had already been made), rearranging the layout, or delaying publication. Such unthinking contempt for individual rights is intolerable from any state official. It is particularly insidious from one to whom the public entrusts the task of inculcating in its youth an appreciation for the cherished democratic liberties that our Constitution guarantees.

IV

The Court opens its analysis in this case by purporting to reaffirm *Tinker*'s time-tested proposition that public school students "'do not shed their constitutional rights to freedom of speech or expression at the schoolhouse gate.'" *Ante,* at 567 (quoting *Tinker, supra,* 393 U.S., at 506, 89 S.Ct., at 736). That is an ironic introduction to an opinion that denudes high school students of much of the First Amendment protection that *Tinker* itself prescribed. Instead of "teach[ing] children to respect the diversity of ideas that is fundamental to the American system," *Board of Education* v. *Pico,* 457 U.S., at 880, 102 S.Ct., at 2814 (Blackmun, J., concurring in part and concurring in judgment), and "that our Constitution is a living reality, not parchment preserved under glass," *Shanley* v. *Northeast Independent School Dist. Bexar Cty. Tex.,* 462 F.2d 960, 972 (CA5 1972), the Court today "teach[es] youth to discount important principles of our government as mere platitudes." *West Virginia State Board of Education* v. *Barnette,* 319 U.S., at 637, 63 S.Ct., at 1185. The young men and women of Hazelwood East expected a civics lesson, but not the one the Court teaches them today.

I dissent.

NOTES

1. The two pages deleted from the newspaper also contained articles on teenage marriage, runaways, and juvenile delinquents, as well as a general article on teenage pregnancy. Reynolds testified that he had no objection to these articles and that they were deleted only because they appeared on the same pages as the two objectionable articles.
2. The Statement also cited *Tinker* v. *Des Moines Independent Community School Dist.,* 393 U.S. 503, 89 S.Ct. 733, 21 L.Ed.2d 731 (1969), for the proposition

that "[o]nly speech that 'materially and substantially interferes with the requirements of appropriate discipline' can be found unacceptable and therefore be prohibited." App. 26. This portion of the Statement does not, of course, even accurately reflect our holding in *Tinker*. Furthermore, the Statement nowhere expressly extended the *Tinker* standard to the news and feature articles contained in a school-sponsored newspaper. The dissent apparently finds as a fact that the Statement was published annually in *Spectrum;* however, the District Court was unable to conclude that the Statement appeared on more than one occasion. In any event, even if the Statement says what the dissent believes that it says, the evidence that school officials never intended to designate *Spectrum* as a public forum remains overwhelming.

3. The distinction that we draw between speech that is sponsored by the school and speech that is not is fully consistent with *Papish* v. *Board of Curators,* 410 U.S. 667, 93 S.Ct. 1197, 35 L.Ed.2d 618 (1973) (*per curiam*), which involved an off-campus "underground" newspaper that school officials merely had allowed to be sold on a state university campus.

4. The dissent perceives no difference between the First Amendment analysis applied in *Tinker* and that applied in *Fraser*. We disagree. The decision in *Fraser* rested on the "vulgar," "lewd," and "plainly offensive" character of a speech delivered at an official school assembly rather than on any propensity of the speech to "materially disrupt[ ] classwork or involve[ ] substantial disorder or invasion of the rights of others." 393 U.S., at 513, 89 S.Ct., at 740. Indeed, the *Fraser* Court cited as "especially relevant" a portion of Justice Black's dissenting opinion in *Tinker* "disclaim[ing] any purpose . . . to hold that the Federal Constitution compels the teachers, parents and elected school officials to surrender control of the American public school system to public school students." 478 U.S., at —, 106 S.Ct., at 3166 (citing 393 U.S., at 522, 89 S.Ct., at 744). Of course, Justice Black's observations are equally relevant to the instant case.

5. We therefore need not decide whether the Court of Appeals correctly construed *Tinker* as precluding school officials from censoring student speech to avoid "invasion of the rights of others," 393 U.S., at 513, 89 S.Ct., at 740, except where that speech could result in tort liability to the school.

6. We reject respondents' suggestion that school officials be permitted to exercise prepublication control over school-sponsored publications only pursuant to specific written regulations. To require such regulations in the context of a curricular activity could unduly constrain the ability of educators to educate. We need not now decide whether such regulations are required before school officials may censor publications not sponsored by the school that students seek to distribute on school grounds. See *Baughman* v. *Freienmuth,* 478 F.2d 1345 (CA4 1973); *Shanley* v. *Northwest Independent School Dist., Bexar Cty., Tex.,* 462 F.2d 960 (CA5 1972); *Eisner* v. *Stamford Board of Education,* 440 F.2d 803 (CA2 1971).

7. A number of lower federal courts have similarly recognized that educators' decisions with regard to the content of school-sponsored newspapers, dramatic productions, and other expressive activities are entitled to substantial deference. See, *e.g. Nicholson* v. *Board of Education Torrance Unified School Dist.,* 682 F.2d 858 (CA9 1982); *Seyfried* v. *Walton,* 668 F.2d 214 (CA3 1981); *Trachtman* v. *Anker,* 563 F.2d 512 (CA2 1977), cert. denied, 435 U.S. 925, 98 S.Ct. 1491, 55 L.Ed.2d 519 (1978); *Frasca* v. *Andrews,* 463 F.Supp. 1043 (EDNY 1979). We need not now decide whether the same degree of deference is appropriate with respect to school-sponsored expressive activities at the college and university level.

8. The reasonableness of Principal Reynolds' concerns about the two articles was further substantiated by the trial testimony of Martin Duggan, a former editorial page editor of the St. Louis Globe Democrat and a former college journalism instructor and newspaper adviser. Duggan testified that the divorce story did not meet journalistic standards of fairness and balance because the father was not given an opportunity to respond, and that the pregnancy story was not appropriate for publication in a high school newspaper because it was unduly intrusive into the privacy of the girls, their parents, and their boyfriends. The District Court found Duggan to be "an objective and independent witness" whose testimony was entitled to significant weight. 607 F.Supp. 1450, 1461 (ED Mo. 1985).

9. It is likely that the approach urged by the dissent would as a practical matter have far more deleterious consequences for the student press than does the approach that we adopt today. The dissent correctly acknowledges "[t]he State's prerogative to dissolve the student newspaper entirely." *Ante,* at 578. It is likely that many public schools would do just that rather than open their newspapers to all student expression that does not threaten "materia[l] disrup[tion of] classwork" or violation of "rights that are protected by law," *ante,* at 579, regardless of how sexually explicit, racially intemperate, or personally insulting that expression otherwise might be.

DISSENTING OPINION NOTES

1. The Court suggests that the passage quoted in the text did not "exten[d] the *Tinker* standard to the news and feature articles contained in a school-sponsored newspaper" because the passage did not expressly mention them. *Ante,* at 569, n. 2. It is hard to imagine why the Court (or anyone else) might expect a passage that applies categorically to "a student-press publication," composed almost exclusively of "news and feature articles," to mention those categories expressly. Understandably, neither court below so limited the passage.

2. The Court quotes language in *Bethel School Dist.* v. *Fraser,* 478 U.S.—, 106 S.Ct. 3159, 92 L.Ed.2d 549 (1986), for the proposition that " '[t]he determination of what manner of speech in the classroom or in school assembly is inappropriate properly rests with the school board.'" *Ante,* at 567 (quoting 478 U.S., at —, 106 S.Ct., at 3165). As the discussion immediately preceding that quotation makes clear, however, the Court was referring only to the appropriateness of the *manner* in which the message is conveyed, not of the message's *content*. See *e.g., Fraser,* 478 U.S., at —, 106 S.Ct., at 3165 ("the 'fundamental values necessary to the maintenance of a democratic political system' disfavor the use of terms of debate highly offensive or highly threatening to others"). In fact, the *Fraser* Court

coupled its first mention of "society's ... interest in teaching students the boundaries of *socially appropriate behaviour*," with an acknowledgment of "[t]he undoubted freedom to advocate unpopular and controversial views in schools and *classrooms*," *id.,* at —, 106 S.Ct., at 3164 (emphasis added). See also *id.,* at —, 106 S.Ct., at 3168 (BRENNAN, J., concurring) ("[n]or does this case involve an attempt by school officials to ban written materials they consider 'inappropriate' for high school students" (citation omitted)).

3. Petitioners themselves concede that "'[c]ontrol over access'" to *Spectrum* is permissible only if "'the distinctions drawn ... are viewpoint neutral.'" Brief for Petitioners 32 (quoting *Cornelius* v. *NAACP Legal Defense & Educational Fund, Inc.,* 473 U.S. 788, 806, 105 S.Ct. 3439, 3451, 87 L.Ed.2d 567 (1985)).

Index

"A Lament for Dr. Rose," editorial, 14
Abortion, 119
Academic Freedom, 4, 12-13, 28
Access, right of, 129, 132-133, 136n.15, 137nn.21,24, 138nn.36,39, 200n.1, 204, 210
"Actual malice," 124-125n.3
"Adams Rule," Alabama's, 13-14
Adventurers, The, 91
Advertising policy, 45-46, 131, 204, 208
Advertisement, anti-draft, 202-210
   anti-Vietnam War, 6, 15-16, 130
   commercial, 16, 46, 128, 130, 136n.18, 182, 202, 205, 211n.8
   editorial, 45-46, 131, 137n.21
   homosexual, 126-129
   military service, 205-206, 209, 211n.7
Advisory board, 19-21
Alcohol, 192
American Civil Liberties Union, 51n.9
American Legion, 73
American Library Association, vi
Anonymous publications, 115
Another Country, 93n.10
Aptheker, Bettina, 12, 14
Arbitrary restrictions, 22, 28n.5
Argus, 24-27
Arrow, 35-38
Associational rights, 129-130, 136n.15
Awakening, 7, 57-64, 67nn.8,9

Balancing interests, 31-32, 46, 63, 76-77, 80, 128, 130-132, 186
Baldwin, James, 91
"Basic educational mission," school's, 214
Biafra, 16
Bible, 64, 69
Birth control, 61, 64, 67n.9, 120, 142-143, 156n.2
Bitburg, 212n.11
"Black Moochie," 19-20, 22
Black Panther flag, 100

Black Power flag, 100
Bloom, Molly, 91
Boards of education, functions of, 13
Boycott, 65n.1
Breach of the peace, 41
Brecht, Bertolt, 191
Broadside, 36-37
Brown, H. Rap, 96
Buckley Amendment, 169

Cafeteria journalism, 6
Calamandrei, Piero, vii
Callow, Andrea, 5
Capote, Truman, 7, 91, 193
Carmichael, Stokely, 12, 14
Cartoon political, 107-108
Catcher in the Rye, The, 93nn.5,9
Catholic Church, 69
Caulfield, Holden, 88
"Censored" across blank page, 12
Chieftain, 165-170
Chilling effect, 3, 5, 43, 65, 125n.5, 146, 160, 195, 222
Christianity, attack on, 68-71
CIA at College: Into Twilight and Back, The, 109
Civil Rights Act of 1964, 97-100
Clear and present danger test, 31, 41, 62, 120
"Closed circuit recipients," students as, 6, 22, 29, 222
College and high school students, 34n.5, 44n.5, 50, 51n.7, 112, 117, 122, 142, 189n.4
Commercial activity, 115-116
Confederate flags, 100
Constitution as a living document, 8, 61
Content discrimination, 129-133
Contraception, 119, 140
Controversial articles, 5-6, 8, 16, 35-37, 61, 64, 68, 153, 175, 185-186
Corn Cob Curtain, 112-117
Cosmic Frog, The, 2, 53, 56n.7
Creation Science, 218
"Crimes against nature," 126, 133n.3

227

228 FREEDOM TO PUBLISH

Curriculum, 15-17, 22-23, 29, 215-217
Cycle, The, 18-22, 89, 93n.6

Daily Mississippian, The, 89
Darwinian evolution, 219
Desecration of American flag, 25-28
Dewey, John, v
Discipline, school, 1-2, 17, 21, 24, 26, 28n.5, 30-31, 46, 52n.11, 54, 59-60, 65, 75, 77, 97, 119-120, 123, 150, 161, 168, 189n.3, 218-219
Disruption, 1-2, 21, 28, 30-32, 41, 43-44, 49-50, 52n.11, 57, 59-62, 64-65, 66n.1, 67n.8, 73-78, 80-82, 85n.3, 97, 104, 111n.6, 112-114, 116, 117n.1, 118, 122-124, 129, 135n.8, 146, 150, 152, 159, 161-170, 173-178, 182, 191, 210, 212n.10, 212n.2, 215, 219-221, 223
Distribution of printed matter policy, 39-43, 48-51, 53-55, 56n.4, 58-59, 63-65, 66nn.1,2, 72, 74, 80-83, 84n.3, 103-106, 113-118, 121-123, 125n.3, 145, 180-182, 182n.2
Divorce article, 4, 8, 214, 218, 221, 224n.8
Dolphin, The, 69
Draft, 8, 16, 205
Draft counseling, 67n.9
Drug Counseling, 67n.9
Drugs, 8, 16, 180-182, 191-192, 217
Due process, 11-12, 63-65, 88-78, 79n.4, 123, 136n.16, 160, 163n.8, 181, 183

"Earthy language," 86-87, 112, 117
Echo, 95-102
Editor-publisher relationship, 5
"Editorial product," 133-134
Editorials critical of state officials, 12
"Emphasis 67, A World in Revolution," 12, 14
"Enclaves of totalitarianism," schools as, 219
Esquire, 199
Establishment Clause, 69-70
Ethics, 36
Evolution, 70

"Fair use" of copyrighted work, 201n.3
Fannon, Frantz, 96
Farm News, The, 140-143
Faulkner, William, 91
Fighting words, 25, 110, 129, 165, 167, 169
Financing school publications, 18-22, 24-27, 35, 68-70, 87-88, 95-96, 101n.1, 127, 131-132, 141, 177, 214
"Fixed star in our constitutional constellation," 9
Flag, picture of burning, 24-26
Flag salute, 9, 34n.6
Forbis, Christopher, 5
"Forecast" rule, 1-2, 31-32, 34n.6, 41, 50, 53-54, 60, 62, 76
Forum, newspaper as, 16-17, 35-37, 68-70, 126; 129-132, 141, 205-206, 208-211, 215-218, 223n.2
    outside speakers', 76-77
    public, 138n.32, 202, 215-217
Forums, types of, 203-210
"Four-letter words," 87-88, 90, 132
"Four Way Test," Rotary International, 185, 189n.5
Fraser, Laura, 6
Free Press Underground, 107
Free speech, function of, 61-52

Gay Alliance, 127
Goddess of Justice, rape of, 107
Godfather, The, 91
"Good taste," 198
Grass High, 1, 30-33, 54
Green Orange, 143-145
Guidelines, lack of, 19, 168-169

Hair length, 67n.11
Hampdens, 9
Hazelwood, reactions to, 5-6
Health and safety of students, 180-183
"Heckler's veto," 44n.6, 158n.9
Homosexual ads, 126-129
Homosexual teachers, reactions to, 172-174, 178-179
Huguenot Herald, The, 15-17
Hustler, 199

Images, 86-90
Immature audiences, 3, 5-6, 34n.5, 143n.2, 149, 153-154, 217-218, 221
Imprimatur of the school, 4, 186
In Cold Blood, 7, 93n.13, 192
Indecent speech, 107, 109n.2, 112, 116
Inquiry, free, 198
Insubordination, 11-13, 186
Insulting language, 104

Jenkinson, Edward, vi
"Jerks," 191-192, 199
Jesus Christ, 69
Joint Effort, 180-182
Journalism II, educational function of, 216-218
Journalism teacher, dismissal of, 185-189
Joyce, James, 91, 93n.16
Judicial opinion, function of, vii
Jury instructions, 162, 164nn.11,13

Kampus Vue, 18
Kennedy, John, 191, 199
King, Martin Luther, 199
Krug, Judith, vi
Kudzu, 90
Kuhlmeier, Cathy, 5
Language, emotive function of, 198
Levin, Alan, 6

Library books, 93n.14
Library censorship, 219, 222
Libelous material, 36, 38, 46, 55, 58, 60-61, 75, 81, 103-106, 109, 115, 121-123, 124-125n.3, 129, 145, 146n.1, 167-170, 172-175, 178, 184n.6, 215
Literary merit, 91, 93n.15
Love Story, 91
Loyalty oath, 101n.2

McEachern Arrowhead, The, 172-179
McMasters, Paul, 6
Magazine, college, 24-28, 86
Mailer, Norman, 91
Malamud, Bernard, 91
Marijuana, 61, 64, 67n.9
"Marketplace of ideas," 21, 41, 59, 92, 190, 200
Meredith, James, 25
Mississippi Gay Alliance, 126-128, 134n.1, 135n.16, 137nn.33,35,39

National Council of Teachers of English, vi
Neutrality, newspaper, 68-71
New Left Notes, 109
Newspaper as extra-curricular, 120, 142-143
Newsweek, 43

Obscenity, 18, 20-21, 31, 40, 43, 46, 55, 56n.7, 58, 60-61, 68-69, 75, 81, 90-91, 103-109, 113, 116-117, 122, 124-125nn.1,3, 129, 135n.6, 145, 146n.1, 165, 167-169, 175, 178, 215
Offensive and objectionable speech, 25, 32, 67n.9, 68, 86-88, 90-92, 108, 129, 135nn.8,9, 220, 222, 223n.4
"Open Forum," 129
Orwellian guardianship, 6, 222

"Pall of orthodoxy over the classroom," 222
Pandering, 88, 92, 111n.6
Pflashlyte, 80
Playboy, 90
"Poor taste," Yearbook quotation in, 192, 198-199
Portnoy's Complaint, 91
Portrait of the Artist as a Young Man, A, 93n.16
Post-publication sanction, 105
"Potentially sensitive topics," 222
Prayers in public schools, 70
Pregnancy article, 4, 7-8, 214, 217, 221, 224n.8
Prior approval, 19-21, 39, 54, 59, 81-82, 85n.4, 105, 113, 122, 146, 182, 186-187, 214
Prior restraint, 2, 8, 20, 23n.4, 27, 40, 42-43, 48-50, 51n.9, 52n.11, 53-54, 56n.5, 59-60, 63, 74-78, 97-98, 103-106, 121-124, 125n.5, 145-146n.1, 147n.3, 152-153, 166-167, 169, 174, 178, 182
Procedural safeguards, 1, 21, 23nn.5,6, 40, 42-43, 50, 83-84, 123, 144-146, 169, 183
Profane language, 3, 75, 80-83, 110, 116-117, 177, 217

Psychological harm to students, 149-156, 157n.2, 168
Public figure, 165, 167, 170-171
Public forum, Yearbook as, 191, 196-197
Publication policy, 36-37
Publisher, university as, 88

Questionnaire, sex, 148-158, 168

Racial and religious slander, 44n.6
Racial and segregationist materials, 95-97
Racial discrimination, 99, 130
Racial tensions, 176
Receive, the right to, 76, 136n.15, 195
Reflector, The, 126-139
Religion, 68-71, 120
Reserve Officer Training Corps, 205
Reston, James, 12, 14
Richmond Times, The, 70
Right to edit, 132, 134
Royal Purple, 45
Rusk, Dean, 12, 14

Salinger, J.D., 91, 93n.5
San Antonio Light, 64
San Diego Committee Against Registration and the Draft (CARD), 202-211
Scalapino, Robert, 12, 14
School newspaper, function of, 15-16, 19
School-sponsored speech, 213-221, 224n.3
"Schoolhouse gate," 2, 8, 74, 174, 181, 186, 215, 219, 223
"Secular religion," 68-69
Selective Service ad, 211n.7
Sex education, 140-143, 157n.3
Sex information supplement, 119, 157
Sexual attitudes survey, 149-157, 158n.7
"Sexuality in Stuyvesant," 149, 157n.2
"Sexually Active Students Fail to Use Contraception," 140, 143
"Shared values of a civilized order," 217, 221-222
Sit-in, 65n.1
Smith, Jeffrey, 5
Socialist Workers Party, 73
Space City, 81
Speakers, outside, 72-73, 76
Spectrum, 2, 7-8, 213-223
"State action," 127, 131-133
State as owner of school newspaper, 13
State sponsored publication, 130-133
Statue of Liberty, rape of, 107
Student Coalition for Peace, 209
Student Committee Against the War in Vietnam, 15
Student-Faculty Relations Committee, 124, 125n.6
Student Nonviolent Coordinating Committee, 12, 14
"Student Responsibilities and Rights," 146nn.1,2
Students for a Democratic Society, 109, 110n.3

Stuyvesant Voice, The, 148
Susceptible readers, most, 5
Suspension and expulsion of students, 11, 30, 48, 53-55, 56n.8, 57-58, 63, 65n.1, 66n.4, 72-74, 77-78, 79n.4, 80-81, 101n.3, 107, 110, 123
Symbolic expression, 26-28, 52n.10, 119

Tenants, The, 93n.12
Texas Bar Journal, 130-131
Time, 43, 64, 190, 201n.3
Time, manner, and place, 54, 104, 106n.1, 107-108, 116, 126, 129, 133, 146n.1, 157n.3, 160, 204
Today's World, 124n.1
Trials, open, 162-163, 164n.14
Tropolitan, The, 12-14
Two-level theory, 138n.35

Ulysses, 91
Underground newspapers, 34n.3, 48, 52n.10, 53, 57-59, 80-81, 90, 144, 169, 180
"Undifferentiated fear or apprehension," 46, 61, 75, 153, 158n.5, 174, 176, 207, 212n.10, 223
Ungrammatical language, 3, 217, 221

"Unnatural intercourse," 128, 130, 136n.6
"Up Against the Wall, M_____F____," 107

Vagueness and overbreadth, 2-3, 42-43, 63-64, 104, 112-114, 117, 121, 123, 145, 160, 161, 163n.6, 182, 199, 212n.10
Valley of the Dolls, The, 91
V.D., 67n.9
V.F.W., 73
Vietnam, 6, 15, 17n.6, 46, 53, 161, 220
"Vietnam Syndrome," 173, 175
Viewpoint-Based Discrimination, 207-208, 210, 222
Vonnegut, Kurt, 4
Vulgar language, 3, 75, 81-82, 165, 169, 175, 215, 217, 224n.4

Washington, George, 199
Welcome to the Monkey House, 4
Wheeler, Earl, 12, 14
Wilkins, Roy, 14
Woodlawn Lampoon, The, 124n.1

Yearbook, 7, 89, 141-142, 190-201